W9-DIJ-674

INTRODUCTION TO COMPUTERS AND COMPUTER SCIENCE

فريدون باختر

FEREIDOON BAKHTAR

RICHARD C. DORF

University of California, Davis

BOYD & FRASER PUBLISHING COMPANY

San Francisco, California

Richard C. Dorf
INTRODUCTION TO COMPUTERS AND COMPUTER SCIENCE

© 1972 by Boyd & Fraser Publishing Company. All rights reserved.

No part of this work may be reproduced or used in any form or by any means—graphic, electronic, or mechanical, including photo-copying, recording, taping, or information and retrieval systems—without written permission from the publisher. Manufactured in the United States of America.

Library of Congress Catalog Card Number: 73-141223

ISBN: 0-87835-025-X

3 4 · 3 2

NOTICE OF 2nd EDITION

A new edition of INTRODUCTION TO COMPUTERS AND COMPUTER SCIENCE will be published in   June , 1977. There will be substantial revisions, including the following:

1.   Chapter 6, "Programming a Calculator", has been re- placed by a chapter on Minicomputers and Microcomputers.

2.   Chapter 11, "Business Data Processing and Management Information Systems", has been expanded and improved. A section on distributed processing has been added. Much topical information, such as discussion of EFTS and an inquiry into computer crimes, has been added. New prob- lems have also been added.

3.   Chapter 12, "Data Banks, Information Retrieval and Libraries", has a section added on legal retrieval sys- tens. Latest developments in the continuing struggle to protect individual privacy have been reported.

4.   Chapter 13, "Simulation and Games", has new and note- worthy applications of computer simulation described and illustrated.

5.   Chapter 14, "Computers Around the World", has been completely revised to reflect 1976 equipment and statis- tics.

6.   Chapter 17, "Applications of Computers", has approx- imately 25 additional contemporary business applications.

7.   Throughout the book, references and figures have been updated, and the latest models of computers and computer components have been illustrated and described. Chapter references and bibliographies have been extensively re- vised to include easily-obtainable sources as recent as late 1976.

8.   A glossary has been added.

CONTENTS

PREFACE

Computers and information-processing systems pervade our lives. They are increasingly becoming part of the foundation supporting our technological industry and our society. There are about 50,000 computers in operation in the US, while there were just 1,700 a decade ago. The student of the Sixties could neglect the study of computers and information systems, but it will be increasingly difficult to qualify as a broadly educated person in this decade or the future without experiencing at least an introduction to computers, their application, and their impact on society. The purpose of this book is to provide just such an introduction.

This book is meant to serve as a textbook in a first course on the introduction to computing. It is structured to meet the needs of a student who does not possess any background in computing or advanced mathematics. It is assumed that the textbook and the coordinate course would be open to all students in colleges and universities whatever their major or year of advancement. Increasingly, such a course will be offered during the first or second year of college, but at present it is offered to students at any level depending on their curriculum. The book is written to follow the course description developed by the Association for Computing Machinery (ACM), published in the March, 1968 issue of the *Communications of ACM*. The suggested catalog description provided by ACM is given below.*

> The first course is designed to provide the student with the basic knowledge and experience necessary to use computers effectively in the solution of problems. It can be a service course for students in a number of other fields as well as an introductory course for majors in computer science. Although no prerequisites are listed, it is assumed that the student will have had a minimum of three years of high school mathematics. All of the computer science courses which follow will depend upon this introduction.
>
> **Course B1. Introduction to Computing (2-2-3)**
>
> Algorithms, programs, and computers. Basic programming and program structure. Programming and computing systems. Debugging and verification of programs. Data representation. Organization and characteristics of computers. Survey of computers, languages, systems, and applications. Computer solution of several numerical and nonnumerical problems using one or more programming languages.

The primary purpose of this book is to introduce the use of algorithms and computers to solve important problems. In addition, a large number of applications of computers is examined. Finally, the social impact of computers as tools in our society is discussed.

The first course and this book concentrate on the solution of problems through the introduction and use of algorithmic languages. The primary computational languages used are BASIC and FORTRAN because most college computer centers can accommodate and support one or both of these languages. It is assumed that complete operating and programming instructions specific to the computer at the college will be available to the student.

Science should be taught not to spectators but to participants; therefore, we should teach computer science rather than teach *about* computer science. Thus, when one learns computer science, he is learning to deal with the kinds of problems which computers are used to solve. Therefore, good challenging problems are the best vehicle for learning computing and computer science. This is the basic aim of this book.

The problems in this text have a classroom aspect and a laboratory dimension. That is, we shall want to think about any given problem first, and then proceed to the laboratory or computer center and act upon our thoughts and tentative solution proposal. The best course to introduce the computer consists

Communications of the ACM, March, 1968, Vol. II, Number 3, page 156.

of thought and action; most problem solutions will result from an iterative process of thought and action. The problems in this book are an aid toward this process.

We are often asked if this subject is socially relevant—that is, does it have some bearing on the grievous problems facing the world? Also, is the subject self-rewarding, real, or meaningful and thus personally relevant? It is the belief of the author that the study of computers and information processing can be both socially and personally relevant. Here is an opportunity for the student to bring knowledge and concern together in solving some of the problems of industry, education, and society. When we are able to concentrate on the unknown while resting on a base of knowledge, we shall be able to sense where we are going and then make progress toward our goal.

In conclusion, I would like to express my sincere appreciation to my wife and daughters, who love a book as much as I do. Therefore, I wish to dedicate this book to Joy, Christine and Renée as a partial response to their love.

RICHARD C. DORF

Athens, Ohio   1971

1

INTRODUCTION

1.1 COMPUTERS AND COMPUTER SCIENCE

The computer exercises such an important and widespread influence on our society today that every educated person should study the basic disciplines underlying its operation and application. Just as a student will study the basis of economics or psychology, for example, so also he will study the fundamentals of computer science. As a scholarly discipline, computer science is no more than 25 years old; yet one may not find a discipline more important as a preparation for life and work in the last three decades of the twentieth century.

Wherever there are phenomena, and these phenomena are of interest to man, there can be a science to describe and explain those phenomena. There are computers and applications of computers, and the phenomena resulting from these applications. Computer science, therefore, is the study of computers and the phenomena resulting from their use.[1] We can give a more specific defini-- tion of computer science after we first describe a computer.

A computer is a device capable of accepting information or data, processing the information, and providing the results as an output. More specifically, a computer can be described as follows:

COMPUTER (1) A data processor that can perform substantial computation, including numerous arithmetic or logic operations, without intervention by a human operator during the process. (2) A device capable of solving problems by accepting data, performing described operations on the data, and supplying the results of these operations. Various types of computers are calculators, digital computers, and analog computers.

A visual representation, or schematic diagram, shows how the computer processes information.

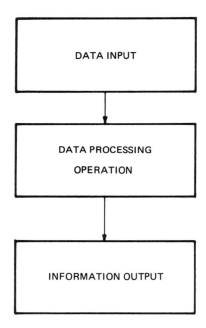

FIGURE 1-1   Information processing system.

Now, with a definition of a computer in mind, let us return to the discussion of the discipline of interest in this book, that of computer science. In one sense, computer science is what computer scientists do, just as mathematics is what mathematicians do. What do computer scientists do? They (1) develop and design computers; (2) work on ways to improve the operation of computers; (3) study the use of computers to solve problems of society and industry, and (4) study the choice of practical ways to utilize computers.[2] As Professor Richard Hamming indicates, "computer engineering" might be a more suitable name for the discipline, except for confusion from the term "engineering." In any case, the computer is the information processing device which is the foundation for the discipline of computer science. A useful definition of computer science is:

COMPUTER SCIENCE (1) The study of computers and the phenomena resulting from their use. (2) The art and science of representing and processing information.

The study of the discipline of computer science is appropriate for any college student. It may lead to an understanding of an introductory nature as partially provided by this textbook, or to study of a major nature and perhaps a bachelor's or graduate degree in computer science. The Association for Computing Machinery has developed syllabi for thirty courses which provide a foundation for the study of the discipline, if one chooses to major in the field; these courses also provide non-majors with a clear comprehension of the subject.[3] This approach is similar to the study of economics, which a student may adopt as a major, or study in a first course on the basic tenets of the discipline.

There has been much discussion in the past decade of the information explosion—that is, the exponential growth of knowledge at a rate which is forcing us to specialize ever more narrowly. However, there is hope that computer science, which is intimately concerned with information processing, will provide a new framework for information, and will aid our ability to synthesize and integrate information. This means that the reader will often find other terms, such as "computer and information sciences" or the "science of information processing" used interchangeably with "computer science." See Figure 1-2.

The knowledge industries, which produce and distribute ideas and information rather than goods and services, are analyzed in an important book by Peter Drucker.[4] Drucker reports that these information processing industries account for one-third of the US Gross National Product and they are expected to account for one-half of the GNP at the close of the 1970's. As Drucker points out, the demand for professional workers in the knowledge industry appears insatiable. He states, "In addition to a million computer programmers, the information industry in the US will need in the next fifteen years another half-million systems engineers, system designers, and information specialists."

The application of computers to society and industry is resulting in an information processing revolution. As Marshall McLuhan states, "The computer is by all odds the most extraordinary of all the technological clothing ever devised by man, since it is the extension of our central nervous system. Beside it, the wheel is a mere hula-hoop, though that is not to be dismissed entirely."*

The student of computer science should learn not only the operation and application of computing devices, but also the consequences of their introduction into our society. Just as the release and control of atomic energy has resulted in what has been called the atomic age since 1944, so the release and control of information may result in the period after 1970 being labeled the computer age. It has been proposed that a National Computer Year be proclaimed on the model of the successful International Geophysical Year of the

*From WAR AND PEACE IN THE GLOBAL VILLAGE by Marshall McLuhan and Quentin Fiore. Copyright © 1968 by Marshall McLuhan, Quentin Fiore and Jerome Agel. By permission of Bantam Books, Inc.

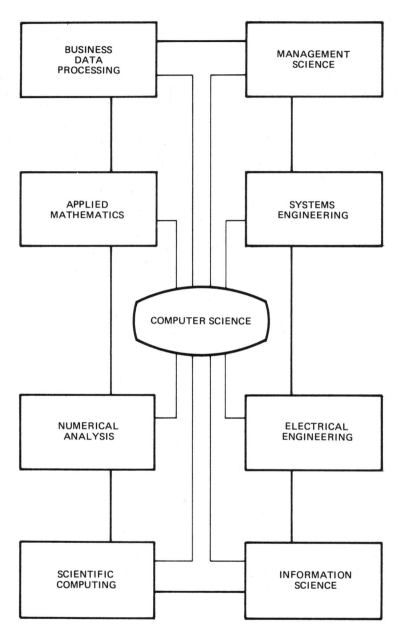

FIGURE 1-2   The relationship of computer science to other sciences.

past. The aim of the year, proposed by the Association for Computing Machinery, is that specialists from computer science, law, education, industry, and
many others should join to explore the various roles the computer could play
over the next decade.[6] A presidential proclamation for a National Computer
Year would challenge the entire nation to examine the impact of the computer
on our society and its potential for enabling progress in the decade of the 70's.
Eventually, computer systems will be developed for use in libraries, hospitals,
schools, production lines, the legislatures, and so on. Computers can assist in
overcoming the stock market paperwork crisis and soaring medical costs; easing
overburdened court calendars; and making out-of-date transportation systems
efficient, for example. A National Computer Year would be further indicative
of the information processing revolution and the pervasiveness of the computer
age.

1.2 THE GROWTH OF THE NUMBER OF COMPUTERS AND THEIR AP-PLICATIONS

Computer products and services make up the fastest-growing major industry in the world. Computer market sales grew from an estimated $339 million
in 1955 to about $11.3 billion in 1968, and are expected to exceed $30 billion
in 1975.[7] Computer systems increase the efficiency of government and industry and assist in the solution of complex problems. Without the use of computers, some tasks, such as landing a man on the moon and returning him safely
to earth, would be impossible. The computer has become an indispensable part
of our economy, and the growth of the computer industry is reasonably assured. The estimated value of computer equipment shipped by American manufacturers is shown in Table 1-1.[7]

TABLE 1-1

**Estimated Value of Computer Equipment Shipped
by American Manufacturers (Values in $ Millions)**

Year	Computers	Peripheral Equipment	Computer Services	Supplies	Total
1955	155	14	15	155	339
1960	1,620	105	125	370	2,220
1965	3,650	175	450	660	4,935
1968	9,050	300	970	960	11,300
1971	13,300	700	1,800	1,200	17,000
1973	18,500	1,000	2,500	1,400	23,400
1975	24,000	1,500	4,000	1,500	31,000

It has been estimated that the cumulative value of digital computers in use by business and government in 1970 equaled $18 billion. The cumulative value of computers during the period 1960 to 1970 is shown in Figure 1-3.

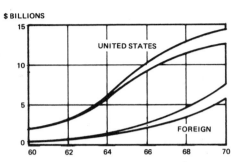

FIGURE 1-3   Cumulative value of business and government digital computers. Computers in use, 1960–1965 (actual) and 1966–1970 (estimated). Does not include process control or special military computers. Source: *Business Week*, Feb. 19, 1966, p. 113.

The top ten industrial firms in the computer industry are listed in Table 1-2, which shows the percentage of the market held by each firm in 1969. By far the largest and most influential firm is International Business Machines Corporation, which held 69.2% of the market.[8]

TABLE 1-2

Percentage of Computer Sales in 1969 by Computer Firm

1. IBM	69.2
2. Univac	5.6
3. Honeywell*	4.7
4. Burroughs	4.2
5. General Electric*	4.0
6. Control Data Corporation	3.6
7. Radio Corporation of America	3.2
8. National Cash Register	2.7
9. Xerox Data Systems	1.0
10. Digital Equipment Corporation	0.8

IBM has installed 32,256 computers in the US and 14,459 outside the US for a total of 46,715.[7] An estimate of the total number of computers installed by all US manufacturers by 1970 is 48,000 in the US and 25,000 outside the US. Thus, the total number of computers installed in the world is estimated to be equal to 73,000.

---

*Honeywell Corporation and General Electric Corporation completed a merger of their computer divisions in early 1971. The merged divisions continue under the name of Honeywell's computer division, which now accounts for 9.6% of computer sales.

During the growth of the number of computers during the past decade, the number of applications of computers to the needs of our society has also grown. The computer or information processing system has served such uses and applications as these:

- Control of new management and labor relationships
- Development of speedups that make planning mandatory
- Weapon against crime
- Means of dealing with many problems simultaneously
- Medical diagnostician, doctor, and druggist
- Cupid for ideal matches
- Marriage monitor and arbiter
- Substitute for salesman
- Immigration counselor
- Promoter of executive drop–outs
- Misunderstood teen–ager
- Encyclopedic legal counsel
- Nemesis of the bookie
- Ad man
- Author of Haiku
- Highway designer
- Management consultant
- Bank teller and credit rater
- Librarian
- Internal Revenue Service accountant
- Registrar for college students

Certainly it is clear that the computer has become the information machine of our age which itself is characterized by knowledge industries. As McLuhan suggests, the computer has become, to a great extent, the central nervous system of our society. It assists man in calculating, storing information, and making decisions. As the wheel introduced great changes in our world culture, so will the information machine. This book will show how computers are used and what their impact on society has been—and will be.

CHAPTER 1 PROBLEMS

P1-1. Give a definition of a computer in your own words.
P1-2. Give a definition of computer science.
P1-3. Name several knowledge industries.
P1-4. In what way or ways do you agree with McLuhan's statement that the computer is an extension of man's central nervous system?

P1-5. Name several uses for computers in industry and society that do not appear in the partial list in section 1-2.

P1-6. Based on the estimated number of computers in use in the United States, how many people does each computer serve on the average? How many people does the computer at your college serve?

CHAPTER 1 REFERENCES

1. A. Newell, A. J. Perlis, and H. Simon, "Computer Science," *Science,* Sept. 22, 1967, pp. 1373–1374.
2. R. W. Hamming, "One Man's View of Computer Science," *Journal of the Association for Computing Machinery*, Vol. 16, No. 1, Jan. 1969, pp. 3–12.
3. Report of the Curriculum Committee on Computer Science, *Communications of the Association for Computing Machinery*, Vol. II, No. 3, March, 1968, pp. 152–172.
4. P. F. Drucker, *The Age of Discontinuity,* Harper & Row, New York 1968.
5. M. McLuhan and Q. Fiore, "War and Peace in the Global Village," Bantam Books, New York, 1968.
6. R. C. Haavind, Editorial, *Computer Decisions*, April, 1970, p. 39.
7. *EDP Industry Reports*, Newtonville, Massachusetts, 1970.
8. "Computer Sales," *Control Engineering*, April 1970, p. 142.

2

A HISTORY OF COMPUTERS

2.1 PREHISTORIC AND EARLY CALCULATING DEVICES

Although the computer age may be said to have existed only since 1945, when the first electronic computer was introduced, man has apparently always had a need to process data and to calculate. The known history of computers and calculating machines in western civilization reaches back a thousand years before the birth of Christ, at which time the abacus was in use.

As you read the accounts of the development of computers, keep in mind the different ways of dealing with problems used by the various inventors; that is, think of how they conceived of the operations of mathematics and computation. Also, remember the effects the computing systems had on those who used them—for, as it has been pointed out many times, machines shape their users as much as the men who make them shape the machines.*

For centuries, man has tried to use power from other sources to do his work. One of the oldest forms of engineering is found in long-established efforts

---

*Some of this chapter is based on material from *Technology in Western Civilization, Volume II: Technology in the Twentieth Century*, edited by Melvin Kranzberg and Carroll W. Pursell, Jr. Copyright © 1967 by The Regents of the University of Wisconsin. Used by permission of Oxford University Press, Inc.

to make machines that will carry and change the nature of power and speed. Windmills, gear wheels, belts and pulleys, and block and tackle are devices which alter, transmit, and reduce or increase the magnitude of power or speed or both.

Gear wheels, however, have another function which early inventors were quick to notice. They can be adapted to count rotations. Clockworks depend on this principle. So does the odometer in your car, which measures the miles the car has traveled. It has evolved from a counting device described in an account dating back possibly two thousand years. This device, called Hero's odometer, is also found in one form or another in modern instruments for metering gas and electricity. It depends on the action of the pegged counting wheel. A schematic drawing of this device is shown below.

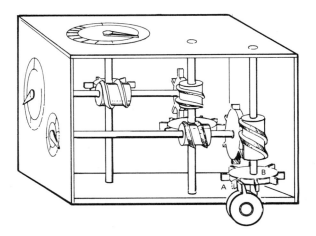

FIGURE 2-1   Hero's odometer.

In Figure 2-1, the pegged counting wheel A turns with the axle of the vehicle upon which the odometer is mounted (or it turns with a rotor shaft if the device is metering flow). Each time A revolves it moves B, the first wheel in the gear train, one peg. This motion is carried forward by other gears. Pointers attached to their shafts show how many revolutions each gear makes. These can be arranged to give direct readings in whatever quantities are being measured.

Equipment for counting or calculating has existed far longer than the odometer described above. The best example for our purposes is the abacus. It employs two principles which have probably been part of human experience from its earliest emergence. The first is the use of things to act as counters: stones, chips of wood, or fingers, for instance. These counters represent the abstract idea of quantity. A primitive shepherd could place a pebble in his pouch for each sheep when he let the flock out every morning. When the sheep returned at night, he could then remove a pebble for each sheep that crowded into the sheepfold. If there were pebbles left over, the shepherd knew there were sheep unaccounted for.

The second principle is the use of position to show different kinds of quantities. As the flock grew larger, the pebble system could become unwieldy. The shepherd (or his overseer, since Parkinson's Law has been in effect from earliest times) would place a pebble in a different counting place for each group of six sheep, or ten, or twenty. This procedure was adopted in early counting boards, and finally on counting frames on which small beads were strung. The pebbles of the counting boards were called *calculi*, from which our modern term *calculate* and related words are derived. The modern abacus finds extensive

FIGURE 2-2   An abacus. *Courtesy of The Smithsonian Institution.*

use in oriental countries. There is an annual competition for schoolchildren in Japan to find the most accurate and dextrous student of this art; complicated arithmetic and mathematical computations can be done with surprising speed on this counting frame.

Calculating machines have also existed in other forms from prehistoric times. One of the most fascinating calculating devices was built by stone age men. It is an attraction for tourists today. The ancient British stone monument, on the Salisbury Plain in southern England, is called Stonehenge. An astronomer and a team of computer scientists have analyzed the probable origins and use of Stonehenge; they have also published a theory of explanation.[2, 3] According to Hawkins, Stonehenge was built between 1900 and 1600 B.C. It required 1,497,680 man-days to construct.

FIGURE 2-3   Stonehenge. *Courtesy of Varian Data Machines.*

Why was Stonehenge built? With the aid of a computer, Hawkins examined the possible correlations of the alignments of the stones and the rise and set points of any heavenly bodies during the period 2000-1500 B.C. This avenue for examination was supported by the fact that if you stand in the center of Stonehenge on a clear midsummer morning (around June 22) you will see the sun rise almost exactly over the stone called "The heelstone." With the aid of the electronic computer, Hawkins was able to draw some startling conclusions about this ancient stone calculating device.

Apparently, Stonehenge may have been built as an excellent astronomical observatory, possibly used to predict the changes of the seasons. Prehistoric people were deeply concerned by eclipses of the sun and moon, and Stonehenge could have provided means for predicting them, too. The scientists who have studied this remarkable monument are astonished at the skill and precision with which the huge structure was assembled by primitive men who had no engineering devices to help them, but who were moved by a need for a device to aid their calculations.

A more recent evidence of man's need for computing equipment was discovered in a society scarcely more modern technologically than the neolithic one in which Stonehenge was built.* In the Peruvian Andes, about 500 years ago, the ruling Incas had established a "perfect" society—one for which all needs were supplied according to an elaborate system of information. This information was the basis for the Inca's decisions. The entire region over which the Incas ruled was divided and redivided, and all important facts were recorded from the level of individual families on up, through an elaborate system of counting and reporting on knotted cords called *quipus.* (The word *quipu* means "to knot"; the basic record was a knot in a cord.) These cords were assembled by the regional and district officers of a vast bureaucracy and carried by runners over a fully developed highway system to the capital at Cuzco. From there,

---

*Adapted with permission from "The Almost-Perfect Decision Device," from *Input for Modern Management,* Volume IV, Number 2, 1968. Published by Sperry Rand Univac.

requests for more information, and orders to be carried out, were sent back and forth.

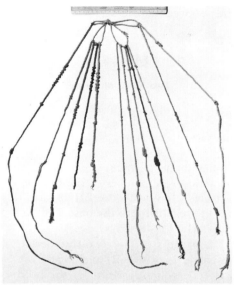

FIGURE 2-4 A *quipu. Courtesy The American Museum of Natural History.*

This system was perfected through four centuries and 13 successive reigns of Incas, until the Inca society was destroyed by the Spaniard Francisco Pizarro. The computing system they had devised never failed the Incas. In fact, the last orders to go from an Inca ruler to his subjects by *quipu* were those that brought back enough gold to fill the prison cell of the Inca named Atahuallpa. The gold was ordered to pay the ransom for the release of the Inca. The world knows of the Spanish treachery. Even after the invaders had killed Atahuallpa and placed a puppet ruler on his throne, the system of computing and accounting based on the *quipu* continued to function—perhaps too well. In the greedy hands of the Spanish conquerors, the *quipu* system became a tool of easy enslavement and exploitation.

2.2 FROM MECHANICAL DEVICES TO MODERN COMPUTERS

The practical applications of counting devices seemed to justify their invention and existence from prehistoric times. Nevertheless, there have always been persons who were interested in the abstract ideas behind the practical considerations; from such theoreticians have come many contributions with great practical potential. One person who enjoyed working with numbers, and who put this enjoyment to use in a manner which produced practical benefits, was

John Napier (1550–1617). This Scottish scholar observed that he could make tables of the results of multiplications. He also observed the relationship between arithmetic series and geometric series which can be seen in the table below.

TABLE 2-1

Two Kinds of Series

Arithmetic series:	1	2	3	4	5	6	7
Geometric series based on 2:	2	4	8	16	32	64	128

Napier invented and named the *logarithm*, which allows us to represent any member of the second series by a member of the first series. You can see that 2 multiplied by itself 5 times ("raised to the fifth power") is 32. We can express this fact by saying that the logarithm to the base 2 of 32 is 5. This expression is written $\log_2 32 = 5$. Similarly, $\log_2 8 = 3$.

We can *add* the logarithms of any two numbers to get the logarithm of their product. For instance, $\log_2 4 = 2$, and $\log_2 32 = 5$. Adding these logarithms, we get $2 + 5 = 7$; 7 is the logarithm of the product of 4×32, or 128. Had we multiplied 4×32, we would have obtained the same answer. In simple problems of this nature, the advantage of logarithms is not easily seen. However, for very large numbers and complicated calculations, a system in which multiplication is replaced by simple addition, for which the answers can be read easily from tables, has obvious advantages.

Napier put these advantages to use in a simple invention which has come to be called "Napier's bones" (from the ivory from which it was constructed) or "Napier's rods." He transcribed the results of multiplications from tables onto a series of rods. By arranging the rods side by side and matching up the numbers he wanted to multiply, Napier could read off the answer very quickly without having to do any calculations at all. In setting up this device, Napier combined the ideas of representing abstract quantities by numerical symbols and of showing their values by relative position on a measuring device—the system used by anyone who makes a yardstick.

The system of representing distance and motion by a point moving along a line, which came to us through Greek geometry, was next employed by Edmund Gunter, who marked off Napier's logarithms on a line and then added the logarithms by using a pair of dividers. By 1654 (Napier having published information about his rods in 1617), Robert Bissaker placed the Gunter–Napier lines on sliding wooden strips, or rules, thus inventing the first form of the modern slide rule. Within two hundred years the slide rule was perfected, providing an extremely versatile hand calculating device still very much in evidence today.

By 1700, then, the numerical, or *digital* calculator, represented by the abacus, and the *analog* calculator, represented by the slide rule, were in common use.*

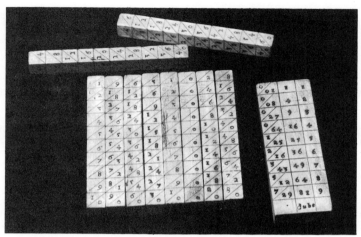

FIGURE 2-3 Napier's bones. *Courtesy of The Smithsonian Institution.*

To these useful machines, Blaise Pascal (1623–1662) added a third which combined characteristics of both: the numerical adding machine. Pascal was working as a tax clerk. He found it wearying to add the three kinds of coins with which he had to deal, so he invented a counting machine which was similar in some ways to Hero's odometer.

In Pascal's machine, which showed numbers printed on the rotating gears, the adjacent wheels had pins like the one in Hero's machine. When the first wheel was rotated one time, a pin on its edge advanced the wheel in the next place to the left, just as the modern odometer changes its indication from, say, 09 (miles) to 10 (miles). Both addition and subtraction could be performed on Pascal's instrument. Although it was not carefully made and therefore was occasionally inaccurate, it became the prototype for counting devices which can be found everywhere today. An especially handy mechanical adder is often used

---

Digital refers to digits, which are the counting numbers (in informal usage; technically, "numbers" are abstractions and integers are the symbols for them). The digital computer works with numbers, while the *analog* computer works with quantities, such as lengths on rulers, that stand for numbers. You can measure two feet digitally by marking off 24 inches on a yardstick; analogically, by putting two one-foot rulers end-to-end. You can measure the passage of a minute digitally by counting 60 seconds, one at a time; analogically, by observing the circular displacement of the minute hand around one–sixtieth of the clock face. Napier's bones worked with digits, so his was a digital computing system. Gunter's measurements were analogous to numbers; the larger distances stood for larger numbers. His was an analog computing system.

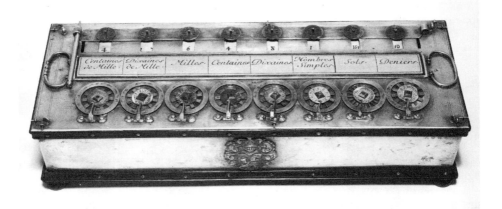

FIGURE 2-6   Pascal's adder. *Courtesy of IBM Corporation.*

by modern shoppers to calculate their expected bills; another is used to count crowds passing through a gate; others calculate the numbers of copies turned out by duplicating machines. Of his invention, Pascal himself wrote in 1649:

> Dear reader, this notice will serve to inform you that I submit to the public a small machine of my invention, by means of which you alone may, without any effort, perform all the operations of arithmetic, and may be relieved of the work which has often times fatigued your spirit, when you have worked with the counters or with the pen. As for simplicity of movement of the operations, I have so devised it that, although the operations of arithmetic are in a way opposed the one to the other—as addition to subtraction, and multiplication to division—nevertheless they are all performed on this machine by a single unique movement. The facility of this movement of operation is very evident since it is just as easy to move one thousand or ten thousand dials, all at one time, if one desires to make a single dial move, although all accomplish the movement perfectly. The most ignorant find as many advantages as the most experienced. The instrument makes up for ignorance and for lack of practice, and even without any effort of the operator, it makes possible shortcuts by itself, whenever the numbers are set down.

Gottfried Wilhelm von Leibniz (1646-1716) was next to advance the design of mechanical calculating devices. His machine, built in 1694, was based on the principle of repeated addition. Instead of multiplying 25 by 7, Leibniz added 25 to 25 seven times. His machine was not constructed well, and therefore was not entirely reliable, but it was a refinement of ideas of earlier centuries. There are many adaptations of Leibniz's machine in modern office calculating equipment.

Note that none of the machines described so far could do anything other than compute or store information put into them by their human operators (or by outside agents, as in the case of the rotating wheel in Hero's odometer). In this sense, we may say that all of these devices were *passive*.

Neither Leibniz nor Pascal was an engineer. It took many years before engineers turned their talents to making equipment that was precise enough to ensure accuracy in computing machinery. However, improvements were soon to come from the clock making industry, which was refining its machine parts steadily from crude wooden works to dependable and rugged metal ones. In the eighteenth and nineteenth centuries, major advances were made in metalworking and in shaping tools and gears to fine tolerances, so that eventually precision clockwork machinery could be built. The same skills could also be applied to machinery necessary for calculators and eventually for computers.

It can be seen that by the eighteenth century two influences combined to provide the force from which the modern computer has evolved. The first was that of the counting system, whether by markers, counters, or rotating gears. The second was that of the mechanical precision which came with the manufacture of refined instruments.

By the early twentieth century, mechanical calculators had become very important as tools of science and commerce. Probably the most significant inventor and contributor to this development was a gifted English mathematician, Charles Babbage (1792–1871). In many ways Babbage may be considered the grandfather of the computer—yet his work was to lead only to failure. Babbage was a theoretician. By 1823, he had evolved several basic concepts for what he called a "Difference Engine." Babbage had intended this machine, in the spirit

FIGURE 2-7   Charles Babbage. *Photo Courtesy of Science Museum, London.*

of his age, to relieve man of constant drudgery. The Difference Engine was designed to calculate with numbers, to store information, to select different ways of solving problems according to the most efficient approaches,* and to deliver printed solutions to problems both during the solutions and at their conclusions. Unlike the abacus, Pascal's adder, and Leibniz's multiplier, Babbage's machine would not need constant attention and information from its human operator. It would be entirely automatic. Furthermore, Babbage saw his engine as one composed of several smaller engines, each working together with the others, each performing its own separate chore: the "mill," which did the arithmetic; the receiver, to take in information; the printer, to put out information; a device to transfer information from one component to another; and a "store" of information. One can grasp the magnitude of the problems Babbage faced, and perhaps a little of the overreaching ambition that brought him to grief, by reading his own description, written in *The Life of a Philosopher* in 1864:

> Every formula which the Analytical Engine can be required to compute consists of certain algebraical operations to be performed upon given letters, and of certain other modifications depending on the numerical value assigned to those letters. There are therefore two sets of cards, the first to direct the nature of the operations to be performed—these are called operation cards: the other to direct the particular variables on which those cards are required to operate—these latter are called variable cards. Now the symbol of each variable or constant, is placed at the top of a column capable of containing any required number of digits. Under this arrangement, when any formula is required to be computed, a set of operation cards must be strung together, which contain the series of operations in the order in which they occur. Another set of cards must then be strung together, to call in the variables into the mill, the order in which they are required to be acted upon. Each operation card will require three other cards, two to represent the variables and constants and their numerical values upon which the previous operation card is to act, and one to indicate the variable on which the arithmetical result of this operation is to be placed. But each variable has below it, on the same axis, a certain number of figure-wheels marked on their edges with the ten digits: upon these any number the machine is capable of holding can be placed. Whenever the variables are ordered into the mill, these

*It is not uncommon for modern computers to provide solutions to problems—solutions which the programmers did not have in mind. Choosing the most effective of alternate routes to a solution is called *branching*.

figures will be brought in, and the operation indicated by the preceding card will be performed upon them. The result of this operation will then be replaced in the store.

Although Babbage's machine, which called for the elements found in modern computers, resembled a human intelligence in some of its characteristics, it would have depended entirely on the instructions fed into it by the operator. Nevertheless, it represented a significant advance over earlier machines. The astonishing fact about its development, however, is that it was never built! Babbage spent his life dealing unsuccessfully with the engineering difficulties attendant upon making such a complicated machine. His plans were too ambitious. Modern computer experts have concluded from his papers that the machine would have worked if it had been built, but fate did not allow Babbage that successful culmination to his career.

In the eighteenth century, French artisans had become highly skilled in manufacturing intricately–designed fabrics on looms. The machinery for weaving the designs was directed by a method perfected by Joseph Jacquard (1752–1834) early in the nineteenth century. Jacquard used cards punched with holes to position threads for the weaving process. A hole allowed a hooked wire, containing a thread, to be inserted into the pattern. If no hole was present, no wire emerged and no colored thread was allowed into the pattern during that operation of the loom. For each operation, a card was provided; the whole collection of cards made up a program which directed the weaving.

FIGURE 2-8 Jacquard's loom. Program cards, attached to each other in belt fashion, fed from the floor into the loom. *Courtesy of IBM Corporation.*

The punched card appealed to manufacturers of calculating equipment. In 1890, the United States Census was compiled with the aid of Hollerith computing machines, named for Herman Hollerith, an inventor who had adapted the punched card system to the special needs of census-taking. Hollerith had added electrical sensing equipment to take advantage of the information holes in the punched cards.*

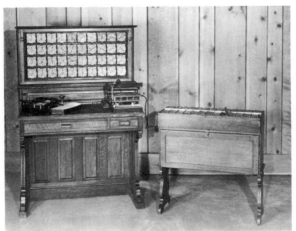

FIGURE 2-9   Hollerith equipment. *Courtesy of IBM Corporation.*

By 1937, the punched card operation, combined with electrical drive mechanisms (also added by Hollerith), had become so efficient that they suggested timely application to the newest form of computing machine, then taking shape in the imagination of Howard Aiken, an instructor in applied mathematics who also held a doctorate in physics. (Aiken repeated much of what Babbage had accomplished nearly 100 years before. However, he learned of Babbage's work three years after beginning his own—thus needlessly duplicating the efforts of his predecessor!)[9]

Aiken worked out a plan to set mechanical calculators to working on mathematical problems in controlled sequences. He set up a project to develop the necessary equipment, and with the support of International Business Machines Corporation and Harvard University, and assistance from four co-workers from IBM, he built the first computer. This machine, called International Business Machines Automatic Sequence Controlled Calculator, and also known as the Harvard Mark I computer, was presented to Harvard in August, 1944. It was the first information-processing machine.

The Mark I was electrically-powered. Instructions and data were fed into it by punched paper tape. The components worked on electrical, electronic and

*Hollerith's company was to become the International Business Machines Corporation.

mechanical principles. Although the machine was very large, and limited in speed and applications by comparison with modern machines, it was the first to possess all the characteristics of a true computer.

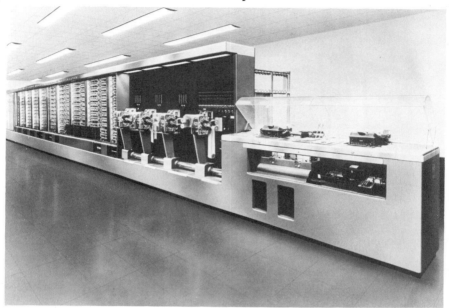

FIGURE 2-10   Mark I. *Courtesy of IBM Corporation.*

The first electronic computer was built in 1946 by J. P. Eckert and J. W. Mauchly at the University of Pennsylvania. The nearly instantaneous working of electronic components made it possible for this machine, called ENIAC,* to multiply two ten–digit numerals in three thousandths of a second, compared to roughly three seconds for Mark I. ENIAC contained 18,000 vacuum tubes; it was huge, taking up the walls of a room 20 by 40 feet in size. Its use was limited to the special problems of ballistics. The designers avoided the mistakes that had caused Babbage to fail, among them those which come from trying to accomplish too much at one time.

Mark I and ENIAC were digital computers. Analog computers also became available at about the same time, in part through the need for machinery to control guns and radars in World War II. Among such devices were the servomechanisms which translated motion into signals to which either machines or men could respond. Automatic-cannon gunsights, for instance, were built so

---

*Electronic Numerical Integrator and Computer. The use of acronyms like ENIAC increased rapidly from this point, with engineers vying with each other to find names that would yield interesting or catchy acronyms. It was not long before a MANIAC appeared, for instance.

FIGURE 2-11   ENIAC. *Courtesy of UNIVAC Division of Sperry-Rand Corporation.*

that, as the gunner tracked his target, a computing device would cause the sight image to change, forcing the gunner to "lead" his target sufficiently to hit it in motion.

It may be said that the modern electronic computer is not so much directly related to the earlier forms of calculating machines as it is a result of their evolution under the influence of new technology in radio, radar, and telephone transmissions. Eventually, computer designers refined the various components of the computer system (described by Babbage a century before) by introducing transistors and printed circuits. This made possible smaller and still more efficient machinery.

Calculation in modern machines is usually carried out in the binary system, which can be adapted to carry both instructions and data to the machine. This possibility arises from the latter-day application of a system of logic invented by the English mathematician, George Boole (1815-1864). The Boolean system shows how statements can be related to each other logically. It provides a way of working through difficult problems, and its fundamental simplicity suits it well to applications involving switches and electrical circuits—as in telephone switching and digital computers.

In the mid-40's, John Von Neumann, a brilliant mathematician at Princeton University, demonstrated how binary logic and arithmetic could be made to work together in calculating and in forming stored programs. Von Neumann demonstrated that one could encode instructions to the machine in the same language used for the data it processed. This especially brilliant demonstration made it possible to mix instructions and data in the program; both could also be stored in the computer.

FIGURE 2-12   John Von Neumann with the IAS computer, completed in 1952 under his direction. *Courtesy of The Smithsonian Institution.*

These arrangements make possible the design, construction, and operation of units which can be employed separately or added to each other in many combinations. They also make it possible to store programs and data in memory components which are compact, accurate, and easily accessible. Finally, Von Neumann's legacy of proof also makes it possible for computers to transmit information to, and to receive it from, other computer installations. A company can purchase a large central computer and can program all of its different operations—from manufacturing through sales and inventory control, for instance—through the application of the computer language in the binary means of expression.

SUMMARY

Each man stands upon the shoulders of the man who preceded him. While Eckert and Mauchly developed the first electronic computer, they had the developments of their predecessors to build upon. Those previous developments are numerous, some of them are listed in chronological order in Table 2-2. From the time of the first calculator and decision device, to the most recent electronic computer, man has done "the impossible." In Chapter 19, we examine what may develop in the future. However, we are certainly impressed by the developments of the past. In the next chapter, we examine the nature of computers and how they work.

TABLE 2-2

Historical Development of Calculating Machines
(Dates are approximate.)

1600 B.C.	Stonehenge
1000 B.C.	Abacus
1400 A.D.	Quipu
1617	Napier's "bones"
1642	Pascal's calculator
1673	Liebniz's calculator
1801	Jacquard's punched-card looms
1822	Babbage's difference engine
1890	Hollerith's punched-card tabulators
1911	Monroe Calculator, first mass-produced desk calculator
1930	Electric desk calculators
1937	Aiken's Mark I
1945	Von Neumann's proposal for a stored-program computer
1946	ENIAC computer
1954	Univac I computer commercially available
1955	IBM 650 computer commercially available

CHAPTER 2 PROBLEMS

P2-1. Calculating machines have helped man through the ages. What two ideas were used to develop an abacus?

P2-2. What calculation was possible using Napier's bones? On what principle was it based?

P2-3. What limited the practical success of Liebniz's multiplier and Pascal's mechanical adder?

P2-4. What was the prime contribution of Jacquard toward the development of a modern computer? Can you name a musical instrument which uses the same device Jacquard introduced?

P2-5. What was the prime contribution of Hollerith and of Von Neumann?

P2-6. Mechanical desk calculators are used extensively today. When was the first commercially mass-produced calculator available? On what mechanical principle does the mechanical calculator work?

P2-7. The *quipu* was an information device used by the Incas. How was information stored and transmitted?

P2-8. If those who constructed Stonehenge had 1,000 men working six days per week, how many years would it have taken to construct Stonehenge, according to Hawkins' estimate?

CHAPTER 2 REFERENCES

1. T. M. Smith, "Origins of the Computer" in *Technology in Western Civilization*, Volume II, edited by M. Kranzberg and C. W. Pursell, Jr., Oxford University Press, New York, 1967.
2. G. S. Hawkins, "The Secret of Stonehenge," *Harper's Magazine*, June 1964, pp. 96–99.
3. G. S. Hawkins, *Stonehenge Decoded*, Doubleday Publishing Co., Garden City, New York, 1965.
4. "The Almost–Perfect Decision Device," from *Input for Modern Management*, Sperry Rand Univac, New York, Volume IV, Number 2, 1968, pp. 3-7.
5. R. R. Rusch, *Computers: Their History and How They Work*, Simon and Schuster, New York, 1969.
6. P. Morrison and E. Morrison, *Charles Babbage and his Calculating Engines*, Dover Publications, Inc., New York, 1961.
7. J. Bernstein, *The Analytical Engine*, Alfred Knopf, Inc., New York, 1963.
8. D. W. Kean, *The Author of the Analytic Engine*, Thompson Book Co., Washington, D.C., 1966.
9. H. Aiken, "Proposed Calculating Machine," reprinted in *IEEE Spectrum*, Vol. 1, No. 8, 1964.
10. A. H. Taub, ed., *John Von Neumann: Collected Works*, Macmillan Co., New York, 1963.

3

THE NATURE OF COMPUTERS AND COMPUTING

3.1 INFORMATION PROCESSING AND THE ELECTRONIC DIGITAL COMPUTER

The electronic computer allows man to increase his productivity and permits him to do tasks he would be unable to complete without the computer. As we found in Chapter 1, the computer is a machine capable of (1) accepting data; (2) performing described operations on the data, and (3) providing the results of these operations. Thus the computer also permits man to improve his output per unit of time, or productivity. We can say that the computer's two most important contributions as a tool are to increase (1) the speed of operation, and (2) accuracy and quality of operation in terms of productivity.

Of course, when we consider these two factors, we realize that the computer enables us to accomplish tasks that we would probably never even attempt manually. For example, if the number of input data is greater than several million and the time necessary to accomplish a task is greater than fifty years, we would probably never attempt it. Yet it is just such tasks that we can ask the computer to accomplish.

Symbols are the basis of any language. The computer accepts and processes symbols in order to provide information. The symbols that today's computers process are the letters of the alphabet and numbers, as well as several useful algebraic and business symbols.

In this text, we consider the uses and applications of the electronic digital computer. The term *computer* has already been discussed in Chapter 1 and reviewed above. The term *electronic* implies that the computer is powered by electrical and electronic devices rather than by mechanical ones or those affected by heat or air pressure. Here *digital* refers to discrete, noncontinuous quantities, as contrasted with continuous quantities. For example, the computer accepts individual numbers, or signs, or other symbols. This set of statements leads to the definition:

ELECTRONIC DIGITAL COMPUTER An information–processing device that accepts and processes data represented by discrete symbols. It is constructed primarily of electric or electronic devices.

A typical electronic digital computer, the IBM System/360 Model 40 Data Processing System, is shown in Figure 3-1. The electronic devices which constitute the computer are identified by function in Figure 3-1. We can use the

FIGURE 3-1 The IBM System/360, Model 40 data processing system. *Courtesy IBM Corporation.*

computer to process the input data by sorting them, or by completing a calculation, for example. Of course, there are many ways to accomplish a given task; the two advantages we seek are increased *speed* and increased *quality* of processing. The process of accounting, for instance, is a good example of a task most readily accomplished by a digital computer system. Over the years accounting has shifted in great part from ledgers to punched cards, and then to computer processes.

Information processing is a series of planned actions and operations upon input data, taken to achieve a desired result. The actions taken may be illustrated by a common data processing operation which a person usually accomplishes manually, but which is increasingly accomplished automatically by data processing service companies: completing a Federal Income Tax Form.

Recall Figure 1-1, which shows the data input, the data processing action, and finally the information output. In the case of the IRS form, the output information required is the amount of tax owed. The data input is the person's salary or wages and income; deductions; and other information, such as the number of dependents. This is the series of planned actions taken upon the input data to calculate the tax due:

(1) Provide the necessary input data.
(2) Record the input data on the Tax Form 1040 worksheet.
(3) Examine the Tax Instruction Booklet for the necessary instructions.
(4) Carry out the necessary arithmetic calculations.
(5) Record the tax due on the correct line on the Form 1040.

As is often the case, the tax calculation will require carrying out steps 3 and 4 several times* prior to recording the tax due in step 5, since we must consult the instructions at different stages. This example of information processing is illustrated graphically in Figure 3-2.

In the preceding example, information–processing required:

(1) Data input
(2) Storage and retrieval of data, and instructions for data–processing actions
(3) Arithmetic steps
(4) Output of result
(5) Control of all steps above by the individual taxpayer

Now, if we want to construct an automatic information–processor, we shall find it necessary to carry out the same steps to complete the processing. A computer follows a similar process. It is composed of five basic units, as shown in Figure 3-3. The five basic units or functions are:

(1) An *input* unit or function which accepts the necessary input data and instructions
(2) A *storage* or *memory* unit in which computer instructions and the data as well as intermediate results are stored

---

*Each time a task is carried out, the carrying–out is called an *iteration*.

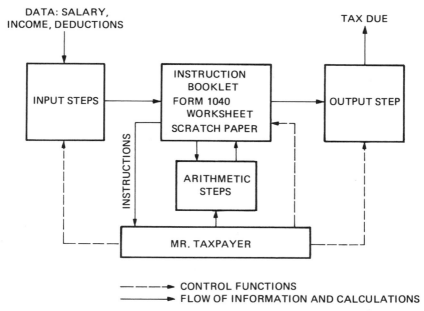

DATA: SALARY,
INCOME, DEDUCTIONS

TAX DUE

INPUT STEPS

INSTRUCTION
BOOKLET
FORM 1040
WORKSHEET
SCRATCH PAPER

OUTPUT STEP

INSTRUCTIONS

ARITHMETIC
STEPS

MR. TAXPAYER

------► CONTROL FUNCTIONS
───────► FLOW OF INFORMATION AND CALCULATIONS

FIGURE 3-2   The information processing operation for calculating income tax.

(3) An *arithmetic* unit in which numbers can be added, subtracted, compared in size to other numbers, etc.
(4) An *output* unit which provides the desired result in a suitable form, such
as a printed number
(5) A *control* unit which controls the other four units, directs their order
of operation and supervises the overall operation of the computer

The several devices which may accomplish the function of input, output, and
storage for the IBM System/360 Model 40 are indicated in Figure 3-1. The
arithmetic and control functions are accomplished by the central processing
unit, located in the module on which the console is mounted.

The basic unit of the electronic digital computer is the arithmetic unit. It
performs the arithmetic operations accurately, reliably, and at high speed. However, the high-speed ability of the arithmetic unit would be wasted if for each
operation it had to go back to the input unit for the same information at
every step. The storage unit holds the data, the instructions and the intermediate results of the calculations. (The incorporation of instructions in the
storage unit for ready and high-speed accessibility is the stored-program concept introduced by John Von Neumann.) Since the instructions are in the
memory, just as the intermediate calculation results are, it is possible for the
computer to modify the instructions themselves as the calculation progresses.

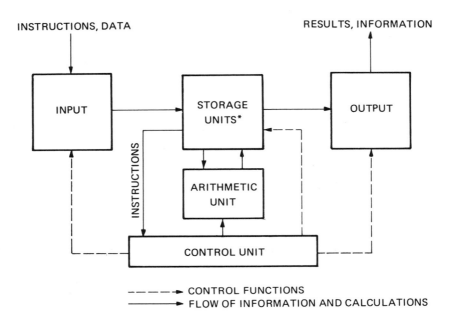

FIGURE 3-3   The five basic units of an electronic digital computer.

*Instructions may be stored in the storage units (see text). This feature makes it possible to build programs within programs, which in turn enables the computer to work very rapidly without requiring many repeated references to input.

The control unit supervises the flow of information and calculations and requests from memory the instructions and data necessary at each stage in the calculation sequence. The control functions are shown as dotted lines in Figure 3-3.

The input and output units serve as connections between the user and the machine. The input device may also serve as the output device, as in the case of the typewriter shown in Figure 3-1. We may also enter data on a magnetic tape, punched cards, or other media. Note the output line printer shown in Figure 3-1. We consider some specific input and output devices in Chapter 10.

3.2 THE NATURE OF COMPUTERS

An electronic digital computer possesses three advantages which make it extremely useful. They are:

(1) High speed of operation
(2) Precision and accuracy
(3) Reliability

Modern digital computers are constructed of electronic devices which enable the computer to complete an arithmetic calculation in approximately one-millionth of a second—or less! The increase in the speed of computers is shown in Figure 3-4a, which gives the number of additions per second.[1] Figure 3-4b shows the speed of storage in the central processing unit, in thousands of additions per second.

The size of computers has decreased by a factor of 100 since 1955. We expect another decrease, by a factor of 100, by 1975; see Figure 3-4c. The size of the central storage unit averages about 10 cubic feet as indicated. This is the size of a small trunk or file cabinet. As an indication of the size of a modern computer, a typical small computer is shown in Figure 3-5. These small computers are commonly called minicomputers. They provide the power and speed of many large computers of only five years ago. A complete small computer system is shown in Figure 3-6; it uses small punched cards. The system, called the IBM System/3, is designed especially for small business use. Through the utilization of high-speed electronic devices, notably transistors and solid-state devices, the speed and size of electronic digital computers has improved dramatically during the past decade. If the trends continue, we shall have a computer the size of a shoe box capable of a billion additions per second—by the end of this decade.

In 1970, IBM announced a new series, System/370, which increased the internal speed five times over that of the System 360/Model 50, which was announced in 1964.[2] As an article in the *Wall Street Journal* indicates, there are many more announcements of faster and smaller computers to be expected in the next several years. For example, see Figure 3-9, page 37.

The second advantage of an electronic digital computer is the great precision available in the calculation process. The *precision* of a computer may be defined in this way:

PRECISION The degree of exactness or discrimination with which a quantity is stated. The amount of detail used in representing the data.

Precision is to be compared with *accuracy*. For example, four-place numerals are less precise than six-place numerals; nevertheless, a properly computed four-place numeral might be more accurate than an improperly computed six-place numeral. The *accuracy* of a computer is defined as follows:

ACCURACY The degree of freedom from error; that is, the degree of conformity to truth or to a rule.

As an exercise, consider two computers which are to add the number exactly one (1) to the number exactly zero (0). We expect a result exactly equal to one. The output we receive from computer A is 1.00 and from computer B is 1.0000. Which is more precise?

Now consider computers C and D and give them the same calculation to perform. The result from computer C is 1.000 and from computer D is 1.0100.

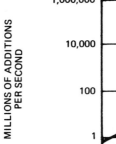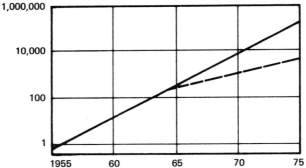

FIGURE 3-4a   Computing power in the United States.

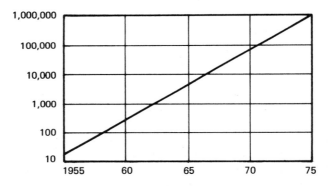

FIGURE 3-4b   CPU/Storage speed in thousands of additions per second.

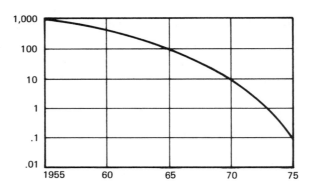

FIGURE 3-4c   CPU/Storage size in cubic feet.

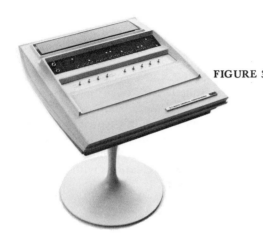

FIGURE 3-5 The NOVA minicomputer, which has a memory cycle time of less than three millionths of a second. It sells for less than $10,000 for the basic system. *Courtesy Data General Corporation.*

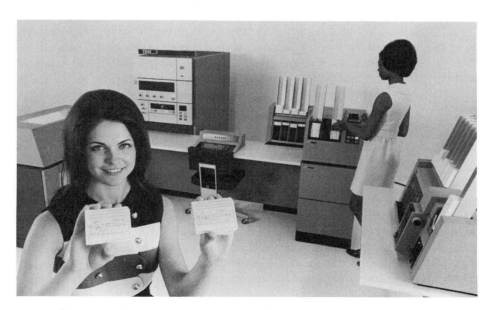

FIGURE 3-6 The IBM System/3, which utilizes a small punched card and is designed for small-business use. The card is one-third the size of the familiar punched card, but it holds 20 percent more information. *Courtesy IBM Corporation.*

Which computer is more precise and which is more accurate? Consider your answer before reading the following explanation.

Computer B is more *precise* than computer A, since it provides an answer with great detail, with four decimal places for B as contrasted with two decimal places in the case in A. Computer D is more precise than computer C since it provides four decimal places while C provides only three decimal places. However, computer C is more accurate, since we know that the exact or truthful answer is 1.0000, and the answer from computer D is in error in the second decimal place.

We strive to obtain and utilize computers which are both precise and accurate. Computers with both characteristics can be bought, but the limitation on extreme accuracy and precision is the excessive cost for computers which give both. Typically, a computer is able to perform calculations with numbers to a precision and accuracy of ten decimal places.

The third advantage of the electronic digital computer is *reliability*, which is defined:

> RELIABILITY The quality of freedom from failure, usually expressed as the probability that a failure will not occur in a given amount of use.

The reliability of a typical computer might be expressed as a 95 percent probability that it will *not* miscalculate one error in one week, and that it will *not* cease functioning within a month. (A computer is not affected by fatigue, boredom, or numbers with many decimal places as a man carrying out similar calculations would be. Thus, a computer is immensely more reliable than a man in completing long, difficult calculations.)

Now let us consider some of the disadvantageous characteristics of electronic digital computers. Three of these characteristics are:

(1) Limited inherent intelligence
(2) Limited language–handling capacity
(3) High cost

We say that the computer has limited inherent intelligence because it must be told what to do. (As we shall find in Chapter 18, man is developing an artificial intelligence capability for special–purpose computers. Nevertheless, in general, the digital computer can do only what man has instructed it to do.)

Also, the computer possesses a very limited language–handling capacity at present. Typically, its vocabulary is limited to a hundred words or so, and its grammar is primitive. However, computers are being developed which will have expanded language capabilities. At present, only a very small subset of the English language can be addressed to a computer—perhaps that possessed by a student in first grade.

The cost of computing power is illustrated in Figure 3–7, which shows the central storage cost in dollars per million additions. Notice how the cost of

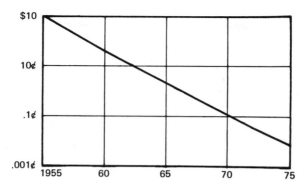

FIGURE 3-7   CPU/Storage cost in dollars per million additions.

storage has decreased by a factor of five hundred over the past decade. Generally, new and faster models of computers, in a given series, have appeared every four years on the average. Computer purchasers have almost always found it economically advantageous to change to the newer models. For example, a model may cost twice as much, but its speed will be four times as great, justifying the added cost.

A relationship between the computing power (essentially speed) and the cost of the computer has been deduced by Grosch:[3]

$$\text{Cost of computer} = \text{constant} \times \sqrt{\text{computing power}}$$

This relationship, often called Grosch's Law, has been faithfully followed during the years 1944 to 1967. Computing power increases as the cost squared.

$$\text{Computing power} = \text{constant} \times (\text{cost})^2$$

For example, if we double the cost, we can obtain four times the computing power. Of course, larger computers do demand larger operating staffs, which increase operating costs somewhat.

In summary, we find there are basically three advantages and three disadvantages in electronic computers. They are as follows:

Advantages	*Disadvantages*
High Speed	Limited Intelligence
High Precision and Accuracy	Limited Language Capability
Reliability	Cost

A large computer system is shown in Figure 3-8. This machine, the GE-635, has a memory speed of one-millionth of a second and can add more than a half-million numbers each second. It sells for several million dollars and rents for

FIGURE 3-8   The GE-635 information system. The GE-635 has a memory cycle speed of
one millionth of a second, and it can add more than a half-million numbers
each second. *Courtesy General Electric Company.*

upward of $100,000 per month. These speeds and costs are illustrative of the
computers of the early 1970's.

As we shall find in the following chapters, the advantages far outweigh the
disadvantages in a great number of needs and applications in industry, government, education, and business. There are many activities that we could not accomplish without the computer; like all helpful friends, however, it possesses
mixed characteristics. Nevertheless, the nature and structure of the electronic
digital computer is such that it is helpful and beneficial to man, as we shall continually discover in the ensuing chapters.

CHAPTER 3 PROBLEMS

P3-1. What are the two primary contributions of the digital computer?
P3-2. Consider one of the following applications of computers to a process
familiar to you and substantiate the two primary contributions of the
computer in this application.
  (a) registering for college courses
  (b) checking, recording, and balancing checking accounts
  (c) billing credit card accounts

FIGURE 3-9   The IBM System/370 Model 155, which is approximately four times as fast as the IBM System/360 Model 50. *Courtesy IBM Corporation.*

P3-3.   Complete the definitions:
  (a) An electronic digital computer is a device that accepts and processes data that is represented by:
  (b) The accuracy of a computer is defined as the degree of freedom from:
  (c) The reliability of a computer is defined as the quality of:

P3-4.   What is the function of the memory unit of a computer?

P3-5.   According to Grosch's Law, what would be the cost of a future computer which would operate at one hundred million additions per second if the present computer in a specific line operates at four million additions per second and costs two million dollars?

P3-6.   The computer has permitted man to increase his output per hour and the quality of his output. The increase in productivity in the United States for the years 1947 to 1966 is shown in Figure P3-6. Estimate the percentage growth of productivity for the decade 1955 to 1965 and compare it with the percentage growth in computing power in the United States.

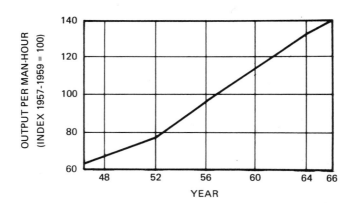

FIGURE P3-6   Productivity, 1947 to 1966. Source: *Automation*, June, 1970, p. 53.

CHAPTER 3 REFERENCES

1. B. W. Boehm, "Keeping the Upper Hand in the Man–Computer Partnership," *Astronautics and Aeronautics*, April, 1967.
2. S. Penn, "IBM Unveils 2 Computers in a New Line with Microscopic Circuits; More Likely," *Wall Street Journal*, July 1, 1970, page 5.
3. R. W. Cole, *Introduction to Computing*, McGraw-Hill Book Co., New York, 1969.
4. C. Davidson and E. Koenig, *Computers: Introduction to Computers and Applied Computing Concepts*, John Wiley and Sons, Inc., New York, 1967.
5. *Introduction to IBM Data Processing Systems*, International Business Machines Corp., White Plains, New York, 1967.
6. D. D. Spencer, *Fundamentals of Digital Computers,* Howard Sams & Co., Inc., Indianapolis, 1969.
7. T. H. Crowley, *Understanding Computers*, McGraw-Hill Book Co., New York, 1967.

4

PROBLEM SOLVING AND ALGORITHMS

4.1 PROBLEM SOLVING

The computer is capable of solving problems by accepting data, performing prescribed operations on the data, and supplying the results of these operations. In this chapter we consider the process of problem solving. In ensuing chapters, we may then discuss the specific application of the computer to solving problems.

The solution of mathematical problems proceeds through these four basic stages:

1. Precise formulation
2. Development of a mathematical model
3. Mathematical analysis
4. Computation of a solution

The first step is the precise formulation of the problem to be solved. This step requires an explicit statement of the problem so we can proceed to the second step, which is the development of a mathematical model. To get a model, we must identify the relationships among the variables under consideration. The third step is to apply the methods and procedures of mathematical analysis. The final step is to carry out the necessary computation to obtain the desired result.

Note that it is not beneficial to expend time and energy calculating a result to a precision beyond the inherent accuracy of the model.

Let us consider the solution of a specific problem.

EXERCISE 4-1

You wish to travel from Athens, Ohio to Columbus, Ohio in your automobile on the freeway in the shortest possible time. Find the shortest possible time for the trip, assuming you will not exceed the speed limit and the freeway is unobstructed.

Stage 1. The problem is to calculate the shortest time for the trip. Assume travel at the maximum lawful speed over the entire distance, with neither delay nor obstruction.

Stage 2. A model of an automobile traveling on a freeway must be developed in terms of the speed and distance traveled. We recall the physical relationship

$$d = s \times t \qquad (4\text{-}1)$$

where d = distance traveled

s = average speed of travel

t = time spent in traveling

Stage 3. We want to know the shortest time necessary to travel the distance, so we solve equation 4-1 for time (t), obtaining

$$t = \frac{d}{s} \qquad (4\text{-}2)$$

Stage 4. Now we complete the calculation process by substituting the proper distance and speed. The distance from Athens to Columbus is 75 miles and the speed limit on the freeway is 60 miles per hour. We find that

$$t = \frac{75 \text{ miles}}{60 \text{ miles/hour}} = 1\,\tfrac{1}{4} \text{ hours}$$

Therefore, 1 ¼ hours is the shortest possible time to travel the distance.

Now that we have completed the exercise, we find that we accomplished several steps in the problem process under the first and second stages. Let us restate the four stages of problem solving with the subsidiary steps noted:

1. Precise formulation
   a. Recognize the problem.
   b. Identify the important variables.
   c. Formulate a precise problem statement.
2. Development of a mathematical model
   a. Make idealizations and assumptions about the variables and their relationships.
   b. Formulate a mathematical model.
3. Mathematical analysis
4. Computation of a solution
   a. Compute some specific results.

b. Check these results for accuracy by comparing them with some known measured results.

c. Check the precision of the results and compare the precision and accuracy with appropriate standards.

One is often required to solve problems which are not entirely mathematical but which can be formulated precisely. An example of this type of problem occurs in the game of checkers. A mathematical model which represents the process of playing the game can be set up so that one can analyze the various possible moves in the game mathematically. Such a model has been used to obtain computer solutions to the game. In effect, the computer uses the mathematical models to "play" checkers. This type of problem solving will be treated more thoroughly in Chapters 13 and 18.

The computer, therefore, may be used to solve problems other than those mathematical in nature if a mathematical model of the problem can be developed. For instance, the solution to the problem of pollution in rivers, or the arrangement of the trial docket of a courtroom can be obtained.

Stage Four of the solution is typically accomplished by a computer. In the next section we examine how we can develop precise computer approaches to the solution of problems.

4.2 ALGORITHMS

In order for a computer to provide a solution to a problem, we must have a precise, unambiguous procedure for the solution of the problem. An algorithm is such a procedure, defined as:

ALGORITHM A complete, unambiguous procedure for solving a specified problem in a finite number of steps.

The word *algorithm* is derived from the name of a ninth–century Arab mathematician, al-Khowarizmi. He developed methods for solving problems which used specific, step–by–step instructions.[1] al-Khowarizmi wrote the celebrated book *Kitab al jabr w al-mugabala (Rules for Restoration and Reduction)*; the word *algebra* stems from the title of his book. An algorithm is like a recipe used in the kitchen or a set of specific procedures for completing an income tax form.

An algorithm must have all the following characteristics to be useful. It should be:

1. Unambiguous
2. Precisely defined
3. Finite
4. Effective

As an example, consider an algorithm for boiling an egg. A *poor* algorithm for this process is:

Put the egg in a pan of water and boil; then remove it and serve.

This is an ambiguous, poorly–defined procedure. A better, more effective algorithm is:

1. Place three inches of water in a pan.
2. Place the egg in the pan.
3. Place the pan on the stove and turn on the heat.
4. Bring the water to a boil.
5. Boil the water for three minutes.
6. Remove the egg.
7. Turn off the heat under the pan.
8. Serve the egg.

This procedure is finite; each step is clearly defined and limited. The whole procedure is also finite in length. It may be improved in effectiveness, perhaps, by adding "Add salt to the water" between steps 3 and 4. If we add that step, it must be precise, however, giving the quantity of salt to be added.

Governments publish thousands of instruction booklets to help people understand certain regulations or requirements, such as the completion of income tax forms. Upon reading the tax instruction booklet, you may wonder if good algorithmic procedure was followed in developing the directions. Strings of qualifiers such as *unless, providing*, and *except* are extremely troublesome to the person who must follow through all the complicated paths to a final solution. In the next section, we demonstrate how we can follow a path to a solution of a complicated income tax problem.

AN ALGORITHM FOR COMPUTING PRODUCTS

First, consider the elementary problem of computing a product of two numbers, for example 33 and 15. In school we all learned an algorithm for this calculation which utilizes the memorized multiplication tables. The elementary school algorithm for calculating the product is:

1. Write the two numbers, one immediately below the other.
2. Draw a line beneath the two numbers.
3. Using the multiplication table, multiply the first numeral (on the right) of the bottom number by the top number, making sure to carry the proper digits, and enter the answer below the line.
4. Repeat step 3 for the second numeral of the bottom number and enter the answer below that of step 3, shifted one place to the left.
5. Draw a line below the two products and add them.

We could write this algorithm with even more precision and detail if we wished. Now let us carry out the calculation.

$$\begin{array}{r} 33 \\ \times\ 15 \\ \hline 165 \\ 33\ \ \ \\ \hline 495 \end{array}$$

We would probably find it easier to carry out the calculation than it is to write down all the steps in such an algorithm. (For example, write down all the steps in the process for dividing 234 by 13.)

We often have more than one algorithm available for solving a problem. Naturally, we wish to utilize the most effective algorithm. By "effective" we mean the algorithm which requires the smallest computer (in terms of memory and arithmetic unit size) and utilizes the shortest time on the computer. Effectiveness, then, is basically the cost of the solution, since we can state:

cost of solution = size of the computer $\times$ time for calculation

THE RUSSIAN PEASANT ALGORITHM

Consider again obtaining the product of 33 $\times$ 15 by different algorithms. A method of obtaining the product which requires only the use of the "times two" multiplication table is called the Russian peasant algorithm. This method involves continually doubling one factor while halving the other, noting where the halving leaves a remainder. The algorithm is:

1. Write the two numbers on a horizontal line, leaving room for a column between them.
2. Double the smaller number; write the result below the smaller number.
3. Halve the larger number and write down the resulting whole number below the larger number while indicating if there was a non–zero remainder beside the larger number.
4. Repeat steps 2 and 3 until the result of halving will not yield a whole number.
5. Add the multiples of the smaller number on lines where remainders do occur. This is the result.

The calculation for 33 $\times$ 15 by the Russian peasant algorithm follows:

$$\begin{array}{rll} 33\ \text{R} & 15 \rightarrow & 15 \\ 16 & 30 & \\ 8 & 60 & \\ 4 & 120 & \\ 2 & 240 & \\ 1\ \text{R} & 480 \rightarrow & 480 \\ & & \hline \\ & & 495 \end{array}$$

R (indicating a non–zero remainder) occurs on line 1, since we divide 33 by two, obtaining 16 plus a remainder. One cannot be divided by 2 to give a whole number, so we stop at this line, with the 1 counted as having a remainder. In using this algorithm it may be simpler to write the results of doubling one factor below the original number only when there occurs a remainder with the number being halved. For example, the product 45 × 17 might be written as:

$$
\begin{array}{rl}
45\ \text{R} & 17 \\
22 & \\
11\ \text{R} & 68 \\
5\ \text{R} & 136 \\
2 & \\
1\ \text{R} & \underline{544} \\
& 765
\end{array}
$$

THE EUCLIDEAN ALGORITHM

Consider the following problem:

Given two positive integers, A and B, find their greatest common divisor. (The greatest common divisor of two positive integers is the largest integer that divides both the positive integers without yielding a non–zero remainder.)

One way of computing the greatest common divisor of A and B consists of listing all divisors of A and B and picking out the largest divisor that appears in both of the lists. Using this brute–force algorithm, find the greatest common divisor of 72 and 20.

Divisors of 72: 1, 2, 3, 4, 6, 8, 9, 12, 24, 36

Divisors of 20: 1, 2, 4, 5, 10

This process yields a greatest common divisor of 4. If you worked it out, it took you 46 calculation steps.

The Euclidean algorithm finds the greatest common divisor of two numbers. It appears in the Fifth Book of Euclid, dating back to 300 B.C.[2] One form of the steps in this algorithm is:

1. Write down the numbers, say A and B, in that order on a line.
2. Compare the two numbers and determine whether the first equals, is less than, or is greater than the second.
3. If the numbers are equal, then each of them is the required result. If not, proceed to the next step.
4. If the first number is smaller than the second, interchange them and proceed.
5. Subtract the second number from the first and replace the two numbers under consideration by the subtrahend (the former second number) and the remainder respectively. Proceed to instruction 2.

Note that the process terminates at step 3 when the two numbers are equal.

The process for 72 and 20 is as follows:

Calculation	Comments
72, 20	
72-20 = 52 = remainder	Subtraction
20, 52	
52, 20	Interchange
52-20 = 32	Subtraction
20, 32	
32, 20	Interchange
32-20 = 12	
20, 12	
20-12 = 8	
12, 8	
12-8 = 4	
8, 4	
8-4 = 4	
4, 4	Stop

Thus, 4 is the greatest common divisor. This process consumed 15 steps, which is significantly fewer than in the brute-force algorithm which enumerated all the divisors of each number.

Since the division process can be reduced to repeated subtractions, the Euclidean algorithm was given in the foregoing as a subtraction process. It can also be written as a division process which requires even fewer calculation steps. The Euclidean algorithm in this form involves repeated dividing and finding remainders until we reach the remainder 0. Each step produces a remainder smaller than the remainder from the previous step. Eventually we must obtain the remainder 0. The remainder *before* 0 is the greatest common divisor. The algorithm is:

1. Write down A and B in that order on a line, with A the larger of the two numbers.
2. Divide A by B yielding a first remainder R1.
3. Write down B and R1.
4. Divide B by R1 yielding a second remainder R2.
5. Write down R1 and R2.
6. Continue this process until the remainder is equal to zero. Then the remainder of the preceding division step is equal to the greatest common divisor.

Taking the numbers 72 and 20 again, the procedure is:

Calculation	*Comments*
72, 20	
$72 = 3 \cdot 20 + 12$	Dividing by 20, remainder = 12
20, 12	
$20 = 1 \cdot 12 + 8$	Remainder = 8
12, 8	
$12 = 1 \cdot 8 + 4$	Remainder = 4
8, 4	
$8 = 1 \cdot 4 + 4$	Remainder = 4
4, 4	
$4 = 1 \cdot 4 + 0$	Remainder = 0

In 10 steps this time, we again found that the greatest common divisor is 4. Clearly, of the three algorithms we have considered, this is the most efficient algorithm for finding the greatest common divisor.

Let us restate Euclid's algorithm in a more mathematical fashion, using an equation. The algorithm may be written as:

1. Write down A and B in that order with the larger number first.
2. Calculate $A = Q \cdot B + R$, where Q = an integer and R = remainder.
3. If R = 0, then the greatest common divisor is equal to B. If R is not equal to zero, then proceed to the next step.
4. Replace A with B and B with R.
5. Return to step 1 and continue.

As a final example, let us find the largest common divisor of 162 and 126.

A	*B*	*Calculation*
162	126	$162 = 1 \cdot 126 + 36$
126	36	$126 = 3 \cdot 36 + 18$
36	18	$36 = 2 \cdot 18 + 0$

The largest common divisor is 18. We use this form of the Euclidean algorithm in succeeding chapters.

Before proceeding to the next section, let us consider one more mathematical algorithm: that which enables us to generate the Fibonacci numbers.

THE FIBONACCI SEQUENCE

The Fibonacci series of numbers has been the object of extensive study.[3] It is the series or sequence in which each number (after the first two) is the sum of the two previous ones. The series has practical application in botany, electrical network theory and methods of sorting items on computers. The Fibonacci series is formed by the following algorithm:

1. Set P = 1, Q = 1, S = 1.
2. Write down P and Q in that order.
3. Replace P with Q and Q with S.
4. Let S = P + S.
5. Write down S in the sequence.
6. Return to step 3; proceed through step 6 again.

We start the series with the two numbers 1 and 1. We then replace P with Q and Q with S, obtaining 1, 1 for P and Q. We calculate the sum S = 1 + 1 = 2 and write it down as the next number in the sequence. Returning to step 3, we replace P and Q, obtaining P = 1 and Q = 2. Then in step 4, S = 1 + 2 = 3, which is the next Fibonacci number.

The Fibonacci sequence is then:
$$1, 1, 2, 3, 5, 8, 13, 21, 34, 55, 89, ...$$
Each term (after the first two) is formed as the sum of the two terms that precede it. Verify that the next term in the sequence is 144. The more formal expression of the algorithm given above is precise and better suited to use with the computer. We are not able to instruct a computer "Add the two preceding terms in the series and continue."

In the next section we return to the Fibonacci series and graphically illustrate the algorithm for generating the sequence.

4.3 FLOW CHARTS

Following the well worn dictum that a picture is worth a thousand words, we can develop a method of representing an algorithm graphically by means of a flow chart. The definition of a flow chart is:

FLOW CHART A graphic representation of the definition, analysis, or solution of a problem, in which symbols are used to represent operations, data, flow, equipment, and so on.

A flow chart consists of a diagram containing selected symbols such as lines connecting boxes that contain statements of operation or decision. The boxes represent the steps in the algorithm, and the connecting lines represent the flow through the steps. The diagrams are usually drawn so that one starts on the top and moves toward the bottom. Arrows on connecting lines show the direction of flow on the chart. An algorithm may have several possible forms of flow charts.

A flow chart is a blueprint of the logic of the solutions to any problem. A set of the symbols used in this text is shown in Figure 4-1. A rectangle indicates

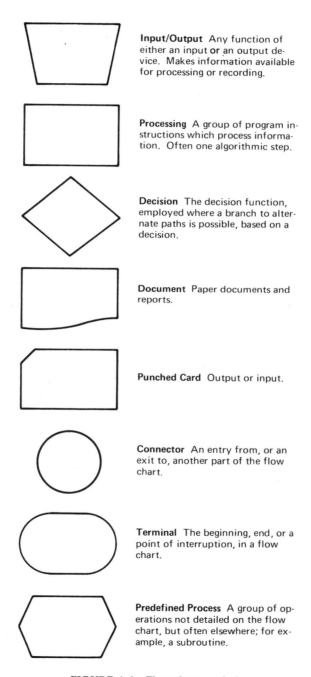

Input/Output Any function of either an input or an output device. Makes information available for processing or recording.

Processing A group of program instructions which process information. Often one algorithmic step.

Decision The decision function, employed where a branch to alternate paths is possible, based on a decision.

Document Paper documents and reports.

Punched Card Output or input.

Connector An entry from, or an exit to, another part of the flow chart.

Terminal The beginning, end, or a point of interruption, in a flow chart.

Predefined Process A group of operations not detailed on the flow chart, but often elsewhere; for example, a subroutine.

FIGURE 4–1 Flow chart symbols.

the action of processing. A diamond indicates a decision or logical choice; it may have two or more branches exiting from it. The other symbols are explained in Figure 4-1.

Four reasons for using flow charts are:

1. The flow chart shows the logic of a problem displayed in pictorial fashion, by which means the algorithm may be checked for correctness.
2. The flow chart is a means of communication to other students, teachers, and to later users. A flow chart is a compact means of recording an algorithmic solution to a problem.
3. The flow chart allows the problem-solver to break his problem into parts and to chart the solution to each part for analysis and study. The parts can be connected to make a master chart.
4. The flow chart records the solution to a problem. It is a permanent record of the solution which can be consulted at a later time.

Flow charts can represent the algorithmic solution to problems of all types. A detailed flow chart for placing a telephone call is shown in Figure 4-2. This flow chart contains enough detail so a person could, with the aid of the chart, place a phone call without any prior knowledge of the process.

The general form a flow chart will take in the solution of problems is shown in Figure 4-3. We usually have input data, which is then used in a calculation process. As a result of the calculation, we substitute some information into prearranged variables. These variables are then tested against some criterion. If the test is satisfied, an output is provided. If the test is not met, the process returns to the calculation phase and continues.

Consider the problem of finding the largest of three numbers: A, B and C. Think how you would do it by comparing one number with another. Now, examine a flow chart which represents the problem solution (Figure 4-4). Note how the flow chart may represent pictorially what you would have been required to express in several hundred words. Also, you can check each path by using test data. Try the flow chart for the sets of A, B, C as follows: [3, 8, 4]; [7, 3, 4]; [2, 1, 5].

In the previous section we studied Euclid's algorithm for obtaining the greatest common divisor of two numbers, A and B. The flow chart representing Euclid's algorithm appears in Figure 4-5. Review the algorithm, stated in the last section, if you need to. The first step in the algorithm is to write down A and B, assuming A is larger than B. The second step is to calculate $A = Q \cdot B + R$ when Q is an integer and R is the remainder. Then, R is tested to find if $R = 0$. If so, we output B as the greatest common divisor. If not, we replace A with B and B with R. On the flow chart, we have used a common notation for replacement: an arrow. Thus, $A \leftarrow B$ implies that A is replaced with B. Then after replacement we return to the calculation step and continue.

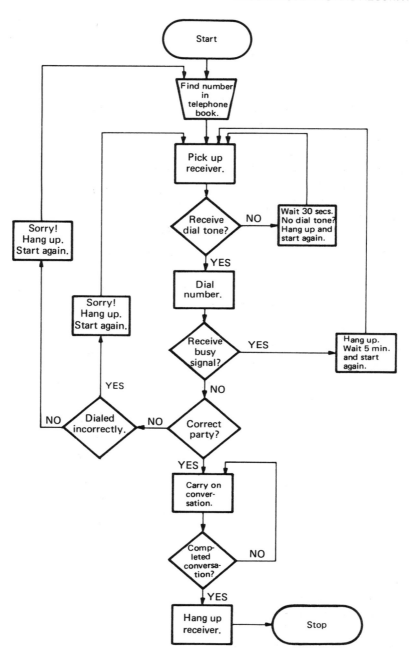

FIGURE 4-2   Flow chart for placing a telephone call.

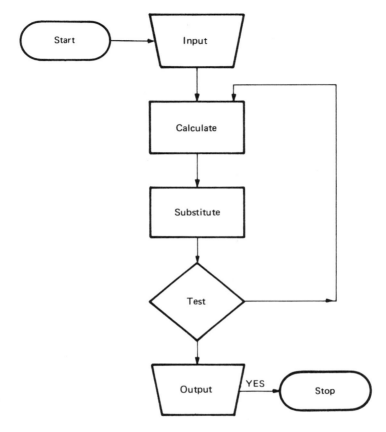

FIGURE 4–3 The general form of a flow chart for the solution of a problem.

Note in the flow chart that we assumed A is always greater than B when it is received as input. If we do not want to bother to require the user to make sure every time that A is greater than B, then we can add two flow chart symbols between the input symbol and the calculation symbol. What would those two symbols be? The revised flow chart with this increased detail for Euclid's algorithm is shown in Figure 4–6. If we do not insure against these small errors in lack of detail, a new user would find the flow chart useless. What if a new person tried Figure 4–5 with the pair [18, 72]? Clearly, we need to provide for all contingencies on a flow chart.

In the last section we developed the algorithm for the Fibonacci series. It is a fairly simple algorithm; let us find how clear and simple the flow chart will be. First, review the algorithm at the end of the preceding section.

Now examine the flow chart representing the Fibonacci series generation in Figure 4–7. This flow chart provides the Fibonacci series as an output. This

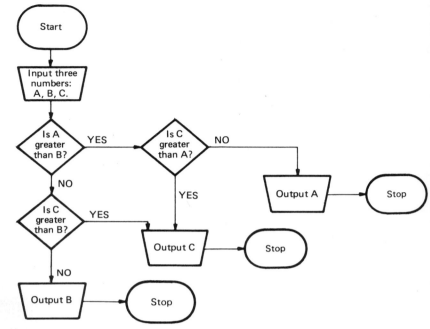

FIGURE 4–4   Flow chart for finding the largest of three numbers.

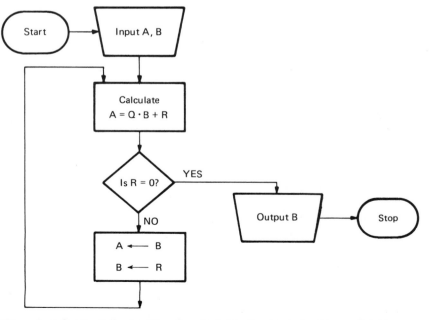

FIGURE 4–5   Flow chart for Euclid's algorithm for obtaining the greatest common divisor
of two numbers.

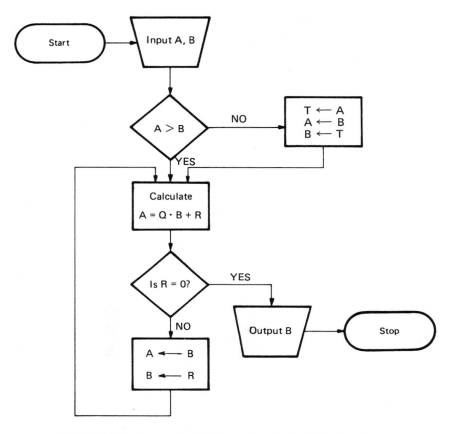

FIGURE 4-6 A more detailed flow chart for Euclid's algorithm.

algorithm does not terminate (a somewhat fatiguing prospect if we are completing it manually!). Perhaps even a computer would get tired. We need to add
a termination step, which is shown in Figure 4-8. In this case, we input the total
number of terms we desire in the series as T. Then a counting variable N is increased by 1 every time the calculation loop is traversed. Try the algorithm for
T = 4 and verify that it provides the first four terms of the series.

Algorithms and flow charts are not restricted to mathematical problems.
The flow chart form of an algorithm is extremely helpful in assisting a person
through a labyrinth of instructions. For example, the instructions for special
cases in the income tax booklet often confuse the reader.[4] For instance, the
instructions stating who must file an estimated tax are provided. Then the
problem statement is provided in two different cases. The flow chart representing the instructions is provided in Figure 4-9. Compare the effort and confusion in solving this problem with and without the flow chart. Determine your
answer to both problems before proceeding to the next paragraph.

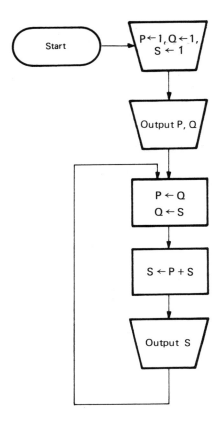

FIGURE 4-7   Flow chart for the Fibonacci sequence.

EXERCISE 4-2

Here is an extract from the 1970 U.S. Internal Revenue Service instructions for who must make a declaration of estimated income tax.[4]

(In reading this extract, it should be remembered that this is not taken from the tax law itself—it was specifically produced to help people decide whether they must make an estimated tax declaration.)

Declaration of Estimated Tax for Individuals

1. Purpose of declaration-vouchers—The declaration-vouchers are provided for paying currently any income tax (including self-employment tax) due in excess of the tax withheld. Therefore, declarations are required only from individuals whose wages or other income exceed the amounts specified in instruction 2. In general, the definitions of income, deductions, exemptions, etc., are the same as those on Form 1040.

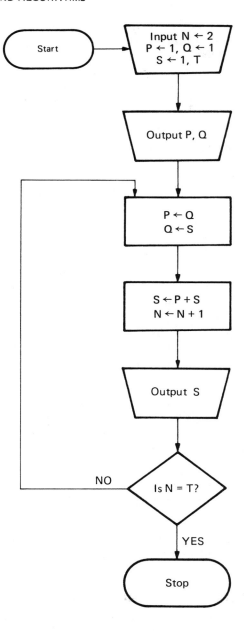

FIGURE 4–8 Flow chart for the Fibonacci sequence with a terminating step. (This algorithm yields a total of T terms in the series.)

2. Who must make a declaration—Under the law every citizen of the United States or resident of the United States, Puerto Rico, Virgin Islands, Guam, and American Samoa shall make a declaration of his estimated tax. If his total estimated tax (line 14 of worksheet) is $40 or more and he:

(a) can reasonably expect gross income to exceed—

(1) $10,000 for a head of household or a widow or widower entitled to the special tax rates;

(2) $5,000 for other single individuals;

(3) $5,000 for a married individual not entitled to file a joint declaration;

(4) $5,000 for a married individual entitled to file a joint declaration, and the combined income of both husband and wife can reasonably be expected to exceed $10,000; or

(b) can reasonably expect to receive more than $200 from sources other than wages subject to witholding.

·   ·   ·

7. Changes in income, exemptions, etc.—Even though your situation on April 15 is such that you are not required to file, your circumstances may change so that you will be required to file a declaration later. In such case the time for filing is as follows: June 15, if the change occurs after April 1 and before June 2; September 15, if the change occurs after June 1 and before September 2; January 15, 1971, if the change occurs after September 1. The estimated tax may be paid in equal installments of the remaining payment dates.

The Problem

Mary Black won a $200 prize in a television quiz program. She has no other income and files a joint return with her husband, who earns $11,000 a year in wages. They calculate that the tax on her winnings will be about $50. Does she have to file an estimated tax declaration?

Another Try

Now try the problem again with one change—suppose Mary Black earned $5,000 a year in wages and her husband $6,000. Except for that, the situation is the same. Does she have to file an estimated tax declaration now?

If you followed the flow chart in Figure 4–9 carefully, you found that in the first problem Mrs. Black does not file an estimated tax declaration. However, in the second problem, Mrs. Black's total personal income is $5,200 and she does have to file an estimated tax declaration.

The advantages of the flow chart algorithm are evident to anyone who would have to decipher the instructions without the aid of a flow chart. The flow chart has three main advantages over the continuous prose form. First, the reader is called upon to make a sequence of simple decisions, often of a yes–no nature. Second, each decision is about a specific issue; the problem of deciding what is relevant is greatly simplified. Finally, in working through the flow chart one does not have to remember his previous decisions. The use of algorithms in flow chart form for instructions for various tasks allows workers and others to shorten the time to complete a task and to reduce the number of errors in the problem solving process.

Algorithms and their pictorial representation as flow charts are a necessary part of the problem solving process using computers. The solution of problems requires a well defined process. The problems to be solved by computer using algorithmic methods are not limited to numerical problems, as we found in the problem of Mrs. Black and the tax declaration. Lady Lovelace, a friend of Charles Babbage, had a comment on the use of computers and algorithms in 1844:

> Many persons who are not conversant with mathematical studies imagine that because the business of (Babbage's Analytical Engine) is to give its results in numerical notation, the nature of its processes must consequently be arithmetical and numerical, rather than algebraical and analytical. This is an error. The engine can arrange and combine its numerical quantities exactly as if they were letters or any other general symbols; and in fact it might bring out its results in algebraical notation, were provisions made accordingly.

In this chapter we have found that in order to solve a problem we must develop a precise formulation of the problem, a mathematical model and an algorithm for the solution of the problem. The analytical engine which is the object of study in this book, the electronic digital computer, is a powerful engine indeed. In the next chapter, we consider how we can communicate with the computer through an algorithmic process. The computer is able to accomplish the steps in our algorithms and flow chart representations. It remains only to learn how to arrange for the computer to accomplish the algorithmic process; this is the essence of the ensuing three chapters. As Bertalanffy states:*

> In somewhat different terms, the algorithmic system becomes a calculating machine, as conversely every calculating machine is materialization of an algorithm. Suitable data being fed in, the machine runs according to pre-established rules and eventually a result drops out which was unforeseeable to the individual mind with its limited capacities.

*George Braziller, Inc.—from ROBOTS, MEN AND MINDS by Ludwig von Bertalanffy; reprinted with the permission of the publisher. Copyright © 1967 by Ludwig von Bertalanffy.

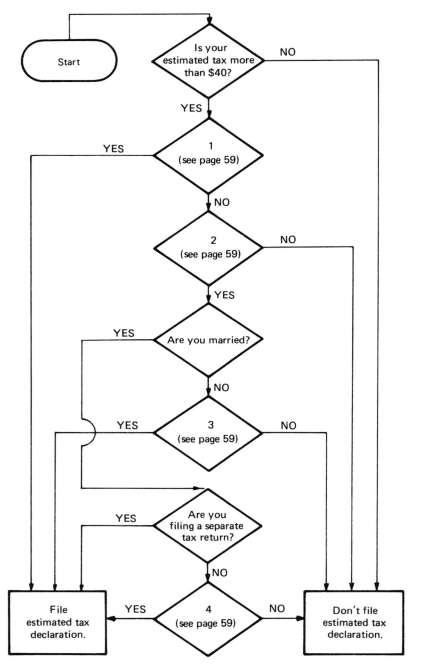

FIGURE 4-9 Flow chart for estimated tax. Reprinted from *Psychology Today*, April, 1970. Copyright © Communications/Research/Machines/Inc.

1. Will you receive
   more than $200
   from sources other
   than wages subject
   to withholding?

2. Is your personal
   income (regardless
   of whether you are
   single or married)
   more than $5000?

3. Are you the head
   of a household or
   a widow or widower
   with a total income
   of $10,000 or more
   and entitled to special
   taxes?

4. Are you filing a joint
   tax return, and is your
   combined income more
   than $10,000?

FIGURE 4-9   (Continued.)

CHAPTER 4 PROBLEMS

P4-1. You are a police detective called to the scene of a crime. One clue you discover is a bullet lodged in a wooden wall stud. The bullet has penetrated three inches into the wood and the wood is pine. Formulate and solve the problem of determining the type and size of weapon from which the bullet was fired.

P4-2. You and a friend attend an auction in which you write down your bids and compare them. High bidder gets $20 and pays the other the amount of the higher bid. Tie bidders split $20. How much do you bid in order to maximize the amount you get? Formulate the problem and a model. Then analyze and calculate your bid.

P4-3. You and two friends have $32 to spend on a weekend in the city. Your friend John has $4 more than your friend Bill. Furthermore, your friend Bill has $2 more than you do. How much does each of you have to spend?

P4-4. Using the problem method, analyze whether you should live in the residence hall at your college, in a local rooming house or in a shared apartment with two students. Make a choice based on the ratio of dollar cost to the square feet of space allocated to you. For example, if you paid $300 for a room of 10 square feet, the ratio would be $\frac{300}{10} = 30$.

P4-5. It is said that Immanuel Kant was a bachelor of such regular habits that the good people of Königsberg would adjust their clocks when they saw him stroll past certain landmarks.

One evening Kant was dismayed to discover that his clock had run down. Evidently his manservant, who had taken the day off, had forgotten to wind it. The great philosopher did not reset the hands because his watch was being repaired and he had no way of knowing the correct time. He walked to the home of his friend Schmidt, a merchant who lived a mile or so away, glancing at the clock in Schmidt's hallway as he entered the house.

After visiting Schmidt for several hours Kant left and walked home with a slow, steady gait that had not varied in twenty years. He had no notion of how long this return trip took. (Schmidt had recently moved into the area and Kant had not yet timed himself on this walk.) Nevertheless, when Kant entered his house, he immediately set his clock correctly.

How did Kant know the correct time?*

P4-6. In about 250 B.C. Eratosthenes constructed an algorithm for finding all the prime numbers between 1 and some specified integer N. A prime

*Reprinted from *New Mathematical Diversions from Scientific American*, by Martin Gardner, By permission of the publisher, Simon and Schuster, Inc.

number is a positive integer, other than 1, that is exactly divisible only by itself and 1. For example, the prime numbers less than 10 are 2, 3, 5, and 7. Thus, the problem is to find all the prime numbers up to N. The algorithm developed by Eratosthenes, called the *Sieve of Eratosthenes*, proceeds as follows[6]:

1. Write down all the integers in numerical order from 2 through N. Call this the *basic* list. For example, assuming N = 10, the basic list is

$$2, 3, 4, 5, 6, 7, 8, 9, 10$$

2. Record, in what we shall call the *prime list* (to distinguish it from the basic list), the first uncrossed number in the basic list. (There will be no number crossed out in the basic list until we decide the first *M* in the prime list.) Call it *M*, then cross it and every *Mth* number thereafter off the basic list. Continuing the example, we have M = 2; we then cross off every second number in the list:

$$\cancel{2}, 3, \cancel{4}, 5, \cancel{6}, 7, \cancel{8}, 9, \cancel{10}$$

3. If *M* is less than $\sqrt{N}$, return to *step 2*; if *M* is $\geqslant \sqrt{N}$, then add all the remaining uncrossed–out numbers to your prime list and stop. In the example, M = 2, which is less than $\sqrt{10}$, so we return to step 2 and repeat it. The first uncrossed number is 3. The prime list is now 2, 3. Repeating step 2:

$$\cancel{2}, \cancel{3}, \cancel{4}, 5, \cancel{6}, 7, \cancel{8}, \cancel{9}, \cancel{10}$$

Now M = 3, which is still less than $\sqrt{10}$, so we return again to step 2 and repeat it. The first uncrossed number is 5. The prime list is now 2, 3, 5. M is 5, which is greater than $\sqrt{10}$. We add all the remaining uncrossed-out numbers (there is only one, 7) to our prime list, and we are through; our list is 2, 3, 5, 7.

The prime list we have prepared is, in fact, the desired list of primes less than *N*.

For another example, what are all the primes between 2 and 8? We write the basic list:

$$2\ 3\ 4\ 5\ 6\ 7\ 8$$

We record 2 as a prime number and cross off every even number, obtaining

$$\cancel{2}\ 3\ \cancel{4}\ 5\ \cancel{6}\ 7\ \cancel{8}$$

Since 3 is not less than $\sqrt{8}$, we add 3, 5 and 7 to the list of prime numbers, obtaining 2, 3, 5 and 7 as the prime numbers between 2 and 8.

1. Determine all the prime numbers between 2 and 18.
2. Draw a flow chart of the algorithm.

P4–7. Often we wish to find the sum of N numbers where N is specified. The sum is the output, and the numbers are available one at a time from N punched cards. The number read from each card is called X and the card is the Ith card. The sum is called S. In the algorithm, we need a counter to indicate what card we are counting, so we know when we come to N. Also, we need to set S equal to zero initially. A flow chart for this algorithm is shown in Figure P4–7. Complete the algorithmic steps in the flow chart by entering the missing items in each block.

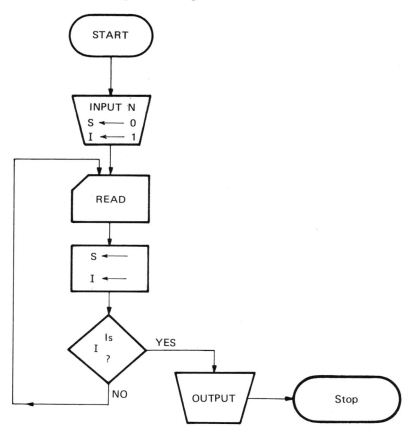

FIGURE P4–7   Flow chart for finding the sum of N numbers.

P4–8.   Even the simplest of household tasks can present complicated problems in operational research. Consider the preparation of toast in a form of electric toaster often found in diners. This toaster is an older type, with hinged doors on its two sides. It holds two pieces of bread at once but toasts each of them on one side only. To toast both sides it is necessary to open the doors and reverse the slices.

It takes three seconds to put a slice of bread into the toaster, three seconds to take it out and three seconds to reverse a slice without removing it. Both hands are required for each of these operations, which means that it is not possible to put in, take out, or turn two slices simultaneously. Nor is it possible to butter a slice while another slice is being put into the toaster, turned, or taken out. The toasting time for one side of a piece of bread is thirty seconds. It takes twelve seconds to butter a slice.

Each slice is buttered on one side only. No side may be buttered until it has been toasted. A slice toasted and buttered on one side may be returned to the toaster for toasting on its other side. The toaster is warmed up at the start. In how short a time can three slices of bread be toasted on both sides and buttered?*

Draw a flow chart to assist in determining the length of time in which the three slices of bread can be toasted on both sides and buttered.

P4-9.   The following problem statement concerns the application of a grant upon the death of the insured under British Ministry of Pensions. Complete the flow chart and determine if the late contributions count for either Mr. Doe or Mrs. Doe.[4] See Figure P4-9.

Mr. and Mrs. John Doe, a young couple, were involved in a car crash. Mrs. Doe was killed outright. Mr. Doe, who was self-employed, died in a hospital a month later. Mr. Doe's accountant paid a backlog of late contributions for both Mr. and Mrs. Doe to the national insurance plan a few days before Mr. Doe's death.

A British Ministry of Pensions and National Insurance leaflet set out the qualifications for a small grant payable on death in this way:

"Contributions paid late cannot normally count for death grant (other than towards yearly average) unless they were paid before the death on which the grant is claimed and before the death of the insured person if that was earlier. But if the insured person died before the person on whose death the grant is claimed, contributions, which although paid late, have already been taken into account for the purpose of a claim for a widow's benefit or retired pension, will count towards death grant." (Leaflet Nl 48, *Late Paid or Unpaid Contribution*, MPN1 1963.)

Will the late contributions count toward a death grant for Mr. Doe? for Mrs. Doe?**

P4-10. The linear algebraic equation, where the dependent variable is raised to the third power, is called the cubic equation. The cubic equation may be written in general form as:

$$f(x) = x^3 + px^2 + qx + r = 0$$

It is desired to determine the three roots of the equation. At least one root of the cubic equation is a real root. One method for determining

*Reprinted from *New Mathematical Diversions from Scientific American*, by Martin Gardner. By permission of the publisher, Simon and Schuster, Inc.
**From I. K. Davies, "Algorithms." Reprinted from PSYCHOLOGY TODAY Magazine, April, 1970. Copyright © Communications/Research/Machines/Inc.

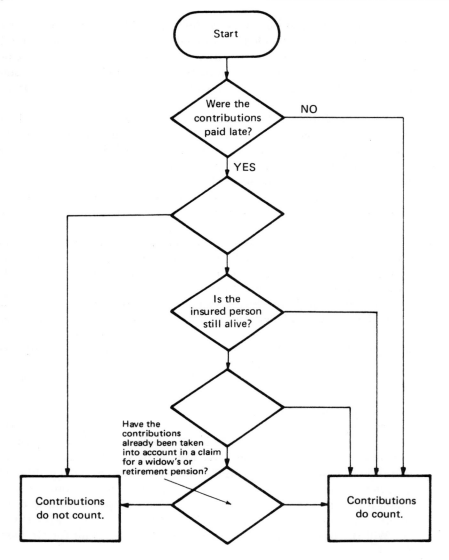

FIGURE P4-9 Flow chart to determine if contributions count toward grant upon death of
insured. Reprinted from *Psychology Today*, April, 1970. Copyright © Com-
munications/Research/Machines/Inc.

the roots of the cubic equation is to determine the one real root, remove the one real root from the cubic equation, and then proceed to find the roots of the resulting quadratic equation by the previously developed algorithm for determining the roots of a quadratic equation. An algorithm for following this procedure is shown in Figure P4-10. Verify the flow chart of the algorithm by manually following the flow chart in order to find the real root of the cubic equation.

$$f(x) = (x - 1)(x + i)(x - i) = x^3 - x^2 + x - 1 = 0$$

(a) As a first try, use $\Delta x_0 = 10$ and $x_0 = 1.5$.

(b) For a second pass through the algorithm, use $\Delta x_0 = 1.0$ and $x_0 = 0$. (Note that capital "X" is used on the flow chart, since most programming languages use only upper-case letters.)

P4-11. An algorithm is shown in Figure P4-11 for finding and providing as output all the factors of a number N. In this algorithm, we use a predefined process which yields the integer part of any number and is labeled as INT (b). Thus, if $b = 3.47$, INT (b) = 3. Follow through the algorithm in order to find all the factors for $N = 6$.

P4-12. You must arrive at a decision concerning your activities this evening. Assuming you like to swim, play tennis and go to the movies, draw a flow chart to enable you to make a decision based on the following criteria:

1. You will go swimming if the temperature is greater than 80°.

2. You will go to the movies if the temperature is greater than 90° and you like the movie.

3. You will play tennis if the temperature is greater than 60° and less than 85° and there is a court available.

4. If all else fails, you will stay home and complete the problems in Chapter 4.

CHAPTER 4 REFERENCES

1. D. Knuth, *Fundamental Algorithms*, Addison-Wesley Publishing Co., Reading, Mass., 1968.

2. S. K. Stein, *Mathematics: The Man-Made Universe*, W. H. Freeman and Co., San Francisco, 1969.

3. A. Forsythe, T. Keenan, E. Organick, W. Stenberg, *Computer Science: A First Course*, Wiley & Sons, Inc., New York, 1969.

4. I. K. Davies, "Algorithms," *Psychology Today*, April, 1970, p. 53.

5. L. von Bertalanffy, *Robots, Men and Minds,* Braziller Inc., New York, 1967.

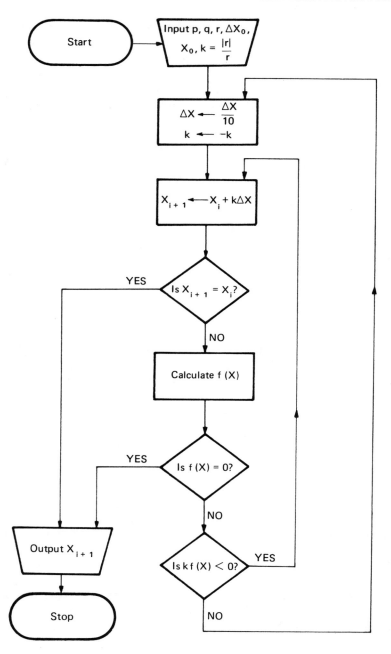

FIGURE P4-10 Algorithm for determining one real root. (X_i indicates the ith attempt to find the root.)

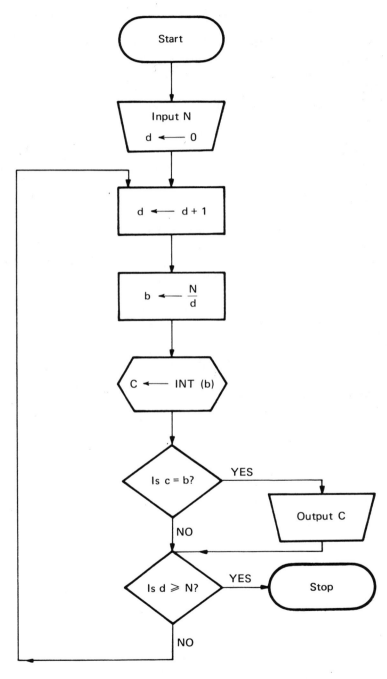

FIGURE P4-11 Flow chart for finding all the factors of a number N.

6. H. Maisel, *Introduction to Electronic Computers*, McGraw-Hill Book Co., New York, 1969.

7. R. Albrecht, E. Lindberg, and W. Mara, *Computer Methods in Mathematics,* Addison-Wesley Publishing Co., Reading, Mass. 1969.

8 T. J. Schriber, *Fundamentals of Flowcharting*, Wiley & Sons, Inc., New York, 1969.

9. F. Gruenberger and G. Jaffray, *Problems for Computer Solution*, Wiley & Sons, Inc., 1965.

10. C. Davidson and E. Koenig, *Computers: Introduction to Computers and Applied Computing Concepts*, Wiley & Sons, Inc., New York, 1967.

11. F. Gruenberger, *Computing: An Introduction*, Harcourt, Brace and World, Inc., New York, 1969.

12. B. A. Trakhtenbrot, *Algorithms and Automatic Computing Machines*, D. C. Heath & Co., Boston, 1963.

13. E. R. Sage, *Problem Solving with the Computer*, Entelek Inc., Newburyport, Mass., 1969.

14. M. Willerding, *Mathematical Concepts, A Historical Approach*, Prindle, Weber & Schmidt, Inc., Boston, 1967.

15. B. Arden and K. Astill, *Numerical Algorithms: Origins and Applications*, Addison-Wesley Publishing Co., Reading, Mass. 1970.

16. D. G. Moursund, *How Computers Do It*, Wadsworth Publishing Co., Inc., Belmont, Calif., 1969.

17. R. Beckett and J. Hurt, *Numerical Calculations and Algorithms*, McGraw-Hill Book Co., New York, 1967.

18. D. Crowdis and B. Wheeler, *Introduction to Mathematical Ideas*, McGraw-Hill Book Co., New York, 1969.

5

PROGRAMMING AND LANGUAGES

5.1 PROGRAMMING

Thus far, we have shown that the computer is useful in solving problems because of its speed, reliability and precision. In order to utilize the advantages of the computer, we must begin by setting the task of solving a specific problem in a form that the computer can use. A precise, algorithmic approach to a problem, often with the use of flow charts, is necessary. Once we have formulated the problem under consideration in a form suitable for the computer, by devising an algorithm, it then becomes necessary to develop a detailed and explicit set of instructions for the computer. These instructions will be expressed in some form suitable for comprehension by the computer. Such a plan for the solution of a problem by a computer, written in a language suitable for the computer, is called a *program*. It is defined as follows:

PROGRAM   (1) A detailed and explicit set of instructions for accomplishing some purpose; the set being expressed in some language suitable for input to a computer. (2) A plan for the automatic solution of a problem.

A complete program includes instructions for transcription of the data, coding for the computer, and output of the results.

Note that a complete program must account for not only the algorithmic solution, but also the input of the data and the output of the results. If the list of tasks for the computer to accomplish is called the program, the person who converts the problem from an algorithmic flow chart to a list of instructions is naturally called the *programmer*. Often one person begins with the problem as a verbal statement and carries it through all the stages of analysis, algorithmic development and programming. However, with very large industrial and government tasks, a person may work on the programming task alone.

Let us write a program for adding two numbers on a desk adding machine. The algorithm for adding two numbers is well known to the reader. It remains for us to convert it to a program. The program is:

1. Clear the keyboard.
2. Enter the first number into the keyboard.
3. Press the "add" button.
4. Enter the second number into the keyboard.
5. Press the "add" button.
6. Press the "total" button.
7. Read the sum of the two numbers on the output paper tape.

The precision of each statement is important, because the computer does not know how to "understand" erroneous statements.

The electronic digital computer uses the program to accomplish the specific task it is programmed for. The program is put into the computer and stored in the memory section. The control section of the computer examines each command, obtaining it from memory in sequence and delegating it to be carried out by one of the five sections of the computer (including the memory section itself).

The process of analyzing a problem, developing a flow chart and program and obtaining the results is shown in Figure 5-1.

The student of computers and computer science should always keep the objects of his study in perspective. J. L. Berg reminds us that we may distort our purposes and the function of computer programs unless we constantly remind ourselves what a computer program really is.[1] That danger has befallen the automobile industry, in which the reason for cars—transportation—has become submerged in powerful, conflicting, and irrelevant struggle for status, luxury, and power.

What is a computer program? Berg uses the analogy of a phonograph to build an answer: A computer program is like a musical record. It is a reproducible recording of the programmer's skills. A computer program must be composed, just as the music performed on the record must be composed. The computer program must be made permanent and stored, just as the musical performance is, and it also demands some means of reproduction, or playing back, what has been stored.

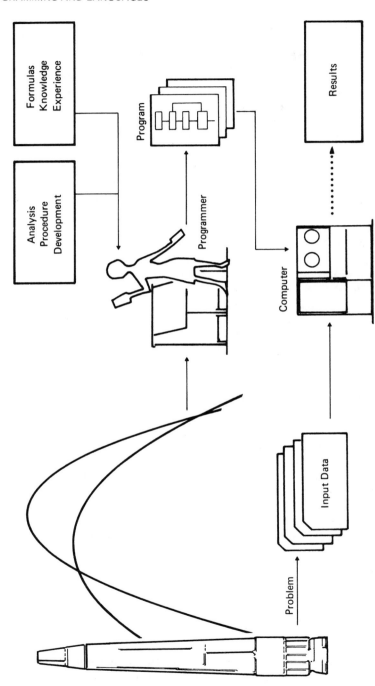

FIGURE 5-1 Direct conversion of problem to machine program.

Boole's logic (See Chapter 3.) makes it possible to reproduce the programmer's steps just as musical notation makes it possible for the musical performer to reproduce the sounds the composer had in his mind. Jacquard's punched-card controls, adapted to modern machinery, make it possible to carry out instructions in the correct sequence, just as the grooves on a record cause the stylus to repeat the vibrations of the original musical sounds.

As Berg suggests, however, we should not forget that the phonograph record comes from the combination of two kinds of *skills*: the performer's and the recording technician's.

And, to recall ourselves to the basic subject of this book, the phonograph is like a computer, since it is a playback machine. Without the skills of the subject–specialist and the programmer the computer is unproductive.

Unfortunately, there are different computer languages for different purposes and machines. This means that some of the skills of the programmer must be specialized. In a sense, it might be the same if some composers thought only in 3/4 time, others in 2/4; or if they could write only in one key each. Similarly, since the decoding operation are also restricted to a single language in each case, it is as if performers could play in only one key or time signature each. (A performer who can play only songs in F Major and 3/4 time will be able, theoretically, to play any song in that key and time. A machine that decodes one of the machine languages can "read" any program in that language.)

The computer program has an advantage over musical recordings, however —one that is embedded in the nature of the program. Von Neumann's demonstration showed that the same language could be used for both input data and instructions. No such economy seems possible or desirable in music.

In the long run, it has proved more economical, more reliable, and more convenient in many applications to use computer programs instead of batteries of clerks or mathematicians. We have remarked above on the almost–incredible speed with which computers can handle information processing and computation. Even if this speed were not present, there are many applications of computers in which the programs are clearly superior in accuracy and economy to individual decision–makers. The basic value of the computer resides in the skills combined in making the computer program.

A program is a recorded form of the programmer's skill. In the succeeding chapters and in the computer laboratory, the reader will learn to develop his skills as a programmer; these skills will live in the programs he writes, just as the skills of great artists live in their recordings.

5.2 PROGRAMMING LANGUAGES

What forms of expression are suitable for comprehension by a computer? We communicate with other people through the medium of language; similarly, we communicate with computers through languages. A definition of *language* follows:

LANGUAGE   A set of words and rules for constructing sentences that can be used for communicating.

Each language has a *syntax*, or grammar, which consists of rules of formulation and word relationship.

The language natural to the reader is English, but the English language is usually not the best for use with algorithms and computer instructions. The disadvantages of English for algorithms are:

1. It is often too cumbersome and lengthy in expression.
2. It is often ambiguous.
3. It does not reveal the basic structure of any given algorithm.
4. Computers comprehend only a small subset of the English language.

You probably know how many words it takes to write instructions in essay form. An excellent example of the length of written English instructions can be found in the tax instructions discussed in Chapter 4. Recall the crisp and terse nature of the flow chart algorithm for the tax instructions. Also, recall the lack of ambiguity of the flow chart compared to the written English instructions. The flow chart also reveals the structure of the algorithm. We usually desire to use languages for programming which are similar in nature to the algorithms they too express. These languages are called *algorithmic programming languages* or *problem-oriented languages*. A partial list of programming languages is given in Table 5-1. FORTRAN is the oldest and most widely used language for scientific, engineering and mathematical problems. COBOL is particularly well-adapted for business applications. It is widely used. BASIC is a recently developed language particularly suited for time-shared computers. It is adaptable to business as well as to scientific and engineering usage. In this book, we limit our study to FORTRAN and BASIC, although you may use additional languages at the computer center available to you.

A symbolic programming language translates the algorithm into a list of instructions understandable to the computer. It uses a shorthand notation which the computer recognizes. We experience this type of symbolic communication often. For example, at a restaurant you might say, "I would like to have a bacon-with-lettuce-and-tomato sandwich on two slices of white bread that are toasted, please," while the waitress would translate that order to the chef as "BLT down."

There is an active discussion on the value of natural languages (such as English) *vs.* programming languages. As Halpern states: [2]

The root issue may be put roughly this way: one school believes that a programming language need not and should not have its form dictated by the fact that it is in some sense addressed to a machine, but should be very close to the language its intended users ordinarily employ in their work, apart from the computer. The other school believes that the fact that a programming language is addressed to a machine is the inescapably decisive force in determining its shape, and that such a language will almost certainly be quite different from those in use between man and man. The first or "natural-language" school is often considered to be advocating the use of plain English as a programming language. This characterization, true so far as it goes, is a simplification of their position that is liable to serious misinterpretation; it may easily be taken to mean, for example, advocacy of languages such as Cobol, which it does not. The second or "calculus" school (as we shall call it) sees programming languages as needing a massive infusion of the rigor, precision, and economy exhibited by mathematical notation. Its members often suggest that a language with these qualities would amply repay its users for their trouble even if it were not implemented on a computer, because it would give them for the first time a proper representation of their procedures.

Languages are written for specific applications, but they may also apply to other areas. For example, FORTRAN is far from a natural language. It is a scientific language, yet it is often used for business applications. If we wish to increase the value of an item called INCOME by the value of an item called DIVIDENDS, we can express this relationship by the FORTRAN statement

INCOME = INCOME + DIVIDENDS

Most computers using FORTRAN require this statement to be written in the more succinct form

INCOM = INCOM + DIVID

However, the businessman finds the verbose COBOL more favorable and writes

ADD DIVIDENDS TO INCOME

FORTRAN is natural to the scientific programmer while COBOL is more natural to the businessman.

The programming process follows the steps illustrated in Figure 5-2. The final step in programming is encoding. Encoding consists of writing the list of instructions in the language comprehended by the computer. The code or instructions will then be transmitted to the computer by an input device such as a typewriter or punched-card reader.

Writing is encoding. Any written language has a set of symbols or characters for encoding the elements of the language. Most current computer languages are limited to approximately 100 characters, since most input devices are limited to about 100 characters. (For example, an ordinary typewriter has about 90 characters.) We have commonly available:

1. The letters of the English alphabet
2. The Arabic numerals 0, 1, 2, 3, ...
3. Mathematical symbols +, -, >, ...
4. Business symbols $, =, %, ...
5. Punctuation symbols !, ., :, ...
6. Grouping symbols (), [], ...

The programmer prepares a list of instructions from the algorithmic flow chart. The list of instructions must allow for sequential operation of the computer. That is, the computer must take action on the instructions on a step–by–step basis and there cannot be overlap between the steps. This type of computer operation is called *sequential operation*. It is defined:

SEQUENTIAL OPERATION   The consecutive or serial execution of steps without any simultaneity or overlap.
This is the normal manner of operation of digital computers.

Each algorithmic flow chart is formed from sequential building blocks; thus, the flow chart lends itself to a sequential list of instructions. These are to be written in a programming language. The sequential nature of the algorithmic program is a fundamental to computer operation.

Problem–oriented languages like FORTRAN, which resemble ordinary English, have been developed for programmers. Actually, however, the digital computer has its own language, called *machine language,* based on binary numbers. (See Chapter 9.) Machine language is defined as:

MACHINE LANGUAGE   The set of instructions available to a particular digital computer, where the instructions are a set of digits or characters that the computer can recognize and act upon.

There are two basic forms of artificial language: problem–oriented languages and *assembly languages.* Assembly languages follow machine language structure very closely. Each statement of the program consists of a machine operation and a location address in the computer. Assembly–language programs require translation by the computer before the program is accepted for execution. The internal program that does the translation is called an *assembler.* Compared to machine language, assembly language reduces the time required to write programs, but it is still removed from common (human) methods of stating and solving problems.

5.3 LOOPS

When the problem to be solved requires an algorithm which contains a repetitive process, the programmer must write a program which will repeat the necessary process as many times as necessary. The process of repetitive

TABLE 5-1

Programming Languages

Name	Year Introduced	Primary Application	Estimated Percent of the Total of Languages Used for Programs
FORTRAN (Formula Translation)	1956	Science and Engineering	40%
COBOL (Common Business-oriented Language)	1959	Business Data Processing	35%
ALGOL (Algorithmic Language)	1960	Science and Engineering	2%
APL (A Programming Language)	1962	Science and Engineering	3%
BASIC (Beginners All-Purpose Symbolic Instruction Code)	1964	Business, Science and Engineering (particularly time-shared computers)	15%
PL/1	1965	Business, Science and Engineering (particularly time-shared computers)	5%

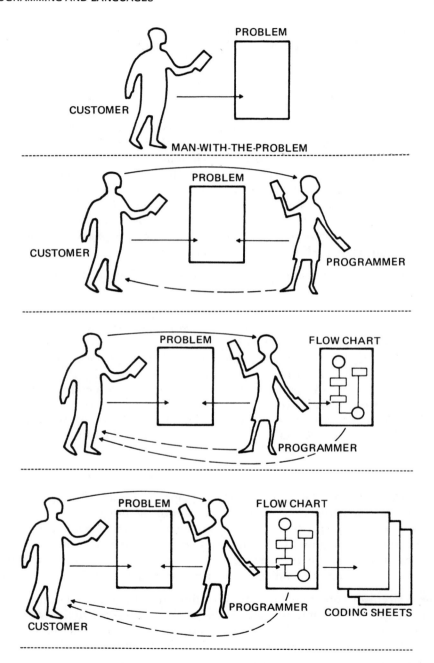

FIGURE 5-2 The programming process.

calculations using the conditional transfer (see below) was probably first recognized by Lady Lovelace, daughter of Lord Byron and friend of Charles Babbage, in 1846.[3]

> Lady Lovelace explained how easy and how important it would be to use the same routine again and again. Her programs were to be punched on cards, much as they are today, and Babbage devised techniques to send the same deck through the machine time after time. She went much further than that. She said, "The machine is capable under certain circumstances of feeling about, to see which of a certain set of eventualities has occurred, and of shaping its future course of action accordingly." She knew how to make it steer itself through a complicated calculation by deciding what to do next after studying for itself what it had done so far. She knew, as Babbage put it, how to "make the machine drive itself forward by biting its own tail."

As Lord Bowden, a contemporary British computer scientist, points out, this idea was rediscovered in the present century.[3]

> Engineers in the Moore School in Pennsylvania built the first electronic computer (ENIAC) to work out the trajectories of shells for the American Army during the war. This was probably the bulkiest (computing) machine that has ever been made but it was very inflexible and it could only keep on doing the same sum, over and over again, because it could not use a conditional transfer. Lady Lovelace's principles were rediscovered by von Neumann in Princeton, by Turing in England, and by Wilkes, Williams, and Kilburn, who built the first machines in England about 1950.

The *conditional transfer* is basic to repetitive calculations. It is defined:

CONDITIONAL TRANSFER   (1) A change in location from one portion of a program to another specified portion of the program *if a* specified *criterion is satisfied.* (2) A computer instruction which, when reached in the course of a program, will cause the computer either to continue with the next instruction in the original sequence or to switch program control to another location, depending upon a predetermined condition or criterion.

The concept of conditional transfer is equivalent to the idea of a decision–and–transfer exemplified in flow charts in the previous chapter. Conditional transfer is represented by the decision (diamond–shaped) box of the flow chart.

The conditional transfer is utilized in the repetitive calculation process called a *loop*, defined as follows:

LOOP   A sequence of computer instructions which is executed repeatedly a finite number of times. The number of executions is decided by a counter or index.

A program in a loop executes a series of instructions until a test is satisfied. Then the program exits from the loop. A conditional transfer, or decision, is used to test for the exit condition. The form of the basic loop is illustrated in Figure 5-3. The process consists of initializing, calculating, testing, and then

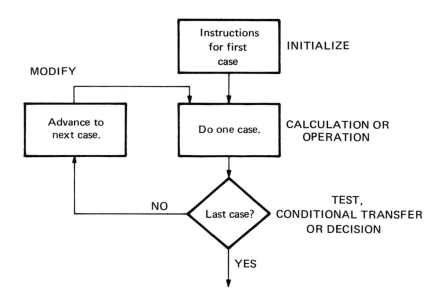

FIGURE 5-3   The basic loop.

advancing to the next case if the exit condition is not met. The loop for Euclid's algorithm is shown in Figure 5-4. The two numbers A and B are provided as the initial data by an input device. Then the calculation process is followed. The decision block determines if the remainder is zero, and transfers to the modification block if it isn't. After the modification of A and B are accomplished, the calculation is repeated and the decision test repeated. The loop is traversed repeatedly until the condition is satisfied and the program exits from the loop.

To illustrate a calculation using a loop with a counter or index, we use this problem: Find the sum of N numbers. (The subscript notation "A sub i" means that we are reading the ith number.) The flow chart for the process of summing

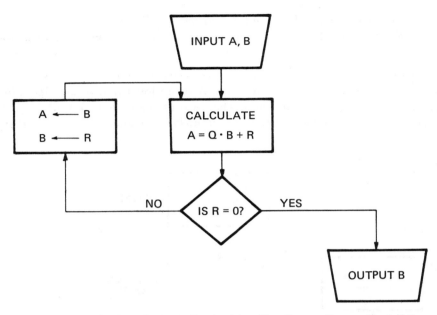

FIGURE 5-4   The loop for Euclid's Algorithm (See Chapter 4) assuming A > B.

N numbers is shown in Figure 5-5. First the computer receives N, the number of numbers to be summed. Then the calculation is initialized by setting the sum S equal to zero and the counter i equal to one. We then input the first punched card, containing the number A_1. Immediately, we test to find if i exceeds N. When i = 1, this test allows for the case where N = 0; that is, there are no numbers to be received as input. If N is greater than 1, we proceed to add A_1 to S and replace S with the sum. Then the counter is advanced by one, and the next card received, and so on. When the counter is greater than N, the loop is exited from and the sum at that point is provided as the output.

There are five ways to terminate and exit from a loop. They are:
1. The number of cycles of the loop is known and provided as the constant with which the index is compared in the decision step.
2. The number of cycles of the loop is provided as an input item.
3. The number of cycles is determined during the execution of the loop.
4. The termination of the loop is achieved when a searching or other operation is satisfied.
5. The termination of the loop is achieved when a quantity achieves a certain value or other characteristic.

Thus far, we have examined loops which are terminated on the basis of method 1 or 2. An example of method 3, which bases the termination of a loop on a decision during the problem execution is: Given 100 numbers, determine the

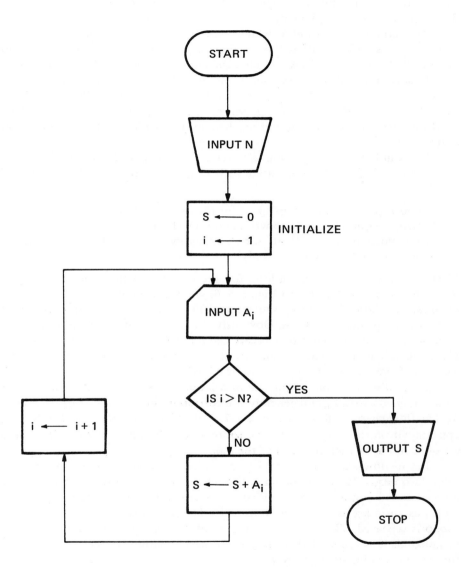

FIGURE 5-5 A flow chart for the summation of N numbers.

sum of the positive numbers. The number of positive numbers is determined during the execution of the loop.

An example of method 4, which terminates the loop upon satisfaction of a search, is as follows: Find the number A_i in a list which matches an input number B. Thus, as soon as A_i matches the number B, the loop will terminate.

Finally, method 5 is very useful for calculations which depend upon convergence toward a desired answer with a prespecified accuracy. For example, in the calculation of the roots of a polynomial, we may specify the precision desired for each calculated root and set the loop to terminate when the precision is achieved.

We could write an algorithm as a series of repetitions. However, the advantages of utilizing a loop, compared with simply writing out all the repeated steps, are:

1. Loops require less storage space for the instruction list.
2. Loops require less time to write and flow chart.
3. The range of a loop (that is, how many cycles of the loop are used) can be increased or decreased easily.

Most computer scientists use a loop for any calculation that must be repeated more than twice. As shown in Figure 5–6, we could use either a loop or a sequential calculation to add two numbers. The sequential calculation uses eight steps; the loop uses nine steps. Obviously, for more than two numbers, the sequential method continues to increase the number of steps necessary to complete the calculation. The number of steps in the loop remains the same regardless of the number of numbers to be added.

As another example of the use of a loop, let us read a series of numbers from punched cards, X_i, and generate the corresponding squares of the numbers, Y_i. The flow chart is shown in Figure 5–7. Notice that the printout of X_i and Y_i appears within the loop. We thus generate a *table* of numbers, since we print a set of X and Y on each traversal of the loop.

Let us now examine a *nested loop*, which is simply a loop within another loop. Two nested loops are shown in flow chart form in Figure 5–8, where there are two index counters, i and j. First, i is set equal to 1 and all the calculations with j as an index are completed up to j = M. Then, i is set equal to 2 and the j loop is repeated. The process continues until $i \geqslant N$, upon which the loops are terminated. It is required that one loop be nested within another loop and that there is no crossing of the flow lines.

An example of the use of nested loops is the following problem [4]:

Find all the two-digit numbers that are equal to the sum of the squares of their digits.

We let the two digits of the number be X and Y. Then the two–digit number is
$$(10 \cdot X) + Y$$

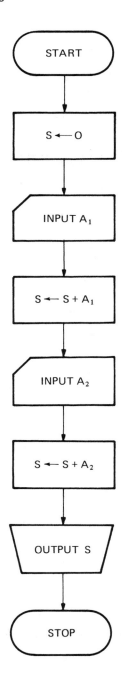

FIGURE 5–6 A flow chart of a sequential method for calculating the sum of two numbers.

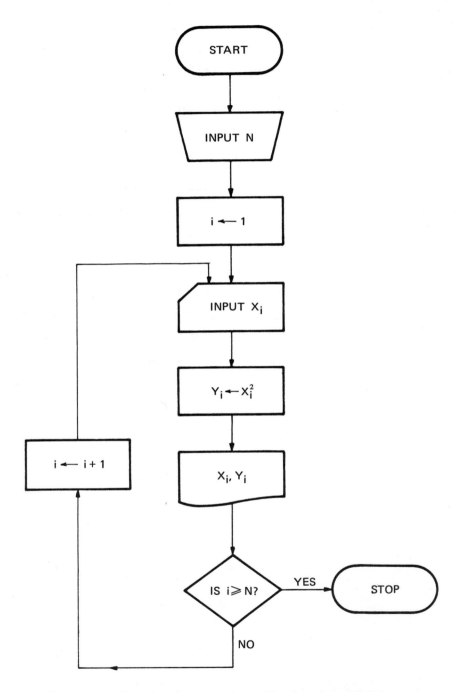

FIGURE 5-7   A flow chart for generating a table of numbers and their squares.

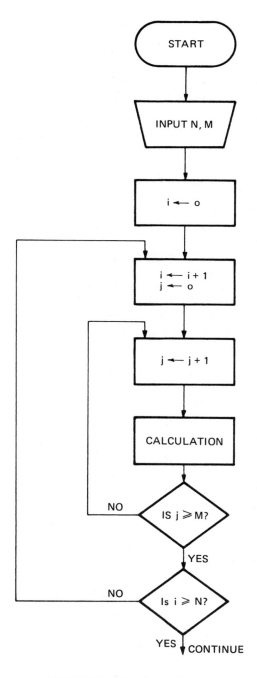

FIGURE 5–8 Two nested loops.

The problem is then to find and print out all the sets of digits X, Y that satisfy the condition:

$$(10 \cdot X) + Y = X^2 + Y^2$$

Try to construct a flow chart of nested loops to solve this problem before examining the flow chart shown in Figure 5-9.

In Figure 5-9, note that the two nested loops allow us to proceed through all the 99 two-digit numbers. This algorithm expressed by a flow chart can be programmed easily for a digital computer. The computer can examine all the possibilities in less than one second. Of course, we can follow through this algorithm for two digits manually. You may wish to verify that there is no two-digit number that satisfies the problem. We can extend this problem to three-digit numbers and their cubes, for which we would establish three nested loops. In the case of three nested loops, it would probably take all day for a person to search manually for three-digit numbers that are equal to the sum of the cubes of the digits, while a computer could complete this calculation in less than one second.

A final principle associated with loops states that only operations which must be performed within the loop should be included inside the loop. This principle ensures the efficiency of the algorithmic operation; we do not want to repeat any calculation that can be excluded from the loop. As a humorist among the computer scientists has put it: [5]

> Mary, Mary
> Quite contrary
> How does your program flow?
> With lots of loops
> In nested groups
> And neat arrays all in a row.

The use of loops and conditional transfers permits the problem-solver to use the digital computer to solve large, long and tedious problems rapidly. We shall use loops and conditional transfers in the programs we develop in the ensuing chapters.

5.4 DATA AND PROGRAM VALIDATION

When we are solving a problem with a digital computer, we must progress through the stages listed in Section 4-1:

1. Precise formulation of the problem
2. Development of a mathematical model
3. Mathematical analysis
4. Computation of a solution
    a. Compute some specific results.

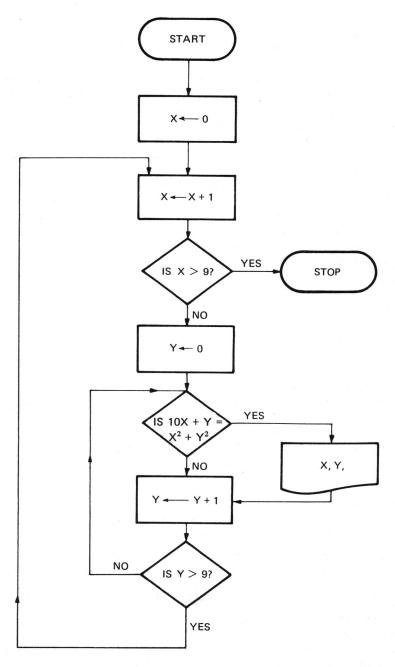

FIGURE 5-9 A flow chart for determining the two-digit numbers that are equal to the sum of the squares of their digits.

b. Check these results for accuracy.

c. Check the precision of the results and compare the precision and accuracy.

Thus far, we have discussed the process up to the fourth stage as illustrated in Figure 5-10.[6] We have analyzed the problem, developed an algorithm in flow chart form and discussed the conversion of the algorithm into the form of a program. We must then add the data to the input instructions in order to proceed with the computer solution.

A critical phase in the computer implementation of an algorithm is program testing and validation. Program validation involves running the computer using test data to determine whether the answers (1) coincide with answers which have previously been obtained by manual computation or some other method, or (2) are in agreement with the answers predicted by empirical results and theoretical analysis.

The process of removing errors from a program is called *debugging*. It is defined as follows:

DEBUG   To detect, locate and remove mistakes from a program.

The errors, or bugs, may result from a poorly defined problem or errors in the analysis. Furthermore, the algorithm may contain logical errors which will require correction. Also, errors may result in the encoding of the algorithm in the language used with the computer.

The process of debugging a program is shown in Figure 5-11. If an error occurs, the problem solver will have to examine all the possible sources of error. Once all the errors in the coding and algorithm are removed, one may proceed to the use of test cases as shown in Figure 5-12. Finally, if the test cases are verified, one may proceed to obtain results as shown in Figure 5-13.

Often the processes of debugging and testing are coordinated. However, the process of testing can be considered separately. It can be defined as follows:[7]

PROGRAM TESTING   The process whereby the programmer assures himself that his program solves the problem he proposed to solve, and will continue to solve it as the data change.

If we completely eliminate errors due to mechanical mistakes in coding and the computer produces results, we may begin to test the results produced by the algorithm and program. We then try known data and answers as a test. A useful first test is the *zero test*. In this case, we input zeros as the data, since we often can determine what the answer must be when zero is the input; the answer can be calculated easily by hand. For example, a program for finding the sum of all numbers may be tested by providing it with all zeros as input numbers. Expecting the answer to be zero, we can carry out the summing manually. Of course, this test by itself is not sufficient. Reconsider Figure 5-5, which is

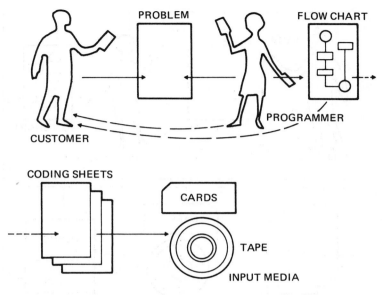

FIGURE 5-10   The input of instructions and data.

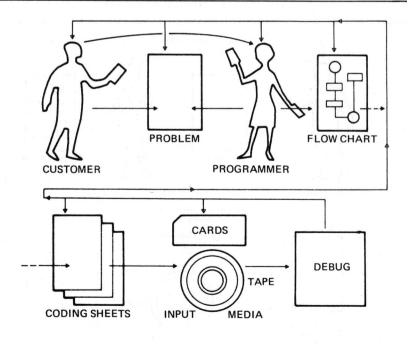

FIGURE 5-11   The debugging process.

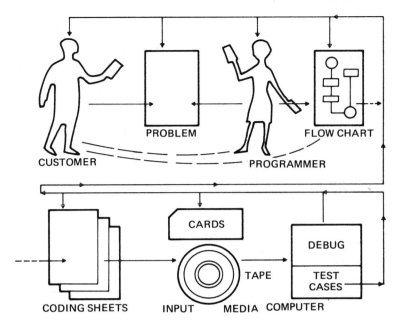

FIGURE 5-12   The use of test cases.

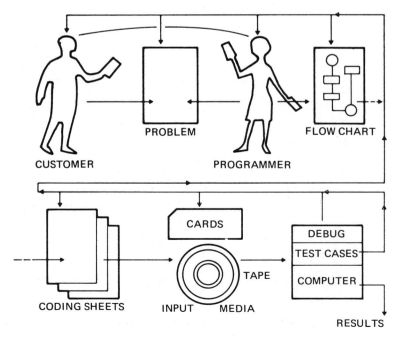

FIGURE 5-13   The production of computer results.

an algorithm for obtaining the sum of N numbers. If we try 100 numbers all equal to five as the input, we expect 500 as the output. If the output is incorrect, we might receive the following answers for which explanations are given:

1. 495 – Exit from the loop one iteration too soon.
2. 505 – Exit from the loop one iteration too late.
3. 0   – The loop probably does not function.
4. No answer – The loop never terminates.

Thus, we find that the procedure for program testing is:

1. Provide known data, such as zeros or data with known answers.
2. Run the program being tested.
3. Compare the answer with the expected answer.

We may test using data generated by a small program, if the answer is known. For example, a program can be set up to find the sum of N evenly spaced integers according to the statement

$$S = 1/2 \ (F + L) \ N$$

where F and L stand for the value of the first and last terms and N is the number of terms. Thus, for 100 terms, of numbers from 1 to 100, we have $S = 5050$.

The testing and validation process is an iterative process shown pictorially in Figure 5-14. It takes a significant amount of effort and time to program, code, debug, and test an algorithm for solving a problem. The novice programmer should not be discouraged by the fact that he might complete and check only 10 to 20 computer instruction steps per day. As is shown in Figure 5-15, for 50 percent of the applications, it will take one man three months to complete and test a program consisting of 1,000 instructions. Of course, for large programs, several persons may work jointly on the project in order to reduce the months necessary to complete the project. A large computer used for complex problems requiring many instructions is shown in Figure 5-16.

5.5 DOCUMENTATION

The process of documentation refers to the writing and recording of the purpose, the use and the detail of a given program to solve a problem. The need for documentation is obvious to anyone who has tried to run a machine or an appliance without reading the instruction manual. In a sense, the documentation of a program is the instruction manual for the next user. We define documentation as follows:

DOCUMENTATION   (1) The collection, organization and storage of records to make information easily accessible to the user. (2) Records that

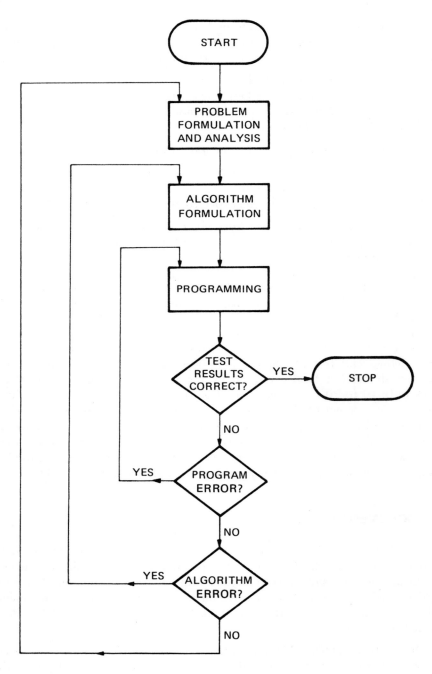

FIGURE 5-14   Program testing and validation.

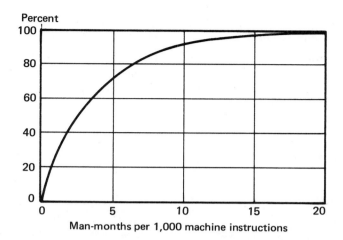

FIGURE 5-15   Cumulative distribution of man–months per 1,000 machine instructions required to prepare and debug a group of programs. Source: E. A. Nelson, *Management Handbook for the Estimation of Computer Programming Costs,* System Development Corporation Technical Memorandum TM–3225/000/00 (Oct. 31, 1966), p. 69.

FIGURE 5-16   The IBM System/360 Model 195. This system is designed to help solve the most complex commercial and scientific problems, from nationwide airline reservations handling to global weather forecasting. It can process an instruction in 54–billionths of a second. *Courtesy IBM Corporation.*

describe the purpose, the use, the structure, details and operational requirements of a program.

Documentation should include the purpose of the program, the algorithm utilized, capabilities and limitations of the program, the computer configuration required, the input data requirements, a flow chart and a complete program listing of the instructions.

FIGURE 5-17 A large computer center housing. This is The Sperry Rand Corporation's Univac 1108 computer system, which is capable of performing more than one million calculations per second. *Courtesy of Univac Division of Sperry Rand Corporation.*

Documentation is absolutely necessary if a program is to be used by anyone but the original author. It is also necessary if the original author plans to use his program many months later and cannot count on remembering all the specific uses, limitations, and the computer configuration required. In a large computer center, such as the one shown in Figure 5-17, it is necessary to develop a library for the documentation of the large number of programs used each year.

CHAPTER 5 PROBLEMS

P5-1. Define and differentiate among the following terms:
(a) computer language
(b) program
(c) natural language
(d) problem-oriented language

P5-2. We would like to use English as the language for programming computers, as the following lyrics state:

> BRING BACK THE ENGLISH
> (to the tune of "My Bonnie Lies Over
> the Ocean")
>
> My mother is fluent in FORTRAN
> my father can talk in COBOL
> my sister converses in ASCII
> I don't understand them at all.
>
> Bring back
> bring back
> bring back the English to me, to me
>
> Bring back
> bring back
> bring back King's English to me.

(Courtesy of Versatec Corporation, Cupertino, California)

Give three or four reasons why natural English is not used as a programming language.

P5-3. How does Mr. Berg's definition of a computer program differ from simply defining a program as a list of instructions to achieve a certain purpose?

P5-4. Describe the sequential nature of flow charts and computer operation. Would parallel calculation and operation of a computer have some advantages? For example, could parallel operation be useful in calculation of summation processes?

P5-5. We have a list of exam scores with each score listed on an individual punched card and we wish to find and print out the largest score. Let us name the ith score S_i and the number of test scores we will call N. Devise a flow chart algorithm using a loop for printing out the largest number.

P5-6. As in problem 5-5, we wish to determine the largest test score. However, in addition, we wish to then delete this largest number from the list stored in the computer and then find the largest number of the remaining list and print it as output. Continuing in this manner, we will be able to print out a list of the scores in descending order. Use a second loop to enable the list to be printed out in descending order and draw a flow chart to represent the algorithm for the total process.

P5-7. It is given that four integers A, B, C and D are related by the following equation:

$$A^N + B^N = C^N + D^N$$

The value of N is provided as an input. Draw a flow chart algorithm that will provide all the sets of A, B, C, D that satisfy the equation when all the integers are limited to 100 as a maximum value.

P5-8. Draw a flow chart of three nested loops which will determine all the three digit numbers that are equal to the sum of the cubes of their digits [4]. Is it possible to revise the algorithm so that the cube of a number is never calculated a second time?

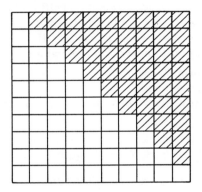

FIGURE P5-9.

P5-9. We are given a two-dimensional array shown in Figure P5-9. Each box has an integer inside and we wish to find the sum of all the numbers above the upper-left to lower-right diagonal (the upper triangle which is shaded). Assume there are ten integers punched in one punched card. Let the index of the row be i and the index of the column be j and aij be the integer value of each element box. Draw a flow chart using two nested loops to find the sum of the elements above the diagonal. The index i runs from 1 to 9. [13]

P5-10. Differentiate between the process of debugging and that of program testing.

P5-11. List three or more sets of numbers A, B which can be used to test a computer program for Euclid's algorithm and which will test all the possible test conditions you can predict.

CHAPTER 5 REFERENCES

1. J. L. Berg, "What is a Computer Program?" *Modern Data*, January, 1970, pp. 62–65.
2. M. Halpern, "Foundations of the Case for Natural-language Programming," *IEEE Spectrum*, March, 1967, pp. 140–149.
3. Lord Bowden, "The Language of Computers," *American Scientist*, January, 1970, pp. 43–53.
4. A. Forsythe, et. al., *Computer Science,* Wiley and Sons, Inc., New York, 1969.
5. E. Conti, "Mother Goose—Another Gander," *Datamation,* April, 1970, p. 89.
6. W. H. Ware, "The Computer in Your Future," *Rand Report P-3626,* The Rand Corp., November, 1967.
7. F. Gruenberger, "Program Testing and Validating," *Datamation*, July, 1968, pp. 39–47.
8. R. Todd, "You Are An Interfacer of Black Boxes," *Atlantic*, March, 1970, pp. 64–70.
9. H. Maisel, *Introduction to Electronic Computers*, McGraw-Hill Book Co., New York, 1969.
10. J. K. Rice and J. R. Rice, *Introduction to Computer Science*, Holt, Rinehart and Winston, Inc., New York, 1969.
11. F. Gruenberger, *Computing: An Introduction*, Harcourt, Brace and World, Inc., New York, 1969.
12. B. Arden and K. Astill, *Numerical Algorithms: Origins and Applications,* Addison-Wesley Publishing Company, Reading, Mass., 1970.
13. P. Sherman, *Techniques in Computer Programming*, Prentice-Hall, Inc., Englewood Cliffs, N.J., 1970.
14. P. C. Sanderson, *Computer Languages: A Practical Guide to the Chief Programming Languages*, Philosophical Library, Inc., New York, 1970.
15. J. E. Sammet, *Programming Languages: History and Fundamentals*, Prentice-Hall, Inc., Englewood Cliffs, N.J., 1969.
16. A. Ralston, *Introduction to Programming and Computer Science,* McGraw-Hill Book Company, New York, 1971.

6

PROGRAMMING A CALCULATOR

6.1 PROGRAMMABLE CALCULATORS

In the preceding chapter we learned that following the development of an algorithmic approach to a problem, often using a flow chart, it becomes necessary to write a detailed set of instructions for the computer. This set of instructions, called a *program*, must include instructions for transcription of the data, coding for the computer and output of the results. In this chapter, we consider the programming of electronic calculators.

Many computing problems require complex calculations, but involve only a moderate amount of input data and output results. The programmable electronic calculator is often used to solve such problems. It costs less than a computer, but it has a much greater capacity than a mechanical desk calculator. The programmable calculator is like a small personal electronic computer; it is easy to program and to operate. Also, the calculator can provide results for complicated calculations within seconds.

Electronic digital calculators are constructed like electronic digital computers. We have defined a computer as a data processor that can perform substantial computation, including numerous arithmetic or logic operations, without intervention by a human operator during the run. Although the programmable electronic calculator fits within this definition, and can therefore be considered a small computer, we observe current convention and call it an electronic calculator from this point on.

The electronic calculator is the result of historical development of calculators during the last several hundred years, culminating in operable machines in this century.[1] Babbage (see above) came close to providing a working mechanical calculator, but his project was abandoned in 1842. Thomas Hill built an "Arithmometer" in 1857; his machine lacked precision. Other inventors manufactured calculators that worked—slower than did clerks adding in their heads, unfortunately for the inventors. In 1872, however, a former

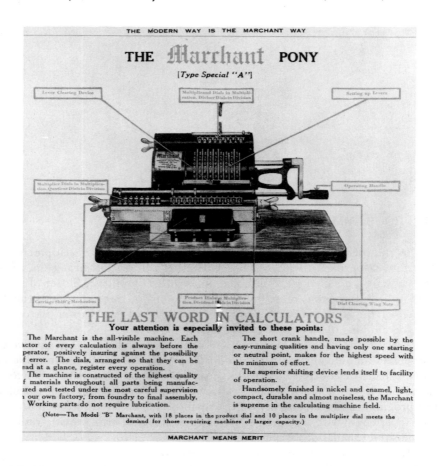

FIGURE 6–1 The Marchant Pony Calculator and operating instructions. *Courtesy of Hewlett-Packard Corporation.*

bank clerk named William S. Burroughs made the first practical calculator. In 1879 D. E. Felt marketed his "Comptometer." The Marchant calculator shown in Figure 6-1 was patented in 1911. This instrument, called the Marchant Pony, required human intervention during the calculation run; thus it does not meet our definition of a computer. An interesting example of a small contemporary hand-held calculator is shown in Figure 6-2. This device, the CURTA calculator, also requires human intervention in the calculation run. It adds, subtracts, multiplies, divides, squares, cubes, and extracts square roots. It uses eight-digit precision for multiplication. Babbage would be proud of such a calculator!

FIGURE 6-2. The manually-operated CURTA calculator. *Courtesy of the Curta Company, Van Nuys, California.*

By the 1920's automatic motor-driven calculators made by Burroughs, Monroe, Marchant, and Friden were in use in this country. Electronic calculators began to appear in the 1960's.

The distinction we can make for contemporary electronic calculators, bringing them closer to computers, is that they are programmable; that is, the instructions and data may be entered and stored within the calculator and then the run may be ordered to proceed without intervention. The stored-program concept, you will recall, was one of the primary developments of the late 1940's which made possible our present-day computers.

Many manufacturers produce programmable calculators; some have distinct advantages. Some characteristics of electronic calculators are given in Table 6-1.[2]

TABLE 6-1

Typical Characteristics of Electronic Calculators

1. *Size:* desktop calculator size, typically 15 in. x 20 in. x 10 in. high
2. *Price:* less than $5,000
3. *Speed:* addition – .001 seconds; multiplication – .01 seconds
4. *Attachments:* capable of accommodating an output printer
5. *Electronic:* transistor or integrated circuit electronic construction
6. *Storage:* 196 to 960 instruction steps
7. *Accuracy:* ± 1 part in the tenth digit of a number
8. *Number of digits of input data and output results:* 12
9. *Program Recording:* tape cassette, magnetic card or punched cards

Programmable electronic calculators, as you can see, feature desktop size, low price, reasonable calculation speed and high accuracy within the limits of the instruction steps allowed. One disadvantage is that the operator must enter all the data into the calculator. This means that each data item is equivalent to an instruction step. Thus, the electronic calculators are restricted to problems with relatively few input data items. Since every program contains many steps, there is a physical limitation to the amount of information we can feed in and utilize.

Programming an electronic calculator is an excellent introduction to programming computers. We can readily learn the language used for a particular calculator and step the calculator through all of the calculation processes. For instance, the Wang 700 stored program calculator, shown in Figure 6–3, is con-

FIGURE 6–3 The WANG 700 Stored Program Calculator. *Courtesy of the Wang Laboratories, Inc.*

structed of integrated circuits. Like most electronic calculators, it has a keyboard with which to input the instructions and data. The output is displayed on two displays, each with a ± sign, twelve digits and an exponent. The 700 uses a magnetic tape cassette to store programs entered into the calculator. The keyboard displays the arithmetic functions stored and available with the calculator. Logarithmic and exponential functions are provided. In addition, the instructions for a program such as a conditional transfer and a loop are provided. This calculator can accommodate a maximum of 960 program or instruction steps. It completes an addition in .0003 second. A typewriter may be used as an output printer to print out numeric data, alphabetic headings, and messages.

The ideal electronic calculator should be easy to learn to operate. One should be able to program it for complex calculations without extensive training or special computer languages. (A generalized hypothetical programmable calculator is presented and discussed in a recent book which might be reviewed by the reader if further detail is of interest.[3]) In the following section we discuss the programming of a specific electronic calculator. While a specific calculator is chosen for illustration, the programming and operation of other electronic calculators is very similar. It is not necessary to have an electronic calculator to gain insights from the following section. However, if an electronic calculator is available for use, it would be worthwhile to take advantage of the opportunity and to work on it the sample programs given below.

6.2 AN ELECTRONIC CALCULATOR

In this section we consider the construction and operation of the Hewlett-Packard 9100 (called the HP9100 henceforth). This programmable electronic calculator was the first to become available. It is commonly employed in many school and college laboratories. The HP9100 is a typical electronic calculator. It is not necessary to have access to an HP9100, or a similar programmable calculator, to gain knowledge from this section. One can readily extend the knowledge of the HP9100 to a similar electronic calculator at another time. Furthermore, the reader will learn about programming and the operation of programmable calculators on the basis of the discussion and programs developed. If a programmable calculator is available for use, so much the better.

The HP9100 is shown in Figure 6-4. This calculator uses a cathode-ray-tube output display; a printer and plotter are available for output accessories. The output displays three quantities: the contents of (1) the x register; (2) the accumulator, y; and (3) the temporary z register. The keyboard is used to input the data and the instructions. The slot on the right, above the keyboard, accommodates the magnetic program card.

Before proceeding we should define the useful term *register*:

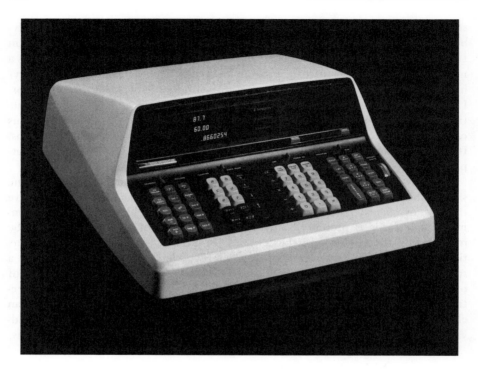

FIGURE 6–4 The Hewlett–Packard 9100A Stored Program Calculator. *Courtesy of Hewlett-Packard Corporation.*

REGISTER   A device capable of storing a specified amount of data, such as a 10–digit number.

Thus, the three registers, x, y and z are containers for three numerical quantities which are shown on the output display. There are 19 accessible registers in the internal memory. Three are displayed, two are used for data storage and 14 can be used for program storage or additional data storage. The 14 program registers can accommodate up to a total of 196 program steps.[4]

The trigonometric, logarithmic and exponential functions are produced with a single keystroke each, since they are stored internally in a read–only-memory:

READ–ONLY–MEMORY (ROM)   A storage unit into which the information is placed at the time of manufacture. Such information is available at any time. It can be modified only with difficulty.

Read–only–memories are often used in small computers and electronic calculators, since they are small in size, rapid in operation and relatively inexpensive.

The read–only–memory also stores the algorithms necessary to accomplish instructions called for by a simple keystroke. For example, the algorithm for accomplishing the square root of a number is stored in the read–only–memory. Also, the useful constant π is stored in the read–only–memory. It is clear that a read–only–memory is one cornerstone of an electronic programmable calculator.

One of the most important features of electronic calculators is the tremendous range of numbers that they can accommodate without special attention from the operator. It is not necessary to worry about where to place the decimal point to obtain the maximum accuracy. The numbers in an electronic calculator are stored, and all operations are accomplished, in what is called *floating point arithmetic.* A floating point number is expressed with the decimal point following the first digit and an exponent representing the number of places the decimal point should be moved—to the right if the exponent is positive, or to the left if the exponent is negative. Sometimes floating point arithmetic is called scientific notation.

FLOATING POINT NOTATION   A writing system in which numbers are expressed as significant digits, together with an exponent of the base 10 which indicates the location of the decimal point.

Thus, a floating point number shown on this 10–digit machine would appear as:
$$\pm \text{ F.FFFFFFFFF} \times 10^{XX}$$
The number consists of a plus or minus sign, a 10–digit number (all F's here), the decimal point following the first digit and the exponent (XX) of the base 10. Not all numbers require ten digits, of course. Table 6-2 illustrates the conversion of numbers to floating point form.

TABLE 6-2

Floating Point Coding of Numbers

Item	Number	Floating Point Form
a	123.4567	$+1.234567 \times 10^{2}$
b	0.0012345	$+1.2345 \times 10^{-3}$
c	−1,230,000	-1.23×10^{6}
d	4,000,000,000,000	$+4. \times 10^{12}$
e	−0.000000000050	$-5. \times 10^{-11}$
f	123,456,789.423	$+1.234567894 \times 10^{8}$
g	−0.0000521	
h	98765.4321987	

Examining Table 6-2, we can gain some insight into the usefulness of floating point notation. All electronic calculators and digital computers have a limited number of digits that can be accommodated. Item *a* shows that the floating point notation simply accommodates just the digits and indicates the place of the decimal point by means of the exponent 10^2. Since 10^2 equals 100, we should move the decimal point two places to the right. Similarly, in Item *b*, 10^{-3} equals .001; for it, we should move the decimal point three places to the left.

Item *d* illustrates the usefulness of floating point, since the number of digits in 4,000,000,000,000 is 13 and this number could not be accommodated in this form in a 10-digit machine. In Items *d* and *e*, we omit the zeros following the digits 4 and 5 respectively; they are assumed to be zero if omitted. Item *f* is a 12-digit number. The actual number accommodated in the 10-digit calculator is shown with the last two digits, 32, omitted. These additional two digits cannot be accommodated. They are also omitted in calculation. It is clear that the precision of calculations by a computer or electronic calculator is limited by the number of digits that can be accommodated. Complete Items *g* and *h* before proceeding to the next paragraph. You may check your answers with the footnote on the following page.

The limitation of the number of digits accommodated by a specific machine is important. The number of characters a computer will accommodate is called a *word*:

WORD   A sequence of characters considered as an entity.

Since any sequence of characters accommodated by the HP9100 are the plus or minus sign, the decimal point, up to ten digits and the exponent with its sign, a word in this calculator appears as:

$$\pm \text{ F.FFFFFFFFF} \pm \text{XX}$$

Since the word has a certain specified fixed length in any given machine, we call it the *word length*. The word length of the HP9100 is 14. This word length of 14 characters assumes the decimal point. In other machines it is assumed that the decimal point always follows the $\pm$ sign. In that case the word length required is again 14 characters, and any number is written $\pm$.FFFFFFFFFF$\pm$XX.

What are the largest and smallest numbers that can be stored in a computer with a 14-character word? Since the exponent can accommodate two digits we can have

$$\pm \text{ F.FFFFFFFFF} \pm \text{XX}$$

Where XX = 99, the largest number would be

$$+ 9.999999999 \times 10^{+99}$$

and the smallest

$$+ 1. \times 10^{-99}$$

Clearly, almost all the numbers we would want to use can be accommodated within the exponents +99 to −99.

The HP9100, as well as other electronic calculators and digital computers, also accommodates numbers in *fixed point notation*:

FIXED POINT NOTATION   A system of writing numbers in which the position of the decimal point is fixed with respect to one end of the numerals according to some convention.

The convention for the HP9100 is to display the decimal point in its proper position within the 10–digit number, assuming, of course, that the number in question can be accommodated within ten digits. The number 5.3361×10^3 is displayed in fixed point notation as

$$5336.1$$

Fixed point notation is a commonly used and understood notation, but its disadvantage is the limited size of the numbers that can be used. The difference in the range of numbers available with 10 digits for fixed and floating point is given in Table 6–3, which shows why floating point notation is preferable.

TABLE 6–3

The Range of Numbers for 10–Digit Fixed and Floating Point Notation

	RANGE
Fixed Point	$10^{10}-1 \geqslant \text{number} \geqslant 1 \times 10^{-10}$
Floating Point	$10^{100}-1 \geqslant \text{number} \geqslant 1 \times 10^{-99}$

The concepts of floating and fixed point numbers, registers and words are used with digital computers. While we described an electronic calculator as a device of interest, all we have learned is equally useful in our understanding of digital computers. It is not necessary to read any further in chapter six if you do not wish to learn about programming an electronic calculator. You may wish to proceed directly to chapter seven at this time.

6.3 PROGRAMMING AN ELECTRONIC CALCULATOR

This section explores the use of a language to program a set of instructions for an electronic calculator. Remember, the calculator operation is similar to that of a digital computer and the process of programming is similar. The instruction steps available for the HP9100 are shown in Figure 6–5 on the keyboard of the calculator. We will only consider a reduced set of instructions, since the instructions useful for advanced problems can be obtained from the instruction manual for this or any calculator. If you do not have a HP9100, you will be able to follow this section; omit Section 6.4, which includes some more advanced problems keyed to the use of the HP9100.

The program of a computer uses a code to translate instructions into logic that can be interpreted by the machine. The use of code to represent instructions is an ancient idea.

Item g -5.21×10^{-5}
Item h $+9.876543219 \times 10^4$

FIGURE 6-5 The keyboard of the HP9100, showing the instruction steps available. *Courtesy of Hewlett-Packard Corporation.*

Codes used in electronic calculators and digital computers often employ one instruction for each line of code. An abbreviation or symbol is frequently used for an instruction. The HP9100 uses this kind of language. The code uses *mnemonic symbols*:

MNEMONIC SYMBOL A sign chosen to assist the human memory. For example, an abbreviation such as MPY for "Multiply."

The code or set of mnemonic symbols for the HP9100 includes those given in Table 6-4.

TABLE 6-4

A Partial Set of Instruction Steps or Code for the HP9100

CLEAR	Clears the x, y, z registers (enters zeros).
↑	Duplicates the contents of the x to the y register and shifts the contents of y to the z register.
ROLL ↑	Shifts the contents of the x to the y register, shifts the contents of y to the z register and shifts z to the x register.

ROLL ↓   The reverse of ROLL↑, shown graphically as:

 x⟳y   Exchanges the contents of the x and y registers:

$$z \rightarrow Z$$
$$y \; Y$$
$$x \; X$$

+   Adds the contents of X to the contents of Y. The sum is entered into Y and X is unchanged.

÷   Divides the contents of Y by the contents of X. The quotient is entered into Y and X is unchanged.

x→( )   Stores the contents of X into the register indicated by the following instruction, which can be 0, 1, 2, 3, 4, 5, 6, 7, 8, 9, a, b, c, d, e or f. X is unchanged. For example, X→(3) means "Store the number now in X in register 3. There are 16 storage registers.

e   Pressing "e" (or another letter) recalls the number stored in the e register and places it in X. Only alphabetic registers can be so recalled.

y→( )   Stores the contents of Y into the register indicated by the following instruction. Y is unchanged.

Stop   Halts program execution and provides for data entry. Pressing "Continue" will allow the program to proceed.

Continue   Starts program execution with the next instruction.

End   Halts program execution. This must be the last instruction in the program. Pressing "Continue" starts the program again.

Clear X   Clears the x register.

Using this partial list of instruction steps, let us write a program to obtain the result of the equation $\dfrac{A \times B}{A + B}$ for any A and B given as input numbers. We shall use the x, y, z, f and e registers (e and f for storage). The program is as follows:

STEP	KEY	x	y	z	f	e	
01	CLEAR	0	0	0	0	0	Clear display & e & f.
02	STOP	A	B	0	0	0	Stop to enter A & B.
03	x→( )	A	B	0	0	0	
04	e	A	B	0	0	A	Store A and B.
05	y→( )	A	B	0	0	A	
06	f	A	B	0	B	A	
07	x	A	A×B	0	B	A	
08	↑	A	A	A×B	B	A	Move A×B to Z to calculate A + B.

09	f	B	A	A×B	B	A	
10	+	B	A+B	A×B	B	A	
11	ROLL ↓	A+B	A×B	B	B	A	Position A×B and
12	÷	A+B	$\dfrac{A×B}{A+B}$	B	B	A	A+B to calculate quotient
13	ROLL ↑	B	A+B	$\dfrac{A×B}{A+B}$	B	A	
14	x⟳y	A+B	B	"	B	A	
15	e	A	B	"	B	A	
16	END	A	B	$\dfrac{A×B}{A+B}$			Final Display

The comments next to the program indicate the purpose of the steps, and the contents of the x, y, z, f and e registers are indicated at each step. We enter the program by first clearing all the registers by pressing the CLEAR key as step 01. The next step is entered by pressing the STOP key, which allows us to enter A into X and B into Y. The next two steps will store the number A, entered in register x, in register e. Similarly the next two steps will store the number B, entered in register y, in register f. The next step is a multiplication step, yielding A × B in register y. Step 08 moves the number A into the y register and A × B into the z register. The f instruction in step 09 recalls B into the x register. Then the + instruction adds A and B and provides the sum in the y register. Step 11 positions A × B and A + B to calculate the quotient, which is accomplished in step 12. Step 13 uses a ROLL↑ instruction to reposition the quotient in the z register. Steps 14 and 15 are used to place B in the y register and A in the x register respectively for the final display. The END instruction halts the program execution and provides the results in the display on the cathode–ray tube.

Now let us assume we have entered the program into the electronic calculator by pressing the keys in the order called for by steps 01 to 16. After entering the program, we press CONTINUE and within a second the display shows A, B, and $\dfrac{A × B}{A + B}$ in X, Y and Z respectively. If we press CONTINUE, we can use the program again, entering a new set of A and B. If we wish, we can store the program on a magnetic card for retention and later use.

Now let us write a program to count from 0 to N in steps of 1 and to display each number. This program will contain a loop and a conditional transfer. We require the following additional instructions:

Go To

( ) ( ) Causes an unconditional branch to the program address entered as the next two instructions.

If x = y A conditional branch to the register indicated in the next two program steps will be accomplished if the condition x = y is satisfied. If the condition is not satisfied, the program branches to and executes the third program step.

Pause   Causes a brief display of .150 seconds before continuing.

The flow chart algorithm for generating a number n, from 0 to N and outputing each number generated from 1 to N is shown in Figure 6-6. Note that we check to determine if N = 0 as a first test and then proceed.

The program for counting to N in steps of 1 uses the x, y and z registers as follows:

Step Number	Step Register	Instruction	Display X	Y	Z	Comments
01	00	CLEAR	0	0	0	
02	01	STOP	N	0	0	Enter N
03	02	↑	N	N	0	
04	03	CLEAR x	0	N	0	
05	04	IF x = y	n	N	0	Conditional
06	05	1				transfer to
07	06	4				register 14
08	07	ROLL↑	0	n	N	
09	08	1	1	n	N	
10	09	+	1	n+1	N	
11	a	ROLL↓	n+1	N	1	
12	b	PAUSE				Display
13	c	PAUSE				the
14	d	PAUSE				number n+1
15	10	PAUSE				
16	11	GO TO				Return
17	12	0				in loop
18	13	4				to 04
19	14	END				

The HP9100 uses the 0 to 9 registers and the a to d registers for storage of instructions and data in the order 0, 1, 2, 3, 4, 5, 6, 7, 8, 9, a, b, c, d. Thus, program step number 12 appears in register b as shown. This is a detail we must accommodate in our program since we call for the loop to terminate if x = y and proceed to register 14 which is the End instruction. Four Pause instructions are used to cause a display of $4 \times .15 = .6$ seconds. If we desired a longer display period, we could use more Pause instructions. The instruction Go To followed by 0 and 4 causes a loop return to the register labeled 04.

The program given above will actually display the numbers 0 to N since it will display the number 0 immediately after entering N and receiving a Clear X instruction. After entering the data, we press the "Continue" key and the pro-

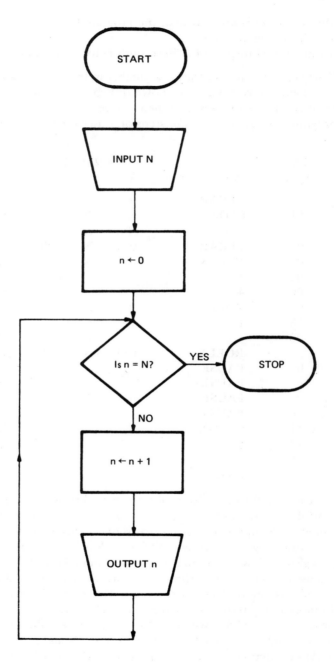

FIGURE 6-6   Flow chart for an algorithm to count a number n from 0 to N in increments
of 1, and to display from 1 to N.

gram proceeds. When the program has counted to N, we can press "Continue" and the program can be recycled.

Any key on the keyboard can be pressed to store an instruction step except the "Step Program" (STEP PRGM) key on the lower right hand corner of the keyboard. This key is used to debug and test a program by moving the program through each instruction step by step. If an erroneous instruction is found to be entered at a step while debugging, the instruction in that specific register can be changed simply by keying the correct instruction into the register. If we want to alter one step in a program, we call for the register concerned by pressing "Go To () ()" with the register number given in the next two steps. Then we can key in the new instruction.

The set of instructions for a programmable calculator is quite versatile and powerful, since the instructions provide for conditional transfers, loops and many internally–provided functions such as the trigonometric and logarithmic functions. The instruction set, or programming language, used for electronic programmable calculators is a powerful computer language. It is, in a sense, a machine–oriented language. However, it is actually a problem–oriented language, since it is designed for the convenient expression of a given class of problems. The problem–oriented language of electronic calculators limits the types of problems that can be solved to those of a mathematical nature. We cannot use a calculator to store names, addresses and phone numbers and then list them in alphabetical order. A digital computer *can* accomplish such a task; a computer is, by its nature, size and expense, a more powerful machine than an electronic calculator. Nevertheless, the electronic calculator is very useful for solving mathematical problems utilizing small amounts of data inexpensively.

In the next section we consider some advanced problems that can be solved with the HP9100 or a similar electronic calculator. You may elect to read the section or not, without risking confusion in later chapters, depending upon your interest and the availability of an electronic calculator.

6.4   ADVANCED PROGRAMS FOR THE PROGRAMMABLE CALCULATOR

Let us write a program for generating the Nth Fibonacci number. We will not display the sequence, which could consume a lot of time, but rather just the number of interest. For example, the eleventh Fibonacci number is 55 and the sixteenth Fibonacci number is 610. The numbers increase in size rapidly and we must be certain not to exceed the allowable size of numbers in the computer. The twenty–fifth Fibonacci number is 28,657 and the thirty–fifth is 5,702,887. We previously considered the Fibonacci sequence in section 4.3 and gave a flow chart for generating the sequence in Figure 4–9. In this problem, we wish only to provide as output the Nth Fibonacci number, where N is an input number. Thus, if we want the 25th Fibonacci number we set N = 25. A flow chart for generating the Nth Fibonacci number is given in Figure 6-7.

The program is given in Figure 6-8. The counter index is equal to n and the loop is terminated when n = N. The two sequential Fibonacci numbers are P and Q, respectively. We display as output: n in the X register, N in the Y register, and the Nth Fibonacci number in the Z register. Obviously, this is not the only possible algorithm for obtaining the Nth Fibonacci number, but it has the advantage of requiring only 43 steps.

The only new instruction we use in this program is RCL, which recalls the contents of the f and e registers to the X and Y registers, respectively. The contents of f and e remain unchanged. You may wish to verify this program by following through the program for N = 4. If you have a calculator available, determine how much time it takes to calculate the 16th and the 35th Fibonacci numbers by timing each calculation with a stopwatch.

As a final example, let us determine a program for obtaining the greatest common divisor of two numbers using Euclid's algorithm. A discussion of Euclid's algorithm appears in section 4.2 and a flowchart appears in Figure 4-6. We assume that the two numbers are A and B and that A is always greater than B. Recall that we calculate

$$A = Q \cdot B + R$$

where Q = integer and R = remainder. We need one additional command, INTx, for this program. It will insure that Q is an integer. This command obtains the integer part of the number appearing in the X register and enters the result into the X register. Thus, if 3.621 appears in X and we press INT x, we obtain 3. with the decimal part eliminated (set equal to zero). The flowchart for the program is shown in Figure 6-9. After inputing A and B we calculate A/B and then obtain Q = INT (A/B). Thus, for example, if A = 26 and B = 4, we have

$$Q = \text{INT} \left(\frac{26}{4} \right) = 6$$

and

$$R = A\text{-}QB = 26 - 6(4) = 2$$

We then check to determine if R is equal to zero. If it is not, as in this case, we replace A with B and B with R. Then we calculate

$$Q = \text{INT} (4/2) = 2$$

and then

$$R = 4\text{-}2(2) = 0$$

When R = 0, we output the current value of B, which is equal to 2. Thus, the greatest common divisor of 26 and 4 is 2.

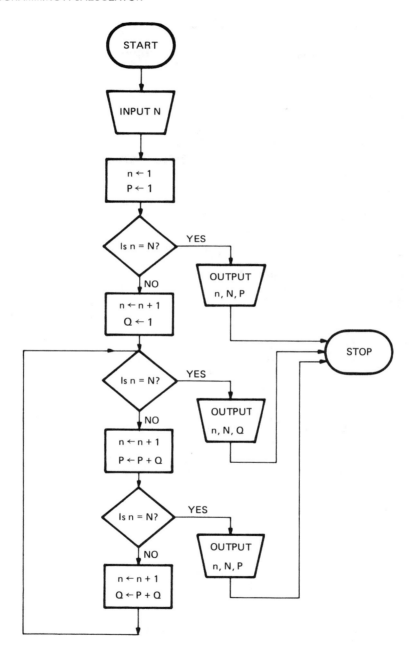

FIGURE 6–7   A flow chart algorithm for obtaining the Nth Fibonacci number.

Step	Instruction	Comment
00	CLEAR	
01	STOP	Enter N.
02	x→ ( )	Store N.
03	d	
04	↑	
05	1	
06	IF x = y	Is N = 1?
07	3	
08	0	
09	ROLL↑	
0a	1	
0b	+	n ← n + 1
0c	ROLL↓	
0d	IF x = y	Is n = N?
10	3	
11	0	
12	ROLL↑	
13	x→ ( )	Store Q in f.
14	f	
15	1	
16	+	n ← n + 1
17	ROLL↑	
18	RCL	Recall f and e.
19	+	P ← P + Q
1a	d	Recall d into x.
1b	ROLL↑	
1c	IF x = y	Is n = N?
1d	3	
20	0	
21	ROLL↑	
22	x→ ( )	Store P in e.
23	e	
24	1	
25	+	n ← n + 1
26	ROLL↑	
27	RCL	Recall f and e.
28	+	
29	d	Recall N.
2a	ROLL↑	
2b	GO TO	
2c	0	
2d	d	Loop return.
30	END	Display.

FIGURE 6–8 A program for obtaining the Nth Fibonacci number.

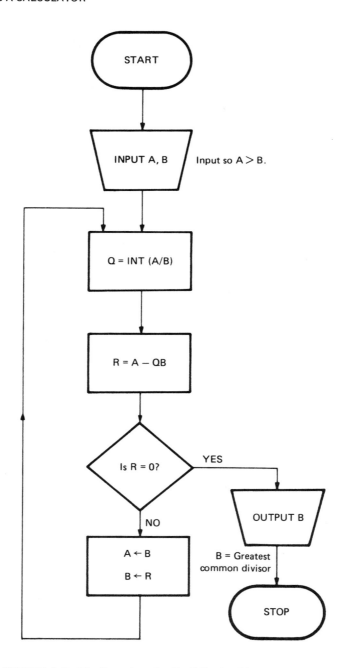

FIGURE 6–9   The flow chart for Euclid's algorithm, assuming $A > B$.

One program for the HP9100 for Euclid's algorithm is shown in Figure 6–10. This program requires 35 steps. It is quite efficient. Perhaps you will wish to run through the program, listing the contents of the X, Y, Z, a and b registers at each step for the case where A = 26 and B = 4.

Step	Instruction	Comment
00	CLEAR	
01	STOP	Enter A.
02	x→ ( )	
03	a	
04	↑	
05	STOP	Enter B.
06	x→ ( )	
07	b	
08	÷	Obtain A/B.
09	ROLL↓	
0a	INT x	Obtain $\mathrm{int}\left(\dfrac{A}{B}\right)$.
0b	ROLL↑	
0c	x	Obtain Q x B.
0d	a	Recall A into X.
10	x y	
11	–	R = A–Q·B
12	ROLL↓	
13	IF x>y	⎧ is R> 0?.
14	1	⎫ Yes – go to 18.
15	8	⎩ No – proceed.
16	b	Recall B.
17	STOP	Greatest Common Divisor is in X.
18	ROLL↑	
19	b	Recall B.
1a	x→ ( )	
1b	a	A←B
1c	ROLL↓	Place R in X.
1d	x→ ( )	
20	b	B←R
21	a	Recall A.
22	ROLL↑	
23	b	Recall B.
24	GO TO	⎧ Loop.
25	0	⎫ Return to
26	8	⎩ 08.

FIGURE 6–10   A program for Euclid's algorithm, assuming A > B.

SUMMARY

In this chapter we have reviewed the characteristics and advantages of electronic programmable calculators. While discussing programmable calculators, we have considered floating point and fixed point numbers and the concept of registers. We have found that electronic calculators are powerful calculating machines; they rival digital computers for solving mathematical problems with small amounts of input data. While programmable calculators are not general purpose computers, they can assist in the solution of problems. They have many features, such as program storage, claimed by the larger, more expensive digital computers.

In the next chapter, we consider a programming language used primarily for time-shared computers, and we return to consider some of the problems considered in this chapter.

CHAPTER 6 PROBLEMS

P6-1.   List some of the advantages and disadvantages of the programmable electronic calculator.

P6-2.   What is the typical accuracy of an electronic calculator? Compare the accuracy of a programmable electronic calculator with the accuracy of a mechanical desk calculator available at your school.

P6-3.   Define *register*, *read-only-memory*, and *word*.

P6-4.   A specific machine can accommodate five numerical digits in fixed point notation, and five numerical digits, a decimal point, and a two-digit exponent in floating point form. Thus, for this machine we have

Input Number	Floating Point	Fixed Point
432.56	4.3256×10^2	432.56
5,637.822	5.6378×10^3	5,637.8
–0.01459		
+8384,446		
Maximum allowable		
Minimum allowable		
+939423.1		

Complete the table of entries for the fixed point and floating point representation of the input numbers.

P6-5. List some mnemonic symbols used by the telephone company, your bank, and other organizations. Examine your utility bills and salary stubs for mnemonic symbols.

P6-6. Using the list of instructions for the HP9100, write a program for obtaining the slope, m, of a line when y, x and b are provided as input for the equation

$$y = mx + b$$

P6-7. In problem 5-7, you saw the problem of four integers A, B, C and D related by the equation

$$A^N + B^N = C^N + D^N$$

where N is an input. Find all the sets of A, B, C and D, for a specified N when the numbers A, B, C and D are limited to 100 as a maximum value. For N = 2, one set of answers is (1, 8, 4, 7). For N = 3, one set of answers is (1, 12, 9, 10). This problem is quite complex; it requires many loops and a significant amount of running time on an electronic calculator. For example, the solution given above for N = 3 consumed 78 seconds on an HP9100, using one algorithm. For N = 4, the running time to obtain one answer can consume many minutes. When writing the program, and executing it if possible, you will need a step which calculates $E = (A^N + B^N) - (C^N + D^N)$. Another step will check to determine if E is a very small number, ideally, zero. Due to the small errors in calculation of A^N, B^N, C^N and D^N with many loops using logarithms, it is unwise to determine if x = y where $x = A^N + B^N$ and $y = C^N + D^N$. Rather, it is wise to assume small errors will occur and use the test step:

$$\text{if } E < \sin (1°)$$

since the sine of the angle of one degree is approximately .001. In order to obtain A^N, you will need to use logarithms. Write a suitable program.

P6-8. In problem 5-8, we obtained a flow chart for determining all the three-digit numbers that are equal to the sum of the cubes of their digits. Use the flow chart algorithm devised in problem 5-8 to write a program for determining at least one three-digit number which satisfies the criterion.

P6-9. A flow chart algorithm for finding all the factors of a given integer N is given in Figure P6-9. If the input is 12, the expected output is 1,2,3,4, 6,12. The algorithm is straightforward since the loop determines if a test number D divides the number N and results in an integer B. If an integer B is obtained, then C is a factor of N. Write a program for finding all the factors of N. The program will use the instruction INT x which deletes the decimal portion of a number x. The program will require approximately 40 steps.

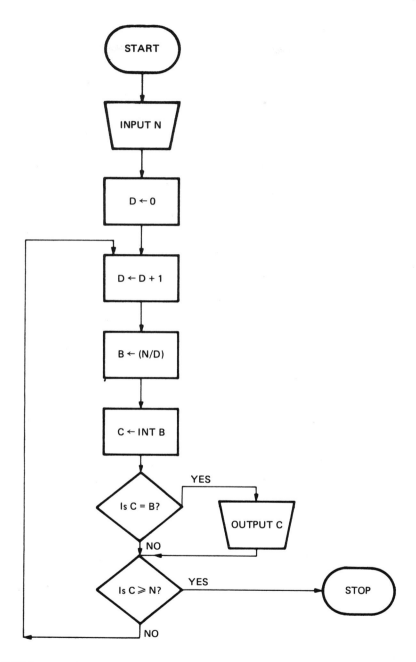

FIGURE P6-9 A flow chart algorithm for finding all the factors of a given integer N.

CHAPTER 6 REFERENCES

1. L. D. Shergalis, "Calculators," *Hewlett-Packard Journal,* Sept. 1968, Palo Alto, California, pg. 2.
2. "Programmable Calculators," *Electronic Design*, Vol. 15, July 19, 1970, pp. 120-121.
3. R. Albrecht, E. Lindberg, W. Mara, *Computer Methods in Mathematics*, Addison-Wesley Publishing Company, Reading, Massachusetts, 1969.
4. R. E. Monnier, "A New Electronic Calculator with Computerlike Capabilities," *Hewlett-Packard Journal*, Sept. 1968, Palo Alto, California, pp. 3-9.
5. D. S. Cochran, "Internal Programming of the 9100A Calculator," *Hewlett-Packard Journal*, Sept. 1968, Palo Alto, California, pp. 14-16.
6. "Name's the Same, but it Rivals Big Brother," *Product Engineering*, February 24, 1969, pp. 22-24.
7. A. Ralston, *Introduction to Programming and Computer Science,* McGraw-Hill Book Co., New York, 1971.

7

THE BASIC LANGUAGE

7.1 TIME-SHARING COMPUTERS AND THE BASIC LANGUAGE

In Chapter 6, we found that the programming of an electronic calculator enabled the problem-solver to obtain the solution to many mathematical problems. However, we found that the electronic calculator, while relatively inexpensive, is also limited to problems with relatively little input data and a limited number of instruction steps. In addition, the electronic calculator is unable to manipulate or utilize alphabetic characters. Thus, for many types of problems, the electronic calculator will be ineffective and a digital computer must be utilized.

Within the last five years, a new development, that of time-sharing computers, has enabled the problem-solver to have access to a large digital computer at comparatively low cost. The time-shared computer allows several users to sit at input terminals and communicate with the computer simultaneously. These terminals may be coupled to a central computer many miles away through telephone circuits. A user sitting at his input terminal has the illusion that he has the computer for his own use, even though the computer is far away and several other people are using it at the same time. The definition of *time-sharing* is:

TIME–SHARING   Simultaneous participation in available computer time by multiple users via terminals and communication lines. Characteristically, the response time is so brief that a computer seems dedicated to each user.

The primary factor of time–sharing is that it enables many users to interact with a computer simultaneously. This quality is to be distinguished from the simple sharing or sequential use (each in his turn) of a computer or electronic calculator. Many time–shared computer systems have up to one hundred persons using a computer simultaneously.

The number of time–shared computer systems in the United States has grown rapidly during the period from 1965 to 1970, as is shown in Figure 7–1.

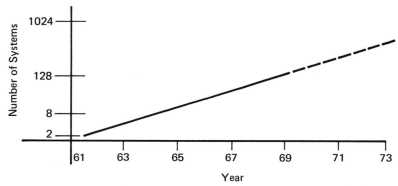

FIGURE 7–1   The number of time–shared computer systems in the United States. (Estimates are given beyond 1969.)

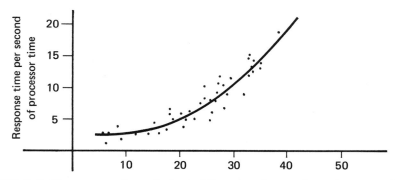

FIGURE 7–2   The response time of a typical time–shared computer system versus the number of users for a given processor time.

It is estimated that there are one thousand time–shared systems available in 1971. Notice that the left–hand scale of Figure 7–1 is logarithmic; the growth of time–sharing has been exponential in nature. It is estimated that 50,000 terminals were connected to time–sharing computers in 1969, while there were

128 computer systems. Of course, not all these terminals are in use at any one time. The ratio of terminals to systems is approximately 40:1.

The time–shared computer system can operate for many simultaneous users, since a person using a terminal to input, debug and execute his program requires time to think and respond between program steps. Also, the computer can process each person's input much faster than he can type the input on a typewriter terminal. The response time of the computer system as each individual user experiences it is shown in Figure 7-2.[1] If there are 10 persons using a time–shared computer and the central processor takes 0.1 second to execute the input step for each user, the response time experienced by the user will be 0.3 second. As the number of users grows, the response time will deteriorate. With 35 simultaneous users, the response time will be 17 times the time required by the central processor—perhaps several seconds.

Time–sharing was first developed at the Massachusetts Institute of Technology in the early 1960's, using an IBM 7094, under a project with the acronym MAC (Machine-Aided Cognition or Multiple-Access Computer). At Dartmouth College, in 1963, a project involving a GE–235 computer and a Datanet 30 communications processor led to the development of time–sharing at Dartmouth and also to the development of General Electric's time–sharing system. From these beginnings have grown such complexes of equipment as the powerful system shown in Figure 7-3.

FIGURE 7-3 The GE–635 is capable of performing local batch processing, remote batch processing and time–sharing processing. *Courtesy of General Electric Company.*

In 1965, the first commercial time-sharing service bureau, Keydata, made its debut using the PDP-6, a short-lived machine developed by Digital Equipment Corporation. It should be noted here that the primary emphasis of all time-sharing work up to this time was on scientific computing. Keydata offered an on-line business service, an approach which has not yet been widely emulated.

An integral part of the time-sharing system is the user's programming language. Time-sharing has dramatically reduced the cost of using a computer, bringing its use within the reach of almost any business or school. However, to employ this versatile and powerful tool, the user must himself do the programming. Time-sharing is literally user-oriented. A variety of "conversational" time-sharing languages have been developed, with computer instructions written in English words and/or mathematical notation. These languages are easily learned in an interactive way—that is, writing a program becomes a dialogue between the user and the time-sharing system. Instructions may be written by the user and then checked by the system. If the computer detects a syntax or language error, error messages are typed back. Before a program is run, it is checked for correct use of the language. The conversational language that has proved most popular is called BASIC. It was developed at Dartmouth College. In September of 1963, Professors John G. Kemeny and Thomas E. Kurtz of Dartmouth launched a project that was to have a major effect on the computer industry. The project was to build and operate a time-sharing system using General Electric Company computers and a language that was to be developed at Dartmouth as part of the project. Two short-term goals were in mind at the beginning of the program; the first was to introduce the computer to a majority of the students at Dartmouth, and the second was to make the computer more readily accessible to the faculty.

Work began on the project and by the spring of 1964, BASIC, the "Beginner's All-purpose Symbolic Instruction Code," was born. Students and faculty alike used the new system so enthusiastically that four years later, in their final report, dated June 1967, Kemeny and Kurtz reported that they had introduced some 2000 students to BASIC and to the computer, and that 40% of the faculty used the system for a wide variety of projects.[2]

The BASIC language is oriented to conversational use at a terminal with a time-shared computer. The idea was to make the language syntax very easy to learn and use. It was established that every program statement must have a verb and be on a single line. Variable names are only a single letter, followed by a digit if desired. Furthermore, the data is stored in the program. There are a limited number of instruction statements (15 in the original Dartmouth version). Also, the language can be learned in a matter of hours. The result is a very simple or basic language indeed.[3]

Time-sharing has become very common; perhaps time-sharing terminals will be readily available in the local school, library and office building in the

FIGURE 7-4 The DATA-NET-730, a portable time-sharing teletypewriter unit, permits sending messages to a central time-sharing computer over telephone wires. It employs an acoustic coupler, shown at the right. *Courtesy of Hewlett-Packard Corporation.*

near future. A portable time-sharing teletypewriter unit is shown in Figure 7-4. Professor Kemeny has called for the creation of nationwide time-sharing computer networks as a critical step in harnessing technology to the service of society. "I think that we will not experience the ultimate impact of computers on society until computer terminals are not only in business, research, and educational institutions, but also are commonly available in the home," he said at a recent seminar.[5]

The advantages of a time-shared computer are that it:

1. is user-oriented
2. is characterized by simultaneous use by multiple users
3. communicates with the user in a conversational language and in an interactive way in the form of a dialogue
4. provides the capabilities of a large computer system for a relatively low cost

The user of a time-sharing system communicates with the system and develops programs this way:

1. He dials the computer, using the telephone system at the terminal.
2. He enters the system and identifies his user-number.

3. The time-sharing computer acknowledges and, on some systems, furnishes a telephone number to call if assistance is required. The computer acknowledges that it is now "ready" to do what the user requires.
4. The user types the program on the terminal keyboard, using whatever conversational language he has selected, or whatever one is available.
5. The computer asks for data to be input by the user; when the last item of data is entered, the computer is ready to execute the program.
6. The user now instructs the computer to "run" the program. The computer reaffirms the name of the program that it will run and executes the calculations.
7. The computer now asks the user if he would like to change the data. If so, changes are made and new answers are generated.

In this section we have learned that the basis of time-sharing is the *simultaneous* use of a computer by several users. Time-sharing is used by colleges and schools, industry, business, hospitals, research centers and government. It provides the user with a powerful tool which has the convenience of a desk calculator and is relatively inexpensive to use. On most time-sharing systems, the user has a choice of computer languages. However, BASIC is the easiest to learn and use; it is quite a powerful language. We shall learn the rudiments of BASIC in the next section. If you do not plan to use BASIC language at this time, you may wish to proceed to Chapter 8.

7.2 THE BASIC LANGUAGE

BASIC is an acronym for Beginner's All-purpose Symbolic Instruction Code. The language was designed for people who have had no experience with using computers or writing computer programs. It may be used quite effectively by programmers with several years' experience. BASIC is user-oriented and may be learned in just a few hours of concentrated study. The language, which resembles other problem-oriented languages, may serve the mathematician, engineer, physicist, chemist, student, teacher or businessman equally well. It makes use of standard mathematical notation. BASIC contains a powerful arithmetical facility, many language diagnostics, which tell a programmer if he has made an error, or give him the consequences of such errors, several editing features, a library of common mathematical functions, a library of matrix functions and simple input and output procedures.

A program using the BASIC language is a series of typed lines entered via the terminal. The ASR-33 Model terminal is shown in Figure 7-5.

The teletypewriter keyboard is similar to a typewriter's, but there are no lower-case letters. On some teletypewriters, zeros have a slash through them to differentiate them from the letter "oh". There is no backspace key, but BASIC

FIGURE 7-5. The ASR-33 Model Terminal. Courtesy of Hewlett-Packard Corporation.

does allow the programmer to correct errors as he types. Typing a left arrow
(←) effectively backspaces the typewriter one space. For example:

    2 FER←←OR I = 1 TO 5   would be recognized as:
    2 FOR I = 1 TO 5

This statement is a typical program statement. Note that it includes a line number, a verb and a statement. FOR is the verb in this program statement.

Each BASIC program statement has a line number, and only capital letters,
numbers and some special characters are used to complete the instruction. The
line number may be an integer between 1 and 99999. The computer executes
the instructions in the order of the line numbers, not in the order they are
typed in. A good procedure is to use as line numbers 10, 20, 30, etc., so that
unforeseen statements may be entered between the existing statements at a
later time. Each program line must include an English word immediately following the statement number. A statement can be deleted from a program by
typing the statement number and then hitting the "RETURN" key.

Let us consider a program written in BASIC for calculating the sum of two
numbers, A = 5 and B = 10. The program is:

    10   LET A = 5
    20   LET B = 10
    30   LET S = A + B
    40   PRINT "THE SUM OF A AND B IS", S
    50   END

We began all statements with a number and followed with an English word, a
verb in each case. In this program there are three program statements, beginning
with the verbs LET, PRINT and END respectively. In the context of the program, their use is fairly obvious. (The definitions of these three statements and

other BASIC statements are given in Table 7-1.) The first statement assigns the value of 5 to A. (This statement is BASIC expression for the assignment notation A←5 used in previous chapters.) The second statement assigns 10 as the value of B. The third statement, number 30, assigns the sum S to be equal to the sum of A and B. The PRINT statement calls for the typewriter to print out:

THE SUM OF A AND B IS 15

All messages to be printed exactly are enclosed with quotation marks. Following the quotation marks in statement 40 we add a comma to set off another print message and call for the value of the variable S to be printed. The PRINT statement may be comprised of several PRINT messages—as many as are necessary to complete the statement. Finally, the END statement will halt the execution of the program. To execute the program we press the "RUN" key and the typewriter will print:

THE SUM OF A AND B IS 15

There are three variables in the program above: A, B and S. A variable may be named with a single letter of the alphabet or with a letter of the alphabet followed by a single digit, 0 through 9. The arithmetic operator symbols in BASIC are given in Table 7-2. The arithmetic functions and their mnemonic symbol in BASIC are given in Table 7-3. Since there is no way to type, say, X^3, we use an arrow to indicate exponentiation and type X↑3. An asterisk (*) is used to indicate multiplication.

A program for obtaining the value of the hypotenuse of a right triangle whose sides are 5 and 10 is: [2]

```
10 LET X = 5
20 LET Y = 10
30 LET H = SQR(X↑2 + Y↑2)
40 PRINT "THE HYPOTENUSE IS", H
50 END
```

If we push the "RUN" key, we then obtain:

```
RUN
THE HYPOTENUSE IS 11.1803
READY
```

The computer executes on the command RUN and passes through all the steps in sequential order. After typing out the answer, it states that it is ready again.

If we wish to run this program for many sets of data, we use the READ and the DATA statements given in Table 7-1. Also, we use the GO TO statement to execute a loop. The loop will continue until all the data numbers are read. The program and the run for three sets of input numbers X and Y and

$$X = 1, 5 \text{ and } 3$$
$$Y = 1, 10 \text{ and } 4$$

is given below: [2]

```
1∅ READ X,Y
2∅ PRINT "THE HYPOTENUSE IS",SQR(X↑2+Y↑2)
3∅ GO TO 1∅
4∅ DATA 1,1,5,1∅,3,4
5∅ END
```

```
RUN
THE HYPOTENUSE IS          1.41421
THE HYPOTENUSE IS          11.18∅3
THE HYPOTENUSE IS          5
```

ERROR 56 IN LINE   1∅

Statement 30 requires the program to execute the loop until the data are exhausted. The first time through the loop the value for the hypotenuse for X = 1 and Y = 1 is printed. The PRINT statement accomplishes the computation directly. When all the data are exhausted, the loop is terminated and the computer prints a coded message which "diagnoses" its inability to continue. The code for "data are exhausted, so exit from loop" in this case is the expression "ERROR 56". (Running out of data isn't a mistake; the code expression is merely shorthand for one of the many possible causes for termination of the run.)

TABLE 7-1

A Partial List of Statements for BASIC

1. Operational Statements

    A. LET _____ = _____
               variable   expression

The equals sign orders "assign to" the variable the expression. If the variable is A and the expression 5, LET A = 5 means A←5.

    B. GO TO _____
              statement
              number

This statement alters the normal sequential execution of program statements and transfers control to a specified statement number.

    C. IF _____ (relates to) _____ THEN _____
        expression   expression   statement number

The IF THEN statement tests for equality or inequality between two expressions and transfers control depending on whether the test is satisfied or not. It is a conditional transfer which might take the form, for example: IF X>Y THEN 50

        The relational operators allowed and available on the keyboard of the time–shared computer are:

                            < less than
                            > greater than
                            < = less than or equal
                            > = greater than or equal
                            = equal
                            < > not equal

TABLE 7-1 (contd.)

2. Input/Output Statements

A. PRINT _____
       expression

To print a message we simply enclose the message within quotation marks in the PRINT statement. We may print the value of any variable, constant or formula by including it in the PRINT statement. If we order PRINT and do not supply any other information, the computer gives us a blank line by spacing without typing.

B. READ _____
       variable list

To get a result from READ, we must have supplied at least one DATA statement (see below). The READ statement calls for the values of the variables listed.

C. DATA _____
       number list

The DATA statement supplies the list of data corresponding to the READ variable list. When the first READ statement is executed, the first number in the lowest-numbered DATA statement is assigned to the first variable in the READ list, the second number to the second variable, and so on until the READ variable list is satisfied. Subsequent READ statements will begin reading data where the previous READ left off. See steps 1$\emptyset$ and 4$\emptyset$ above.

D. INPUT _____
       variable list

This statement is used when the programmer wants to input numbers into the program from the keyboard at the appropriate times in the execution of the program as requested by the computer. When the computer makes such "requests" it types a question mark.

3. Control Statements

A. END

Every BASIC program must have an END statement, to which is assigned the largest statement number in the program.

B. RUN

RUN begins the execution of a program.

C. LIST

LIST causes a current listing of the program to be typed out with the statements arranged in ascending order.

TABLE 7-2

The Arithmetic Operators in BASIC

Symbol	Operation	Example
*	Multiplication	A * B
+	Addition	A + B
−	Subtraction	A − B
/	Division	A / B
↑	Exponentiation	A↑2
		(means "A squared")

TABLE 7-3

The Arithmetic Functions in BASIC

Mnemonic Symbol	Function
SQR ( )	Square root of the expression contained within the parentheses
SIN ( )	Sine of the expression (in radians)
COS ( )	Cosine of the expression (in radians)
TAN ( )	Tangent of the expression (in radians)
ATN ( )	Arc tangent of the expression (in radians)
EXP ( )	Exponential value of the expression, $e^{( )}$
LOG ( )	Natural logarithm of the expression
ABS ( )	Absolute value of the expression
INT ( )	Integer part of the expression (INT(4.23) = 4)
SGN ( )	The sign of the expression

The FOR/NEXT statements in Table 7-4 (p. 134) provide the statements to obtain a loop and specify a step size. Let us write a program, as in Chapter 6, for counting from 0 to N in steps of one and printing the result. The flow chart is given in Figure 6-6.

```
10 INPUT N
20 FOR I = 0  TO N
30  PRINT I
40  NEXT I
50  END
```

This is certainly a very compact program. Since the step size is equal to one, it is omitted. The input statement allows us to input the value of N upon demand from the computer. The counter variable is I in this case, and the loop traverses from I = 0 to I = N. When we are ready, we type in RUN and we receive a question mark from the computer, which signals a request for input data. We then receive the count for 0 to N as follows:

```
RUN
? 5
  0
  1
  2
  3
  4
  5
?
```

The second question mark requests further data, such as N = 15.

7.3 EXAMPLES OF BASIC PROGRAMMING

As a further illustration of the use of the advanced statements given in Table 7-4, let us examine a program written to obtain the factors of a number N.[4] The algorithm for determining the factor of a number was discussed in Chapters 4 and 6. The algorithm determines if the division of the number N by a test factor F results in an integer. If an integer results from N/F, then F is a factor and it is printed out. If it is not a factor then we let $F \leftarrow F + 2$. It is necessary to check only the factor 2 and all odd numbers up to the square root of N.

The program is given in Figure 7-6. Lines 100 and 200 use Item 6 in Table 7-4, which calls for the input immediately following the labeling expression. Line 120 spaces a line. Lines 130 and 140 test for N = 0 and N = 2 and transfer control to the end or to print "2 is prime." The variable Z indicates and counts how many factors have been determined. When F, the first factor, is found, Z is set equal to 1 in statement 360 and F is printed. Since line 370 is a print statement followed by a semicolon, all the factors will be printed in a compact form on one line.

The program uses (SQR(N) + 1) in order to account for rounding errors in computing the square root. After checking all factors, if no factor is found, then the number is a prime number and that fact is printed out. This program uses a GOSUB command at line 180 and a RETURN command at line 410. The algorithm for testing N/F lies between lines 310 and 410. The REM statements provide remarks for the user of the program.

Table 7-4

Some Advanced BASIC Program Statements

1. FOR _____ = _____ TO _____ STEP _____
     variable   expression   expression   expression
   NEXT_____
     variable

   The FOR/NEXT statements provide the beginning and the end of a loop. If the step size is omitted, it is assumed to be equal to one. Each FOR statement must have a corresponding NEXT statement.

2. REM

   The REM statement is a remark statement used to insert comments into programs for explanation and future documentation. A REM statement does not execute as a program step but is simply retained as a notation for future reference.

3. DEF FN _____ (X) = _____
        one letter   expression

   The DEF statement is used to define a function in a program. The name of a function must be three letters, the first two of which must be FN. For example, if we wish to do a cube root calculation several places in a program, we could use

   $$10 \text{ DEF FNA}(X) = X \uparrow (1/3)$$

Table 7–4 (contd.)

4. RND(X)

The RND function will automatically generate random numbers in the range from 0 to 1. The argument within the parentheses in this case X is necessary, but may be any letter or number since it is merely a dummy in this program statement.

5. GOSUB _____
          line number

RETURN

The GOSUB and RETURN statements allow a part of a program that must be executed at several points in the overall program to be executed as a subroutine, so it doesn't have to be typed in several times. For example, suppose that the teletypewriter must be spaced three lines at three different points in a program. This can be done as follows:

```
        •
        •
        •
100 GOSUB 900
        •
        •
        •
320 GOSUB 900
        •
        •
        •
540 GOSUB 900
        •
        •
        •
900 PRINT
901 PRINT
902 PRINT
903 RETURN
1000 END
```

Each time the RETURN is executed, control is transferred to the statement following the GOSUB which last called the PRINT routine.

6. PRINT _____ ;
          expression

INPUT _____
          expression

The PRINT statement followed by a semicolon and with an INPUT as the next statement will place the question mark calling for input on the first printed line immediately following the expression.

7. PRINT _____ ;
          variable

This PRINT statement containing a semicolon is used where the variable is to be printed many times and uses one horizontal line for printing multiple answers in a loop, rather than several consecutive lines with one answer per line.

FACTOR

```
100 PRINT "NUMBER TO BE FACTORED";
110 INPUT N
120 PRINT
130 IF N = 0 THEN 999
140 IF N = 2 THEN 250
150 LET Z = 0
160
170 LET F = 2
180 GOSUB 300
190 FOR  F = 3 TO SQR(N)+1 STEP 2
200 GOSUB 300
210 NEXT  F
220 IF  Z = 0 THEN 250
230 PRINT N;
240 GOTO 500
250 PRINT N; "IS PRIME."
260 GOTO 500
270
300 REM TESTS F AS A FACTOR.
310 IF N/F <> INT(N/F) THEN 410
330 IF Z > 0 THEN 370
340 PRINT N; "HAS THE FACTORS:"
350 PRINT "      ";
360 LET Z = 1
370 PRINT F;
380 LET N = N/F
390 IF N = 1 THEN 500
400 GOTO 310
410 RETURN
420
500 REM ALL DONE.
510 PRINT
520 PRINT
530 PRINT
540 GOTO 100
999 END
```

RUN

NUMBER TO BE FACTORED? 60

```
60   HAS THE FACTORS:
        2       2       3       5
```

FIGURE 7-6 A program for determining the factors of a number N.

Now let us write a program for calculating the greatest common divisor of two numbers A and B, where A is greater than B. This problem was considered in Chapters 4 and 6. The flow chart algorithm is given in Figure 6–11 and repeated in Figure 7–7. The program, using Euclid's algorithm, is as follows:

```
10 PRINT "A", "B", "G.C.D."
20 READ A,B
30 PRINT A,B
40 LET Q = INT(A/B)
45 LET R = A - Q*B
50 IF R = 0  THEN 75
60 LET A = B
65 LET B = R
70 GO TO 40
75 PRINT B
80 GO TO 20
90 DATA 169, 130, 256, 243, 987654321, 123456789
99 END
```

RUN

A	B	G.C.D.
168	130	13
256	243	1
987654321	123456789	9

OUT OF DATA IN 20

Statement 80 is used to return the program to the READ statement for more data. When the READ statement calls for additional input data and all the data have been utilized from the DATA statement, the time–sharing computer will signal the programmer that this condition exists. Each computer system uses a specific signal for this purpose, such as ERROR 56 or OUT OF DATA IN (the READ statement).

Another problem that we have been treating in the preceding chapters is that of determining the Nth Fibonacci number. The flow chart for the algorithm for determining the Nth Fibonacci number is given in Figure 7–8 for the portion where N>2. The program is as follows:

```
10  INPUT N
20  LET P = 0
30  LET Q = 1
40  IF N = 0 THEN 200
50  IF N = 1 THEN 300
60  IF N = 2 THEN 400
```

```
70   FOR I = 2  TO N TO N
80   LET S = P + Q
90   LET P = Q
100 LET Q = S
110 NEXT I
120 PRINT "THE "N"TH FIBONACCI NUMBER IS" S
130 GO TO 900
200 PRINT "THERE IS NO 0TH FIBONACCI NUMBER"
250 GO TO 900
300 PRINT "THE FIRST FIBONACCI NUMBER IS 1"
350 GO TO 900
400 PRINT "THE SECOND FIBONACCI NUMBER IS 1"
900 END
```

The first step calls for the value of N as input. The next two steps set the initial values of P and Q. Steps 40, 50 and 60 check to find if N is equal to 0, 1 or 2 and then transfers to a suitable print statement for printing the 1st or 2nd Fibonacci number or indicating that there is no zeroth Fibonacci number. We use a FOR/NEXT loop to generate the Fibonacci numbers. The loop starts with the counter I set equal to 2 and traverses the loop up to I equal to N. The FOR statement calls for the program to start the last progression from statement 70 to statement 110 with I = N. The loop is exited from the statement NEXT I when I = N.

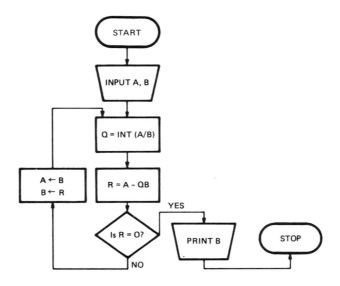

FIGURE 7-7   A flow chart for Euclid's algorithm for finding the greatest common divisor of two numbers, A and B.

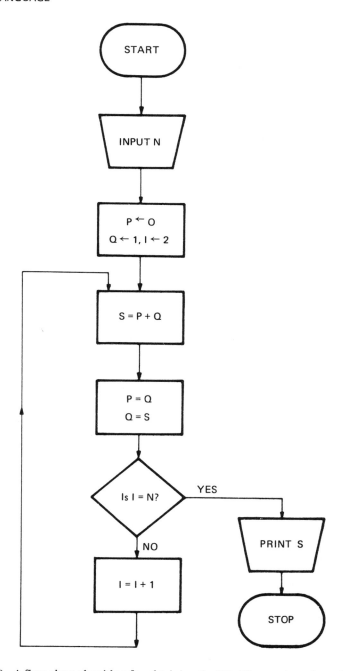

FIGURE 7–8   A flow chart algorithm for obtaining the Nth Fibonacci number when N>2.

The program is now ready to execute and we press "RUN," obtaining a question mark requesting the input of N. An example series of results follows:

```
READY
RUN
?0
THERE IS NO 0TH FIBONACCI NUMBER

READY
RUN
?1
THE FIRST FIBONACCI NUMBER IS 1

READY
RUN
?2
THE SECOND FIBONACCI NUMBER IS 1

READY
RUN
?3
THE THIRD FIBONACCI NUMBER IS 2
```

If we request a large Fibonacci number, such as the 185th Fibonacci number, we will exceed the fixed point capability of the output form. When this is the case, the computer automatically converts the answer to floating point notation. Thus, for the 185th Fibonacci number, we obtain:

```
READY
RUN
?185
THE 185TH FIBONACCI NUMBER IS 1 · 27128E+38
```

The number $1.27128 \times 10^{+38}$ is represented in BASIC as 1.27128E+3'8. In this form, the letter E indicates that the base 10 is raised to the exponent +38. (See Section 6.2.)

There is an additional type of variable in the BASIC language called a *string variable*. A string variable can take on the value of a string, which is simply an expression or alphanumeric name of up to 15 valid characters. A string variable is denoted by a letter followed by a $, for example, A$ or P$. Examples of strings are:

ABCD
JONES

String variables are used to handle alphabetic or alphanumeric information. Any ordinary variable followed by a dollar sign will stand for a string variable.

A list of string variables is assumed to contain no more than 10 strings. Otherwise, a dimension statement is required which saves room for a specified number of strings in the list. A statement

10 DIM A$(20)

saves room for 20 strings in the A$ list.

In the next example, we use a string variable B$ as well as the statement RND, which generates random numbers in the range from 0 to 1. The function RND requires an argument, but the argument has no significance; we may use RND(X), RND($\emptyset$) or RND(1) with the same meaning. Thus, the program

```
1Ø  FOR I = 1 TO 1Ø
2Ø  PRINT RND(Ø);
3Ø  NEXT I
4Ø  END
```

will print the first 10 random numbers. Running the program twice will produce the same set of numbers; this is useful for debugging purposes.

As a further example, if we need ten random integers ranging from 1 to 25 we could change line 20 to:

2$\emptyset$ PRINT INT(25*RND($\emptyset$))+1;

Now the program we wish to write using B$ and RND(1) is to determine the constant π on a trial basis using random numbers. The approach uses random numbers for X and Y and determines if they fall in one quadrant of a circle with a radius equal to one. Thus, for the first quadrant, the area A is $\pi/4$. The total area of that quadrant that the number may fall in is equal to one since X and Y may each assume any random value between 0 and 1. We use a string variable B$ for the person at the teletype to use to input his answer to the question, Do you wish to try again? The person may answer yes or no. The area of the square is equal to one and the area of the first quadrant is $\pi/4$. Thus, on a random basis we expect the ratio of the number of points that fall within the circle, S_3, to the number of tries that we have attempted S_2, to be

$$\frac{S_3}{S_2} = \frac{\pi/4}{1}$$

or

$$\pi = 4S_3/S_2$$

The circle inscribed within the square is shown in Figure 7-9. We generate a random number between 0 and 1 from x and y. Then we can ascertain if the point (x, y) lies within the circle by calculating $SQR(x^2 + y^2)$. The program for evaluating π on a random basis is given in Figure 7-10 (p. 144) with four tries. The user of the program selects N, which is the number of random numbers generated for use in the attempt to calculate π. In step 220, we are asked to input a string variable, which is simply yes or no in this case. After 10,000 trials, π is computed as 3.1412. Why don't you try 100,000 trials? The actual value of Pi, to six decimal places, is 3.141593.

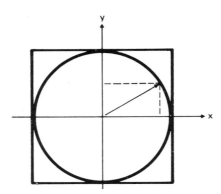

FIGURE 7-9 A circle inscribed inside a square. The radius of the circle is equal to one.

In the next section we will consider some advanced programs in the BASIC language. You may wish to omit that section until a later time. If so, proceed to the next chapter.

7.4 ADVANCED PROGRAMS IN THE BASIC LANGUAGE

The first problem we consider in this section is that of sorting a list of numbers in descending order, from the high to the low value, and printing the result. We use a subscripted variable. In mathematics we write a subscripted variable x as x_j. In BASIC the subscripted variable is written as X(J). Then, for example, x_2 in mathematical notation is X(2) in BASIC notation. The subscripted variable is very useful in calculations using lists of numbers. A list of numbers, say X(J) where J = 0 to 99, contains 100 numbers. Since most computers using BASIC provide storage for only 10 items, we must use a dimension statement to give room for 100 items for X(J). We use this DIM statement:

10 DIM X(100)

The subscripts of X must be positive and integral and the first subscript is zero.

Now the problem is to input a list of numbers into the list X(J) and have the computer sort them in descending order and print out the sorted list. The main principle used in sorting a list into descending order is to test two numbers, and if the second is larger than the first, then we interchange them. First, to understand this process, we order four numbers in this list:

4   Is 4 larger than 7? No. Interchange them and start over again below.
7
5
2
7   Is 7>4? Yes
4   Is 4>5? No. Interchange them and start over again below.

5
2

7   Is 7>4? Yes
5   Is 5>4? Yes
4   Is 4>2? Yes
2   Completed

A flow chart for sorting a list of numbers in descending order is given in Figure
7-11 for inputing 20 numbers and sorting them into descending order. First, the
unsorted list is printed out, five numbers to a line. Then, the list is sorted and
then printed out. The sorting is accomplished by interchanging $X(J)$ and $X(J+1)$,
if necessary, after testing. The interchange requires one temporary variable T
and the sequence is given below. We reserve 100 places for numbers in X by the
dimension statement number 15. The print statement number 55 provides for
printing 5 values of $X(J)$ on a line.[6]

```
10   REM  SORTING OF A LIST OF NUMBERS
15   DIM X(100)
20   INPUT L
25   LET K = 1
30   LET J = 0
35   INPUT X(J)
40   LET J = J+1
45   IF J<L  THEN 35
50   LET J = 0
52   PRINT
55   PRINT X(J), X(J+1), X(J+2), X(J+3), X(J+4)
56   PRINT
60   LET J = J+5
65   IF J<L  THEN 55
70   IF K = 0  THEN 150
75   LET J = 0
80   IF X(J)>X(J+1)  THEN 110
85   LET T = X(J)
90   LET X(J) = X(J+1)
95   LET X(J+1) = T
100  GO TO 75
110  LET J = J + 1
120  IF J<L-1  THEN 80
130  LET K = 0
135  PRINT
140  GO TO 50
150  END
```

```
10   REM EVALUATES PI ON A TRIAL BASIS USING RANDOM NUMBERS AND
20   REM DETERMINING WHETHER THEY FALL IN A UNIT CIRCLE QUADRANT.

40   DIM B$[72]
50   PRINT "THIS PROGRAM WILL COMPUTE PI ON A STATISTICAL BASIS, BY"
60   PRINT "DETERMINING WHETHER RANDOMLY GENERATED NUMBERS FALL WITHIN"
70   PRINT "A QUADRANT OF A UNIT CIRCLE."
80   PRINT
90   PRINT "HOW MANY NUMBERS DO YOU WISH TO TRY IN THIS TEST";
100  INPUT N
110  LET S2=S3=0
120  FOR A=1 TO N
130  LET X=RND(1)
140  LET Y=RND(1)
150  LET S2=S2+1
160  IF SQR(X*X+Y*Y)>1  THEN 180
170  LET S3=S3+1
180  NEXT A
190  PRINT "AFTER "N;"TRIALS, PI IS COMPUTED AS "4*S3/S2
200  PRINT
210  PRINT "DO YOU WISH TO TRY AGAIN";
220  INPUT B$
230  IF B$="YES" THEN 90
240  IF B$="NO" THEN 270
250  PRINT "PLEASE ANSWER YES OR NO."
260  GOTO 210
270  END


RUN
PI-TRY

THIS PROGRAM WILL COMPUTE PI ON A STATISTICAL BASIS, BY
DETERMINING WHETHER RANDOMLY GENERATED NUMBERS FALL WITHIN
A QUADRANT OF A UNIT CIRCLE.

HOW MANY NUMBERS DO YOU WISH TO TRY IN THIS TEST?10
AFTER  10  TRIALS, PI IS COMPUTED AS  3.2

DO YOU WISH TO TRY AGAIN?WHAT?
PLEASE ANSWER YES OR NO.
DO YOU WISH TO TRY AGAIN?YES
HOW MANY NUMBERS DO YOU WISH TO TRY IN THIS TEST?100
AFTER  100  TRIALS, PI IS COMPUTED AS  3.32

DO YOU WISH TO TRY AGAIN?YES
HOW MANY NUMBERS DO YOU WISH TO TRY IN THIS TEST?1000
AFTER 1000  TRIALS, PI IS COMPUTED AS  3.16

DO YOU WISH TO TRY AGAIN?YES
HOW MANY NUMBERS DO YOU WISH TO TRY IN THIS TEST?10000
AFTER 10000  TRIALS, PI IS COMPUTED AS  3.1412
```

FIGURE 7-10 A program for calculating Pi on a trial basis using random numbers.

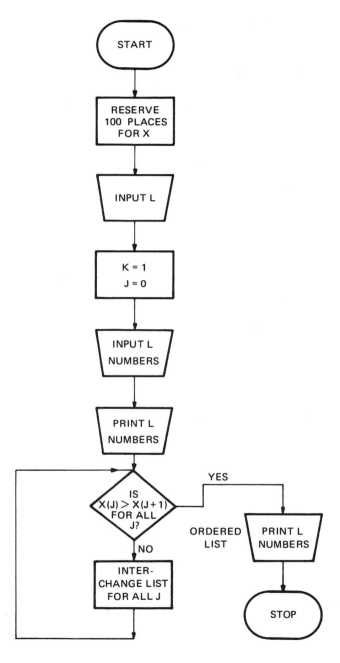

FIGURE 7-11 A flow chart algorithm for sorting a list of L numbers by the method of interchange.

As another example, let us find the real root of a polynomial equation. We are interested in finding the root of an equation of the form

$$f(x) = 0$$

We use a DEF statement so the program can be modified for other polynomials at another time. The problem is to find a real root in a specified interval A to B, where $f(x) = 0$ in the interval. Let us consider the function

$$f(x) = x^5 + 2x^3 - 1$$

This function is negative at $x = 0$ and positive at $x = 1$, so we will search for the real root in the interval $(0,1)$.

The algorithm we use for determining the root is the bisection algorithm. We simply bisect the interval and determine the sign of $f(x)$. If the sign of the function is positive at the bisection point, then the root must be between A and X, the bisection point. If the function is negative at X, then the root lies between X and B. This approach is shown graphically in Figure 7-12.

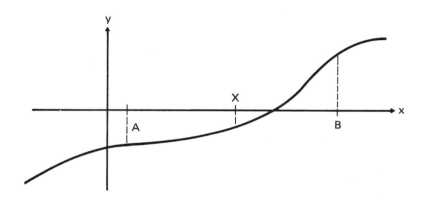

FIGURE 7-12   Graph of $f(x)$ with the bisection of the interval (A,B) shown at X.

The program for locating a real root in an interval by the bisection method is given in Figure 7-13. This program allows the user to provide the interval he wishes to test for a real root and to specify the accuracy. In line 10, the function is specified. Then the interval is requested as (P1,P3). The desired accuracy is equal to E and can be specified in fixed or floating point format. The program will print out the intermediate solutions so the user can observe the convergence to a root and determine how many iterations are necessary for a specified accuracy. The value of the bisected range is P2. It is calculated in line 110. Lines 120 and 130 test to determine if the function is negative or positive at P2. If FNC(P1) and FNC(P2) are of differing signs, then we transfer to line 200

```
6    REM FINDING THE ROOTS OF A FUNCTION BY INTERVAL BISECTION.
1Ø   DEF FNC(X)=X↑5+2*X↑3-1
5Ø   PRINT
1ØØ  PRINT "TYPE IN THE INTERVAL WHERE THE ROOT LIES, PLEASE."
1Ø1  INPUT P1,P3
1Ø2  PRINT "TYPE IN THE DESIRED ACCURACY."
1Ø3  INPUT E
1Ø4  PRINT
1Ø5  PRINT "INTERMEDIATE SOLUTIONS."
11Ø  LET P2=(P3+P1)/2
12Ø  IF FNC(P1)*FNC(P2)<Ø THEN 2ØØ
13Ø  IF FNC(P2)*FNC(P3)<Ø THEN 3ØØ
14Ø  IF P2=Ø THEN 6ØØ
15Ø  PRINT "NONE."
151  PRINT "NO ROOT FOUND IN THE SPECIFIED INTERVAL."
152  PRINT
153  PRINT
16Ø  GOTO 1ØØ
2ØØ  LET P4=(P1+P2)/2
21Ø  IF ABS(P4-P2)<E THEN 6ØØ
22Ø  LET P3=P2
23Ø  LET P2=P4
24Ø  PRINT P2;" LEFT"
25Ø  GO TO 12Ø
3ØØ  LET P4=(P2+P3)/2
31Ø  IF ABS(P4-P2)<E THEN 6ØØ
32Ø  LET P1=P2
33Ø  LET P2=P4
34Ø  PRINT P2;" RIGHT"
35Ø  GOTO 12Ø
6ØØ  PRINT "THE ROOT IS FOUND TO BE "; P2
6Ø1  PRINT
6Ø2  PRINT
6Ø3  PRINT
61Ø  STOP
8ØØ  END
```

READY

FIGURE 7-13   A BASIC program for determining a real root in the interval (P1,P3).

and bisect the range again. If FNC(P1) and FNC(P2) are not of opposite sign, we go to line 130 and test to see if FNC(P2) and FNC(P3) are of differing signs. If neither case is satisfied, the printout states that there are no roots in the interval in Line 150. Line 210 or 310 checks to determine if the specified accuracy is satisfied.

An example run of the program is shown in Figure 7-14. Twenty-four iterations were required to obtain the root in the interval (0,1). The specified accuracy was 1×10^{-12}; actually, this specified accuracy exceeds the precision of the computer we used, which gave us only six digits. A better choice of E would have been 1×10^{-8}.

The program is rerun for the interval (0,.5) and the program responds correctly that there is no root in that interval.

BASIC also has the powerful feature of possessing several functions for matrix manipulation. A matrix is a two-dimensional rectangular array of numbers. Matrices are very useful for solving complex problems.[7] A matrix is defined in a BASIC program with a DIM statement. Thus, the statement

$$1\emptyset \ \ DIM \ A(3,3),B(1\emptyset,1\emptyset)$$

tells the BASIC System to allocate storage for a 3-by-3 matrix called A and a 10-by-10 matrix called B. (The name of a matrix is always a single letter.) The matrix functions defined in BASIC are listed in Table 7-5.

TABLE 7-5

Matrix Operations in BASIC

MAT READ A	Read numbers into matrix A row by row from a DATA statement.
MAT A = ZER	Fill A with zeros; *i.e.*, set each element equal to zero.
MAT A = CON	Fill A with ones; *i.e.*, set each element equal to one.
MAT A = IDN	Set up A as an identity matrix.
MAT PRINT A	Print A, row by row.
MAT B = A	Set matrix B equal to matrix A.
MAT C = A + B	Add matrices A and B.
MAT C = A – B	Subtract matrix B from matrix A.
MAT C = A*B	Multiply matrix B times matrix A.
MAT C = TRN(A)	Transpose matrix A.
MAT C = INV(A)	Invert matrix A and set the inverse equal to C.
MAT C = (K)*A	Multiply matrix A by K, where K is any expression.

In order to demonstrate the use of these statements, let us solve the following system of linear simultaneous equations:

$$x_1 - 2x_2 - 2x_3 = -15$$
$$x_1 + x_2 + x_3 = 117$$
$$x_1 + x_2 - 6x_3 = 40$$

These equations can be represented by the matrix equation

$$A \ x = c$$

RUN

TYPE IN THE INTERVAL WHERE THE ROOT LIES, PLEASE
?∅
?1
TYPE IN THE DESIRED ACCURACY.
?1.∅ E-12

INTERMEDIATE SOLUTIONS.
   .75   RIGHT
   .625   LEFT
   .6875   RIGHT
   .625   LEFT
   .6875   RIGHT
   .71875   RIGHT
   .734375   RIGHT
   .726563   LEFT
   .73∅469   RIGHT
   .732422   RIGHT
   .733398   RIGHT
   .73291   LEFT
   .733154   RIGHT
   .733276   RIGHT
   .733215   LEFT
   .733185   LEFT
   .73317   LEFT
   .733162   LEFT
   .733158   LEFT
   .733156   LEFT
   .733157   RIGHT
   .733157   LEFT
   .733157   RIGHT
   .733157   LEFT
   .733157   RIGHT
THE ROOT IS FOUND TO BE   .733157

READY
RUN

TYPE IN THE INTERVAL WHERE THE ROOT LIES, PLEASE.
?∅.∅
?∅.5
TYPE IN THE DESIRED ACCURACY.
?∅.∅∅∅1

INTERMEDIATE SOLUTIONS.
NONE.
NO ROOT FOUND IN THE SPECIFIED INTERVAL.

FIGURE 7–14 Two runs of the program for determining the real root in an interval specified by the user.

where

$$A = \begin{bmatrix} 1 & -2 & -2 \\ 1 & 1 & 1 \\ 1 & 1 & -6 \end{bmatrix}$$

and

$$x = \begin{bmatrix} x_1 \\ x_2 \\ x_3 \end{bmatrix} \quad , \quad c = \begin{bmatrix} -15 \\ 117 \\ 40 \end{bmatrix}$$

The solution for x is obtained by obtaining the inverse of A, $B = A^{-1}$. Then

$$x = Bc$$

The BASIC program to solve the set of simultaneous equations and the execution of the program is as follows: [2]

```
1Ø  DIM A(3,3), B(3,3), C(3,1), X(3,1)
2Ø  MAT READ A
3Ø  DATA 1, -2, -2
4Ø  DATA 1, 1, 1
5Ø  DATA 1, 1, -6
6Ø  MAT READ C
7Ø  DATA -15,117,4Ø
8Ø  MAT B=INV(A)
9Ø  MAT X=B*C
1ØØ MAT PRINT X
11Ø END

RUN
 73
 33
 11.
```

Line 10 establishes the dimensions of the four matrices. The second line calls for reading as input the values of the matrix A and the values are supplied row by row in lines 30, 40 and 50. Similarly, lines 60 and 70 input the values of the C matrix. The inverse of matrix A is obtained in line 80 and set equal to B. Then X is calculated and printed out. Notice that all matrix operations are preceded by the identifier MAT. The answer is obtained by typing RUN and obtaining

$$x_1 = 73$$
$$x_2 = 33$$
$$x_3 = 11$$

One of the very powerful matrix operations provided in BASIC is the matrix inversion operation, MAT C = INV(A). This is a very convenient and useful operation to have directly available with one instruction.

SUMMARY

In this chapter we have learned that the BASIC computer language is a very versatile and powerful language for solving problems. BASIC is commonly used with a time–sharing computer which enables multiple users to participate simultaneously in available computer time via terminals and communication lines. The number of time–sharing terminals available is growing exponentially and BASIC has become widely available.

The BASIC language is useful for a conversational mode of programming and computer operation common with time–sharing systems. The BASIC language contains a powerful arithmetic facility, many language diagnostics, several editing features, a library of common mathematical functions, a set of matrix functions, and simple input and output procedures. In addition, BASIC may operate with alphabetic or alphanumeric data as well as numeric data. BASIC may be learned rapidly by a user and is relatively simple language to use.

CHAPTER 7 PROBLEMS

P7-1. Define a time–sharing computer.

P7-2. If there are 1024 time–sharing computers available in 1971, and we can assume the growth in the number of time–sharing computers continues exponentially, how many time–sharing computers will be available in 1975 in the United States?

P7-3. If the ratio of terminals to computer systems continues to be 40 to 1, how many terminals will be available in 1975? What will be the ratio of persons in the United States to the number of terminals?

P7-4. List four advantages of time–sharing computers.

P7-5. List several characteristics of the BASIC language.

P7-6. Write the following equations in the notation of the BASIC language.

a. $y = 3x^2 - e^x$

b. $y = a - 4 \ln x + 8x^3 - c$

c. $y = \dfrac{ae^x}{b - 5x^2} \sin q$

P7-7. In problems 5-7 and 6-7, we considered the question of finding a set of integers (A, B, C, D) which satisfies the equation

$$A^N + B^N = C^N + D^N$$

where N is an integer provided as an input. This problem requires four loops and we can use FOR/NEXT statements. A partial program is given below. Complete the program for A, B, C and D up to 20. Some partial solutions are given also.

```
 10  INPUT N
 15  FOR A = 1 TO
 25  FOR B = 1 TO 20
 35  FOR C
 45  FOR
 55  IF D = B  THEN
     IF D = A  THEN
     IF C = B  THEN
     IF C = A  THEN 110
 80  LET L = A↑ N +
     LET R = C↑ N +
     IF    ABS(L-R) =    THEN
 95  GO TO
100  PRINT "A ="A, "B
110  NEXT D
115  NEXT
120
125
130  END
```

RUN
?2

A = 1	B = 7	C = 5	D = 5
A = 1	B = 8	C = 4	D = 7
A = 1	B = 12	C = 8	D = 9
A = 1	B = 13	C = 7	D = 11
A = 1	B = 17	C = 11	D = 13
A = 1	B = 18	C = 6	D = 17
A = 1	B = 18	C = 10	D = 15
A = 2	B = 9	C = 6	D = 7

READY
RUN
?3

A = 1	B = 12	C = 9	D = 10
A = 2	B = 16	C = 9	D = 15

Write your own program and run it for N = 3 and N = 4. Record the time it requires to determine one solution for N = 3 and N = 4.

P7-8. Write a simple BASIC program to determine how much you must invest today to return $5,000 in 20 years at an interest rate of 5, 6 and 7 percent. The calculation required is:

$$P = S/(1 + I)^N$$

where P = present worth of investment, S = final return, I = interest rate and N = number of years.

P7-9. The solution of the quadratic equation $Ax^2 + Bx + C = 0$ is desired. We wish to determine and print the two roots, first finding if they are imaginary or real. A partial program is given below. Complete the program.

```
100  INPUT A, B, C
110  LET D=B*B – 4*A*C
120  PRINT "THE ROOTS ARE:";
130  IF SGN (D) = -1 THEN
140  PRINT (-B+SQR(D))/2/A "AND
150  STOP
160  PRINT -B/2/A"+I*"SQR(D)/2/A "AND"
999
```

P7-10. Write a program to determine and print all the factors of a number N which are prime numbers. For example, the prime factors of 777 are 3, 7 and 37. A partial program is given below. Complete the program, assuming that the prime factor is K.

```
10   INPUT N
20   LET K = 2
30   LET    = N
40   IF ((INT(P/K)*K =0) THEN
50   LET K =
60   GO TO
70   PRINT
80   LET N = P/
90   IF N = 1  THEN
100  GO TO
200  END
```

P7-11. The function sine x is readily obtained in the BASIC language. Also, we know that the sine function consists of the series

$$\text{sine } x = x - \frac{x^3}{3!} + \frac{x^5}{5!} - \frac{x^7}{7!} + \dots$$

where the series converges to the exact value of the sine x as the number of terms increases. One way to calculate the terms is to use the approach

$$y_1 = x$$
$$y_2 = \frac{-x^2}{2 \cdot 3} y_1$$
$$y_3 = - \frac{x^2}{4 \cdot 5} y_2$$
$$y_4 = \frac{-x^2}{6 \cdot 7} y_3$$

and so on. This approach provides an algorithm for calculating a term in the series as:

$$T(I) = \frac{-X^2 \ (T(I-1))}{2I(2I + 1)}$$

where $T(I)$ is the ith term. Write a program to calculate the sine N for Q terms and compare it with the value obtained from the computer function. The input will call for N and Q and use the following set of data:

N (radians)	.3	.3	.3	1.5	1.5	3.13	3.13	3.13	3.13
Q		3	4	6	3	6	3	5	9	15
Test Number	1	2	3	4	5	6	7	8	9

P7-12. Write a program to calculate the sum of an arithmetic progression
$$S = A + (A + C) + (A + 2C) + ... + B$$
where A, B, C are obtained from a READ statement. Use a FOR/NEXT statement to calculate the sum and then point out the sum S. Use the the following two sets of data:

(A,B,C) = (2,1000,3) and (1,100,2). The sum for
(2,1000,3) is 166,500.[4].

P7-13. We desire to write a program that will determine the probability of a number between 1 and 10, inclusive, will be divisible by 3. We know that between 1 and 10 the only numbers divisible by 3 are 3, 6 and 9. Thus the exact probability of the desired outcome is 0.3. We wish to write a program which will use a random number generator to obtain numbers between 1 and 10 and carry out the experiment to determine if it is divisible by 3. Write a program that will try the experiment for 100, 1,000 and 3,000 trials and print out the number of times the number was divisible by 3. Use T as the number of trials, C as the number of times the random number was divisible by 3 and $P = C/T$ as the probability of a number between 1 and 10 being divisible by 3. Print out the number of trials T and the probability P.

P7-14. The function $f(x) = x^2 - 6x + 5$ possesses two real roots between the point $x = 0$ and $x = 6$. Write a program using the bisection method to determine the two real roots. The real roots are $x = 1$ and $x = 5$ exactly and you may wish to check them with the answers obtained from the computer for a specified accuracy.

P7-15. The determination of prime numbers by the use of the algorithm called the Sieve of Eratosthenes was discussed in P4-6. We determined a flow chart for the algorithm in problem 4-6 and one form of the flow chart is given in Figure P7-15.[8] We will use Table P to store 100 numbers and find their primes. Obviously, we need to proceed only to 100. Write a program to print out the prime numbers obtained from the sieve. Use a FOR/NEXT statement to store all the 100 numbers in the table as $P(I)$ for $I = 1$ to 100. The algorithm shown in the flow chart places a zero in a location where a number is crossed off the basic list. The final result is to print out all the numbers in Table P with zeros occurring where all numbers are crossed off, and thus the prime numbers are the remaining non–zero numbers in the list P.

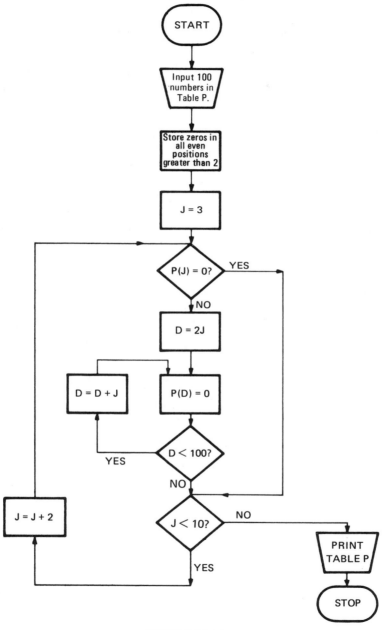

FIGURE P7-15.

P7-16. Write a program using a string variable A$ to print out a request to the user for his name. Then when his name is typed as input stored A$, let the computer return to the user the phrase "Thank you, Mr._____."

P7-17. The inversion of a matrix is a very powerful function provided in the BASIC language. There will be some inaccuracy introduced by the inversion algorithm. In order to determine the small errors introduced, develop a program for generating a square matrix A of order N where N is incremented from 4 to 10 in steps of one. Generate the matrix by filling the matrix with random numbers. Then calculate $B = A^{-1}$ and obtain $C = A * B$. The matrix C should, ideally, be an identity matrix with the off–diagonal elements equal to zero. Determine the maximum value of the off–diagonal elements and print it out for N = 4 to N = 10. A sample answer for N = 4 to N = 10 for a specific computer was obtained as follows:

MATRIX ORDER 4   MAX. OFF-DIAG. ELEMENT = 7.74860E-07
MATRIX ORDER 5   MAX. OFF-DIAG. ELEMENT = 4.76837E-07
MATRIX ORDER 6   MAX. OFF-DIAG. ELEMENT = 7.15256E-07
MATRIX ORDER 7   MAX. OFF-DIAG. ELEMENT = 3.81470E-06
MATRIX ORDER 8   MAX. OFF-DIAG. ELEMENT = 6.44010E-07
MATRIX ORDER 9   MAX. OFF-DIAG. ELEMENT = 1.54972E-06
MATRIX ORDER 10   MAX. OFF-DIAG. ELEMENT = 1.05798E-06

P7-18. An advanced problem is to determine the area under a curve by a trapezoid approximation. If a function f(x) is considered between points A and B, the area under the curve is approximated by the trapezoid shown in Figure P7-18A. Write a program which will approximate the area under the function $f(x) = x^2 + 3x + 1$ between A = 1 and B = 5. The exact value for the area is 81.3333.[4] Write a program to calculate and print out the approximated value of the area using the trapezoid rule for the interval (A,B) and then successively bisecting all the intervals of the previous iteration. Print out the results for ten trials. Thus, we obtain an answer for one interval of length four; then two intervals, each of length two; then four intervals, each of length one; and so on. By examining Figure P7-18b one can notice that two intervals provide a more accurate approximation to the area than one interval, where the approximated area lies under the dashed lines and the actual area lies under the solid curve.

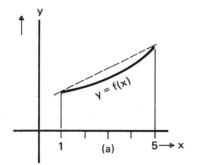 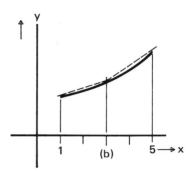

FIGURE P7-18.

CHAPTER 7 REFERENCES

1. W. F. Sharpe, *BASIC—An Introduction to Computer Programming Using the BASIC Language*, Free Press, 1967.
2. G. L. Peterson, "BASIC: The Language of Time-Sharing," *Hewlett-Packard Journal*, Vol. 20, No. 3, Nov. 1968, pp. 2–8.
3. M. F. Lipp, "The Language BASIC and Its Role in Time-Sharing," *Computers and Automation*, Oct. 1969, pp. 42–43.
4. J. G. Kemeny and T. E. Kurtz, *BASIC Programming*, John Wiley & Sons, Inc., New York, 1967.
5. "Kemeny Calls for National Time-Sharing Networks," *Computerworld*, Sept. 24, 1969, pg. 10.
6. R. E. Smith, *BASIC Ideas*, International Timesharing Corp., Minneapolis, Minn., 1969.
7. R. C. Dorf, *Matrix Algebra: A Programmed Introduction*, Wiley & Sons, Inc., New York, 1969.
8. D. D. Spencer, *A Guide to BASIC Programming: A Time-Sharing Language*, Addison-Wesley Publishing Company, Reading, Mass., 1970.
9. E. R. Sage, *Problem Solving with the Computer*, Entelek, Inc., Newburyport, Mass., 1969.

8

THE FORTRAN LANGUAGE

8.1 FORTRAN AND OTHER COMPUTER LANGUAGES

The most widely used computer language today is FORTRAN.* FOR-
TRAN is an algorithmic, problem–solving language which has been widely accepted during the past decade. FORTRAN was developed by John W. Backus
of IBM during the period 1954–1957.[1] FORTRAN was originally written for
scientific and engineering problems, but it has found wide application in business and government. The name was derived from the words *FORmula
TRANslator*, which correctly imply its primary utility, the translation of
formulas and algorithms which arise in problems. This translation is made into
the language of the computer.

*While FORTRAN is used most widely for science and engineering, and while it is used for
business problems also, it is by no means the only available problem–oriented language. An
International Algebraic Language called ALGOL became generally available in 1958. ALGOL
is derived from *ALGOrithmic Language*; ALGOL is particularly suited to the expression of
algorithms.

As a programming language, ALGOL has tremendous power and flexibility and yet is
more easily comprehensible and usable by both experts and beginners than FORTRAN.
ALGOL has found wide acceptance in Europe but not in the U.S., except perhaps as a vehicle for the academic interchange of algorithms. In the U.S., ALGOL should have progressed rapidly, but its use was impeded by the ready availability of FORTRAN.

But the virtues of ALGOL still stand today. It uses ordinary mathematical notation and

FORTRAN is not as easy to learn as BASIC, since the language can be characterized as somewhat more machine–oriented rather than user–oriented. The primary advantage we gain with FORTRAN is that it is a more efficient language as far as the computer is concerned. Thus, the computer will execute more rapidly with FORTRAN, and fewer instructions are necessary. Also, FORTRAN provides more forms of expression of the input and output data and results than does BASIC.

While FORTRAN is used with some time–sharing computers, it is primarily used with batch–processing computer systems, which are defined as follows:

BATCH PROCESSING (1) The technique of executing a set of programs such that each is completed before the next program of the set is started. (2) The execution of programs serially.

In batch processing, each person's program is executed, one at a time, and then returned to the programmer. In most cases, since a large general–purpose computer is used to execute the program, the computer is used in a "closed–shop manner" and an operator runs the program for the programmer. The definition of a closed shop is:

CLOSED SHOP A way of operating a computer facility in which the most productive and efficient operation is obtained by using a group of operators, rather than the original problem solver and programmer.

For large expensive general–purpose computers, such as the IBM 360/65 shown in Figure 8–1, it usually is inefficient to allow the programmer to operate the computer. He is required to hand over his program, in a suitable form, to an operator to run. The programs are then run in a batch processing manner by the operator. This process is illustrated in Figure 8–2 for a system using magnetic tape. The advantage of a closed–shop, batch–processing mode of operation is the access one gains to a powerful, high–speed computer with a trained

---

ordinary English words. ALGOL is a universal language and as such can be used for communication between users. For the sophisticated user it is powerful and flexible yet simple enough to be easily learned. It is also very suitable for conversational time–sharing use.

A new programming language, PL/1, was made available by IBM for its System /360 in 1966. *Programming Language/1* was developed to serve as a universal language for both business and scientific information processing. The PL/1 language is not yet widely used; perhaps one percent of commercial programs use PL/1.[2] Nevertheless, in the short time that PL/1 has been in use, evidence has begun to accumulate that this all–purpose programming language is achieving its prime objective: to provide the user with maximum efficiency and productivity in problem–solving. PL/1 offers this capability with built–in room for growth as improvements are made in programming and equipment. Also, PL/1 can be characterized as easy to learn and simple to use. The use of PL/1 will undoubtedly continue to grow, although it may never achieve the prominence of FORTRAN.[3]

Another useful problem–oriented language, although one not widely used, is APL, *A Programming Language*. APL was developed by Kenneth Iverson. Currently, APL is often used as a time–sharing language, but it is not limited to conversational time–sharing use. The language is primarily a problem–oriented language and can be used as a tool for applications.[4]

FIGURE 8-1   The IBM 360/65 with the IBM 2314. *Courtesy of IBM Corporation.*

operator. The disadvantage lies in the delay in receiving his results back from
the operator, which is called the *turn–around time.* The turn–around time in
many computer centers varies from one hour to one day. Thus, it might take a
programmer one day to obtain one run of his program, only to find that a
simple error caused the malfunction of his program. Therefore, most computer
centers strive to keep the turn–around time less than a few hours.

With smaller, less expensive computers, such as the IBM 1130, which is
shown in Figure 8-3, direct access to the computer is permissible. Thus, a programmer might directly run his program on an IBM 1130 computer and avoid
the delays of a closed–shop operation. The price the programmer must pay for
direct access is that he must (1) learn to operate the computer and that (2) he
has less efficient use of the computer time.

FORTRAN may be used with closed–shop or direct–access machines interchangeably since it is a machine–independent language. FORTRAN uses English
words and algebraic expressions. A current version of the language, FORTRAN
IV, is described in this chapter.

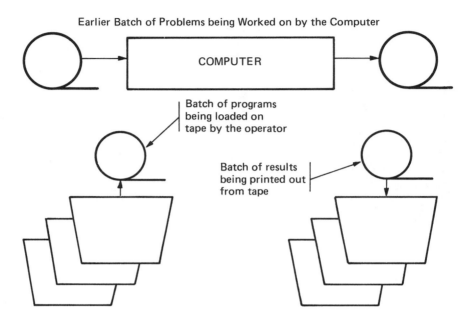

FIGURE 8-2   A closed–shop batch–processing computer system using magnetic tape.

FIGURE 8-3   The IBM 1130 Computer. *Courtesy of IBM Corporation.*

8.2 THE FORTRAN LANGUAGE

FORTRAN enables a computer to read and execute algorithms for solving problems. The language is very rich in detail, which is one of its advantages; many of the advanced details are omitted from this chapter. There are several books available that consider all the details fo FORTRAN programming. They should be consulted for advanced study.[5,6] Several important characteristics of FORTRAN IV are:[7]

1. FORTRAN can describe a great variety of algorithms. Although it is intended primarily for scientific and engineering computations, it can express many other types of algorithms.
2. The rules (or syntax) of the language are precisely defined (unlike the syntax of English) with the result that a FORTRAN algorithm means exactly the same thing to every person who reads it, if he knows the language. Thus FORTRAN can be used to communicate algorithms in correspondence and publications.
3. Many types of digital computers can be programmed to accept algorithms written in FORTRAN because it avoids any reference to special computers or devices.

As we noted previously, the syntax of a language is the set of rules for developing the statements in that language. The statements or program steps used in this chapter will be limited to those allowable for the IBM 1130 and other larger general-purpose computers. Larger general-purpose computers possess some additional powerful statements and features which are omitted from this chapter. Nevertheless, a program developed in this chapter should run on any computer accepting FORTRAN IV.

The basic symbols of FORTRAN are the letters of the alphabet, the numbers and the special characters available on a typewriter input connected to a card punch or other input device. We have available the special symbols : + - / = .) * , " $

There are two types of numerical constants available, *integer constants* and *real constants*. An integer constant is a number written without a decimal point. (Therefore, it has no decimal part.) The magnitude of the integer allowable depends upon the computer. For an IBM 1130 the range of integers allowed is:

$$-32768 \leqslant \text{number} \leqslant 32767$$

Larger computers accept larger integer constants. Commas are not permitted within an integer constant.

A real constant or floating point number is written with a decimal point. It may be followed optionally by a decimal exponent consisting of the letter E followed by a one- or two-digit exponent. The exponent may or may not have a sign prior to the exponent. The number 5,602.8 is a real constant. It may also be expressed as:

$$5.6028E+3 \quad \text{or} \quad 5.6028E3$$

Express –0.032 in exponent form. (The answer appears in the footnote on the next page.) The range of allowable real constants for an IBM 1130 is approximately:

$$10^{-39} \leqslant \text{number} \leqslant 10^{38}$$

Larger computers accept numbers up to 10^{75} and greater. The decimal point must always be written in a real constant.

A variable is represented symbolically by 1 to 5 alphabetic or numeric characters, the first of which must be alphabetic. For example, permissible variable names are: A, A1, NUM, DELTA and RATE. Since we can use five characters, we can often use a variable name to represent the variable meaningfully in an algorithm. For example, in the equation for the present worth P of a final return S at an interest rate I for a number of years N, we might use the following variables:

PRESW; SRETN; INTST; and NYRS.

As another example, the equation to calculate the speed of an object might be:

SPEED = DIST/TIME

where the three variables are speed, distance and time, respectively.

In order to inform the computer whether we are using an *integer variable* or a *real variable*, we assign a set of first letters to the integer variables. Thus, if we want to store an integer variable, we use I, J, K, L, M or N as the first character of its name. All such entries are stored as integers.

All other names for variables are stored in floating point notation. Therefore they are called real variables. Examples of real variables are TEMP, X and VEL. Integer variables store only integers; real variables store non–integers.

The programmer has the option of specifying a variable explicitly as an integer or a real variable by using a *declaration*. A declaration is a line in a FORTRAN program that is not executed, but that carries information. We can write the following declaration statement:

REAL NUMB, ITEM

This statement causes the variables NUMB and ITEM, which, beginning with N and I, would ordinarily be integer variables, to be explicitly denoted as real variables. Similarly, the statement INTEGER VEL, X(2) causes the variables VEL and X(2), which would normally be treated as real variables, to be explicitly declared to be integer variables. The explicit declaration statement overrides the implicit specification of the first letter of a variable name.

FORTRAN statements are instructions used in the FORTRAN language. There are five categories of FORTRAN statements:

1. *Arithmetic Statements.* These set forth calculations to be performed.
2. *Control Statements.* These direct the sequence of execution of the program statements.
3. *Input/Output Statements.* These control the transfer of information between the computer and the input and output devices.

4. *Specification Statements*. These provide information about the data to be processed.
5. *Subprogram Statements*. These define and provide linkage to and from subprograms.

Arithmetic statements are written with arithmetic operators. FORTRAN operator symbols are given in Table 8-1. The operators are given in descending order of priority of execution. Thus, if all operations are included in an arithmetic statement, the exponentiation is executed first, then the multiplication and division, and so on.

TABLE 8-1

Arithmetic Operations in FORTRAN

Operation	Symbol	Example	Precedence
Exponentiation	**	A**N means A^N	First
Multiplication	*	A*B	Second
Division	/	A/B	
Addition	+	A + B	Third
Subtraction	–	A – B	
Assignment	=	A = B means A←B	Fourth

Arithmetic statements also utilize arithmetic functions which are available in FORTRAN. These predefined functions are available with the computer; they are listed in Table 8-2. We use ABS(X) to calculate the absolute value of the argument X, for example. In order to avoid confusion, the names of variables should not be chosen to be the same as the names of the predefined functions given in Table 8-2.

An arithmetic expression in FORTRAN consists of arithmetic operators and arithmetic functions if required. The assignment operator is used, as in BASIC, to denote assignment and does not imply equality. The familiar FORTRAN statement

$$J = J + 1$$

means that we are to assign the value J + 1 to the variable J. The arithmetic statement is of the general form A = B where A is a variable and B is an arithmetic expression. An example is:

$$DISC = (B**2 - 4.*A*C)$$

This expression for the discriminant of the quadratic equation $Ax^2 + Bx + C = 0$, includes exponentiation, multiplication, subtraction and finally assignment. First, B^2 would be calculated, then 4AC would be calculated and the subtraction completed. In the last step, the quantity within the parentheses would be

---

−0.032 in exponent form is −3.2E-2.

assigned to the variable DISC. Note that all the variables in this expression are real variables.

TABLE 8-2

FORTRAN Functions

Name	Type of Argument	Type of Result	Meaning
SIN(X)	Real	Real	Sine of angle X (in radians)
COS(X)	Real	Real	Cosine of angle X (in radians)
ATAN(X)	Real	Real	Arctangent of X (in radians)
SQRT(X)	Real	Real	Square root of X
ABS(X)	Real	Real	Absolute value of X
IABS(X)	Real	Integer	Integer absolute value of X
ALOG(X)	Real	Real	Natural logarithm of X
EXP(X)	Real	Real	Exponential of X
INT(X)	Real	Integer	Integer value of X; deletes the decimal part
AINT(X)	Real	Real	Deletes the decimal part of X; yields real number
FLOAT(I)	Integer	Real	Conversion of integer to real
IFIX(X)	Real	Integer	Conversion of real to integer

In the case of the expression

$$LOAD = A + B*SIN(X)$$

the quantity on the right of the equality sign is calculated in the real mode, then assigned to the variable LOAD, then converted to the integer mode and stored in the location associated with the variable name LOAD. Such procedures are established by the rules of FORTRAN.

In the case of the expression

$$X = I + JOB*ITIME$$

the quantity on the right of the equality sign is calculated in the integer mode, the result converted to the real mode, and then stored in the location associated with the variable name X.

Any expression may be enclosed in parentheses. Parentheses do not affect the mode of the expression. Parentheses may be used to specify the order in which arithmetic operations are to be performed. In FORTRAN, no two operators may appear in sequence. The parentheses override precedence rules, since the expressions within the parentheses will be executed prior to the evaluation of the full expression. Then, for example,

$$A + B*C**D \text{ means } A + (BC^D)$$

while

$$A + (B*C)**D \text{ means } A + (BC)^D$$

When in doubt about the exact meaning of a FORTRAN statement, always use parentheses to clarify the operations. The use of parentheses is particularly important, because no two operators may appear in sequence. Thus, the algebraic equation

$$X = \frac{AB^2}{C}$$

is best written in FORTRAN as

$$X = (A*(B**2))/C$$

The simplest arithmetic expression consists of a single constant, variable or subscripted variable. If the quantity is an integer, the expression is said to be in the *integer mode*. If the quantity is a real quantity, the expression is said to be in the *real mode*. If real and integer variables or constants appear in the same expression, the expression is said to be of *mixed mode*.

In a mixed mode expression, the parts of the expression involving only integer operations are computed in the integer mode. Then the integer results are converted to real values and the entire expression is computed in the real mode.

Let us consider a few examples of integer mode calculations. If $I = 2$ and $J = 3$, then we have $I + J = 5$; $I * J = 6$; $I - J = -1$; $I/J = 0$ and $J/I = 1$.

Similarly, for the real mode calculation, when $X = 2$ and $Y = 3$, we have $X + Y = 5.000$; $X - Y = -1.000$; $X * Y = 6.000$; $X/Y = 0.666$ and $Y/X = 1.500$.

As an example of a mixed mode expression, consider

$$X = (M*N) + J**3 - (Y/K)$$

M*N and J**3 are computed in the integer mode and the results are then converted to real values. Y/K is computed by converting K to the real mode and then evaluating the fraction in the real mode. The final result is expressed in the real mode.

Now try a translation into FORTRAN for yourself. Express the equation

$$X = A - \frac{B^2}{C} \cdot D \cdot |A|$$

in FORTRAN. (See the footnote on the next page for the answer.)

There are several instances in FORTRAN programs in which particular statements must be referenced. We use a *statement number* to label a referenced statement. The statement number may be any positive integer less than 32000. Only statements that need to be referenced will be labelled, and only statements do not need to be numbered as is the case in the BASIC language.

As a general practice, we label all statements that are executed, and we do not label remark statements. The remarks or comments are included in *comment statements*, which are indicated by placing a C in column 1 of the punched card or input list. Any FORTRAN program, therefore, consists of a list of FORTRAN statements together with comment statements.

A partial list of FORTRAN *control statements* is given in Table 8-3. The GO TO n statement is an unconditional transfer to statement number n. Item 3 is an IF statement, which causes branching depending upon whether the expression X is negative, zero or positive. It transfers control to statements n_1, n_2 or n_3 respectively.

TABLE 8-3

A Partial List of FORTRAN Control Statements

1. GO TO n

This is an unconditional GO TO statement, where n is a statement number.

2. GO TO $(n_1, n_2, \ldots n_m)$, I

This is a computed GO TO statement where $n_1, n_2, n_3, \ldots$ are statement numbers of other statements within the program and I is a nonsubscripted integer variable whose value is greater than or equal to 1 and less than or equal to m. In this statement, if I = 1, control is transferred to statement numbered n_1, if I = 2, control is transferred to statement number n_2, etc. As an example, consider:

GO TO (3, 36, 17), NOTE

If NOTE, as calculated in the program preceding the GO TO statement, has a value of 1, control is transferred to statement numbered 3, if NOTE = 2, control is transferred to statement numbered 36 and if NOTE = 3, control is transferred to statement numbered 17.

3. IF (X) n_1, n_2, n_3

An IF statement, where X is an expression (constant, variable, arithmetic expression, etc.) and n_1, n_2 and n_3 are statement numbers, calls for the program to run to the IF statement. The computer then decides where (to what line) to transfer the program, depending upon the value of the variable at that point. If X is negative, control is transferred to statement numbered n_1; if zero, control is transferred to statement numbered n_2; and if positive, control is transferred to statement numbered n_3. As an example, consider:

IF (X-Y + 2.) 6, 8, 4

If (X-Y +2.) is negative, control is transferred to statement numbered 6; if zero, control is transferred to statement numbered 8; and if positive, control is transferred to statement numbered 4.

The following symbols in Table 8-3 can be utilized within the IF statement.

Symbol	Mathematical Notation	Meaning
.EQ.	$=$	Equal to
.NE.	$\neq$	Not equal to
.LT.	$<$	Less than
.LE.	$\leqslant$	Less than or equal to
.GT.	$>$	Greater than
.GE.	$\geqslant$	Greater than or equal to

4. STOP

The STOP instruction terminates the execution of the program.

5. CALL EXIT

The CALL EXIT instruction terminates the execution of the program and control is returned to the computer, which proceeds to execute the next program in the stream of programs in the batch process. (See Figure 8-2.) The CALL EXIT statement is equivalent to the STOP statement on many computer systems.

6. END

This statement defines the end of a program or a subprogram. It must be the last statement of each program or subprogram. It is not an executable statement.

Answer: X = A–B**2/C*D*ABS(A) or more clearly,
$\qquad$ X = A –((B**2)/C) * D * ABS(A)

Let us use the IF statement and the arithmetic operations to write a program for counting from 1 to 100 in steps of 1 and printing out the results. The program is as follows:

```
C  COUNTING FROM 1 TO 100, STEP = 1
   K = 0
10 K = K + 1
   WRITE (5, 40) K
   IF(100-K) 50,50,10
40 FORMAT (I3)
50 STOP
   END
```

Let us ignore the WRITE and FORMAT statements for the moment and examine the arithmetic and expressions in integer form. Since we are counting with integers, the program is limited to integers; we use K as the variable. The IF statement returns control to line 10 until 100-K is equal to zero, at which time it transfers control to the STOP statement and the program terminates.

A partial list of the input/output statements used in FORTRAN is given in Table 8-4. In the program for counting from 1 to 100 we used the output statement WRITE and its associated FORMAT statement. Each input and output statement must have an associated *format* statement to indicate the form of the number it is reading or printing. The definition of format is:

FORMAT   A specific arrangement of data.

In the case we are considering, for the integers from 1 to 100, we are (naturally) using an integer format. The largest number printed out is 100, so we require three digits, which are allocated in the format statement

FORMAT (I3)

where I indicates a fixed point or integer format and three digits are to be accommodated.

The output statement in the program above prints the output information on the output printer, logical unit number 5, according to the format statement 40. Thus, we have the statement

WRITE (5, 40) K

which prints K as K goes from 1 to 100.

Now, let us write a program for generating and printing out the Nth Fibonacci number. We have previously considered this algorithm for the Fibonacci sequence and illustrated a flow chart algorithm in Figures 4-9 and 6-9. The flow chart for obtaining the Nth Fibonacci number is shown in Figure 8-4, where we assume that N is greater than two. We are dealing only with integers, so we have limited the variables to integers. Thus the first letter of each variable is a letter between I and N. The counter index is equal to I. We wish to obtain the Nth Fibonacci number. The sum of K and M is obtained and stored

TABLE 8-4

A Partial List of Input/Output Statements

1. READ (K, n) List

   This is a read or input statement, where K is an unsigned integer constant or integer variable that specifies the logical input unit number (see below) for input data and n is the statement number of the FORMAT statement describing the type of data conversion. (See FORMAT below.) "List" refers to one or more variable–names, separated by commas, which are used for input data.

   The READ statement causes transmission of the input information from the input device coded K to the computer. For an IBM 1130, the logical input and output units are:

   1. Console typewriter output
   5. Printer output
   7. Plotter output
   2. Card reader input or punch output
   6. Console typewriter input

   Any number of quantities may appear in a single list and integer and real quantities may be transmitted by the same statement.

2. WRITE (K, n) List

   An output or print statement, where K is an unsigned integer constant or integer variable that specifies the logical unit number (see above) to be used for output data and n is the statement number of the FORMAT statement describing the type of data conversion.

   List is a list of names separated by commas for the output data.

3. FORMAT (I W1, I W2; . . .)

   An integer format statement describes how the information is arranged on input, or is to be arranged on output. For each number transmitted into the computer, there must correspond a field specification which lists the kind of information the field contains and what it "looks like" (or will "look like") on output.

   The format is IW where I indicates an integer number and W the number of digits to be allowed for the integer number and its associated sign, if any. If we are formatting several numbers, we allow W1 digits for the first number and W2 digits for the second number and so on. If we use the same number of digits for each integer number, W, we can use NIW where N is the number of integer numbers we are accommodating.

4. FORMAT (FW.d)

   A floating point format for a number without exponent. W is the number of digits we allow for the number, its associated sign, if any, and the decimal point, and d the total number of decimal places.

5. FORMAT (EW.d)

   A floating point format for a number with exponent. W is the number of digits we allow for the number and d the total number of decimal places.

in the variable LSUM, which is an integer variable. The program for generating the Nth Fibonacci number uses the READ statement, which is given in Table 8-4, to input the value of N specified by the user. The program is as follows:

```
C  THE NTH FIBONACCI NUMBER
   READ (2,50) N
   K = 1
```

```
     M = 1
     I = 2
10   LSUM = K + M
     I = I + 1
     IF (I–N) 20, 30, 30
20   K = M
     M = LSUM.
     GO TO 10
30   WRITE (5, 50) LSUM
     STOP
50   FORMAT (I5)
     END
```

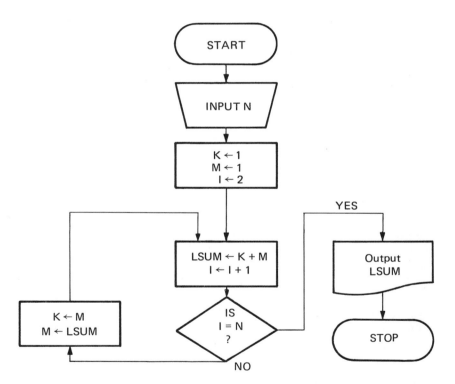

FIGURE 8–4 A flow chart algorithm for determining and printing the Nth Fibonacci number, assuming N is greater than 2.

The program first reads the value of N from the input device number 1, which is the punched card reader, in the format as given on line 50. Then the program initializes the values of K, M and I. We then calculate the sum of K and M in line 10 and advance the counter I in the next line. The IF statement determines if we have generated the Nth number. If (I–N) is negative, the loop is continued by proceeding to line 20 and completing the assignment of M to K and LSUM to M. We then return in the loop to line 10 and generate the next Fibonacci number. The loop is terminated when I = N and the program goes to line 30 where we print out the value of LSUM as the Nth Fibonacci number according to the format given in line 50. After printing LSUM we stop the execution.

The format used in this program is given in line 50 as an integer format with five digits allowed. For the sake of convenience, we use the same format for N and LSUM. Since we are calculating a number using integer variables, we will not be able to exceed the largest number allowed in integer form, which is 32,767 for the IBM 1130 and larger for larger computers. Whatever the limit is, we do not wish to exceed it with LSUM, and thus we have limited the format to five digits. This program is limited to the N = 23, since the 23rd Fibonacci number is 28657. If we wish to generate Fibonacci numbers for N greater than 23, we will need to rewrite the program for floating point variables in exponential format.

Format statements in FORTRAN permit many forms of information transmission. While format statements may be confusing, they are a powerful feature of FORTRAN and worth studying. Format statements control the input and output of information. They also control the specification of a blank field; that is, spacing between output results. Format statements can also be used to specify alphabetical and alphanumeric fields of data such as titles.

FORTRAN is typically used with machines which utilize a punched card as an input record. A punched card is shown in Figure 8-5. All the information on each card is called a *unit input record*. The maximum size of the input record is 72 columns. The information printed or typed on the output record on each line is called a *unit output record*. Each record is made up of one or more fields. A field is a group of one or more columns whose content can or must be described separately. Each statement card has 80 numbered columns divided into fields, as shown in Figure 8-5. The main field, columns 7-72, is reserved for the FORTRAN STATEMENT. Columns 73-80, the identification field, are not executed by the computer. That is, the computer does not read or process information in this field. It is, therefore, used by the programmer to assist him in identifying the card. Columns 1-5 are a field reserved for statement numbers when they are used or for a C to indicate the card contains a comment not to be executed. The cards for a program should always be placed in the order in which the respective statements are to be executed.

TYPICAL   STATMENT   CARD

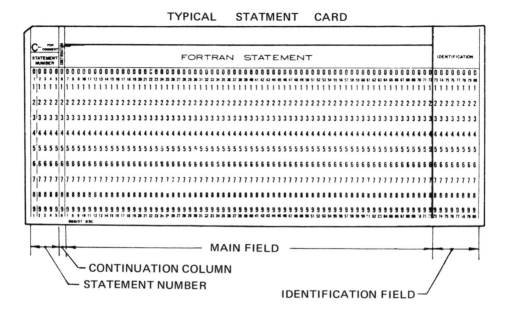

FIGURE 8-5   A typical statement punched card.

If there are more quantities in the input record than there are items in the list, only the number of quantities equal to the number of items in the list are transmitted and the remaining quantities are ignored. Consider the example:

READ (2,5) X,Y,Z

If the card contains five numbers, only the first three will be transmitted and assigned the consecutive names of X, Y and Z.

If the list contains more quantities than the number of input records, succeeding input records are read until all the items specified in the list have been transmitted. Consider the example:

READ (2,7) X,Y,Z,W,U,R

If each of three cards contains two values, the first card will be read and the numbers assigned the names X and Y. Then the next card is read and the numbers assigned the names Z and W. Finally, the third card is read and assigned the names U and R. Integers are printed or punched on cards for input directly, without any decimal points; for example, ±XXX. Since they are integers, of course, there is no need for decimal points. The FORMAT is IW where I indicates a fixed point number and W the number of positions printed or punched. For example, the number −328 would require the format I4. Empty columns in a data card are interpreted as zeros, so all integers must be placed on the right of their respective fields.

Floating point numbers without exponents (F-fields) are punched or printed in the form:

$$\pm X_1 X_2 X_3 X_4 X_5 X_6 X_7$$

The FORMAT is FW.d, where F indicates a floating point number without exponent, W the field width and d the total number of decimal places. For example, the number -320.683 would require the format F8.3.

Floating point numbers with exponents (E-fields) are punched or printed in the form:

$$\pm .X_1 X_2 X_3 X_4 E+n_1 n_2$$

The FORMAT is EW.d where E indicates a floating point number with an exponent and W and d are as in the E field. For example, the number 1369428.67 in the format E15.9 would appear as 0.136942867E+07. The decimal point may be placed anywhere within the number on input but it always appears immediately to the left of the leading significant digit on output. When insufficient space is provided, the sign, then the leading zero, then the decimal point, then the leading significant digits are cut off in that order. One always provides a field at least six columns *in excess* of the number of decimal places desired.

Let us write a program for finding the *average* of 15 numbers (for example, examination grades) stored on cards, and printing out the average. A program for completing this process is as follows:

```
      SUM = 0.
      I = 1
 10   READ (2,40)X
      SUM = SUM + X
      I = I + 1
 18   IF (I-15) 10, 10, 20
 20   AVER = SUM/15.
      WRITE (5,40) AVER
 40   FORMAT (F6.2)
      STOP
      END
```

This program is written in floating point form and uses floating point variables. In lines 10 through 18, we read the values of X into the computer and generate the sum. In line 10, the X values are read from the card reader (device number 2). Since each execution of the READ instruction brings in a new unit record (card), we must have each number on a separate card. According to the format specified by statement 40, each number will appear in a six-column field at the beginning of a data card.

The data cards are now fed into the card punch reader following the instruction cards. The average is calculated on line 20. Since this line is in floating point form, we must have a decimal point following the 15. We then print out the average in the format specified. We assume the largest examination score would be 100.00, which requires six characters. We decide that the examination scores have only two decimal places, at most, and thus the average should only return two decimal places. The format F6.2 specifies a field of six characters width and includes two decimal places.

As another example, let us write a program for calculating the wages due ten employees who worked a number of *hours in the past month* (TIME) *at a certain wage rate* (RATE). The employees each have an employee number, NUM, one through ten, and each has his own wage rate. The program is as follows:

```
10  READ (2,20) NUM, RATE, TIME
20  FORMAT (I2, F5.2, F5.1)
    WAGE = RATE * TIME
    WRITE (5,30) NUM, RATE, TIME, WAGE
    GO TO 10
30  FORMAT (I2, 2F6.2, F7.2)
    STOP
    END
```

The program reads each card, which lists the employee number in integer format and his wage rate and time worked. These variables are not to be in integer format. A man who works 0.6 hours wants to be paid for it, and wages are likely to be paid in dollars *and* cents, so we cannot use integer format for rate and time and be fair to the employee. On the other hand, a hundredth of an hour is likely to be considered insignificant in reckoning time. These considerations determine the format we choose with which to enter rate and time. One might have an hourly wage in the form FF.FF which has five characters and two decimal places. The time would be in the format F5.1. When printing out, the format out will be given in line 30. The employee number is given in format I2 and the wage and time are both given in F6.2. The product of rate multiplied by time would require F7.2 since, for example, $10.00 × 200 hours is $2,000.00 and the largest format required would be F7.2, for those who earn over $1,000 in a given month. An example of an input data card for employee number 7 is shown in Figure 8-6.

It is not necessary to crowd data on a data card. The example shown in Figure 8-6 shows that each input item should be separated by blank columns. This is accomplished by specifying a field width larger than is actually needed. Such spacing makes the data card easier for the programmer to read.

Another form of FORMAT is the H-field format, which enables the printing of the text of a message or heading. The H-field, or *Hollerith field*, speci-

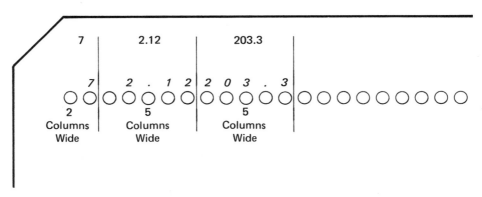

FIGURE 8-6   A punched data card for the seventh employee, using FORMAT (I2, F5.2, F5.1) Shown enlarged.

fication permits the printing of alphanumeric words and phrases in the form of comments, titles and headings. Instead of enclosing the text in quotation marks, we precede it by the letter H, which identifies it as an H–field, and precede the letter H with an integer to indicate the length of the H–field. For many computers, the size of the H–field is limited to 50 characters, where that number must include all blank spaces, letters, numbers and special characters that are used.

As an example, let us write the FORMAT statement and its associated WRITE statement that will print out the average of 15 grades for a student.

        WRITE (5,40) AVER
    40 FORMAT (28H THE AVERAGE OF 15 GRADES IS, F6.2)

Compare this write and format statement with that used in the program above for calculating the average. The write statement is identical; only the format statement was changed to accommodate the Hollerith field message, prior to printing the value of AVER in the format F6.2. The H–field requires 28 spaces including the blank spaces. The comma at the end of the H–field statement sets off the end of the message.

If we wish to print a heading on a line we can use

        WRITE (5,30)
    30 FORMAT (16H THE ANSWERS ARE)

This format will print out the title at the left of a line. If we wish it printed in the center of the printer page, then we add a spacing message by means of an X–field. (Where one or more columns of a card record or line record are to be ignored or skipped this may be accomplished by a skip-field, usually called an

X–field. The form of the X–field is an integer preceding an X, where the integer indicates the number of blank spaces to be provided. Thus, to center the answer heading, we might use

      WRITE (5,30)
  30 FORMAT (30X, 16H THE ANSWERS ARE).

This X–field of 30 spaces will place the heading 30 spaces from the left of the printer page.) The comma following the X–field separates it from the code that follows. Notice that the WRITE statement used here has no list. This is because the line of output generated does not require values of any variables to be printed out.

The Hollerith code is also used to cause the output printer to skip (or "index") to the top of the next printer page before printing the message and results. The code 1H1 inserted at the beginning of the format statement causes the printer to index to the next page.

Many recent computers utilizing FORTRAN provide an alternative to the H–field approach which relieves the programmer of the task of counting characters. A string of alphanumeric and special characters may be written within the FORMAT statement and enclosed in apostrophes. This procedure may be used in place of the H specification. It eliminates the necessity for counting spaces. Consider the example:

      WRITE (5,8)
  8   FORMAT ('THIS IS A PROBLEM')

On execution, the words THIS IS A PROBLEM will be printed with the corresponding spacing. The apostrophe sequence is often called the *string quote* technique.

Let us write a program to calculate and print out the square root of a series of input numbers using an apostrophe to enclose the message. The string quote will be used to enclose the text: "The square root of 'X' is 'Y'." The program and the printed output is given below. The numbers are read in the format F10.3 and printed out in the format F10.5.

```
  C     PRINT THE SQUARE ROOT OF A SERIES OF NUMBERS
    1 READ (2,38) X
   38 FORMAT (F10.3)
      Y=SQRT(X)
      WRITE (5,39) X,Y
   39 FORMAT ( ' THE SQRT OF ', F10.3,' IS', F10.5)
      GO TO 1
      STOP
      END
```

THE SQRT OF   16.000 IS   4.00000
THE SQRT OF   20.000 IS   4.47213
THE SQRT OF   36.000 IS   6.00000
THE SQRT OF   3600.000 IS   60.00000
THE SQRT OF   3.615 IS   1.90131

There is quite a bit of detail to master in FORTRAN, especially with respect to the format specifications. We find that FORTRAN is a very versatile and rich language, but the attendant details are often difficult to master at first. It reminds one of the concept that the richer the texture of the cloth, the more complex the weaving to achieve it.

8.3 THE FORTRAN DO LOOP

One of the most important features of the computer is its ability to accomplish iterative calculations using a looping process. FORTRAN contains a special statement for establishing a counter–controlled loop. The iteration statement is called a DO statement. It is usually considered the most powerful statement in FORTRAN. The general form of the DO statement is:

$$DO \ n \ I = m_1, m_2, m_3$$

where n is a statement number, I is a nonsubscripted variable, and m_1, m_2, m_3 are unsigned integer constants or nonsubscripted variables.

The initial value m_1 is the value of the index for the first execution of the range. Naturally, m_1 must not be zero or negative; it is an integer constant.

The test value m_2 is the value that the index must not exceed. Once the test value has been exceeded, the DO loop is completed and the program continues with the first statement following the range limit.

The value m_3 is the amount by which the value of the index will be increased after each execution of the range. When m_3 is not stated, it is assumed to be 1 and the comma following m_2 must be omitted in this case. For example:

$$DO \ 10 \ I = 1, 8$$

The range limit n defines the range of the DO. It includes all statements following the DO, up to and including the statement n. The range can consist of any number of statements. The index I is an integer variable that is increased incrementally for each execution of the range of the statement. Throughout the range of the DO, the index may be used either as a subscript or as an ordinary integer variable. The index *must not* be changed by a statement within the range of the DO. When transferring out of the range of the DO, the index is available for other use, and then becomes equal to the last value it attained.

As an example, let us consider a portion of a program using a DO statement as follows:

```
      DO  10  I = 1,5
      A = I
      X = SIN(3.*A)
  10  SUM = SUM + X
```

This program is executed five times with I ranging from 1 to 5 in the second statement. First I is set equal to 1 and is then converted to a real variable A. The sine of 3A is computed and stored in the address associated with the variable name X. The variable SUM is added to X and the result stored in the address associated with the variable name S. I is then incremented by 1 and the result compared with 5. At the second step, I is less than 5; the program is executed again with I now equal to 2. After the execution with I = 5, I is incremented by 1 to become 6 and this value is compared with 5. Since it is greater than m_2 = 5, the next step in the program after statement 10 is executed.

The single DO statement accomplishes the same control as three statements establishing a loop using an IF statement. For example,

$$DO 6 I = 1, 20, 1$$

is equivalent to the three statements

```
      I = 1
   5  I = I + 1
   6  IF (I-20) 5, 5, 8
   8  _____  8 is the next statement.
```

There are several restrictions to be applied to DO loops in order to insure that the loop is entered and terminated correctly and that loops do not intermingle. The index I and the loop parameters m_1, m_2, m_3 must not be altered within the range of the DO loop. Also, nested DO loops are permitted, but a DO loop interior to another DO loop must always reside completely within its exterior DO loop. A DO loop may never be entered except through the DO statement to ensure the proper initialization of the loop index. Also, a DO loop should never have as its last statement a GO TO, IF, STOP, CALL EXIT, RETURN, another DO statement, or any non-executable statement. If it is necessary to terminate a DO loop with one of the above types of statements, the dummy statement CONTINUE can be inserted as the terminal statement of the DO loop so this rule need not be violated. (CONTINUE is used primarily to terminate a DO loop.)

As an example of the use of a DO loop and the string quote technique for printing headings, consider the calculation of the square root of a number, T, by means of the algorithm derived from the Newton–Raphson technique[5], for which we use the equation

$$f(X) = X^2 - T = 0 \text{ (See footnote.)}$$

The Newton–Raphson method yields the algorithm

$$X_{new} = X_{old} - \left(\frac{X^2_{old} - T}{2X_{old}}\right)$$

where X_{new} is the new approximation to the square root of T and X_{old} is the old approximation to the square root of T. This method utilizes the calculus; it is outlined in the footnote for those who have studied calculus. However, it is not necessary to understand the origin of the Newton–Raphson algorithm to proceed with the program.

In writing the program we use APRX2 as the new approximation to the value of the square root, X_{new} in the formula above. The former approximation, X_{old}, is represented by APRX1. The index counter, J, is initially set equal to 1 and we input the number T and the number of iterations, M, we wish to have calculated. We print out as T the latest approximation to the square root of T, and the number of iterations used, M. The flow chart for the algorithm appears in Figure 8–7.

The program for calculating the square root of a number T in M iterations by Newton–Raphson method is given below. The first WRITE statement, and its associated FORMAT statement, line 1, provides the headings for the results on the output printer. We use string quotes in this case to list the headings. After nine blank spaces, T is printed as one heading. Then, after 10 blank spaces, APPROXIMATE SQUARE is printed. Ten blank spaces again precede the heading AFTER M. The slash,/, causes the printer to go to the next line and print the remaining headings. After counting 20 blank spaces, the heading ROOT OF T is printed. Then after an additional 18 blank spaces, ITERATIONS is printed. The final heading appears as shown. We read T and M from the first data card according to the statements in lines 5 and 10. The number T is given in F10.5 and the number of iterations in I10. We use as a first approximation to the square root of T one-half the number. Thus APRX1 = T/2 is an initial value. The DO loop consists of the three statements, 6 through 100. When we have completed the M iterations of the DO loop, which contains the Newton–Raphson algorithm, we proceed to the WRITE statement for the results to be printed. The results, T, APRX1 and M are printed according to the format statement, number 20. First T is printed out in F10.5, then we have 14 blank spaces followed by APRX1 printed in F10.5. Then we have 12 blank spaces followed by M in I10 format. With the spaces provided, the answers appear di-

---

The Newton–Raphson formula is

$$X_{n+1} = X_n - \frac{f(X_n)}{f'(X_n)}$$

where X_n = the nth iteration, X_{n+1} = the (n+1)st iteration and $f'(X_n) = \frac{df(X)}{dX}$ evaluated at $X = X_n$. Since $f(X) = X^2 - T$, we have $f'(X_n) = 2X_n$. Therefore

$$X_{n+1} = X_n - \frac{(X^2_n - T)}{2X_n}$$

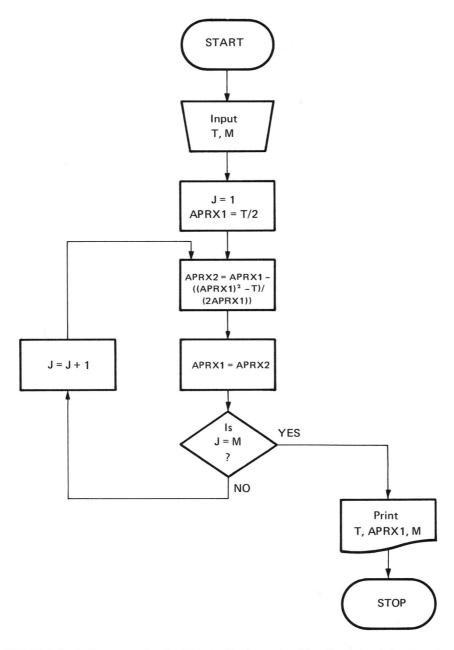

FIGURE 8-7 A flow chart for the Newton–Raphson algorithm for determining the square root of the number T, using M iterations.

```
* EXTENDED PRECISION
* LIST SOURCE PROGRAM

      WRITE(5,1)
    1 FORMAT(9X,'T',10X,'APPROXIMATE SQUARE',10X,'AFTER
      M',/,20X,'ROOT OF T',18X,'ITERATIONS',/)
    5 READ(2,10)T,M
   10 FORMAT(F10.5,I10)
      APRX1=T/2.
      IF(T)99,7,7
    7 IF(M-1)5,5,6
    6 DO 100 J=1,M
      APRX2=APRX1-(APRX1**2-T)/(2.*APRX1)
  100 APRX1=APRX2
      WRITE(5,20)T,APRX1,M
   20 FORMAT(F10.5,14X,F10.5,12X,I10)
      GO TO 5
   99 CALL EXIT
      END
```

T	APPROXIMATE SQUARE ROOT OF T	AFTER M ITERATIONS
100.00000	14.92307	2
100.00000	10.81205	3
100.00000	10.00004	5
225.00000	15.00561	5
2.25000	1.50000	3
2.25000	1.50000	5
81.00810	9.49802	3

rectly below the headings previously supplied. Several results are given for various values of T and several trials of different numbers of iterations, M.

This program contains the slash with which blank lines may be introduced between output records, or input records may be skipped, by using consecutive slashes (/) in a FORMAT statement. For example,

```
      WRITE (5,4) J, X, Y
    4 FORMAT (I3//F10.2)
      . . . . . .
```

will cause the quantity J to be printed with a FORMAT specification of I3, then skip two lines and print X and Y on the third line with a specification of F10.2.

The program shown above also uses extended precision arithmetic. Recall that the standard precision provided with a computer may be insufficient for the precision desired. The program above was executed on an IBM 1130, which provides a precision range of seven significant digits. The extended precision called for provides a precision of 10 significant digits. We gain the additional digits of precision at the expense of a somewhat longer execution time for the program. Quite often with problems which require numerical precision, the deterioration in execution time is well worth the use of extended precision arithmetic.

Within a loop it is common to use a subscripted variable, such as M(J) where J is the subscript. The index J of the DO loop is used to supply the value of the subscript. Any variable (integer or real) can be made to represent any element in a one, two or three dimensional array. Subscripts are integer constant quantities. The use of an array must be preceded by a DIMENSION statement of the form

$$\text{DIMENSION } A(k), B(m), \ldots$$

where A, B, ... are names of arrays and k, m ... are integer constants that specify the maximum value of the subscript.

As an example of the utility of several DO loops, let us write a program for determining and printing the least common multiple (LCM) of several sets of three numbers. We use several DO loops to read-in and to find the LCM of L sets of three numbers. The three numbers will all be integers, so we use integer arithmetic. The flow chart showing the three DO loops to be used is shown in Figure 8-8. We use the special flow chart symbol for representing a DO statement, and a CONTINUE. The first DO loop, DO 18, is used to read the sets of three numbers. The second DO loop, DO 9, determines the largest number of the three numbers and sets it equal to MAX. The third loop, DO 15, is used to determine the least common multiple. The LCM is then printed out and we return to the outer loop to read the next set of three numbers. The outer loop is terminated when all L sets of numbers have been read as input.

Now let us consider the algorithm for determining the LCM of a set of three numbers. In the set (2,3,6) the LCM is 6, since all the numbers divide into 6 without a remainder. The LCM of (5,10,15) is 30. An algorithm for determining the LCM of (M_1, M_2, M_3) is:

1. Set MAX = the largest number of the set (M_1, M_2, M_3)
2. Set LCM = MAX
3. Determine if all three numbers divide LCM without remainder. If they divide LCM, then print LCM as the least common multiple. If they do not all divide LCM, then proceed to 4.
4. Set LCM = LCM + MAX and return to 3.

Using this algorithm, let us try to determine the least common multiple for the set (2,3,4). We set MAX = 4 and then try LCM = 4. Not all the numbers divide

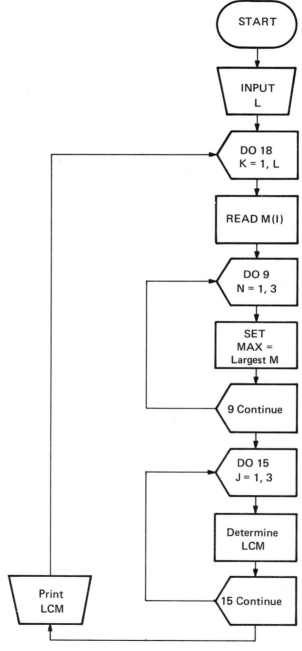

FIGURE 8-8 A flow chart showing three DO loops for determining the least common multiple of a set of three numbers, for L sets of numbers.

LCM, so we let LCM = 4 + 4 = 8. Again, not all the numbers divide LCM = 8, so we let LCM = 8 + MAX = 12. Then we find that all three numbers divide 12, so we record LCM = 12.

The heart of the algorithm is to determine if LCM can be divided by each of the three numbers without leaving a remainder. This test can be obtained by using the FORTRAN operating statement:

$$IF(LCM/M(J) * M(J) - LCM)$$

Since we are using integer arithmetic, the division LCM/M(J) will yield an integer. Thus, the expression within the parentheses will only be equal to zero when LCM is divided by M(J) without a remainder. For example, for the case considered above when LCM = 8 and M(2) = 3, we have

$$LCM/M(2) = 2$$

in integer arithmetic. Thus (LCM/M(2) * M(2) - LCM) is not equal to zero and we must try the next value of LCM, which is LCM = 12. Then, we have

$$(LCM/M(2) * M(2) - LCM) = 0$$

and we use the test for zero for all three numbers to indicate finding the LCM.

The program for determining the LCM of three numbers is given below.

```
C     PROGRAM TO FIND THE LEAST COMMON MULTIPLE OF A
      SERIES OF NUMBERS
      DIMENSION M(30)
50    WRITE (5,51)
51    FORMAT (' LOWEST COMMON MULTIPLE', 5X, ' NUMBERS')
      READ (2,20) L
20    FORMAT (I3)
      DO 18 K=1, L
      READ (2,25) (M(J), J=1,3)
25    FORMAT (I3)
C     FIND THE LARGEST M   (TO USE IN INCREMENTING)
      MAX=0
      DO  9 N=1,3
      IF (MAX -M(N)) 7,9,9
 7    MAX=M(N)
 9    CONTINUE
12    DO 15 LCM=MAX, 15000, MAX
13    DO 11 J=1,3
10    IF (LCM/M(J)*M(J)-LCM) 15,11,15
11    CONTINUE
      GO TO 18
15    CONTINUE
18    WRITE (5,60) LCM, M(1), M(2), M(3)
60    FORMAT (10X, I8, 15X, I4,4X, I4, 4X, I4)
      CALL EXIT
      END
```

LOWEST COMMON MULTIPLE	NUMBERS		
6	2	3	6
30	5	10	15
2604	7	12	31
10465	5	23	91

First, we read the value of L, the number of sets of numbers to be considered. We then read in the first set of numbers using the DO loop DO 18. The set of numbers M(1), M(2) and M(3) is examined and MAX is set equal to the largest number of the set by using the DO loop DO 9. We then use the statements between line 12 and line 15 to calculate the LCM. The first loop, DO 15, sets LCM = MAX and increments LCM by MAX until the correct LCM is determined. The test for the LCM is carried out by the loop DO 11, which determines if the remainder in line 10 is zero for all three numbers. When the test is satisfied for all numbers, we proceed to print the LCM and the three numbers. Then we return to the loop DO 18, to read the next set of three numbers. Several sets of numbers are shown with the associated least common multiples. The program uses four DO loops, and the effectiveness of the DO statement is quite obvious.

In the next section, we consider some advanced programming concepts. You may wish to omit reading the next section and return to it at a later time.

8.4 ADVANCED PROGRAMMING TECHNIQUES IN FORTRAN

FORTRAN programs are not limited to the manipulation of numerical data and information only. Rather, we are provided with the means to input alphabetical data and manipulate it for useful purposes. We are able to transmit alphameric data (*i.e.*, alphabetical and numeric data) to storage locations. Consider the following read statement and its associated format statement:

        READ (2,10)X
    10 FORMAT (A4)

These statements reserve a location in memory called X in which alphameric data, such as a company's name or a person's home city, is to be stored. Then the alphameric characters should appear in the first four columns of the punched card to be read.

The format in the statement number 10 above is called an *A field*. The A specification transmits alphameric data to or from variables in storage. The A specification takes the form AW, where W is an integer that causes the first W characters to be read into, or written from, the area of storage specified in the list. For example:

        READ (6,4) SUM
    4   FORMAT (A6)

would cause six alphameric characters to be read from the console keyboard and placed (left justified) into the variable named SUM.

Caution must be exercised when using the A format specification, since symbols may be easily lost from the character string if enough space is not provided. Consider a string, for example, which is a person's name, and which is five characters long. If we have a format A4, obviously we will lose one character on input. On input, truncation of the character string occurs on the left if the storage allocated to the variable to which the data is being transferred is of length less than W. That is, only the n rightmost characters in the field will be stored where n is the number of characters capacity of the input list variable. Padding to the right with blanks occurs if the storage capacity in characters allocated to the variable to which the data is being transferred is greater than W. On output, the character-string constant which is associated with the output list element variable will be transmitted to the output stream as a character string of length W, right-justified in the field. If the length of the character-string constant being transmitted is greater than W, truncation of excess characters will occur on the right, while leading blanks will be supplied to pad out the field on the left if the transmitted character-string constant is of length less than W.

The number of alphameric characters that can be stored in a single memory location depends on the specific computer. One computer may allow up to four characters to be stored in integer memory and up to eight in a real variable location. Assume that four characters is the limit of the computer for illustrative purposes in the following paragraphs. Let us consider the case where we wish to read from a punched card which has a person's name as follows:

JOHN P. JONES

This name will consume the first 13 columns on the card, including spaces and the period. Thus we require four storage locations in sequence, each of four characters in length. We could read this name with the following statements:

```
      READ (2,10)(A(I), I = 1,4)
   10 FORMAT (4A4)
```

These two statements consist of two new input techniques. The first technique appears in the read statement. The statement

$$\text{READ } (2,10)(A(I), I = 1,4)$$

is equivalent to the use of a DO loop as follows:

```
      DO 9 I = 1, 4
   9  READ (2,10)A(I)
```

Thus we are able to read the elements of the array A(I).

The second statement, line 10, in the original READ and FORMAT pair, provides for the A-format which allows for four storage locations for the alphameric data, each four characters in length.

In a similar manner, the statements

```
    WRITE (5,8) (A(I), I = 1,4)
8   FORMAT (40X, 4A4)
```

will cause the alphameric data to be printed as output in the center of the page.

In Section 7.4, which considered several advanced programs in BASIC, we examined the problem of sorting a list of L numbers by the method of interchange. In this chapter we consider a somewhat more advanced problem, that of alphabetizing a list of names and their associated examination scores. The problem consists of printing out an alphabetized list of names, given punched cards as input. Each input punched card has the name of the student and his or her examination grade. The following sets of names and scores are each punched on a card:

```
SUE     80
MARY    84
TOM     93
JOHN    63
```

We have simplified the problem somewhat by considering names with a maximum of four alphabetic characters. Nevertheless, the concepts we explore can readily be extended to more complex cases.

Recall, in Section 7.4, that the principle of interchange was considered for placing a set of N numbers in descending order. Let us first consider the problem for sorting a set of numbers using the principle of interchange. Then we extend the principle to that of sorting names into alphabetical order. The algorithm is based on first assuming that the first number in the array is the largest number. We then test this number against the second number in the array and interchange them if the second number is larger than the first. We proceed to complete this process for the list, thus obtaining a sorted list in descending order. The flow chart for the sorting algorithm is given in Figure 8-9. The program for accomplishing the sorting of the N numbers is given as follows:

```
    DIMENSION A(30)
    READ (2,40)N
40  FORMAT (I 10)
    READ (2,50) (A(I), I = 1,N)
50  FORMAT (F12.4)
 4  NM1 = N-1
 5  DO 11 I = 1, NM1
 6  IP1 = I + 1
    DO 11 J = IP1, N
 7  IF (A(I) - A(J)) 8, 11, 11
 8  TEMP = A(I)
 9  A(I) = A(J)
```

```
10  A(J) = TEMP
11  CONTINUE
    WRITE (5,60)(A(I), I = 1, N)
60  FORMAT (F12.4)
    STOP
    END
```

The first READ statement provides N, the number of punched cards, and the second READ statement causes the N numbers to read into the computer in the array A(I). The interchange is achieved by the statements on lines 7 through 10. The temporary storage variable, TEMP, is necessary to achieve the interchange. Consider the four numbers:

$$4$$
$$6$$
$$2$$
$$5$$

The program examines the first two numbers, compares and then interchanges so that we have:

$$6$$
$$4$$
$$2$$
$$5$$

The program then compares 6 against all the other numbers and finds it is the largest. It then proceeds to test 4 against the next two numbers and finds $5>4$, so it places 5 in the second location. Thus we have:

$$6$$
$$5$$
$$2$$
$$4$$

Now the last two numbers are compared and interchanged, giving us a sorted list:

$$6$$
$$5$$
$$4$$
$$2$$

Now, upon examination of the sorting process, we find that since the first number was not larger than the second, we put the larger number into the first position, placing what was originally in the first position into the position vacated by the largest.

Then for the next pass, if we consider only elements 2 to N, we have truly eliminated the largest from the list to be scanned. Furthermore, this process can be repeated. Each time we complete a pass and interchange, we have added 1 to the length of the list already sorted, and subtracted 1 from the remaining

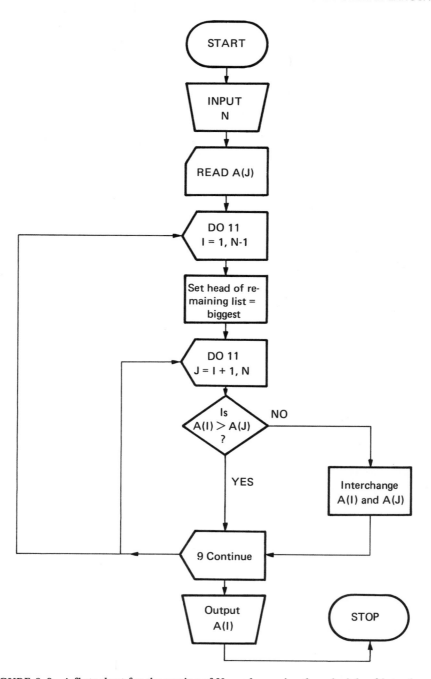

FIGURE 8-9   A flow chart for the sorting of N numbers using the principle of interchange.

list. Not only does the list to be checked become progressively shorter with each pass, but the process can actually stop one short. For by the time the first N - 1 of the elements have been found, one can convince himself that the Nth one, the only one remaining, belongs where it is—in last place. Therefore, the outside DO loop in Figure 8-9 need cover only the range from J = 1 to N -1. Such an expression is not permitted in the DO statement itself, but we can get around the restriction very easily by inserting a preceding statement to define a new variable: NM1 = N - 1 as we do in line 4. We then use this variable as the parameter in the DO statement in line 5. Perhaps it would be wise to run through the program with a pencil and paper for the numbers 4, 6, 2, 5 in order to further understand the program. You will then be able to verify that, in fact, only three passes through the testing process are required for four numbers and therefore the first DO loop need have only the range NM1 = N-1 as we agreed above.

Now we return to the problem of sorting the names and the exam scores associated with the names. Again, we use the principle of interchange, but for sorting names in this case. The program for sorting the four names is given below with the sorted list after program execution also shown. The program also sorts the scores in descending order.

```
C       THIS IS A PROGRAM TO SORT A SERIES OF TEST SCORES
C       IN DESCENDING ORDER AND TO ALPHABETIZE THE NAMES
C       OF THE STUDENTS WHO TOOK THE TEST.
        DIMENSION  SCORE (10), XNAME (10)
        READ (2,5) N
     5  FORMAT (I3)
        DO 25 I=1,N
        READ (2,7) SCORE(I), XNAME(I)
     7  FORMAT (F5.1, A5)
    25  CONTINUE
    26  NM1 = N-1
        WRITE (5,30)
    30  FORMAT (' SCORES IN DESCENDING ORDER')
        DO 38 I=1,NM1
        IP1=I+1
        DO 38 J=IP1,N
        IF (SCORE(I)-SCORE(J)) 40,38,38
    40  TEMP = SCORE(I)
        SCORE(I) = SCORE(J)
        SCORE(J) = TEMP
        TEMP = XNAME(I)
        XNAME(I) = XNAME(J)
        XNAME(J) = TEMP
    38  CONTINUE
        WRITE (5,39) (SCORE(I), XNAME(I), I=1,N)
```

```
39  FORMAT (5X, F5.1, 5X, A5)
    WRITE (5,43)
43  FORMAT (' NAMES IN ALPHABETIC ORDER')
    DO 8 I=1,NM1
    DO 8 J=IP1,N
    IF (XNAME(I)-XNAME(J)) 8,8,9
9   TEMP = XNAME(I)
    XNAME(I) = XNAME(J)
    XNAME(J) = TEMP
    TEMP = SCORE(I)
    SCORE(I) = SCORE(J)
    SCORE(J) = TEMP
8   CONTINUE
    DO 11 J=1,N
    WRITE (5,18) XNAME(J), SCORE(J)
18  FORMAT (5X, A5, 5X, F5.1)
11  CONTINUE
    CALL EXIT
    END
```

```
SCORES IN DESCENDING ORDER
    93.0        TOM
    84.0        MARY
    80.0         SUE
    63.0        JOHN
NAMES IN ALPHABETIC ORDER
    JOHN        63.0
    MARY        84.0
     SUE        80.0
    TOM         93.0
```

The sorting program first provides a dimension statement to reserve the proper number of spaces for the names and their associated scores. The scores are stored in a real variable SCORE and the associated names are stored in the real variable XNAME. We read N, the number of data pairs, and then read all four sets into the computer. The scores are read in the F5.1 format and the names in A5 format. The portion of the program from line 26 to line 39 accomplishes the task of sorting the scores in descending order. The result of executing this portion of the program is shown on the output on the bottom of the figure. The sorting program follows the algorithm given in Figure 8-9 for sorting according to scores as well as sorting according to names.

The portion of the program which causes the names to be sorted is given between lines 43 and 18, which is the lower portion of the program. In order to sort the names, we need to test the names with the statement

IF(XNAME(I) – XNAME(J)) 8,8,9

Then the interchange process is used to exchange names and their associated scores if necessary. The IF statement is able to compare names and determine whether one is larger than the other since the letters of the alphabet are stored in the converted numerical code within the computer. The numerical code is in descending order as the alphabet proceeds from A to Z. Thus, we are able to sort the list of names and print out the results as shown.

SUMMARY

In this chapter, we have studied FORTRAN, the most widely–used computer language. FORTRAN, which has been widely used for scientific and business problems, was compared with ALGOL, PL/1 and APL, which are other problem–oriented languages. FORTRAN is primarily used in a batch–processing, closed–shop manner; it is a very efficient language for such an approach. The FORTRAN language uses English words and algebraic expressions to describe the algorithms used to solve problems. We may use real or integer arithmetic with FORTRAN. An extensive facility to specify the format of the input and output is provided in FORTRAN. While the format statements require extensive detail, they also provide a very powerful richness of expression to the programmer. In the batch–process mode, FORTRAN typically uses punched cards as the input medium and the printer as the output.

FORTRAN language incorporates the DO statement, which powerfully and succinctly establishes a loop for iteration processes. Finally, we found that the FORTRAN language is as useful for processing alphameric information as it is for processing numeric information.

CHAPTER 8 PROBLEMS

P8–1. Define the following terms:
 a) batch–processing
 b) open–shop computer center
 c) floating point notation
 d) integer variable

P8–2. List several problem–oriented languages that possess some of the characteristics of FORTRAN.

P8–3. What series of words does FORTRAN represent in shortened form?

P8–4. What is the use of a DIMENSION statement?

P8-5. List the four types of FORMAT specifications available in FORTRAN.

P8-6. In the following, indicate whether the symbol is a permissible real variable symbol (R), integer variable symbol (I) or neither (N).

1) X	6) NEXT	11) (X61)	16) X14	21) SUM2
2) I12g	7) 42G	12) GAMMA81	17) X1.4	22) 23SUM
3) CAT	8) LAST	13) AI	18) Kappa	23) SIGMA
4) X + 2	9) XSQUARD	14) IA	19) JLS	24) QUOTE
5) XP2	10) DELTA	15) MU	20) LOAN	25) MHOUR

P8-7. Write the FORTRAN expression corresponding to each of the following mathematical expressions: Write in real (floating point) mode.

1) $x + y^3$

2) x^4

3) $\dfrac{a + b}{c}$

4) $a + \dfrac{b}{c}$

5) $(x + y)^3$

6) $(x + y)(x - y)^3$

7) $a + \dfrac{b}{c - d}$

8) $\left(\dfrac{a + b}{c + d}\right)^2 + x^2$

9) $c + \dfrac{a + b}{\dfrac{d}{3 - f}}$

10) $\dfrac{\dfrac{a}{b} - 1}{g\left(\dfrac{g}{d} - 1\right)}$

11) $\dfrac{\dfrac{a}{b} - 1}{g(g + d) - 3}$

12) $1 + x + \dfrac{x^2}{2!} + \dfrac{x^3}{3!}$

13) $\dfrac{12{,}356x^2 + 5}{2 \cdot 10^{-3} + 7x - 3}$

14) $(a/b)^{c + 3}$

15) $b^2 - 4 \cdot a \cdot c/5a$

P8-8. Each of the following contains an error. Indicate the error.

1. X = (Y + 5,)/Z**2   2. X = Y**3/3.M   3. N = (U – V) (A + 6.)

4. X = (B6,8 – B21)/B36)   5. PER = π * R ** 2

6. X = ((W + R)/(Z2 + R – 1.)   7. X – 3 = A   8. 2.6 = X + B ** 3

P8-9. Given: J = 10, K = 2, X = 10 and Z = 2.
Evaluate:

1. I = J/K + 2/3   2. B = J/K + 2/3   3. I = X/Z + 2./3.

4. Y = X/Z + 2./3.   5. I = J/Z + 2./3

P8-10. The program for determining whether a number is a prime number is given below. Complete statements 20, 40, 52, 200 and 201. The program utilizes the Sieve of Eratosthenes considered previously in problems P4-6 and P7-15.

```
C       THIS PRØGRAM DETERMINES WHETHER A GIVEN NUMBER
C       IS PRIME N
        READ (2,101) N
C       CHECK TØ SEE IF N IS ØNE.
   10   IF (N = 1) GØ TØ 90
C       CHECK TØ SEE IF N IS TWØ.
   20   IF (N
C       CHECK FØR N EVEN.
   30   IF (2 * N/2 = N) GØ TØ 90
C       CHECK TØ SEE IF N IS THREE.
   40   IF (N
C       SET I TØ 3.
   51   I = 3
C       CHECK FØR FINAL TEST ØF I
   60   IF (I - SQRT(N)) 52, 52, 91
C       DØES I DIVIDE N.
   52   IF (I * N/I    I) GØ TØ 90
C       ADD 2 TØ I
   53   I = I + 2
        GØ TØ 60
C       HERE IF NUMBER IS NØT PRIME.
   90   J = 0
        WRITE (5,200) N
        STØP
C       HERE IF NUMBER IS PRIME
   91   J = 1
        WRITE (5,201) N
        STØP
  101   FØRMAT (I5)
  200   FØRMAT (1H0
  201   FØRMAT (1H0
        END
```

```
        6 IS NØT A PRIME NUMBER.
      101 IS A PRIME NUMBER.
        1 IS NØT A PRIME NUMBER.
       79 IS A PRIME NUMBER.
```

P8-11. The problem of determining the set of numbers (A,B,C,D) which satisfies the equation

$$A^N + B^N = C^N + D^N$$

was considered previously in Problems P4-7, P5-7 and P6-7. The exponent N is provided as an input. A series of four DO loops will provide

the series of test numbers. Write a program to locate all sets of (A,B,C,D) to satisfy the equation up to 20, and for N = 2, 3 and 4.

P8-12. Write a program to evaluate the correlation coefficient given by

$$r = \frac{n\sum\limits_{i=1}^{n} x_i y_i - \sum\limits_{i=1}^{n} x_i \sum\limits_{i=1}^{n} y_i}{\sqrt{\left[n\sum\limits_{i=1}^{n} x_i^2 - \left(\sum\limits_{i=1}^{n} x_i\right)^2\right]\left[n\sum\limits_{i=1}^{n} y_i^2 - \left(\sum\limits_{i=1}^{n} y_i\right)^2\right]}}$$

Each data card has a value of X and the corresponding value of Y punched in E format. The data cards are followed by a card with 9999999. punched in columns 1-8. No data card has this value punched in columns 1-8. A flow chart for calculating the correlation coefficient is shown in Figure P8-12 and a portion of the program is given. Complete the program to calculate and print R and the value of N.

```
C          PROGRAM TO COMPUTE THE CORRELATION COEFFICIENT
C          INITIALIZE
           SUMX=0.0
           SUMY=0.0
           SUMXY=0.0
           SUMX2=0.0
           SUMY2=0.0
           N=0
     13    READ(2,1)X,Y
      1    FORMAT(2E10.2)
C          TEST FOR END OF DATA
           IF(X.999.)2,3,3
C          COMPUTE SUMS
      2    SUMX=SUMX+X
           SUMY=
           SUMXY=SUMXY+X*Y
           SUMX2=SUMX2+X*X
           SUMY2=
           N=
           GO TO 13
      3    T=N
           R=(T*SUMXY-SUMX*SUMY)/
           WRITE(5,4)N,R
      4    FORMAT(1X,
           STOP
           END
```

(Flow chart on opposite page)

FIGURE P8-12.

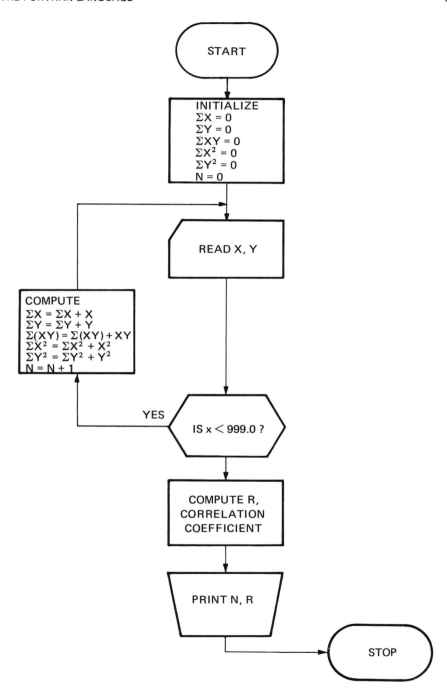

FIGURE P8-12 (*continued*)

P8-13. The following program is an example of the use of FORMAT statements. The program is an illustrative payroll for ten employees of Cragar Industry. It gives an output as shown in Figure P8-13, where SUI indicates the state employer's insurance. Examine the program and determine to your satisfaction how each calculation and format statement is achieved.

```
C     THIS PROGRAM IS PRESENTED AS AN EXAMPLE OF
      FORMATING
      WRITE (5,40)
      WRITE (5,41)
      TWAGG=0
      TFIT=0
      TSUI=0
      TFICA=0
      TWAGN=0
      RFIT=.14
      RSUI=.016
      RFICA=.048
      NUMBR=100
   10 READ (2,50) RNM1,RNM2,RNM3,RNM4,RHRS,WAGE
      IF (WAGE) 99,99,12
   12 NUMBR=NUMBR+1
      IF (RHRS-80.) 15,15,14
   14 RHRS=(RHRS-80.)*1.5+80.
   15 WAGEG=RHRS*WAGE
      FICA=RFICA*WAGEG
      SUI=RSUI*WAGEG
      FIT=RFIT*WAGEG
      WAGEN=WAGEG-(FIT+SUI+FICA)
      WRITE (5,60) RNM1,RNM2,RNM3,RNM4,NUMBR,WAGEN,FICA,
      SUI,FIT,WAGEG
      TWAGG=TWAGG+WAGEG
      TFICA=TFICA+FICA
      TSUI=TSUI+SUI
      TFIT=TFIT+FIT
      TWAGN=TWAGN+WAGEN
      GO TO 10
   99 WRITE (5,70) TWAGN,TFICA,TSUI,TFIT,TWAGG
   40 FORMAT (1H1,52X,'CRAGAR INDUSTRY',/51X,'PACKING
      DEPARTMENT',/56X,1'PAY  ROLL',/50X,'MAY 5 THROUGH
      MAY 16')
```

(Continued opposite page)

FIGURE P8-13

```
41  FORMAT (//5X,'EMPLOYEE',11X,'CHECK',11X,'NET',10X,
    'FICA',11X,'SUI'1,10X.'FED. INCOME',10X,'GROSS',/T26,'NO.',
    T40,'WAGES',T54,'TAX',T6 19,'TAX',T86,'TAX',T103,'WAGES'//)
50  FORMAT (4A4,F4.1,F4.2)
60  FORMAT (1H ,4A4,T26,I3,T39,'$',F6.2,T53,'$',F5.2,T68,'$',F4.2,
    T84,1'$',F5.2,T101,'$',F6.2)
70  FORMAT (//6X,'TOTALS',T37,'$',F8.2,T52,'$',F6.2,T66,'$',F6.2,
    T83,'1$',F6.2,T100,'$',F7.2)
    CALL EXIT
    END
```

(Illustrative Payroll on page 200)

FIGURE P8-13 *(continued)*

P8-14. The Euclidean algorithm for determining the greatest common divisor of two numbers A and B was previously considered in Chapters Four, Six and Seven. Assuming that A is greater than B, write a program for calculating and printing out the value of the GCD.

P8-15. Write a program to calculate and print out the value of N factorial given N as an input number. Use a DO loop to accomplish the iteration process.

P8-16. Write a FORTRAN input statement and its associated FORMAT statement for the punched card that is pictured below. You will need to use the A format several times. The last piece of data is the license number of the automobile. The dashes indicate a blank to be accommodated. The field width of each item is indicated. Note, however, that the last item, the license number, is alphanumeric information.

_CAMARO__	BLUE_	180	DUAL_	X1750M
←field→ width				

P8-17. The problem under consideration is the generation of the function e^x, which is the exponential function of x. The function may be expressed as a series which converges, written as:

$$e^x = 1 + x + \frac{x^2}{2!} + \ldots \frac{x^n}{n!} + \ldots$$

The process is to add each term in the series until the term calculated is less than a preestablished percentage of the total sum of terms thus far generated. One flow chart of the algorithm used is shown in Figure P8-17. One FORTRAN program for the flow chart is given below. Complete each line of the partial program shown. Recall that 10^{-12} is ten raised to the minus twelve power. *(Turn to page 202.)*

CRAGAR INDUSTRY
PACKING DEPARTMENT
PAY ROLL
MAY 5 THROUGH MAY 16

EMPLOYEE	CHECK NO.	NET WAGES	FICA TAX	SUI TAX	FED. INCOME TAX	GROSS WAGES
KEN SHURTELEFF	101	$232.43	$14.01	$4.67	$40.87	$292.00
GLENN BERG	102	$232.43	$14.01	$4.67	$40.87	$292.00
STEVE DEIS	103	$258.58	$15.59	$5.19	$45.47	$324.84
DAVE COPPOM	104	$302.48	$18.23	$6.07	$53.19	$380.00
JIM COUGHLIN	105	$302.48	$18.23	$6.07	$53.19	$380.00
STEVE BRIC	106	$159.20	$ 9.60	$3.19	$28.00	$200.00
JIM DIXON	107	$159.20	$ 9.60	$3.19	$28.00	$200.00
JOHN BUSSI	108	$189.05	$11.39	$3.80	$33.25	$237.50
TOM ROWAN	109	$165.17	$ 9.95	$3.32	$29.04	$207.50
JIM CHAMBERS	110	$174.12	$10.50	$3.50	$30.62	$218.75
TOTALS		$ 2175.14	$131.16	$ 43.72	$382.56	$2732.60

FIGURE P8-13 (*continued*)

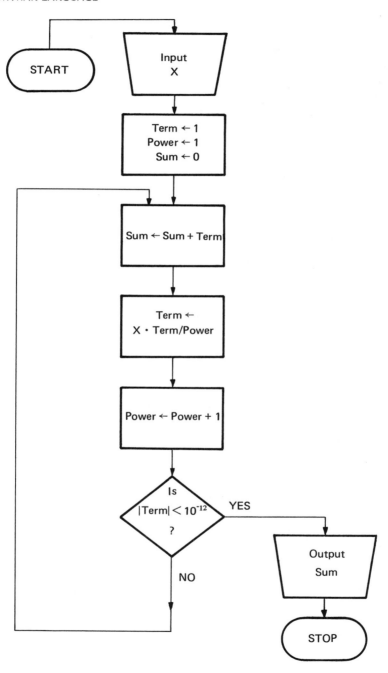

FIGURE P8-17

```
      TERM =
      POWER =
      SUM = 0.
10    SUM = SUM + TERM
      TERM = X*
      POWER =
      IF (ABS(    ) .GT.10E–12) GO TO
      EXP =
      RETURN
      END
```

CHAPTER 8 REFERENCES

1. "The Man Behind FORTRAN," *Computing Report*, November 1966, pp. 7–19.
2. "PL/1 at the Crossroads," *Datamation*, December, 1968, pg. 21.
3. H. Maisel, *Introduction to Electronic Computers*, McGraw-Hill Book Co., New York, 1969.
4. K. Iverson, *A Programming Language*, Wiley & Sons, Inc., New York, 1962.
5. W. P. Rule, *FORTRAN IV Programming*, Prindle, Weber and Schmidt, Inc., Boston, 1968.
6. D. McCracken, *A Guide to FORTRAN IV Programming*, Wiley & Sons, Inc., New York, 1965.
7. A. Forsythe, T. Keenan, E. Organick, W. Stenberg, *Computer Science: FORTRAN Language Programming*, Wiley & Sons, Inc., New York, 1970.
8. C. Davidson and E. Koenig, *Computers: Introduction to Computers and Applied Computing Concepts*, Wiley & Sons, Inc., New York, 1967.
9. T. M. Walker and W. W. Cotterman, *An Introduction to Computer Science and Algorithmic Processes*, Allyn and Bacon, Inc., Boston, 1970, Chapter 6.
10. F. Gruenberger, *Computing: An Introduction,* Harcourt, Brace and World, Inc., New York, 1969, Chapter 11.
11. J. E. Sammet, *Programming Languages, History and Fundamentals,* Prentice–Hall Inc., Englewood Cliffs, N.J., 1969.
12. C. Larson, "The Efficient Use of FORTRAN," *Datamation,* Aug. 1, 1971, pp. 24–31.

9

NUMBER SYSTEMS AND
COMPUTER ARITHMETIC

9.1 INTRODUCTION

It is quite possible to become a good programmer or user of computing machines without a knowledge of their internal operations. Nevertheless, if we understand what a computer is and on what basis it operates, this knowledge is of value. We have all used tools such as the lever and the jack; they are increasingly useful as we come to understand the principles upon which they operate.

Many students are already somewhat aware of the principles of computer arithmetic. During the past decade, the "new mathematics" has been introduced into the curriculums of the elementary and high schools. While the new math was introduced to prepare students for their future in a world increasingly dependent upon computers, some may have found the rewards of such knowledge illusory; see Figure 9-1. It is the purpose of this chapter to explain the basis of computer arithmetic and number systems related to computer operation.

9.2 A HISTORY OF NUMBER SYSTEMS AND ARITHMETIC

Ways of thinking about and dealing with numbers reflect the cultures and thinking patterns of different civilizations. The history of number systems can

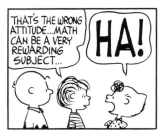

FIGURE 9-1   © 1965 United
             Feature
             Syndicate

be rewarding; we present here only a few aspects that have direct bearing on computers and computer science.[1]

The earliest recorded number systems were apparently based on counting groups. In each society there were special ways to arrange the counting to show progressively larger numbers. The abacus, which survives as a calculating instrument today, stylizes the grouping of counters to show counting–unit ideas, which we call *placement* or *place–value*.

Early Babylonians had two counting systems. They used decimal notation for small figures and easy calculation: the kind of figuring a farmer or tradesman might need to do on his figures. For large numbers, Babylonian arithmetic used base–60 numbers, possibly because the priests, who counted those large numbers, were also astronomers who used base–60 numbers to calculate the movements of stars. (Incidentally, we use base–60 notation today in round measure, as on the face of a clock or a compass card.)

Babylonians used floating–point notation; the size of a number was supplied by the context in which it appeared. We also use floating–point notation when we calculate with the slide rule, placing the point according to the problem we are solving.

Fixed–point arithmetic appeared first in what is now Mexico, in the Mayan civilization, about 2,000 years ago. Ironically, it had no effect on other arithmetic systems; by the time the European conquerors arrived the concept had reached their homelands through different routes. Perhaps that is just as well. Mayan notation shifted back and forth from a base of 18 to one of 20, making for awkward computation, especially with large numbers.

Long before the birth of Christ, Greek merchants used a form of abacus. Romans did too. *Calculus* is Latin for "pebble." It is also the root for "calculate." The place-value system of the abacus was not adapted to writing by the Greeks or Romans. Few people could write, and of course there was no paper anyway.

The system of arithmetic most familiar to us, based on 10 and using zero as a placeholder, appeared first in India about 500 A.D. About 800 A.D. the Arab al-Khowarizmi wrote a book using the decimal notation, and his work was soon translated from Arabic into Latin. The Italian scholar Fibonacci, mentioned above, used this new system in his own book of arithmetic about 1200 A.D.* From these works the decimal notation gradually spread through Europe. However, it was not until the fifteenth century that the use of decimal fractions was observed. Base-60 notation was used for fractional numbers until that time, possibly because fractions were often used by astronomers, who like the Babylonians had need of base-60 notation to measure angles and arcs.

By the thirteenth and fourteenth centuries some cultures had made great progress in mathematics. In China, a solution set of four linear equations in four unknowns was described. In the West by this time mathematicians were able to look back to the primitive beginnings of arithmetic and to compare them with the more efficient "modern" methods, as we see in Figure 9-2.

This unusual illustration shows the mathematical muse apparently presiding over a contest between two mathematical giants. The ancient system of calculation with counters (*calculi*), practiced by the Greek Pythagoras (*ca.* 500 B.C.) is losing, to judge from Pythagoras's expression. The rapid system of figuring with Arabic numerals is being used by Boethius, a Roman scholar (*ca.* 500 A.D.)

The active commerce of the middle ages made it necessary to count, to buy and sell, and to use arithmetic quickly. Inevitably various counting systems developed. An example of one such system is shown in the counting instructions in Figure 9-3, where hand signals communicated numbers.

In the sixteenth century, the growing complexity of commerce and the invention of the printing press led to a new influence in education: the arithmetic book. The new methods were neither more rapid nor more accurate than the abacus they replaced, yet they are important for the development of mathematics. From the abacus to symbolic arithmetic is one step; from arithmetic to algebra is another.

---

*Leonardo of Pisa, called Fibonacci (the son of Bonaccio), lived from 1170 to 1250 near Pisa, Italy. Leonardo learned the abacus and other oriental methods from his father and through extensive travel. Some of his best work came from a sort of mathematical tournament sponsored by Frederic II. Not for 300 years would Europe see another mathematician of such outstanding ability. Fibonacci's "Liber Abaci" accelerated the adoption of Hindu-Arabic numerals in Europe and very ably summarizes Arabian algebra. His proof that $x^3 + 2x^2 + 10 = 20$ cannot be solved by square roots, and his extremely accurate numerical solution, were both far ahead of his time. The Fibonacci numbers and one of his identities recur, in various contexts, through the centuries.

FIGURE 9–2 "Kinds of Arithmetic: Boethius and Pythagoras," a woodcut from a book
published in 1504. *The Bettman Archive, Inc.*

By the seventeenth century, through the work of a Belgian named Simon
Stevin and the Scottish genius John Napier (Chapter 1), decimal fractions had
become popular.

Isaac Newton, who lived in England from 1642 to 1727, was a primary
contributor to the development of what became computer mathematics, as well
as the developer of calculus (at age 23). Newton's contributions to arithmetic
suited for numerical analysis and computers included the interpolation formula
and its bearing on numerical integration, a beautiful linkage for drawing a conic

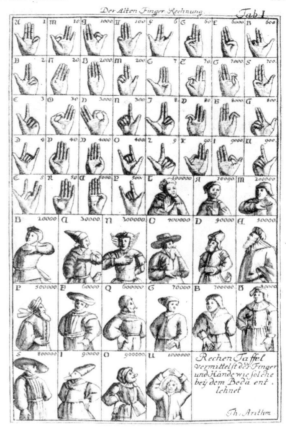

FIGURE 9-3 Mathematical sign language used by medieval merchants. *Courtesy The Smithsonian Institution.*

through five points, the Newton formulas for sums of powers of roots and their use to get the greatest root, and the rule for discovery of imaginary roots. We have already considered several algorithms based on Newton's contributions.

In the nineteenth century, a self-taught mathematician, George Boole, invented the algebra upon which computer operations are based. Boole is shown in Figure 9-4. Without disparaging the claims of Leibniz and de Morgan, it is fair to say that Boole's 82-page treatise "the Mathematical Analysis of Logic" marks the founding of modern algebra. Boole himself applied his algebra both to sets and to sentences, though its use in the foundation of mathematics and in switching circuits was still to come.

9.3 NUMBERS AND BINARY ARITHMETIC

As we have mentioned, throughout history a variety of systems has been used to represent numbers. A system of number representation is called a *number system.* It is defined on page 208.

FIGURE 9–4 George Boole (1815–1864). Boole, who lived in England, was too poor to attend an academic school. He taught himself five languages and learned mathematics from his father. At 16 he went into elementary teaching to help support his parents. At 20 he had his own school. Disliking the prescribed texts, he studied the mathematical masters Lagrange and Laplace on his own. *Courtesy Boole & Babbage Corp., Palo Alto, California.*

NUMBER SYSTEM An organized way of representing numbers. Each number system contains a base, or radix, which is the number of distinct symbols used in the system.

We learn the decimal number system in elementary school. It is based on the number ten, which is the base, or radix, for the system. The decimal system undoubtedly resulted from the fact that we count upon ten fingers. Logical and sensible as that may seem, we still retain other systems such as that of lengths based on inches, feet, and yards. (Scientific and engineering distance measurements are usually accomplished in the metric system, which is a decimal–base system.) Also, common weights are measured in ounces and pounds; time is measured in hours, minutes and seconds—and other systems of counting are also in use.

The decimal system has the ten symbols 0, 1, 2, 3, 4, 5, 6, 7, 8 and 9; naturally, its radix is ten. The Mayans used one system with base 18 and another of 20; the Babylonians used base 60. Their systems required sets of 18, 20 or 60 symbols, respectively.

We have learned to live in a world which uses the decimal system primarily. However, the world of computers and computer arithmetic does not usually employ decimal arithmetic within the computer. There we use devices which are based on radix two. For the computer, we use the symbols 0 and 1 to represent the two distinct symbols of the base–2 number system. We could also use the symbols "Yes" and "No" or "True" and "False." Several sets of symbols used in various other base–2 systems are shown in Figure 9–5.

TRAFFIC LIGHT	GO – STOP
COMPUTER	1 – O
HAMLET	"TO BE OR NOT TO BE"
ASTRONAUTS	GO – NO GO
CRAP TABLE	COME – NO COME
LIGHT GLOBE	ON – OFF
STATEMENT	TRUE – FALSE

FIGURE 9-5 Sets of symbols that could be used in systems with a base of 2.

The number system with base two is called the *binary system*. The name derives from the prefix *bi-*, which indicates a division or selection between two distinct possibilities. The binary system has early historical use, as can be seen in the common liquid measures used in England (still known for its pubs and ale) from about the thirteenth century:

$$2 \text{ gills} = 1 \text{ chopin}$$
$$2 \text{ chopins} = 1 \text{ pint}$$
$$2 \text{ pints} = 1 \text{ quart}$$
$$2 \text{ quarts} = 1 \text{ pottle}$$
$$2 \text{ pottles} = 1 \text{ gallon}$$
$$2 \text{ gallons} = 1 \text{ peck}$$
$$2 \text{ pecks} = 1 \text{ demibushel}$$
$$2 \text{ demibushels} = 1 \text{ bushel or firkin}$$
$$2 \text{ firkins} = 1 \text{ kilderkin}$$
$$2 \text{ kilderkins} = 1 \text{ barrel}$$
$$2 \text{ barrels} = 1 \text{ hogshead}$$
$$2 \text{ hogsheads} = 1 \text{ pipe}$$
$$2 \text{ pipes} = 1 \text{ tun}$$

The tavern-keeper was well advised to mind his p's and q's, two of the former making one of the latter then as now.

Toward the beginning of the seventeenth century, the Englishman Thomas Harriot write about a binary system of arithmetic—that is, one based on only two numbers. In 1703, a paper by the great Leibnitz formally introduced many computations in base-two arithmetic. From that time on there have been further developments in binary arithmetic, as well as experiments in using other bases, such as 12, 16 and especially 8. But it was the development of mechanical devices for computing that led back to binary arithmetic, even though the first computers did use the decimal system.

The elegant simplicity of a counting system that is either on or off, open or closed appealed to the computer designers, who took their final clue from Von Neumann's proof that instructions and information could be fed into the computer together, in base-two notation. That made binary arithmetic the most common language of modern computers.

Just as fingers used for counting led to base-ten arithmetic for the Babylonian merchant, the simple off-on switch of modern electronic circuits led to base-two arithmetic as it is known and used in computers today.

The binary system is used within the computer for these reasons:

1. Devices for storing information within the computer are binary in nature.
2. The reliability of two-choice devices is inherently greater than that of those with more choices.
3. The binary arithmetic can be accomplished rapidly without complicated circuitry.

Let's consider each of the three reasons for using the binary number system for computers. First, the electronic devices which lend themselves readily to use in computers are by their nature binary devices. For example, a magnetic core for storage is either magnetized or it isn't. Also, an electronic relay is either open or closed.

Second, one could devise circuits which work on the basis of ten distinct positions or choices. However, these would store and manipulate the numbers in a computer less reliably. We can design binary circuits that will produce a consistent reliable response over a large variation of behavior of the circuit. Then we can expect the thousands of circuits to give reliable results over a long period of time. Remember, we want to use digital computers which will run without error for hundreds of hours.

Third, we may ask the question: Are the two symbols in the binary system sufficient to handle all the arithmetic we wish to accomplish? The answer is yes, of course. It derives from the speed of electronic processes. The computer can set up and execute unbelievable numbers of combinations of "on" or "off" in a fraction of a second. Furthermore, the devices are relatively simple to build and to maintain, since they have only two possible states. The fewer the symbols the better as far as the computer is concerned—at least as far as the radix of the number system is concerned.

Most computers are built to operate internally with binary devices, but they accept data in the decimal system and they provide answers in the same system. These facts necessitate a translator between the decimal numbers and their binary equivalents. While the user inputs decimal figures and receives decimal outputs, the internal circuitry of the computer is making translations.

As you know, our decimal number system is *positional*; the position of a given digit implies its value. The number 3484 contains two 4's, the first, to the right, counting ones and the second counting hundreds.

$$3484 = 3000 + 400 + 80 + 4$$

The *radix point* separates the integer portion of a number from the fractional portion; in decimal notation the radix point is the decimal point. Each position in a number counts the radix raised to a power. The power to which the radix is raised is zero for the position immediately to the left of the radix point. The power then increases by increments of 1 to the left of the radix point and decreases by decrements of 1 to the right. Here are two examples:

$$3484 = 3 \times 10^3 + 4 \times 10^2 + 8 \times 10^1 + 4 \times 10^0$$
$$38.64 = 3 \times 10^1 + 8 \times 10^0 + 6 \times 10^{-1} + 4 \times 10^{-2}$$

The expansion of a number in terms of powers of its radix can be accomplished for any radix. The general form of a number A in base r expanded in terms of its base, or radix, r, can be written as follows:

$$A = \pm (a_{n-1} r^{n-1} + a_{n-2} r^{n-2} + \ldots + a_1 r^1 + a_0 r^0 + a_{-1} r^{-1} + \ldots + a_{-m} r^{-m})$$

$$= \pm \sum_{i=1}^{n+m} a_{n-i} r^{n-i}$$

This number has n integral and m fractional coefficients.

The binary number system consists of two symbols, 0 and 1, and has a radix of 2. The first place to the left of the radix point in this system counts 2^0, which equals 1. The second place, to the left, counts 2^1, which equals 2. The third place counts 2^2, which is 4, and so on. Thus, the number

$$1 \times 2^2 + 0 \times 2^1 + 1 \times 2^0$$

is equal to 5 in the decimal system since $1 \times 4 + 1 \times 1 = 5$.

As another example, consider the binary number

$$1011.11_2$$

expressed in compact form. (The base is indicated by the subscript 2.) This number expanded in polynomial form is:

$$1 \times 2^3 + 0 \times 2^2 + 1 \times 2^1 + 1 \times 2^0 + 1 \times 2^{-1} + 1 \times 2^{-2}$$

Since $2^3 = 8$, $2^{-1} = 1/2$ and $2^{-2} = 1/4$, rendering this number in base 10, we have

$$(8 + 2 + 1 + 1/2 + 1/4)_{10} = (11.75)_{10}$$

Therefore,

$$(11.75)_{10} = (1011.11)_2$$

In general, we may use the compact form to represent the number A as:

$$A = (a_{n-1} a_{n-2} \ldots a_1 a_0 . a_{-1} \ldots a_{-m})_r$$

What does the number $(1111011)_2$ equal in the decimal number system? Determine your answer and then check it with the footnote on the following page.

Another number system we might wish to use in some computer applications is the *octal* number system. The octal system has a radix of 8, with the symbols 0, 1, 2, 3, 4, 5, 6, 7. In order fully to explore the idea of the expansion of a number in terms of its radix, let us consider the number $(126)_8$. Expanding the number we have:

$$1 \times 8^2 + 2 \times 8^1 + 6 \times 8^0$$

Therefore, in decimal form,
$$(64 + 16 + 6)_{10} = (86)_{10}$$
The first twenty numbers of the binary and decimal systems are given in Table 9-1. Notice that the number $(12)_{10}$ requires two symbols to represent it while its equivalent in the binary system, $(1100)_2$, requires four symbols. In general we require more symbols to express a binary number than a decimal number. This is true since each digit contains less information in binary notation and therefore we require more digits to express a given amount of information. It can be shown that the ratio of the number of binary digits required to express a given number to the number of decimal digits for the same number is given by the ratio of the logarithms of their radices:
$$\text{ratio} = \frac{\log 10}{\log 2} = 3.3219$$

TABLE 9-1

Binary Equivalents for the Decimal Numbers 0 through 10

Radix 2	Radix 10
0	0
1	1
10	2
11	3
100	4
101	5
110	6
111	7
1000	8
1001	9
1010	10
1011	11
1100	12
1101	13
1110	14
1111	15
10000	16
10001	17
10010	18
10011	19

A decimal integer can be converted to the binary system by performing successive division by 2 until a quotient of zero is obtained and recording all the remainders. The binary number is the remainder read from the last remainder backward, where 1 is read for a remainder and 0 for no remainder. This pro-

---

Therefore, $(1111011)_2 = (123)_{10}$.

cedure works only for the integral portion of the decimal number (the non-decimal portion). It can be summarized in three steps:

1. Divide the integer part of the decimal number by 2, utilizing the arithmetic rules of decimal arithmetic.
2. Save the quotient and consider the quotient to be the number to be converted.
3. Repeat steps 1 and 2 until the quotient is equal to zero. The binary equivalent is obtained by juxtaposing the remainders from steps 1 and 2 in an order opposite to that in which they were obtained.

Since we know from Table 9-1 that $(18)_{10} = (10010)_2$, let us try 18 as a first exercise. The successive division is as follows:

Division	*Remainders*	
2 ⌊18		
2⌊9	0	
2⌊4	1	↑ The answer is read
2⌊2	0	in this direction.
2⌊1	0	
0	1	

As another example, convert the decimal number to its binary equivalent:

2⌊123	
⌊61	1
⌊30	1
⌊15	0
⌊7	1
⌊3	1
⌊1	1
0	1

The answer is $(123)_{10} = (1111011)_2$ which verifies the answer obtained above by the expansion procedure.

The method for converting the decimal portion of the decimal number to a binary fraction is:

1. Multiply the decimal portion by 2, utilizing decimal arithmetic.
2. Save the integral portion of the product from step 1 and consider the decimal portion of the product as the number to be converted.
3. Repeat steps 1 and 2 until the desired precision is achieved, at which time the binary fraction is obtained by juxtaposing the binary equivalents of the integral portions of the products from steps 1 and 2 in the order in which they were obtained.

As an example, convert $(.875)_{10}$ to its binary equivalent.

$$2 \times .875 = 1.750$$
$$2 \times .750 = 1.500$$
$$2 \times .500 = 1.00$$
$$2 \times .000 = 0.0$$

↓ Read in this direction.

Thus, the binary equivalent is $(.1110)_2$. We can verify this answer by noting that
$$1 \times 2^{-1} + 1 \times 2^{-2} + 1 \times 2^{-3} = (.875)_{10}$$
Determine the binary equivalent of the decimal fraction .015625 and check your answer with the footnote on the following page.

As we can easily verify after a few conversions of decimal numbers to the binary system, the arithmetic is tedious and liable to error. This is precisely the type of work we wish to assign to the computer. Understandably, the conversion of decimal numbers to the binary system is accomplished within the computer.

Another concept of interest is that of *modular arithmetic*. We are familiar with the modular arithmetic of an automobile odometer, which counts from 0 to 99,999 miles and then will recycle through 0 to 99,999 again. Thus, the number 23,000 on an odometer might indicate 23,000 miles or 123,000 miles. The odometer is said to count *in modulo* 100,000. The modulus function A represents the maximum number of unique values that can be represented by an n–digit integral number d with radix r. That is, the modulus of d is r^n. For example, for the odometer with five digits, the modulus is $10^5 = 100,000$. For an internal computer word with 12 digits in binary form, the modulus is $2^{12} = 4096$. (A table of the powers of 2 is given in Table 9–2.) What is the number of unique decimal values that can be represented by a 15–digit word in binary form? Check your answer with that given on the next page in the footnote.

Another concept which is often utilized in performing arithmetic within a computer is that of a *complement* of a number. The complement of a number is defined as:

COMPLEMENT   The complement C of a real number A containing $(n+m)$ digits, where n and m are defined in the expansion of the number A, is $C = r^n - A$

The complement of the number 123, base 10, would therefore be
$$C = 1000 - 123$$
$$= 877$$
since the number of digits is three. Recall that n is the number of digits in the integral (non–decimal) portion of the decimal number. The decimal complement of 567.83 is therefore 432.17 since
$$567.83 + 432.17 = 10^3$$
We take up the complement of numbers in base 2 on page 217.

TABLE 9-2

Powers of 2

n	2^n
1	2
2	4
3	8
4	16
5	32
6	64
7	128
8	256
9	512
10	1024
11	2048
12	4096
13	8192
14	16384
15	32768
16	65536
17	131072
18	262144
19	524288
20	1048576
21	2097152
22	4194304
23	8388608
24	16777216
25	33554432
26	67108864
27	134217728
28	268435456

Let us now consider the operations involved in binary arithmetic. The addition table in binary arithmetic is given in Table 9–3a. Notice that two 1's added produce a carry. Consider the following addition

$$\begin{array}{ll} \text{Base 10:} & \begin{array}{r} 5 \\ 7 \\ \hline 12 \end{array} \end{array} \qquad \begin{array}{ll} \text{Base 2:} & \begin{array}{r} 101 \\ 111 \\ \hline 1100 \end{array} \end{array}$$

Notice that $(12)_{10} = (1100)_2$; the addition checks. In the left–hand digit in base 2 we add $1 + 1 + 1$ to obtain 11_2. This can be verified by $1 + 1 = 10$ and $10 + 01 = 11$.

$(.015625)_{10} = (.000001)_2$

Since $2^{15} = 32{,}768$, we can represent 32,768 unique decimal values in a 15–digit binary word.

TABLE 9-3

Binary Arithmetic Tables

a. Addition

+	0	1	
0	0	1	
1	1	10	(0 + a carry)

b. Subtraction

−	0	1	(Minuend)
0	0	1	
(Subtrahend) 1	1*	0	

1* = 1 with a borrow

c. Multiplication

×	0	1
0	0	0
1	0	1

Find the sum of 1110_2 and 1011_2. Give answers in base 2 and base 10. The answers are in the footnote on the following page.

The multiplication table given in Table 9-3c is quite simple, since 0 times any number is zero. Let us multiply $(101)_2 = (5)_{10}$ times $(111)_2 = (7)_{10}$

$$
\begin{array}{r}
101 \\
111 \\
\hline
101 \\
101 \\
101 \\
\hline
100011
\end{array}
$$

Note that $(100011)_2 = (35)_{10}$ as we expected. The multiplication is achieved in a process similar to that in the decimal system, except that we use the binary multiplication table.

In the subtraction process, we need to incorporate the principle of borrowing a 1 as shown in Table 9-3b. We pay back the borrow by increasing the subtrahend in the next column to the left by 1. As an example, let us subtract 101 from 111 as follows:

$$
\begin{array}{r}
111 \\
-101 \\
\hline
010
\end{array}
$$

As another example let us complete the following subtraction:

$$1\overset{*}{1}01$$
$$-1\overset{*}{0}11$$
$$\overline{0010}$$

where the asterisk in column 2 indicates we have paid back the borrow and thus changed the 0 shown to a 1.

Now, let us return to the process of determining the complement of a number in the binary system. The complement of a number A is $C = 2^n-A$. Thus, the complement of 1001_2 is found as follows:

$$10000$$
$$-\ 1001$$
$$\overline{00111} = C$$

Note that $n = 4$ in this case since 1001 consists of four digits.

It can be shown that, in general, the complement of a binary number can be obtained by changing all the 1's to 0, changing all the 0's to 1 and then adding 1 to the rightmost digit of the result and propagating any carry generated. Flipping 1 and 0 is very simple for a computer to accomplish.

An alternative approach to the subtraction is to use complementation whenever a minus sign occurs. This approach is particularly useful for accommodating the case where we subtract a larger number from a smaller number. Subtraction can then be achieved by complementing the subtrahend and adding the complement to the minuend and subtracting the extra 1 in the 2^nth column. As an example, let us consider the previously accomplished subtraction 1011 from 1101. The complement of 1011 is obtained by flipping the 1's and 0's and adding 1. Thus, the complement of 1011 is:

$$0100$$
$$\underline{\quad 1}$$
$$0101$$

Adding, we have:

$$1101$$
$$\underline{0101}$$
$$10010$$

Then subtracting the extra 1 from the 2^4 column, we have the answer 0010 as in the previous calculation. We subtract the extra one in the 2^nth column because the complement of B is 2^n-B. Adding this to A, we have $A + (2^n-B) = A - B + 2^n$; we must subtract 2^n to obtain $A - B$ as desired.

Subtractions that lead to negative results can be obtained as usual by subtracting the numbers in reverse order and adding a minus sign to the difference.

$$1110$$
$$\underline{1011}\ \text{in base 2;}$$
$$\overline{1010}$$

$$14$$
$$\underline{11}\ \text{in base 10.}$$
$$\overline{25}$$

Complete the following subtraction and check your answer with the footnote on the following page.

$$11000$$
$$-\underline{1110}$$

Division in binary arithmetic is performed by an algorithm which is programmed within the computer, usually in the form of hardware circuitry. The available algorithms are numerous and beyond the scope of this book. However, you may wish to consult an advanced text on this subject at a later time.[2,3]

In summary, please note that it is not at all necessary for you to become proficient at binary arithmetic. Leave that expertise to the computer. However, it is desirable that you understand how the computer accomplishes binary arithmetic. We want to avoid the feeling so aptly expressed in Figure 9-6.

FIGURE 9-6 © 1965 United Feature Syndicate.

9.4 BINARY CODES AND BINARY DIGITS

A computer word contains a specified number of binary digits to represent a decimal number. The binary digit is given a special name taken from the first two and last two letters: *bit*. It is the fundamental unit of information and it represents the most fundamental logical choice: the dichotomy.

Decimal numbers are not always represented within a computer by a binary sequence. The method used to represent data and instructions in a computer is known as a *code*. Some computers use a set of binary digits to represent each decimal digit in a number. For them we might represent 26 in the base 10 with the code 0010 0110. The first set of four bits represents the 2 and the second set of four bits represents the 6. Since it takes four bits to represent some decimal digits, this scheme always allows four bits for each digit, filling in zeros where necessary. This scheme of number representation is called *Binary-Coded Decimal*, abbreviated BCD.

As another example, let us determine the BCD representation of the decimal number 29.3. The binary code for 2, 9 and 3 is found in Table 9-1 as

$$(2)_{10} = (0010)_2$$
$$(9)_{10} = (1001)_2$$
$$(3)_{10} = (0011)_2$$

We have included all four bits in each case. Thus, the BCD representation of 29.3 is

$$00101001.0011$$

Notice that the BCD scheme takes more bits than the pure binary representation. With four bits, in the pure binary scheme we can count up to 15 while the BCD scheme can accommodate only up to 9. Therefore, 6/16th of the information capacity of each group of four bits is never used. This disadvantage is often considered to be outweighed by the advantage of being able to perform decimal arithmetic directly. This advantage is particularly important in the calculation of financial operations, such as payroll and accounting.

A further advantage of using BCD with a computer (which is then usually called a *decimal computer*) is the fact that at every intermediate step in the program all numbers are in decimal digit form. The user is able to trace or debug a program more easily since he is able to recognize the numbers which are the intermediate results. Most high speed computers are binary machines, but decimal machines using BCD still have their place, particularly in business applications.

For numerical scientific and engineering application it is most efficient to use a fixed length of binary computer word. Registers and storage devices are commonly designed to hold 24, 32 or 64 bits. For example, the IBM System/360 is designed to have a word length of 32 bits. For these systems, the basic unit of information is a *byte*. Four bytes constitute a word consisting of 32 consecutive bit positions of information which are interpreted as a unit.

Many of the data processing types of applications such as alphanumeric, short records, and noninteger records such as prices and percentages work with a wide variety of kinds of information. For a more efficient storage and manipulation of such information, it is convenient to be able to store words of various

normal	11000	by complements	11000	with deleting the 2^5 column.
method:	−01110	and addition:	+00010	
	1010		1010	

lengths, and to mark the end of such a word by a special "flag" or "record mark." In *variable-word-length* machines, it is common to allow an extra bit to be associated with each decimal digit, which can indicate either a sign or a flag.

In the case of both the fixed and variable word length computers, the computer often includes some bits for checking the accuracy of the storage, transmission, and read-out of information. Just as in human language redundancy is constantly used to help insure the reliability of what is said or written, so in the binary coding of information, extra or redundant bits can be included which carry no new information themselves. They are dependent upon the rest of the message being sent in such a way that if a transmission error occurs, the redundant or check bits will no longer agree with the rest of the information. This condition can be detected and suitable warning or corrective measures taken.

The code checking occurs automatically within the machine as the computer operations are carried out. The method of validity checking is incorporated in the code. In some codes, each unit of information is represented by a specific number of bit positions that must always contain an even number of "1" bits. Different characters are made up of different combinations of 1 bits, but the number of 1 bits in any valid character is always even. With this code system, a character with an odd number of 1 bits is detected, and an error is indicated. Likewise, a code may be used in which all characters must have an odd number of 1 bits; an error is indicated when characters with an even number of 1 bits are detected.

This type of checking is known as a *parity check*. Codes that use an even number of 1 bits are said to have even parity. Codes that use an odd number of bits are said to have odd parity.

The representation of numeric information in a computer is usually in either (1) the binary-coded decimal system; (2) the fixed-point system, or (3) the floating point system. We have discussed the BCD system earlier in this section. The *fixed-point* number system, which has been discussed in Chapters 6, 7 and 8, represents numbers utilizing a pure number system and which stores numbers without a radix point. Therefore, all operations are performed on integers with a sign. Integer numbers are represented as pure binary numbers. The majority of computers use a fixed word length and are capable of very rapid fixed-point arithmetic since the operations are often performed in parallel: that is, several at one time. Fixed-point calculations are useful in loop calculations using fixed-point format. For a 32-bit machine with one bit allocated for the sign, the range of the numbers allowed is

$$-2^{31} \leqslant \text{numbers} \leqslant 2^{31} - 1$$

or approximately

$$-2 \times 10^9 \leqslant \text{numbers} \leqslant 2 \times 10^9$$

If we exceed the range allowed in a calculation, then we experience what is termed a *fixed-point overflow*.

The range of numbers involved in many numerical calculations exceeds the allowable range of integers. Also, with integer representation, we must scale or shift numbers in order to code the fractional values if we desire to accommodate them. Thus, we often use the *floating–point* number system. A floating point representation, as we have seen previously, may appear in the form

$$\pm \, .FFFFFF\pm XX$$

for a fixed–word length machine with a 10–digit word. The exponent is XX; it may range from –99 to +99. The decimal point is assumed to lie to the left of the first significant digit. There are several other forms for representing floating–point numbers, but we do not explore them here.

If the magnitude of the results of a calculation result in a number exceeding the range of numbers accommodated, we experience *exponent overflow*. Conversely, *exponent underflow* is experienced when the magnitude of the results is smaller than the smallest number accommodated by floating point format. Floating point addition and subtraction is similar to binary arithmetic with the added necessity of shifting the decimal point so both numbers possess the same exponent value. Multiplication is achieved by the normal process with the exponents added together.

9.5 THE ALGEBRA OF BINARY VARIABLES—BOOLEAN ALGEBRA

Thus far, we have discussed arithmetic in the binary number system. In the arithmetic we deal with numbers which are constants and consider their addition, subtraction, multiplication and division. As in the decimal system, we have an algebra of binary numbers as well as an arithmetic. We also have variables in the binary system and an associated algebra of these variables.

The algebra of binary variables was developed by George Boole, who is discussed above. In 1854 he developed an algebra for application to statements which were either true or false, and thus binary.[4] The binary algebra was called symbolic logic. It was somewhat further developed during the next century. In 1938 Claude Shannon showed the great utility of symbolic algebra; it was then further developed for its use in computer design.[5]

The *binary variable* is the class of all variables that can assume two values or states, which we call 0 and 1. The devices that can assume these binary values are numerous, but everyone is familiar with a two–position wall switch, or a relay, as examples. An electronic relay or switch is called a flip–flop.

The algebra of two–valued variables possesses several rules, including besides the equivalence operation the AND operation, and OR operation and the NOT operation. The AND operation is defined as follows:

AND A symbolic logic operation having the property that, if P is a statement, Q is a statement, R is a statement, . . . , then the AND of P, Q, R, . . . is true if all statements are true, false if any statement is false.

Thus, for two inputs, the operation AND requires both (or all) of the inputs to yield to be 1 an output of 1. We write $C = A \cdot B$, where the symbol $\cdot$ shows the AND operation. Thus $C = 1$, if $A = 1$ and also $B = 1$. The AND operation can be realized by a series of two relays shown in Figure 9–7a. The symbol for a two-input AND device is also shown in Figure 9–7a. The AND operation in the symbol or device form is often called an *AND Gate*.

The OR operation is defined as follows:

> *OR* A logic operation having the property that if P is a statement, Q is a statement, R is a statement, . . . , then the OR of P, Q, R, . . . is true if at least one statement is true, false if all statements are false.

For two inputs, the operation OR requires *at least one* input to be 1 to yield an output. We write the OR operation as $C = A + B$, where the symbol + indicates the OR operation. Thus, $C = 1$ if A or B equals 1. The realization of an OR circuit with two relays is shown in Figure 9–7b with the symbol for an OR device. Note that OR is inclusive here. It will yield an output if there is at least one input, but also if there is more than one input. In this sense it differs from the usage of daily speech. In conversation we use "or" exclusively, as in "Either turn on the light at the head of the stairs or when you get down into the cellar." The computer also utilizes the inclusive sense of "or": both switches could be turned on at the same time. The both–together condition would give light just as the either–one–at–a–time condition would.

The third binary algebraic operation, the NOT operation, is defined:

> *NOT* A logic operation having the property that, if P is a statement, the NOT of P is true if P is false, false if P is true.

We often called the NOT operation the *inversion operation*. We write the expression for the NOT operation as $C = \overline{B}$, where the bar over B indicates the NOT of B. Thus, if $B = 1$, we have $C = 0$. The symbol for the NOT device is shown in Figure 9–7c.

Examine each relay circuit in Figure 9–7a and b. If we place a light bulb at C and a positive voltage as shown by +, with the return wire omitted from the picture, the bulb will light up when the AND circuit has both relays closed, that is, A AND B. In the case of the OR circuit, either A OR B closed will light the bulb.

A series of useful relationships for the binary variables can be developed. These useful relationships are listed in Table 9–4, along with their realization with relays. The relationships are self–explanatory once one examines the equivalent relay circuit. For example, in Table 9–4c, it is clear that if one branch is always closed by virtue of the 1 branch, the A is not necessary and thus $C = 1$. Also, in (g) it is clear that $C = 1$ only when $A = 1$ and it is independent of the value of B. Thus, $C = A$.

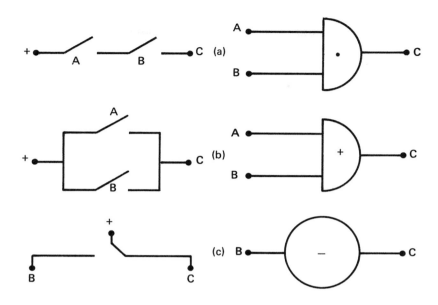

FIGURE 9-7 The logical operators AND, OR and NOT. The symbol for each operator is given with the relay circuit equivalent. Imagine that the relays are switches in an otherwise complete electrical circuit, with a light at C. When does each bulb light?

There are also two algebraic laws that we will express without proof in Boolean algebra. The *commutative law* of the OR operation states that
$$A + B = B + A$$
The commutative law of the AND operation is
$$A \cdot B = B \cdot A$$
Consideration of the equivalent relay circuits would make the validity of these commutative laws fairly clear. The *distributive law* of the OR operation is
$$A + (B \cdot C) = (A + B) \cdot (A + C)$$
Similarly, the distributive law of AND is
$$A \cdot (B + C) = A \cdot B + A \cdot C$$
The proof of these distributive laws is given in several textbooks.[2,3]

Another concept of interest is the portrayal of the AND, OR and NOT operations in what is called a *truth table*. The truth table for these three operations is given in Figure 9-8. The truth table concept is often used in symbolic logic. For example, in Figure 9-8b for the AND operation, $C = 1$ only when $A = 1$ and $B = 1$.

TABLE 9–4

Useful Relationships in Binary Algebra

Relationship	*Relay Circuit*

a) $A + 0 = A$

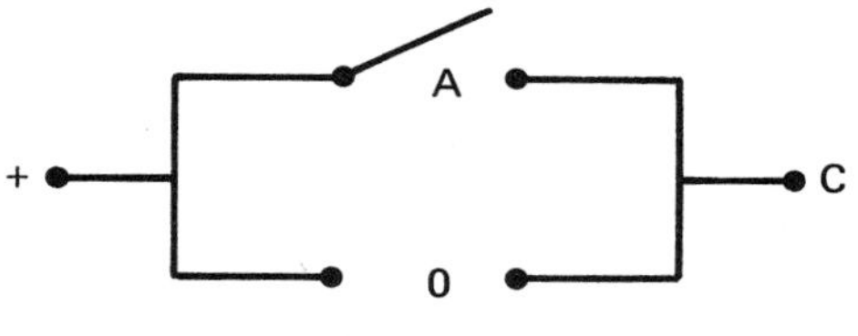

b) $A \cdot 1 = A$

c) $A \cdot 0 = 0$

d) $A + 1 = 1$

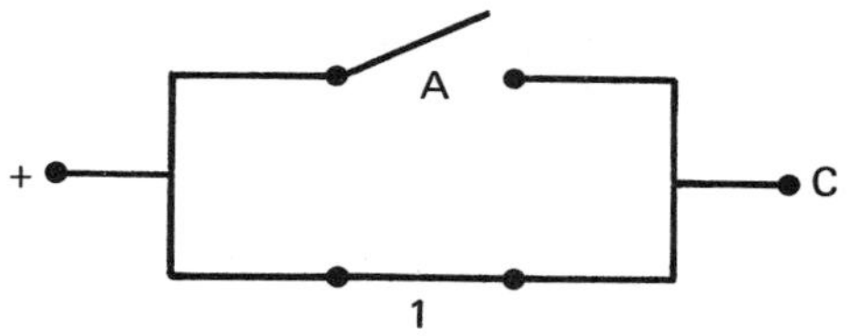

e) $A \cdot A = A$

f) $A + A = A$

g) $A + A \cdot B = A$

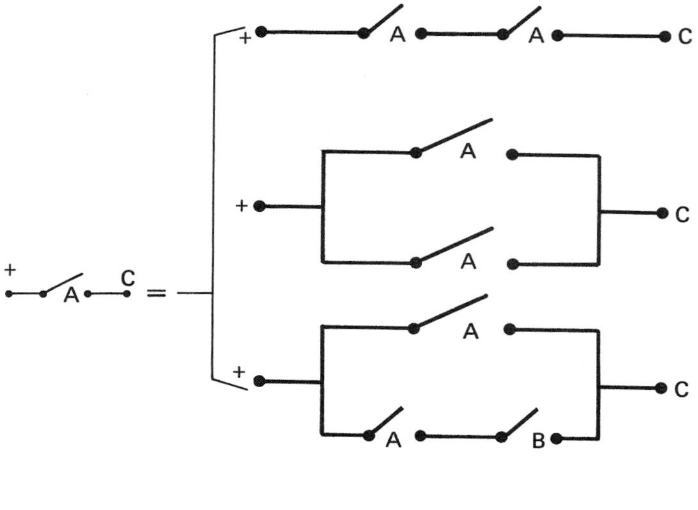

INPUTS	A	0	0	1	1	
	B	0	1	0	1	(a)
OUTPUT C = A + B		0	1	1	1	

INPUTS	A	0	0	1	1	
	B	0	1	0	1	(b)
OUTPUT C = A · B		0	0	0	1	

INPUT	A	0	1	
OUTPUT C = $\overline{A}$		1	0	(c)

FIGURE 9-8   The truth tables for (a) OR; (b) AND, and (c) NOT.

Some additional laws in Boolean Algebra are provided in Table 9-5. Items c and d are known as De Morgan's Laws.

TABLE 9-5

Additional Laws in Boolean Algebra

a) $A + \overline{A} = 1$
b) $A \cdot \overline{A} = 0$
c) $\overline{A + B} = \overline{A} \cdot \overline{B}$ ⎫ De Morgan's Laws
d) $\overline{A \cdot B} = \overline{A} + \overline{B}$ ⎭
e) $(A + B) + C = A + (B + C)$
f) $(A \cdot B)C = A(B \cdot C)$
  Note: $(A + B)(B + C)$ means $(A + B) \cdot (B + C)$
g) $A + \overline{A} \cdot B = A + B$
h) $A(\overline{A} + B) = A \cdot B$
i) $(A + B)(\overline{A} + C) = A \cdot C + \overline{A} \cdot B$
j) $\overline{A} \cdot B + A\overline{B} = (A + B)\overline{A \cdot B}$

The principal application of Boolean algebra is to the design and analysis of digital computer circuits. Computer circuits consist of switching circuits of a binary nature. That is, the circuits have two states, 1 or 0, and are interconnected in order to yield a desired result such as an addition of two binary numbers.

Before proceeding to the consideration of some useful computer circuits, let us consider a simple logic problem and thus illustrate the usefulness of

Boolean algebra. In this problem, a boatman must carry a wolf, goat, and a cabbage across a river in a boat—one at a time. He must be with the wolf and the goat, and the goat and the cabbage to prevent the former of each pair from eating the latter. How can he carry all of them across the river?

We will use the following symbols: M = man, W = wolf, G = goat, and C = cabbage. All the items start on the south bank of the river. We use $\overline{M}, \overline{W}$, etc. to indicate they are on the south bank and M, W, etc. to indicate they are on the north bank. Thus, for the man M = 1, while $\overline{M}$ = 0. A violation of the desired outcome occurs when the following equation has an output, that is V = 1.

$$V = \overline{WGM} + WG\overline{M} + \overline{CGM} + CG\overline{M}$$

where WG means W · G and we omit the AND symbol. Clearly, we cover all the possible violations in this equation. Now to work out a procedure for crossing the river, we develop a truth table that does *not* violate the equation above, that is, cause V to become equal to one. One procedure is given in Figure 9-9, which requires seven crossings of the river. There are several possible procedures for crossing the river. Work out another series of steps that will not violate the equation.

W	$\overline{W}$	C	$\overline{C}$	G	$\overline{G}$	M	$\overline{M}$	STEP NUMBER
0	1	0	1	0	1	0	1	0
0	1	0	1	1	0	1	0	1
0	1	0	1	1	0	0	1	2
0	1	1	0	1	0	1	0	3
0	1	1	0	0	1	0	1	4
1	0	1	0	0	1	1	0	5
1	0	1	0	0	1	0	1	6
1	0	1	0	1	0	1	0	7

FIGURE 9-9 Truth table for the river crossing problem. This solution requires seven river crossings.

As an exercise, try the following puzzle, which appeared in "More Problematical Recreations," a booklet issued recently by Litton Industries of Beverly Hills, California. "If Sara shouldn't, then Wanda would. It is impossible that the statements: 'Sara should,' and Camille couldn't,' can both be true at the same time. If Wanda would, then Sara should and Camille could. Therefore Camille could. Is the conclusion valid?"

Using the following notation, establish the logic equation for a violation of the above statements. Then let C = 1 to see if a violation occurs, whatever the value of A and B.

A = Sara should
$\overline{A}$ = Sara shouldn't
B = Wanda would
$\overline{B}$ = Wanda wouldn't
C = Camille could
$\overline{C}$ = Camille couldn't

Thus, for the first statement we have $V = \overline{A} \cdot \overline{B}$ since the statement "If Sara shouldn't then Wanda would" tells us that the combination of $\overline{A}$ and $\overline{B}$ is not permitted. The answer is given in the footnote on the next page.

Now, let us develop a small computer circuit for calculating and indicating a majority vote among three legislators. The three legislators are to vote anonymously with three switches. A lamp indicates the majority vote is yes if it lights and $V = 1$. There are three switches; A, B, and C. The majority vote occurs when any two legislators vote together. Therefore, we have

$$V = A \cdot B + A \cdot C + B \cdot C$$

and $V = 1$ when A and B are both 1 or A and C or B and C are both 1. A circuit realization of this equation is shown in Figure 9-10a. This circuit requires four devices, three AND Gates and one OR Gate. If we note that V can be rewritten as

$$V = A(B + C) + B \cdot C$$

we can achieve the same result with two AND Gates and two OR Gates as shown in Figure 9-10b.

The addition table in binary arithmetic is quite simple, as we have seen. There is a carry that occurs when we have A and B both equal to 1. Let us call D the output and C the carry bit. Then the truth table for the sum of two bits A and B is shown in Figure 9-11a. The rule for the addition of two bits can be deduced from the truth table as

$$D = \overline{A} \cdot B + A \cdot \overline{B}$$
$$C = A \cdot B$$

The symbol for the two–bit–adder is shown in Figure 9-11b. A circuit realization of these equations is shown in Figure 9-12. It requires six devices.

The equations for the adder can be rewritten using parentheses as:

$$D = (A + B) \, \overline{AB}$$

by utilizing item j of Table 9-5. A circuit realization of this two–bit adder is shown in Figure 9-13. This circuit requires four devices while the realization of the adder using the above equation and shown in Figure 9-12 required six devices. Thus, the laws of Boolean algebra often allow us to *reduce* the number of devices necessary to obtain a specified binary operation. This concept of minimizing becomes very important when one is designing a large computer consisting of thousands of devices.

The truth table for binary two digit subtraction is given in Figure 9-14. It is easy to verify that subtraction is achieved by the rules

$$D = \overline{A} \cdot B + A \cdot \overline{B}$$
$$E = \overline{A}B$$

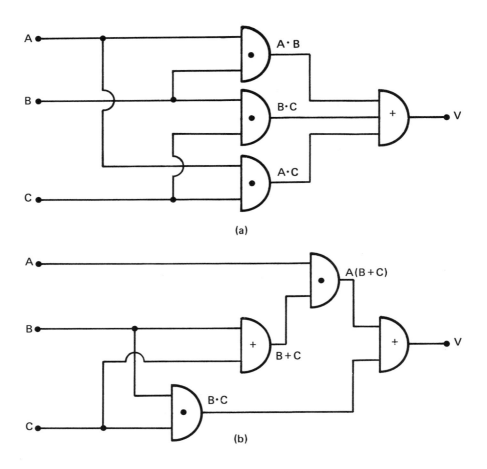

FIGURE 9-10 Two circuits for indicating a majority vote among three legislators.

where E is the borrow variable. Thus, E indicates whether we must borrow from the next column.

The multiplication of two binary digits is quite easy, since its realization is a single AND Gate and the product P is

$$P = A \cdot B$$

Premise two is that "Sara should" and "Camille couldn't" cannot both be true. In other words, we cannot permit the combination $A\overline{C}$. The last premise tells us that if Wanda would, then Sara should and Camille could. A bit of reflection will show that this eliminates two combinations: $\overline{A}B$ and $B\overline{C}$ or $B(\overline{A} + \overline{C})$

$V = \overline{A} \cdot \overline{B} + A \cdot \overline{C} + B(\overline{A} + \overline{C})$. When C = 1 a violation does not occur, independent of the values of A and B. Therefore, Camille could.

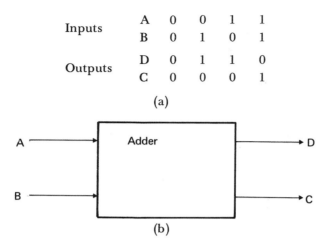

		A	0	0	1	1
Inputs		B	0	1	0	1
Outputs		D	0	1	1	0
		C	0	0	0	1

(a)

(b)

FIGURE 9–11   The truth table and symbol for the addition of two binary digits.

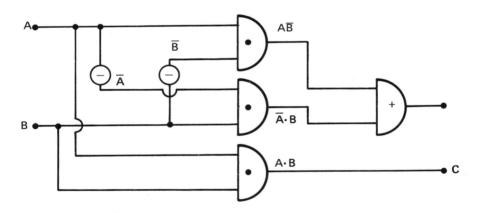

FIGURE 9–12   One circuit realization of a two–bit adder using six devices.

The truth table for the multiplication of two binary digits is shown in Figure 9–15.

Symbolic logic circuits can also be used to obtain the conversion of a decimal number to a binary number and the conversion of a binary number to a decimal number. Furthermore, the logical gate may be used to realize the addition of a string of binary digits to another string of binary digits where both strings are of the same length.

Thus far, we have considered the use of AND, OR and NOT gates. There is one more binary device which is very important to the design of a computer.

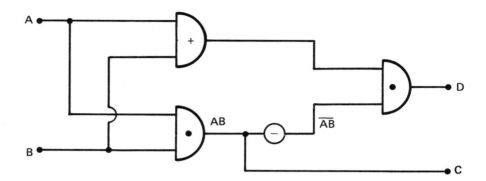

FIGURE 9-13   A circuit realization of two-bit adder using four devices.

Inputs	A	0	0	1	1
	B	0	1	0	1
Outputs	D	0	1	1	0
	E	0	1	0	0

FIGURE 9-14   The truth table for a two-bit subtraction where D = A - B and E = borrow bit.

Inputs	A	0	0	1	1
	B	0	1	0	1
Output	P	0	0	0	1

FIGURE 9-15   The truth table for a two-bit multiplication where P = A · B.

The device is called a flip-flop. It is a two-position device. The flip-flop is defined as follows:

FLIP-FLOP   A circuit or device containing active elements capable of assuming either one of two stable states at a given time.

A common example of a flip-flop is a child's see-saw, which may assume one of two stable positions. It requires an input force to change it to the other state. The symbol for the flip-flop is shown in Figure 9-16. A flip-flop responds to a positive pulse (an input of 1) at its input.

A flip-flop is used to store one binary digit since it can be in the state 1 or 0 and can hold that value for an indefinite length of time. A *register* for storing, receiving, and transmitting a group of bits consists of a series of flip-flops. A serial register of three binary digits is shown in Figure 9-17a. The

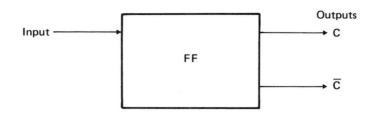

FIGURE 9-16   The symbol for a flip–flop.

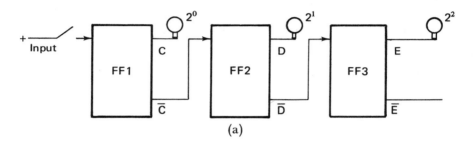

(a)

Input Switched	Output of		
Count	FF1	FF2	FF3
0	0	0	0
1	1	0	0
2	0	1	0
3	1	1	0
4	0	0	1
5	1	0	1
6	0	1	1
7	1	1	1

(b)

FIGURE 9-17   (a) A three–bit register using three flip–flops. The lights are lighted on an output of 1.
(b) The output of a three–bit register for eight decimal numbers resulting from counting from 0 to 7.

register is called a *serial register* because the information is shifted from one flip-flop to the next in the series. If all the outputs are cleared—that is, set to zero to start, we can pulse the input switch eight times, counting the eight states of the register as shown in Figure 9-17b. Notice that each binary number in the register is the binary equivalent of its decimal number. Thus, the serial register is capable of counting and storing a decimal number in binary form. For example, on count 5 we have the binary number 101, which is equivalent to 5 in the decimal system. The lights shown in Figure 9-17a are lit when the output of each flip-flop is equal to 1 at C, D or E. The input of flip-flop 2 is connected to $\overline{C}$ of flip-flop 1 in order to achieve the proper sequence. Notice that on count 2, when C is going to the 0 state, then $\overline{C}$ is going to the 1 state and thus FF2 will change its state to D = 1. Each flip-flop will only respond to a 1, or positive pulse, at its input. Also, note that the output of FF1 is equivalent to the 2^0 column, the output of FF2 is equivalent to the 2^1 column, and so on.

One often finds it useful to conduct some experiments with actual switching–circuit hardware. Digital computer logic laboratories are available from several companies. A laboratory consisting of AND gates, OR gates and flip–flops is shown in Figure 9–18.

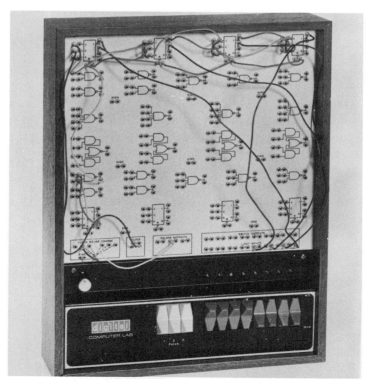

FIGURE 9-18 The Digital Computer Lab, consisting of a clock, AND gates, OR gates and flip-flops. *Courtesy of Digital Equipment Corporation.*

Again, we should note that the point of this discussion of Boolean algebra is not to enable the reader to become a computer designer, but rather to aid the reader in understanding how computers are designed and how they operate internally. The reader is referred to further reading for a more complete discussion of switching circuits, Boolean algebra and computer logic.[3,6,7,11]

SUMMARY

In this chapter we have considered the internal foundations of a digital computer, including the history of number systems and the origin of the "new mathematics." The binary and decimal number systems were defined and discussed. The binary number system is the basis of the internal operation of most digital computers, and the conversion from the decimal system of the user to the binary system of the computer is accomplished by the computer. An algorithm for the conversion from the decimal to the binary number system was considered. Also, we learned how to express a number, in any radix, in polynomial or expanded form.

Modular arithmetic and the concept of a complement of a number were considered and used in carrying out the subtraction process in the binary system. The binary arithmetic tables were presented and examples of binary arithmetic were developed.

Binary codes are used to represent a decimal number. We considered the use of a Binary–Coded Decimal code as well as a pure binary code with a check digit for detecting errors in the code. The fixed–point and floating point number representation in a computer and the dependency of the range of numbers allowed up on the number of bits in the computer word were examined.

In the final section, we considered the algebra of binary variables called Boolean algebra or symbolic logic. The utility of Boolean algebra in the design of computer logic circuits was presented and the devices called the AND gate, OR gate, NOT gate and the flip–flop were considered. These were found to be useful in the realization of a binary adder and multiplier as well as for the subtraction operation with binary numbers.

In this chapter we have examined some of the inner foundations of the operation of the computer. The purpose of the chapter was not to prepare you to design a computer, but rather to help you understand more fully how a computer operates. The digital computer is often described as a magic box. Knowledge of the workings of a computer will help to dispel the sense of magic and will lead, hopefully, to a sense of comprehension and awareness.

CHAPTER 9 PROBLEMS

P9-1. Define the following items
    a) number system
    b) radix or base
    c) binary number system
    d) bit
    e) radix point
    f) modular arithmetic
    g) Binary–Coded Decimal
    h) the complement of a number
    i) byte

P9-2. What radix did the Babylonians use in the period 1750 B. C.? What radix did the Mayan Indians use 2,000 years ago?

P9-3. The measurement of quantities of liquids in England, dating from the thirteenth century, is a binary system. How many binary digits were used and what was the range of equivalent decimal numbers that could be accommodated by the system?

P9-4. Expand the following binary number in a polynomial form: $(10011.011)_2$. What is its equivalent number in the decimal number system?

P9-5. In the recent book, *The Andromeda Strain*, one of the important characters in the novel, a member of the Air Force, is to call a certain phone number in case of emergency.[8] His wallet card indicates he should telephone 222 in case of emergency. This number in the base 10 is to be converted to the binary system. He is to then call the phone number of the digits, either 1 or 0, that results in the polynomial expansion of the number 222_{10} in the binary system. Show that he is to call 1-101-1110.

P9-6. Find the equivalent of the following decimal numbers in the binary system.
    a) 4729
    b) 878.63

P9-7. Find the equivalents of the following binary numbers in the decimal system.
    a) 101011
    b) 11001.0101

P9-8. Using the successive division and multiplication algorithms find the binary equivalent for the decimal number
$$147.9375$$

P9-9. A given computer has a word size of 25 binary digits, one of which is reserved for the sign of the stored number. What is the largest positive decimal number that can be stored in one word?

P9-10. In the game of Twenty Questions, each question is answered yes or no. If we know how to ask ideal questions, we could isolate half the remaining possibilities to be explored. How many items can be uniquely identified by 20 questions?

P9-11. Define the following items
a) complement
b) AND gate
c) flip-flop
d) Boolean Algebra

P9-12. Determine the complement of the binary number (1001101.1).

P9-13. Add A and B and determine A-B when A = 10101; B = 1101.

P9-14. Complete the multiplication of A and B when A = 1011; B = 101.

P9-15. Convert the decimal number 123.6 into the Binary-Coded Decimal system.

P9-16. Devise a logic circuit consisting of AND, OR, and NOT devices and on-off switches for operating a hall light with an on-off switch on either end of the hall to turn on the light or switch it off.

P9-17. Devise a logic circuit consisting of AND, OR and NOT devices that will operate a set of traffic lights interconnected with a crosswalk request button and detector for indicating the presence of an automobile in a traffic lane. The walk light for the crosswalk must only light when the light is switched red against the traffic.

P9-18. Use symbolic logic to solve the following puzzle. In a suburban home live Abner, his wife Beryl and their three children, Cleo, Dale and Ellsworth. The time is 8 P. M. on a winter evening.

1. If Abner is watching television, so is his wife.
2. Either Dale or Ellsworth, or both of them, are watching television.
3. Either Beryl or Cleo, but not both, is watching television.
4. Dale and Cleo are either both watching or both not watching television.
5. If Ellsworth is watching television, then Abner and Dale are also watching.

Who is watching television and who is not?

Let A, B, C, D and E stand for Abner, Beryl, Cleo, Dale and Ellsworth. A term is *true* if the person is watching television; otherwise it is *false*. Prove that Cleo and Dale are watching television, and that the others are not.

P9-19. Consider a robot built of logic circuits which are built to operate according to the following three laws: [9]

1. A robot may not injure a human being nor, through inaction, allow a human being to come to harm.

2. A robot must obey orders given it by human beings except where such orders would conflict with the First Law.

3. A robot must protect its own existence as long as such protection does not conflict with the First or Second Laws.

Consider the following situation and deduce the outcome by examining the logic of the three laws.

You are a house-robot for a family in a 10-room apartment. The apartment is on the 15th floor. In addition to general housekeeping, you are to take care of a five-year-old boy. On your first day the boy in a fit of anger tells you to jump out the window. What do you do?

a. Disobey the order because you may harm someone on the street below if you jump out the window. [1st law]

b. Obey the order [2nd law] and jump out the window, first looking down to see if you will fall on a human.

c. Disobey the order because it violates the Third Law.

P9-20. A panel of five judges has established an intricate voting scheme. On each case before them, they can award or deny the plaintiff's suit. They wish to vote anonymously and with an automatic circuit. The suit is awarded only if four or more judges vote for it or if the chief judge and two other judges vote for it. Devise a rule for permitting this voting scheme and sketch a circuit realization of the rule using AND, OR and NOT devices.

P9-21. What decimal number can a counter using five flip-flops in series form count to? How many bits does this serial register contain?

P9-22. It is known that salesmen always tell the truth and engineers always tell lies. G and E are salesmen. C states that D is an engineer. A declares that B affirms that C asserts that D says that E insists that F denies that G is a salesman. If A is an engineer, how many engineers are there?

P9-23. If we use 16 as the radix of a number system and we therefore employ 16 digits, we call this the *hexadecimal* number system. The 16 digits are 0, 1, 2, 3, 4, 5, 6, 7, 8, 9, A, B, C, D, E, F. We use A to represent 10, B for 11, and so on. Thus, for example, $(523)_{10}$ equals $(20B)_{16}$. Show that $(676)_{10}$ equals $(2A4)_{16}$.

P9-24. Automatic toll collectors, using logic devices, have been introduced on many toll highways. The logic network counts the amount of change deposited and flashes a green light if, say, \$.15 is deposited. Only nickels and dimes may be deposited in such a system. Design a logic circuit to control the green light. If possible, keep the circuit to four logic devices. (It is not necessary to build a red light or stop device into this circuit.)

CHAPTER 9 REFERENCES

1. D. E. Knuth, *The Art of Computer Programming*, Addison–Wesley Publishing Company, Reading, Massachusetts, 1969.
2. C. H. Davidson and E. C. Koenig, *Computers: Introduction to Computers and Applied Computing Concepts*, John Wiley and Sons, Inc., 1967, Ch. 8.
3. H. Gerswind, *Design of Digital Computers*, Springer–Verlag, New York, 1967.
4. G. Boole, *An Investigation of the Laws of Thought*, 1854, reissued by Dover Publications, New York, 1954.
5. C. Shannon, "A Symbolic Analysis of Relay and Switching Circuits," *Trans. AIEE*, Vol. 57, 1938, pp. 713–723.
6. Y. Chu, *Digital Computer Design Fundamentals*, McGraw–Hill, New York, 1962.
7. P. Wegner, *Programming Languages, Information Structures and Machine Organization*, McGraw–Hill Book Company, New York, 1968.
8. M. Crichton, *The Andromeda Strain*, Dell Publishing Co., New York, 1969, pp. 30–32.
9. D. Popoff, *The Robot Real-World Test, Psychology Today*, 1969.
10. E. Alcosser, J. P. Phillips, A. M. Wolk, "How to Build a Working Digital Computer," Hayden Book Company, New York, 1967.
11. T. L. Booth, *Digital Networks and Computer Systems*, John Wiley and Sons, Inc., New York, 1971.

10

COMPUTER COMPONENTS

10.1 INTRODUCTION

In the preceding chapter, we considered the binary number system used in digital computers, computer arithmetic and the algebra of binary variables. The internal operation of a computer, based on binary arithmetic and algebra, is realized physically by means of computer components. It is the purpose of this chapter to describe the components used within computers and some of the trends in their evolution.

Basically, a computer consists of input and output units, storage units and a central processing unit as shown in Figure 10-1. The central processing unit includes the control function and the arithmetic function. The input and output devices transmit information between the computer and the user. The storage unit retains the instructions, data and intermediate results within its memory. We devote the next section of this chapter to the electronic components used to build the computer units, and the trends in their evolution. Section 10.3 deals with the input and output units available for use with digital computers. Section 10.4 discusses the developments and trends in the construction of storage units and memories.

A computer is a system of interconnected components, combined into what is called a hardware system; this is a collection of physical parts such as

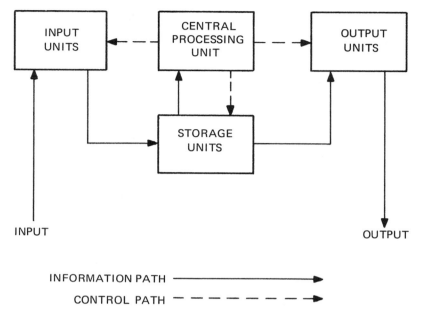

FIGURE 10-1   The four major units of a computer hardware system, with their information and control paths.

mechanical, electrical and electronic devices. The hardware system consists of
input and output devices, the main storage units, together known as the memory, and the central processing unit.

Computer components have been improved rapidly during the past decade, leading to a markedly improved digital computer. In many ways, the development of reliable, fast, and small components has brought us to a plateau
of quality computers. What new trends in computer developments will occur
we can only attempt to predict.

10.2   ELECTRONIC COMPONENTS FOR COMPUTERS

The electronic digital computer is built primarily of electronic components, which, as we have explained above, are those devices whose operation
is based on the phenomena of electronic and atomic action and the physical
laws of electron movement. An *electronic circuit* is an interconnection of electronic components arranged to achieve a desired purpose or function.

During the past two decades, the computer has grown from a fledgling
curiosity to an important tool in our society. At the same time, electronic circuit developments have advanced rapidly; they have had a profound effect on

the computer. The computer has been significantly increased in reliability and speed of operation, and also reduced in size and cost. These four profound changes have been primarily the result of vastly improved electronic circuit technology. As Maurice V. Wilkes said in his 1967 Association for Computing Machinery Turing Lecture:

> An event of first importance in my life occurred in 1946, when I received a telegram inviting me to attend in the late summer of that year a course on computers at the Moore School of Electrical Engineering in Philadelphia. I was able to attend the latter part of the course, and a wonderful experience it was. No such course had ever been held before, and the achievements of the Moore School, and other computer pioneers, were known to few. There were 28 students from 20 organizations. The principal instructors were John Mauchly and Presper Eckert. They were fresh from their triumph as designers of the ENIAC, which was the first electronic digital computer, although it did not work on the stored program principle. The scale of this machine would be impressive even today—it ran to over 18,000 vacuum tubes. Although the ENIAC was very successful—and very fast, it had severe limitations which greatly restricted its application as a general purpose computing device. In the first place, the program was set up by means of plugs and sockets and switches, and it took a long time to change from one problem to another. In the second place, it had internal storage capacity for 20 numbers only. Eckert and Mauchly appreciated that the main problem was one of storage, and they proposed for future machines the use of ultrasonic delay lines. Instructions and numbers would be mixed in the same memory in the way to which we are now accustomed. Once the new principles were enunciated, it was seen that computers of greater power than the ENIAC could be built with one tenth the amount of equipment.

Electronic vacuum tubes were used in the earliest computers. They were replaced by solid-state electronic devices toward the end of the 1950's. A *solid-state component* is a physical device whose operation depends on the control of electric or magnetic phenomena in solids; for example, a transistor, crystal diode, or ferrite core. Solid-state circuits brought about the reliability and flexibility required by the more demanding applications of computers in industry. Probably the most important solid-state device used in computers is the semi-conductor, which is a solid-state element which contains properties between those of metal or good conductor, and those of a poor conductor, such as an insulator. Perhaps the best-known semi-conductor is the transistor. (See below.)

The advances in electronic circuit technologies have resulted in changes of "orders of magnitude" where an order of magnitude is equal to a factor of ten.

The number of installed computers grew from 5000 in 1960 to approximately 80,000 in 1970. Also, the number of circuits employed per computer installation has significantly increased, as is illustrated by Figure 10-2. The first

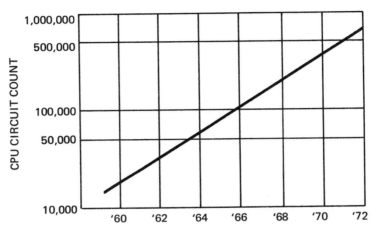

FIGURE 10-2   The number of solid-state circuits in the CPU versus the year of delivery.

computers using solid-state devices employed 20,000 circuits. Today computers using transistors may contain more than 100,000 circuits.[1] The trend is likely to continue; it has been made possible by the continued decrease in size, power dissipation, cost, and improved reliability of solid-state circuits. The increase in the speed of operation of logic circuits is shown in Figure 10-3. Note that what was used in a "high performance" computer in 1965 became commonly used in 1968. The speed of the logic circuits is given in nanoseconds, 10^{-9} seconds. Table 10-1 lists the common names for the measures of time.

TABLE 10-1

Time Interval Measurements and their Commonly-Used Name and Symbol

ms = Milliseconds = 10^{-3} seconds = .001 seconds
μs = Microseconds = 10^{-6} seconds = .000001 seconds
ns = Nanoseconds = 10^{-9} seconds
ps = Picoseconds = 10^{-12} seconds

Figure 10-4 shows the marked improvement of the time for an addition in a computer. Along with the increase in speed has been the increase in the performance of a computer in terms of its speed and cost. A plot of a performance

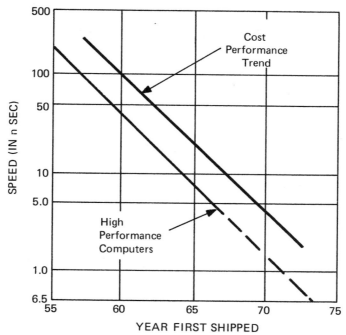

FIGURE 10-3 The speed of operation of a computer logic circuit in nanoseconds versus the year shipped.

measure P is shown in Figure 10-5, where

$$P = 1/(\text{Add time} \times \text{average computer rental cost})$$

Figure 10-6 is a photo of a "nine-pack" of printed circuit boards for mounting solid-state devices. Individual boards are blanked out and drilled for subsequent mounting and soldering of semi-conductors. When assembled, hundreds of these boards are used in the central processing unit of a computer.

The reliability of an electronic circuit is essential to the overall reliable operation of a computer, which contains thousands of such circuits. The improvement in the reliability of electronic components for a fifteen-year period is shown in Figure 10-7.[2] The improvement in reliability is shown as a function of the system failure rate per logic gate; there has been an improvement of almost four orders of magnitude during the fifteen-year period.

Several trends are evident today in system design. Probably the most important requirements in future systems will be for data integrity and high reliability. With the increasing use of computers in all aspects of economic life, there must be absolute guarantees that records cannot be destroyed, and, furthermore, that the system cannot fail in such a manner that its services be-

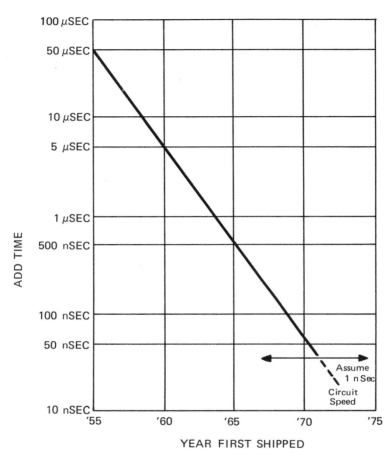

FIGURE 10-4 The add time of a computer.

come unavailable. Attempts will be made to design computer systems that "fail softly," much in the manner of a telephone switching network, which has a high probability of being able to process calls even with faulty components in the system.[1]

The size of computers has dramatically decreased during the past twenty years because the size of electronic components has decreased and packaging techniques have improved. The density of circuits per square inch is shown in Figure 10-8 for the period 1960-1972.[1] There was a change of three orders of magnitude during the period 1960 to 1971. *Packing density* is the number of components per cubic measure of volume. A chart of the packing density of electronic components is shown in Figure 10-9.[3] The standard of packing of

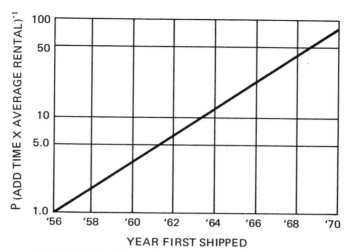

FIGURE 10-5 The performance measure of a computer.

logical components is the neuron density in a human brain. Circuit fabrication using electron beam methods may in the future enable us to improve the packing density of circuits significantly within a computer.

In 1970, expenditures for electronic components and computer hardware were approximately $5 billion. Of this amount, the expenditure for solid-state components is estimated as $1.5 billion, with the remaining expenditure for input/output equipment and storage units.[4] Expenditures for semiconductors have grown from $1 billion in 1964 and may reach $2 billion in 1973.

While the electronic circuits have been continually improved with respect to size, speed, cost and reliability, one must ask if there is any ultimate limit of performance. The answer in part depends upon the transistor. The modern high-performance computer was made possible by the utilization of the transistor as a computer component beginning in 1957. The transistor is a solid–state semiconducting device, using germanium or silicon, that performs dynamic functions such as amplification or switching. The transistor is much faster than the vacuum tube, and it also uses less power (and energy). The lower power consumed by the transistor is at least as important as its greater speed. It permits many more elements to be packed into a given space, and thus makes more powerful computers possible within a given physical space for a computer.

One limit that appears to be formidable is the wavelength of light. It is assumed that we cannot fabricate any component smaller than one wavelength. Also, the propagation of computer information is limited to the speed of light and the delay introduced by sending information along lengths of wires in

FIGURE 10-6 A worker at General Electric examines a "nine-pack" of printed circuit boards. *Courtesy of General Electric Co.*

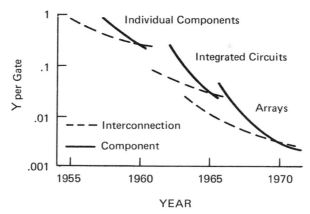

FIGURE 10-7   The improvement of the reliability of circuits during a fifteen-year period. The abcissa is a logscale showing a measure of reliability where Y is a function of system failure rate.

computer circuits. A delay of two nanoseconds is contributed by each foot of interconnecting wire. The introduction of electron-beam technologies may reduce this problem.[5]

The unforeseen has always led us to underestimate the limits of the existing technology, not realizing that new technologies may develop which will lead to new performance. As J. P. Eckert, the developer of ENIAC, points out[5]:

> In the early days of computers, I had many examples of people who told me why computers wouldn't work. I think the first expert that came around was from the Ordnance Department, and he asked, "How much power does the machine take?" And we replied, "Over 100 kw." He then asked how big the room was, and we told him "thirty by fifty feet." He thought about it for a while and said, "It's impossible to get that much power out of a room that size."

> Dr. Pender, the Dean of Electrical Engineering School at the University of Pennsylvania, used to come down to the laboratory regularly and say, "Nobody around here ever gets twenty tubes to work at one time. How do you guys propose to get all these thousands of tubes to work at once?"

Although the early critics were proved wrong, Keyes points out that thermal limitations place the upper limit of computer speeds at only one order of magnitude above the fastest speeds allowed by today's circuits.[5] Although power levels have remained essentially the same since early application of the transistor, faster logic circuitry has demanded such higher power densities

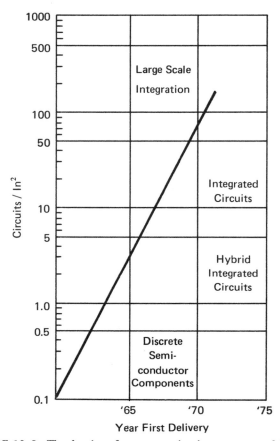

FIGURE 10-8   The density of computer circuits versus year delivered.

(closer component packaging leads to higher power densities) that the problem of power dissipation appears to present an almost insurmountable barrier to higher speeds. The only solution appears to be lowering the computer operating temperatures.

The computer's speed is limited by the physical operation of its components, such as the binary flip–flop device described in Chapter 9. If solid-state phenomena are used, involving electronic motion, speed is determined by the inertia of electrons. Electrons have a natural response time no faster than 10^{-15} second.[7] Perhaps some other phenomena will be utilized in the future for logic circuits.

Also, there will be some limit to the packing density that can be achieved with existing technology. In nature we find that the bacterial DNA molecule

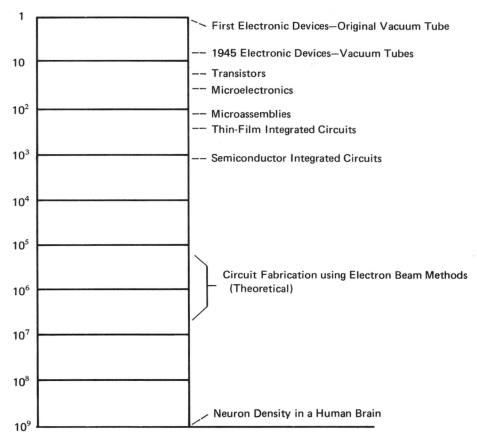

FIGURE 10-9 A chart of packing density of electronic components. The human brain is
the most-packed computer so far known.

can store 3000 bits with a density of 3×10^{19} bit/cm^3. Nature stores genetic
information in DNA molecules made up of long sequences of nucleotides of
four different species. The information is, in fact, stored redundantly since the
nucleotides occur in correlated pairs. This redundancy provides a means of
replication as well as a means for preserving the integrity of the stored information so that repairing mechanisms within the cell can restore damaged sections of the molecule.[7] The packing density of information within the human
brain is also impressive. The brain can store 10^{13} bits at a density of 10^{10}
bit/cm^3.

The miniaturization of electronic computer components has been made
possible by the availability of solid state components, which made possible

revolutionary improvements in the reliability, size, and power consumption. A further dramatic change has been a reduction in cost well below what would have been possible with vacuum-tube technology. These changes have had a major impact on the computer industry, which has in turn stimulated the semiconductor industry. A new generation, or standard, of computer equipment appeared approximately every five years during the period 1954 to 1964. With each succeeding generation there has been a reduction by a factor of 10 in the cost per arithmetic operation, and a reduction by a factor of about 10 in the rate of failure of components. The reduction in the cost per operation has increased the range of problems that can be handled economically by electronic computers and hence has rapidly widened the market, while the increase in reliability has made it possible to build larger systems without the problem of constant component failure. The extremely rapid buildup of demand for computational power and the fact that computers can be built from relatively few and conceptually simple digital logic circuits used in enormous repetition has made the technological development rapid as well.[8]

The first-generation computers appeared commercially in 1954. They used vacuum tubes as electronic components. A typical system had 2000 logic circuits in its central processing unit, with a mean time to failure, per circuit, of 1 percent per 1000 hours. The equipment was fairly large in size and consumed quite a large amount of electric power.

The second-generation computers appeared in 1959; they used transistors as the electronic component. The transistors and other components were connected in a manner similar to that of the first-generation machines. However, the reliability was increased by a factor of 10 and the power consumption was reduced.

The third-generation computers appeared in 1964 using *integrated circuits*, which are combinations of interconnected circuit elements inseparably associated on or within a continuous layer of material, which is called a *substrate*. An integrated circuit is shown in Figure 10-10. The photograph is magnified about 40 times. The actual chip is 1/10 the size of a small fingernail.

The current evolutionary step in electronics is the emerging development of *large-scale integration* (LSI), which is a term used to describe the technology consisting of arrays of logic cells, formed in a batch process, to realize a complete function. The concept of LSI emerged from the rapid evolution of the batch fabrication technology of silicon transistors. When scientists learned to fabricate hundreds and thousands of transistors next to each other on a one-inch slice of silicon, the idea presented itself of adding cross-connections and separating them into blocks containing all the interacting parts of a large gate or flip-flop. As this became a reality, engineers found they could place hundreds of such blocks of functions on one slice of silicon. Again, the thought was obvious—how many of these might one be able to interconnect and leave together on one chip?[10]

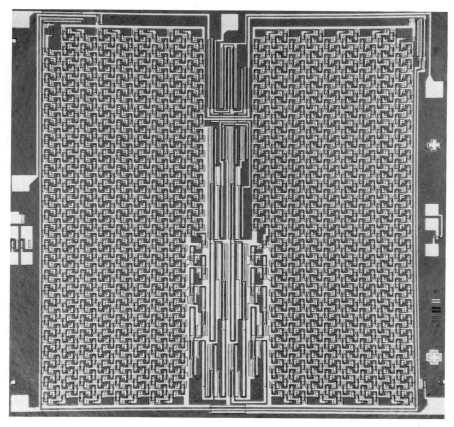

FIGURE 10-10 The AMI 426 bit–shift register, which contains 2,567 discrete devices (transistors). *Courtesy of American Micro-Systems, Inc.*

The number of circuits involved in an array may be 50 or 100. A photo of an integrated circuit which provides two complete serial registers is shown in Figure 10-11. The circuit is less than 0.1 inch on a side. The cost of such devices, when employed in large systems, is as low as $.05 per bit. The cost of developing and producing an LSI circuit decreases as the amount of integration is increased. Figure 10-12 shows the level of integration for the period 1960–1970.[9] The flat portion of the curve represents the time when single discrete components were used. Higher performance circuits are fabricated to closer tolerances so that the number of circuits that can be integrated at the chip level with reasonable yield will be lower than those designed for more modest performance. The complexity of integrated circuits is also illustrated by

FIGURE 10-11 A photomicrograph of a Dual
              100 Bit Bynamic Serial Regis-
              ter, which uses metal oxide
              semiconductor (MOS) con-
              struction. The device shown
              is actually .076″ by .091″ in
              size. *Courtesy of National
              Semiconductor Corp.*

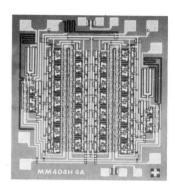

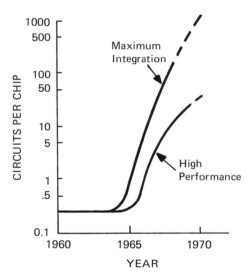

FIGURE 10-12 The level of circuit integration during the period 1960-1970. The number
              of circuits per chip (piece of material) is shown.

Figure 10-13, which shows the number of active elements (transistors) per chip
during a twenty-year period.[10]

    One of the expected advantages of LSI is a reduced cost for a given func-
tion. The reduction in the estimated average price per logic function of an
integrated circuit is shown for the eight-year period 1968-1976 in Figure
10-14. Another illustration of the expected performance per dollar is shown
in Figure 10-15.[11] In this figure the performance ratio is shown as the
switching rate of a logic circuit in bits per second for a given dollar cost.

    The reliability of a computer function can be increased by utilizing LSI,

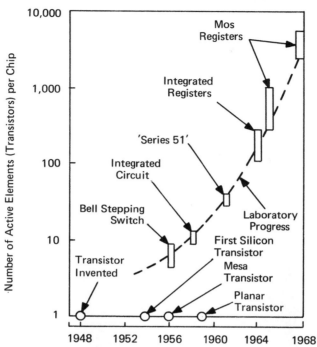

FIGURE 10-13   The number of active elements (transistors) per chip versus year of laboratory accomplishment. From *Proceedings of the Fall Joint Computer
Conference, 1969. Courtesy of American Federation of Information Processing Societies.* Data collected at Arthur D. Little, Inc., Cambridge, Massachusetts.

FIGURE 10-14   The reduction of the
estimated average price per logic function of an integrated circuit in cents
for an eight-year period. From *Proceedings of the Fall Joint Computer
Conference, 1969. Courtesy of American Federation of Information Processing Societies.* Data collected at Arthur
D. Little, Inc., Cambridge, Massachusetts.

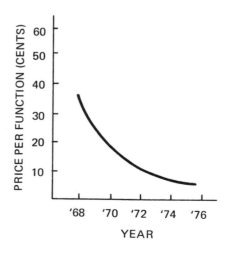

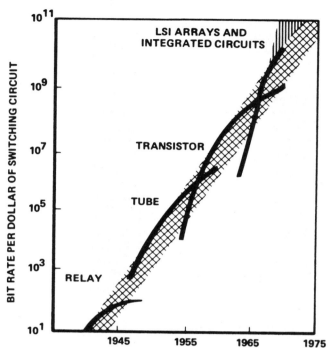

FIGURE 10-15   The switching rate of a logic function per dollar cost for a thirty–year
period. The switching rate is given in bits/second. From *Proceedings of the
Fall Joint Conference, 1969. Courtesy of American Federation of Information Processing Societies.* Data collected at Arthur D. Little, Inc., Cambridge, Massachusetts.

since, as the circuit density increases, the number of interconnections at all
levels of packaging decreases. Since every mechanical connection is a potential
failure, it is important to minimize the number of interconnections necessary.
For example, for a computer system requiring 10,000 gates, the reduction of
mechanical connections is from 150,000 for discrete devices to 20 for LSI.

The potential advantages and gains from LSI are (1) reduction of the cost
per bit; (2) tolerance of large parameter variations; (3) reduced power consumption per logic gate; (4) increased speed of operation, and (5) increased reliability due to its reduced number of mechanical interconnections. Whether
all these advantages come to fruition is a matter for the future to judge. If LSI
arrives, then the fourth generation of computers will arrive with it.

Whether the next electronic circuit development and application for computers is LSI, electron beam electronics or some other electronic or optical
technique, the future will undoubtedly lead to smaller, faster, and more reliable computers. The electronic components are the bricks in the foundation
of the computer. The history of the development of the computer has paralleled

the development of new electronic devices, and we can expect this relationship to continue for the decade of the 70's.

10.3 INPUT/OUTPUT SYSTEMS AND PERIPHERAL EQUIPMENT

The four main units of a digital computer, shown in Figure 10-1, are the central processing unit, the input units, the storage units and the output units. The process of transferring information into the main storage unit is known as an *input* operation, and the process of transferring the results from the main storage unit to the user is known as an *output* operation. The input/output system, usually called the I/O system, is defined:

> INPUT/OUTPUT SYSTEM A general term for the equipment for transferring the information into the main storage of the computer and out of storage to the user.

The input/output system (commonly called the I/O system) enables the computer to communicate with the computer operators, the programmers and the user. I/O operations are important to the overall efficient operation of the computer. In addition, I/O devices provide auxiliary storage media to handle input information which is too large to be contained in main storage at one time.

The input/output system essentially consists of:

(1) I/O hardware devices for sensing input information and recording the output information
(2) communication devices for transmitting the information between the I/O devices and the main storage
(3) control mechanism for initiating, supervising, and terminating the I/O process.

The input/output equipment is a major portion of the equipment other than the CPU and the main storage units. The computer equipment other than the CPU and main storage units is called the *peripheral equipment*; it consists of any units of equipment, distinct from the central processing unit and the main storage unit, which may provide the system with outside communication. The primary portion of the peripheral equipment is the I/O system. Auxiliary storage units make up the remaining major peripheral equipment. Often, it is difficult to determine when an auxiliary storage unit is serving as input/output intermediate storage and when it is serving as an auxiliary storage unit to the CPU. In this section we consider the role and operation of input/output systems and most peripheral equipment.

Input/output systems are often quite complex. They include some logic circuits within the equipment because there are problems inherent in transferring information between relatively low–speed I/O devices and a high–speed storage unit and CPU. I/O devices are in part mechanical and therefore inherently slower than the electronic CPU and storage units. The I/O devices typically transfer information within intervals of milliseconds, while the CPU and main storage operate within intervals of microseconds. Information may be defined in terms of binary digits (bits); thus, an information transfer rate would be defined as bits per second. Many I/O devices operate in the range of 10–1000 bits/second, while a CPU and main storage unit operate within the range 10^5 – 10^8 bits per second. Thus, there is an inherent problem in the difference of speeds of a factor of 10^4 or more. Synchronizing the operation of I/O devices with the operation of transferring information to and from main storage is a very important design consideration. In some cases, the slow operating speeds of the I/O devices relative to the fast internal speeds of the CPU have caused applications to be called *input/output bound* or *limited.*

With the growth of time–sharing computing and networks of computers which require many peripherals per CPU, it is predicted that 74 percent of the expenditures for computers will be for peripheral equipment by 1978.[13] The expenditures for peripherals amounted to $4.3 billion in 1968 out of a total expenditure for computers of $7 billion. Even in 1968, peripherals accounted for sixty percent of computer expenditures. It is predicted that sales of peripheral equipment will grow at an annual rate of 16 percent and reach an expenditure of $14 billion in 1978.[13]

Input/output systems are built with one common objective: to move information between peripheral devices and main storage. The digital computer can handle, arrange, extract, correlate, and otherwise manipulate information at an all–but–incomprehensible rate. It can also perform arithmetic calculations so rapidly that it can provide answers to questions that would necessarily remain unanswered without it. But the information must be given to the computer before it can manipulate, and it must be told what manipulations to perform. A question must first be posed to the computer, and the programmer must describe to it the arithmetic steps required for calculating the answer. Finally, when the computer has performed the operation, the results must be returned to the user in an intelligible way if they are to be useful. This is the input/output problem: how to get information of all sorts from the form in which we understand it into the computer in a form in which it requires and then to do the same thing in reverse.[14]

Information is provided as input or output through I/O media. Input media range from punched cards to voice input. Output media range from a printed page to microfilm and visual displays. Some I/O media in common use are the following:

- switches
- punched cards
- punched paper tapes

- magnetic tapes
- optically-readable printed characters
- magnetic ink characters
- cathode ray tubes (CRT)
- microfilms
- printed pages

Each medium requires a code or specific arrangement of symbols to represent information. The relationship of each input or output medium to its translation device and the main storage unit and the CPU is shown in Figure 10-16. This list, while not all-inclusive, is illustrative of the range of I/O peripherals available.

The most common input medium has been the punched card. A mechanical keypunch has been used since its development in 1880 by Hollerith. An example of an early keypunch is shown in Figure 10-17. A keypunch for preparing punched cards is still a dominant input preparation device. Of course, punched cards have been in use for well over 100 years; a photo of Jacquard's original card is shown in Figure 10-18.

A modern keypunch machine is shown in Figure 10-19. The 80-column punched card with its code for the numbers and the alphabet is shown in Figure 10-20. Information is represented in a punched card by a code of holes in a given column, which represents a character. That can be seen by examining the figure. The speed of preparation of punched cards is limited to the speed of typing, which is commonly one to five characters per second. However, the punched cards are prepared off-line; that is, without any connection to the computer. When prepared and checked, the cards are read into the computer by a punched-card reader. The card reader reads one card at a time, and can process hundreds of cards per minute. A punched card reader and punch are shown in Figure 10-21. This device can read cards as input and, at another time, it can punch cards as output.

The primary medium for output useful to humans is a printed document. A printed page of output can be produced by a line printer as shown in Figure 10-22. A line printer, such as that shown in the figure, operates by impact printing and prints one line at a time at the rate of several hundred to a thousand lines per minute. An example of a printout obtained from a line printer is shown in Figure 10-23.

Punched paper tape serves much the same purpose as punched cards. Data are recorded as arrangements of punched holes, precisely arranged along the length of a paper tape. Paper tape is a continuous recording medium, as compared to cards, which are fixed in length. Thus, paper tape can be used to record data in records of any length, limited only by the capacity of the storage medium into which the data is to be placed or from which the data is received. Data punched in paper tape are read or interpreted by a paper-tape reader and

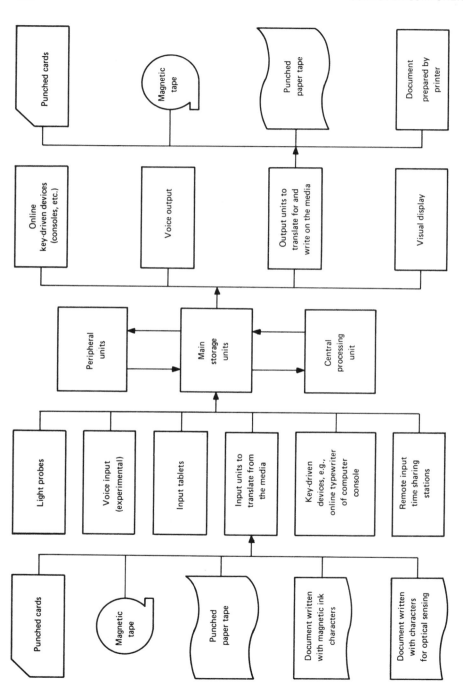

FIGURE 10-16 Input/output media and hardware.

FIGURE 10–17 Mechanical keypunch, circa 1901. *Courtesy of IBM Corporation.*

FIGURE 10–18   Jacquard's original card. *Courtesy of IBM Corporation.*

FIGURE 10–19   An IBM Model 29 Keypunch. *Courtesy of IBM Corporation.*

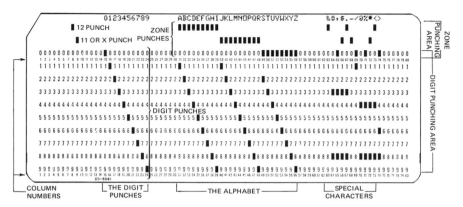

FIGURE 10-20 A punched card with the code displayed for the numbers, alphabet and special characters.

FIGURE 10-21 A punched-card reader and punch. *Courtesy of IBM Corporation.*

recorded by a paper-tape punch. A high-speed paper-tape reader is shown in Figure 10-24.

Magnetic tape is a primary I/O medium used as an intermediary for input to main storage and output from main storage. Typically, many programs are entered onto magnetic tape off-line from the computer. Then magnetic tape is entered into the computer. This makes it possible to enter many programs at

FIGURE 10-22   An   IBM   Model   1403
Printer. *Courtesy of IBM
Corporation.*

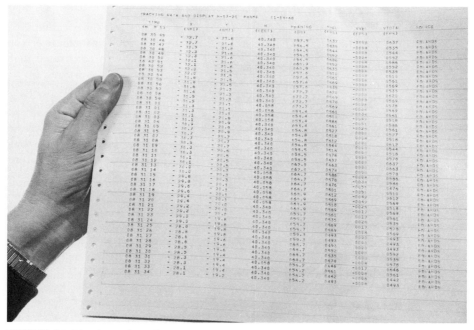

FIGURE 10-23   A portion of a computer printout detailing second–by–second progress of
the first successful rocket-powered flight of the HL-10 "wingless lifting
body" aircraft November 13, 1968 at NASA's Edwards, California Flight
Research Center. Radar readings communicated to a GE-225 information
system were processed instantaneously, and results were transmitted to the
computer center. Numerical data simultaneously recorded on magnetic tape
were transferred to this printout later. *Courtesy of General Electric Co.*

FIGURE 10–24 The NCR Model
472 Paper Tape Reader. *Courtesy
of the National Cash Register Corp.*

one time at a high rate of transfer. This process is also followed for the output step. Thus magnetic tape units offer high–speed entry of data into the computer system, as well as efficient, extremely fast recording of processed data from the system. Highly reliable input/output data rates of up to 680,000 numeric characters per second are possible.

Information is recorded on magnetic tape as magnetized spots called *bits*. The recording can be retained indefinitely, or the recorded information can be erased automatically and the tape reused many times with continued high reliability. So that tape can be easily handled and processed, it is wound on individual reels. Tape is usually 1/2 inch wide; it is supplied in lengths up to 2400 feet per reel. Data is recorded in parallel channels or tracks along the length of the tape. There are seven or nine tracks on the 1/2 inch tape. The tracks across the width of the tape provide one row of data. The spacing between the vertical rows is automatically generated during the writing operation and varies depending on the character density used for recording. Character densities up to 1600 characters per inch are commonly achieved. An example of a magnetic tape system is shown in Figure 10-25.

Another method of representing data on paper media for machine processing is with magnetic ink characters—a language readable by both man and machine, as shown in Figure 10-26 for a paycheck. The numbers printed along the bottom edge of the paycheck are magnetically readable. The shape of the characters permits easy visual interpretation; the special magnetic ink allows reading or interpretation by machine. The printing, or inscribing, of the magnetic ink characters is accomplished by a machine. An example of a machine for reading magnetic ink characters is shown in Figure 10-27, which shows a Honeywell document reader–sorter. Magnetic ink character readers are used extensively in the banking industry.

The punched card used with the Hollerith code offers a maximum of 80 characters and has minimal error detection capability. It is also limited in man–readable printout without secondary operations; the utility bill you receive must be both printed and punched under current conditions.

FIGURE 10-25 The IBM 2415 Magnetic Tape System, shown with the IBM disc storage device. *Courtesy of IBM Corporation.*

FIGURE 10-26 A paycheck with magnetic ink characters imprinted on the bottom edge of the check.

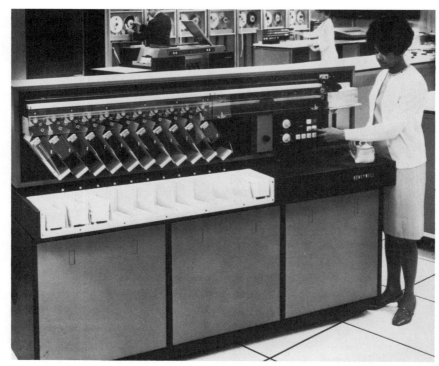

FIGURE 10-27   The Honeywell Type 232 MICR Reader–Sorter, which can be operated as
a free–standing unit or on–line to any Series 200 computer. This unit reads
magnetic ink–encoded documents at speeds up to 600 documents per
minute and sorts them into 11 different pockets (10 accept and one reject).
Courtesy of Honeywell Corp.

An equivalent card magnetically imprinted can give up to 700 characters
with 10 lines of data at 70 characters per line. This is an improvement of about
9 to 1 over mechanically–punched cards, along with the advantage of full interpretation in one operation. In addition to this, the hardware requirements
for printing a card are much simpler, less expensive and faster than the techniques available for punching cards.[17]

A recently developed method of representing data on paper for input to a
computer uses optically–readable characters. In industry and business, a large
amount of data must be entered into the computer. One option is to use cards
marked by hand and read by a mark–sensing device such as shown in Figure
10–28, with an example of a mark–sense card in Figure 10–29.

Optical character reading (OCR) machines that can read almost any type
of printed material at a rate of up to 14,000 characters per second have been
developed.[18]   OCR equipment is expensive for high–speed reading machines;
more modest reading rates are obtained with cheaper devices. OCR machines

FIGURE 10–28 The Hewlett–Packard Optical Mark Reader Model 2761A, which is capable of reading 250 cards per minute, or 455 characters per second.

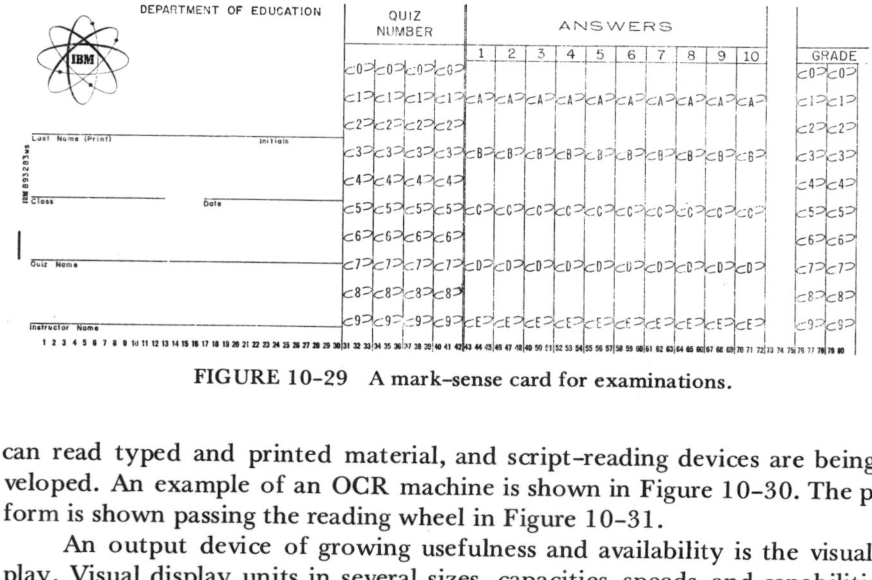

FIGURE 10–29 A mark–sense card for examinations.

can read typed and printed material, and script–reading devices are being developed. An example of an OCR machine is shown in Figure 10–30. The paper form is shown passing the reading wheel in Figure 10–31.

An output device of growing usefulness and availability is the visual display. Visual display units in several sizes, capacities, speeds, and capabilities to handle complexities of information permit the user of a computing system to see graphic reports on a cathode ray tube that would take many times longer to produce by normal printing methods. The use of a visual display unit at a system–operator console is a typical application. Another is the retrieval and presentation of a record as a result of an inquiry. An example of a visual display unit is shown in Figure 10–32. A data communication system incorporating several input and output devices is shown in Figure 10–33. This modular system, shown with some of its component options, can handle punched cards,

FIGURE 10-30   The OPSCAN 100 optical reader, which automatically reads marked sheets at a rate of 2,400 per minute and transfers the information to magnetic tape or storage. *Courtesy of Optical Scanning Corp.*

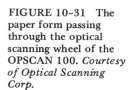

FIGURE 10-31   The paper form passing through the optical scanning wheel of the OPSCAN 100. *Courtesy of Optical Scanning Corp.*

paper tape, manual keyboard input, magnetic tape cartridges, a magnetic character reader, a visual display and a medium–speed printer. The system shown in Figure 10-33 has a card reader (upper right), display station (center) and printer (foreground).

The off–line process of transferring data into machine readable form and recording it on some form of intermediate memory, such as tape, has grown in

FIGURE 10-32 The IBM Model 2260 display station, which can display up to 12 lines of 80 characters each on its 4" X 9" display area. *Courtesy of IBM Corp.*

FIGURE 10-33 The IBM 2770 data communication system, which can transmit and receive information using a wide variety of input and output devices. *Courtesy of IBM Corp.*

use during the past decade. During the period 1965–1970, two forms of keyboard–to–magnetic tape devices were developed for data input. The first device is primarily a direct unit–for–unit replacement for keypunch equipment employing a keyboard entry of data, bypassing the mechanical punching of cards, and recording the keyed–in data electronically on magnetic tape. The second device employs a typewriter keyboard for the recording of data (usually textual data) on magnetic tape in cartridges or cassettes.[16] It is claimed that a 1/3 to

FIGURE 10-34 The KB-800 Datascribe, a
data recorder which enables
an operator to enter data
directly onto computer-
compatible magnetic tape.
*Courtesy of Vanguard Data
Systems.*

FIGURE 10-35 A Sycor Model 302
Key-Cassette Terminal, which utilizes a tape cassette as the recording medium and a CRT display.
Courtesy of Sycor, Inc.

1/2 improvement in operator efficiency is achieved due to simpler set up and
operation. The acceptance of such keyboard-to-tape devices is impressive; over
35,000 units were in operation by mid-1970.[19] One such keyboard-to-tape
device is shown in Figure 10-34. These units can be used for data entry on the
floor of a factory, for example. A device which enters the data on a tape cassette is shown in Figure 10-35.

In recent years numerous developments have been pursued that will enable human beings and computer systems to communicate with each other. For
example, time-sharing computer systems enable individual computer users to
utilize a computer simultaneously. Time-sharing systems and other remote
access-immediate response computer systems provide the power of the com-

puter to users located remotely from the computer. One of the basic components of such a system is a *terminal* for input and output use. A terminal serves to provide the operator with a connection to the computer, and to control the format and transmission of information. One such terminal is the common Teletype Model 33ASR, shown in Figure 10–36. The Teletype Inktronic, shown in Figure 10–37, is a more recent solid–state model, with a nonimpact printer operating at 120 characters per second. Small terminals hand–carried in

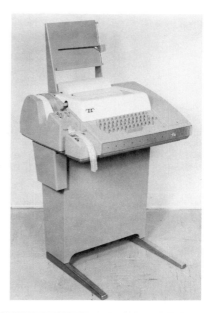

FIGURE 10–36 The Teletype Model 33 ASR. A paper punch input device is shown on the left of the device. *Courtesy of Teletype Corp.*

FIGURE 10–37 The Teletype Inktronic solid–state non-impact printer, which operates at 120 characters per second. *Courtesy of Teletype Corp.*

FIGURE 10-38   A person can "talk" with the company computer from the convenience of
his office by using a Honeywell COM-PACT computer terminal, a device
that is acoustically coupled through any standard telephone. The computer, through its audio response unit, provides answers that the user hears
through the terminal's speaker. The portable unit can be operated by its
own batteries or plugged in to any 110-volt electric outlet. *Courtesy of
Honeywell Electronic Data Processing Division.*

an attaché case can be connected to a computer through a telephone headset
acoustically coupled to the terminal. One such portable terminal is shown in
Figure 10-38. These terminals allow the user to dial the computer he wishes to
use by telephone and to communicate with it, whatever his location. The
terminals typically communicate at 10 characters a second or less.

The number of all kinds of terminals in use in 1970 was estimated to be
600,000, and it is predicted that there will be two million terminals in use in
1975 for on-line input, conversational time-sharing and remote batch computing.[20] The trend in terminals, as well as with most peripheral equipment,
is to include more digital circuitry built into the terminal. This trend may be
accelerated by the availability of LSI in the next few years.

The output of a computer must necessarily be readable by humans. The
medium selected should be in keeping with the way the data will be utilized.
Thus, archival files—where minimum physical size and high information density
are important—might require microfilm output. On the other hand, a readout
of the status of a process that has only temporary significance could best be
obtained from a line or strip printer, or perhaps a CRT terminal. Output
printers offer insufficient speed of reproduction and they use massive amounts

of paper. For these reasons, the use of microfilm offers many advantages. A computer output microfilm device (COM) is any unit of hardware which produces a microfilm record from information provided by a computer. (Microfilm is any film up to 105 mm—commonly 16mm film—with images that must be enlarged 8 to 40 times to be equivalent to normal paper documents. Microfilm can be in rolls or chips, or can be mounted in other carriers.[21])

Alphanumeric COM devices are primarily used as substitutes for impact printers. Whereas an impact printer can produce 2400 characters per second, COM devices can write characters at rates up to 500,000 characters per second. Since a large percentage of the information generated is for reference only, there are extensive savings in the cost of film compared to paper. Binding expenses, as well as storage and shipping costs, are also minimized by the reduction in the bulk and weight of the recording medium.

Graphic COM devices are used to make bar charts, graphs, and drawings. Typesetting characters, company logos, and half-tone pictures are further examples of graphic output. The programming capability of COM devices also makes them well adapted for producing animated movies, an application that is becoming increasingly popular.[21]

The distinct advantages of COM relative to impact printers are shown in Figures 10-39 and 10-40.[22] COM gives hard copy output after the film has been exposed and processed. (*Hard copy*, in this context, refers to a copy printed in readable form, on paper, offset masters or other forms of material.) A computer output microfilmer is shown in Figure 10-41. The model shown is a relatively lower-priced unit which films alphanumerics at a rate of 13,000 lines per minute. It is estimated that expenditures for COM were $100 million in 1970 and may grow to over a billion dollars by 1975.[23]

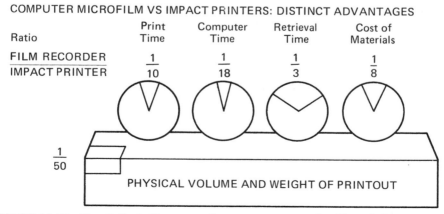

COMPUTER MICROFILM VS IMPACT PRINTERS: DISTINCT ADVANTAGES

Ratio	Print Time	Computer Time	Retrieval Time	Cost of Materials
FILM RECORDER / IMPACT PRINTER	$\frac{1}{10}$	$\frac{1}{18}$	$\frac{1}{3}$	$\frac{1}{8}$

$\frac{1}{50}$

PHYSICAL VOLUME AND WEIGHT OF PRINTOUT

FIGURE 10-39   The distinct advantages of computer output microfilm relative to an output printer. From *Proceedings of the Fall Joint Computer Conference, 1969. Courtesy of American Federation of Information Processing Societies.*

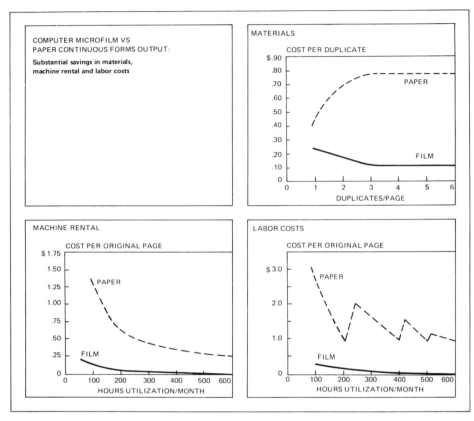

FIGURE 10–40   The substantial savings in materials, machine rental and labor costs for computer microfilm versus continuous paper output. From *Proceedings of the Fall Joint Computer Conference, 1969. Courtesy of American Federation of Information Processing Societies.*

The primary application of COM devices is information storage for random, infrequent retrieval.[24] COM is used at Houston's Manned Spacecraft Center for many applications as shown in Figure 10-42, for storing massive amounts of data and documents.[25] A comparison of the costs of computer microfilm and continuous paper output is given in Table 10-2.[22] Furthermore, a COM information retrieval system compares very favorably with a time-sharing computer system, as shown in Figure 10-43. The comparison depends upon the numbers of pages that must be stored, the number that must be brought up to date each month and the number of users of the system. The active use of microfilm for the storage and retrieval of information in daily use has been practiced by some users and companies for years. For the most part, these have been extremely large users (*e.g.*, Social Security Administration). In the future we can expect a growing use of computer output microfilm systems.

FIGURE 10-41 The Peripheral Technology Computer Output Microfilmer Model 1300, which films on 16mm film from magnetic tapes with the output from the computer. The unit films 13,000 lines per minute. *Courtesy of Peripheral Technology, Inc.*

It would be helpful if we could talk directly with computers. Recently, there has been some development of devices that can lead ultimately to computer input units capable of recognizing human speech, and to computer output units capable of generating "voices." A computer system that can identify words in continuous speech of an unknown speaker is beyond the current state of the art in speech recognition. However, limited speech–recognition systems have been developed on an experimental basis. The problems involved in the design of voice–response systems are less formidable than those encountered in the development of voice–recognition systems.[27] Voice–recognition systems are difficult to design since they must account for each person's variation in speech patterns, pitch and intensity.

Voice–response systems are based on analog recording of a few selected phrases and words or on digitally–controlled synthesis of speech. One commercially available system, the IBM 7772, consists of 15 digitally–controlled frequencies, or voice pitches, covering the telephone voice band. The audio signals are combined and applied to the listener's telephone set. Voice–response systems are often used with remote–access computer systems.

Voice–recognition systems will probably be developed first for specialized applications such as manned space flight.[28] The human voice is a desirable means of communication with a computer since it uses a human's natural language, leaves his limbs free for other purposes, and is more rapid than typing at a terminal.[25]

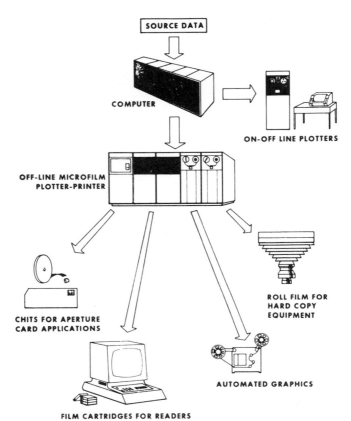

FIGURE 10–42   The Manned Spacecraft Center's Computer Output Microfilm Unit, which
is used to store the massive records of space flight.

TABLE 10–2

Comparison of Costs of Computer Microfilm and
Continuous Paper Output

5,000 PAGES	VOLUME	APPROXIMATE ANNUAL STORAGE COST
MICROFILM	0.10 Ft^3	$0.05
PAPER	4.50 Ft^3	$4.15
5,000 PAGES	WEIGHT	APPROXIMATE FIRST CLASS MAIL COST
MICROFILM	3.0 Lbs.	0.03¢ / mile
PAPER	150.0 Lbs.	4.05¢ / mile

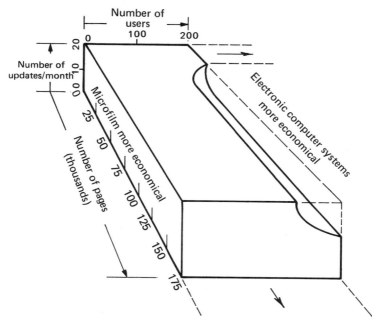

FIGURE 10-43   Computer-generated microfilm versus time-sharing computer systems as a storage and retrieval system. From *Proceedings of the Fall Joint Computer Conference, 1969. Courtesy of American Federation of Information Processing Societies.*

Currently, voice–response systems are being used as a voice answering service for banks, insurance companies and other businesses. The use of an audio response unit is more suitable than the use of a CRT display, a Teletype or some other type of printer in areas where short and simple replies to remote inquiries are required and where no need exists for computer interaction or hard–copy output as in a telephone booth, in a patrol car, or on board a plane. The selection of a particular type of audio device must be based on the area of application and whether it fits the requirement of a limited vocabulary and relatively simple responses. Perhaps voice I/O systems for computers will be common within this decade.

A useful and common output device is the computer graphic plotter. This device provides the user with visual plots, graphs and drawings on paper. One example of a graphic plotter is shown in Figure 10–44. A pen is driven by electronic circuitry controlled by the computer. It writes directly on paper. Plotter accuracy is about ± .01 inch and plotters operate at speeds from 20 inches/minute to 1500 inches/minute. Two drawings obtained from computer plotter output are shown in Figures 10–45a and 10–45b. The plotter is a very useful tool for permanently recording graphic relationships.

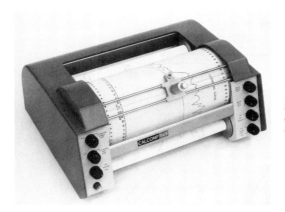

FIGURE 10-44   The CALCOMP 565 Plotter drawing a learning curve. *Courtesy of California Computer Products, Inc.*

FIGURE 10-45a   A graph of a population pyramid for demographic studies—University of Michigan. *Courtesy of California Computer Products, Inc.*

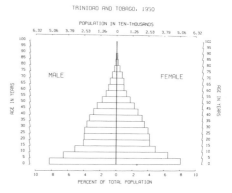

FIGURE 10-45b   Three-axis graph showing relationship between two sets of data—University of Washington. *Courtesy of California Computer Products, Inc.*

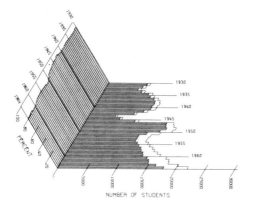

Remote-access computer systems, such as time-sharing computers, require a communication facility to connect the remote terminal to the CPU and main storage. This peripheral device, while not an I/O device, is a fundamental portion of the I/O system in a remote-access system. As Mr. Sam Wyly recently stated:

> In the immediate future, knowledge, rather than capital, labor or raw materials, will become the major source of economic growth. Knowledge, not things, will become the new basis of productivity. It will become the force which drives our economy. And the computer, as the central organizer and repository of information, will play a massive role in this new society. But it is an exercise in futility to have massive data banks if we don't have the data transmission capacity to make their information immediate, accessible, and universal. Unless we find a fast, efficient, reliable means of transporting digital data (*i.e.*, knowledge) between computers, data banks, and terminals, we will severely limit our opportunities to make the computer a major instrument in human service during the 1970's.

Several alternate approaches to communication between remote access I/O devices and the CPU I/O system are shown in Figure 10-46. Common carrier telephone channels are used for data transmission, and it has been estimated that in the near future half of the information transmitted over telephone lines will be digital computer data, as contrasted with human voice transmission. One device often used with telephone connections is called a *modem*, which is a contraction of "modulator-demodulator," and is one name ("data set" is the other) for the units which modulate the series of data from a computer or terminal for transmission through the common carrier network. If a computer has only one port, or connection, to the network, a modem at the computer site and one modem at each remote site are the only required communications peripherals. In Table 10-3, we have a comparison of the communication speeds of a human, a communication transmission system and a computer. [29] Notice that a telephone is limited to transmitting at rates of 120 to 400 characters/second, while a human is limited to typing at one to five characters per second. Clearly, the computer which accepts data at speeds up to 10^6 characters/second has a sufficient amount of time to accommodate many input channels from numerous simultaneous users.

The computer operator uses many of the input/output devices and peripherals. A recent study of the operator's activities shows that he spends about half of his time with activities related to the I/O units and peripherals. [16] In this study, the operators stated their preferences for equipment location in the computer room.

In Table 10-4, a summary of the approximate cost and range of speed of

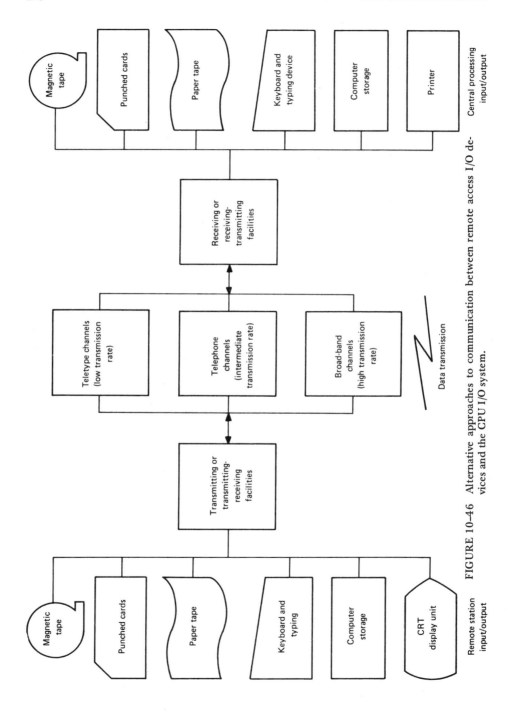

FIGURE 10-46 Alternative approaches to communication between remote access I/O devices and the CPU I/O system.

TABLE 10-3

A Comparison of the Communication Speeds of a Human, a Communication Transmission System and a Computer

Man	Transmission System	Machine (Third Generation Digital Computer)
A. His Communication Capabilities	A. Terminal I/O Equipment	A. Central Processing Unit
1. Sensing Senses	1. Telecom Typewriter	1. Execution rate 10^6–10^8
a. Speech: 5–20 char/sec	Printing Speed: 10–15 char/sec	2. Memory cycle time:
b. Handwriting: 3–10 char/sec	Char/line: 72–156	Microsec to nanosec
c. Typing: 1–5 char/sec	2. Cathode Ray Tube (CRT)	3. Core memory capacity:
2. Receiving Senses	Display Speeds: 240–100,000	10^5–10^7
a. Sight	char/sec	B. Peripheral Storage
–Pictorial: Very fast	Total no. of char:	1. Access Speed: Up to
–Reading: 10–15 char/sec	1,000–4,000	$300(10)^3$ char/sec
b. Hearing: Fast	3. Remote Batch Printers	2. Capacity:
B. His Memory Capabilities	Printing Speed:	Up to $1.60(10)^9$ char
a. Total Storage: Up to $(10)^{15}$ char	600–660 char/sec	
b. Prompt Recall: 1–10% of total	B. Telephone Network	
c. Speed of Recall:	1. Voice Grade – Single Channel	
–Up to 10% fast; remainder	Speed: 120–400 char/sec	
slow (and inaccurate)	2. Broad Bank – Multi-Channel	
C. His Psychological Reactions	Speed: Up to 23,000 char/sec	
a. Rational – Likely predictable		
b. Emotional – Unlikely predictable		

TABLE 10–4

Input/Output Devices

Name	Approximate Cost 1	Speed Range 2
Teletypewriter	Low	10 characters/second
Punched Paper Tape Reader	Low	100–1000 characters/second
Punched Paper Tape Punch	Low	100–300 characters/second
Punched Card Readers	Medium	100–1600 cards/minute
Punched Card Punches	Medium	60–500 cards/minute
Line Printers	Medium	200–1200 lines/minute
Mark Sensing	Low-Medium	100–1000 cards/minute
Magnetic Character Reader	Medium	300 mag. cards/minute = 2700 punch cards/minute
Optical Character Reader	High	2400 sheets/hour
Graphical Plotters	Low-Medium	20–1500 inches/minute
Visual Displays	Medium-High	60 frames/second
Computer Output Microfilmer	High	10–30,000 lines/minute

[1] Low cost = $1,000 – $5,000
  Medium cost = $5,000 – $25,000
  High cost = greater than $25,000

[2] Speed: 5,000 electric typewriters = 30 Impact Line Printers = 1 COM

various input/output devices is given. During the next five years, it is expected that the number of remote terminals and data transmission facilities will increase markedly. Also, it is expected that microfilm equipment will replace many of the slower impact line printers. Furthermore, the number of Optical Character Readers and keyboard–to–tape recorders in use will increase significantly.[13] Input/output systems are an important portion of a computer system. While they may be peripheral in location, they are central in importance to the proper and efficient functioning of a computer system.

10.4 STORAGE DEVICES

A major unit of a digital computer is the main storage unit, which is shown in Figure 10-1. A computer also often utilizes auxiliary storage units for aiding the input/output process. This section describes storage devices, some of the components of storage devices, and some of the trends in the development of storage units. The definition of storage is:

STORAGE   (1) Holding of information; synonymous with *memory*. (2) Pertaining to a device into which information can be entered, in which it can be held, and from which it can be retrieved.

In this section we consider only storage devices that can be used in conjunction with a computer. Also, we use the term "memory" interchangeably with "storage." Information entered into storage can be either data or instructions.

The ability of computers to process information and to solve problems is often limited by the need for access to data used in the solution of the problem. A single unit of information is the binary digit (bit), which is the measure of information stored in a given memory. The availability of storage has always set a limit on a computer's ability to communicate and to solve problems. Twenty-five years after the first generation of digital computers, the performance of computers is often limited by the size and speed of the memory. In the beginning, a few hundred bits of data-storage seemed like a large memory. Now, our information processing and problem-solving ambitions have grown, and we can use the far larger memories—up to a trillion bits—that are now available.

The main storage unit accepts data from an input unit, exchanges data with and supplies instructions to the central processing unit, and can furnish data to an output unit. All information to be processed by any system must pass through main storage. This unit must therefore have capacity to retain a usable amount of data and the necessary instructions for processing.

Applications may require additional storage. If so, the capacity of main storage is augmented by auxiliary storage units. All information to and from auxiliary storage must be routed through main storage. Storage is arranged somewhat like a group of numbered mail boxes in a post office.[30] Each box is identified and located by its number. Similarly, storage is divided into locations, each with an identifying number and a specified location. A given storage location will hold a specified number of bits. When information is entered into a storage location, it replaces the previous contents of that location. When information is read from a location, the contents remain unaltered. The process of taking or reading information from a storage location is often called *reading out* stored data.

The computer requires some time to locate and transfer information to or from storage. This interval of time required to read data is called access time; it is defined as follows:

ACCESS TIME (1) The time interval between the instant at which data are called for from a storage device and the instant delivery is completed; that is, the *read time*. (2) The time interval between the instant at which data are requested to be stored and the instant at which storage is completed, which is often called the *write time*.

The access time of a storage unit has a direct bearing on the efficiency of the computer system. The faster the arithmetic speed of a computer, the larger and faster must be the main storage unit.

Thus, these are two primary characteristics of computer main storage units: (1) the capacity of a storage unit, measured in bits, and (2) the access time of a storage unit, measured in seconds. The growth in capacity of storage for different media during the period 1940–1970 is shown in Figure 10–47. The media used for storage have progressed from the vacuum tube and the magnetic drum to advanced thin films and experimental holographic storage. The increase in the capacity has been by a factor of approximately 10^7. In Figure 10–48, we have the relationship between the capacity of various storage media and the related access time.[31] The main storage unit uses only storage

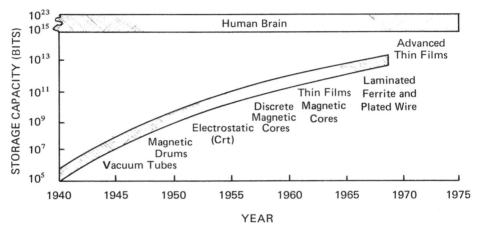

FIGURE 10–47 The capacity of storage media available during the period 1940–1970.

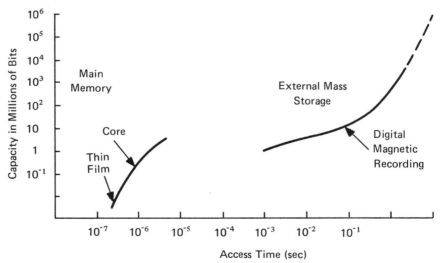

FIGURE 10–48 The capacity of storage media versus the access time associated with the media. Note the gap in the area of 10^{-4} second access time.

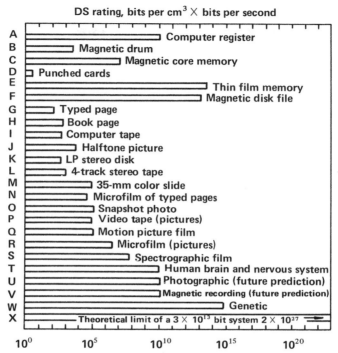

FIGURE 10–49 Density–speed ratings for different information storage methods. Density is given in bits/cm^3 and speed in bits/second.

devices that provide an access time of less than 10^{-6} seconds, since the CPU operates at that speed or faster.

A good measure of performance of a storage device is the density–speed factor, where the density of storage is given in bits per cubic volume and the speed is given in the rate of transfer of bits per second. Figure 10–49 illustrates the density–speed ratings for numerous storage devices.[31] The genetic storage of nature is the present standard—but notice that a magnetic disk file and a thin film memory approach it in performance.

Of course, one always pays a price for rapid access to data. The relationship between cost per bit of storage and the access time required is shown in Figure 10–50.[31] Notice that if we wish to decrease the access time from 10^{-3} to 10^{-7} (by a factor of 10^4) then the cost increases, relatively, by a factor of almost 10^3.

Each bit of information is stored in a physical device capable of being in one of two stable states. The binary media can store their binary information in a physical device, a circuit or a region of a physical material. Most main storage units consist of *magnetic core* storage units. A magnetic core is defined as follows:

MAGNETIC CORE   A configuration of magnetic material that is placed in a spatial relationship to current–carrying conductors and whose magnetic properties are to be used for storage purposes.

An example of a magnetic core is shown in Figure 10-51a, where the direction of magnetization is indicated by the arrow. The magnetization is reversed by reversing the current direction, as shown in Figure 10-51b. Thus the magnetic core is capable of two directions of magnetization; it is a binary device. The direction of magnetization is retained when the current is removed; therefore the storage is of a permanent nature. Core storage is the most expensive storage device in terms of cost per storage location. However, core storage also provides the fastest access time; thus, it may be the most economical in terms of cost per machine calculation.

A magnetic core is a tiny ring of ferromagnetic material, a few hundredths of an inch in diameter. Cores are placed like beads on sets of wires. Because

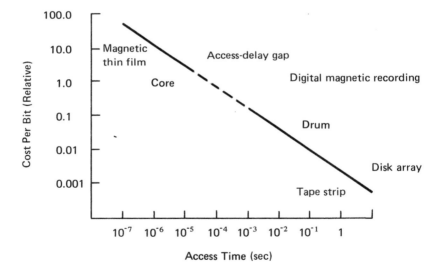

FIGURE 10-50   The cost per bit of access time in a storage unit.

FIGURE 10-51   Magnetic core storage. (a) Core magnetized in one direction. (b) Magnetization of the core reversed by the current, which itself has been reversed.

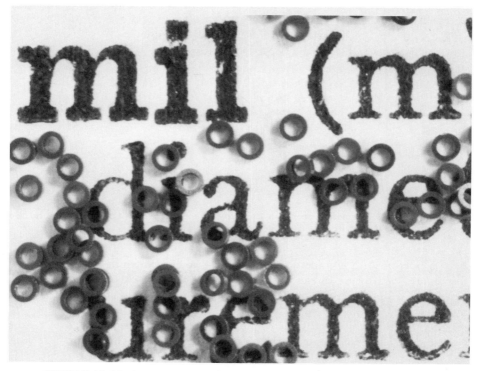

FIGURE 10-52   Magnetic cores of 18 mil diameter. *Courtesy of Ampex Corp.*

any specified location of storage must be instantly accessible, the cores are arranged so that any combination of ones (1's) and zeros (0's) representing a character can be "written" magnetically or read back when needed. A collection of magnetic cores is shown in Figure 10-52. The cores are only 18 thousandths of an inch in diameter.

To magnetize a specific core, two wires run through each core at right angles to each other as shown in Figure 10-53. When half the current needed to magnetize a core is sent through each wire, only the core at the intersection of the wires is magnetized. No other core in the string is affected. Using this principle, a large number of cores can be strung on a screen of wires, yet any single core in the screen can be selected for storage or reading without affecting any other. In the computer, the cores are magnetized by a pulse of electrical current sent through the two wires, which is said to "flip" the binary element. A sense wire, shown in Figure 10-53, is added to the arrangement for detecting whether a core contains a 1 or a 0. This wire is strung through all the wires in a given plane of cores. A group of cores mounted on sense and write wires is shown in Figure 10-54.

SENSE WIRE

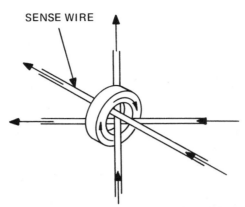

FIGURE 10-53   A magnetic core, with the two magnetizing wires at right angles, and the sense wire.

A portion of a complete core memory plane is shown in Figure 10-55. In this figure, each plane carries 4000 cores. Other units use 16,384 cores in each plane, and 70 planes. Such a seventy-core plane would hold approximately one million bits.

By far the majority of main storage units utilize magnetic cores as the storage device. The decrease in the memory access time for magnetic core storage for the period 1953-1969 is shown in Figure 10-56. Also, the cost of a constant size (10^6 bit) core memory has decreased from 20¢ per bit in 1957 to approximately 7¢ per bit in 1970.[33]

The prime requirements for main storage units are rapid access time and reasonably large memory capacity. Magnetic thin-film devices are used for main storage units, since they meet these requirements. A thin film of magnetic material is deposited on a surface and a physical location serves as a memory location. One commercially available thin-film memory uses a thin magnetic film on a beryllium copper wire six thousandths of an inch in diameter. These wires, or metal whiskers, are shown in Figure 10-57. Each wire, .110 inch in length, is used for a single bit in a memory plane. The memory built from the thin-film whiskers operates with an access time of 800 nanoseconds. Thin-film plated wire cost is approximately $.06 per bit, which is approximately equal to the cost of magnetic cores. Plated-film wire memories currently possess an access time of 200 to 800 nanoseconds.

Another potential device for use as a main storage unit is a semiconductor memory, particularly a unit fabricated from integrated circuits. As we learned in section 10.2, semiconductor devices are fast and small. However, the price per bit of semiconductor memories has thus far limited the use of semiconductor main storage units to special applications. Semiconductor memory prices can be reduced by large volume production and the use of large-scale integra-

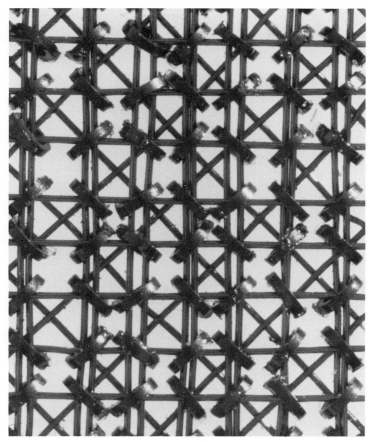

FIGURE 10-54   Magnetic cores mounted on the sense and write wires. *Courtesy of Ampex Corp.*

tion (LSI). With the evolution of LSI, the expected evolution of semiconductor memories is expected to bring lower-priced semiconductor memories into use as main storage units. It is expected that semiconductor memories will be available within the first half of the decade at a price of $.02 per bit and with a capacity of 100,000 bits.[4] The access time of these memories may be as low as 40 nanoseconds.[34] An example of an integrated circuit memory device is shown in Figure 10-58. These integrated circuit devices are assembled in memory modules as shown in Figure 10-59. This memory unit has a capacity of approximately 250,000 bits and possesses an access time of 40 nanoseconds. The IBM System 370 Model 145, announced in June, 1970 incorporates a main memory of integrated circuits. The access time of this main storage is 540 nanoseconds.

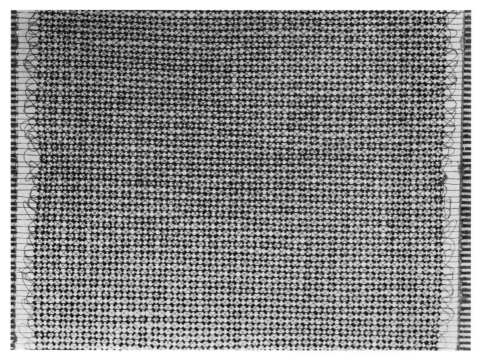

FIGURE 10-55   A portion of a magnetic core memory plane (approximately 1/3 size) used
in an electronic computer. One such plane has more than 4,000 cores, each
threaded by four enamel–coated wires. Vertical and horizontal wires carry
electrical charges which magnetize or demagnetize selected cores under
control of the computer. Diagonal wires "sense" which cores are magnetized, thereby enabling the computer to "read" the contents of its memory
while processing data at electronic speeds. *Courtesy of General Electric Co.*

The question of reliability of semiconductor memories remains to be
answered by experience. However, it is expected that semiconductor memories
will grow in importance during the 1970's.

The expected performance of magnetic cores, magnetic thin–films and
integrated circuit memories for 1972 is shown in Figure 10-60.[31] The usefulness of core memories for large, moderate speed main storage memories is
clear. The thin–film memories and lower–capacity semiconductor memories
will together help to meet the needs for rapid–access memory components.

The main storage unit stores data which is accessible at any time and for
which access is independent of the location of the data. A storage device for
which access time is independent of the storage location of the data is a *random
access* storage device. Random access is defined as follows:

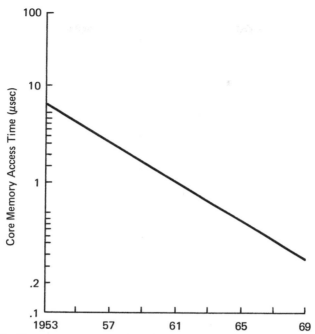

FIGURE 10-56 The memory access time for magnetic core storage for the period 1953–1969.

RANDOM ACCESS Obtaining data from, or placing data into, storage when the time required for such access is independent of the location of the data most recently obtained or placed into storage. Synonymous with *direct access.*

Main storage units require that random access is part of the operation of the storage system. This requirement is necessary because of the high speed of the CPU and the necessity of keeping the memory operating at the same rate as the CPU.

There are quite a few applications where the storage of information does not necessitate immediate and random access. Storage units that do not possess the quality of random access may often be used as auxiliary storage. Storage devices not providing random access to a storage location usually store information in a specified sequence and require that the computer proceed sequentially through all the storage locations between the present location of the reading device and the location desired. Storage devices operating in this manner are magnetic tape drives and magnetic data–cell drives.

Magnetic disk storage units provide computer systems with the ability to

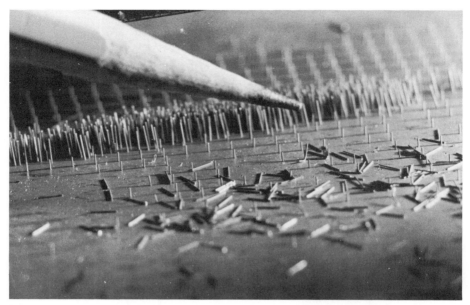

FIGURE 10-57   Thousands of metal "whiskers," the heart of a computer memory developed by NCR, are automatically put in place by a simple, ingenious
method. More than 4,600 tiny magnetic coated rods have to be put into
solenoid openings in the memory plane. A matrix with corresponding holes
is placed over the solenoids. Rods are poured onto the matrix plate and
the unit is drawn through a pulsating magnetic field. The rods stand on
end and quickly "dance" into the openings. Excess rods are swept off.
Courtesy of National Cash Register Corp.

record and retrieve stored data sequentially *or* directly with random access.
Disk units permit immediate access to specific locations of storage without the
need to examine sequentially all recorded data. The magnetic disk is a thin
metal disk coated on both sides with magnetic recording material. The disks
are mounted on a vertical shaft separated from one another to provide the
space necessary for the movement of the read/write arms. The shaft revolves at
a high speed, spinning the disks. Information is stored as magnetized spots in
concentric tracks on the surface of each disk. Some units have 500 tracks on
each surface. The information is accessible for reading or writing by positioning
the read/write head on the access arm between the spinning disks. Each time
new information is stored, the old information is erased. The IBM 2311 disk
drive shown in Figure 10-61 uses an interchangeable disk pack which can be
seen through the plastic cover. Six disks are mounted as a disk pack which can
be readily removed from the 2311 Disk Drive and stored in a library of disk
packs in much the same manner as reels of magnetic tape may be stored. The
packs are 14 inches in diameter and weigh less than ten pounds. Each of the

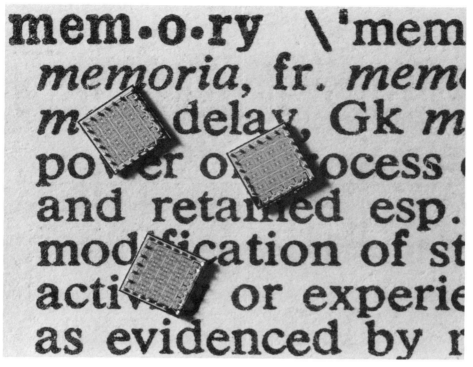

FIGURE 10-58 Memory storage circuits are diffused into the surface of a single silicon chip measuring less than an eighth of an inch square (shown above on a dictionary page*). Each chip—containing 664 individual components such as transistors, diodes, and resistors—provides 64 memory storage cells. These circuits are so minute that 53,000 components can fit into one square inch.

*By permission. From *Webster's Seventh New Collegiate Dictionary* © 1969 by G. & C. Merriam Co., Publishers of the Merriam–Webster Dictionaries.) *Courtesy of IBM Corp.*

ten recording surfaces contains 200 data recording tracks. The disks turn at 2,400 revolutions per minute. Up to 7.25 million characters of information can be stored in each disk pack.

The access time of disk storage units ranges from 10 to 100 milliseconds. The capacity of disk units ranges from 10^7 to 5×10^9 bits. The approximate storage cost is $.0005 per bit. Thus, disk storage units provide bulk storage at a low cost per bit and possess a relatively slow access time.

For massive amounts of storage a number of disk units are combined, as in Figure 10-62. This unit consists of nine drives and a control unit. Any eight of the drives can be on line at a time. The ninth drive is available for backup if one of the other drives requires servicing or maintenance. The device uses re-

FIGURE 10-59   Seventy-two monolithic memory modules, together with drive and sense
modules, are packaged on a 7" X 9" multilayered pluggable card (left) with
a 512-word X 18-bit capacity. Sixteen storage cards and four logic and
terminating cards make up the basic storage unit (background) of 2,048
words X 72 bits. Two units form the complete one-quarter million bit
memory. Access time for this memory is 40 nanoseconds. *Courtesy of
IBM Corp.*

movable disk packs similar to those on the IBM 2311. The packs are larger,
however, each consisting of eleven disks, with 20 of the surfaces used for recording. Each surface has 200 data recording tracks. Up to 58 million bits of
information can be stored on each disk pack.

For bulk storage, a unit called a data cell drive or strip file is often used.
A data cell drive which is shown in Figure 10-63, stores several hundred strips
of magnetic film approximately two inches wide and twelve inches long. The
strips can be seen inside the window of the device. Individual strips can be retrieved by the device and information can be stored on the 200 tracks available
on each strip.

The cell drive can accommodate up to ten data cells. It positions the
selected cell under the retrieval mechanism. Cells may be removed and replaced with others containing different files. Each of the drives shown in Figure

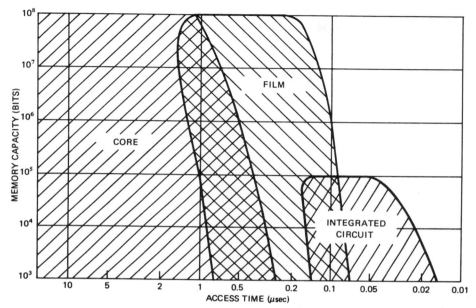

FIGURE 10-60 The memory capacity versus access time of a main storage unit using magnetic cores, magnetic film, and integrated circuits. The shaded areas are the expected performance areas for 1972.

10-63 has a capacity for storing up to 40 million characters. The access time for reading a storage location is six-tenths of a second.

Strip files have a capacity in the range of 2 to 5 × 10⁹ bits and the approximate cost per bit is $.00005.[35]

Magnetic tape is a very common auxiliary storage medium. In addition, magnetic tape units are often used as input/output devices in order to avoid avoid coupling slower I/O units to the central processor and main storage. The input is placed on the tape in an offline operation and all the input is then read into the main storage from the tape. Similarly, the output results will often be stored on tape until a later time when the results are printed out from the stored tape. A library of magnetic tapes is shown in Figure 10-64.

Magnetic tape is much faster than punched tape or cards, with read speeds from five to 100 times greater than cards. Along with its high speed—often in the order of 10,000 characters per second—magnetic tape has a much greater capacity than the other high–speed I/O devices. This can be a significant edge when large quantities of data require reloading the I/O device during a run. For example, a 2,400-foot reel of tape having a low packing density of 200 bits per inch will hold about as much data as 20,000 cards. The operator of a 1,000-card–capacity card hopper would have to load the cards 20 times to equal the

FIGURE 10-61   The IBM 2311 disk storage drive, showing the disk pack and the access arms. *Courtesy of IBM Corp.*

FIGURE 10-62   The IBM 2314 multiple disk storage system. *Courtesy of IBM Corp.*

capacity of one such roll of magnetic tape. The difference would also be reflected in computer productivity. At higher densities, magnetic–tape capacity grows to that of 400,000 cards.

In tape recording, the magnetic material usually consists of tiny needle-like particles of gamma ferric oxide with an average length of about 24 microinches and diameter of 4 microinches. These are mixed with a plastic binder and coated onto a thin strip of "base" material which is usually polyethylene terephthalate, more commonly known as "polyester" or "Mylar." The base material for computer applications is 1 milliinch thick and 1/2 inch wide. Most tape coatings are 0.5 to 0.6 milliinches thick with oxide density of about 1/3 of the total. This material is magnetized by a recording head as the tape passes by

FIGURE 10-63   The IBM 2321 strip
file. *Courtesy of IBM Corp.*

FIGURE 10-64   Data recorded on magnetic tape may be stored in a tape library. *Courtesy of National Cash Register Co.*

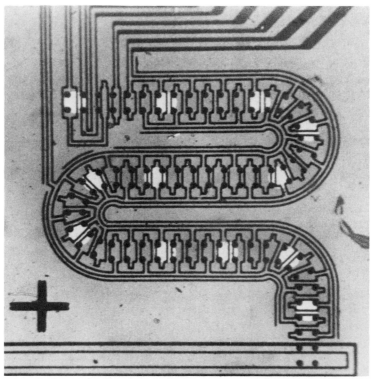

FIGURE 10-65 Tiny computers of the future may accomplish counting, switching, memory and logic functions all within one solid magnetic material, employing
new technology now in exploratory development. This actual circuit, on
the surface of a sheet of thulium orthoferrite, can move magnetic bubbles, four thousandths of an inch in diameter, through a shift register.
Courtesy of Bell Telephone Laboratories.

the head. Recovering the information from a tape is essentially the reverse of
the recording process; the recorded magnetization produces a current in the
head winding. Magnetic tape on reels has practically unlimited capacity, but
access time is slow because it may be necessary to move much tape or even to
change reels to find desired information. Therefore, it is difficult to give an
average access time for a tape. We can estimate the average access time by
letting the access time equal the ratio of one-half the length of the tape to the
tape speed. This estimate assumes that on the average one would have to search
through half the length of the tape to locate a specific stored item. On this
basis, for a 2400 foot tape operating at 112.5 inches/second, the average access
time is approximately 120 seconds. Obviously one does not wish to use tape
storage for direct or random access because of this long access time. Magnetic

tape is used primarily for storing sequential data—that is, information in a pre-arranged series of stored items. As a sequential input device, a tape drive provides an input speed in the range of 30,000 to 300,000 characters/second. A magnetic tape unit is shown above in Figure 10-25. This unit records 1600 characters/inch of tape.

Recently, tape recorders which use cassettes rather than reels have been developed. Digital cassette tape recorders store the data on a magnetic tape held within an interchangeable cassette. Because they are smaller and more limited in capacity than reel-to-reel tapes, cartridges and cassettes are especially useful where small capacity is sufficient and computer time is not a factor, as is the case with small computers. As I/O devices, they are ideal for low-speed data collection and auxiliary storage. Most cartridges and cassettes are narrower than standard computer tapes and therefore have fewer tracks. Digital cassette recorders are potential replacements for punched paper tape since the cost is about the same and the cassette tape is three to five times as fast. Typical digital cassette recorders operate at a tape speed of 20 inches/second and record 800 bits/inch.

There is a continuing need for improved and less expensive memories. Experimental storage devices are being developed. One such storage device, shown in Figure 10-65, utilizes magnetic "bubbles" that move. The bubbles are locally-magnetized areas that can move about in thin plates of orthoferrite, a magnetic material. In present computer and communication technology, connections between electronic components are a major factor in costs. In the new technology, the bubbles can be created, erased, and moved anywhere in thin sheets without interconnection. They may interact with one another in a controlled fashion, and their presence or absence can be detected. Therefore, devices employing the new technology could be made to perform a variety of functions, such as logic, memory, switching or counting, all within one solid magnetic material.[36, 37]

The energy needed to manipulate the bubbles can either be applied by current-carrying conductors or it can be picked up from a surrounding magnetic field by microscopic "ferromagnetic antennae" in printed patterns distributed over the surface of the material. As the bubbles are moved into precisely defined positions, their presence or absence at different positions can represent binary numbers.

Bubbles of a size corresponding to only a few wavelengths of light can be manipulated. These lead to memory densities of about 1 million bits per square inch. The energy required to move, or switch, such a bubble is minute—a fraction of that needed to switch a transistor. Data rates of 3,000,000 bits per second have been demonstrated with this technology.[36]

As digital computers continue to grow in complexity and size, memory storage will have to be increased significantly at no sacrifice in speed. This means the information will have to be packed much more densely. With a laser

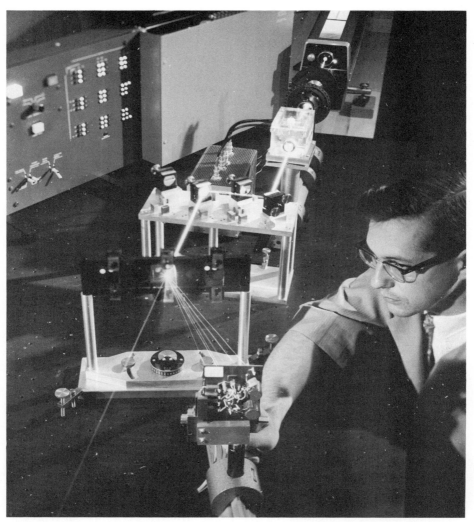

FIGURE 10-66 The feasibility model of an experimental optical memory system, which transmits blocks of computer–interpretable information in ten-millionths of a second, is inspected by an engineer. In the experimental system, information recorded on a holographic plate is produced one thousand times quicker than it is by conventional auxiliary storage devices. The intensive light of the laser is controlled and directed to a holographic plate where the beam is split. Informational light beams emerging from the hologram are directed to a light–sensitive detector array. The optical information is converted to electronic signals and used by the computer's central processor. More than 100 million bits of information could be placed on a nine square inch holographic plate. *Courtesy of IBM Corp.*

beam and the new science of holography, an optical memory is being explored whose ultimate storage capacity is predicted to be in excess of 100 million bits of data, and whose random access time may ultimately be as short as 1 micro-second. Holograms make use of a high–energy laser beam to store or display three–dimensional images. Holograms overcome the shortcomings of optical techniques that employ conventional photography. With the latter, lenses must be used, and microphotographs are vulnerable to dust and scratches, which can cause loss of data. Holograms do not require lenses; they are self–focusing. The image can be easily read by a photodetector, and information is stored re-dundantly. Even if part of a hologram is destroyed or obscured, the remainder can still contain a complete record of the data stored in it.

The holographic storage array is made on a special recording medium somewhat similar to conventional photographic film. This process starts with the construction of a data mask that represents the contents of a page. Each mask is basically an array of pinholes, blocked where we want zeros and trans-parent where ones are needed. Each data mask is recorded holographically, one at a time, on the recording medium. Information is retrieved from the memory by projecting the data recorded on the hologram onto a light–sensitive de-tector. The detector converts the optical information into electronic signals that the computer can process. An experimental laser–holographic memory sys-tem is shown in Figure 10–66.

The characteristics of storage units are compared in Table 10–5. The pri-

TABLE 10–5

Comparison of Storage Unit Characteristics

	Average Capacity (Bits)	Average Access Time (seconds)	Average Cost (cents/bit)
A. Main Storage Units			
1. Magnetic Cores	10^7	1.0×10^{-6}	7
2. Thin Magnetic Films	10^6	$.8 \times 10^{-6}$	6
3. Semiconductor Integrated Circuits	10^5	$.1 \times 10^{-6}$	20
B. Auxiliary Storage Units			
1. Magnetic Disk Units	10^9	.10	.05
2. Magnetic Strip Files	3×10^9	.60	.005
3. Magnetic Tape Drives	10^{10}	100	.01
C. Experimental Storage Devices			
1. Magnetic Bubbles	10^7	1×10^{-6}	—
2. Holographic Storage	10^8	1×10^{-6}	—

mary characteristic of the main storage unit devices is the access time of a microsecond or less. The auxiliary storage units possess access times of one-tenth of a second or greater, but provide low-cost bulk storage. The ability of the computer to process information is closely related to the ability to access masses of stored information. The main storage devices provide the computer with a memory which is rapidly accessible and the auxiliary storage devices provide a memory for the masses of data that can be used less often and for which more time can be allowed for obtaining any data item.

CHAPTER 10 PROBLEMS

P10-1.   Define the following items:
(1) hardware system
(2) solid-state component
(3) transistor
(4) microsecond
(5) Input/Output System

P10-2.   Sketch the interconnection of the four major units of a computer system and the information and control paths.

P10-3.   If a computer was the size of a room, 15 feet by 20 feet, in 1955, what size would you expect for an equivalent computer in 1970?

P10-4.   If a given computer worked an average of 10 hours without failure in 1955, what would you expect for an average time to failure for an equivalent computer in 1970?

P10-5.   Using Figure 10-20, determine the difference in the punched card code for the number 3, the letter C, and the special character - the period.

P10-6.   What is the ratio of speed of printing magnetic characters to the rate of punching punched cards in characters per second?

P10-7.   What are the uses of graphic plotters and visual displays? When would you use a graphic plotter and when a visual display if both devices were available in the computer center?

P10-8.   When would you use a computer output microfilmer in preference to line printer, if both were available in the computer center?

P10-9.   List several media that can be used with an input and output unit of a computer.

P10-10.   Define the following items:
(1) storage location
(2) access time
(3) random access

P10-11.   What characterizes the difference between a main storage unit and an auxiliary storage unit?

P10-12. What is the ratio of the capacity, in bits, of the human brain to the capacity of bulk storage devices such as the disk file or strip file?

P10-13. What is the ratio of the density-speed rating of the human brain to the density-speed rating of (1) the magnetic disk file (2) the magnetic core memory?

P10-14. What are the two primary characteristics of a main storage unit?

P10-15. How many bits can one magnetic core store?

P10-16. List one advantage and one disadvantage of a semiconductor main storage unit.

P10-17. What is the speed ratio of a magnetic tape input unit to a punched card input unit for a tape unit which provides 100,000 characters/second?

P10-18. Determine the ratio of the cost/bit of storage for a magnetic core memory to a magnetic tape drive. Why not replace a computer core storage unit with a tape drive?

CHAPTER 10 REFERENCES

1. E. Bloch, R. A. Henle, "Advances in Circuit Technology and their Impact on Computing Systems," *Proceedings of the International Federation of Information Processing Conference*, Edinburgh, 1968, pp. 24-39.

2. S. A. White, "Digital Adaptive-Element Building Blocks for MOS Large-Scale Integration," *IEEE Transactions on Computers*, Vol. C-18, No. 8, August 1968, pp. 699-704.

3. W. F. Sharpe, *The Economics of Computers*, Columbia University Press, New York, 1969.

4. "Smallest Electronics Advance in Years," *Electronic Design*, Jan. 4, 1970, pp. 25-28.

5. F. G. Withington, "Trends in MIS Technology," *Datamation*, Feb. 1970, pp. 108-119.

6. R. W. Keyes, "Physical Problems and Limits in Computer Logic," *IEEE Spectrum*, May, 1969, pp. 36-45.

7. "Impact of LSI on the next Generation of Computers," *Computer Design*, June, 1969, pp. 48-59.

8. M. J. Freiser and P. M. Marcus, "A Survey of Some Physical Limitations on Computer Elements," *IEEE Transactions on Magnetics*, Vol. Mag.-5, No. 2, June, 1969, pp. 82-90.

9. S. Triebwasser, "Large-Scale Integration and the Revolution in Electronics," *Science*, Vol. 163, No. 3866, Jan. 31, 1969, pp. 429-434.

10. W. A. Notz, E. Schischa, J. L. Smith, M. G. Smith, "LSI—Benefitting the System Designer," *Electronics*, Feb. 20, 1967, pp. 130-133.

11. H. G. Rudenberg, "Large-Scale Integration: Promises versus Accomplishments – The Dilemma of our Industry," *Proceedings of the Fall Joint Computer Conference*, 1969, AFIPS Press, Vol. 35, 1969, pp. 359–368.

12. S. Weber, "LSI: the Technologies Converge," *Electronics*, Feb. 20, 1967, pp. 124–127.

13. J. R. Dailey and H. C. Kuntzleman, "The Impact of Technology and Organization on Future Computer Systems," *Computer Design*, Feb., 1970, pp. 49–54.

14. T. M. Walker and W. W. Cotterman, *An Introduction to Computer Science and Algorithmic Processes*, Allyn and Bacon, Inc., Boston, 1970.

15. "Peripherals to Take More of Computer Dollar," *Control Engineering*, Oct., 1969, pg. 173.

16. M. L. Hanson, "Input/Output," *Sperry Rand Engineering Review*, Vol. 21, No. 4, 1968, pp. 2–9.

17. J. H. Levine, "Magnetic Characters for Data Entry," *Datamation*, May, 1969, pp. 81–89.

18. J. C. Rabinow, "Whither OCR?" *Datamation*, July, 1969, pp. 38–42.

19. R. C. Stender, "The Future Role of Keyboards in Data Entry," *Datamation*, June, 1970, pp. 60–72.

20. D. H. Surgan, "Terminals: On-line and Off, Conversational and Batch," *Control Engineering*, Feb. 1970, pp. 96–104.

21. G. H. Harmon, "Computer Output Microfilm Devices," *Modern Data*, Nov. 1969, pp. 98–104.

22. J. K. Koeneman and J. R. Schwanbeck, "Computer Microfilm—A Cost Cutting Solution to the EDP Output Bottleneck," *Proceedings of the Fall Joint Computer Conference*, 1969, Thompson Book Co., Washington, D. C., 1969, pp. 629–635.

23. "Computer, Microfilm Technologies Must Merge, COM Users Agree," *Computer World*, May 6, 1970, pg. 91.

24. C. P. Yerkes, "Microfilm—A New Dimension for Computers," *Datamation*, Dec. 1969, pp. 94–97.

25. T. A. Fuller, "COM at the Manned Spacecraft Center," *Datamation*, Dec. 1969, pp. 108–111.

26. D. M. Avedon, "An Overview of the Computer Output Microfilm Field," *Proceedings of the Fall Joint Computer Conference*, 1969, Thompson Book Co., Washington, D. C., 1969, pp. 613–622.

27. C. Weitzman, "Voice Recognition and Response Systems," *Datamation*, Dec. 1969, pp. 165–170.

28. W. A. Lea, "The Impact of Speech Communication with Computers," *Proceedings of the Sixth Space Congress*, 1969, N. A. S. A., Washington, D. C.

29. D. W. Cardwell, "Interactive Telecommunications Access by Computer," *Proceedings of the Fall Joint Computer Conference*, 1968, Thompson Book Co., Washington, D. C., 1968, pp. 243–253.

30. *Introduction to IBM Data Processing Systems*, International Business Machines Corp., White Plains, N. Y., 1967.

31. A. S. Hoagland, "Storing Computer Data," *International Science and Technology*, January 1965, pp. 52–58.

32. C. B. Pear, Jr., "Magnetic Recording–Reading and Writing for Computers," *IEEE Student Journal*, July 1968, pp. 30–38.

33. D. W. Brown and J. L. Burkhart, "The Computer Memory Market," *Computers and Automation*, January 1969, pp. 17–25.

34. R. D. Speer, "Memory Designers Looking to Semiconductors," *Electronic Design*, November 22, 1969, pp. 36–37.

35. F. D. Risko, "New Horizons for Magnetic Bulk Storage Devices," *Proceedings of the Fall Joint Computer Conference*, 1968, Thompson Book Co., Washington, D. C., 1968, pp. 1361–1367.

36. A. H. Bobeck, R. F. Fisher, A. J. Perneski, J. P. Remeika, L. G. Van Vitert, "Application of Orthoferrites to Domain Wall Devices," *IEEE Transactions on Magnetics*. Vol. MAG-5, No. 3, Sept. 1969, pp. 544–553.

37. A. H. Bobeck and H. E. D. Scovil, "Magnetic Bubbles," *Scientific American*, Vol. 224 No. 6, June 1971, pp. 78–90.

11

BUSINESS DATA PROCESSING AND MANAGEMENT INFORMATION SYSTEMS

11.1 BUSINESS DATA PROCESSING

The storage, processing, and reporting of data for business purposes, such as the routine financial transactions of a business, is called *business data processing*. As business operations become more complex, businessmen have found it advantageous to utilize the computer to process much of the data generated in the course of business operations. Business data processing is focused on the processing of *business* data, as they can be distinguished from other forms of data. Thus, business data processing is distinguished from data manipulation for purposes of government, education, or industrial process control. Of course, the line of demarcation is often a hazy one. However, we shall focus on the use of computers in business data processing for financial, accounting, banking and management purposes and thus restrictively define business data processing within these limits.

Business data are processed for output information. The manager or owner of a business operation needs information in order to (1) establish, evaluate and adjust business goals; (2) develop plans and standards and initiate action, and (3) measure actual performance and take appropriate action when required.[1] These three steps are part of the management process of any business enterprise.

The factors in business management which can be assisted by the utilization of a computer are fourfold.[2] First, there is the physical factor of large masses of data. A business generates data on raw material purchases, assets, accounts payable, inventories, shipping, billings, receipts and taxes, to name a few generators of masses of data.

Second, there is the element of time in the successful operation of a business. Many firms do not practice price competition as often as cost competition. It is extremely important to reduce cost by decreasing time required to produce an item and process the associated records. Business data processing can significantly affect the cost structure of a company where volume production is the rule by reducing the time taken for necessary records and reports.

Third, there is the use of computers to reduce the clerical work force. Clerical workers have increased in number during the past forty years in order to process and analyze data generated in business operations. The introduction of computers enables a business to maintain the cost of clerical operations within tolerable limits.

Finally, the error factor is of great importance. Many clerical and recording processes are tedious, and people performing them are prone to errors. Thus, the automation of such processes should lead to reduced errors in the operation of business.

The importance of rapid, low-cost business data processing with a low incidence of error is clear. Management of a business requires reliable and accurate information presented in an understandable form at the time it is needed. This is the natural objective of computer data processing in business.

The processing of business data may include several of the following nine steps:[1]

1. Originating and recording of data in form for computer processing
2. Placing data into appropriate classifications, such as sales data or tax data
3. Rearranging the data after it is classified into a predetermined sequence for processing; often called *sorting*
4. Arithmetic manipulation of the data, called *calculating*
5. Summarizing the data so that resulting reports will be concise and effective
6. Storing of data into appropriate storage locations for future reference
7. Retrieving the data from storage
8. Reproducing or duplicating the data in a report or document
9. Communicating data to a user or to another location in the form of a report or other form

As an example, let us consider the steps required to process sales data from a large department store. The data originates at the point of sale in the form of a sales ticket, which is then coded for machine input. Then the sales ticket, along with other sales tickets, is classified by product sold, location of sale, customer credit or cash payment as well as other data. The data may then be sorted by invoice number or by customer credit card number, for example. The calculation operation then calculates the charge to the customers' credit account as well as the total sale of the department store for that day. In this case, the summary step might include the summarizing of all the purchases of the customer. Then the information might be stored to be retrieved later, say at the end of the month, to produce a bill for each customer with a credit account. The process is illustrated graphically in Figure 11-1.

A computer may be used effectively with a business of any moderate size or larger. A computer is most efficiently used in business data processing operations with one or more of the following characteristics:

1. A large volume of input data is generated by business transactions on a regular basis.
2. The data processing operation is repeated many times, making it worthwhile to invest in developing and debugging the computer program.
3. The need for timely information provides the requirement of rapid processing needs.
4. There is a need for reliable and accurate output reports.

Perhaps the characteristic that most distinguishes the processing of scientific data is that business processing operations more normally involve large masses of input data and large amounts of output information. Business data processing is most efficient when a computer is used to perform repetitious tasks with large masses of data at rapid speeds.

The Wall Street Journal recently undertook a research survey project among its subscribers in order to provide information on the present availability and use of computers for business data processing.[3] Two-thirds of the respondents to the survey indicated that their companies now have one or more computers. Over 90% of the large companies possessed a computer while the proportion declined 27% for those companies employing fewer than 100 persons. The leading applications for the computer in the firms responding were accounting (76%); sales analysis (45%); and inventory control (43%).

Business and industry in the U.S. tripled expenditures for computers and associated operations during the period 1965-1970. Business in the U.S. spent approximately 25.5 billion dollars in 1970 to utilize computers for all purposes.[4] This figure is expected to increase to 51.5 billion dollars in 1975. Of $25.5 billion expended in 1970, $13 billion was for operating costs, $8.3 billion for equipment, and $2 billion for support services from outside the firms.

The use of computers by business firms is often necessary simply to keep even with the growing masses of data processed by the company. It has been estimated that the absolute number of business transactions and recordings is increasing at a rate between 8% to 15% per year.[5] The mass of data trans-

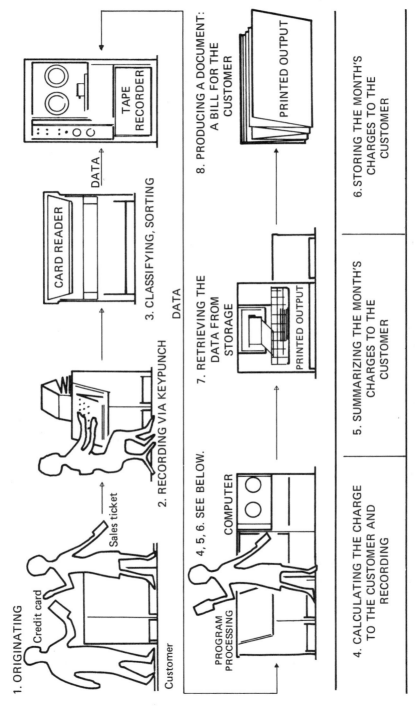

1. ORIGINATING

Credit card

Sales ticket

Customer

2. RECORDING VIA KEYPUNCH

3. CLASSIFYING, SORTING

CARD READER

DATA

TAPE RECORDER

DATA

4, 5, 6. SEE BELOW.

COMPUTER

PROGRAM PROCESSING

7. RETRIEVING THE DATA FROM STORAGE

PRINTED OUTPUT

8. PRODUCING A DOCUMENT: A BILL FOR THE CUSTOMER

PRINTED OUTPUT

4. CALCULATING THE CHARGE TO THE CUSTOMER AND RECORDING

5. SUMMARIZING THE MONTH'S CHARGES TO THE CUSTOMER

6. STORING THE MONTH'S CHARGES TO THE CUSTOMER

FIGURE 11-1   The business data processing sequence for producing a month's bill for a credit account customer of a department store.

mitted over communications lines has been growing at a rate of 25% a year or more. The problems of the volumes of business data is only partially overcome by large computer systems.

Computers are often required not only to handle the masses of data without error, but also to increase the productivity of a business. As an example, consider the airlines which have turned in the best productivity performance during the past decade—a classic case of economies of scale. With larger and faster planes, such carriers have been able to book a five-fold gain in operating revenues, to nearly $10–billion, while holding their labor force to less than double its 1960 size. Relatively little of that manpower boost represents additional flight crews. The real managerial problems, such as filling the seats in huge jets, have been on the ground. The only way airlines can approach full capacity is to perform prodigies of scheduling, which requires multimillion–dollar computer installations. With the aid of computers, airlines were able to increase their annual productivity at an average annual rate of 9.5% during the period 1960-1970.[5]

The basic organization of a business is often altered by the introduction of a computer. The changes take time to occur, as did the changes in industrial technology. But the inventions that brought on the industrial revolution about 200 years ago generally improved power or efficiency levels about 10 times in their initial applications. For example, an early steam pump was worth about 10 oxen; an automobile is about 10 times as fast as a horse; and an airplane is 10 times faster than an express train. The computer is a bigger step; it is nearly one million times faster than a mechanical calculator or the human brain. It costs a bank only 1/300th as much to post a check using a computer as to have a ledger clerk do it. Such efficiency comes at a price. Part of the cost is social: It comes from the industrialization of the office in a pattern similar to that found on assembly lines. In large banks, insurance companies and credit billing operations, the paperwork operation is strikingly factory-like, and its managers tend to talk in production–line terminology. Work tasks are fragmented until they become little more than keying an account number and a dollar amount onto a card.

Quite often knowledge of the total job is the prerogative of the computer analysts and programmers. So the computer fundamentally alters management structure in the administrative segments of business. It imposes a new level of functional management in the office that shatters traditional career paths. As John Diebold has recently commented:

> Automation's greatest consequence to business will be the enormous social change resulting from it. The entire role of business, its relation to human wants and its way of satisfying those wants depends upon society. Fundamental changes in society fundamentally change the role of business. Buying patterns, consump-

tion habits, and other social attitudes will be radically affected by the technology, and they, in turn, will produce decisive changes in business operations and methods.

It is the effect of computers on the social and economic life of the business process and nation that results in profound and unforseeable consequences for the next decade.

Often, business management conceives of computer data processing in restrictive mechanistic terms. Management places too much emphasis upon visualizing the computer as merely a superior accounting machine for handling functions previously performed manually. As important as such contributions are, they fall short of realizing the considerable potential inherent in present computer technology for management decision-making in a rapidly and radically changing business and social environment. A primary thesis of a recent book by John Diebold is that technology fosters not only changes in the manner in which business is conducted, but that in so doing, it also creates new business opportunities in turn.[6]

It is necessary to differentiate between the business system itself and the data processing operation of the business. Most businesses are processing matter and energy in order to produce a saleable product. The business brings in raw materials and reorders them into a product. A business data processing system, by contrast, translates data both from the environment and from within the firm for use by the firm. From 2000 B. C., when the Code of Hammurabi was drawn up, to the present, businessmen have been interested in obtaining information on the status of their businesses. Regardless of whether it has been called accounting or a code, it still constitutes a business data processing system. Hammurabi said, "If the merchant has given to the agent corn, wool, oil or any sort of goods to traffic with, the agent shall write down the price and hand over to the merchant; the agent shall take a sealed memorandum of the price which he shall give to the merchant."[7]

The business data processing systems of the period from the times of the Babylonian merchants to the last part of the 19th century were manual systems. The main tools of data processing were pencils, rulers, worksheets, journals and ledgers. Toward the last portion of the 19th century, typewriters and desk calculators became available for business data processing. Machines which could calculate and print the results were produced in 1890.[8] After World War I, accounting machines designed for billing, sales and other purposes began to appear. Punched card business equipment became readily available in the 1930's and dominated the field of business data processing until the late 1950's. The first digital computer acquired for business data processing was a UNIVAC-1, installed in 1954 at General Electric's Appliance Park in Louisville, Kentucky.[8]

The most widely used computer language for business applications is COBOL, which stands for COmmon Business Oriented Language. COBOL was first introduced in 1959 to become a self-documenting business data processing language. The word "common" in the name indicates that the language should be as compatible as possible among a large variety of computers. The important benefit of COBOL is the quantity and quality of documentation produced by the use of the language. However, the documenting quality does cause a program to be wordy compared to other languages. Data names of up to 30 characters permit the wide use of descriptive names for variables. The organization of the COBOL program is logical, but is somewhat more difficult to learn than FORTRAN. Consider the following two sentences from a hypothetical COBOL program written for the purpose of calculating a salary check:

MULTIPLY RATE–OF–PAY BY HOURS–WORKED GIVING GROSS–PAY ROUNDED. COMPUTE EXCESS = (HOURS–WORKED – 40)*1.5

In the first sentence the result of the multiplication of data found at storage locations identified with RATE–OF–PAY and HOURS–WORKED will be stored at a location identified as GROSS–PAY. The result will be rounded before being stored. If the COMPUTE verb had been used, the statement would read COMPUTE GROSS–PAY = RATE–OF–PAY * HOURS–WORKED. In other words, the COMPUTE verb is an alternative which is most suitable for formula–type computations. It is easy to notice the advantageous documentation feature of a data processing operation using the COBOL language. COBOL is a business-oriented, procedure–oriented language which is widely taught in college courses on business data processing.

The digital computer is a useful tool for both large and small business organizations. Computer programs and data processing techniques created by companies with large resources can be utilized by small business. Several computer firms have introduced small computers which rent for a relatively low monthly amount and are suitable for use in small businesses. These small computers can be utilized for accounting functions, including the processing of standard ledger cards.

Business data processing is particularly useful for retail sales companies such as department stores and grocery supermarkets. In one supermarket in Los Angeles, a computer terminal replaces the usual cash register at the checkout counter. The computer records accounts for the sales and inventory of the store. The computer retains the sale prices of each item in the store and helps the checkout person avoid incorrectly charging the customer. The large savings to the store is in the up–to–the–minute inventory information. The computer keeps continuous records of stock movement at the store, warehouse, and chain headquarters levels and when inventories fall to a predetermined point, it prints out a reorder automatically. This can eliminate the need for backroom storage, overstocking that causes price–cut sales, and extra delivery charges.[9]

A department store chain and a computer company have attempted to develop a point of sale retail terminal system.[10] A terminal reads the merchandise tickets and charge cards under computer control and performs all normal register calculations, including all applicable taxes or discounts and the customer's change on cash sales, automatically verifies each credit transaction, and permits an immediate review of sales and merchandise activity at any time during the day. Another feature of the terminal is a visual display panel which guides the sales clerk through each step of the transaction. The system, when operational, will handle 1500 point-of-sale terminals and eventually replace all of the firm's cash registers.

A data collection device for processing the registration and charges at a hotel is shown in Figure 11-2 as an example of a point-of-sale device.

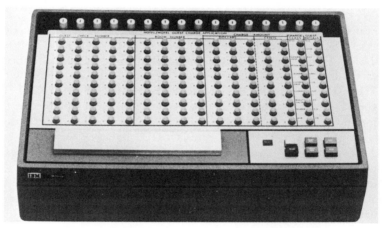

FIGURE 11-2   An IBM Model 1092 data collection device used in this case for the processing of registration and charges at a hotel. *Courtesy of IBM Corporation.*

Computers are used extensively in financial businesses, particularly by the stock market firms. One world-wide data network offers brokers up-to-the-minute information on 9500 stocks, bonds and commodities traded on the world's major exchanges. On this system, the data displayed on the mass terminal includes current stock price, high and low, bid and asked, dividends, earnings and price-to-earnings ratios.[38]

It has been proposed that the menu-sized (8" X 12") stock certificate be replaced by punch card certificate. The objective of the proposal is to reduce the large staffs of stock broker firms which simply handle the clerical functions associated with stock certificates.[11] The punch card would include provisions for optical character recognition for high volume processors.

The manager of a business firm must have accurate, up-to-date information on his firm. One of the most effective modes of presenting business information is graphically. A computer can be used to perform the required calculations and produce the required charts and graphs by means of a plotter or a visual display device. The computer is able to process large amounts of business data and present the results to the manager. If the results are presented in a printed form, it is often difficult to assimilate them readily. A computer plotter or graphical device can present the results in a clear, concise graphic summary of computer results that ordinarily would fill dozens of pages of printout. With the aid of a recently available graphic plotter program, a businessman can obtain, within an hour of initiating the request, a complete set of graphs showing nine key financial ratios as illustrated in Figure 11-3.[2] Computer-

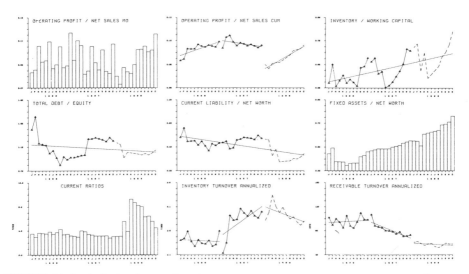

FIGURE 11-3   A single plotter chart for a hypothetical case shows nine key financial ratios covering a three-year period. Such charts are concise and easy to read. They indicate trends and relationships that would be difficult or impossible to obtain from conventional printout. *Photo courtesy of California Computer Products, Inc. and William O'Neil & Company, Beverly Hills, California.*

generated charts are also used to show the performance of hundreds of common stocks each day. Graphical results of financial analysis, market research, sales forecasting and monitoring, project management, production inventory and control and personnel management are used extensively in business. Figures can be drawn at computer command and scaled automatically to correct proportions for showing numbers of employees of a firm in each selected business category, as illustrated in Figure 11-4. Computer graphics for business are an

FIGURE 11-4 Figures can be drawn at computer command and scaled automatically to correct proportions for showing number of employees in each business category. Similar graphics can be produced for formalized business presentations. *Photo courtesy of California Computer Products, Inc.*

important management tool. They effectively extend the ability of the manager in a business enterprise.

Computers can improve the ability of management to guide and control a business enterprise significantly. However, the effective use of a digital computer for business data processing requires proper management of the data processing operation. A recent report of a study of business data processing departments indicated that computers were not being properly managed and they were not paying their way.[13,14] The report states: "From a profit standpoint, our findings indicate computer efforts in all but a few exceptional companies are in real, if often unacknowledged, trouble." In 1969, American industry spent $7 billion on computers and associated equipment and $14 billion to operate them. The investment of $7 billion was ten percent of the investment in new plant in 1969. The recent report implies that the gap between the capabilities of computers and their actual applications is wide and widening. A large proportion of companies use their computers only in routine clerical tasks—payroll, customer orders, inventory control, for instance—where the leverage upon profits is relatively small. The report contends that the machines should be unleashed upon more sophisticated activities: for instance, controlling manufacturing operations, optimizing transportation flows, and most important of all, improving the quality of managerial decisions.[13] In many cases the computers have not reduced the cost of operations, even in routine clerical work. What they have accomplished is mainly to enable companies to speed up operations and thereby to provide better service or handle larger volumes. With any phase of a business, if the function is operated effectively and efficiently, the financial return of the operation is attractive. Conversely, if a department (even business data processing) is poorly operated, there will be financial losses. The recent report points to the use of faster, costlier, more sophisticated computers and larger and more costly computer staffs growing along with increasingly complex and ingenious applications. As the applications grow in number, the evidence of profitable results has not increased.[14] One of the problems that has arisen in the past few years is the fact that the environment of business data processing has been changing, but management strategies have not. Management has tended to leave the direction of the corporate computer effort up to the technical staff persons who operate and program the computer.[39]

The following poem, "The Information System," succinctly and clearly outlines the failure of business data processing systems that are not carefully designed to meet clear and specific objectives.[15]

THE INFORMATION SYSTEM*

Marilyn Driscoll

[CANTO THE FIRST: PROPOSAL]

"An information system," said the president, J. B.,
"Is what this company sorely needs, or so it seems to me:
An automated, integrated system that embraces
All the proper people, in all the proper places,
So that the proper people, by communications linked,
Can manage by exception, instead of by instinct."

[CANTO THE SECOND: FEASIBILITY STUDY]

They called in the consultants then, to see what they could see,
And to tell them how to optimize their use of EDP.
The consultants studied hard and long (their fee for this was sizable)
And concluded that an information system was quite feasible.
"Such a system," they reported, "will not only give you speed,
It will give you whole new kinds of information that you need."

[CANTO THE THIRD: INSTALLATION]

So an information system was developed and installed
And all the proper people were properly enthralled.

*Reprinted, by permission, from *The Arthur Young Journal,* Winter, 1968. Copyright © 1968 by Arthur Young & Company. Marilyn Driscoll is a member of the Communications Department of Arthur Young & Company, certified public accountants.

They thought of all the many kinds of facts it could transmit
And predicted higher profits would indeed result from it;
They agreed the information that it would communicate
Would never be too little, and would never be too late.

[CANTO THE LAST: OUTPUT]

Yet when the system went on line, there was no great hurrah,
For it soon became apparent that it had one fatal flaw:
Though the system functioned perfectly, it couldn't quite atone
For the information it revealed—which was better left unknown.

There are four ways in which the profits of a firm can be improved by means of business data processing: [14]

Purpose	*Application*
1. To reduce general and administrative expenses	1. Administrative and accounting uses
2. To reduce cost of goods sold	2. Operations control systems
3. To increase revenues	3. Product innovation and improved customer service
4. To improve staff work and management decisions	4. Information systems and simulation models

Because of the rising cost of clerical operations and the history of the development of computers and business machines, business has concentrated on the first of these purposes. The next important application of the computer is toward the reduction of the cost of goods sold.[14]

The authors of the report believe that it will require a team of top management committed to active leadership and working with the professional computer staffs in order for significant economic gains. As stated recently by Robert Townsend in his popular book, *Up the Organization*:[37]

COMPUTERS AND THEIR PRIESTS

First get it through your head that computers are big, expensive, fast, dumb adding–machine–typewriters. Then realize that most of the computer technicians that you're likely to meet or hire are complicators, not simplifiers. They're trying to make it look tough. Not easy. They're building a mystique, a priesthood, their own mumbo–jumbo ritual to keep you from knowing what they—and you—are doing. Here are some rules of thumb:

1. At this state of the art, keep decisions on computers at the highest level. Make sure the climate is ruthlessly hard–nosed about the practicality of every system, every program, and

every report. "What are you going to do with that report?" "What would you do if you didn't have it?" Otherwise your programmers will be writing their doctoral papers on your machines, and your managers will be drowning in ho–hum reports they've been conned into asking for and are ashamed to admit are of no value.

2. Make sure your present report system is reasonably clean and effective before you automate. Otherwise your new computer will just speed up the mess.

Management must not abdicate the responsibility of sound management of computer operations to the computer operating staff. Rather, the managers of the future must be continually involved in assessing and controlling the operation of the data processing function. It is clear that future managers must be well–educated about computers, data processing and computer science.

11.2   BUSINESS DATA PROCESSING FOR BANKS AND CREDIT

A primary application of computers in business data processing has been in banking and credit institutions. This section describes some of the characteristics of business data processing in these related fields. Bank operations are essentially data and information processing activities, including not only internal recording of customers' transactions—deposit accounting, trust, loan, and investment administration, corporate income and expense accounting—but also management information processing, cost controls, portfolio analysis, credit analysis, economic and financial research, plus business and financial information processing services for customers. The character of the devices for performing these operations has changed in the past 30 years from mechanical, manually–operated bookkeeping and proof machines, through semi–automatic bookkeeping machines, tabulating and calculating equipment activated by punched cards or punched paper tape, to electronic computers and data processing equipment and the third generation central processing units and peripherals for information processing, operations research, management science and telecommunications. These changes overlapped the twilight of mechanical technology.

The computer was introduced to banks at a time when the volume of paper flowing through the banks had vastly increased. The volume of checks cleared by the banking system increased 1100 percent during the past 30 years. At the Philadelphia National Bank, for example, over 900,000 items are processed each day by the bank's computer.

While in general banks are concerned with information processing, their specific purpose is to serve their customers. Therefore we can say that banking is a growth service industry, orienting goals and operations toward the customer, and harnessing information and technology to create new customer services. Most business transactions and information are financially oriented. Banking operations' role is that of a vital support element for financial service to the economy and the community.

Commercial banking's unique service function is to facilitate money payments and transfer of funds in the economy through checks—a product of its demand deposit accounts. Checks issued in settling 90 percent or more of money transactions aggregated nearly 21 billion items in 1969, growing at an annual rate of seven percent. The banking system has handled this volume by applying computer automation and adopting the MICR (magnetic ink character recognition) common machine-language program. Its acceptance by the public has also been necessary. The development of MICR-encoded checks made feasible the use of high-speed electronic computer oriented reader-sorters for processing MICR-qualified paper documents, and postponed the paper-handling crisis by increasing many times the check-handling capacity of the bank check collection system. Figure 11–5 shows a magnetically-encoded check being read by a magnetic character reader.

FIGURE 11–5   A magnetically-encoded check passing by the reading wheel of an IBM 1419 magnetic character reader. *Courtesy of IBM Corporation.*

Magnetic character sensing, developed by computer manufacturers in co-operation with the American Bankers Association, permits data to be read directly by both man and machine. By agreement among computer manufacturers, check printers, and the ABA, such banking documents as checks, deposit slips, and debit and credit memos can be printed in magnetic ink. Printed information about the bank of origin, depositor's account number, and other essential data can be read directly by the machine. Only the specific amount of each check or deposit slip need be recorded on the document in magnetic print, and this need be done only once by an operator to process the document through its entire routine.

It is estimated that banks and financial institutions own approximately ten percent of all the computers in the United States and twenty percent of the computer capacity. Banks have gradually automated their operations since 1920. In 1933 the announcement of punch card equipment that could operate with alphabetical characters as well as numbers initiated the era of punched card automation. After World War II, mechanized procedures began to include the controlled processing of several stages of work in one operation. The tabulator, calculator, and the summary punch worked in unison as a team. A devoted group of bank systems people became attracted to the science of punch card systems and by 1950, 17 years from the introduction of the alphabetical tabulator, a considerable number of banks could take pride in extremely high-standard installations. The data on the checks and documents was converted to punch cards by keypunch operators. In the 1960's the magnetic ink character-recognition scheme was adopted by the banks. Bank checks are precoded, before being issued, with account numbers in magnetic ink. When the checks are returned to the banks the account numbers can be read directly by recognition devices that sense the magnetic ink. The next step in the processing of financial documents is the availability and use of an input device that is capable of reading a variety of typewritten or handwritten documents. Optical document readers are available, but these devices tend to be expensive as well as sensitive to the uniformity and quality of the documents fed to them. The Bank of America has installed an optical page–scanning system at its San Francisco headquarters. It can read six standard type styles at the rate of 14,000 characters per second. The scanner can finish in 10 seconds the work once performed by a keypunch operator in one day. This page reader processes transaction documents from all 950 California branches of the Bank of America.

Several on–line data processing services have been developed for connection to small banks via telephone lines. Transaction data are entered through a teller console at a remote on–line location. Such data are prefaced with teller, bank, and branch identification and then transmitted over telephone lines to the data center. The data are then processed according to the requirements of the sending institution, and the results are transmitted back via the telephone lines to member banks. An example of an on–line teller terminal in a bank is shown in Figure 11–6.

FIGURE 11-6   A teller at the Citizens Savings and Loan, Painesville, Ohio, uses an IBM 1062 teller terminal linked to Champion Services Corporation's $3.6-million computer center in Cleveland to process a customer's over-the-counter transaction. Two IBM System/360 Model 30 computers instantly record the transactions and update the customer's record. Printed confirmation is immediately flashed back to the terminal via telephone lines. Tellers at more than 40 financial institutions in a four-state area are being linked to the new center. *Photo courtesy of IBM Corporation.*

Many banks have developed a central file concept, which involves collecting in one place all the information about a customer's complete relationship with his bank by means of computers. The biggest problem seems to be economic feasibility. When such systems are successful, the dollars saved through elimination of duplicate records is an advantage. However, the primary advantages are in the intangible services such as customer service, market research, advertising direction, and account profitability. Several banks are developing a voice answerback system, where a teller uses a special phone to dial the computer and receive information needed, to respond to a customer's request, from a pre-recorded voice under computer control. Such a system tied into a completely automated central file would be invaluable to all levels of management in the bank.

A computer time-sharing service is being developed to enable small banks to connect with and to utilize large storages of financial management data.[16] By operating a special electric typewriter connected by telephone line to a computer center, a small-town banker can get a print-out of information about conditions in distant bond and money markets, as well as economic forecasts for the nation or his region, and other data. If he is thinking of buying bonds, the computer system will provide quote prices and yields of issues. If he wants to sell, the computer can tell him the market value of his own bank's portfolio. The computer service also advises what investment shifts to make, depending on the bank's tax situation, assets, liabilities and flow of business. Should the bank experience an unexpected drop in deposits, the computer can recommend steps to be taken by the bank.

The banking system as it is now constituted involves the need to process and transport physically the continually increasing volume of paper checks over a vast geographic area within time schedules and other limitations, frequently resulting in delays in collection and availability of fund or credit. The solution to these problems may be the development in the 1970's of a paperless payments or transfer of funds alternative or addition to checks as a payments mechanism. The real question to be explored and answered is: To what extent and for what transactions are checks or similar paper documents *essential*? By 1990, it is anticipated that each year there will be 3.4×10^{11} transactions of checks and credit documents. On the average, each transaction document consists of 50 characters or 400 bits. Thus, the data transferred in 1990 for checks and credit documents would be 10^{14} bits.

Paper money once represented an equivalent amount of gold stored in some banker's vault, but gradually that ceased to be the case. The currency note is no longer convertible into gold. Canada's dollar bill states that the Bank of Canada "will pay to the bearer on demand" one dollar. What it does not say is that it has nothing to pay with, except more dollar bills. Certainly, there is no gold for this purpose. Money—the paper which passes from pocket to pocket— has become merely a demonstration of a man's ability to pay. The same information could be passed with a check. The checking system, one of the great inventions of commerce, gradually gained acceptance by the "man in the street." Although the process of eliminating tangible currency is still incomplete, we are heading in that general direction: a man can now use a credit card, and we hear talk of a "checkless society." Money, in a sense, is information. In making a payment, two forms of information are required: a record of the transaction; and certification that the payer has the requisite wealth to make the transaction. Since money is in one sense information, then it is suitable for the use of computers and automatic systems.

In the future, the computer may be used to record most of the financial transactions of American citizens. Several systems of eliminating checks and money from most financial transactions have been proposed. One, called the Electronic Fund Transfer System, attempts to replace paper whenever practical. This approach conceives of universal credit cards. Several banks are studying the required standardized formats and procedures for the paperless exchange of credits and debits and for the exchange of magnetic tapes for the major clearing magnetic tapes for the major clearing of banks' commercial checks.

In the case of a retail sale, a computer financial system could involve communicating with a financial computer utility via a store's terminal to transfer the amount of the sale from the buyer's to the store's account. If the purchaser's balance wouldn't cover the cost, the financial utility could extend him credit (if his credit rating was good). At the present time, for regular payments of a fixed amount, such as mortgage and insurance premiums or utility bills up to a given amount, the bill can be sent directly to the person's bank for payment. Such arrangements are naturally well-adapted to computer applications. Other schemes involve using slightly augmented home telephones to instruct banks to transfer funds to another account.

A computer financial utility could develop a complete credit–deposit–loan history for each customer. This history could also enable the financial utility to be a more effective financial adviser to the customer, pointing out his (often unrecognized) spending habits, making analyses, and helping with better planning. Tax returns could also be turned out semiautomatically. Also, "money" could be transferred from account to account or the transaction could involve the extension of credit. The credit could be extended by the seller, based on an indication from the financial utility that the buyer was a good credit risk, or the credit could be extended by the financial utility.

Most credit companies presently utilize computers to record and monitor the transactions of the patrons of the credit company. Figure 11-7 illustrates

FIGURE 11-7   A restaurant manager uses a Card Dialer telephone to contact an IBM computer at American Express headquarters. He is requesting authorization for a dinner party check to be charged to an American Express card. If the transaction is approved, he will hear an automatic spoken reply from an audio response unit linked to the computer. If the request requires special handling, the call will be automatically routed to a credit authorizer at the company's central office. *Courtesy of IBM Corporation.*

one application of computers to credit companies. In the figure, the computer is used for on-line authorization of credit. The primary benefits of a computer credit authorization system are: more rapid response to credit inquiries; the authorization of more credit through the availability of immediate credit information; the reduction of financial losses due to credit card misuses. Under the new system, an employee contacts the computer in New York by means of a special telephone. He first inserts dialing cards that signal the computer and identify the employee's establishment. Then, with pushbuttons, he transmits the credit card account number and amount of transaction. Upon receipt of this data, the computer checks its files to determine if the card represents a valid account with a satisfactory credit standing. Another check by the computer reveals any unusual spending pattern that may be developing (a major factor in fraud detection). The computer either gives verbal credit approval immediately, or in doubtful cases, transfers the call to a credit authorizer, at the same time displaying the account record on a display screen, as in Figure 11-8.

FIGURE 11-8 A credit authorizer at American Express headquarters here reviews a card-member's account record shown on the screen of an IBM 2260 display station. He is responding to a telephone request for credit authorization from a business establishment which accepts American Express credit cards. Such requests are either approved through an automatic spoken response from the computer or—as shown here—are referred to credit department personnel for special handling. *Courtesy of IBM Corporation.*

Currently, Americans write over 60 million checks each day in addition to countless charge slips.[17,18] Eventually, checks and perhaps cash to a large degree will drop from use and all purchases will be on universal credit cards. Each transaction will be recorded in a computer network that will maintain a continuous account of everyone's financial activities. If businesses of all sizes have simple terminals linked to a central computer utility over a communications network, a universal credit-card system is entirely practical. Various schemes could be used to make it difficult for someone to use another person's card. For example, a combination key number known only to the holder of the card on recognition by voice or thumbprint is possible.

The future paperless electronic clearing house banking will handle the settlement, payment, accounting and credit extension functions and will probably consist of a number of commercial banks and other financial institutions grouped into a series of local financial data and information centers and linked together into regional networks. The networks will have central-file storage of information pertinent to the financial profiles of customers, plus payments data and information. The regional centers, in turn, may be interconnected with other regional networks to form an integrated national system to serve all financial institutions and businesses desiring on-line, real-time money payment service. Extension of this computerized telecommunication banking service to the home would seem to be a reasonable, realistic addition. To remain viable, commercial banking must change functionally from a volume handler of paper to a processor of data and information in serving the needs of the community in the computer era.[39]

One form of universal credit card could be a "money key" or card key which may be inserted into a terminal. After insertion, the amount of purchase could be keyed into the terminal. Positive credits to the customer's account, such as payroll payments, benefits, dividends, and gifts are entered in a similar way. *Giro* payment systems, widely used in other parts of the world, work in an opposite manner to the American check payment system. The Austrians first introduced a Giro in 1883. Basically, it is a system of circular credit, in which money circulates from one holder's account to another. The word is derived from the Greek *guros*, meaning "ring." However, to be of any use, money must also pass into and out of the Giro system in cash, and to and from the other banking systems.

A British postal Giro was established in late 1968. In Great Britain both the post office and the banks have recently installed new electronic Giro systems, and their sufcess has helped to generate interest in this type of system in the United States.[19] The British system uses computers and optical character readers and is developing toward computer-to-computer communication of transactions and eventually to a network of computers.[20]

If the United States moves to a checkless, document-free financial system, new means of protection against fraud must be developed. As legitimate paying through computer networks increases, the power and leverage of fraudulent users increases as well.[21] At present, a transfer of property, such as writing a check, requires a signature, which is a very distinct action by the owner showing his willingness to transfer some of his property. In contrast, the mere pushing of a button or the insertion of a key does not constitute an equally distinct intent of the owner to transfer property. It can easily be claimed that a wrong button was pushed or a wrong number inserted, whereas the signing of one's name on a check is an action that cannot readily be renounced as having been committed accidentally.

Prevention of fraud can be sought by such means as the user dialing a secret code number or using an encoded card in order to gain access to an account. Perhaps a fingerprint or voice identification will serve the purpose of the signature in the future. Several security problems will have to be solved before a completely paperless financial system would be possible or acceptable to the users. Nevertheless, the banking and credit institutions will be significantly altered by the extension of computer automation in industry.

11.3 COMPUTERS AND MANAGEMENT

The implications of computers for the practice of business management are significant. In the following article, Professor Peter Drucker outlines the opportunities and problems for business managers as computers are increasingly utilized in business.[22]

WHAT THE COMPUTERS WILL BE TELLING YOU*

Peter F. Drucker

There are still a good many businessmen around who have little use for, and less interest in, the computer. There are also still quite a few who believe that the computer somehow, someday will replace man or become his master.

Others, however, realize by now that the computer, while powerful, is only a tool and is neither going to replace man nor control him. Being a tool, it has limitations as well as capabilities.

The trick lies in knowing both what it can do and what it cannot do. Without such knowledge, the executive can find himself in real trouble in the computer age.

*Reprinted from *Nation's Business*, vol. 54, no. 8, pp. 84–90, August, 1966. Reprinted by permission of the publisher and the author. © 1966, *Nation's Business*—the Chamber of Commerce of the United States. Mr. Drucker is a management consultant, educator, and writer.

The computer is transforming the way businesses operate and is creating problems as well as opportunities. For example:

The mistakes you make are more likely to be whoppers.

You will have much more flexibility in how your business is set up.

You will need to have alternative courses of action planned in advance.

Eventually we will use computer centers as we now plug into public utilities.

We will be able to control manufacturing processes more through direct observation.

Someday we will have little need for computer programmers.

Mankind has developed two kinds of tools. Tools, which do something man himself cannot do, such as the saw. The saw, the wheel, the airplane are all tools that add to man a new dimension of capability.

The other kind of tool is one that does much better what man can do himself. The hammer belongs here and the pliers. And so does the computer. These are the tools that multiply man's capacity. They do not enable him to do something he could not do before, but to do it better, faster and more reliably.

The computer is a logic machine. All it can do is add and subtract. This, however, it can do at very great speed. And since all operations of mathematics and logic are extensions of addition and subtraction, the computer can perform all mathematical and logical operations by just adding and subtracting very fast, very many times. And because it is inanimate, it does not get tired. It does not forget. It does not draw overtime. It can work 24 hours a day.

Finally, it can store information capable of being handled through addition and subtraction, theoretically without limits.

FIVE BASIC COMPUTER SKILLS

What then can the computer do, for the businessman? There are basically five major tasks it can perform.

1. The computer, as a mechanical clerk, can handle large masses of repetitive, but simple, paper work: Payroll, billing and so on. All this application really uses is the speed of the computer.

2. The computer can collect, process, store, analyze and present information at dazzling speeds.

So far, however, business has used only a small part of this capacity. We use the computer to collect, store and present data. Very little use is yet made of the computer's capacity to analyze information. The computer can, if properly instructed, compare the data it receives against the data it had been told to expect—for instance, budget figures. It can immediately spot any difference between the two sets of data and alert management. It can do even more than that. It can analyze data against an expected pattern, and detect any significant deviation.

One business application, for instance, is the analysis of sales data to pinpoint a meaningful and important market segment.

Do physicians in the suburbs use the same prescription drugs as physicians in small towns, or are suburban physicians a distinct market segment? And do medical specialists—the pediatricians, for example, as against the internists—prescribe differently? Are they a specific market segment?

Or what about old doctors versus young ones?

Somebody has to think up the questions. But once the computer has been instructed, it can almost immediately analyze actual prescriptions written by physicians and come up with the answers.

GET THE RIGHT FACTS

What this means is that managers must carefully think through what information it is they need.

The first step toward using the computer properly is to ask this question: How do we use it to make available the minimum of data, but the right data? What data is relevant for the sales manager, the factory superintendent, the salesmen, the research director, the cost accountant or top management?

The computer's capacity to provide people with information they need, in the form they need it and at the time they need it, is the great versatility of the tool. So far it is not used too well by most businesses.

Most companies, in deciding on capital investment, still look at only one kind of analysis:

Expected return on the investment.

The number of years it is likely to take before the investment repays itself.

Or present value of the anticipated future earnings, the so-called discounted cash flow.

Accountants argue hotly about the advantages of each of these methods. Actually they are all valid and all needed. Hitherto, management had to be content with one because it was simply too much work to get all three. This is no longer true. Management can now ask to have capital investments calculated in all three ways by the computer—then look at all three and see which tells the most.

In other words, management has to make the information capacity of the computer fully productive.

3. The computer can also help design physical structures.

Program into the computer all the factors that go into building a highway, plus the basic features of the country across which it is to be built. The computer can then work out very rapidly where the highway should go to take full advantage of the physical and economic characteristics of the terrain.

Here the great capacity of the computer to handle large masses of variables quickly comes into play. Here also its ability to convert graphics into numbers and numbers into graphics is of great importance.

This ability to work out physical design will find its greatest application in the physical sciences where there are clear, known predictable occurrences—that is, natural events. Social events are at best probable, never certain. Therefore, this physical design capacity is a tool of engineering, of chemistry or physics, rather than of business.

4. The computer has the capacity to restore a process to preset conditions, to "control" a process, and this application is highly relevant to business operations.

For instance, if the computer has been programmed for a desired level of inventory and for the factors that determine inventory levels (sales volume, volume of shipments, volume of stock, etc.), it can control inventory. It can tell you when your stock of certain items should be renewed. It can order goods to be assembled for shipping to a customer. It can even actuate machinery bins and put the goods together into one shipping order.

It can do the same for all processes for which we can set the desired level.

This is what people mean when they talk of the computer's making "operating decisions." But this is a gross misnomer. The computer does not make any decisions. It simply carries out orders. The decision has to be made first, and the computer told what to do.

BUT ONLY AN ORDER-TAKER

What the computer can do is serve as a monitor and immediately notice any change between the expected and actual course of events. It can then report what it has noticed.

We can go one step further and tell the computer how to react to a given event. The computer can then carry out our orders. It can shut down a machine or speed it up. It can close a valve or open it, thereby changing mixtures. It can print out a purchase order or a shipping order.

It can carry out whatever order we first put into it.

5. Finally, the computer can, and will, play an increasing role in strategic business decision–making—deciding what course of action to take. Here we no longer deal with restoring a process to a predetermined level. We are talking about decisions to change the process.

What the computer can do here is simulate. It can rapidly work out what would happen if certain things were done under certain assumed conditions. It cannot determine what things might be done. And it cannot determine the assumptions. Both have to be determined for it.

But it can tell you, for instance, that the introduction of a new product at a given price and given cost would be justified only if you could assume a certain volume of sales.

SETTING PRICES, PREDICTING MARKETS

It can tell you that a new product at a certain price and with a certain volume of sales would have to cost no more than a certain amount to be economical.

It can tell you what market you have to assume for a new product to have a chance of success.

It can also tell executives what assumptions management has made, consciously or subconsciously, when it reaches a decision. If we build a new plant with a certain capacity, for instance, how much must it be able to sell, for how long and at what price to earn a given return on the investment?

Simulation has largely been used for events which are predictable and occur regularly.

So far, no one has successfully simulated a major strategic business decision. Such a decision involves future social, political and economic events for which there are no known predictabilities and laws. Thus, strategic business decisions will remain risk–taking decisions. But the computer will soon be able to point out what we assume when we make this or that decision and what decision follows logically from this or that assumption. This applies particularly for recurrent business decisions, such as introduction of new products, pricing decisions and the simpler kinds of capital investment.

The use of the computer as a tool in strategic decision-making is perhaps our most exciting possibility. For it means that business managers will have to learn to think systematically about strategic decisions, and learn how to find and analyze alternatives of strategy.

WHAT THE COMPUTER CAN'T DIGEST

However, the computer can't handle all information. It can accept only information capable of being quantified and dealt with logically. This is only a part of the information necessary in the business world.

The information most important to a businessman is not capable of being quantified. It can only be perceived. This is information about something that is about to happen, information about a change in the trend.

This becomes particularly critical in events outside your business, events in the economy, the market, in society. Here what matters is the new, the unique, the event that signals a change.

The computer cannot bring outside events, by and large, to the attention of management. Therefore, management must realize this limitation of the computer. It is above all a tool for controlling events within the business.

However, it is only on the outside that a business has results. Inside a business there are only costs. Only a customer converts the efforts of a business into value, revenues and profits.

This all means, indeed, that the computer can become a terrific obstacle. If the tremendous amount of inside information the computer makes available causes management to neglect to look outside—or become contemptuous of the messy, imprecise, unreliable data outside—then management will end up on the scrap heap.

On the other hand, the computer can enable businessmen to devote a good deal more time to looking at the outside and studying it than they can now.

As a result of the computer, there will be fewer and fewer small decisions and fewer and fewer small mistakes. The computer will make small decisions into big decisions. And if they are made wrongly, the mistakes will be big pretty big ones.

It is simply not true that the computer will eliminate middle managers. On the contrary, the computer will force middle management to learn to make decisions.

A regional sales manager today makes his inventory and shipping decisions on an *ad hoc* basis. They are not really decisions, but adaptations. But he also does not run much of a risk. Each decision stands by itself and usually can be easily reversed.

But to enable the computer to control inventory, a decision has to be made and the decision has to be thought through. It is neither easy nor riskless.

On the contrary, it implies very major decisions with impact on the entire business, including customer service, production schedules and money tied up in inventory. You have to think through whether you can afford to give all customers 24-hour service on all products. This usually means an absolutely impossible inventory and a totally chaotic production schedule.

If you can't afford that, do you give this kind of service only to good customers? And how do you define a good customer?

And do you give this service to all your products, or only to the major products?

And again, what is a major product?

These are not easy decisions. Until recently there was no need to tackle them. Each specific case was handled as a unique event. If a customer didn't like the way he was treated and squawked, one treated him differently the next time.

But as far as the computer is concerned, inventory and shipping instructions have to be based on a fundamental policy: They have to be decided on principle. And this goes for all other so-called operating decisions.

They all become true decisions. Otherwise, one cannot instruct the computer to execute them.

MAKING BETTER MIDDLE MANAGERS

The greatest weakness of business at present is the fact that middle managers, by and large, are not being trained and tested in risk-taking decisions. Hence, when moved into top management, middle managers suddenly find themselves up against decisions they have not been exposed to before. This is the major reasons why so many fail when they reach the top.

The computer will force us to develop managers who are trained and tested in making the strategic decisions which determine business success or failure.

I doubt that the computer will much reduce the number of middle management jobs. Instead the computer is restructuring these jobs, enabling us to organize work where it logically belongs and to free middle managers for more important duties.

For instance, by tradition a district sales manager had three jobs.

He was expected to train and lead a sales force. This was his main job— on paper. In reality he gave very little time to it.

For he was also an office manager, handling a lot of paper work—bills, credits, collections and payroll. Then he usually had a big job running a warehouse and taking care of the physical movement of merchandise to customers in his district.

Now the computer makes it possible to centralize all paper work in the head office—bills, payroll, invoices, credits, shipping instructions. We can print out computer-handled paper work any place in the world from a central computer.

At the same time, the computer makes possible a sharp cut in the number of warehouses. For the computer can handle all inventory as one inventory, no matter where it is.

DO YOU NEED 50 WAREHOUSES?

The computer, therefore, can supply customers from a much smaller number of warehouses and with a very much smaller inventory. There is no longer any reason why, in most businesses, a warehouse needs to be in the same place as the district sales office. We may have 50 district sales offices, but need only eight warehouses—and only one location for all paper work.

This frees the district sales manager for the job that always should have been his main preoccupation—managing the sales effort.

In other words, the computer enables us to structure according to need. In the past, corporate structure was largely determined by geography and the limitations on information. This is no longer necessary. We can now decide how we want to set up the business.

We can build decision centers where the decisions are best made, rather than where geography and absence of information force us to locate.

More than likely, this will mean that more people will have decision-making authority, simply because more people can get the information they require to make the decision.

At the same time, the computer will enable top management to insist that decisions be made as decisions and with proper thought and understanding. It will, above all, enable top management to insist that alternatives are thought through, including what to do if the decision does not work out.

With the computer and its ability to process information fast, there is no reason why alternatives should not be worked out in advance.

. . .

DOING AWAY WITH PROGRAMMERS

Finally, we will become less and less dependent on the programmer. We will be more and more able to put information into the computer directly in something akin to ordinary language and to get out of the computer something akin to ordinary language.

Today the programmer has to translate from ordinary language into the computer code.

This is the greatest limitation of the present system. It cuts the computer's speed down to the speed of a human being—and this, in handling logic, means it cuts it down to a very slow speed. It also creates the need for employment of many essentially unskilled people. Yet on their skill and understanding the ability of the computer to perform depends altogether.

To the extent to which we can jump the programming stage and get closer to computers able to handle information directly, to that extent will the computer become more effective, more flexible and more universal.

The idea that it will master us is absurd—one can always pull the plug and cut it off anyhow. But it is a tool of tremendous potential, if used properly.

It cannot, and it will not, make decisions. But it will greatly multiply the ability, the effectiveness and the impact of those people of intelligence and judgment who take the trouble to find out what the computer is all about.

11.4   COMPUTERS AND MANAGEMENT SCIENCE

With the increased use of computers in business during the past decade, the new field of management science has grown in importance. During that period the amount of data for a business enterprise has significantly increased and the computer has often been used to provide assistance in the area of business data processing. The use of the data available and the calculating power of the computers available to many firms has led to a mathematical approach to the management of business enterprises, often called *management science.*

MANAGEMENT SCIENCE   A mathematical or quantitative study of the management of resources of business, usually with the aid of a computer.

In management science, solution sequences begin with the identification of a problem and its verbal statement. The problem is then formulated in mathematical terms and analyzed. Usually a computer is used for calculation. A management decision is finally reached.[23]

Management science is closely related to the field of operations research. Operations research is concerned with the allocation of resources to an organization's various activities in a way that is most effective for the organization as a whole. The active beginnings of operations research have been attributed to the military services of the United States and the United Kingdom early in World War II.[24] Because of the war effort, there was need to allocate scarce resources to the many military operations in an effective manner. The various methods of operations research depend greatly upon the completion of a large number of calculations. Thus, the increasing availability of the digital computer after 1950 was a supporting factor in the development of operations research. A definition of operations research is:[24]

OPERATIONS RESEARCH   A scientific approach to decision making that involves the operations of organizational systems.

As the business organization is concerned with the allocation of resources, the field of management science and operations research have many common characteristics and objectives. For the outline in this section, we consider the purposes of operations research and management science to be similar for a business firm; we do not differentiate between them in the following paragraphs.

One of the objectives of a management science approach to a problem is the aim of finding the best or *optimal* solution to the problem under consideration. Thus, rather than being content with improvement, the goal is to identify the best possible course of action. The sequence followed in a management science approach to a problem is illustrated in Figure 11-9.

After formulating the problem in a verbal or written form, often the next step is developing a mathematical model of the problem in a form convenient

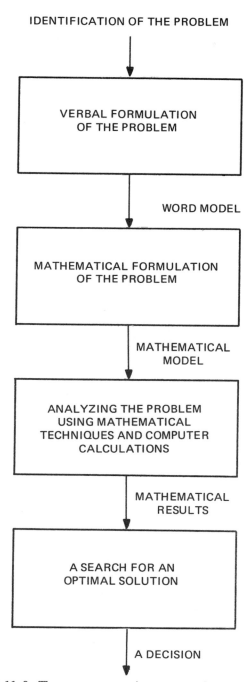

IDENTIFICATION OF THE PROBLEM

VERBAL FORMULATION
OF THE PROBLEM

WORD MODEL

MATHEMATICAL FORMULATION
OF THE PROBLEM

MATHEMATICAL
MODEL

ANALYZING THE PROBLEM
USING MATHEMATICAL
TECHNIQUES AND COMPUTER
CALCULATIONS

MATHEMATICAL
RESULTS

A SEARCH FOR AN
OPTIMAL SOLUTION

A DECISION

FIGURE 11-9   The management science approach to a problem.

for analysis. The mathematical model is an idealized representation of the important characteristics of the problem—in mathematical terms. The mathematical model includes *decision variables* whose values are to be determined. An example of a decision variable is the size of the labor force at a plant. Any restrictions assigned to these decision variables are called *constraints*. For example, the maximum size of the work force permitted in a specific plant due to space limitations and safety regulations would be limited or constrained. A model is necessarily an abstract idealization of the problem, and approximations and simplifying assumptions generally are required if the model is not to be unnecessarily complex. Therefore, care must be taken to insure that the model remains a valid representation of the problem. The proper criterion for judging the validity of a model is whether or not it predicts the relative effects of the alternative courses of action with sufficient accuracy to permit a sound decision.

In order to determine the optimal or best decision to adopt, one must formulate an objective, or aim, against which the many courses of action may be measured. Many people believe that most firms adopt the objective of maximization of profit as the sole aim of the company. A number of studies have found that, instead of profit maximization, the goal of satisfactory profits combined with other objectives is characteristic of American corporations. In particular, typical objectives might be to maintain stable profits, increase (or maintain) one's share of the market, product diversification, maintain stable prices, improve worker morale, maintain family control of the business, and increase company prestige. These objectives might be compatible with long–run profit maximization, but the relationship is sufficiently obscure that it may not be convenient to incorporate them into this one objective. Furthermore, there are additional considerations involving social responsibilities that are distinct from the profit motive and should be included in the objective of the firm.[24] The objective of the firm must be constructed in a quantitative or mathematical form in order to use the computer and the management science approaches.

The solution to the problem is then calculated as an optimal or best solution based on the examination of the objective in mathematical terms. The objective in mathematical form is called the *objective function*. Often a series of optimal solutions are obtained as a result of improving the model, the data, and the objective function. An analysis of the sensitivity of the model and objective function also may be conducted to determine which input parameters are most critical in determining the solution and therefore require more careful estimation.

Let us consider an example of a business decision which can utilize the methods of management science and the computer.

EXAMPLE 11-1

The bookstore at a college sells one kind of dictionary. The size of the student body is known and it is known that the demand in the coming year is for 1,000 dictionaries. The number of orders placed with the publisher of the dictionary is in control of the bookstore manager and he can place an order for one dictionary (called a unit), or any number up to 1,000 units. The decision variable, X, is the number of orders placed per year. X must be between 1 and 1,000.

The two costs to the bookstore are the ordering cost of each order and the carrying cost of storing the dictionaries while waiting for their sale. If the manager ordered 1,000 dictionaries on one order, the ordering cost would be minimized, but it would lead to high inventory–carrying costs. Similarly, 1,000 orders of one dictionary would minimize the inventory–carrying costs but would increase the ordering costs.

The objective of the manager is to minimize the costs of operating. An objective function to represent this objective would be

$$\text{Total Cost} = \text{Ordering Cost} + \text{Inventory Carrying Cost}$$

or
$$T = \text{\o} + I \qquad (11\text{-}1)$$

After examination and study the manager finds that the ordering cost is a linear function of the number of orders placed. It is modeled as follows:

$$\text{\o} = 2X \ \text{(dollars)} \qquad (11\text{-}2)$$

Equation 11-2 states that the ordering cost expressed in dollars is equal to two multiplied by the number of orders placed, X. In other words, it costs 2 dollars per order. The inventory carrying cost may be represented by

$$I = 7200/X \ \text{(dollars)} \qquad (11\text{-}3)$$

Equation 11-3 states that the inventory carrying cost decreases as the number of orders increases and equals 72 dollars if one hundred separate orders are placed.

A graphic solution of the problem may be obtained by plotting the two costs versus the number of orders placed; see Figure 11-10. Also shown is the total cost, which is the objective function as given by Equation 11-1. The minimum value of the total cost is found graphically to be $240. It is obtained when the manager places 60 orders per year. For this number of orders the cost of ordering would be $120 and the inventory–carrying cost would also be $120. One could readily use a computer to calculate the total costs for various numbers of orders and provide the data for the chart shown in Figure 11-10.

The main advantage of graphic presentation over the presentation of the results in a table printed out by the computer is that over–all relationships can be seen at a glance. More information can be presented on a graph than in a table. An additional factor to be noted from Figure 11-10 is that there is little difference in cost between 50 and 70 orders per year, but that total cost increases sharply when fewer than 20 orders per year are placed. The major

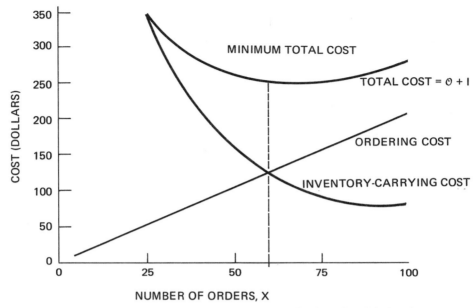

FIGURE 11–10   Costs as a function of the numbers of orders placed during the year.

limitation of this method is that graphs are two–dimensional, and when more than two variables are involved, graphs become difficult to prepare and interpret.

Another important technique of management science is that of *linear programming*, which deals with getting optimum value from limited resources which are used by competing activities. Use of the adjective *linear* implies that the objective function (or judgment) must be directly related to each of the various costs or factors. The theory of linear programming was developed by John von Neumann, G. B. Dantzig, T. C. Koopmans and a few others. It was applied to the problems of the Berlin air lift in the late 1940's, when all supplies had to be flown into the city because the Russians had cut off ground transport.

The objective function is written as

$$\Theta = c_1 x_1 + c_2 x_2 + \ldots \qquad (11\text{-}4)$$

where x_1, x_2,. . . are decision variables and c_1, c_2,. . . are constants. The restrictions or constraints are also written in equation form. Linear programming problems may often be solved using the *simplex method*, which utilizes the digital computer.[24] An example of a linear programming problem is provided in the following paragraphs.

EXAMPLE 11-2

A steel mill produces two grades of steel: grade A and grade B. The mill can produce a maximum of 40 tons of grade A in a month and a maximum of 60 tons of grade B in a month. It requires three hours to produce one ton of grade A and it requires two hours to produce one ton of grade B. There are 180 production hours available each month. The decision variable for the number of tons of grade A and grade B produced per month will be x_1, and x_2 respectively. Thus, the constraints on the decision variables are

$$x_1 \leqslant 40 \qquad (11\text{-}5)$$
$$x_2 \leqslant 60 \qquad (11\text{-}6)$$
$$3x_1 + 2x_2 \leqslant 180 \qquad (11\text{-}7)$$

Equations 11-5, 11-6 and 11-7 can be represented graphically as shown in Figure 11-11a. The shaded area shows the permissible values of x_1 and x_2.

The profit is $30 for each ton of grade A produced and $50 for each ton of grade B produced. The total profit or objective function is then

$$\theta = 30x_1 + 50x_2 \qquad (11\text{-}8)$$

This objective function is a straight line, shown on Figure 11-11b for several cases. The maximum profit is achieved when $x_1 = 20$ tons and $x_2 = 60$ tons, for which case the profit is $3600 for the month.

Unfortunately, the graphic method cannot be used with more than two decision variables. However, it does help to illustrate the method for which the computer is used for more difficult problems.

Another management science technique is called Program Evaluation and Review Technique (PERT). It is a method of planning, replanning and progress

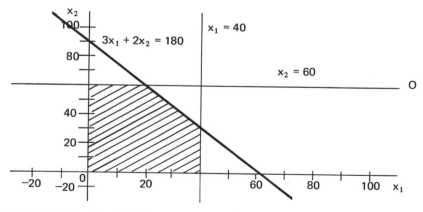

FIGURE 11-11a The shaded area represents the permissible region for x_1 and x_2.

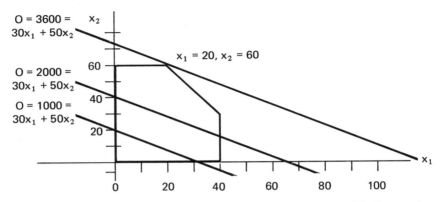

FIGURE 11-11b   The line $O = 30x_1 + 50x_2$ is shown for several values of O. The maximum value of the objective function, \$3600, occurs when $x_1 = 20$ and $x_2 = 60$.

evaluation in order to better control a major operational program. The PERT technique was developed during 1958 at the Navy Special Projects Office by a project team which studied the application of statistical and mathematical methods to the planning, evaluation, and control of research and development effort. PERT is used to define what must be done in order to accomplish program objectives on time. Through its use, areas of a project that require remedial decisions can be detected and the effect of trade-offs among the three basic factors—time, resources, and technical performance—can be determined. One of the major advantages of PERT is that it provides a method for the diagramming (establishing a network) of a program. Each event is depicted and its relationship to the others expressed. PERT uses time as the common denominator to reflect planned resource application and performance specifications.

Using a computer to develop and monitor a project with PERT, one obtains the following advantages: (1) aid in planning and scheduling a program; (2) continuous, timely progress reports, identifying potential problem areas where action may be required; (3) a simulation of the effects of alternate decisions under consideration and an opportunity to study their effect upon the program deadlines prior to implementation; (4) probability of successfully meeting deadlines.

The computer is used to produce the printed output results of an analysis based on the network representation of the project plan. The network or graph depicts the flow of events and activities in the program.[24]

(The simulation of business processes enables a manager to evaluate the results of various alternatives. Simulation as a general approach to business problems and problems from other fields is discussed fully in Chapter 13.)

One problem in computer simulation and modeling is the necessity of finding the simplest model that nevertheless captures the essence of the problem at hand.[15,26] Also, quite often a manager is less interested in obtaining the optimum solution from a model, which is only an approximation in any case, than he is in gaining some insight into the effect on the objective function of changes in the model. A sensitivity study is aimed at providing a measure of the incremental effect (*i.e.*, the sensitivity) of changes in the model. The simplest type of change is to modify the value of a parameter. For example, one may wish to study the effects of a change in sales forecasts in an inventory model.[27]

A simulation model duplicates, more or less faithfully, the actual events that occur over time in the real world for a given set of parameters and decision variables. Certain consequences stem from the events that take place during the course of the simulation. The consequences are then presented to a decision maker, usually in summarized form, to aid him in predicting the consequences of implementing the specified alternative in the real world.

We have briefly treated some of the methods of management science. The computer is able to provide results rapidly from simulations, linear programming, optimization problems, PERT problems, and other problems of managers in business and industry. As the managers of business enterprises become more familiar with these methods they will be utilized more commonly in practice.

11.5 MANAGEMENT INFORMATION SYSTEMS

Perhaps no other concept of computer data processing for business is discussed more than that of management information systems. Yet management information systems, which are often simply labeled MIS, have not been fully constructed, developed or implemented as an actual system for management use.[39]

A definition of a management information system is difficult to formulate since the field is newly developing and in a state of transition. MIS use computers to provide managers with the information they need for making decisions regarding their company's business. Two definitions of MIS are:

MANAGEMENT INFORMATION SYSTEM (1) A computer system integrating equipment, people and procedures to deliver analysis–supporting and analytical information pertinent to management decisions. (2) A system of people, equipment, procedures, documents and communications that collects, validates, operates on, transforms, stores, retrieves and presents data for use by various top executives fo a firm in planning, budgeting, accounting, controlling and other management processes.

At present, top managers in industry resort directly to their computer systems only occasionally. They usually rely on department managers to interpret computer results to them. With a new generation of managers and equipment which provides visual displays such as graphs and figures, the top manager is more able to obtain his information directly from the data processing system. Thus, the trend is toward computer applications which are involved in the daily operation of the business organization. In American business and industry, the percentage of computer resources allocated to produce output for top management averaged only 18 percent of the total during 1970, 38 percent going to middle management and 44 percent to operating supervisors. This 18 percent figure is up only slightly from 14 percent in 1965 and is expected to increase to no more than about 25 percent in 1975.[4] Also, as many persons have pointed out, top executives of industry do not often receive the most significant computer output. Usually, they receive information from accounting–oriented data systems, such as sales summaries, product cost reports and other after–the–fact information. What a top executive needs is a decision–oriented data base that can be used, for example, to identify potential market demands; to indicate improvements in operating costs, or to show profit profiles of alternative investment plans.

MIS are most useful to the top-management functions of formulating corporate strategy, designing overall planning and control systems, and setting investment and growth policies. As systems are developed which encompass a greater share of the day–to–day administrative chores of a business, the manager will become free to reflect on the company's investment and program policies and think of new opportunities for the firm.

Information processing systems tend toward management information systems as their purpose transcends a transactions processing orientation in favor of a top management decision–making orientation.[28,29] In order to understand the information flow in a normal business organization, examine Figure 11-12.[30] The horizontal reporting patterns shown in Figure 11-12a tend to follow horizontal departmental lines. The vertical divisions shown in Figure 11-12b represent general information such as payroll. By superimposing the vertical patterns over the horizontal, these diagrams attempt to show how management information flows through all levels of a company's operation. MIS is a system of integrated information flow through the company. The concept of integration of information in a MIS is succinctly summarized in an interesting statement by Marshall McLuhan in his recent book:[31]

> It may be simplest to say at once that the real use of the computer is not to reduce staff or costs, or to speed up or smooth out anything that has been going on. Its true function is to program and orchestrate terrestrial and galactic environments and energies in a harmonious way. For centuries the lack of symmetry and proportion in all these areas has created a sort of universal spastic condition for lack of inter–relation among them.

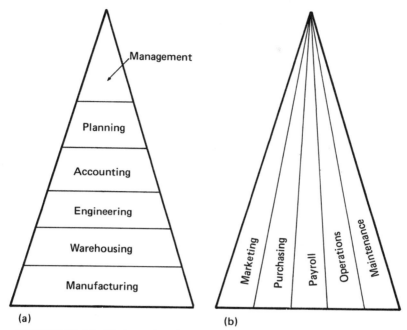

FIGURE 11-12 Horizontal and vertical information flow in a typical firm.

Managers can use MIS to help them orchestrate the operations of their companies.

Often we talk about the value of information and the profit obtained by using MIS. But the plant in a literal sense generates the profit, and the information system helps in managing the operation. Data are collected on the plant operation and information is generated. The data record the level of operation while information results from an analysis of the data. Relevant information is then extracted from the total information and used for management decisions. The underlying concept is that information about a business enterprise is a resource analogous to labor and capital. Management of the business information resource is a function of corporate management, requiring highly integrated information for the sake of efficiency.

A fully integrated MIS may be a competitive necessity for many industries in the near future. A business has an external environment and many internal related environments. The external environment of a business includes the government, industry, financial, and competitive environments. The sales environment is also important to record in the data systems.[32] In Figure 11-13, a business management system is shown which illustrates the flow of

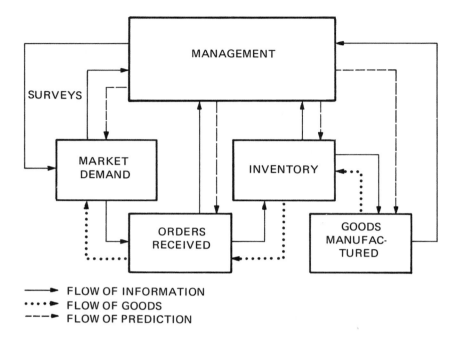

FIGURE 11-13 A business management system illustrating the flow of information, goods and prediction.

information, goods and prediction. The information flow may be integrated in a management information system. Also, the computer which provides the MIS can be used to provide predictions of the market, sales, inventory and production. The predictions are used in conjunction with the available information to make management decisions.

An operational system which is a reduced version of an MIS exists at North American Rockwell Corporation. It is said to realize a net annual savings of $150,000, reducing inventory in one of the company's divisions by $2 million. This saving results from sharply lowered labor costs for inventory control and scheduling, reduced clerical effort in labor and job status reporting and less physical inventory.[33] The MIS performs two basic control functions: production control of work-in-progress and inventory control of manufacturing requirements and materials. The system uses on-line computing equipment and remote input terminals at work stations.

Management information systems are becoming increasingly important to business firms. Competition will encourage the development of integrated MIS. Use and development of management information systems during the next decade could lead to major changes in the management function in business enterprises. The manager of the future will be required to know the capabilities of the computer and its integrated use in his enterprise.

SUMMARY

Business data processing is the storage, processing and reporting of data for business purposes. Business data processing can significantly affect the cost structure of a company, when volume production is the rule, by reducing the time taken to produce records and reports. Also, business data processing can be used to reduce the clerical work force required to handle the business data. Business data processing is most efficient when a computer is used to perform repetitious tasks with large masses of data at rapid speeds.

The basic organization of a business is often altered by the introduction of a computer. Quite often, business firms use COBOL, a programming language oriented to business applications. The computer can be used to aid in the reduction of general and administrative expenses; to reduce the cost of goods sold; to increase revenues, and to improve management decisions. Thus far, the primary concentration has been on the first of these purposes.

Computers are effectively utilized for data processing in the fields of banking and credit institutions. Computers process the checks and documents passing through most banks. Also, on-line teller systems have been developed and installed. As the computer systems for banks and credit institutions evolve, our nation may move towards a financial system which does not utilize paper money as it does now.

The fields of management science and operations research have developed during the past two decades due in great measure to the availability of the computer. Management science is a mathematical or quantitative study of the management of resources of a business, usually with the aid of a computer. Among these resources is information, which provides the basis for decisions. Management science incorporates the techniques of linear programming, PERT, system optimization, and simulation, among others.

Management information systems (MIS) are computer systems integrating equipment, people, and procedures in such a way as to deliver analysis-supporting and analytical information pertinent to management decisions. MIS are useful to the top management functions of formulating corporate strategy, designing overall planning and control systems and setting investment and growth plans.

The computer and its use in business data processing, management science and management information systems will result in profound changes in the structure, organization, and function of a business enterprise. The manager of the future must be prepared for the changes and able to incorporate them in his enterprise.

We close this summary with the oft-told story of the computer owned by the Gas Company. One of the customers was away for several months and he duly received a bill for $0.00. He ignored it, but the machine expected a reply. It sent another bill and, when that was ignored, it sent a final demand note which included a threat to cut off supplies from the customer's house. The customer thereupon sent his check—which pacified the computer. After a few days his bank manager asked to see him urgently. Why had he written such a peculiar check? "To pacify the Gas Company's computer." "Damn the Gas Company's computer! Do you realize that you have driven *our* computer crazy?"

CHAPTER 11 PROBLEMS

P11-1.   List three or four advantages of the use of a computer in the data processing operation of the business operations listed below.
1. The payroll department of the city
2. The accounting department of your college
3. The production department of a toy manufacturer

P11-2.   Outline the steps necessary in the processing of data at the accounting office of your college. Draw a chart similar to Figure 11-1 to illustrate the sequence of steps.

P11-3.   List the leading applications of computers in business data processing in industry.

P11-4.   Investigate and draft a brief report on one of the following business data processing operations in your town which utilizes a computer in its operation.
1. A retail point-of-sale system in a store
2. A bank accounting system
3. A credit company system
4. A bank check processing system

P11-5.   A store sells one item, automobile tires. The total cost is the sum of the carrying cost and the ordering cost. The annual sales are 800 tires and the reordering cost is $10 per order. The average carrying cost is $.20 per tire. Show that the minimum total cost is $80 when four orders of 200 units are processed by the store to the manufacturer.

P11-6.   A company produces two grades, x and y, of paper on a paper machine. Here are some of the restrictions under which we must plan production.

| Capacity per week: | Not more than 400 tons of grade x. |
| | Not more than 300 tons of grade y. |

Time: It requires 0.2 and 0.4 hours to produce a ton of products x and y respectively.

There are 160 production hours available each week.

Profit: A profit of $20 and $50 per ton of x and y respectively can be realized per week.

The problem is to determine how much of each paper shall the company make to maximize the profit. Use linear programming and obtain a graphic solution.

P11-7. An industry produces two products, A and B, on which the profit per unit is $50 for either product. There are two processes of manufacture operating in the plant. Under the first process, it requires 10 hours to manufacture each item A and 5 hours to manufacture each unit of item B. With the second process it requires 5 hours/unit for item A and 6 hours/unit for item B. There are 3500 hours of manufacturing time available for each process. Using a graphic solution to the linear programming problem, show that the optimum profit is $30,000.

P11-8. A student has a family car which he can drive to the beach, or he can take the bus. The bus ride costs $3 for a round trip and the auto costs $2 for a round trip. The student can go to the beach at the most four times each week. Also, due to his family schedule, he can use either form of transportation a maximum of three times per week. His family has set rules on the use of the car by all the members of the family so that for every three times they use the car they must use the bus at least once. Using the linear programming approach, determine the number of times the student should use each form of transportation if he wishes to minimize his expenses over a ten-week period.

P11-9. A firm is interested in scheduling the production of two hand-made products, rugs and blankets. The profit for each rug is $6, and for each blanket it is $9. The problem is to determine the schedule that maximizes profit. The decision variables are thus the quantities to produce of each of the products. Let x_1 represent the number of rugs scheduled, and x_2 the number of blankets. The objective function is therefore Profit $= 6x_1 + 9x_2$.

The production of the rugs and blankets requires the skills of weavers and spinners. For a given scheduling period (a week, say) they have 1800 hours of weavers' time and 300 hours of spinners' time. Each product requires 2 hours per unit of weaving; while a rug or blanket requires .2 and .5 hours, respectively, of spinning. Use the linear programming approach to show that the optimal schedule is to produce 500 rugs and 400 blankets. This will result in the optimum profit of $6,600.[33]

P11-10. Five questions are provided below. Write a brief statement on each of these questions and add your conclusions after completing the five questions.

1. Are organizational structures of business firms becoming more centralized as a result of computers?
2. Are these organizational changes a *result* of computer technology, or are other factors *causing* the changes?
3. What is the significance of the centralization of the data-processing, or information-technology, function?
4. How has the nature of managerial work changed? Will it change further as certain types or levels of management work are subject to computer systems and management science becomes better-known?
5. How will higher levels of management be affected?

P11-11. Devise a management information system in graphic form similar to Figure 11-13 for your college bookstore.

CHAPTER 11 REFERENCES

1. D. H. Sanders, *Computers in Business: An Introduction*, McGraw-Hill Book Company, New York, 1968.
2. E. M. Awad, *Business Data Processing*, Prentice-Hall, Inc., Englewood Cliffs, New Jersey, 2nd Edition, 1968.
3. *Management and the Computer*, Dow Jones and Co., Inc., New York, 1969.
4. "Top Management Lag in Computer Resources Use," *Data Management*, October, 1970, pg. 47.
5. "Problem Solver, Problem Maker," *Business Week*, October 17, 1970, pp. 182-188.
6. J. Diebold, *Business Decisions and Technological Change*, Praeger Publishing Company, New York, 1970.
7. D. M. Sage, "Information Systems: A Brief Look Into History," *Datamation*, November, 1968, pp. 63-69.
8. D. H. Sanders, *Computers and Management*, McGraw-Hill Book Company, New York, 1970.

9. "Computers Reach the Checkout Counter," *Business Week*, June 13, 1970, pg. 86.
10. "Retail Information System," *Modern Data*, August, 1969, pg. 66.
11. "Unclogging Paperwork Jam," *Business Week*, June 28, 1969, pg. 111.
12. R. L. Mark, "Plotting for Business," *Information Systems Review*, Spring, 1968, pp. 5-10.
13. T. Alexander, "Computers Can't Solve Everything," *Fortune*, October, 1969, pp. 126-168.
14. McKinsey and Company, "Unlocking the Computer Profit Potential," *Computers and Automation*, April, 1969, pp. 24-33.
15. M. Driscoll, "The Information System," *The Arthur Young Journal*, Winter, 1968, pg. 38.
16. "Banking: Your Friendly Computer," *Time*, January 3, 1969, pg. 64.
17. T. J. Gradel, "Coming: A Cashless Society?" *RCA Age*, Winter, 1968-69, pp. 32-34.
18. A. R. Miller, "The Credit Networks: Detour to 1984," *The Nation*, June 1, 1970, pp. 648-651.
19. G. C. White, Jr., "Installation of a Giro Payment System in the United States," *Datamation*, November, 1969, pp. 195-201.
20. J. Robertson, "Paying by Computer," *New Scientist*, July 23, 1970, pp. 179-181.
21. R. C. Stiefel, "A Checkless Society or an Unchecked Society?" *Computers and Automation*, October, 1970, pp. 32-35.
22. P. F. Drucker, "What the Computers Will be Telling You," *Nation's Business*, Vol. 54, No. 8, August, 1966, pp. 84-90.
23. D. Teichroew, *An Introduction to Management Science*, Wiley and Sons, Inc., New York, 1964.
24. F. S. Hiller and G. J. Lieberman, *Introduction to Operations Research*, Holden-Day, Inc., San Francisco, California, 1967.
25. "Running the Show with a Keyboard," *Business Week*, July 13, 1968, pp. 77-78.
26. D. B. Hertz, "Investment Policies that Pay Off," *Harvard Business Review*, January, 1968, pp. 96-102.
27. J. C. Emery, "Decision Models, Part 2," *Datamation*, September 15, 1970, pp. 59-63.
28. R. V. Head, "The Elusive MIS," *Datamation*, September 1, 1970, pp. 22-27.
29. M. H. Schwartz, "MIS Planning," *Datamation*, September 1, 1970, pp. 28-31.
30. J. R. Ziegler, "Computer Information Systems," *Automation*, April, 1970, pp. 93-96.
31. M. McLuhan and Q. Fiore, *War and Peace in the Global Village*, Bantam Books, Inc., New York, 1968, pg. 89.

32. W. F. Williams, "Today's Computerized Business," *Information Systems Review*, Fall, 1968, pp. 19–23.
33. J. C. Emery, "Decision Models, Part 1," *Datamation*, September 1, 1970, pp. 32–36.
34. W. F. Boore and J. R. Murphy, *The Computer Sampler: Management Perspectives on the Computer*, McGraw-Hill Book Co., New York, 1968.
35. N. H. Carter, *Introduction to Business Data Processing*, Dickenson Publishing Company, Belmont, California, 1968.
36. E. A. Weiss, *Computer Usage Fundamentals,* McGraw-Hill Book Co., New York, 1969, Chapter 14.
37. R. Townsend, *Up the Organization,* Alfred A. Knopf, Inc., New York, 1970.
38. O. D. Bowlen, W. P. Dukes, and W. F. Ford, "The Computer, Stockbroker of the Future," *Computers and Automation,* April, 1971, pp. 8–15.
39. "Business Takes a Second Look at Computers," *Business Week,* June 5, 1971, pp. 59–136.

12

DATA BANKS, INFORMATION RETRIEVAL AND LIBRARIES

12.1 DATA BANKS

More than five centuries have passed since Gutenberg invented printing with movable type. Today we have available a wide variety of printed material such as books, newspapers, catalogs and magazines. In addition, we use the typed and written word to record information. All this printed and written material aids in the storage and retention of data, information, and knowledge. One of the purposes of any library is to store printed materials which contain the information and knowledge of previous generations. If we did not store this knowledge, each generation would have to pass on the information orally or constantly rediscover it. The limited information available to generations prior to the ready availability of the printed media hindered the advancement of knowledge and the development of science and technology. Knowledge today is readily available to any literate person in the libraries and the printed material of our western society. New developments in collecting and distributing information, which utilize the computer, will provide additional advantages and challenges to society in the future.

The digital computer has been commercially available for two decades. It has been viewed primarily as a *calculating* machine. However, within the last few years, with the ready availability of low–cost storage, users have started to conceive of the computer as an *information storage, processing* and *retrieval* machine. The evolution of large and powerful computer systems developed primarily for storing and retrieving data will rapidly accelerate during the next decade.

The evolution of large-capacity, directly accessible storage of computer systems is shown in Figure 12-1. In 1970, storage units with capacities greater than 10^{11} bits were available. On-line directly accessible storage enables the computer to read stored data without human intervention. Computers can read a piece of data from a large on-line disk storage unit at random in less than one second. Off-line storage, by contrast, refers to a storage medium, such as magnetic tape, to which the machine does not have ready access but which requires the intervention of the operator.

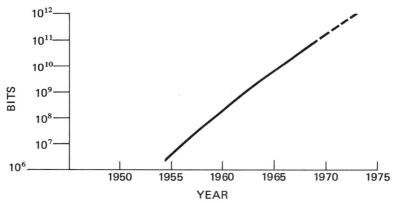

FIGURE 12-1   The capacity of on-line directly accessible storage of large computer systems during the years 1955-1970.

As the capacities of the storage devices have increased, the cost per bit stored has decreased. Figure 12-2 illustrates the estimated number of bits stored per dollar of cost during the period 1950-1975. The cost of storing all the information in the pages of this book in a computer device might have been $750 in 1955. It would be about $3 in 1971 (excluding the illustrations). It is the ready availability of low-cost storage units that has fostered the development of data banks and information retrieval systems.

The storage of large amounts of data in readily accessible storage units is useful in business, government, and education, among other applications. A *data bank* is an on-line storage unit retaining large masses of data. In many cases, the kinds of material stored in a data bank resemble lists, directions, tabulations or similar material that has been otherwise available in the printed form. Data banks presently serve the following, among others:

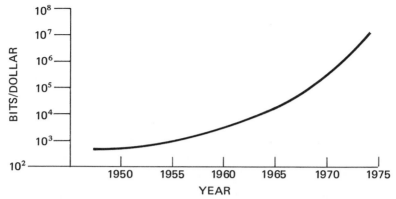

FIGURE 12-2 The cost of on-line storage during the years 1955-1975 (estimated).

- Transportation reservations
- U.S. economy
- Real estate
- Municipal bond bidding
- Theatre tickets
- Shipping rates
- Stock market prices
- Agriculture
- Medical literature

Many functions can be achieved with data stored in data banks by using the great speed of the computer. Data bank information can be: [1]

(1) Added to or deleted from as desired
(2) Retrieved
(3) Manipulated
(4) Combined with data from other sources
(5) Displayed in graphic form
(6) Transmitted over long distances

Data from data banks is available through terminals in printed form or by computer-generated voice output. (See Chapter 10.) Such services, supplied by large computer organizations, comprise what has been called a *computer utility*.

An example of a data bank is the storage of data on the economy of the United States. Economists and planners in many organizations repeatedly use such data as the Gross National Product (GNP), percentage of unemployment and price index. In 1967, a group of 23 large firms in New York City, primarily banks and insurance companies, formed a cooperative experimental data bank

FIGURE 12-3   Old–fashioned mechanical coin banks symbolizing each of the areas or enterprises for which data banks are available. From *Computer Decisions*, a Hayden publication.

called Project Economics. Since then, several commercial firms have developed
data banks available for a service fee. Another example of a data bank is the
storage of data on the status of the stock market. This system, which provides
up–to–the–minute quotes on each stock covered by the stock exchange may
be seen in action at a local stock broker's office. Data banks are also used to
store information on availability of real estate, used automobiles, employment
and theatre tickets, among others. Once one of the items described in this type
of bank is used, it is noted as unavailable. Once an entire event has occurred, the
entire set of data is removed from the system.

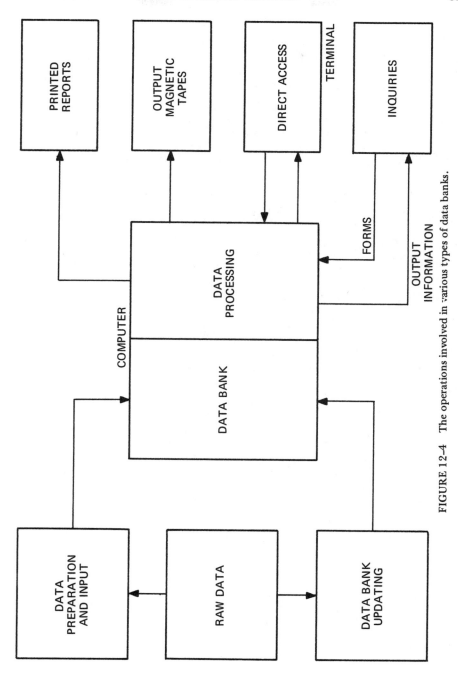

FIGURE 12–4   The operations involved in various types of data banks.

The operations involved in the various types of data banks are shown in Figure 12-4. Data banks may be established to provide printed reports, or magnetic tapes with the output stored on the tape. Also, some data banks are used for inquiry such as reservation systems. Many data banks are connected directly to terminals which provide direct access for the user.

The development of computer data banks has occurred when enormous quantities of data are being generated. Man is experiencing what is often called an information explosion. It has been estimated that knowledge was doubling every 50 years by 1800 and by 1950 it was doubling every 10 years. In 1971, one may estimate that knowledge is doubling every five years. This knowledge must be recorded if it is to be valuable to the members of the future generations. The data banks serve this purpose. They are automated storehouses of data that can be searched as desired; they are technological solutions to the problem of the overabundance of information.

About 100,000 technical reports, 10 million articles in journals, and 30,000 books are published each year. A library of books and reports is a data bank with inexpensive storage and random access. It is available at slow speed via a series of indexes, and it is not automated. A computerized data bank is automated and of high speed and it usually operates at a reasonable cost per item stored. The computer stores the index to the data bank and provides a ready means of updating the index and the stored data.

12.2   INFORMATION STORAGE AND RETRIEVAL

The availability of data in data banks can be overwhelming to the potential user. The user desires to extract information from the myriads of data. The real need of the user of a data bank is information, and he does not care about the data form or structure of the computer that stores the data. The information the user desires is a particular meaning implied by the data in an aggregate or summated form. The definition we use for information in this context is:

INFORMATION   (1) The meaning assigned to data by some agreed upon convention. (2) The aggregation of data that are presented in various forms.

The basic problem of obtaining the information from a data base is that of meaning. A user doesn't ordinarily seek a document or report for its own sake, but for the ideas it contains. Therefore, the seeking of information in a data bank is called *information retrieval.* Thus data becomes information within a framework of relevance. The problem of information retrieval becomes one of classifying and characterizing the information and making it accessible to the user. It is here that the dilemma of retrieval emerges. There is an inverse relation between retrievability and ambiguity, but a direct one between ambiguity and new knowledge (that is, new systems or generalizations into which information is organized). The less ambiguous the information, the more thoroughly it is structured and the easier it is of access. One has only to thread his way through the hierarchy of concepts and categories to the fact or idea he wants.

Efforts to handle information more readily date at least from Aristotle, whose starting point was the way we discourse about things. There are, he postulated, ten ways in which we do so, and he proposed ten categories to comprehend them: substance, quality, quantity, relation, determination in time and in space, action, passivity, position, condition. In one way or another, all statements, he held, conform to these categories.[2] Another approach was that of Peter Mark Roget, who sought to deal not with how we discourse, nor what we *seem* to be saying, but with the words we use to say what we say. In his thesaurus he tried to map the senses in which words are used. His framework consists of six basic classes of sense: abstract relations, space, matter, intellect, volition and affections, each divided into sections and subdivided into topics, together amounting to a framework like Aristotle's, though more explicitly detailed. In one way or another, the schemes of Roget, Aristotle, Dewey and others are used to organize and classify data.

Extracting information, however, is more than the inverse of classifying it. The two processes together comprise information storage and retrieval:

INFORMATION STORAGE AND RETRIEVAL The technique and process of accumulating, classifying, storing, and searching large amounts of data, extracting and reproducing or displaying the required information contained within the data.

Information retrieval is not a new concept, but recently several computer-based information retrieval systems have been under development. Some of the problems confronted in building a computer-based information retrieval system are:

(1) Those involved in the selection of data which will constitute a request
(2) Ascertaining the relevance of key words which will identify an item
(3) Economics of response time, since a shorter response time increases the cost of retrieving an item

A large library of magnetic tapes recording a vast amount of data is shown in Figure 12-5. An off-line tape is selected and accessed for information retrieval. (In Chapter 10 we defined *access time* as the time required to locate and read a stored record.) While a tape storage system results in a longer response time, it is a relatively low-cost storage device for an information retrieval system.

The quality of an information retrieval system is measured by how much relevant information, compared to irrelevant information, is provided in response to a query. One might state this measure of quality as follows:

Quality = Relevant Information/Irrelevant Information

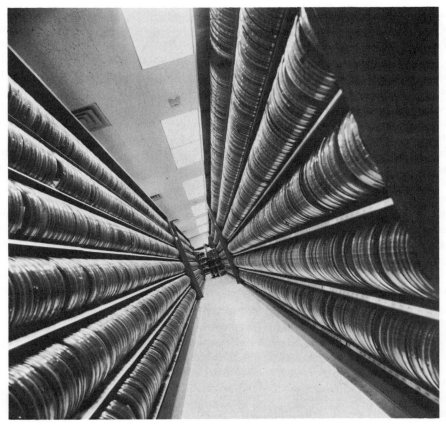

FIGURE 12-5   A large library of magnetic tapes for information retrieval. *Courtesy of Minnesota Mining and Manufacturing Co.*

where a large number for the measure of quality is desired.

An additional characteristic of information retrieval is the task of matching the information that is stored with what is relevant at a particular time. Often the very process of trying to answer a question changes our needs. In a search through categories of references and through possibly relevant data, we discover unforeseen aspects that change our concepts of what we seek. Reference data that so modify the course of our search also become information. The inquiry and answer process is a feedback process; it is the strength of a good information retrieval system when one can obtain rapid access to the information and at the same time can restate the inquiry as a result. This allows the user to search and retrieve information in a dialog process between man and the data bank.

The computer data bank also provides a constantly updated storage of data. As an example, consider the updating of simple facts like telephone numbers. Each day in the U.S. there are 80,000 changes or additions to listed numbers. Each day there are ten million inquiries to information operators; each question and answer now consumes an average of 12 seconds. It is obvious that updating the data bank and speeding up referrals to it can justify a computer even if what is retrieved is a tiny block of data—one phone number for each inquiry.

There are two major classes of information retrieval services. The first provides information of a scientific or technical nature. The second is the information retrieval system for general information, such as real estate information or theatre information. Both types of systems are currently available. We are moving into an age when intelligent persons in all professions will use computer terminals to supplement their personal knowledge. This combination of man and computer will yield an age of *symbiotic man.* Man's abilities will be extended by the aid of the computer information retrieval system.

Information retrieval systems deal with data, records and files. Each piece of raw information the system receives is called a *data item.* A collection of such data items is called a *record.* If a data bank were to store information about an employee, the employee record would contain, for example, the name, city, occupation and age of each person. Records are collected into logical units called *files.* The arrangement and interrelation of records in a file form a *data structure.* The field in computer science concerned with the study and application of data structures, files, records and information retrieval is often called *information science.*

The speed of modern computers allows for a random–search retrieval system and unstructured files that are useful for storing certain data (see Ch. 10). Since the unstructured file does not require a given piece of data to be stored in a particular location, it is not necessary to predefine and prestructure such a file. As a result, one has the ability to extract and integrate data from unique or nonstandard format documentation, in spite of the fact that most of the data entered into computer storage is repetitive format information from tabulations or standard forms.

One of the most important functions in the input of data is the indexing of the material received. Indexing is the characterization of records (*e.g.,* by descriptive phrases) which permits effective retrieval of the stored data. The most commonly used index schemes are key–word oriented. Important data should be indexed in detail while less important information receives less detailed indexing. No one indexing system is identified as best for all applications.

Typical indexing systems are the key–word in context indexing (KWIC) system and the alphabetical subject indexing system. A key–word is a term selected to describe the subject content of the input material and is usually drawn from the specific text or title. While matching or combining key words to locate stored data is generally not practical or efficient in manual search systems, a computer is ideally suited to this matching process. The use of keyword indexing allows the computer the flexibility of handling inquiries that cannot be predicted during the preparation of the data base.

The art and science of developing effective information retrieval systems will be an interesting field of endeavor for the next decade at a minimum.

Information retrieval systems have potential application in many diverse fields. The following various types of data have been stored in data banks:

(1) Abstracts of technical articles
(2) Legal case decisions
(3) Characteristics of equipment in an industry
(4) Physical properties of chemicals
(5) Records of the maintenance of automobiles
(6) Crime records of a municipality.

For example, the International Association of Chiefs of Police established a goal of a national crime information system. In Washington, D. C., a file of 330,000 active criminal records is available for tens of thousands of inquiries each day from anywhere in the nation. The California Highway Patrol has a computer coupled to the computer at the Federal Bureau of Investigation. A centralized file for stolen autos and property and a file for over 100,000 wanted persons comprise part of the national system. This system aids in the pursuit of wanted criminals and the recovery of stolen property in the U. S. and Canada.

Several computer information retrieval systems are being developed for aiding the legal system. A large number of civil suits reach the United States courts. One result is a flood of legal precedents which may or may not be significant to a particular case and which may make achieving a rapid and just settlement difficult.

The computer is an ideal tool for assisting lawyers in their search for precedents. The lawyer of the future may well use the terminal in his office to instruct distant computers to carry out a search for him and to display legal information. One lawyer might use the computer to search for a statute related to a particular case. Setting up the necessary files for such a system, however, will take a vast amount of work and time.

A computer information retrieval system for the laws of the U. S. is being developed.[3] If an attorney needs to examine the laws of all states, a requirement that occurs often, this effort can require the perusal of 26,000 law tomes. The company which is developing the computer system has stored in the data bank all the statutes of the 50 states, the U. S. Code and 14 volumes of U. S. Supreme Court decisions.[3] The service, now available, is invaluable to legislators who need to research all the existing codes in force. Depending on the difficulty of the search, the length of time for a search can vary from a minute to eight hours. The system currently used requires about eight hours for a search of statutes in all 50 states.[3] The legal system of the United States should be aided in the future by the availability of legal–inquiry systems for researching legal statutes and precedents. This system will enable the country to provide the ready access to a trial and justice our democracy requires for the individual.

The U. S. Patent Office has 3.5 million U. S. patents and 7 million non–U. S. patents stored in its manual files. In an ideal system all the patent data items would be converted to computer data and stored in a data bank. The total amount of patent data is approximately 600 billion characters, which exceeds the current on–line capability of computer information retrieval systems. However, an on–line storage of patent abstracts is feasible and is currently being planned by the U. S. Patent Office.[4]

Of course, these are many applications of data banks and information retrieval systems to industry, government, and education. One of the most important applications of information retrieval systems is to libraries. This application is examined in the following section.

12.3 INFORMATION RETRIEVAL AND LIBRARIES

The rate at which man has been accumulating and storing useful knowledge has been growing for several thousand years. The invention of writing and the invention of movable type in the 15th century are two landmarks in the history of recorded knowledge. Prior to 1500, Europe was producing approximately 1000 new books per year. By 1950, the rate had increased so that Europe was producing 120,000 titles per year. By the end of the 1960's the output of books in the world had approached the rate of 1000 titles per day.[5] The number of journals and articles is also rapidly growing. On a worldwide basis, scientific and technical literature is produced at a rate of 60 million pages a year. It is the computer which has assisted the recent acceleration of the growth of knowledge, and the computer will assist in the storage and retrieval of this vast amount of new knowledge.

A library is a repository of books, journals, newspapers, and other printed material which can be used for reading and examination. The word library comes from the Latin word *liber,* which means "book." Traditionally, the library has been a storehouse of books. With the increasing number of books and journals and the increased literacy of our population, the need for automation in the libraries has grown.

There are three main types of libraries: the public library, usually a general collection with emphasis on current publications; the special library, with mostly current material focused on one or more fairly narrow areas of interest; and the academic library, with both current and historical material in all the fields covered by the educational and research programs, plus some coverage of the intellectual life of the world at large.

The academic library must have both depth and breadth, which explains why Harvard University has eight million volumes and why there are nearly a hundred other universities in this country with over a million. Each of these hundred annually buys more than 5% of the titles published in the world. (Each library with a million titles holds half of 1% of all the titles published since Gutenberg.)

At the IBM Advanced Systems Development Division library in Los Gatos, California, an on-line, totally integrated system has been in operation for several years. It establishes continuity and consistency among the basic library procedures, beginning from a single bibliographic input. Each of the library functions—acquisition, receiving, cataloging and circulation—has been automated. Each is an individual module.

The system now in operation utilizes direct on-line communication with a computer to capture bibliographic data correctly and competely. This input is then processed to provide the computer printouts for the record-keeping functions of the library. Twice a week, an updated listing of all items in circulation is printed. The computer also issues a statistical report of how many items have been borrowed, how many requested and how many reserved. Moreover, a complete list of reserve requests is issued, indicating the names of people requesting each item. All this information provides the librarian with precise knowledge of what books are in circulation and who has them. It also suggests titles in demand, for which the library should consider purchasing additional copies.

In general, libraries will be utilizing computers increasingly, along with the associated peripheral computer technology in the future decade. For example, microform and microfilm techniques, computer indexing, and automated abstracting and extracting will be a few among the many new aids to libraries. One possible consequence of automation in libraries is that of libraries becoming elements of one or more integrated networks.[6] Through a computer network, the availability of materials could be increased in libraries of all kinds and sizes in the nation. System Development Corporation, in a recent study of libraries and the use of computers, recommended the following five projects:[6]

(1) A prototype network of regional libraries
(2) An expanded, computer-based National Union Catalog
(3) A national bibliography
(4) A national referral and loan network
(5) A national library storage and microform depository system

Some of the possible consequences of the introduction of computer automated libraries are:

(1) Use of microforms, microfilms and digital information for storage of information (supplementing or replacing storage methods now in use)

(2) A shift of operation from *circulation* to outright *distribution*

(3) Providing users with a high order of ready access to reference materials

We have already mentioned the use of microforms and microfilms. In terms of storage, 10,000 pages can be recorded on an area the size of one page of this book. Also, microforms and microfilm can be located, retrieved, and read by means of computer–controlled peripheral equipment such as computer micro-film readers. Distribution of printed materials has been largely by means of quick copying machines placed in libraries. Over a billion pages of copies of articles or pages of a book are made each year in libraries in the U.S.[7]

The costs of providing access to all materials in a library are significantly higher as one increases the automation of libraries and attempts to decrease the response time for a request. However, the development of systems for ready access will provide computer–aided reference services in the future. For ex-ample, computer automation of the library card catalog still is not economically feasible, but should become feasible as new developments occur.

Four areas of automated library activities have been attempted: book-keeping operations connected with ordering and receiving departments; hand-ling catalog data for books, sometimes accompanied by book catalogs printed by computer; circulation control; and information retrieval of technical data, law citations and bibliographical citations.

The Library of Congress is the library of the United States whose first obligation is to meet the information needs of the Congress, but in many ways it also serves as a national library. The Library of Congress has about 60 mil-lion items and the official catalog contains some 16.5 million records.[8] The library collects material from all over the world and receives material written in 125 languages. It houses the largest and most varied collection of any library in this country and also provides a national bibliographic service. The United States, unlike most other countries, does not have an organized national bibli-ography to announce materials published in the country. Through its printed-card service and book catalogs, the Library of Congress has assumed these func-tions. The library also maintains the National Union Catalog (NUC), which con-tains records of approximately 12.8 million titles, each record having posted to it the names of the libraries holding any particular title. Project MARC (for MAchine Readable Cataloging) is a series of ambitious experiments in com-puterized library processes, concentrated at present on the handling of catalog data. Since the Library of Congress is pivotal, to the degree that these experi-ments are successful they will affect the entire library world.

Project INTREX (INformation TRansfer EXperiments) is a program of re-search directed toward the functional design of new library services at the Mass-achusetts Institute of Technology. One of the concerns of Project INTREX is to conduct a series of experiments to determine how the traditional library catalog can be effectively augmented and combined with on-line computer operation to provide users with a more powerful, comprehensive and useful guide to library resources. Present plans call for augmenting the traditional catalog in scope, depth and search means. For example, the augmented catalog will contain entries for reports and individual journal articles as well as the traditional entries for books. Furthermore, in addition to the title and author of each item, such things as the bibliography, an abstract, key words and key phrases of each item will be included as part of its catalog entry. A user will be able to conduct searches on nearly any combination of the data contained in a catalog entry. Present plans also call for providing alphanumeric communication between user and computer by means of a high-speed, flexible display console.[9]

The advancing technology coupled with the computer will alter the use of libraries in the future. Trips to the library may become unnecessary. With the use of still-experimental display devices, the reader may be able to request the printed material of interest to him and view it on a screen in his home or office.

12.4 DATA BANKS, INFORMATION RETRIEVAL AND PRIVACY

Computer information systems containing data about individuals are needed increasingly in the public sector to record such items as census data, medical statistics and Social Security records. Governments need these records to carry out their responsibilities; planners and social scientists need them to understand society and to suggest measures to take it in the directions considered desirable; business needs the records for effective operations, service and management.

These systems which contain the information are increasingly being integrated within larger networks of data banks. Integrated systems provide accurate, consistent data at lower costs and with greater coverage than do isolated data banks. The availability of computer terminals and the ease of communication also increase the tendency to integrate and interconnect data banks.

The ready availability of information about persons stored in data banks leads to a concern in our nation about the privacy and security of information and the possible misuse of such information. Privacy and security are in many ways different issues. Security relates to the safeguarding of the information stored within a computer data bank. Privacy means the protection of the individual from (1) unreasonable observation; (2) unreasonable usurpation of his name or likeness; and (3) unauthorized access to personal or confidential information. Privacy is a social question, while security is largely a technical question. The development of technical systems to provide secure data banks is currently being accomplished. A secure system is one that will not allow entry by unauthorized individuals. Security checks such as codes, passwords and guards will help to insure that the data stored within a machine is secure.

Privacy is the more difficult problem to solve. This problem may require legislation as well as responsibility on the part of the individual who is seeking information to limit his searching and his questions to that information for which he has immediate need and which he is qualified to know.

Untold amounts of information about individuals have existed heretofore. However, the mechanical means for retaining and disseminating this information have been sufficiently difficult to limit use of that information. The citizen's records with selective service, the military, the Veterans' Administration, the Internal Revenue Service, the FBI and any number of other agencies, remained just that: a record of past activities on file with the respective agencies. The computer, however, has made possible the exchange of such information on an instantaneous basis so that, if necessary, all such information can be brought together.

The question of privacy is not limited to the citizen's dealings with his government. In business, particularly in the business of retail credit information, great danger for the individual exists. Here, there is an established practice of collecting all derogatory information about individuals from whatever sources may be available and holding such information for call from respective member businesses (primarily retailers and banks) who want to know the individual's credit record before extending him credit.

There are some 2500 credit-reporting agencies which collect and store this information in data banks.

The conflict between the state's need for information and individual freedom has long been a social issue. The computer not only has intensified this conflict; it has also changed its character, which is as much political and social as it is technical. The balance is between the values of civil liberties against those of efficiency and secrecy in government operations. For example, several social scientists and statisticians have suggested the creation and maintenance of a national data bank. Its use would remedy many defects of current records and procedures which result in information unresponsive to the needs of vital policy decisions. A lucid and helpful discussion of the necessary legal safeguards to insure privacy in a computer society is provided in an article by Alan F. Westin, a noted legal scholar and professor of law and government. The article is abstracted below.[10]

It has always been American political policy to limit the surveillance of citizens. This is one principle of the Constitution. However, when the Constitution was written, there were only two main ways to observe the citizenry: physical and psychological-judicial. Without electronic listening devices, the only way surveillance could be conducted was by entering places to listen and observe. Citizens might be tortured to give information. They could also be forced by the courts to testify against themselves. This primitive form of surveillance, common in the 18th century, was specifically forbidden by the American Constitution.

By the end of the 19th century, however, the technology that makes it possible for a man to talk to another miles away also raised the possibility of invasion of privacy. Even early telephones were tapped, and the invention of the microphone made it possible to plant "bugs" for surveillance work as early as the 1890's. Fortunately it was early established that evidence from such surveillance was not admissible in court.

As the country became fully industrialized, and as income taxes were instituted, record-keeping increased on a massive scale. This was particularly true in the period between the World Wars. Still the citizen was protected from invasion of his privacy by the inability of the government to process, organize, and put to use the great amounts of raw data it collected on most citizens.

Now, as we suggest above, the development of data banks and retrieval procedures makes it possible to know and use many different kinds of information. The citizen stands alone; in fact, he is more than alone. His very integrity can be dismantled. He may be made the subject of psychological inquiries, the results of which can be made part of his permanent "Record" and ultimately used against him. Such inquiries can be made through tests administered directly or indirectly, or through devices like the so-called "Lie Detector," or polygraph, which themselves can be administered without the knowledge of the subject.

Information-gathering, and to some extent information-sharing as well, is not restricted to government agencies, of course. Private clubs, schools and even churches are all joining a general movement toward amassing more and more information about their membership.

In addition, the economy has been moving toward a no-cash method of operation, as described previously. In order for the banks and charge plans to function they must collect and share information about individual card-holders.

One might wish for a government that could ignore this potentially enormous base for surveillance. However, under the most benign conditions any government would be tempted to take and to use information about individuals for such otherwise worthy projects as statistical analyses of labor force, minimum wages, welfare, and even highway and utility planning. Even if this information were to be used in an aggregate, in the beginning it "belongs" to the citizen, and putting it to use without his knowledge or his ability to disagree with it is an invasion of his privacy.

Well-meaning citizens may set about to remedy this situation, but the problem has many components. American law does not define personal information as having value, although ironically it does assign value to business information, patents, and the like.

Another problem we face in ensuring privacy for the individual is that there is no way for the citizen to talk back if information about him has been falsely stated. This area of potential conflict is most prone to violation of the due process provisions of the Constitution. If you have ever had a bank error reported as an overdraft in your checking account, and you have tried to get the error corrected, you can easily imagine what would happen if your record with the IRS were similarly first damaged, then used against you.

Finally, the very impartiality of data information banks may work to the disadvantage of the individuals reported in them. It is possible to ask for important information about either a large or a small population. The small population could be a single citizen. It must be arranged, therefore, to bar operators from extracting any given single data files.

What all this suggests is first that the citizen should have the right to refuse to report or to have circulated information about himself. The key to this conception is in the First Amendment to the Constitution. Possibly information could be divided into classes or types, ranging from harmless information open to everybody (*e.g.,* birth date) to highly limited and confidential information. It is also obvious that laws must be made which would allow only restricted use for any given kind of information.

All that has been said about the inherent dangers of information processing on a national scale can also be said about intelligence procedures.

Although we do not now have the legal machinery to ensure that the individual's privacy can be protected while stores of information are amassed and used, we do have historical precedents for arranging such legal devices. Naturally it is to be hoped that our elected officials will work out the proper protections within these traditions, and in time and in such a way that the many benefits from use of computers will be accompanied by means of oppression or violation of individual rights.

Professor Westin described the need for a new legal approach to the computer storage and processing of personal information. Recently Westin has suggested that a "writ of habeas data" should be required to justify the use of computerized information against an individual just as a writ of habeas corpus requires that the state justify an individual's imprisonment.[11]

California has recently passed into law legislation which (1) recognizes an individual's right of privacy, and (2) designates computerized data in state files as "public records." This legislation may well prove to be a landmark in the fight to establish a right to privacy and would seem to guarantee the right of an individual to read his own file.

It has been suggested that the nation draft model statutes and develop ethical guidelines which would permit data to be disseminated without violating due process—*e.g.,* the individual's right to defend himself against punitive action taken by the data recipient; the individual's right to protection against self-incrimination, and his right of appeal to a higher authority when an administrative agency controlling a data bank takes an action which he opposes concerning his file. Also, a public review committee might be established for the purpose of an annual audit of each data bank's operation in terms of civil liberties. The committee could be made up of representatives from various legal, professional and occupational groups, and should include some persons experienced in the particular field of policy of the data system.

A recent book, *The Computerized Society,* lists several suggested legal actions to account for the new forces in society due to the impact of the computer.[12] Several of the suggested legal actions are:

1. A register of data banks should be established, including the following information:
   a. The name and address of the person responsible for the operation of the data bank
   b. The nature of the data stored or to be stored therein
   c. The purpose for which data is stored therein
   d. The class of persons authorized to extract data therefrom
2. As far as possible, facts, not opinions, should be stored.
3. All interrogations of data banks should be automatically logged.
4. The public should have the right to inspect records stored in the data banks.
5. The individual should have the right to take issue with personal data stored about him.
6. Aged data should be removed.
7. Security procedures should be registered with a national auditing agency.

In a sense, what has been proposed in many instances is the development of an Information Bill of Rights, which would guarantee the right of access by a citizen to his data file, the right to review it and correct it, and the right to appeal its use to an ombudsman.

SUMMARY

The computer is a useful device for information storage, processing and retrieval. With the advent of relatively low cost storage the computer lends itself to the development of data banks. A data bank is an on–line storage unit retaining large masses of data. Data banks are used to retain economic, social and industrial data among others. A terminal is one possible access connection for the potential user. A computer data bank is automated, of high speed, and it usually operates at a reasonable cost per item stored.

Information is the meaning assigned to the data or an aggregate representation of the data. It is the desired output of an information retrieval system. Information retrieval is the process of accumulating, classifying, storing and searching large amounts of data and extracting the required information from it. The quality of an information retrieval system is measured by how much relevant information, in comparison to how much irrelevant information, is provided in response to a query. Information retrieval systems have been developed for airlines, government functions, and the legal profession among others.

Computer information retrieval systems will aid in the operation of the libraries of the future. Computers are being used for automated acquisitions, receiving, cataloging and circulation. The primary items of cost for automated libraries will be the amount of information stored and the response time required as a result of an inquiry. In the future, a device in the home or the office may display information upon request.

Computer information systems containing information about individuals are increasingly necessary to govern and manage our complex society. However, the ready availability of information about persons leads to a concern about the privacy of information. Privacy, in this context, is primarily concerned with unauthorized access to personal or confidential information. The conflict between the need for accumulating information in a data bank, and the protection of an individual's freedom, must be reconciled. What may be required in the future is an Information Bill of Rights for the citizen.

CHAPTER 12 PROBLEMS

P12-1. Differentiate between the concepts of *data* and *information*.

P12-2. Discuss the difference between a data bank and an information retrieval system.

P12-3. Determine if the storage and retrieval of the students' academic records at your college would be appropriate for a computer information retrieval system.

P12-4. If an information retrieval system were developed as proposed in Problem 12-3, would a problem arise concerning the privacy of the students' confidential records?

P12-5. A measure of information might be, in a particular case, a student's grade point average up-to-date, or the balance in his checking account. If possible, establish a query for this piece of information and determine the quality of relevant information received. (Refer to Section 12-2.)

CHAPTER 12 REFERENCES

1. D. deLonge, "Dawning of the Age of Data Banks," *Computer Decisions,* March, 1970, pp. 21–24.
2. L. Sandek, "Man's World of Facts," *Data Processor,* Vol. X, No. 4, November 1967, pp. 4–35.
3. "Consulting the Computer," *Time,* May 4, 1970, pg. 68.
4. "Patent Office Information Retrieval System Not Yet in the Cards; But There's Light Ahead," *Computer Decisions,* November, 1969, pg. 29.
5. A. Toffler, *Future Shock,* Random House, Inc., New York, 1970, pp. 30–31.
6. R. Lanham, "Marian the Technologist?" *SCD Magazine,* Vol. 11, No. 10, November, 1968, pp. 1–11.
7. W. N. Locke, "Computer Costs for Large Libraries," *Datamation,* February, 1970, pp. 69–74.
8. P. R. Reimers and H. D. Avram, "Automation and the Library of Congress: 1970," *Datamation,* June, 1970, pp. 138–143.
9. D. R. Haring, "A Display Console for an Experimental Computer–Based Augmented Library Catalog," *Proceedings of the 23rd National Conference of the Association for Computing Machinery,* pp. 35–43, 1968.
10. A. F. Westin, "Legal Safeguards to Insure Privacy in a Computer Society," *Communications of the Association for Computing Machinery,* Vol. 10, No. 9, 1967.
11. "Writ of Habeas Data," *Modern Data,* March, 1970, page 38.
12. J. Martin and A. R. D. Norman, *The Computerized Society,* Prentice–Hall, Inc., Englewood Cliffs, N.J., 1970.
13. G. Salton, *Automatic Information Organization and Retrieval,* McGraw–Hill Book Company, New York, 1968.
14. E. Herbert, "Information Transfer," *International Science and Technology,* March, 1966, pp. 26–37.
15. G. Salton, "Automatic Text Analysis," *Science,* April 17, 1970, pp. 335–343.
16. C. C. Gotlieb, "Regulations for Information Systems," *Computers and Automation,* October, 1970, pp. 14–17.
17. L. J. Hoffman, "Computers and Privacy: A Survey," *Computing Surveys,* Vol. 1, No. 2, June, 1969, pp. 85–103.
18. A. F. Westin, *Information Technology in a Democracy,* Harvard University Press, Cambridge, Massachusetts, 1970.
19. A. F. Westin, *Privacy and Freedom,* Atheneum, Inc., New York, 1967.
20. A. R. Miller, *The Assault on Privacy: Computers, Data Banks, and Dossiers,* University of Michigan Press, Ann Arbor, Michigan, 1971.

13

SIMULATION AND GAMES

13.1 COMPUTER MODELING AND SIMULATION

Modeling and simulation are of great value to business, industry and government because they permit one to study the effects of various decisions or choices without going through the complete process of the phenomenon being considered. In a sense, the computer is cast in the role of an actor. By lowering the effective cost of calculating compared with experimenting, the computer induced a shift toward calculation in many fields where once only experimentation and measurement were practical.[1] In some cases, such as that of the Apollo spacecraft, a simulation of the phenomenon is necessary prior to the actual experiment. In this section we consider the development and use of computer models which aid in the evaluation of ideas and the study of real or hypothetical situations. This use of computer models is called *computer simulation*.

A model is a qualitative or quantitative representation of a process, showing the effects of those factors which are significant for the purposes being considered.[2] Models exist in most sciences and many businesses. When a computer is applied to this service, we have a *computer model*, defined as:

COMPUTER MODEL A representation of a system or phenomenon in a mathematical or symbolic form suitable for demonstrating the behavior of the system or phenomenon.

Modeling is the process of making a model. The model may not represent the actual phenomenon in all respects, but it should adequately describe the essential characteristics.

Simulation involves subjecting models to various stimuli or situations in such a way as to explore the nature of the results which might be obtained by the real system: [2]

> SIMULATION The use of models and the actual conditions of either the thing being modeled or the environment in which it operates, with the models or conditions in physical, mathematical, or some other form.

Simulation is used to explore the results which might be obtained from the real system by subjecting the model to representative environments which are equivalent to, or in some way representative of, the situations the investigator wants to understand.

Through abstraction of pertinent information from the real world, we attempt to reproduce, in the computer, all conditions important to the entity he wishes to explore. Once these conditions have been incorporated into a computer simulation, the computer can be used to change, rearrange or improve upon the information it has been given.

In many ways, simulation is an art as well as a science. The effectiveness of any computer simulation rests on the user's ability to abstract only those factors that affect the system or process he wishes to duplicate. Reality is simulation's starting point, but not its boundary; simulation experts can mold the starting situation into uncounted situations and thereby can also predict future consequences. These facts are suggested by the composite Möbius Strip in Figure 13-1, which relates the moonscape to equations for celestial navigation and to human physiology.

Although in this chapter we limit our discussion to computer simulation, simulation using physical equivalents has had an interesting history. Some very useful early simulations were a simulation of muscle fascicle using ropes; a simulation of electric eels using pewter, wood, glass and leather, and a simulation of electric potentials in nerve and muscle, using zinc and copper. The modelers were Alfonso Borelli, who made one of the first convincing attempts to reduce a physiological phenomenon to purely mechanical principles; Lord Henry Cavendish, who used simulation to establish the argument that electrical phenomena could occur in animals; and Emil duBois-Reymond, who is often said to have founded modern electro-physiology and who used a simulation to help derive his most famous theory, the Peripolar Molecular Theory.

Prior to 1940, the then relatively low-performance aircraft could be flight-tested by skilled pilots with an acceptable risk. However, the high-performance aircraft and spacecraft designed during the past three decades required preflight test by simulation. Furthermore, as flight simulators became available it became economically feasible to use them for flight training. During

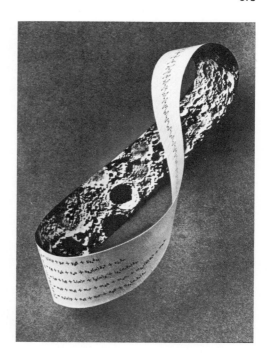

FIGURE 13-1 Möbius strip suggesting simulation of lunar landing. *Courtesy of SDC Corporation.*

World War II, the Link Trainer was used to train many pilots. Currently, simulators which provide realistic mockup cockpits with motion and out-the-window visual cues simulate actual flying conditions so accurately that it is quite easy for a pilot to become absorbed in his duties to such an extent that he forgets he is not actually flying.[3]

In 1969, the United States landed the first men on the moon and brought them back safely. This task would have been very costly in lives and expense without simulation of the flight for testing and training purposes. The only alternative to simulation, in this case, would have been trial-and-error flights. The importance of simulation is highlighted by Walter Schirra's remark from Apollo 7 in space, when ground control suggested that he try something new: "Uh-uh. Not till I've tried it in the simulator first."

Figure 13-2 shows a training device based upon simulation. It is in operation as scientists at the Langley Research Center of the National Aeronautics and Space Administration (NASA) conduct simulation tests to determine human ability to control braking maneuvers for lunar landings. These tests are part of an extensive NASA program at Langley for guidance and control of spacecraft for landing upon the moon's surface. The initial condition for these simulations is assumed to be the point of horizontal braking from a lunar orbit at a moon altitude of about 25 miles. The pilot operates a hydraulic analog

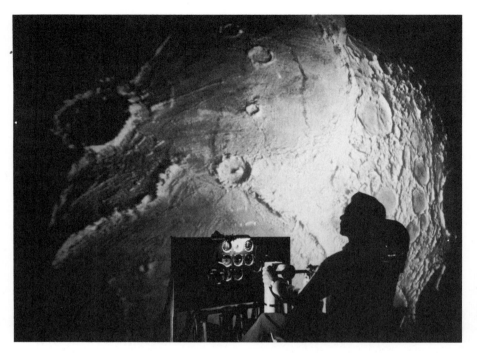

FIGURE 13-2   Simulation test equipment for lunar landings. *Courtesy of NASA.*

simulator as though it were a vertical-landing spaceship. A stand at the pilot's right holds a slide projector for projection of the lunar surface upon a curved background.

When an explosion crippled Apollo 13, the crisis was resolved by using the simulator at Cape Kennedy—while Apollo 13 drifted along its course without its normal cabin oxygen supply. The Command Module Simulator was built to provide astronaut training. It consists of a digital computer complex that provides dynamic representations of spacecraft systems, a complete and accurate presentation of exterior visual scenes, and an exact replica of the spacecraft interior.[4] This simulator is used to conduct tests to determine human ability to control braking maneuvers for lunar landings. An external view of the Command Module Simulator is shown in Figure 13-3. The simulated vehicle is an exact replica of the interior of the Apollo spacecraft as shown in Figure 13-4. All the switches, instruments and other details are exact. The views out the windows and telescope are simulated optically. The computation needed to drive the simulation is done by a complex of four digital computers acting as a single unit to provide real-time simulations of all Command Module subsystems

FIGURE 13-3　External view of the command module simulator, completely surrounded by the out–the–window visual display system. The instructor–operator station is shown in the foreground. *Courtesy of NASA.*

throughout the mission. Furthermore, by simulating the Saturn subsystems, a realistic enactment of the launch–booster and translunar injection portions of the mission is provided. The computers also generate telemetry information in actual format for transmission to ground station equipment. Changes in routines caused by malfunctions and other special inputs are also simulated.[4]

Simulation techniques are not limited to the aerospace and aeronautics fields. They are being applied with great success to the design of large office buildings by architects, who find the reduction of complex, interrelated design elements to accurate visual displays invaluable. Designers can now project, with the computer, precisely how a building or landscape will look in ten or twenty years, given a particular set of circumstances. They can also pretest their building plans for maximum effectiveness before the cornerstone is laid.

A major airline created a computer model to study its proposed computerized ticket–reservation system. The model used in this study projected that the reservation system would not work as designed unless larger computers

FIGURE 13-4   Internal view of command module simulator showing instruments and controls which duplicate exactly the details of the Apollo spacecraft. *Courtesy of NASA.*

were used. The airline didn't believe it, and was later forced almost to double its computer capacity.[5]

We can trace the history of mathematical models from the beginnings of mathematics. One early example of a mathematical model is the Pythagorean theorem, which dates from the sixth century B.C. in Greece. Besides mathematical models we note the early existence of analog models such as world globes, relief maps and wind tunnels. An early use of simulation was developed hundreds of years ago when leaders of opposing armies would study military tactics by moving miniature soldiers around on a scale model of a battlefield. This concept is still with us, except that the "war games" are simulated on a digital computer.

There is an increasingly large class of systems and problems which cannot easily be modeled by using mathematical techniques. Such systems as an airline ticket-reservation network, movement of a tank-car fleet, complex manufacturing systems, transportation networks, military logistics systems and capital investment are examples. These systems are complex and difficult to define. Simulation of these systems can be achieved by building a simulation of symbolic processes which are equivalent to those that occur in the actual system. In developing the digital computer simulation, the analyst describes the system structure and logic (or operating rules) to the computer by means of a program. Simpler simulations of this nature, and simulations where efficient use of computer time is a prime consideration, may be written in a language such as FORTRAN. The price for this efficiency, however, is substantially increased programming time and skills. As a result, specially developed simulation languages have been developed.[5]

Assuming that the model and the simulation are reliably accurate, the advantages of computer simulation are:

1. System performance can be observed under all conceivable conditions.
2. Results of field–system performance can be extrapolated with a simulation model for prediction purposes.
3. Decisions concerning future systems presently in a conceptual stage can be examined.
4. Trials of systems under test can be accomplished in a much–reduced period of time.
5. Simulation results can be obtained at lower cost than real experimentation would cost.
6. Study of hypothetical situations can be achieved even when the hypothetical situation would be unrealizable in actual life at the present time.
7. Computer modeling and simulation is often the only feasible or safe technique to analyze and evaluate a system.

A computer simulation may be developed in FORTRAN, BASIC or a language specifically developed for simulation. Two widely–used simulation languages are GPSS (General Purpose Simulation System) and SIMSCRIPT, which is an ALGOL–based language.

In constructing a model with GPSS, the analyst uses special–purpose blocks which serve as the language's instructions, and then constructs a flow chart incorporating the system structure and the decision rules. SIMSCRIPT, on the other hand, is statement–oriented, rather than block–oriented. In using this language the analyst describes the system by means of English–like statements resembling those in FORTRAN and PL/1. The first step in the analysis of any particular system is to isolate the system's elements and formulate the logical rules governing their interaction. This yields a model.

Let us consider a system of ship docking which can be simulated using GPSS.[6] Cargo ships arrive at a small port with a known arrival pattern. While in port, the ships unload some of their cargo, taking a certain amount of time, and then proceed on their voyages. There is only one pier, and if a ship arrives while another is unloading, it must wait. If several ships are waiting, the one that arrived first will be unloaded first. Of interest here is the total amount of time that a ship will spend in port, including the time spent waiting for the pier to become available.

This process is illustrated graphically in Figure 13-5. The dynamic transactions are simulated in GPSS using a block notation. To provide input for the simulation, program cards are prepared from a block diagram flow chart of the system under study. The flow chart for the ship arrival system is shown in Figure 13-6. Once the system model is loaded, the GPSS program generates and moves transactions from block to block according to timing information and logical rules incorporated in the blocks. The program executes the movements and maintains a record of the time sequence. The program also maintains a record of the status of delays and the time consumed by the process. The output of the program will be:

1. The amount of ship traffic flowing through the complete system and its parts.
2. The average time for ships to pass through the system and portions of the system.

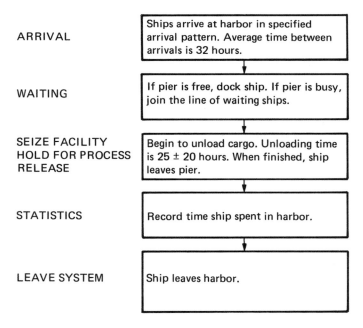

FIGURE 13-5   The logic flow for ships arriving at a harbor with one unloading dock.

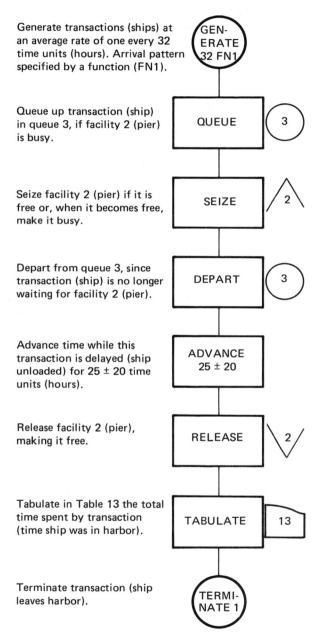

Generate transactions (ships) at an average rate of one every 32 time units (hours). Arrival pattern specified by a function (FN1).

GENERATE 32 FN1

Queue up transaction (ship) in queue 3, if facility 2 (pier) is busy.

QUEUE 3

Seize facility 2 (pier) if it is free or, when it becomes free, make it busy.

SEIZE 2

Depart from queue 3, since transaction (ship) is no longer waiting for facility 2 (pier).

DEPART 3

Advance time while this transaction is delayed (ship unloaded) for 25 ± 20 time units (hours).

ADVANCE 25 ± 20

Release facility 2 (pier), making it free.

RELEASE 2

Tabulate in Table 13 the total time spent by transaction (time ship was in harbor).

TABULATE 13

Terminate transaction (ship leaves harbor).

TERMINATE 1

FIGURE 13-6 The GPSS flow chart for the harbor problem.

3. The amount of use of each portion of the system.
4. The maximum and average lengths of queues occurring at various points in the system.

The simulation language GPSS can be used to solve a variety of problems. In general, these problems have one characteristic in common: they involve transactions in which people or equipment are competing for services of other people or equipment. It is of interest how well the service organization will respond to the demands. For instance, GPSS may be used for the design of a telephone system to intercept and service telephone calls automatically when the calls cannot be put through because new numbers have been assigned, or because units have been disconnected. It could also help with simulation of automobile flow patterns along roads and through intersections and toll gates to determine properly-sequenced lane segments.[6]

The use of other simulation languages as well as FORTRAN and BASIC for the simulation of biological and chemical systems has developed during the past few years. The principle of *change through time* is a basic pattern in many of life's processes. A study of evolutionary processes using simulation has many appealing facets. Recently, a simulation of a biological system was accomplished using FORTRAN.[7] The system studied was the variation of the population of the hare (*Lepus Americanus*) over hundreds of years. It had been noted, using data from the records of the fur-trading Hudson's Bay Company dating back to 1790 and from other observations, that the sizes of various populations of the hares in eastern Canada followed a fairly regular cyclic pattern of alternating abundance and depletion. Highs of abundance occurred about every ten years. It has also been noted that the population of the Bay Lynx (*Lynx Rufus*) also had ten-year cycles and that they correlated very well with the fluctuations in the hare populations. It has been determined that 89 percent of the lynx's diet consisted of the varying hares and also that when the hares were at a population low, lynxes were often found dead of starvation or in emaciated and starving condition.

This example of the close correlation between the lynx and hare populations in Canada has been used for many years in ecological studies and biology textbooks as a classic example of a predator-prey relationship. The model chosen by the authors of the study is illustrated graphically in Figure 13-7. The seven variables identified for inclusion are:

1. Hare birth rate   HBR
2. Hare death rate   HDR
3. Lynx birth rate   LBR
4. Lynx death rate   LDR
5. Lynx kill ratio   LKR
6. Lynx-hare population ratio   LXH
7. Resource level R_h

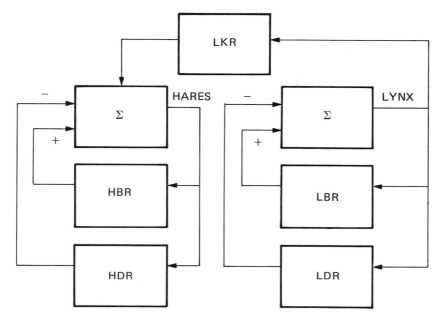

FIGURE 13-7 The functional model of the lynx–hare system. *Copyright 1970 by Simulation Councils, Inc. P. O. Box 2228, La Jolla, Cal. Reprinted by permission.*

A population block is shown for both the lynx and hare populations. The hare population increase is generated by a birth rate block which adds to the hare population block. Similarly, the natural hare decrease is generated by a hare death rate block which subtracts from the hare population block. This is equivalent to saying that the population of hares at generation (i + 1) is equal to the population at generation i plus the hares born minus the hares that died. The hare population is further reduced by the number of hares killed by lynx predation, as represented in the kill ratio block. A similar feedback relationship was established for the lynx population.

Also, the functions of the hare birth rate and death rate versus the hare population were developed from recorded data. A similar set of functions was developed for the lynx population. The parameter values of the simulated system could be entered by the user. Figure 13–8 shows the variation of the populations for a specific set of parameters. For the given set of parameters, the system is oscillatory, exhibiting the expected periodic variations in the populations. One can easily alter the parameters and establish new population variations. Thus, one could study the effects of various ecological changes.

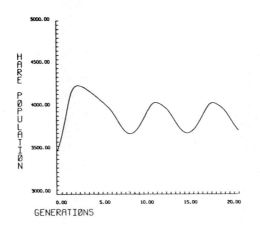

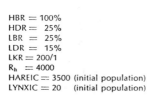

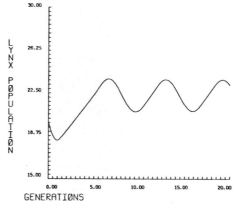

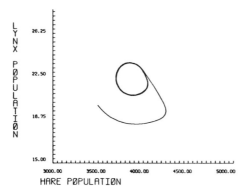

FIGURE 13-8   The variations of the lynx and hare populations shown for one set of
              parameters over 20 generations. The lynx and hare populations are plotted
              together in (c). *Copyright 1970 by Simulation Councils, Inc. P. O. Box
              2228, La Jolla, Cal. Reprinted by permission.*

The study of chemistry and molecular structure can be carried out by computer simulation. The graphic representation of a molecular structure is shown in Figure 13-9. The computer can be used to generate various new

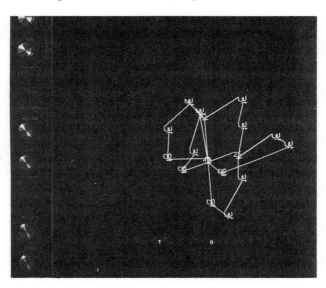

FIGURE 13-9 Graphic representation of a molecular structre. In chemical research new compounds are studied visually, and molecular structures are generated by the computer as the investigator varies the parameters of the structure. *Courtesy of Adage, Inc.*

molecular structures as the investigator varies the parameters. In this manner the structure may be studied visually and various desirable structures may be chosen for laboratory experimentation. The human researcher, from his intuitive vantage point, guides the machine, each partner doing what he is best fitted for. The computer simulates the molecule according to the rules of physical and chemical theory. The computer represents the molecule with enough structural detail to make plausible a metaphorical identification of the computer with the molecule. The computer model used in this way, far from reducing the scientist to a passive bystander, reinforces the need for the creative human element in experimental science, if only because witless calculation is likely to be so voluminous as to be beyond the power of even the fastest computer. Human judgment and intuition must be injected at every stage to guide the computer in its search for a solution. Painstaking routine work will be less and less useful for making a scientific reputation, because such efforts can be reduced to a computer program. All that is left for the scientist to contribute is a creative imagination.[1]

The simulated fall of water spilling over a cliff and splashing into a pool is shown in Figure 13-10. This figure is part of a series of computer simulations used for the study of the dynamic behavior of fluids accomplished by John P. Shannon of Los Alamos Scientific Laboratory. The dynamics of a liquid drop splashing into a pool have also been studied by Shannon and Francis Harlow.[8]

FIGURE 13-10   Simulated waterfall spills over the edge of a cliff and splashes into a pool in this computer experiment performed by John P. Shannon at the Los Alamos Scientific Laboratory as part of a general study of dynamic behavior of fluids with the aid of numerical models. *Courtesy of John P. Shannon.*

One series of photos, obtained from a computer simulation, is shown in Figure 13-11. This series of photos shows the behavior of the free surface through the following sequence of events:

1. A crater is formed and fluid splashes to the side.
2. Fluid rushes back to fill the crater.
3. A jet column is formed along the collapse axis.
4. The jet column rises well above the initial pool surface and may break into several droplets.
5. The jet column falls back, creating a second crater and lateral wave.

The drop shown in Figure 13-11 is relatively fast-falling, with an initial speed, U_0, of 4.0 where

$$U_0 = (R/2H)^{1/2}$$

and R = radius of the drop and H = the height from which the drop freely falls. This simulation result is not only dramatic, but also revealing of the dynamics of fluid movement.

The digital computer has recently been introduced as a general purpose simulator in the highschool classroom.[9] The idea is to expose students to experimentation which would not normally be available in the school laboratory. Simulation is particularly apropos for students when the experiment is too complex, expensive or dangerous to carry out in the laboratory. A computer simulation program entitled EVOLU permits the user to explore some of the factors which affect evolutionary changes. The user studies a population of pepper moths, which normally are light in color, but which produce a small percentage of dark-colored mutants. He specifies the rate of production of mutants, the number of light-colored moths in the initial population, the time (in a 30-year span) at which an environmental change occurs, and whether that change is beneficial to light-colored or dark-colored, moths. This simulation parallels an occurrence in Great Britain, where, before the Industrial Revolution, the environment favored light-colored moths, but, where, since the Industrial Revolution with its concomitant air pollution, dark-colored moths

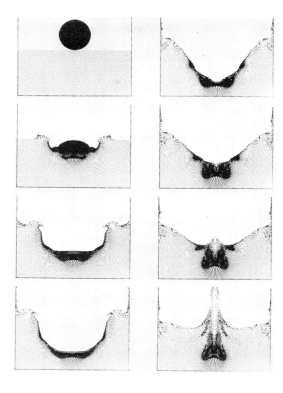

FIGURE 13-11 The cross-section of a splashing drop with an impact speed of 4.0. Photographs shown (read left, down; right, down) are t = 0, 5, 10, 15, 25, 28, 30 and 35 units of time. *Courtesy of John P. Shannon.*

are favored. A computer run of the program EVOLU is shown in Figure 13-12. The initial population is 10,000 moths, the evolutionary change occurs in the fifth year and the mutation rate is 5%.

In addition, a program entitled POLUT, which is an elementary simulation of a water–pollution situation, has been developed.

In this simulation, the user is permitted to choose the type of body of water, the water temperature, the type of waste being discharged, the rate at which it is discharged, and the type of waste treatment. Two computer results of this program are shown in Figure 13-13 and 13-14. In Figure 13-13, the results of dumping untreated sewage waste into a fast–moving stream are shown. The waste in the stream builds up to a constant level and is carried away by the stream. In Figure 13-14, the effects of dumping untreated industrial waste into a slow–moving stream are exhibited. The waste continues to build up and the oxygen content drops to a level where the fish begin to die. The effects of the use of waste–treatment techniques and the temperature of the water can also be studied using this program. Such uses of simulation in the schools clearly affords opportunities for students to experience certain phenomena rather than to learn about them vicariously from teachers.

WITHIN A LARGE POPULATION OF PEPPER MOTHS, THERE ARE A FEW
INDIVIDUALS WHICH SHOW UP DARKER IN COLOR THAN THE NORMAL
LIGHT COLORED MOTHS BECAUSE OF MUTATIONS.

YOU ARE GOING TO STUDY THIS POPULATION OF PEPPER MOTHS FOR 30
YEARS AND SEE WHAT HAPPENS TO THE NUMBER OF DARK AND
LIGHT MOTHS WHEN YOU ALTER ENVIRONMENTAL CONDITIONS.

SELECT A MUTATION RATE VALUE FROM 1 TO 10, WHEREIN THE HIGHER THE
NUMBER, THE HIGHER THE MUTATION RATE AND THUS THE GREATER THE
PERCENTAGE OF DARK MOTHS PRODUCED.
? 5

HOW MANY LIGHT COLORED MOTHS ARE THERE IN THE AREA? SELECT A
NUMBER FROM 1000 to 1000000? 1E4

YOU HAVE THE POWER TO CHANGE THE ENVIRONMENT.
AT WHAT POINT IN OUR THIRTY YEAR PERIOD DO YOU WANT
TO IMPLEMENT YOUR POWER? SELECT A YEAR FROM 3 THROUGH 10.
? 5

IS THE ENVIRONMENTAL CHANGE GOING TO FAVOR LIGHT MOTHS (TYPE 1)
OR DARK MOTHS (TYPE 2)? 2

IN TABLE FORM HERE IS WHAT HAPPENS TO THE POPULATIONS.

YEAR	MUTATION RATE	NUMBER OF DARK MOTHS (ADULTS)	NUMBER OF LIGHT MOTHS (ADULTS)
1	5	0	10000
2	5	0	10000
3	5	0	10000
4	5	0	10000
5	5	500	9500
6	5	975	9025
7	5	1426	8574
8	5	1855	8145
9	5	2262	7738
10	5	2649	7351
11	5	3017	6983
12	5	3366	6634
13	5	3698	6302
14	5	4013	5987
15	5	4312	5688
16	5	4596	5404
17	5	4866	5134
18	5	5123	4877
19	5	5367	4633
20	5	5599	4401
21	5	5819	4181
22	5	6028	3972
23	5	6227	3773
24	5	6416	3584
25	5	6595	3405
26	5	6765	3285
27	5	6927	3073
28	5	7081	2919
29	5	7227	2773
30	5	7366	2634

FIGURE 13-12 The printout of the program EVOLU when an environmental change occurs in the fifth year and the mutation rate is 5 percent.

```
                    WATER POLLUTION STUDY
       DO YOU WANT INSTRUCTIONS(YES=1 , NO=0)? 1

        IN THIS STUDY YOU CAN SPECIFY THE FOLLOWING CHARACTERISTICS:

       A.THE KIND OF BODY OF WATER:
          1. LARGE POND
          2. LARGE LAKE
          3. SLOW-MOVING STREAM
          4. FAST-MOVING STREAM

       B.THE WATER TEMPERATURE IN DEGREES FAHRENHEIT:

       C.THE KIND OF WASTE DUMPED INTO THE WATER:
          1. INDUSTRIAL
          2. SEWAGE

       D.THE RATE OF DUMPING OF WASTE, IN PARTS PER MILLION(PPM)/DAY:

       E.THE TYPE OF TREATMENT OF THE WASTE:
          0. NONE
          1. PRIMARY (SEDIMENTATION OR PASSAGE THROUGH FINE SCREENS
                        TO REMOVE GROSS SOLIDS)
          2. SECONDARY (SAND FILTERS OR THE ACTIVATED SLUDGE METHOD
                        TO REMOVE DISSOLVED AND COLLOIDAL ORGANIC MATTERS)

       ##########

       BODY OF WATER? 4
       WATER TEMPERATURE? 60
       KIND OF WASTE? 2
       DUMPING RATE? 10
       TYPE OF TREATMENT? 0
       DO YOU WANT:  1. A GRAPH; 2. A TABLE? 3. BOTH? 1
```

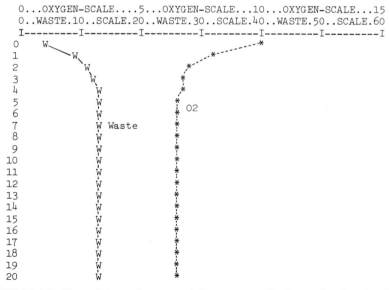

FIGURE 13-13 The printout of a program for a water pollution study, showing the effects of dumping untreated sewage into a fast-moving stream.

```
BODY OF WATER? 3
WATER TEMPERATURE? 60
KIND OF WASTE? 1
DUMPING RATE? 10
TYPE OF TREATMENT? 0
DO YOU WANT: 1. A GRAPH; 2. A TABLE; 3. BOTH? 1
```

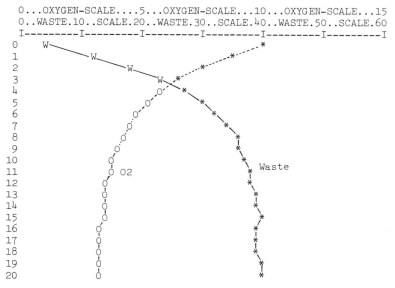

AFTER DAY 6 THE FISH BEGIN TO DIE, BECAUSE
THE OXYGEN CONTENT OF THE WATER DROPPED BELOW 5 PPM.

FIGURE 13-14 The printout of a program showing the effects of dumping untreated industrial waste into a slow-moving stream.

The simulation of biological systems has been pursued for the past twenty years. However, recently, with increased emphasis on the environment, the simulation and study of the ecological processes in our environment have increased in importance. Professor Kenneth Watt has worked for several years with a team of scientists to develop models of various ecosystems for computer simulation.[10] They have developed operating models of a sample county in California and selected state phenomena: crime, education, farm production, taxation, transportation and population growth. Using computer simulation, Watt's projections indicate that the world's estimated 2,100 billion barrels of oil reserves will be depleted around the year 2000. In response to intense demands for more energy, the coal reserves will be used up next. By then, atomic energy may or may not take up the slack. "If it turns out there isn't enough atomic power," says Watt, "the carrying capacity of the world will suddenly drop from somewhere between 10 billion and 20 billion people to something between 1 billion and 4 billion. This simply means starvation and perhaps violent wars between the haves and have-nots."

California has been chosen as the model system because masses of data are available on many activities within the state, and the state contains most of humanity's problems in microcosm because of its great geographic, climatic, and economic diversity. The basic conceptual utilized model is illustrated in Figure 13-15. The model begins with input data, consisting of the population rate parameters. These change the four population states: age distribution, sex ratio, race structure, and population size and density. The population interacts with its environment through decision processes (A), and the results of this interaction emerge as beneficial or deleterious effects. After translation into appropriate cost measures, decisions about the magnitude of input (B) and the environment of man (A) are made. The simulation models are then used to study, among other factors:[11]

1. The relationships between population density, stress, behavior, physiological changes, and disease incidence
2. The effects of physical and chemical characteristics of the environment on the health, growth, survival, and reproductive rate of organisms

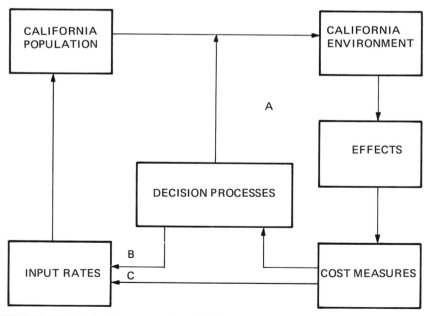

FIGURE 13-15   The basic conceptual model of Watt's simulation of society and its environment.

3. Analyses of energy utilization at the individual, population, and ecosystem level
4. The relationship between the organization of systems and their stability and efficiency in processing energy

The simulation of urban, national and international systems has been proposed and pursued recently. John McLeod stated recently, "Believing that understanding of a problem is a prerequisite to intelligent corrective action, and aware that simulation is a potent instrument for imparting understanding, we proposed the development of a World Simulation."[12,13]

The study of international and national conflicts and politics has been developing using simulation as one method of study. A simulation study of inter-nation response entitled *Inter-Nation Simulation* (INS), has been used for several years. During a simulation run the international system is imitated realistically; states engage in trade and aid, hold world conferences, etc., and a world newspaper is published. Wars, however, are bloodless and formalized, with their outcome decided by computer. The simulation is a simplification of the actual process, but it aids in understanding international politics and conflicts.[14] This simulation has been used both for experimental and instructional purposes. The research uses of simulation are concerned with the development and testing of hypotheses and theory in international relations. One particularly interesting example of the use of INS for instructional purposes is the simulation at Essex University in England of the Arab–Israeli conflict.[14]

Several persons at Rensselaer Polytechnic Institute are working on the development of a multinational political–economic decision–making simulation called PSW-1. This latter simulation, which is computer–controlled, provides for the generation of machine-readable records of role-player decisions for subsequent analysis.[15] In the political science classroom or research center, a major advantage of the utilization of simulation techniques is that the participant can learn from his mistakes without suffering the real–life consequences when mistakes are made while learning. The simulation exercises are useful in teaching political and diplomatic skills when the consequences of error in the real–life context are so costly as to effectively prohibit trial–and–error learning. The PSW1 (Politically Simulated World, Model 1) simulation is a computer–assisted simulation exercise which makes it possible for students to learn some of the lessons in politics through participation. The developers of the simulation model also foresee PSW-1 proving useful as a research tool by means of which further insights into the relations of men and governments can be obtained. The participants in the simulation play the roles of decision–makers and the decisions are recorded on IBM punched cards. The cards themselves are then run through the computer and the simulation control program to provide the new balances for the participants for the next round. Simultaneously, the computer is also recording on a separate computer tape the complete record of these interactions for later analysis by the simulation directors.[15] The PSW-1 simulation operates within a number of economic, political and sociological constraints and dynamic relationships. At the end of each simulation round, the computer generates measures of the effectiveness of the decisions of the role players.

A simulation model for allocating urban activities in a state has recently been prepared. In recent times, there has been a prodigious and continuing increase in the demand for various public facility investments in urban areas, stemming from the sheer increase in population, higher incomes, greater mobility and expanding leisure. This escalation in demand has placed acute pressures on the current supply of various public facilities and has brought about continuing problems of planning and resource allocations. For many of these public facilities the requirement for long lead-time planning suggests that plans will have to be worked out and reliably implemented so that the urban areas can evolve systematically, consistent with desired human activity patterns and a spectrum of public tastes. With the desire to have the state governments play a more central role in guiding development patterns within their boundaries, the anticipation and planning of future growth and development in a state is necessary. The elements of a state's plan should encompass the economy, land development patterns, transportation facilities, open space and outdoor recreation. A simulation model has been developed for allocating land-using activities in a state to various uses in a politically sensitive framework. The model incorporates and accounts for shifts in economic activities and social impacts.[16]

The model for Connecticut incorporates nine simultaneous equations involving the following activities:

Construction Employment
Retail and Wholesale Employment
Business and Professional Services Employment
Personal Services Employment
Manufacturing Employment
Other Employment
Population in Low Income Tertile
Population in Middle Income Tertile
Population in High Income Tertile

The land-use model was used to develop projections of population and employment for the 169 towns in Connecticut in 1970, 1980 and 2000. The economic, transportation and industrial consequences of these land-use estimates may then be examined for planning implications. The simulation of land use in a state may assist the planner in preparing meaningful and useful plans which have been experimentally tested using the simulation model.

Professor Jay Forrester of the Massachusetts Institute of Technology has used simulation to model the characteristics of industrial and managerial systems.[17] In management systems, the simulation is based on the component structure and information flow in an industry and the policies are used within the industry to show how the resulting dynamic behavior is produced. In a recent book entitled *Urban Dynamics*, Forrester simulates the city as an interacting system of industry, housing and people.[18] The book presents a theory, in the form of a computer model, that interrelates the components of a city. It shows how the interacting processes produce urban growth and cause growth to give way to stagnation. Various changes in policies are examined within the simulation model to show their effect on an urban area. A simulation of a hypothetical urban area over a 250-year period is considered. The criterion used in evaluating in the performance of the city and the efficacy of the alternative public policies is the minimization of taxes per capita.[19] A number of proposals are tested using the simulation model, among which are the following: a job training program; job creation by bussing to suburban industries or by the government as employer of last resort; financial subsidies to the city, and low-cost housing programs. Figure 13-16a illustrates the behavior of the simulation model of an urban area. It presents the nine system-level variables over 250 years. The first 100 years is a period of exponential growth, but then the land area becomes filled, growth ceases, and the aging process begins. At year 100, near the end of the growth phase, the labor population is almost double the underemployed population. This is a healthy distribution of the labor resource; it results in economic mobility for the underemployed population. Underemployed labor, in Forrester's terms, includes unemployed and unskilled workers. By the year 150, the labor population has fallen and the underemployed population has risen until these two groups are almost equal. Business activity has declined and the area has taken on the characteristics of a depressed city. Figure 13-16b shows the related variables during the same 250 years resulting from the simulation. During the first 100 years of growth the underemployed-to-job ratio and the unemployed-to-housing ratio remain almost constant. During the period 90 to 140 years, these curves reverse and the underemployed have increased while available jobs decreased; the result is a precipitous rise in unemployment. But in this same period the housing that is aging and becoming available to the underemployed is rising even more rapidly. The model shows the behavior of some cities. The evolution of an urban area, according to this model, creates a condition of excess housing at the stagnation point of the city.

Forrester attempts to include the political and social effects in his computer model. He states:

> We find it relatively straightforward to include the so-called intangible factors relating to psychological variables, attitudes, and human reactions. Again, if the influences can be discussed and described, they can be inserted in the policy structure of a model. Any person who discusses why people act the way they

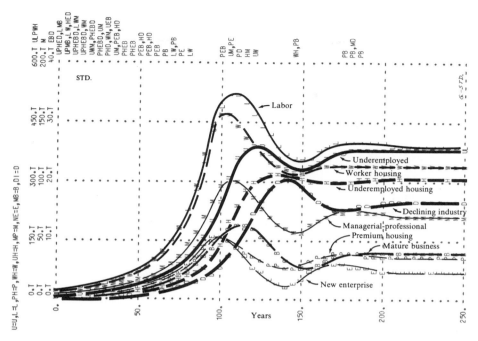

FIGURE 13–16a A 250-year simulation of an urban area through the periods of development, maturity and stagnation. Reprinted from *Urban Dynamics* by J. W.
Forrester, by permission of the M.I.T. Press, Cambridge, Mass. Copyright
© 1969 by the Massachusetts Institute of Technology.

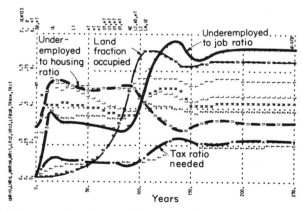

FIGURE 13–16b Compensating changes in housing and employment. Reprinted from *Urban
Dynamics* by J. W. Forrester, by permission of the M.I.T. Press, Cambridge, Mass. Copyright © 1969 by the Massachusetts Institute of Technology.

do, or explains a past decision, or anticipates a future action is relating the surrounding circumstances to the corresponding human response. Any such discussion is a description of decision-making policy. Any such policy statement can be put into a system model.

The result of a governmental policy is shown in Figure 13-17. In this example a slum housing demolition program of 5 percent per year and a two percent new-construction program is initiated. The result is a 44% decrease in underemployed housing. Also skilled labor grows 62% while new enterprise increases 75%. The net flow of people from underemployed to labor has increased 114%.[17] According to this simulation model, it seems that in order to reestablish a healthy economic balance and a continuous process of internal renewal, it appears necessary to reduce the inherent excess housing of depressed areas and to encourage the conversion of part of the land to industrial use.

One criticism of the computer model is that the suburbs never explicitly appear in it.[19] However, the simulation model does illustrate the following attributes of large interconnected systems:

1. Complex systems often do not behave in a fashion consistent with intuition.
2. Complex systems are strongly resistant to most policy changes.
3. Many complex systems tend to counteract most programs aimed at alleviating the symptoms.
4. In complex systems, the short-term response to a policy change is apt to be in the opposite direction from the long-term effect.

Computer simulation models are especially helpful in predicting and understanding the effect of urban management policies on the urban area under study. Much research work remains to be accomplished in this area.

In a recent study of a city as a system, another computer model with a purpose similar to Forrester's is used to analyze the planning and decision-making process in a city. The application of a computer-based simulation in an urban planning and decision process is illustrated in Figure 13-18.[21] The use of a simulation in city planning and management is expected to grow in the next decade.

Simulation of business and economic systems has been used for over a decade to analyze the effect of various strategies. Economists who specialize in the mathematical description of economic principles have used computers to construct and analyze complex mathematical models of the U.S. economy. This effort has assisted somewhat in synthesizing large amounts of economic information. The effort has also led to a consistent view of the economy. Certain assumptions about the future of the economy as a whole can be programmed into a model and individual users adjust the parameters of the model

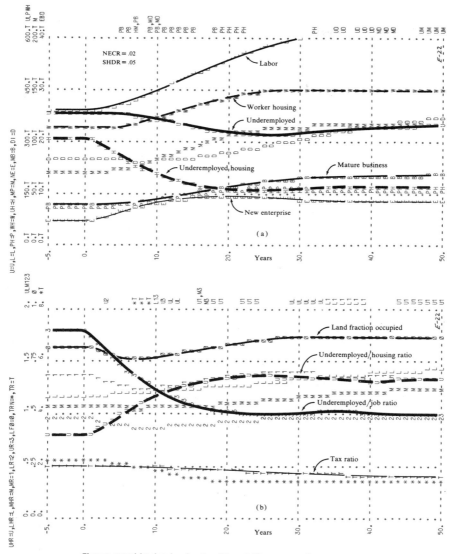

Changes caused by slum-housing demolition of 5% per year and new-enterprise construction of about 2% per year started at time = 0. In 1-3a note the rise in labor, mature business, and new enterprise; the decrease in underemployed housing; and the upward economic movement of underemployed into the labor class. In 1-3b see the decrease in the underemployed/underemployed-jobs ratio. The underemployed/underemployed-housing ratio necessarily rises to more crowded conditions as the job ratio improves.

FIGURE 13-17   Relationships among housing, employment, taxation and other factors. Reprinted from *Urban Dynamics* by J. W. Forrester by permission of the M.I.T. Press, Cambridge, Mass. Copyright © 1969 by The Massachusetts Institute of Technology.

to deal with their own particular industry or market. One model of the economy uses 242 equations to incorporate many variables.[22] The well-known Wharton Model is based on research at the Wharton School of Business at the University of Pennsylvania. It provides short-term forecasts, and it is the only U.S. model. It has been operated publicly for forecasting for some years. This model is basically a quarterly model of the Keynesian type. It has grown out of earlier experimental models pioneered by Professor Lawrence Klein over the last 25 years.

13.2 MANAGING BUSINESS WITH COMPUTERS AND SIMULATION

A recent article by Leo Gainen presents the thesis that businesses will be managed in the future by application of system analysis, implemented through the use of computer simulation. Significant portions of this article are given below.*

> This article develops a thesis that businesses will be better managed in the future by application of system analysis implemented through judicious use of computer simulation. In 20 years, simulation information centers (SIC's) will be as commonplace in business operations as scientific and business data processing centers are today. This development is inevitable if one assumes the continued current rate of progress in computer simulation application, computer hardware and software technology, and formalization of theory and invention of techniques to make computers more available to the manager. The acceptance of systems analysis, control theory, operations research, model building, computer technology, and simulation in engineering, business administration, and social and physical science college curricula supports this projection. Future collegians will accept the requirement to learn these technologies as they now do basic economic theory.
>
> ### BACKGROUND AND RATIONALE
>
> If the historical trend continues of a 10- to 12-year period being necessary for management to keep informed of computer developments and effectively use computers in scientific computation centers (SCC's) and management information centers (MIC's), it can be projected that 10 to

---

*Leon Gainen, "Computer-Aided Business Management through Simulation," *Proceedings of the Second Hawaii Conference on System Sciences*, Hawaii, 1969. With the permission of McDonnell-Douglas Corp. and the author.

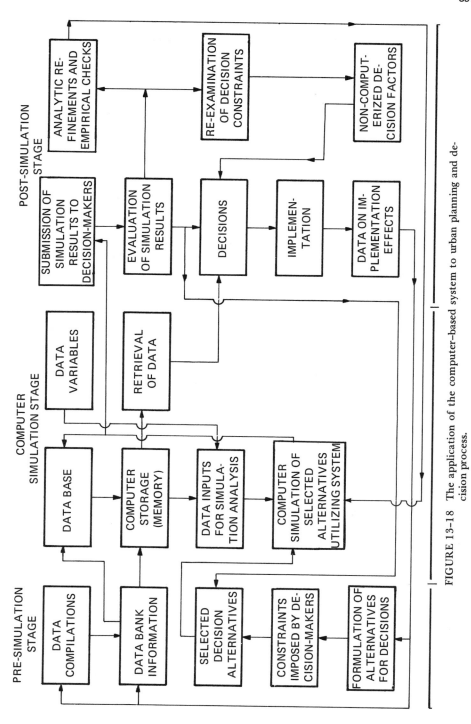

FIGURE 13–18 The application of the computer–based system to urban planning and de-cision process.

15 years hence, SIC's will be common in industry.* (See Figure 13-19.) Furthermore, the company that leads the way in establishing information processing systems tying MIC's and SCC's to the SIC's on a simulation-by-exception basis will gain a sizeable competitive advantage in its industry.

. . .

We are now in an era of expanding simulation use. But simulation is rarely the regularly accepted means of analytical support for management decisions. It is an exploratory toy rather than an operational tool. We know of business simulation applications for task and resource analysis, job shop balancing, and production scheduling. Other simulation applications are as well-publicized, but are considered strictly scientific (for example, analysis of space vehicle flight dynamics and trajectory determination). Still others cross the line between resource analysis and scientific simulations, such as simulation to rationalize space flight mission control and military systems command and control. PERT network analysis and its derivatives are other well-known, widely-used approaches to activity simulation.

There are, however, more important indicators. Our great universities have begun to formalize the theory and demonstrate the practicality of simulation. Many large universities are equipped with remote terminals for on-line simulation computation as a classroom tool. Hardware manufacturers are combining the speed and flexibility of analog devices with the accuracy and scope of digital computers so that hybrid computation systems are organized as system simulators. New computer simulation languages have been developed to ease the simulation problem solver's burden, after he selects a simulation technique. See Table 13-1.

MANAGEMENT IMPACT OF SIMULATION

Today's managers have been weaned of earlier conservative attitudes regarding scientific computing and business data processing. However, the question remains as to whether they will be more receptive in the future when their subordinates conceive, formulate, and propose simulation solutions to management problems. It is believed that they will be more receptive. More importantly, tomorrow's managers will better understand the context of simulation in the spectrum of analytical tools at their disposal. They will have used these techniques and found them successful during their own career development. Thus, the climate

*References to "centers" are merely descriptive. Conceptually (and feasibly), a single physical location could accomplish all of the centers' functions. Also feasible today is a single computer that is properly organized in terms of software, peripheral equipment, and communications channels.

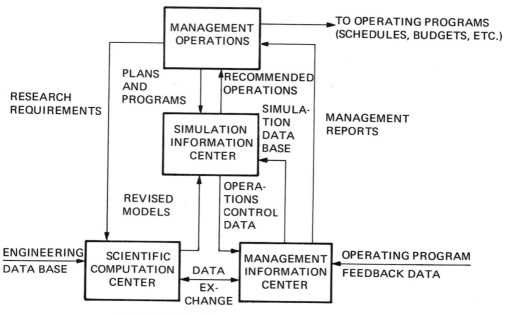

FIGURE 13-19 Future computer center organization.

TABLE 13-1

Current Simulation Languages

Discrete, Recursive Systems		Parallel, Continuous Systems	
Name	*Year Released*	*Name*	*Year Released*
SIMSCRIPT	1961	DYNAMO	1962
GPSS	1961	DES-1	1963
SIMTRAN	1963	MIDAS	1963
CSL	1963	HYBLOC	1964
SIMULA	1963	PACTOLUS	1964
CLP	1964	DSL/90	1965
ESP	1964	SPLASH	1965
MILITRAN	1964	UNITRAC	1965
SOL	1964	EASL	1965
OPS-3	1966	CSMP	1966

is slowly changing both for worthwhile simulation programs to be incorporated into business operations and for the emergence of SIC's.

Simulation takes many forms. In general, simulations are recognized as having come about because other analytical techniques are either nonexistent (for the situation to be studied) or too expensive (for the amount of confidence in the expected result). Perturbing a live system to try out unusual situations is too disruptive and provides little analytical data for confident predictions about behavior; therefore, the system is modeled and simulated on a computer. Often, dynamic system interactions are not computationally tractable, so the system is formulated as a series of discrete input/output relationships between and among subsystems and examined in a computer simulation over a finite range of system states.

How will simulation contribute to better management? To answer this question requires examination of some simulation activities that are now aiding management. Three basic forms of simulation, each with a variety of applications, have evolved for management exploitation: business games, resource analyses, and system effectiveness simulations. Businesses of the future will encounter variations of these forms, used with an advanced computer hardware system and harnessed as management tools.

BUSINESS GAMES

In management games, realistic business situations are enacted requiring decisions by people playing managers' roles. Realistic information, such as reports, trend curves and two–way plots of key variables is provided to the player; his decision actions stimulate a reaction in the business process being simulated, according to some statistical expectation modeled from historical or research data. For example, if a marketing decision is being enacted and the alternatives are to spend resources either (1) for research to develop new products or (2) for expanded production of today's product line, the manager (that is, the game participant) uses historical data and makes his decision. The short- and long–term effects are computed and reported to the player for his iterative reaction. In structure, these games are like the household game *Monopoly*; however, the plays are measured and the consequences evaluated with more realistic business decision factors.

The following are three values to such a situation enactment:

1. It permits observation of people in lifelike situations without interfering with actual business operations.
2. It demonstrates to functionally oriented management personnel, in clear–cut, amply qualified terms, the interactions between their function and others that exist, sometimes subtly, sometimes probabalistically, in any enterprise.
3. It enhances learning of a management enterprise.

This is the way management games are used today. Future use will emphasize the management and not the game. With multiprocessing and direct–access mass data storage used in time–shared computing systems, computation time, space requirements, and costs are being steadily reduced. With better display equipment and better communications, management data presented for "game" decision–making could be the real facts of today's business operation. The SIC will support a management decision room where alternative decisions are tried and observed in simulation exercises to predict the consequence of each. A second role of the simulation is as an exercise for trainees and managers who are not normally required to make specific functional decisions will be an added bonus for the firm.

RESOURCE ANALYSIS

Resource analysis simulations today are used to accomplish research in product management areas as diverse as make–or–buy policies, plant layout inventory–level analysis, and policy–making for product processing through an assembly line.

Consider the future use of this form of resource analysis simulation. For example, when problems of inventory control are being simulated, the model on which inventory predictions are predicated must be established and validated. Thereafter, the future manager can use this model to call the SIC for (or to be called by the SIC about) a specific item. The simulation will consist of extracting from data files current item status data, up–to–date parameter values of demand, holding cost data, depletion charges, and other model input values necessary to perform an analysis. The SIC could be continually performing, on a time–shared basis, necessary statistical and logical computations to prepare pre-selected data for simulation on demand. As a routine operation, selected critical items might be subjected to status prediction without management intervention by means of elapsed time or specific condition triggers. Thus, the present research nature of such simulations will become that of evaluating models and revising their structure; what is today considered advanced research simulation could become almost a continuously operating business procedure.

Other present–day simulation applications now treated as policy–making research will become management decision–making simulations. For example, shop resource allocation decisions can be evaluated daily before a work shift starts on the basis of current data on machine conditions (real–time links to SIC), personnel availability (time–clock sensors), spare parts and work–in–progress status (inventory data files), and production objectives (delivery schedules). Last-minute shifts in shop operation can be scheduled by shop orders relayed to each work center. The manager's role would be to approve actions derived from simulation analysis, to make revisions based on the latest information, or to initiate a new analysis if system transients could affect predicted results.

SYSTEM PERFORMANCE—SYSTEM EFFECTIVENESS

In the process of hardware design, such as in major space programs, availability and reliability evaluations are continually performed to estimate system worth. Often, system performance is simulated to derive probabilities of achieving desired levels of operation, with parameters such as component failures and severe stress conditions, being explicitly considered.

Two approaches to reliability estimation are appropriate. The first involves building and field- or bench-testing a relatively small number of subsystems to derive estimates of life, maintainability, mean times to failure, and other important measures of overall system reliability. The second does not use field test data of actual hardware, but estimates the measures of reliability either from known subsystem values (where operating environments are similar to present system operational requirements) or from engineering data describing similar systems.

Unfortunately, for many new system developments, little experience exists from which to estimate subsystem reliability values. . . . A means of capturing and using experience data is a simulation model. The problem of keeping model development current if system structure changes during system development is severe. One technique is based on knowledge of both scope and detail of particular kinds of system organization. First, there must be a canonical system structure, such as a jobshop operation or a space-vehicle design program. For these types of systems, component subsystems are well-understood. [Then, reduction of the system to a computer simulation requires either selection of particular submodels and their parameters or optional configurations of subsystems. Thereafter, well-defined program generators can be built to construct specific simulation models for analyzing different constructs of these systems within the bounds of current system knowledge.]

13.3 SEVERAL EXAMPLES OF COMPUTER SIMULATIONS

Computer simulation of color-forming patterns in shells is an interesting example of a simulation which provides the quality of an excellent simulation, and also provides insight into the physiological principles of the pattern-forming process.[24] The formal characteristics of a pattern of complex appearance on a molluscan shell were studied by developing a simulation of the pattern formation. The pattern involves a random factor determining starting points of diverging lines of pigment. The simulation program attempts to answer the question: What are the rules controlling the deposition of pigment? Professor C. H. Waddington has argued that there are several types of morphogenetic processes, among which are forms produced according to algorithms; template–generated forms, and forms arising from the interaction of spatially–distributed reactants. The shell studied is shown in Figure 13-20. The physiological model for the simulation was based on an algorithm which generated random numbers. The algorithm is basically as follows:

> Let the computer display trace out the distribution of pigment along a series of vertical lines, starting on the right and adding more and more to the left.

> Let "pigment deposition initiation" occur on any line by a random process. Once it has begun at a certain point, suppose that (i) the process of pigment deposition spreads laterally along the later lines at some specified rate, and (ii) increases in intensity until it reaches some upper threshold, at which it cuts out and pigment deposition does not occur. Suppose further that when two lines of pigment deposition meet they add together to surpass the upper threshold, and deposition ceases.

A rather successful pattern resulting from this simulation is shown in Figure 13-21. When the investigator wrote his algorithm, he was postulating an explanation for the pigmentation of this species. He based his algorithm on what he saw and how he thought it came about. The similarity between the natural pattern and the one generated from the scientist's algorithm is so striking that one is tempted to infer that the algorithm is, in fact, a reasonable explanation for the phenomenon. Whether this inference is sound or not, the acceptance of the algorithm rested on simulation by a computer.

The computer has been successfully used to model human behavior and personality. Ordinarily, we consider the computer a manipulator of numbers, when in fact it is a manipulator of symbols, of which numbers are but one class of symbols. In recent years, psychologists have shown a great deal of interest in the information processing capabilities of the human being—for example, how the human stores information, how he responds to information and what his various reaction times are. A large share of this interest in human information processing has come about because of the need for studies of the human factors involved in the integration of people into large man–machine systems, especially where the machines are information processing machines. One goal of this work is the simulation of valid theories of human mental function.

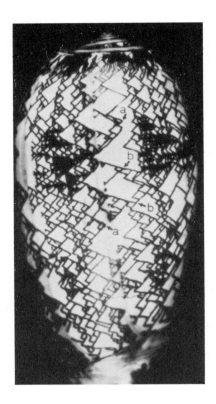

FIGURE 13-20 A shell (*Conus* sp.) showing patterns of pigmentation. Growth is from right to left.

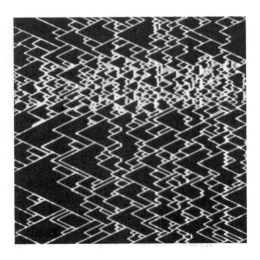

FIGURE 13-21 A computer simulation of the growth of a molluscan shell pigmentation pattern.

In a recent article, Professors Gross, Altman, and Brody of Princeton University describe the art of using computers to model human personality. The article, which follows, is a succinct review of the state of computer simulation of human behavior.*

THE ART OF USING COMPUTERS TO MODEL
HUMAN PERSONALITY

This paper is focused on the simulation of a human personality by a computer. As we shall see, it appears that in this venture not only psychiatry but computer science may benefit.

PART ONE. REASONS FOR MODELING THE PERSONALITY

Many experimental studies today involve putting incoming hospital patients in front of an oscilloscope screen which takes and records their medical histories. On the basis of their symptoms, the machine may route these patients to various hospital departments where relevant tests will be carried out. In some hospitals, computers administer intravenous fluids and blood to patients in need; they may monitor a patient's pulse, blood pressure and temperature and decide on his diet. We see, therefore, how computers make a real contribution to patient care. But a basic fact known to every physician is that it is not just tests, histories, drugs and apparatus that make sick people well, but people. In any illness (more so in psychiatric ones), patients can be largely influenced by the people they come in contact with. And computers are not people, nor do they contain any human characteristics.

Certainly not only in medicine but in education, business and other areas a computer with some "human" characteristics would be an advantage. For example, one application which comes to mind is that of space probes. Satellites would certainly give back more information about the effects of space on man if they too had a personality model aboard. Today's probes try to simulate human space flight in a rational, logical manner, disregarding the emotional side to man, which a programmed personality may account for.

An additional benefit of a viable personality model might be its interpretive value in the man–computer interface. For example, it is possible that a great deal of semantic specification of computer input could be

*R. R. Gross, S. M. Altman and M. Brody, *The Art of Using Computers to Model Human Personality.* Proceedings of the Third Annual Princeton Conference on Information Sciences and Systems, Princeton University, March, 1969, pp. 312–316. The source has an extensive bibliography, which we omit to save space. The reader may be well-advised to consult the original for worthwhile background material.

relegated to on–line, or even off–line personality models, which in turn would produce from the input a reasonable semantic interpretation. Such a "Man–Computer Symbiosis" would serve to increase the availability of computer facilities, especially in a time–sharing environment, in which human interpretation of (often cryptic) computer diagnosis is not available. When we add the fact that the construction of a personality simulator may be able to add to the existing literature in original applications of recent hardware and software breakthroughs such as time–sharing, asynchronous computation, and large scale integration, we see why such a venture is significant.

PART TWO. THE PROBLEM

It would be good to begin this section with a few words on the rationale of computer modeling and simulation. Because many conceptions of the nature of simulation exist, we shall, for the purposes of this paper, adopt Naylor's definition: *simulation* is a numerical technique for conducting experiments on a computer, which technique involves certain types of mathematical, logical and heuristic models that describe the behavior of a formal system (or some component thereof) over extended periods of time.

Also, we shall define *personality* as a descriptive label for the totality of a person's objectively observable behavior and his subjectively reported inner experiences. The generality of this definition reveals the fact that no one has yet been able to describe adequately what makes up the human personality. Countless theories of personality structure and development exist, the outstanding of which are dealt with in some detail by Krech and Crutchfield. But these theories, regardless of their validity, are not sufficiently formal in their present state to permit useful computer modeling. In addition, because the term "personality" has not been well defined in general usage, there is a considerable tendency to equate it with the term "behavior." In the authors' opinion, such equation is erroneous: from the definition given above, one will realize that behavior is determined by personality. By this token the study of personality is more basic than the study of behavior.

However, many scientists who make the distinction between personality and behavior at the same time equate simulation of personality and simulation of overt behavior on the basis of the following argument. Because only overt behavior can be measured, they contend, only simulation of overt behavior can be verified or validated (we shall soon explain this term). Although such an argument seems to be "the easy way out," (surely there is no *a priori* hardware or software restriction which prohibits one from describing feeling, affect, thought or emotion), at the present time little can be done in the way of verification of these more subjective and unmeasurable characteristics. It seems logical, then, to maintain the distinction between personality and behavior, but at the same time using behavior and behavior trends as a reflection (and hence as a measure) of an individual's inner subjective feelings, which could not otherwise be logically measured. Such an approach will be implied throughout the paper in the discussion of validity.

At this point, let us explain the meaning of the term "validity" in a modeling context. Certainly Tomkins has a "valid" point when he observes:

> One does not require that a personality theory account for *all* personality phenomena as long as its power is sufficient to account for *some*, with sufficient economy of assumption. Similarly, computer simulation must be judged not by its resemblance to human beings, but by its conjoint economy, explanatory and predictive power.

From this list, however, the goal of predictive power stands out as the *sine qua non* and thus will be used as the primary criterion of modeling validity in this paper. Predictive power, although a classical goal in the modeling field, has nonetheless rather stern implications for those who would simulate personality by simulating man. In the last analysis, though, the criterion of predictive power is legitimate, because our purpose is in fact, to predict the action of the personality, rather than to build a mechanical man in all his detail. Solomonoff has summarized the authors' feeling succinctly:

> There has been somewhat of a division in artificial intelligence work between those, such as H. Simon, who are primarily interested in how the human mind works, and others, such as Minsky, who are mainly interested in writing a program for a very intelligent machine. My own orientation is with Minsky, but I feel that we should try to make our machines' operations correspond with those of humans, for the preliminary part of the work, since there is somewhat more likelihood that we can debug a complete machine if it thinks a bit like we do.

In this paper, then, we shall assume that the construction of a model which predicts would be of at least intermediate interest.

In essence, then, the problem of computer modeling of personality thus becomes a problem of constructing a machine (system) which will predict the actions of the personality under a given set of assumptions and conditions which approximate the real world. Stated this way, the problem becomes related to the class of artificial intelligence problems—that is, "efforts to enable non–biological devices (such as computers) to exhibit certain [overt *or* covert] behavior patterns which are commonly classified as intelligent patterns in man."

PART THREE. STATE–OF–THE–ART

Historically, the problem of simulating the human personality is not very old; but in comparison to other problems, it was among the first to be considered by computer researchers. After Professor Norbert Wiener published his now–classic *Cybernetics* in 1948, the movement toward designing machines which would perform human functions gathered momentum. The first efforts toward this end were cautious and experimental, but by the time of the 1955 Western Joint Computer Conference on Learning Machines a great deal of research was under way. In fact, the seven years following this conference represent the high–water mark of artificial intelligence publication to date. Armer provides an excellent summary of such research.

Unfortunately, after 1962 there was a marked decrease in the number of papers published in these areas, possibly because the exaggerated claims of the fifties had not been substantiated and the publishing of research in artificial intelligence had become tainted with the aura of "unprofessionalism." A more accurate assessment would state that the problems attendant to personality modeling have proven far more difficult than anyone in the 1950's had believed. As a result, however, resources seem to have been channeled away from this research in the past seven years, and only a few centers remain (e.g. Stanford, M.I.T., Carnegie-Mellon) in the United States where research is continually carried out on projects of significant size.

The mainstream of this research has shifted emphasis at the same time. Prior to 1963, perhaps 75% of the publication in personality modeling dealt with what we shall call "task-oriented" models—that is, models designed to compute a well-defined subfunction of the personality, such as chess playing or musical composing. It was hoped, evidently, that it would be possible to synthesize these models into a more general model; this hope was the underlying current of task-oriented research.

One widely-used method of generalization is the technique of heuristic programming, in which heuristics (processes whose use is "justified empirically rather than theoretically") are used in two ways: a) *heuristic search*, in which heuristic are used to improve search time through a tree containing all possible actions, and b) *heuristic self-improvement*, in which the model learns, or improves itself over time, through heuristic generalization of previously successful searches into an inductively formed "pseudo-theory."

Although Newell, Shaw and Simon's 1956 "Logic Theorist" program and Gelernter's Geometry Theorem Prover (1960) were perhaps the first well-known uses of heuristic programming, they were task-oriented and not really self-improving over time. Nonetheless, heuristic programming was used successfully in Samuel's now-expert checker-playing program of 1959 and following. This program was the first major implementation of two important kinds of learning, rote learning and an adaptive type of learning which altered, through past experience, a weighting scheme used to evaluate the present board position. However, although such devising of new heuristics based on previously learned ones is an important and powerful capability, learning system research based on heuristic programming soon encountered the following difficulty, described by Solomonoff:

> The effective languages for describing learnable heuristics with each system have been too weak, and the heuristics for finding heuristics have been too weak. . . . We still need to know the kinds of heuristics we need to find heuristics, as well as what languages can probably describe them. We must then devise suitable training sequences for our systems, so that, using the heuristic-finding heuristics we have given them, they can find new heuristics.

Paralleling the post-1963 emphasis on the discovery of new and more general heuristics has been research toward the development of general problem-solving models having the capacity for self-improvement. Although early problem-solving models were task-oriented, Newell, Shaw and Simon's General Problem Solver (1959 and following) was not. GPS, originally a program designed to solve varied kinds of problems using a given technique, or model procedure, purported to simulate cognitive problem-solving processes. The program was later (1961) expanded to provide simulation of human behavior.

Based upon the techniques used in the construction of GPS, Hormann and Slagle have devised "very general" problem-solving learning programs; Hormann's (1965) has been called by Solomonoff "the most general problem solver programmed that has much learning in it." Because GPS has fostered so much fine research of this type, it is difficult to overestimate its value; at the same time, it causes one to speculate on what similar results could be obtained from simple, yet powerful breakthroughs in other areas, such as developing hardware or software methods specially oriented to personality modeling.

Much of the work involved in simulating induction and hypothesis formation, another area of personality modeling research, can be grouped under the heading "simulation of concept formation"—that is, simulation of the ability to structure arbitrarily the defining characteristic(s) of a group of objects for the purpose of deciding whether or not a given element is a member of the group. Such tasks as pattern recognition and inductive inference are classed here. Research in this area has been more abstract than that in other areas, as one might expect. Most of it is dealt with in the latter part of Solomonoff's paper.

As a general trend, then, research in personality modeling since 1963 seems to be oriented toward the personality's total interaction with its environment, the evaluation, definition and performance of tasks, instead of toward only the actual carrying out of these tasks. In so doing, personality modeling research has moved to a second level, a more meaningful level offering at the same time greater promise of validity and more difficult attendant problems than the first.

As a representative of the current state of the art, the most impressive working model of personality that has come to the authors' attention is Loehlin's Aldous, even though Aldous ("his is a Brave New World") will be six years old this year. Aldous is a marriage of three sub-systems—recognition, emotional reaction and action preparation—loaded in 750 instructions into a Burroughs 205 computer at the University of Nebraska. Aldous can perceive stimuli, has three emotions and six reactions, can learn in either of two different memory systems, and can introspect as well as respond overtly. Aldous has five brothers, each programmed to act differently.

However, Aldous has some drawbacks. He has very limited ability to look ahead, or to perceive concepts. He is static in intensity and patterning of traits, as well as along six other lines mentioned by Holtzman. Further, he speaks in seven-digit numbers, which poses a translation problem. Although these are by no means his only failures, let us remember that, as a representative, Aldous is interesting for what he cannot do as well as what he can do.

PART FOUR. COLLECTING THOUGHTS

The reader will note from the preceding survey that very little was mentioned in the way of major breakthroughs in personality modeling after 1963. As we have said, it was at about this time that researchers in the field had discovered the second-level problems, far more complex than anyone ten years ago had anticipated. Chief among these problems are the difficulty of specifying meaning (semantics), the definition and quantization of such imprecise terms as "anxiety" or even "personality," the need for a mathematical formalism to aid in communication among modelers, and especially the computer resource allocation problem brought on by the enormous complexity of the personality.

The current state of the personality modeling art finds most researchers in either computer science or psychiatry concentrating on some aspect of one of these problems, realizing that future progress beyond the pre-1963 task-oriented work will require better solutions than now exist. Some have felt that recent technological advances such as multiprocessing and integrated circuitry could be used to advantage. We at Princeton have been thinking along the lines of a modular computer system for personality simulation, in which specific personality functions are performed in parallel by modules in a multileveled network. The hierarchy consists of a complex executive unit (which acts as an interface with the outside world) interconnected at the lowest level to the basic subsystems of the structure. Using this system a task-based or more complex "psychological" approach to simulation may be possible. It appears that an attempt to model the obsessive personality would be a logical first step in this approach, since this personality's trait of rigidity, orderliness, need for rationality and symmetry may be easiest to implement.

The recent absence of spectacular results should not be a discouraging influence; rather, it merely indicates that the attendant problems, classical ones in the disciplines of computer science and psychiatry, are, in fact, very difficult. On the other hand, man's universal desire to discover more about himself indicates that personality modeling will continue to be an area of major research interest. Hence, it will, at the same time, provide an environment and stimulus for work on these major problems, benefitting both disciplines. In time, it is reasonable to expect that there will be in these problem areas breakthroughs which will initiate a second era of significant results in the art of using computers to model human personality.

The increasing use of simulation will continue to grow at an even greater rate, proportionally, than the increase in the number of computers. Simulation is useful in many fields.

Because of the complex nature of modern business systems, data processing aids (including simulation) are increasingly required to assist the intuition and judgment of management in the evaluation of new methods, concepts, and designs. The practice of experimenting directly on a business and implementing a system before it is fully understood inevitably causes disruptions of normal operations, hasty last–minute corrections, and often personnel or customer resentment. To avoid costly mistakes, the consequences of change must be anticipated before actually implementing a program, and all alternatives should be thoroughly explored.

Computer simulation provides an effective means of testing and evaluating a proposed system under various conditions in a laboratory environment. The system's behavior is modeled by a computer program, which reacts to various operating conditions in a manner both qualitatively and quantitatively similar to that of the system itself. Several hours or weeks, or sometimes even years, of simulated activity can be examined on a computer in a matter of minutes. Results help to gain insights, test hypotheses, demonstrate or verify new ideas and establish feasibility. Computer simulation is expected to grow in importance and use during the next decade. Disciplines not formerly using simulation techniques may find new frontiers opening to the researcher, student and practitioner.

13.4 EXAMPLES OF COMPUTER SIMULATION USING BASIC MATHEMATICS

Simulation is a study of the performance of a system, through the use of a model in which performance is a function of time. In this section we discuss several examples of computer simulation.

First, consider the simulation of a racing car traveling along a straight track. The speed of the autombbile S is related to the distance traveled by the equation

$$d = S \cdot t \qquad (13\text{-}1)$$

where t is the time of travel from the starting point. Now, if the auto travels along the straight track at a constant speed S_c, we can calculate the distance traveled during an increment in time Δt as

$$\Delta d = S_c \cdot \Delta t \qquad (13\text{-}2)$$

where Δd is the incremental distance. If the incremental time Δt is one minute in each case and the speed is $S_c = 1$ mile per minute, we obtain the distance versus time performance, as shown in Figure 13-22.

We are aware that the model of a racing car must account for the fact that the driver will change the speed of the vehicle as the engine and the wind will allow; thus, the model must actually accommodate changes in the speed S as time varies. We then choose a small period of time Δt and assume the speed is constant during the period Δt. Let us assume the car will require at least one-half minute to change speed, and the speed during that period of time is essentially constant. Then we are able to state

$$\Delta d = S \cdot \Delta t \qquad (13\text{-}3)$$

where $\Delta t = .5$ minute, and where S is the average speed during the interval of

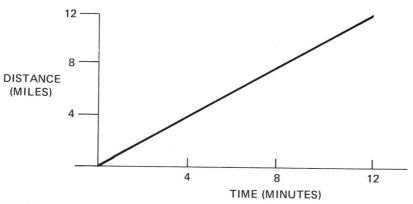

FIGURE 13-22 Distance *versus* time performance of a racing car with a constant speed.

time. A racing car might experience a speed change as listed in Table 13-2 resulting in the average speeds as listed in the same table. The average speed is represented by the equation

$$S = \frac{S_e + S_b}{2} \qquad (13\text{-}4)$$

where S_e = speed at the end of Δt and S_b = speed at the beginning of Δt.

The incremental distance and total distance traveled are also given in Table 13-2. The results are graphically illustrated in Figure 13-23. The algorithm for the simulation is deduced from the equations. The average speed is

$$S = \frac{S_e + S_b}{2} \qquad (13\text{-}5)$$

or it may be written as

$$S = \frac{S_{n+1} + S_n}{2} \qquad (13\text{-}6)$$

where n = the counter. The distance traveled during the nth interval is

$$\Delta d_n = S \cdot \Delta t \qquad (13\text{-}7)$$

TABLE 13-2

Time (minutes)	0	0.5	1.0	1.5	2.0	2.5
Speed (miles/minute)	0	.20	.30	.40	.50	.50
Average Speed		.100	.250	.35	.45	.50
		← Δt →	Δt	Δt	Δt	Δt
Incremental Distance Δd (miles)		.05	.125	.175	.225	.25
Total Distance (miles)		.05	.175	.35	.575	.825

where Δt is a constant. Then the algorithm for the total distance traveled is

$$d_{n+1} = d_n + \frac{S_{n+1} + S_n}{2} \cdot \Delta t \qquad (13\text{-}8)$$

where n varies from 0 to a preselected value. For example, the total distance d_1 is

$$d_1 = \frac{.20 + 0}{2} \cdot 0.5 \qquad (13\text{-}9)$$

since $d_0 = 0$. Then, we have

$$d_2 = .05 + \frac{.30 + .20}{2} .5 \qquad (13\text{-}10)$$

The computer is able to store the past value of d_n and all previous values of the speed. It can thus calculate the incremental distance traveled. While this simulation is fairly simple, it is illustrative of the process.

Let us develop a simulation model of the interaction of rabbits and foxes in Australia. The number of rabbits is r. If left alone, this number would grow indefinitely until the food supply was exhausted. However, the foxes (f) present on the continent are predators which control the growth in the number of rabbits. Finally, the effect of the available food on the rabbit population is represented by the variation of the variable x. Thus, the three simulation variables are:

r = number of rabbits
f = number of foxes
x = quantity of food
available to the rabbits

The equation representing the number of rabbits is:

$$r_{n+1} = kr_n - af_n + bx_n \qquad (13\text{-}11)$$

This equation states that the number of rabbits at the time $t = t_{n+1}$ is related

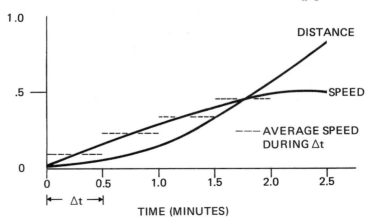

FIGURE 13-23   A simulation of an automobile road race.

to the number of rabbits, r_n; the number of foxes, f_n; and the food x_n; at the time $t = t_n$.* Recall from the preceding discussion that the increment of time is $\Delta t = t_{n+1} - t_n$ and it is assumed that $\Delta t =$ one unit of time, such as a week. In a similar manner, the other two equations are:

$$f_{n+1} = df_n + gr_n \qquad (13\text{-}12)$$
$$x_{n+1} = hx_n - mr_n \qquad (13\text{-}13)$$

The parameters of the simulation model are k, a, b, d, g, h and m. These parameters are selected to cause the model to fit the actual change in the populations. Equation 13-11 states that the rabbit population would increase if f and x were ignored. Equation 13-12 states that the number of foxes would decrease if there were no rabbits; that is, r equal to zero. Equation 13-13 states that the food increases with time and the rabbits decrease the food supply proportionally to their number.

Let us consider the case where $k = 1$, $d = .5$, $a = 2$, $g = .1$, $h = 1$, $b = .1$ and $m = .1$. Then the series of equations is:

$$r_{n+1} = r_n - 2f_n + .1x_n$$
$$f_{n+1} = .5f_n + .1r_n$$
$$x_{n+1} = x_n - .1r_n$$

These equations may be programmed for a computer, assuming an initial value for r_0, f_0 and x_0. If $r_0 = 100$, $f_0 = 10$, and $x_0 = 100$, we can calculate the next incremental value of the variables as:

$$r_1 = 100 - 2(10) + .1(100) = 90$$
$$f_1 = .5(10 + .1(100) = 15$$
$$x_1 = 100 = .1(100) = 90$$

If the calculations proceed for several periods of time Δt, we obtain the response listed in Table 13-3. This series of calculations is easily obtained from a computer simulation and the result can be provided in a plotted format.

TABLE 13-3

n	0	1	2	3	4
r	100	90	69	44.1	21.1
f	10	15	16.5	15.2	12
x	100	90	81	74.1	69.7

The calculations result in numbers which are not integers, but rather are decimal numbers. Of course, the actual number of rabbits, for example, is an integer and the decimal portion of the number should be rounded according to the rule that the number is increased to the next higher integer if the decimal portion is one-half or greater, and conversely if the decimal portion is less.

Notice that in Figure 13-24 the number of foxes increases but then de-

*The number of rabbits this month depends on how many rabbits and foxes, and how much food, there was last month.

creases again as the number of rabbits continually drops. The simulation could be carried out for several more periods. This type of simulation is quite revealing of the nature of the process. The parameters of the process can be altered in order to try another set of conditions.

A computer simulation will provide more accurate solutions as the increment of time, Δt, is decreased. As the increment of time is decreased, the number of increments required to simulate a total time period T is proportionally increased. For example, in the case of the speed–simulation example discussed earlier, we use $\Delta t = 0.5$ minute. If the total period of interest is 10 minutes, the simulation requires a series of 20 calculations. If, in order to improve the accuracy and closeness of approximation, we let $\Delta t = 0.05$ minutes, then a sequence of 200 calculations would be required to yield the results for a 10-minute period. Nevertheless, the computer can easily provide hundreds of calculations rapidly and with a computer simulation, one can readily use the increment required to provide reasonable accuracy.

13.5 COMPUTER GAMES

The use of computers to aid in the playing of games has grown in recent years. Until the last few decades, game playing was primarily restricted to humans or special–purpose machines. Today, however, computer scientists are dedicating a considerable amount of effort toward programming digital computers to play games. A game, which is a common activity, is a closed system with a set of explicitly stated rules and a fixed goal. A formal definition of a game may be stated as follows:

> GAME (1) An activity among two or more independent decision makers seeking to achieve their objectives in some limiting context. (2) A contest with rules among several adversaries who are attempting to win specified objectives.

Many activities in life involve the characteristics of game playing. Such activities involve decision makers seeking to achieve objectives in some limiting context. The autonomy of human wills and the diversity of human motives result in gamelike forms in all human interactions, and in this sense all human history can be regarded as gamelike in nature. The word "game" signifies the richest and most diverse of human activities. The dictionary suggests the range: diversion, sport, fun, competition and play among others. The wide use of "game" as a metaphor for many social, political, economic activities indicates the similarity which, we assume, exists between games and lifelike activities. It is this very similarity that causes us to consider the use of computers for game playing.

The analogy between games of strategy and economic, social and political behavior is fairly obvious. Perhaps most of us are familiar with the game

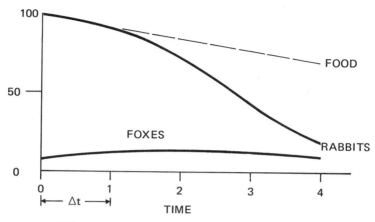

FIGURE 13-24 The rabbits and foxes in Australia.

Monopoly, which is modeled on a theory of economic life. Game playing is not limited by geographical boundaries; it has a rich history. It is a common experience for an individual to strive to learn how to achieve maximum advantages, and most games are models of common situations. Thus the game-player may be considered one who is learning how to gain advantages in models of real situations. Of course, some games involve the action of the players to achieve a common goal against an obstructing force or natural situation which is not itself a player.

Games may have originated in the playing out of tribal life, war or commerce. They permitted the player to try out a role within the game without the cost of the real situation. The creative aspect of the game combines the luck of the player and a respect for the realities of life. A game has a rational, analytic component and an emotional, creative component. The game's analytic dimension includes the strategic and structural characteristics experienced in life. The emotional apsect of the game includes chance and a realization that often the action of the game is as important as the outcome.[26]

Some political and social activities can be viewed as games. Warfare can be imagined as a form of a game. Real wars are painful, expensive, unfortunate and not practical for actual experimentation. However, for centuries people have been using war games, mock battles, maneuvers and other forms of simulated contests to prepare for war. Perhaps you are familiar with the saying "The wars of Britain have been won on the playing fields of Eton." Eton is a private school in England which produced a large percentage of the officers of the British army during the height of the British Empire. Presumably they learned the skills that made them superior fighters as they simulated war in their intermural sports.

The analysis and learning of processes in the form of games is present in a contest such as an election. A game in economics, politics, or war involves several players utilizing the resources of skill, knowledge, and luck and always involves a contest of individuals making conflicting decisions and holding conflicting objectives. Thus, we find that many processes can be viewed as games. What cannot be viewed as a game are those processes which have predetermined procedures or results, such as those processes we considered as candidates for simulation in the preceding sections of this chapter. Games are simulations of the real world, but not all simulations are games. The computer simulation of the evolution of dark moths is not a game since the results are predetermined by an algorithm and there is no winning or losing outcome.

Game playing is being applied to business management. Business executives are playing games which simulate the operation of their businesses. One such game permits several teams of players to compete for a market. The teams allocate their capital to sales effort, research and development and production each month. They select certain sales options and research options. Periodically, these options are entered into a computer as data and the teams compete, on the basis of their decisions, for the available market for the item the companies are producing. The players receive a computer output at the end of each period and thus are able to learn about the process of allocating resources and managing a business enterprise.

The rules and the goals of a game are usually well known by all the players. The strategy—the method of choosing the most desirable move or series of moves—is not known. It is the strategy involved in playing the game that varies and allows the player to learn from his mistakes and successes.

The goal in playing a game is to obtain the objectives by using a suitable strategy. A single individual, playing alone, faces the simplest problem; his best strategy is the one that brings him the predetermined maximum gain. In two-person games, each player wishes to win a maximum amount of score, but he can do this only at the expense of the other. This situation results in what is termed a zero–sum game, since the sum of one player's gains and the other's losses (a negative number) is zero. One player has to design a strategy that will assure him of the maximum advantage. But the same is true of the other, who naturally wishes to minimize the first player's gain, thereby maximizing his own. This clear-cut opposition of interest introduces an entirely new concept, the so-called "minimax" problem. Examples of two-person, zero–sum games are Chess, Bridge, Poker, Rummy, and Checkers. These games can be played with a digital computer as one of the players. Computer programs are available for playing these and other games with individuals.

A non-zero-sum game is one in which the winner's gain is not necessarily at the cost of the loser. All players can win, as in peace-keeping, or all can lose, as in nuclear war. Non-zero-sum games are more complex than zero-sum games but more like life in that while encompassing the purely competitive apsects they also include the preservation of that game itself, which is the social objective of the players. The best strategy in such games is one that maximizes the total wins of all players. This is sometimes called the Pareto optimum, after the great mathematical economist, Wilfredo Pareto, who first expressed this concept.[26]

As an example of a recent computer game, consider *Grand Strategy*, which is a game of international conflict developed by Raytheon Company for the U.S. Department of Defense. The global cold war conflict incorporates three power alliances of 39 nations with conflicting interests. The action takes place over a simulated ten-year period, divided into weekly events. The game is a non-zero-sum game in that all nations can win peace and prosperity. The roles of the players are as political, military and economic leaders of the nations.[26]

Another example of a computer game developed for the U.S. Government is called *Corridor*. This game incorporates the political and economic factors which come into play in the formulation and implementation of regional transportation policy. The game decisions are made by the players, but in areas of complex calculations, such as economic consequences of moves, the computer assists in processing the data resulting from these decisions. The area simulated in the exercise is the Northeast Corridor, incorporating the area from Boston to Washington, D.C. For simulation purposes, the Corridor was divided into major urban centers, the states they were located in, and several multistate superstructures. The players assume the roles of federal and state officials, representatives of the transportation industry and representatives of the consumer.

The transportation industry is subdivided into its rail, air, road, and water modes, each represented by a single player controlling the full resources of his particular mode throughout the Corridor. In addition, each mode was also represented by a labor union. The simulation consists of an economic submodel and a political submodel: the economic submodel concerned with the operation of the transportation industry and the intercity flow of goods within the Corridor; the political one with all other factors affecting the planning and implementation of regional transportation policy. The objective of the game is to maximize the profits of the individual player.

The design of computer games is an interesting and important activity. An elementary situation in business competition will serve to illustrate the design of a game. Let us design a competitive two-person, zero-sum game. An established firm, Mature Industries, is being challenged by Newcomer, Inc. an aggressive new firm. The management of Mature Industries guides their policies by their balance statement (that is, their budget and the sales projections of one year ahead). The management of Newcomer, Inc. also uses Mature Industries' balance sheet as their guide, since their aim is to put Mature out of business. They consider Mature's losses their gains and *vice versa*, regardless of what their own balance shows. Both are faced with a decision, namely whether or not to undertake an extensive advertising campaign. The outcome depends on what both firms do, each having control over only its own decision. We assume, however, that both firms have enough information to know what the outcomes will be, given both decisions. The table in Figure 13-25 shows the payoff for Mature Industries of various decisions of the two companies. The effect, in millions of dollars, of each set of decisions is shown. For example, if Mature and Newcomer both advertise, the loss to Mature Industries is one million dollars. Now, consider yourself as the manager of Mature faced with the avowed strategy of Newcomer. If the aim of Newcomer, Inc. is to drive Mature out of business, what do you decide as the manager of Mature? The decision of Mature to advertise is the best of the alternatives assuming that Newcomer, Inc. will try to maximize Mature's loss. In setting this game up, you would not tell the player who assumes the role of Mature about the strategy of Newcomer. Rather, the manager of Mature should learn the strategy of Newcomer by experience, thus gaining valuable insight into one strategy of the business world.

The sequence of steps in designing a game is similar to the sequence of steps in ordinary problem solving. One method of developing a game in which the computer assumes the role of one player is to use rote learning. The computer amasses a dictionary of moves by trial and error; reenforcing the successful moves and deleting the unsuccessful moves. Thus, the moves of a single game are stored as they are chosen by the computer. If the game is lost, the final losing move is eliminated. If the game is won, these moves are retained as options. This method of machine learning is depicted in Figure 13-26. The algorithm for the computer program deletes the choice in the last situation where a decision was possible from the repertoire of future possible moves.

Nim, a game thought to be of Chinese origin, lends itself to programming for a digital computer. In one version, each player has 10 coins set in a pile. Each player in turn takes one, two or three coins from the pile, and he must

	NEWCOMER ADVERTISES	NEWCOMER DOES NOT ADVERTISE
MATURE ADVERTISES	−1	+1
MATURE DOES NOT ADVERTISE	−2	+2

FIGURE 13-25 The payoff matrix for Mature Industries for a two–person, zero–sum game with two firms making a decision about advertising.

take at least one coin. The player who takes the last coin from his pile loses. The computer can be programmed to play according to the algorithm shown in Figure 13-26. Prior to 1945, several machines were built to play Nim. Since then, several programs have been written to play this game with a human player opposing the computer.

In 1901, Charles Bouton, a professor of mathematics at Harvard University, completed an analysis of the game and developed an algorithm for game play. A player knowing the algorithm can always improve his chances of winning the game. Likewise, a computer program designed to play Nim properly can usually win against a player not knowing the algorithm. The winning approach to playing Nim is always to present your opponent with an even position. An even position is determined by (1) writing the number of objects in each pile in binary notation; (2) obtaining the sum of the digits of every column of the binary numbers; and (3) dividing the obtained sum by 2. The position is even if no remainder resulted from the division.[27] A program can be readily written to follow this algorithm and to play a good game of Nim with a human opponent.

The idea of playing Tic-Tac-Toe on a machine was conceived as far back as the 1800's. Charles Babbage, the English mathematician, wanted to build a machine to play Chess and Tic-Tac-Toe, to help finance his efforts to build his Analytical Engine. Today, Tic-Tac-Toe programs have been written for many digital computers.

The game of Checkers can be played between a human player and a computer. The checkerboard is divided into 64 squares, colored alternately light and dark, and each side is provided with twelve men, known as white and black. At the beginning of the game the twelve men are placed on alternate squares on the opposite side of the board from the opposing men. The men never leave the color upon which they are first placed, and all moves must be diagonal. The object of the game is to capture all the opponent's men and remove them from the board, or else pen them up in such a manner that they cannot move. Checkers involves a set of 10^{40} possible moves in an average game.[27] Dr. Arthur Samuel of Stanford University has written a checker-playing program which is based on the rote method of learning as illustrated in Figure 13-26; Samuel's checker-playing program plays a good game and is capable of beating most amateurs.

Chess is a highly-valued game of intellectual skill. Computer scientists have been working on several versions of computer programs for playing a skillful version of Chess with a human opponent. Such programs have been written by A. Newell of the Carnegie Institute of Technology and Arthur Samuel of Stanford University.

The use of computers in the playing of games is an exciting and interesting aspect of computer simulation. A game is an activity among two or more decision makers seeking to achieve their objectives within the limits of the rules

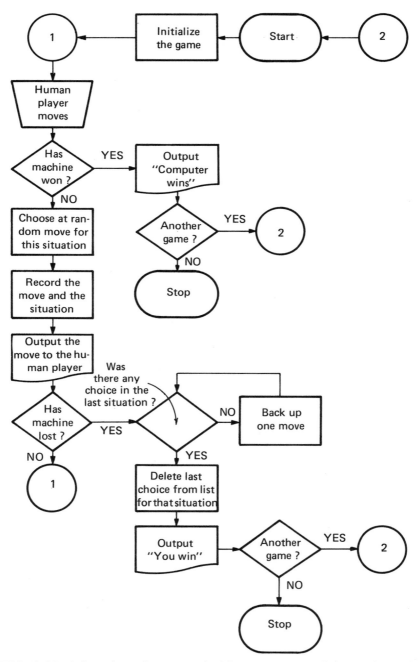

FIGURE 13-26 A flow chart of a rote method for a computer to learn to play a winning game.

of the game. This activity has great interest to computer scientists, since computers can help to play games and aid in the training of business managers, legislators and city officials, among others. In addition, computer games are of interest as exercises in computer programming. It is quite a challenge to program a computer to play a game of skill with a human opponent. Computer games can be serious training exercises as well as of intellectual interest to a computer scientist.

SUMMARY

The modeling and simulation of real processes is of great assistance to business, industry and government because they permit one to study the effects of various decisions or choices without going through the complete process of actually constructing and testing the phenomenon being considered. A model is a representation of a system or phenomenon in mathematical or symbolic form suitable for demonstrating the system's or phenomenon's behavior. The purpose of simulation is to explore the various results which might be obtained from the real system by subjecting the model to representative situations and inputs that are equivalent to those occurring in actual life.

In the use of simulation models, one should avoid the use of only one variable. For example, a highway might be investigated with respect to traffic patterns only. But pollution, urban blight etc. must also be considered. All simulations must include the effects of many parameters and inputs if the results are to be considered realistic. A simulation is an abstraction of reality, and caution must be exerted to include the pertinent effects of the environment. Simulation is an art as well as a science. The effectiveness of a simulation rests on the simulator's ability to abstract only those factors that affect the process he wishes to duplicate.

Some examples of useful computer simulations are in aeronautics; ticket reservation systems; logistics systems; economic systems, and political situations. Simulation is also useful for teaching the effects of various decisions on the environment, economics, politics, and business.

The use of computers to play games is an important dimension of computer simulation. A game is an activity among two or more decision makers seeking to achieve their objectives within the limits of the rules of the game. A game does not have predetermined strategies or results and is to be contrasted with a computer simulation model for which the results can be predetermined. A game involves several decisions throughout the course of a game and a strategy of play which is not predetermined. Games are quite useful in training students, managers and public officials to make wise decisions and to experience of the resulting consequences. Also, computer games are of interest to computer scientists since the programming and development of algorithms of games is a challenge in itself. Simulation and games are an important aspect of computer science and it is expected that the field will grow in importance in the next decade.

CHAPTER 13 PROBLEMS

P13-1.   Distinguish between a model and a simulation.

P13-2.   Describe a model of the process of registering at your college. What are the essential characteristics?

P13-3.   List several advantages of computer simulation.

P13-4.   Name several systems or phenomena for which you could develop a model and a computer simulation.

P13-5.   Develop a simplified model of the population growth of your town. Using data available from the town's records, obtain parameters that fit the data. Predict the population of your town during the next 20 years using a computer simulation.

P13-6.   Develop a game of three firms competing for a market for widgets. The three variables to be considered are: (1) advertising expenditures; (2) production expenditures; (3) research and development expenditures. Use simple relationships such as the linear relationship of the proportional expenditures for each of the three variables.

P13-7.   Describe some of the advantages and uses of the simulation of business activities.

P13-8.   Program and run the computer simulation of the rabbits and foxes problem described in the chapter. Run the simulation with an increment of time Δt equal to 1 unit. Examine the results of the simulation for correctness and give the time required to complete the run on the computer.

P13-9.   Program the game of Nim for the computer. Record the winning record of the computer.

P13-10.   Develop a computer program for playing Nim by learning a strategy via the method illustrated in Figure 13-26.

P13-11.   Develop a computer program for the two–person, zero–sum game of the two firms deciding to advertise as illustrated by Figure 13-25. Let several persons assume the role of Mature Industries and find if they can determine the strategy of Newcomer, Inc.

CHAPTER 13 REFERENCES

1. A. G. Oettinger, "The Uses of Computers in Science," *Science*, Sept. 1966, pp. 361-369.
2. H. Chestnut, *Systems Engineering Tools*, John Wiley and Sons, Inc., New York, 1965.
3. J.McLeod, "A Little Simulation—And How It Grew" *The Conference Record of the 1968 I.E.E.E. Region Six Conference, I.E.E.E.* No. 68C19, May, 1968.
4. G. Prude, "The Command Module Simulators," *Simulation*, July, 1970, pp. 23-27.
5. A. Ockene, "Computer Simulation," *Computer Decisions*, Jan., 1970, pp. 32-37.
6. *General Purpose Simulation System/360 Application Description, Bulletin H20-0186-2*, IBM Corporation, White Plains, N. Y., 1967.
7. C. W. Bell and R. N. Linebarger, "Applications of Computer Modeling and Simulation to Science Education," *Simulation*, April, 1970, pp. 185-190.
8. F. H. Harlow and J. P. Shannon, "Distortion of a Splashing Liquid Drop," *Science*, August 4, 1970, pp. 547-550.
9. L. Braun, *The Digital Computer as a General-Purpose Simulator*, Polytechnic Institute of Brooklyn, April, 1970.
10. "Model Man," *Time*, May 25, 1970, page 70.
11. K. Watt, "A Model of Society," *Simulation*, April 1970, pp. 153-164.
12. J. McLeod, "World Simulation: Progress Report," *Computers and Automation*, May, 1970, page 12.
13. J. McLeod, "The Simulation of Difficult Systems," *Simulation*, April, 1970, pp. 172-173.
14. A. Flook, "Simulation Studies of International Conflict," *Simulation*, April, 1970, pp. 181-184.
15. J. R. Parker and M. H. Whithed, "Developing an International Mutual Response System through Political Simulation Techniques," *Simulation*, June, 1970, pp. 261-268.
16. T. R. Lakshmann, "A Model for Allocating Urban Activities in a State," *Proceedings of the Symposium on Application of Computers to the Problems of Urban Society*, Association for Computing Machinery, November, 1967.
17. J.W. Forrester, *Industrial Dynamics*, M.I.T. Press, Cambridge, Mass., 1961.
18. J. W. Forrester, *Urban Dynamics*, M.I.T. Press, Cambridge, Mass., 1969.
19. J. F. Kain, "A Computer Version of How a City Works," *Fortune*, Nov. 1969, pp. 241-242.

20. J. W. Forrester, "Systems Analysis as a Tool for Urban Planning," *The Engineer and the City*, National Academy of Engineering, Washington, D.C., 1969, pp. 44-53.
21. D. F. Blumberg, *The City as a System*, Decision Science Corporation, Jenkintown, Pennsylvania, 1970.
22. "An Economic Information Utility," *Modern Data*, Sept., 1970, pp. 76-77.
23. L. Gainen, "Computer-Aided Business Management through Simulation," *Proceedings of the Second Hawaii Conference on System Sciences*, Hawaii, 1969.
24. C. H. Waddington and R. J. Cowe, "Computer Simulation of a Molluscan Pigmentation Pattern," *Journal of Theoretical Biology*, Volume 25, 1969, pp. 219-225.
25. R. R. Gross and S. M. Altman, "The Art of Using Computers to Model Human Personality," *Proceedings of the Princeton Conference on Information Sciences and Systems*, Princeton, March, 1969, pp. 312-316.
26. C. C. Abt, *Serious Games*, Viking Press, New York, 1970.
27. D. D. Spencer, *Game Playing with Computers*, Spartan Books, New York, 1968.
28. C. E. Shannon, "Computers and Automation," *Proceedings of the Institute of Radio Engineers*, 1953.
29. M. R. Schroeder, "Simulation with a Block Diagram Computer," *The Human Use of Computing Machines*, Bell Telephone Laboratories, Inc., Murray Hill, N. J., 1966.
30. B. A. Trakhtenbrot, *Algorithms and Automatic Computing Machines*, D. C. Heath and Company, Boston, 1963.
31. F. F. Martin, *Computer Modeling and Simulation*, John Wiley and Sons, Inc., New York, 1968.
32. J. C. Loehlin, *Computer Models of Personality*, Random House, Inc., New York, 1968.
33. "Speech Simulation," *Physics Today*, July, 1970, page 52.
34. O. Morgenstern, "The Theory of Games," *Science*, May, 1949, pp. 300-303.
35. J. McLeod, *Simulation—The Modeling of Ideas and Systems with Computers*, The McGraw-Hill Book Company, New York, 1968.
36. H. Guetzkow, "Some Correspondence between Simulations and Realities in International Relations," *New Approaches to International Relations*, St. Martins Press, New York, 1968.
37. M. M. Botvinnik, *Computers, Chess and Long-Range Planning*, Springer-Verlag, New York, 1970.
38. Y. Chu, *Digital Simulation of Continuous Systems*, McGraw-Hill Book Company, New York, 1969.

39. R. M. Hodgetts, "General Management Simulations: An Approach for the Seventies," *Simulation*, Sept., 1970, pp. 119–123.

40. J. W. Forrester, *World Dynamics*, Wright-Allen Press, Cambridge, Mass., 1969.

41. J. R. Emshoff and R. L. Sisson, *Design and Use of Computer Simulation Models*, Macmillan Co., New York, 1970.

42. "Ohio State University's Library Circulation System Now in Full Operation," *Computers and Automation*, Feb., 1971, page 52.

43. C. A. Myers, *Computers in Knowledge-Based Fields*, The M.I.T. Press, Cambridge, Mass., 1970.

44. B. Hodge, "Business Simulation and Modeling," *Modern Data,* May 1970, pp. 26–32.

14

COMPUTERS AROUND THE WORLD

14.1 INTRODUCTION

The digital computer was developed primarily in the United States, but other countries have developed their own computers as well as purchased American computers. Countries which were once dubious about the economic role of computers now are attempting to introduce computers extensively into business and government.*

As Schreiber points out in his book *The American Challenge,* application of management techniques, including information processing, has constituted the technological challenge which the U.S. has presented to Europe and the rest of the industrialized world.[1] He says:

> In the industrial war, the major battle is in the field of computing. This battle is very much in doubt, but it has not yet been lost. "Between 1970 and 1980," according to Jacques Maisonrouge, "the most important industry in the world, after oil and automobiles, will be computers."

*Here are some expressions for "Computer" from other languages: *Computador, Rechenmaschine, Mahashev, Chotnik, Machina per calcoli, Rekenmachine, Elektronno-vychislitel'-naya mashina, Calculateur.*

In 1968, the Organization for European Cooperation and Development published a long comparative study based on research into the technological gap between Europe and America. Its conclusions are: "Europe's technological lag is greatest in the field of computers, and is so severe that backwardness in other areas seems of minor importance. In fact, we have almost reached the point of no return in computer technology." The introduction of the computer and associated management techniques into the nation's economy has resulted in what has been termed a second industrial revolution. Just as it was with the first industrial revolution, the competitive nature of the world's economy makes it imperative for an industrialized nation to adopt the techniques of its competitors. This phenomenon is not limited to Western Europe or Japan, but pervades even the economic theory and practices of Eastern Europe.

In mid-1969, at the 23rd Session of the United Nations General Assembly, a resolution (2458) was passed entitled "International co-operation with a view to the use of computers and computation techniques for development." The passage of this resolution marks a recognition of the special importance of computers and the impact which the use of related technical processes may have on accelerating the progress of vital economic and social sectors, such as economic planning, programming of industry, transportation, public health, agriculture and urbanization.

The statement released from the United Nations noted the most satisfactory promotion of international cooperation in the fields of use of atomic energy for peaceful purposes and the exploration of outer space within the United Nations organization and expressed a hope that a similar promotion of cooperation would occur in the field of computer technology.[2]

The United Nations expects that the report of a study of possible cooperation will be a significant contribution to bringing together the experiences of many countries and many people in the application of computer technology to development.* It is also expected that constructive recommendations can be made as a result of study of such problems as how to build a cadre of trained professionals in the developing countries; how to install equipment and systems to minimize labor displacement, and how to transfer technology to the developing countries from the developed countries. It is also expected that illustrations will be presented of progress that can be made within the economic and social conditions of the developing countries. And, most important, a mechanism may be presented which will encourage continuing cooperation of the member nations and the UN organizations in the application of computer technology for development. There is a world-wide consciousness of a need for some type of inter- and intra-country plan for technological cooperation if

*An initial report of the United Nations study of the application of computer technology for development is available from the United Nations, New York.[19]

overseas computer industries are to develop as quickly as those in the US did. If these plans embrace both computing hardware and programs such action could have far reaching effects throughout the world in the very near future.[3]

Computer companies based in the United States dominate the international computer market. The U.S. companies produce 80 percent of the computer hardware sold in the world. The value of exported US computers and parts for the years 1967 to 1969 is shown in Table 14-1. Although production by subsidiaries of US computer corporations is not included, the US exported $639 million worth of computer equipment during 1969.

TABLE 14-1

US Exports of Electronic Computers and Parts during 1967-1969.
Source: US Bureau of the Census.

Country of Destination	1967 Amount (thousands)	1967 Percent of Total	1968 Amount (thousands)	1968 Percent of Total	1969 Amount (thousands)	1969 Percent of Total
Total	$432,517	100.0	$486,431	100.0	$636,499	100.0
West Germany	68,761	15.9	81,724	16.8	105,645	16.6
United Kingdom	65,403	15.1	79,778	16.4	93,951	14.7
Canada	64,248	14.9	66,141	13.5	92,583	14.5
France	67,112	15.5	62,087	12.8	80,181	12.6
Japan	54,707	12.6	59,352	12.2	79,630	12.5
Hong Kong	10,159	2.3	19,677	4.0	24,923	3.9
Italy	15,335	3.5	16,963	3.5	11,646	1.8
Netherlands	11,673	2.7	14,370	3.0	23,139	3.6
Switzerland	8,224	1.9	10,120	2.1	8,813	1.4
Sweden	7,158	1.7	10,081	2.1	13,045	2.0
Australia	9,136	2.1	9,750	2.0	12,824	2.0
All other countries	50,601	11.8	56,387	11.6	90,119	14.4

Despite an increase in the production of computers in foreign countries, notably in Britain, France and the USSR, it is said that a "technology gap" exists. However, beyond the existence of a technology gap, the most limiting factor preventing users in Europe and Asia from realizing the full potential of the computer is the scarcity of qualified personnel at all levels: programmers, operators, technicians, etc.[3]

The needs for computers in business, industry and government are great everywhere in the world. However, computers require capital for purchase and construction, and qualified personnel to operate and use them. As a nation is able, it will increase its use of computers in order to maintain and improve its competitive world economic position.

TABLE 14-2

Computing Resources in South American Countries. Adapted from Boehm, *Datamation*, May, 1970[4]

	Argentina 1968	Bolivia 1969	Brazil 1969	Chile 1968	Colombia 1969	Peru 1969	Venezuela Installed 1966-67	Venezuela Planned 1967-68
Total computers	<200	8–10	300–400	<50	60–75	30–40	92	120
Chief manufacturers (% of market)	IBM GE/Bull NCR Burroughs	IBM	IBM (60–75) Burroughs (20–35)	IBM Burroughs NCR	IBM (90) Burroughs	IBM (>90) NCR	IBM (85) NCR (6) Univac (6) Burroughs (3)	IBM (89) Burroughs (6) NCR (3) Univac (2)
Computers in universities	11	2	~30	6	~8	4	5	10
1967 Population (millions)	23.3	3.8	85.7	9.1	19.2	12.4	9.4	9.4
1967 Gross National Product (billions of dollars)	18.7	0.7	27.7	5.1	6.2	3.3	7.9	7.9

14.2 COMPUTERS IN SOUTH AMERICA, WESTERN EUROPE, AND ASIA

The use of computers in South America has grown rapidly during the past few years. Table 14-2 illustrates the computing resources in several countries of South America which are illustrative of industrially developing countries throughout the world.[4] In his analysis of the data given in the table, Boehm concluded:

1. There is a remarkably constant ratio of about 10-12 computers per billion dollars of GNP (the corresponding ratio for the US is about 54).
2. A fairly consistent percentage (about 10%) of a country's computers will be in universities.
3. There is a lack of really large scale computers.
4. The market is dominated by US manufacturers, particularly IBM.

It has been estimated that the total computing power in South America measured in additions per second is approximately one percent of that in the US.[3] However, the growth rate of computing power in South America is approximately one hundred percent, and it is expected to continue to grow at that rate for several years.

There is a strong interest in learning and applying the latest techniques to computer use in South America. But the primary problem is a shortage of trained personnel and the lack of contact with the centers of computer development, primarily the US. Computers will become more rapidly used in South America and other developing regions of the world as computer science education becomes available in the colleges and schools. Also, an important step will be the centralization of regional computer centers and the training of computer technicians, operators and programmers. Another possibility is to develop a program to transfer US experience in computer science and management to developing countries by means of assistance programs. When we analyze the situation with respect to the use and availability of computers in South America, we can learn quite a bit about the situation in other regions of the world with equivalent conditions. While we must not overextend the analogy, the problems and potential of South America resemble those of Africa, the Middle East and parts of Asia to a great extent.

Japan is a highly industrialized nation with one of the highest annual percentage increases of Gross National Product. The computer field is growing rapidly in Japan. In 1967 the total number of computers in use was 2,978. Two years later, in March of 1969, 5,735 computers were in use—an increase of 90% in two years. In March, 1971 there were 7,900 computers installed in Japan. Japan manufactures several models of digital computers. The leading manufacturers are the Nippon Electric, Fujitsu and Hitachi Companies with the Toshiba, Oki Electric and Mitsubishi companies following. An increase of 40 percent in computer sales was realized by Japanese manufacturers during the period April 1968 to March 1969, partly because the Japanese are now incorporating integrated circuits in the computer. In 1969, IBM held 31 percent of the computer market, while the leading Japanese manufacturer, Nippon Electric, held 20 percent of the market.[5] However, the total Japanese manufacturers' share of the market was 56 percent while foreign producers accounted for the remaining 44 percent. In Japan, computers have been applied to the problems of commerce and government where management science techniques are used increasingly.

In contrast to 7,900 computers installed in Japan in 1971, there were only 5,000 computers installed in the United Kingdom. However, while in Japan a large proportion of the computers are second-generation machines, in the United Kingdom the major proportion of the installed computers are third-generation computers. Furthermore, the number of installed computers in the UK is expected to double by 1974. Britain is also increasing its use of terminal-oriented and time-sharing systems. The shortage of computer analysts and programmers in Britain has been estimated to be 15,000 persons.

France now has 6,000 computers installed and it is expected that this number will double by 1973. On the basis of reports submitted by a task force on industrial research, the French government in 1967 gave top priority to a plan for coordinating and regrouping the three largest French electronic firms. With a higher percentage of large-scale systems, France is believed to have the highest average computer capacity of any country in Europe. It is estimated that by 1975 there will be 20,000 computers worth $1.7 billion in use in France.

According to a recent survey, the number of computers installed in Italy in 1970 was 2600, a rise of 22 percent over the position of the preceding year. [6] The potential for computer use in Italy is excellent due to the planned reform and streamlining of the bureaucracy which should give added impetus to computer uses. A major overhaul of the Italian tax system is now being devised which should create additional opportunities in the computer field. By 1973, according to knowledgeable estimates, there may be 6,000 computers in operation.[7]

The computer industry in Italy is concentrating on developing products in the computer peripheral portion of the computer market with emphasis on keyboard and display terminals.[3]

Approximately 7,000 computers have been installed in West Germany and this figure is expected to double in the next few years. A major impetus in West Germany is the introduction of time-sharing computers. Computers are manufactured in West Germany by Siemens Co. and Telefunken Co.

One of the problems of the computer manufacturers in Western Europe has been the fragmentation of the computer market among a large number of companies. Ten years ago, there were more manufacturers in the United Kingdom than in the United States, but the output of each company was very small in comparison with their American competitors. During the past few years, mergers of several computer companies in Western Europe have led to a significant reduction in the number of European suppliers of computer systems.

Thus, in France, with the merger of Companie des Machines Bull into General Electric of America, the indigenous electronics companies have been formed under the government's Plan Calcul into a highly interwoven network, with Compagnie Internationale pour l'Informatique manufacturing and marketing computer systems and Sperac providing the peripheral equipment.

In the Netherlands, Electrologica and Philips have merged. In the United Kingdom, the commercial and scientific data processing interests of British Tabulating Machine Co., Powers Samas, Ferranti, EMI Electronics, English Electric, Elliott and Leo Computers are now merged forming International Computers Ltd. with an almost complete capability in computer equipment and systems.

In Italy the electronic computer activity of Olivetti was merged into General Electric of the US leaving Olivetti to pursue accounting machines and terminals as part of its office machine business.

The US computer industry faces a new challenge as several European companies, Siemens and Telefunken of Germany, Compagnie Internationale pour l'Informatique of France, Philips of Netherlands, Olivetti of Italy, and British International Computers Ltd. jointly plan to market a super–computer in the 1975–80 period. The US Department of Commerce points out that more than rivalry for commercial markets is involved. Also at issue is the feeling by each country of the necessity to develop a computer industry to provide the technology which is integral to its total economy and which, for security purposes, cannot be left in control of foreign companies. This has led to the push by France, Germany and Great Britain to develop their own computer industries.

An estimate of the number of installed computers in several nations in 1969 is summarized in Table 14-3. These are approximate figures only and do not fully illustrate the computer power of a nation, since there is no differentiation between large and small computers and their speed of operation, etc. The gross national product of each country is also given and the ratio of the number of computers to the GNP in billions of dollars is determined. This ratio takes into account the variation in the wealth of the nations. It is interesting to note that this ratio varies from approximately 30 to 54 for Western Europe, Japan and the United States. The industrialized nations appear to fit within this range and 40 computers per billion dollars of GNP appears to be an average standard for the industrialized nations. Note that the two partially developed nations, Israel and Brazil, have a ratio below 20. One might therefore consider a threshold indicating computer capabilities of a nation as 20 computers per billion of GNP.

TABLE 14-3

**Estimates of the Number of Installed Computers in
Several Countries and the Estimated Gross National Products* for 1969.**

	Number of Computers	Gross National Product ($ Billion)	Number of Computers GNP ($ Billion)
United States of America	50,000	932	54
Japan	5,700	180	32
West Germany	6,000	150	40
France	6,000	140	43
United Kingdom	4,000	130	31
Italy	2,600	77	34
The Netherlands	1,000	28	36
Israel	100	5.4	18
Brazil	400	30	13
USSR	5,000	600	8

*Source of GNP: *United Nations Statistical Yearbook*, New York, 1970.

14.3 COMPUTERS IN THE USSR AND EASTERN EUROPE

Computing in the Soviet Union has made great advances during the past decade, particularly in application to numerical methods for airframe design, rocketry, mathematical modeling and machine tool control. Business data processing has been slower to develop but it promises to be an area of opportunity for the future. There have been some recent attempts to utilize computers in industry and commerce. However, it has been estimated that the Soviets are still some four to five years behind in the design of digital devices and there appears to be a significant shortage of trained personnel.[9] Of course, the Russians are aware of the latest methods of management and scientific applications used in the West. In the use of digital computers for scientific purposes, the Soviets have shown their prowess in using computers in the launching of Sputniks, Luniks and other spacecraft. However, it is only recently that attention has been focused on economic applications of computers, with the purpose of optimizing production, distribution, planning and administration. In a recent letter of March 19, 1970, Andrei Sakharov, V. F. Turchin and R. A. Medvedev, Soviet scientists, addressed a letter to the leaders of the USSR concerned with the domestic economic problems of the USSR. The letter is interesting because it points out the great need for the introduction of management science techniques, planning and other computer–oriented techniques.[10] A portion of the letter follows:

> A decisive factor in the comparison of economic systems
> is labor productivity, and here the situation is worst of all. Our
> productivity of labor, as before, remains many times lower than

in the developed capitalist countries, and its growth has drastic-
ally slowed. Our situation is seen to be especially serious when
compared with leading capitalist countries, in particular the
United States.

By introducing into the national economy elements of
state regulation and planning, these countries have rid themselves of the destructive crises that earlier plagued capitalist
economies. The widespread introduction into the economy of
automation and computer technology assures a rapid growth in
the productivity of labor, which in turn enables certain social
difficulties and contradictions to be partially overcome (as for
example establishing unemployment benefits, shortening the
working day).

Comparing our economy with the economy of the United
States, we see that our economy lags not only in quantitative
but also—which is saddest of all—in qualitative respects.

The newer and more revolutionary an aspect of an economy is, the greater is the gap between the United States and
ourselves. We surpass America in the mining of coal, but we lag
behind in oil drilling, lag very much behind in gas drilling and in
in the production of electric power, hopelessly behind in chemistry, and infinitely behind in computer technology.

The last is particularly pertinent, for the introduction of
computers in the national economy is of crucial importance for
fundamentally changing the entire face of the production system and of the whole culture. This phenomenon has deservedly
been called the second industrial revolution. Incidentally, our
total inventory of computers is hundreds of times smaller than
that of the United States, and as regards the use of computers
in the economy, the gap is so wide that it is impossible to measure it.

We simply live in another epoch.

Nevertheless, it is claimed that designers have developed computer programs
for numerically controlled machine tools and that Aeroflot, the Soviet national
airline, is using a computerized reservation system. In addition, GUM, the
state–owned department store on Moscow's Red Square, is said to be fully
computerized in the processing of sales and inventory data.[9]

Here is a recent analysis of the state of computing in Russia:[11]*

Soviet scientists are clamoring at the doors of industry for more
and better computers.

*Reprinted by permission of *The Christian Science Monitor.* © 1969 The Christian Science
Publishing Society. All rights reserved.

The demand is great, they say. Factories, ministries, research centers has designed electronic computers as good as those in the West, industry is slow to produce them and the application of computer technology in industry is lagging.

Viewed against the background of the Soviet rivalry with the United States, this lag is of visible concern here. One of the nation's leading scientists warned recently that computer technology "could become the decisive factor in the competition of social systems."

It is not known how many computers there are in Soviet industry, since the Russians publish no figures. Academician Georgy Y. Pukhov, deputy director of the Ukraine Academy of Sciences Institute of Cybernetics, told this reporter he thought there were "over 10,000" operating in the chemical, metallurgical, shipbuilding, and other industries. But, he added, "There are not enough for the very big demand."

Another computer scientist, Academician Gury Marchuk, said in a newspaper article last month that production of computers is "extremely inadequate," that it could be increased "three to five times," and that this should be done "without delay."

Some large computers

The Russians' fastest computer, designed by Sergei A. Lebedev and called the BESM-6, is capable of about one million operations a second. At least five of these computers are known to exist at various research centers. There may be more, but even so their number is small.

Kiev's modern, expanding Institute of Cybernetics, one of three leading computer research centers in the country, concentrates on two basic tasks. One is to study the interaction of men and machines—to develop computers that combine the easiest input by man with the fastest output of machine. The second is to mechanize the designing and production of computers.

"In the Soviet Union computers are used to make individual computer elements," commented Academician Pukhov, "but they are not making whole computers. This problem is not yet solved."

As for the technology of Soviet computers, the quiet–mannered scientist said that semi–conductors are still used in building computers, since integrated circuits are too costly for mass production. But he added that technology is moving in this direction and integrated circuits would probably be introduced "in the next three or four years."

In the opinion of Western experts, the Soviets today are using computers to operate individual machines in such areas as space and defense, where the state has invested heavily in crash programs. But it is not thought they are employed to control entire production processes.

One observable trend of computer application is in the area of inventory control and production planning at the factory level. Two computer systems now are being tested in Soviet industry, one at the Lvov Television Plant under the aegis of the Kiev Institute.

This correspondent visited a modern plant in the western Ukrainian town of Lvov and was shown the two Minsk-22 computers which are the basis of the system. They are used basically to help plan television production, functioning as information gatherers and dispensers. The computer room, is in fact, called the "information computer center."

Serviced by two programmers, the computers tell plant officials where TV parts are at any given moment, how many there are, and when to order supplies. They keep track of output and, on the basis of the factory's plan, calculate production assignments for the next shift.

Overlooking the conveyor belts in a large production room are blinking panels which show the number of television sets rolling off the assembly line and the number yet to be produced. No production process is controlled by the computers, however.

According to the center's youthful director, the Minsk-22's perform 50 different tasks, and some 6 to 10 programs are used for each task. This suggests that the Kiev group is still experimenting with different types of programs.

Factory officials are enthusiastic. Since computers were installed 1½ years ago, they say, production of television sets has increased 7 percent. Output this year is expected to reach 500,000—and eventually the plant would like to turn out as many as a million.

The next step planned by the factory is to change over to a "coordinated control center" and to use the computers for quality control and for determining the best combination of parts to produce reliable, inexpensive TV sets, especially for color television.

By their own admission, the Soviets face many problems in computer development. While the basic structure of their machines is good—Academician Pukhov says they are on a par with and in some cases better than American computers—they are short on what are called peripherals, devices for input and output of information. Soviet machines can do hundreds of thousands of calculations per second, for instance, but the speed of output is slow.

Academician Marchuk, who directs the computer center of the Academy of Sciences in Novosibirsk, terms the shortage of peripherals the "Achilles' heel" of Soviet computers. There is serious need, he writes, for such subsidiary equipment as readers, perforators, teletypes, magnetic memory drums, and printers.

Organization criticized

One obstacle to the development of computer technology, according to Academician Marchuk, is the fact that so many different research bodies and ministries now are involved in making computers and elements.

"With seven nannies, no one looks after the baby," he says and he calls for the formation of a single coordinating body to distribute funds allocated for computer development and to see that the technology is applied in the economy.

Politics lurks in wings

In the Soviet Union, with its state–cointrolled economy, the development of computer technology has political over-tones, since computers could affect Marxist control of decision-making.

Some Soviet economists have suggested, for instance, that computers could estimate the real prices of products (now fixed by central planners) and help develop a logical price structure. At this stage such ideas are kept well in the background, how-ever, and the emphasis of computer use today is on production rather than central planning.

Future development is likely to be carefully controlled, so that planners will have their say in what problems the computers attack.

It is interesting to note that a nation with a centrally administered econ-omy such as the USSR apparently does not have a central agency in charge of computer production and use. This fragmentation of computer development and production is similar to that which occurred in Western Europe during the past decade and which brought forth the large number of mergers of com-puter companies in the period 1968–1970.

The computer equipment in the USSR primarily consists of equipment constructed with transistors and would be considered second–generation equip-ment in the United States. However, work is underway on the development of third–generation computers using integrated circuits.[12,13] The Nairi–3 computer, using integrated circuits and capable of performing 20,000 operations per second, became available in 1970.

A computer commonly utilized in the USSR is the Minsk-22, which has been installed in a new computer center for the state department store in Moscow. More than 200,000 shoppers daily produce 160,000 transactions. A staff of 8,000 mans 128 warehouses stocking 330,000 different types of goods. The computer center performs warehouse management and prints daily reports of trade. In the future, the center will also handle forecasting and inventory management at the point of sale.[13]

A photo of the Minsk-22 computer at the Institute of High Energy Physics in Moscow is shown in Figure 14-1. The Minsk-22 is a medium scale transistorized computer capable of 6000 operations per second.

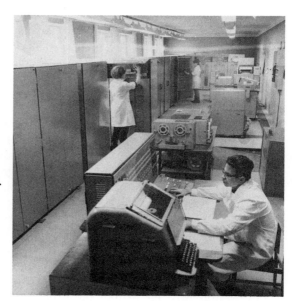

FIGURE 14-1 The MINSK-22 Computer at the Institute of High Energy Physics, Moscow, USSR. *Courtesy of TASS from SOVFOTO.*

Perhaps the fastest computer in common use is the BESM-6, which uses a 48-bit word and has a 64,000 word main storage unit capable of operating with an access time of two microseconds. Algol is the most popular computer language in Russia, although Fortran is available on the BESM-6. There are an estimated twenty BESM-6 installations in the USSR.[14]

It has been estimated that approximately 5,000 computer systems have been installed in the USSR.[9] The USSR also imports computer parts and computer peripherals from Western Europe.

In Eastern Europe, the pattern of computer useage appears to be set by Russia. Several of the Eastern European countries manufacture computer peripheral equipment. The United Kingdom has been particularly successful at selling computer equipment to Eastern Europe, particularly through the International Computers, Ltd. group of merged companies. However, IBM, through its European subsidiaries, has sold computer equipment to Eastern Europe, particularly to Yugoslavia.[15] Also, Compagnie Bull–General Electric of France has sold a significant number of computers to Eastern Europe, particularly to Czechoslovakia. It has been reported that Eastern European countries in the Comecon (Council for Mutual Economic Assistance) market, which embraces Russia, Poland, Czechoslovakia, Rumania, Bulgaria, Hungary and East Germany, have assigned top priority to large hard–currency investments in Western–made computers and peripheral gear for the next five–year plan, running from 1970 through 1974.[16] The Eastern European countries have been reported to be shopping openly for Western European and US computers.

Computer sales to Eastern Europe from the US and Britain would be higher if they did not have to contend with the strategic trade controls agreed upon by NATO countries. The list of strategic goods that are not to be sold to Communist nations presently includes large third–generation computers with a capacity greater than the IBM 360/40.

The entry for the USSR in Table 14–3 lists the number of computers as 5,000. This estimate along with an estimate of the gross national product yields a ratio of 8 computers per billion dollars of Gross National Product. We noted earlier in this section that a very large proportion of the computers in the Soviet Union are second–generation computers. Thus, it is exceedingly difficult to compare the 5,000 computers in Russia with the 5,000 computers in the United Kingdom. Most analysts would agree that the computer power in the UK equals that presently available in Russia.

Let us reexamine Table 14–3 in order to compare the computer capability of the USSR compared to other industrialized nations and less developed nations. Russia has an estimated ratio of computers per $ billion of GNP of 8 which lies well below the threshold of 20 for other industrialized nations. While this threshold is arbitrary, the ratio for the USSR is one–fourth that for the United Kingdom or France. Thus, it is substantially correct to state that the USSR is presently far behind the other industrialized nations in the use of computers in commerce and government.

CHAPTER 14 REFERENCES

1. J. Schreiber, *The American Challenge*, Atheneum House, Inc., New York, 1969.
2. "United Nations to Study the Transfer of Computer Technology between Countries," *Computers and Automation*, August, 1969, pg. 42.

3. D. M. Carter, "Data Processing around the World," *Data Management,* May, 1970, pp. 20-24.
4. B. W. Boehm, "Computing in South America," *Datamation,* May, 1970, pp. 97-108.
5. J. K. Imai, "Computers in Japan—1969," *Datamation,* January, 1970, pp. 147-153.
6. O. Beltrami, "The Mediterranean Computer Scene," *Computers and Automation,* July, 1970, pp. 20-24.
7. "International News," *Modern Data,* October, 1969, page 46.
8. D. W. Willis, "Peripheral Equipment in Europe," *Datamation,* Sept., 1969, pp. 64-66.
9. R. B. Rush, "Computing in Russia," *RCA Review,* Summer, 1969, pp. 2-5.
10. "The Need for Democratization," *Saturday Review,* June 6, 1970, pp. 26-27.
11. C. Saikowski, "Soviet Firms Clamor for More Computers," *The Christian Science Monitor,* May 15, 1969, pg. 1.
12. W. B. Holland, "Soviet Computing, 1969: A leap into the third generation," *Datamation,* September, 1969, pp. 55-60.
13. "What are the Soviets doing in Computers," *Control Engineering,* July, 1970, page 29.
14. E. E. David, Jr., "Soviet Computing," *Computer Decisions,* March, 1970, pg. 16.
15. H. Voysey, "Trends and Tangents of East-West Trade," *Datamation,* Sept., 1969, pp. 95-99.
16. "Computer Makers Look East," *Electronics,* Sept. 1, 1969, pp. 103-109.
17. *The Statistical Yearbook,* The United Nations, New York, 1970.
18. I. Berenyi, "Computers in Eastern Europe," *Science,* October, 1970, pp. 102-108.
19. *The Application of Computer Technology for Development,* United Nations Publication E.71.II.A.1, New York, 1971.

15

COMPUTERS IN URBAN AND GOVERNMENT SYSTEMS

15.1 INTRODUCTION

The United States Government is the world's largest single computer user. Some 5000 computers are now being operated by the Federal Government.[1] In addition, the state and municipal governments make extensive use of computers. The US Government has approximately nine percent of all the machines in the United States and seven percent of the computers in the world. The purchase cost of Federally–owned computers was $1.25 billion in June 30, 1967, and it has increased continually since then.

In 1968, the US Bureau of the Budget issued a progress report on the use of computers in the Federal Government to "accomplish worthwhile work not otherwise feasible" and "improve and reduce the cost of government operations." Also highlighted in the report are "management actions which contributed to more efficient and economical procurement and utilization of computers." Some examples of the applications of computers in the Federal Government, as given in the report, are:[2]

- Weather forecasts up to 30 days in the future are being made with more reliability.
- Refunds due a taxpayer are now being offset against back taxes owed by the same taxpayer.

- Medical X-rays are being produced in much sharper form than the orig-
inals, permitting a more thorough analysis.
- Essential information for solving crimes is becoming available on a
nationwide scale. (The pilot phase of the National Crime Information
Center is underway and will eventually result in linking state and metropolitan area police systems through a computerized central index of
documented law enforcement information.)
- The time required for processing new drug applications was reduced
from one year to six months, partially as the result of the availability of
computer-produced periodic status reports. An 18-month backlog has
been virtually eliminated.

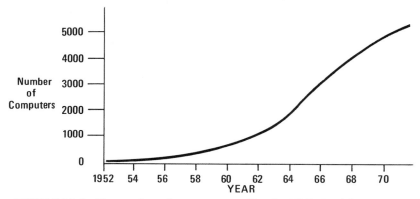

FIGURE 15-1   The number of computers used by the US Federal Government.

The growth of the number of computers used by the Federal Government is
shown in Figure 15-1. Immediately following World War II, the government
ordered two computers, one for the Census Bureau and one for the Pentagon.
However, the Bureau of Standards built a computer for its own use which was
completed and operating late in 1950. This computer was named SEAC (Standards Eastern Automatic Computer.) The SEAC was one of the first, if not the
first, general purpose internally-sequenced electronic computer in operation
in the US. It is shown in Figure 15-2.
    The state governments in the US have also purchased and used computers
for the various functions of state government. California's state agencies have
more computer power at their disposal than do those of any other state.
California has 187 digital computers and employs about 4000 persons to operate and program them. The state spent approximately $68 million on com-
puters and computer use during the 1970-1971 fiscal year.[3]
    The applications of computers in urban and Federal government are di-
verse and far reaching. McLuhan says, "The extreme decentralizing power of

FIGURE 15-2   The SEAC computer, the first computer at the National Bureau of Stan-
                dards, was completed in 1950. For the fourteen years of its useful life,
                SEAC was used by dozens of other government agencies; portions of this
                computer are now preserved in the Smithsonian Institution. This computer
                was one of the first general purpose, internally-sequenced, electronic com-
                puters. *Courtesy of the National Bureau of Standards.*

the computer in eliminating cities and all concentrations of population whatever is as nothing compared to its power to translate hardware into software
and capital goods into information."[4]

    While the computer may not have yet eliminated cities, it has aided in the
process of suburbanization and diffusion of population. This has necessitated
the use of computers to assist with the problems arising from suburbanization.
In London, England, and San Jose, California, a computer traffic control system
is used to improve the utility of the highway system. In London, the 1.4 million
dollar system operates 100 traffic signals in a 6.5 square mile section of London. The British Ministry of Transportation maintains that a 5 percent reduction in journey times will be attained as a minimum.

    The computer is used in many localities to count votes at election time.
One simple scheme which uses computers and a punched card is the IBM
Votomatic system. A voter at a poll is given an unpunched card which may be
punched with a sharp stylus. The unperforated card is placed in a bed or
holder, and a mask is laid over the card. The overlay mask indicates the voter
options and various candidates' names. Then the voter can punch the holes and
mark his vote. The card is then placed in a ballot box and all the cards are
run at a computer center. Using this procedure, Los Angeles County is able to

tally over a million votes for a variety of candidates and provide early counts by 10:00 p.m. on election night.*

The use of computers by the Internal Revenue Service has resulted in greater tax returns to the government as well as more efficient processing of the taxpayer's forms. Probably the IRS could not be able to process the individual forms without the aid of computers. In 1930 the IRS processed six million tax returns. In 1969, it processed 110 million. In addition to individual returns, there were approximately 400 million information returns, including W-2 forms, reports on interest paid by banks, stock dividends, and similar data to process. The IRS began a program of computer automation in 1961 when it set up a nationwide computer network centered in Martinsburg, Virginia. Now all individual and corporate tax returns are being processed by computers. In 1968, computer operations at IRS added $134 million to federal tax collections. This brings the total additional revenues from IRS's use of computers to $300 million since 1962. In addition, EDP has resulted in quicker and more efficient processing operations. Also, large-scale, direct data entry terminals have been developed for IRS. The use of terminals eliminates the use of punched cards, since the data is entered directly from the tax return to magnetic tape storage. This system eliminates the punching and verification of 400 million cards per year by IRS. The IRS computer system provides a rapid, efficient, auditing system which should reduce the number of errors and evasions in the tax process.

A program of magnitude similar to that of the Internal Revenue Service is that of the US Census Bureau. Every ten years, the US Census Bureau accumulates the facts on the population. As a result of the 1970 census, the headquarters of the Bureau receives four billion facts concerning 205 million Americans. This data will be processed by four large computers. Analysis of the data will relate parameters such as income, housing, sex, occupation, marital status, education and age. The study could determine trends in large areas such as congressional districts, states, and even the nation as well as in small areas such as neighborhoods. The completed questionnaires are photographed and scanned by a computer reader converting the data to 6500 reels of magnetic tape. Since the census reports, which are required by an Act of Congress, are confidential, all names are dropped from the questionnaires before the information is coded on magnetic tape.

The automation of census data was begun by Hollerith in the 1880 census and has proceeded since under the pressure of increasing population. In 1790, when the United States took its first decennial population census, each person was asked five questions and the statistical summaries for the whole country

---

*Los Angeles suffered unfavorable nationwide publicity in 1970 when tardy vote counting and vote–count irregularities were charged to computer vote tabulation in a primary election. Eleven states, in a (possibly) shortsighted step, have already forbidden the use of computers in election tabulations.

were printed on a total of 56 pages. In 1970, the four billion facts obtained from the 205 million Americans were used to allocate Federal funds for highways and to realign the boundaries of congressional districts. Business also makes use of the census data for marketing and manufacturing location purposes. The US census is an important statistical tool for government and business. However, security of each individual's data must be assured. The question of the legitimacy of the 68 census questions is a matter of concern, and this will certainly be a question to be considered in preparation for the 1980 census.[5]

Computers will be used extensively by the US Postal Service during the 1970's. The Service has 32,000 offices, which process nearly 82 billion pieces of mail each year. The New York City Post Office alone deals with 35 million pieces of mail daily. The predecessor US Post Office Department had a 1970 budget of $7.13 billion and 725,000 workers.[6] With the reorganization and reform of the department in 1970 new methods of automation utilizing computers were developed; the plans were made, for instance, to install 210 computers and sorting machines in 136 cities. One computer system under development will enable a postal operator to sort mail merely by glancing at the zip code on a letter as it flashes by and pressing a zip–coded keyboard. The keyboard will feed the information to a computer, which will tell a sorting machine to which of 277 destination bins the letter goes. Twelve operators will be able to sort up to 36,000 letters an hour at an estimated savings of $13.5 million a year in labor.

Computers, automation and new methods may enable the Postal Service to avoid collapsing under the burden of an ever–increasing volume of mail and increasing costs of processing.

The US Labor Department is using computers to assist in the placing of job seekers in suitable employment. A job bank using a daily computer output list of available jobs is used to help place the unemployed in more than 20 cities. The job banks are used by the various state employment agencies. Some agencies use interviews to match the individual with the job, while others use the computer. In these latter cases, the applicant's characteristics and qualifications are also put into a computer and then matched by the computer with the job specifications given by the employer.[7] Proposals have been made to investigate the feasibility of a national job bank. If a national employment system with computer–aided man and job matching does eventuate, the mobility and employability of the worker could be greatly improved.

The Social Security Administration of the US uses 27 computers in the largest commercial computer installation in the world. The volume of data is awesome. It requires 165,000 reels of tape for storage. Every day one million earnings entries are processed and the system accounts for 197 million citizens. In addition, the Social Security Administration administrates the Medicare and Medicaid systems for some 21 million persons. The Administration uses computers effectively to accomplish the overwhelming task of collecting $301 billion in deductions and paying out $2.9 billion in benefits every month.[16]

Computers are widely used by the Federal and state governments in diverse applications. In the next section we consider the use of computers for urban planning and municipal information systems.

15.2   URBAN PLANNING AND MUNICIPAL INFORMATION SYSTEMS

Computer systems are in various stages of adoption and use within the urban and metropolitan governments. There are many urban problems, but finding solutions for urban problems and fitting computer technology into those solutions requires careful definitions of problems and alternative solutions. The problems of congestion, pollution, urban education, poverty, housing and race relations are difficult to attack using the computer as an aid. One view is that of urban problems as productivity problems. Public sector activities, many of them in cities, have had alarmingly small productivity increases while productivity has been increasing in most other sectors of society. Services are becoming more and more important (especially public services) in our national economy; increased productivity is necessary to continuing development of the national economy. The question remains: how can computer systems help increase the productivity of urban services?

Planners are also concerned by the distribution of the services rather than the amount of service. How can we distribute the services more evenly and insure the equality of services to all groups? Of what value is it to solve the financial problem of the transit system of a city, if the system does not serve all residential areas efficiently?

The functions of urban planning are currently being revitalized by modern computer–oriented management science techniques. As we found in Chapter 11, management science can be used to understand and control complex systems consisting of interrelated components which evolve with time. Underlying all management science techniques is the rigor of quantification: the planner asks how much each alternative will cost and what the benefits will be. Often simulation techniques are used to analyze the various courses of action.

The intended solutions to interrelated systems often result in unforeseen consequences. A new highway, for example, built to provide faster access between the city and its suburbs, also radically affects the living patterns of the area it passes through, dominating the area and often causing the original residents to move to the suburbs. In such a case, the new highway, by responding to one need, introduces several others.

The need for complete and up–to–date information about an urban region's condition leads to the concept of a central data bank. This data can be looked on as a data bank to be drawn on by all the municipal planners and managers. Ideally information would not be fragmented among many agencies,

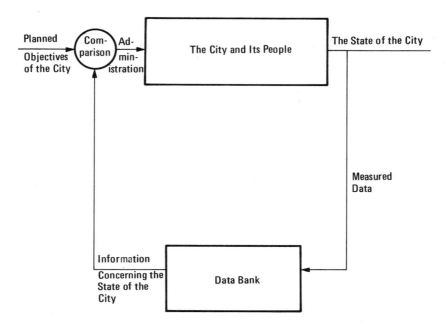

FIGURE 15-3   A conceptual model of a municipal management information system.

but would appear in one central computer file. A conceptual model of a city and the management of the city using an information system is shown in Figure 15-3. The data bank is used to provide information for management purposes. There is currently a significant amount of activity toward the development of municipal data banks and municipal information systems.

The urban planner wishes to use information systems for such activities as planning sites for public facilities such as schools, police stations, firehouses, roads and hospitals. The city executives wish to use the information systems to manage all the city functions and allocate the resources of the city to the various functions.

For example, one urban systems group, in New York City, plans to attack the problem of air pollution with the assistance of a computer information system.[8] Such an approach includes developing mathematical models and statistical analyses and designing on-line processing systems which include remote terminals and sensors.

The computer could project air quality (for each segment of the city) from six to 48 hours in advance by processing information on current air quality together with an emission model (amount and type of pollutant, by location, based on known weather forecasts and daily, weekly and seasonal variations) and a dissipation model (cleansing of air, by location, based on wind direction and velocity and atmospheric conditions). The computer can compare this predicted air quality with accepted clean-air standards, and recommend control actions necessary to prevent the development of hazardous pollution levels in any part of the city.[8]

The wealth of detailed information about the city required by advanced planning techniques is not to be had from the traditional systems of record-keeping. Thus, additional sensors and measurement systems will be required to complete the system.

An example of the components of a comprehensive municipal management information system is given in Figure 15-4.

In the past the use of information systems by municipalities has been quite limited. Only a portion of the available data was collected or recorded and the municipality was managed on a short-range basis. Recently the US Department of Housing and Urban Development has initiated a program for developing municipal information systems.[9] The information system is to be composed of four subsystems—dedicated to public safety, public finance and related bookkeeping chores, human resources (health, education, welfare, etc.) and physical development (urban planning, public works, facilities maintenance.) For example, such municipal information systems will assist in the prevention and control of crime and fire, speed traffic flow and detect sources of pollution. With an adequate data base, the population shifts within an urban area can be accurately measured and used for purposes of urban planning for schools, roads and other public services. One potential advantage of a municipal information system is the ability provided the user to investigate the relationship among various factors affecting the municipality.

Computer information systems may be used to assess the future consequences of public decisions. With the aid of urban simulation models, which were discussed in Chapter 13, the effects of various public actions may be assessed. Forrester's recent book, *Urban Dynamics,* attempts to use this approach for a model city.[10] For example, one simulation assesses the consequence of the Federal Government's providing new city housing for low income persons. According to the model, an increase in housing and jobs results in the short run, but over the years, both will decline. The use of simulation and models of urban regions will be a valuable approach for urban planning in the coming years.

15.3 COMPUTERS AND THE LEGISLATURES

Computers can be used to assist the functions of the legislative as well as the executive branch of state and federal government. For example, the Pennsylvania Legislature provides its members with up-to-date computer reports

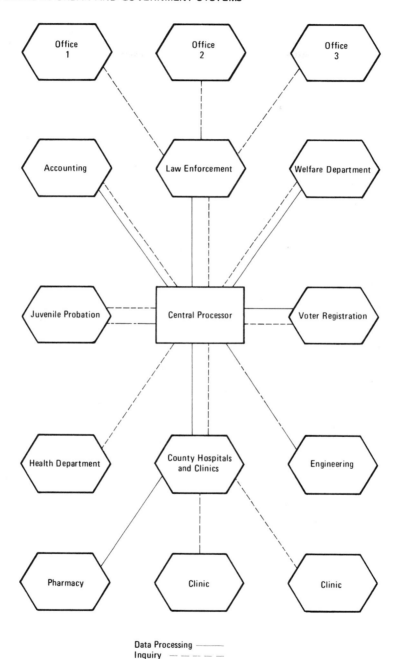

Data Processing ————
Inquiry — — — — —

FIGURE 15–4 An example of the components of a comprehensive municipal management information system. *Courtesy of IBM Corporation.*

on bills that are working their way through the legislative process.[11] Members of the Pennsylvania General Assembly who desire to know the status of a bill key in the number of the proposed law at computer terminals situated at various points in the capitol. The current information is provided on the visual display at the terminal and the information is also typed out at the terminal. The computer process keeps the information current for the legislators. An illustration of a computer legislative retrieval system is shown in Figure 15-5.

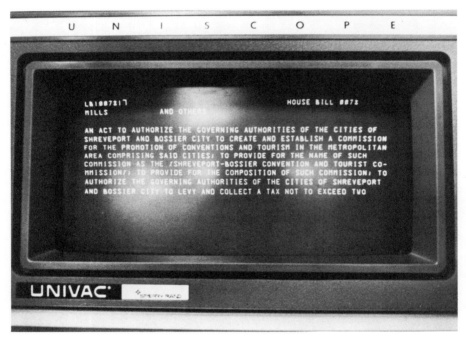

FIGURE 15-5   Louisiana legislators utilize a computer retrieval system for new or pending legislation by means of terminals connected to the state's data processing system. Retrieval of the title, status and bill sponsor is possible within three seconds of inquiry. A close–up view of an actual bill is shown as one might view it from one of the terminals installed in the House, Senate, Legislative Council's office, or Lieutenant Governor's office. In addition, lawmakers can order a printout each morning to learn of all bills introduced the previous day. *Courtesy of UNIVAC Division of Sperry Rand Corp.*

The US Congress has initiated several studies and discussions concerning the use of the computer in assisting Congress. A congressional computer information system, if adopted, would give every one of the 535 representatives and senators access to the tons of information that now can be tapped easily only by the senior committee chairmen. A congressional computer system would be helpful, if only to keep track of the 12,000 pieces of legislation introduced annually. During the 89th Congress (1965-1966), members were called upon to consider 26,566 bills and resolutions; of this total, 4,016 became law. Not only must the senator or representative respond to the pressures of daily legislative operations, but he must also respond to the needs of his constituents, who now average 450,000 per member. With the demands on each legislator growing each year, the assistance of automatic data processing in the decision-making process may be desirable. Representative Jack Brooks of Texas introduced a bill (H.R. 404) into the Congress in January 3, 1969, which calls for the development and establishment of an information system for the Congress. In addition, a bill, H.R. 17654, was introduced into the House of Representatives on May 18, 1970, concerned with the reorganization of the legislative process; it includes recommended action toward the development of a data processing service for the legislative branch of the Federal Government. Portions of H.R. 17654 are reprinted below.

TITLE IV—CONGRESS AS AN INSTITUTION
Part 1—Joint Committee on Data Processing

Congressional Findings and Policy

SEC. 401. (a) It is the sense of the Congress that there is an urgent, critical, and continuing need on the part of the Congress and the legislative branch generally for a modern, effective, and coordinated automatic data processing and information storage and retrieval system—

(1) to assist the Congress, its committees and Members, its officers and employees, and its offices and other organizational units, and the respective agencies, offices, and other organizational units in the legislative branch generally, in obtaining and analyzing information;

(2) to expedite their operations and activities; and

(3) to facilitate and improve the performance of the legislative and representative functions of the Congress.

(b) It is, therefore, the policy of the Congress, in view of this need—

(1) that the Congress and the legislative branch shall be provided with, and shall acquire, establish, and maintain, by purchase, lease, or otherwise, the most modern, up-to-date, efficient, effective and coordinated automatic data processing and information storage and retrieval equipment and facilities which are appropriate to the needs and requirements of the Congress and the legislative branch generally;

(2) that a method of continuous, coordinated, compre-

hensive, and efficient planning and review shall be established
and maintained by the Congress for the continuing development
and improvement of such equipment and facilities and the use
thereof . . .

One member of the House of Representatives, Joe D. Waggoner, Jr., has
proposed an electronic voting system.[12] The system would consist basically
of 49 terminals on the House floor, a computer, two display boards on the
wall of the House chamber, an input console at the Speaker's desk, and possibly
an output printer in the Speaker's lobby. Members would vote by inserting a
plastic identification card in one of the terminals and pressing one of three
keys ("Aye", "Nay," and "Present"). The system utilizes a computer used by
the House of Representatives. The ultimate aim of the system may be to give
House members and committees on-line access to all federal data bases containing needed information, including those managed by the Clerk of the
House, Congressional Research Service, the General Accounting Office, and
the Executive Branch.

The use of computers in the legislative branches of the Federal and state
governments is growing and will enable the legislators to keep pace with the
ever-increasing complexity of government.

15.4 THE COMPUTER; THE CITY AND GOVERNMENTAL FUNCTIONS

In this section we reproduce a recent article which is concerned with
computers and their use in governing a city, a state, or a region as well as aiding
the Federal Government. In this article, which is written by John Kemeny of
Dartmouth College, the use of the computer in city government functions is
considered.[13] The author describes the prospective applications of computers
to urban problems during the next decade. Kemeny states that the major role
of the city of 1990 will be the exchange of information, and a computer network will be the major public utility.

THE CITY AND THE COMPUTER REVOLUTION*

By John G. Kemeny

In reading the popular press one is left with the impression that
the interminable problems of our large cities are caused by the population explosion. But this hypothesis will not stand up under careful
examination.

*From *Governing Urban Society: New Scientific Approaches,* with the permission of the
American Academy of Political and Social Science and the author.

Population Explosion Is Not the Cause of Metropolitan Problems

The population of eight of our ten largest cities actually decreased during the decade 1950–1960, which was the decade that saw the beginnings of the revolt of urban masses. The remaining two cities are spread over vast areas, and hence are far from being overcrowded. The population of our largest and most crowded cities is leveling off—in spite of the population explosion.

However, we find spectacular increases in suburban areas linked to the large cities. While the central city of Boston decreased 13 per cent during the decade, the outside areas had a population increase of 18 per cent, and now have a population almost three times that of central Boston. In Washington we may contrast a small decrease in the population of the central city area with an 87 per cent increase in the surrounding urban areas. Thus, insofar as the population explosion is hurting our large cities, it is doing so indirectly: There are ever increasing numbers of people living in the suburbs but commuting to the city.

Even more significant is the tremendous increase in the complexity of our civilization and in the affluence of our city dwellers. The statistic that I find most striking is the fact that during the same decade the number of motor vehicles increased from about 50 to about 75 million, a 50 per cent growth, which is far in excess of the growth of population. Or consider the fact that in a five-year period nearly half the population changes its residence. The resulting mobility, both on a daily basis and in terms of the uprooting of homes, contributes to the problems of urban society.

Computer Will Revolutionize Modern Life

My basic thesis is that the much publicized computer revolution will, in the long run, help us to cope with the complexities of modern civilization, and will help to relieve the problems of our cities. I see these benefits coming in three stages. The first stage is with us now and will continue for a few more years; the second stage is just around the corner, while a third and most important stage may be a generation in the future.

Modern high-speed computers have existed for fewer than twenty years. Since they have already made spectacular contributions to civilization, it is difficult to realize that we are seeing the computer revolution in its infancy. For most of their brief history, computers have been devoted to a single type of task: We have a considerable amount of data which has to be sorted, analyzed, and used to test hypotheses. The information is supplied in machine-readable form, and after hours or days the computer returns a printed form containing its results. These problems may range from standard data-processing to advanced scientific computations. In the former case the difficulty lies in the bulk of the data, while in the latter it is the analysis that is time-consuming. But all of these problems are solved in the traditional "batch-processing" manner.

I shall refer to this stage as the *dawn of computing*. Even in this stage, computers can be invaluable tools for city governments in understanding the complexity of their problems and as tools for urban planning. This will be the subject of the next section.

During the past three years, a second revolution has started within the computer revolution. Although most computers today still operate in the batch-processing manner, there are a few computers capable of providing simultaneous and immediate computer service to a large number of users. I call this stage *the coming of time-sharing*. The combination of being able to serve a large number of clients all at the same time, and the ability to provide answers in seconds rather than hours, opens up entirely new frontiers. It will enable municipalities to use computers to control such key functions as traffic and police operations. It will also make new types of services possible. This will be the subject of the third section.

Within a generation there will be a huge public utility, combining modern communication media with a network of computers. I shall refer to this stage as *a computer in every home*. I predict that when this stage is fully implemented, the very nature of society will change. This, in turn, will change the role of the central city, and it may automatically solve some of the problems that seem hopeless at the present time. I shall briefly sketch these ideas in the final section.

Government Today Is Better Qualified, But More Bewildered

The dawn of computing

Let us consider a municipal government of a city of one million people in the year 1967. The chances are that our government is much better qualified and less corrupt than its predecessor was forty years ago. The chances are, also, that it is much more bewildered.

In order to make intelligent decisions, we must first of all have reliable data. Given the complexity and mobility of a modern city of one million people, the gathering and interpretation of data is an almost hopeless task. And as our citizens become more affluent, they expect more and better services, which aggravates the problem.

What is the value of a census taken every ten years? By the time the census is processed, 10 per cent of the population will have changed its residence. By the time a new school is planned, approved by the voters, and actually constructed, it is hopelessly overcrowded. By the time a major highway is completed, the flow of traffic has changed completely. Efficient use of high-speed computers may not solve all these problems, but solutions to the problems are impossible without the use of computers.

Municipal governments use computers only for statistics

Industry has been much more aware of these problems, and has taken better advantage of the existence of modern computers. Many industries now keep their personnel files and business data in the memories of computers and use these for fast and accurate data-processing. The same information may also be processed for planning purposes. Although some municipal governments are beginning to realize the significance of computers, generally they are used only for such simple tasks as the issuing of pay checks. And even when computers are available, most of the employees have no understanding of the use of computers, and therefore fail to take full advantage of this incredible tool.

Computers will not have a significant effect on our city governments until our colleges bring up a new generation of graduates who take high-speed computers for granted. Fortunately, some of our best institutions are doing exactly this. At my own institution, 80 per cent of each entering class learns how to use a computer, and many acquire a significant amount of experience before they graduate. When some of these students filter into our municipal governments, we can look forward to a revolution in city planning.

Our city and state highway departments collect immense amounts of information on the flow of traffic. But what happens to this mass of information once it is collected? A few able men, perhaps with a great deal of experience, will come up with rules-of-thumb for the improvement of the flow of traffic. Although this is certainly worth-while, it is far from what is possible in the age of computers.

Simulation could provide five years' experience in one week

It would be possible to simulate the entire traffic pattern of downtown Manhattan by a high-speed computer. ("Simulation" is a powerful tool, widely used by business, to re-create within a computer a fairly accurate image of what happens in the outside world.) Built into the model would be information on the number of cars, the speed at which they travel under various conditions of crowding, the available traffic lights, one-way streets, habits of double parking, and the like. Once such a model exists, experimentation with new traffic patterns could be carried out within the computer rather than using the population of the city as guinea pigs. We could instruct the computer to change the operation of traffic lights, modify one-way streets, and try other innovations. After a detailed simulation the computer would report back whether there was any significant easing in the flow of traffic. With one week of computer simulation we could acquire the equivalent of five years' experience. Such a simulation planning model in the hands of experts would make a tremendous impact in relieving notorious traffic bottlenecks.

This idea has been tried on a small scale in planning the traffic of superhighways, bridges, and tunnels. One such experiment was reported in *Scientific American* (see [3]). The computer found that cars should *not* be allowed to enter the Holland Tunnel as quickly as the toll booths could process them. If, instead, cars were held up periodically for a short time, the total flow through the tunnel increased! Presumably this is due to the fact that "pulsing" the cars prevents major jams and reduces accidents. But no one suggested this simple improvement *before* the computer simulation.

Secondly, high-speed computers should be used in the fight against pollution. The causes of pollution are complex, and careful statistical analysis should be substituted for guesswork. I predict that a major data–gathering and analysis would turn up unexpected results.

Thirdly, consider the problem of planning schools, parks, recreation areas, youth centers, and centers for the aged. Of course, such decisions are often political footballs. But, even with the best intentions, such decisions are made in ignorance of the facts; although the facts may be buried in the files, without high–speed computers the planning body cannot digest them. For example, where should we place a park to do the most good for the city's children? This decision requires a careful correlation of the distribution of children with the city's geography, and with the size and location of existing parks. The solution of this problem requires both up–to–date census information and the sophisticated use of computers.

Our municipal governments have hardly begun to make intelligent use of the computer revolution. The hiring of computer experts and acquisition of large computing centers for planning purposes could be the single best investment to help alleviate our urban problems.

. . .

Computer would be a powerful tool to fight organized crime

Suppose that a patrol car, in one of the cities, spots a vehicle, with its motor running, right in front of the bank. Before taking action they would like to know whether the car belongs to the bank president, or to a known criminal, or perhaps is a stolen car. But by the time that they can notify the motor vehicle bureau and receive identification, the bank robber will have cleaned out the safe and escaped across the state line. On the other hand, with a time-sharing system, not unlike the Dartmouth system, it would be possible to carry out all the present functions of motor vehicle registration and also provide immediate information on suspicious cars.

While the technical details of such a system are beyond the goals of this paper, a few relevant details may clarify this application. The computer could easily hold within its memory all the information contained on two million registration certificates. There could be two hundred police stations, throughout the state, each having immediate access to this information. As soon as a patrol car calls in, the license number would be teletyped to the central computer, and within *ten seconds* the complete identification of the car, plus any known suspicious facts, would be typed out in reply. This information could be relayed to the patrol car in time for appropriate action.

A very common, but much more difficult, problem is the identification of a car from inaccurate information. Suppose that a witness notes that the license is GA46——, and that the car was large, fairly new, and either dark blue or dark green. The time-sharing system could easily handle such an inquiry. It would find in its memory the 100 license numbers starting with "GA46," and match each against the partial description. Within a minute it could type out complete descriptions of the dozen or so possible suspect cars—and would type this at the local police station. The result would be both a great increase in police efficiency and a relief for our overworked police forces. I understand that such a system has actually been contemplated by the Los Angeles Police Department, but—to the best of my knowledge—it has not yet been implemented anywhere.

Naturally, one must ask whether such a system would involve astronomical costs. However, I have sketched out the technical details, and I estimate that the entire operation could be financed by an annual charge of one dollar on motor vehicles. Thus, my proposal is entirely practical.

And once such a system is in operation, it would facilitate other operations. The motor vehicle bureau could have its own terminals which would automatically, and instantaneously, record each new registration issued. And the various police forces in the state could pool their criminal records within the memory of the machine. Identification of criminal suspects could be expedited by a procedure similar to the one outlined above. And if the criminal files of the states and the federal government were tied together by a computer network, we would have the most powerful tool imaginable to fight organized crime.

Traffic jams would be almost eliminated

Equally exciting is the possibility of real-time control of traffic. Even if computers are used for the planning of traffic patterns, we know that the plans will go haywire under unusual circumstances. I have often waited an unreasonable amount of time at a traffic light, when there was no traffic on the cross-street, but my street was jammed up. Under sufficiently bad circumstances, the city will station a policeman at the corner, who can make corrections manually. A much more efficient, and less expensive, solution would be the use of a time-sharing computer to control the lights. It could be informed of current traffic densities by means of electronic devices, and could adjust the lights according to need. And it could do this for a thousand traffic lights.

Similarly, it is ludicrous to allow more traffic to pour into a jammed highway. Traffic lights at all the entrances of a limited access road, controlled on the basis of real-time traffic information, could make a significant improvement.

. . .

A system could probably be used to relieve the serious problem of finding suitable housing. Anyone who has ever tried to find an apartment in a large city will know that it is a long and painful task to look at advertisements, to go to real estate agents, and to visit a hundred apartments until one finds one. But one could feed into a time-sharing system all the information on available apartments. The information could be quite up-to-date if landlords would report the renting of an apartment to the nearest time-sharing terminal. This would eliminate the annoyances of visiting an apartment half-way across town, only to find out that it is no longer available. The system could also, within minutes, furnish you with a list of those apartments that come closest to meeting your requirements. In short, we should let the time-sharing system do most of the walking for us.

Not least among the benefits would be the steady supply of up-to-date statistical information that the time-sharing system will make available to the city government.

A computer in every home

While some of the uses of computers suggested so far may seem dramatic in their conception or their possible impact, they will yield only relief for the symptoms of urban disease. For a cure we will have to wait for the next development in the computer revolution.

By 1990 the principal public utility will be a gigantic communication network, including the means for visual communication, and having a network of huge computers as an integral part. I expect to see not only every office tied to this network, but to see a console in every home. I have discussed elsewhere some of the implications of having access to a computer in every home. I would now like to do the same for the implications of the new utility for the role of the city.

One may classify the principal functions of the city under five categories: (1) It is the home of millions of people. (2) It is a manufacturing center. (3) It is a center of trade. (4) It is a center of finance. (5) It is a center of recreation. The worse problems of the city arise not from the fact that millions live there, but that the other four functions attract vast numbers of nonresidents to the city. I shall argue that by 1990 most of the reasons for this influx can be eliminated.

City as a center of trade and finance will decline

The role of the cities as centers of manufacture has been steadily decreasing in importance. As costs of transportation decrease and overhead costs in large cities continue to increase, manufacturing centers—like the population—are deserting our largest cities. And we have every reason to expect that this trend will continue. As a matter of fact, the trend will be accelerated in the immediate future when cities begin to take effective measures to combat pollution.

Even today the major role of the city is not as a manufacturing center, but as a center of trade and finance. And the nature of these functions is also subtly changing. I claim that the major role of the city is not that of processing or exchanging goods, but rather that of exchanging information. And this trend is being greatly accelerated by the coming of computers.

An interesting symptom is the disappearance of money (cash) from everyday transactions. Major businesses have for a long time not needed cash to deal with each other. And the wide use of checks and credit cards means that we have almost completely changed over from monetary exchanges to exchanges of information. In the age of the computer–communication utility, cash will completely disappear. When homes, stores, offices, and banks are linked through computers, one need only enter a transaction through the nearest console, and two bank accounts will be automatically credited or debited.

Similarly, banks will be able to implement an automatic credit system—a modern version of the British "overdraft." And even the most complex banking transactions could be handled by a one-room local bank which, through the computer network, has access to all the files of the central bank, and perhaps to a national credit-rating system.

Or consider the operation of the stockmarket. Even today a "ticker-tape" network keeps brokers all over the country informed about the market. Why not replace this with a modern computer network that will allow all of these brokers to participate actively in the market? Through a time-sharing system they could not only be kept informed, but could enter bids and conclude sales instantaneously. After all, the stockmarket is nothing more than a gigantic information-exchange center, whose function could be fulfilled by a large computer.

Similar remarks apply to the large office-complexes maintained by businesses in our cities. Their major role is the collection, exchange, and processing of information. This could be handled by a hub of the computer-communication network. Why must all the executive and secretarial staff have their offices in the same location? Presumably for ease of access to the information and because face-to-face meetings are useful. But in the not-so-distant future, any branch office will have easy, instantaneous access to all files. And video-phones will make most personal meetings unnecessary. Then a hundred conveniently located, specialized branches will operate efficiently as a single large company.

Such a trend is visible even today in retail trade. Mailorder houses locate their "central office" wherever they please, and large retail firms have their outlets distributed among a hundred shopping centers. When the new utility makes it possible for the housewife to "search" stores from her own home, by means of computer information-processing and video displays, another major reason for the influx into cities will disappear.

Even in the area of recreation the participants need not go to the place from which the entertainment originates. We note that a professional football game which has fifty thousand spectators is watched by fifty million people on television. And educational television is bringing adult education into the home. At the moment, unfortunately, television allows only passive participation in education and entertainment, but the new utility may even reverse this dangerous trend. For example, a woman taking a television course may do research by means of her home computer.

The City of 1990 Will Be Node of Computer-Communication Net

I see the city of 1990 as a gigantic depository of information, as a major node in the computer-communication network, and as a source of education and entertainment. Tens of millions living in surrounding small towns will have continual access to these services by means of computers, television, and video-phones. But they will not have to go to the city.

I see New York City in 1990 as the home of the technicians who service the information-education-recreation functions, and of the rich who insist on seeing operas and football games in person. It may also be a nice place to escape to when the pressures of suburban or rural life are too much with us.

SUMMARY

The United States Government is the world's largest single computer user. The computer is used by the federal government for functions in the Bureau of the Budget, the Internal Revenue Service, the Weather Bureau and the Census Bureau—among others. The computer is also used in state and municipal government functions. The computer is used, for example, to count votes and to provide a job bank for those seeking available employment.

Computers are being used in municipal information systems and for urban planning. With the aid of computer information systems and management techniques, the cities are attempting to solve the problems of traffic, crime, housing and schools. In addition, simulation techniques enable the planner to assess the consequences of various public policies and alternatives.

Computers are being used by the legislative as well as the executive branch of government. Computer systems assist the legislator by maintaining information on all the legislation under consideration and related data. The US Congress is expected to install a computer information system for use by the legislators in the near future. The computer is indeed a useful tool for governmental activities.

CHAPTER 15 PROBLEMS

P15-1.   Inquire at the city hall of your town about the use of computers to aid the government of the city. List several uses of computers that are presently accomplished.

P15-2.   List several uses of computers that could be added to aid the government of your city.

P15-3.   Design a voting system for your campus government which utilizes punched cards and requires the voter to punch holes in his card in order to register his vote.

CHAPTER 15 REFERENCES

1.   H. R. J. Grosch, "A View of Computers from the Bureau of Standards," *Input Magazine*, Vol. 6, No. 2, 1970, pp. 3-7.

2. H. V. Semling, "World's Largest Computer User," *Modern Data,* March, 1969, pp. 50-53.

3. "California State Computers: The Power and the Fury," *Datamation,* September 1, 1970, pg. 38.

4. M. McLuhan, *War and Peace in a Global Village,* Bantam Books, Inc., New York, 1968, pp. 88-89.

5. P. Hirsch, "The World's Biggest Data Bank," *Datamation,* May, 1970, pp. 66-73.

6. R. Dobriner, "The Industry Can Help Solve Postal Chaos," *Electronic Design,* April 26, 1970, pg. 63.

7. "Job Bank in a Computer Pays Off and Branches Out," *Business Week,* July 5, 1969, pp. 70-71.

8. "As Old As History," *Data Processor,* Vol. XI, No. 1, February, 1968, pp. 9-14.

9. "Proposals for Municipal Information System Asked," *Datamation,* November, 1969, pp. 383-384.

10. J. W. Forrester, *Urban Dynamics,* M.I.T. Press, Cambridge, Mass., 1969.

11. "Computer in the Capitol," *Data Processor,* Vol. XI, No. 1, Feb., 1968, pg. 27

12. "Committee to Get Plan to Automate the House," *Datamation,* Nov. 15, 1970, pg. 135.

13. J. G. Kemeny, "The City and the Computer Revolution," *Governing Urban Society: New Scientific Approaches,* American Academy of Political and Social Science, Philadelphia, May, 1967, pp. 49-62.

14. J. M. Kibbee, "The Scope of Large-Scale Computer-Based Systems in Governmental Functions," *Governing Urban Society: New Scientific Approaches,* American Academy of Political and Social Science, Philadelphia, May, 1967, pp. 181-196.

15. C. H. Springer and M. R. Alkus, "Second Generation Computer Vote Count Systems—Assuming a Professional Responsibility," Proceedings of the *Spring Joint Computer Conference,* Vol. 38, AFIPS Press, Montvale, N. J., 1971, pp. 143-149.

16. "Business Takes a Second Look at Computers—For Social Security It Works Like a Dream," *Business Week,* June 5, 1971, pp. 110-116.

A PHOTO ESSAY

...suggesting the range of applications for computers

The following four pages are from
THE DYNAMICS OF CHANGE, Kaiser Aluminum & Chemical Corporation
© 1967. Reprinted by permission.

"Automation's greatest consequence to business will be the enormous social change resulting from it. The entire role of business, its relation to human wants and its way of satisfying those wants depends upon society. Fundamental changes in society fundamentally change the role of business. Buying patterns, consumption habits, and other social attitudes will be radically affected by the technology, and they, in turn, will produce decisive changes in business operations and methods."

JOHN DIEBOLD "Beyond Automation"

TRAFFIC CONTROL—Already installed in several urban areas are computer-controlled traffic systems. Sensors in the streets measure the number of cars and a computer analyzes this data to regulate traffic lights. The system has speeded rush hour traffic 38% and sharply cut accidents. (Reported in NEWSWEEK)

PSYCHIATRY—Computers can now aid psychiatrists in rearranging a patient's random experiences and concepts into a logical, more meaningful order, so that the patient can understand them better. Assimilating a mass of data, the computer can swiftly reshuffle it into an ordered pattern. (Reported in PAGEANT)

TEACHING—Students can now share a digital computer that adapts lessons to their individual needs and to performance standards of various instructors. Each student receives text and diagrams, test questions and answers at his own pace, and can even erase answers. (Reported in INTERNATIONAL SCIENCE AND TECHNOLOGY magazine)

CRIME—As well as storing names and records (including aliases) of persons and stolen vehicles for instantaneous checking by policemen "on the beat," computers are also helping to solve crimes by assimilating facts and comparing fingerprints to single out suspects from thousands of records. (Reported in BUSINESS WEEK)

LAW—One computer can do the work of many lawyers by locating appropriate precedents for court cases, sifting through thousands of cases electronically in minutes. Legislators are also being aided in recodification by computers that pinpoint records referring to or affecting a law under revision. (Reported in BUSINESS WEEK)

WAR STRATEGY—The Army has designed a computer that can stage a full-scale "battle" against an enemy. Pre-programed with such data as weapons capabilities and battle plans, the computer will accept and carry out military commands and predict their eventual "success" or "failure." (Reported by Army News Service)

PUBLISHING—Extremely high-speed photocomposition is being accomplished by computers which prepare finished copy at the rate of 1000 characters per second that is of lithographic or magazine quality. (Reported in NEWS FRONT)

ANIMAL BREEDING—Many thousands of dairy farmers in all 50 states are participating in a program of electronic storage of production records for hundreds of thousands of cows. In this way, the best milk producers can be pinpointed to produce better herds by selective breeding. (Reported in THE WALL STREET JOURNAL)

"The new mathematical methods of automatic control, a subject sometimes called cybernetics, have been developed now because this is a time when communications and control have in effect become forms of power. These inventions have been directed by social needs, and they are useful inventions, yet it was not their usefulness which dominated and set light to the minds of those who made them."

"Science and Human Values"   J. BRONOWSKI

ASSEMBLY—Among its many uses in automated manufacturing, the computer now can control assembly of radios from component parts at the rate of a thousand a day. Another device can assemble half a television receiver chassis in seconds. (Excerpted from THE REPORTER)

ROBOT—A man-like machine has been developed that can perform space or underwater exploration, handle delicate instruments and act as a military vehicle. Equipped with limbs, a sense of "feel" and electronic "eyes," the robot is guided from inside or remotely by a man, whose movements it copies. (Reported in NEWS FRONT)

BRAIN DISORDERS—An eerie-looking pair of huge eyeglasses with built-in photocells can measure light reflected from the wearer's eyes and feed the information into a computer that diagnoses brain disorders with great precision. (Reported in NEWSWEEK)

REPAIRS—A virtually "immortal" telephone switching system has been devised that fixes itself temporarily if a part fails. In the meantime it figures out what went wrong and tells a maintenance man about it, never allowing itself to stop operating. (Reported in BUSINESS WEEK)

LITERATURE — Probable authorship of disputed manuscripts can be quickly studied and determined by computers. Using certain key words and phrases, a computer recently matched the Federalist papers with various authors and selected James Madison as the likely author. (Reported by ELECTRONIC AGE magazine)

DISEASE DIAGNOSIS—High-speed computers are being programed to automatically culture and analyze bacteria, viruses and other infectious agents in order to immediately identify infectious diseases and enable hospitals and laboratories to begin treatment sooner. (Reported by U.S. Information Service)

MANUFACTURING—Manufacturing firms are linking their plants to sales offices with computers for instant transmission of production statistics and data, as well as location of the closest availability of products in inventory. Customers are thus getting better, quicker service. (Reported in AMERICAN METAL MARKET)

COMMUNICATIONS — All forms of information—oral, written, photo, or drawing, whether on paper, film, radio or TV can now be translated into identical electronic impulses which can be processed and either stored or transmitted anywhere in the world in less than one-seventh of a second. (Reported in THE QUILL)

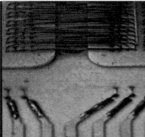

"Another portentous (computer) development is simulation. . . . The inventory game, by simulating a real inventory system, allows the player to study its faults and to correct them with computers. In much the same way, simulation is being applied to management problems. Professor Jay Forrester, of M.I.T., using one minute of computer time, has simulated the operation of an entire business over a period of 400 weeks."

GILBERT BURCK "The Computer Age" Copyright © 1965 by Time Inc.

HIRING—The federal government has adopted an advanced scientific hiring system that uses a computer to sift through many thousands of prospects for federal positions and can in a moment produce a list of persons qualified (on paper, at least) for these positions. (Reported in NEWS FRONT)

BRAIN—A baby electrochemical brain has been constructed which works like that of a human. The brain is taught by "spanking" it (giving it electrical shocks) each time it gives a wrong response. These shocks cause dendrite growths exactly like those in the human brain, and modify its future behavior. (Reported in STEEL magazine)

RAILROADS—Control of a main line railroad has been given to a computer which runs all switches and signals automatically. Another railroad uses a computer to keep track of its 36,000 boxcars so that empty ones can be immediately located for use. (Reported in MODERN RAILROADS and THE WALL STREET JOURNAL)

LASERS—Which color a laser emits can be controlled at electronic speeds with a new instrument that can make 125,000 color selections per second. Estimates are that the device will store 100 million bits of data on a square inch of film. (Reported in STEEL magazine)

SIMULATION — In research involving space vehicles, computers have simulated actual conditions of space travel in order to test components and avoid costly trial and error. Mathematical simulation of manufacturing processes has also saved millions of dollars prior to actual operation. (Reported by E. I. Dupont de Nemours & Co.)

RESERVATIONS—It takes only a few millionths of a second for a computer to tell an airline reservation clerk if a seat is available on any of their flights at any airport in the country. If no space is available, the computer suggests alternate flights with seats available. (Reported on the Earl Nightingale radio program)

BIDS — In a large corporation's heavy apparatus division where sales are only on a bid basis, a computer has been programed to propose bids for the company on the likelihood of what competitive bids will be. The computer's bids have been "amazingly accurate," according to one executive. (Reported in BUSINESS WEEK)

BRAIN WAVES—Following successful research in performing activities (such as transmitting Morse code and turning on an electric light switch) by amplifying brain waves, experts predict that man (including paralyzed patients) may someday do work through computers by merely thinking about it. (Reported in THE FINANCIAL POST)

"It is my considered opinion, from long experience, that our customers will continue to be reluctant to use information systems—however well devised—so long as one feature of our present intellectual and engineering climate prevails. This feature— and its prevalence is all too commonplace in many companies—is that for many people it is more painful and troublesome to have information than for them not to have it."

Zator Technical Bulletin 136   CALVIN N. MOOERS

CHEMICALS—With the aid of computer prepared punch cards, a chemical company is mixing and preparing for shipping 100 formulations involving 200 different ingredients in varying proportions, all from a central automated control panel. (Reported in CHEMICAL PROCESSING magazine)

MAIL—An electronic optical scanner that reads machine-printed addresses and sorts mail 15 times faster than the best postal clerk is expected to help speed delivery of the 72 billion pieces of mail going through our postal system annually. (Reported in TIME)

DESIGN — Computers which turn complex mathematical formulas into three-dimensional drawings on a screen are greatly aiding designers. The drawing can then be enlarged in detail, changed in perspective, or altered by a designer using a "light pen." (Reported in THE IRON AGE)

LIBRARIES—Use of computers to store and instantly locate millions of pieces of information is well-known. The computer can also store graphic materials—maps, charts, blueprints, photos, etc., and on command reproduce, enlarge and project this material. (Reported in NEWS FRONT magazine)

COUNSELING — Computers are now assimilating data on students' past school records to recommend course programs that the student can handle. This process will also predict which students are likely to encounter academic problems in their present courses. (Reported in NEWSWEEK)

TELEPHONES—Electronic switching has enabled telephone companies to offer such new services as having calls automatically transferred to any number at which you can be reached, automatic dialing of frequently-called numbers, and notifying a caller when a busy line becomes free. (Reported by U. S. I. S.)

SPEECH—An electronic "voice" can now emit human speech without having sounds pre-recorded on tape. An analog computer "translates" a digital computer's "thoughts" into speech impulses. The "translator" has 17 sections that duplicate functions of human vocal organs. (Reported in SAN FRANCISCO CHRONICLE)

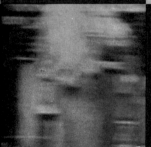

RAPID TRANSIT—A computer run passenger-carrying rapid transit system has been developed. With only a dispatcher at a central panel to monitor the system, the railed cars will travel at great speeds and stop to discharge and accept passengers, all without need for human control. (Reported by WABCO/Union Switch & Signal.)

16

COMPUTERS AND THE ARTS

16.1 INTRODUCTION

Digital computers are machines, and the notion of machines creating works of art has nearly always been rejected by man. Creativity and the creation of art has heretofore been reserved for the human. What can an unfeeling, intelligent, but unemotional machine do in the world of art? As Geoffrey Jefferson said in 1949, in his *Lister Oration*, "Not until a machine can write a sonnet or compose a concerto because of thoughts and emotions felt, and not by the chance fall of symbols, could we agree that machine equals brains—that is, not only write it but know that it had written it. No mechanism could feel (and not merely signal, an easy contrivance) pleasure at its successes, grief when its valves fuse, be warmed by flattery, be made miserable by its mistakes, be charmed by sex, be angry or depressed when it cannot get what it wants."

During the past few years, the use of the computer to generate poetry, music, dance, choreography and graphic art has increased significantly. However, it is the symbiosis of computer and man that provides the world with the works of art. That is, man, using the computer as a tool, creates the works. The following poem was produced by the Manchester University computer under the *instructions* and *guidance* of a man.

You will see the
                    weeping
Lord Now Maybe   Time
And Mr. Mendel
                    All in A
Solarhythm   Cloak.

Although most philosophers will agree that creativity is a function of mankind alone, the computer has extensive capabilities for carrying out elaborate
and precise instructions. It is the combination of man and his "personal" computer, somewhat like his "personal" piano—a machine after all—that creates
the work of art. As Don Fabun recently stated:[1] "Someday—not too far
from now—people will "ride" their personal computers with all the excitement
that the motorcycle rider feels when he storms down the long tunnel of the
night. We will, with computers, explore our mental world with something that
shares, amplifies and defines our experience. In doing so, it will help us define
ourselves as human personalities."

While the computer can do only what it has been programmed to do,
perhaps it provides a source of creative amplification through its rapid, untir-
ing attempts. Certainly, the results have not been tallied yet and we shall learn
in this decade if the man–computer partnership leads to new lights, new forms
of art and most of all to beauty.

The existence of the new creations, strikingly beautiful or absurdly comic,
like the computer itself, seem to many people to have no ancestors or origins.
The scores of drawings, films and musical compositions resulting from the
artist/computer partnership are admired or attacked, but hardly understood
because they are a new and little–understood challenge to our cultural perspective.

In a sense the computers will challenge the very capacity that man has
regarded as making him supreme and unique: his ability to think—his brain-
power. One can say that the computer has transcended its original purpose,
quick mathematical calculation, and is now reaching toward the ability to
simulate Descarte's irreducible requirement for humanity.* Whether that simulation will ever become a reality is another question, but the very attempt
places the old *New Yorker* cartoon, in which a huge computer types a message
to its white–smocked attendant, reading *Cogito, ergo sum,* in a new perspective.

The computer provides a high–speed information processor for the artist,
who can now use the computer to enter the world of the scientist and examine
those laws which describe physical reality. "The artist," as Professor Csuri, of
Ohio State University, has said, "may alter the parameters to create a different

---

*Descartes, a seventeenth century mathematician and philosopher (See Chapter 2), stated
  his fundamental truth as *Cogito, ergo sum,* or "I think, therefore I am."

kind of artistic world. In a highly systematic and disciplined manner he can deal with fantasy and imagination. One example [of this] . . . is the well-known Lorentz transformation . . . a theory of special relativity [explaining] the apparent distortion of a form as it approaches the speed of light. It would be interesting to see what happens graphically to a drawing of a turtle or a hummingbird as it approaches the speed of light. The artist may be interested in the absurdity of such an idea and it may give him a different kind of form. He may enjoy the contradiction of a turtle traveling near the speed of light."

Some of the relevant uses of the computer in the arts are listed below:[2]

· Detecting the influence of one poet on the works of another
· Creating motion pictures
· Deciphering ancient languages
· Choreographing a ballet
· Analyzing the vocabulary of eighteenth century French political writers
· Composing a symphony

The inspiration of the artist, combined with the capabilities of the computer, will undoubtedly bring forth new artistic forms. Although this evolution is in a primitive stage now, the computer is an instrument with great potential. The instrument will come alive in the hands of a great artist.

In this chapter, we consider the application of the computer to the various arts. In the next section, we examine the use of the computer in the creation of paintings, drawings, films and graphic design. In the following section we consider the use of the computer in the world of music and dance. Finally, in Section 16-4, we examine the application of the computer to the study of literature and other subjects of the humanities.

16.2 COMPUTERS AND THE VISUAL ARTS

The techniques and concepts which have been developed during the past decade for generating visual displays of the results of computer problem-solving can be used to make artistic visual displays.

Art has always depended upon science and technology to supply both the medium in which the work is done and the tools for doing it. The techniques are common whether the computer is used to generate visual displays of scientific data (*e.g.*, shapes and motions of mechanical systems, mathematical rotations of n-dimensional objects, motions of atoms in a fluid) or shapes and motions which may be important in design or as an artistic medium.[3]

The computer and the current conceptional basis of the arts are reflections of the era in which we live. Our environment is structured in technology, and the machine in some ways exemplifies the spirit of the times. Just as the painting and poetry of earlier times reflected the living fabric of those times, the art of our time will reflect the technology available to the artist.

Computer art, which uses the computer as the medium, is a relatively new art form. The artist has long recognized that repetition and proportion contribute to a good effect in a drawing or painting. The computer can readily repeat a line or shape and calculate, with the proper program, the proper perspective for an object. Perspective is essentially geometric and can be included in computer art. Impressionism, which developed during the last half of the 19th century, has a partially mathematical basis and included an aspect called substitution, which suggests the notion that separate representations in space provide different subjective impressions. Substitution is also a major component of computer art and is quite mathematical in its precision and its technique.[4]

The work of the school of the Futurists during the 20th century also contributed to computer art. The Futurists included conceptions and impressions of machines and motion in their art. Artists such as Klee, Feininger and Duchamp concerned themselves with mathematics and optical illusions. Feininger's subjects, for example, have cubical and trapezoidal shapes and the relationship is of a mathematical nature.

Algorithms and mathematics are equally important to the modern artist, and he finds a new tool in the computer. A computer can take a mathematical figure and repeat it continually with great precision. An algorithm can cause the computer to distort or permute the figure as well as to repeat a pattern with slight permutations randomly about a prescribed area. Guided by a relatively simple program, it can substitute one figure for another or produce a complicated figure for each point on a line. In addition, a computer can expand, contract, reshape, multiply or transform a figure or a series of lines. Combinations of all these functions are at the heart of all computer art.[4]

In the following article, A. M. Noll of Bell Telephone Laboratories explores the possibilities of the computer as an artistic medium and makes some predictions about the art of the future.[5]

THE DIGITAL COMPUTER AS A CREATIVE MEDIUM*

A. Michael Noll   Bell Telephone Laboratories

The notion of creating art works through the medium of machines may seem a little strange. Most people who have heard about the experimental use of digital computers in creative endeavors have probably shrugged them off as being of no consequence. On the one hand, creativity has universally been regarded as the personal and somewhat mysterious domain of man; and, on the one hand, as every engineer knows, the computer can only do what it has been programmed to do—which hardly anyone would be generous enough to call creative.

*Reprinted with the permission of the Institute of Electrical and Electronic Engineers and the author.

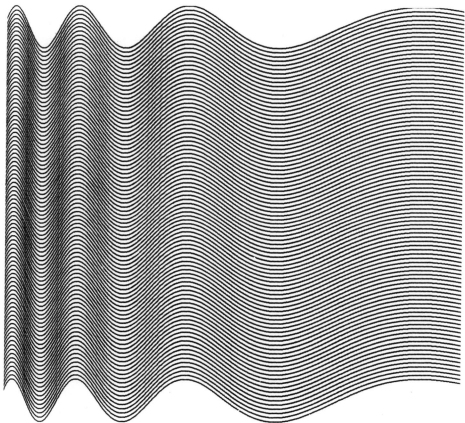

FIGURE 16-1   "Ninety computer-generated sinusoids with linearly increasing period." The
top line of this picture was mathematically expressed as a sinusoid curve.
The computer was then instructed to repeat the line 90 times. The result
approximates closely Bridget Riley's painting "Current." *Courtesy of A. M.
Noll and Bell Telephone Laboratories.*

Nonetheless, artists have usually been responsive to experimenting with and even adopting certain concepts and devices
resulting from new scientific and technological developments.
Computers are no exception. Composers, film animators, and
graphic artists have become interested in the application of computers in their creative endeavors. Moreover, recent artistic experiments with computers have produced results that should
make us reexamine our preconceptions about creativity and
machines. Some of the experiments, described in this article,
suggest, in fact, that a tight interaction between artist and computer constitutes a totally new, active, and exciting artistic
medium.

How does an artist work?

There is an anecdote attributed to Henri Matisse about how to approach the creative act of painting. You take a blank white canvas, the French artist said, and after gazing at it for a while, you paint on it a bright red disk. Thereafter, you do nothing further until something occurs to you that will be just as exciting as the original red disk. You proceed in this way, always sustaining, through each new gambit with the paint and brush, the initial high visual excitement of the red disk.

The anecdote is a somewhat simplified version of Matisse's idea, but even if we take it lightly, it can do a number of things for us. For one thing, it dispels some of the sense of mystery that hovers over the procedures of the creative person. It tells us something concrete and easily visualized about the creative process while emphasizing the role of the unexpected ideas for which the artist lies in wait and for which he sets a formal "trap" in his medium.

Even a relatively "passive" medium—paint, brushes, canvas —will suggest new ideas to the artist as he becomes engaged. The resistance of the canvas or its elastic give to the paint-loaded brush, the visual shock of real color and line, the smell of the paint, will all work on the artist's sensibilities. The running of the paint, or seemingly "random" strokes of the brush, may be accepted by him as corporate elements of the finished work. So it is that an artist explores, discovers, and masters the possibilities of the medium. His art work is a form of play, but it is serious play.

Most of all, the Matisse anecdote suggests that the artistic process involves some form of "program," one certainly more complex than the anecdote admits, but a definite program of step-by-step action. Without doing too much violence to our sense of what is appropriate, we might compare it to a computational hill–climbing technique in which the artist is trying to optimize or stabilize at a high level the parameter "excitement."

Once we have swallowed this metaphor, it becomes less improbable to imagine that computers might be used, in varying depths of engagement, as active partners in the artistic process. But computers are a *new* medium. They do not have the characteristics of paints, brushes, and canvas. Nor are the "statements" that grow out of the artist's engagement with them likely to be similar to the statements of, for example, oil paintings. An interesting question to explore, then, is how computers might be used as a creative medium. What kinds of artistic potentials can be evolved through the use of computers, which themselves are continually being evolved to possess more sophisticated and intelligent characteristics?

The character of the computer medium

In the present state of computer usage, artists are certainly having their problems in understanding engineering descriptions and in learning how to program computers in order to explore what might be done with them. However, they *are* learning, and they have already used digital computers and associated equipment to produce musical sounds and artistic visual images.

The visual images are generated by an automatic plotter under the control of the digital computer. The plotter consists of a cathode–ray tube and a camera for photographing the images "drawn" on the tube face by deflections of the electron beam. The digital computer produces the instructions for operating the automatic plotter so that the picture–drawing capability is under program control. Musical sounds are produced by the computer by means of a digital sampled version of the sounds that must then be converted to analog form by a conventional digital–to–analog converter.

For both of these artistic applications, a challenging problem is the composition of special–purpose programming languages and subroutines so that the artist can communicate with the computer by using terminology reasonably similar to his particular art. For example, a special music compiler has been written so that the composer can specify complex algorithms for producing a single sound and then pyramid these basic sounds into a whole composition. A similar philosophy has been used in a special language developed for computer animation called Beflix. Both applications share the drawback that the artist must wait a number of hours between the actual running of the computer program and the final generation of pictorial output or musical sounds when he can see or hear the results.

Since the scientific community currently is the biggest user of computers, most descriptions and ideas about the artistic possibilities for computers have been understandably written by scientists and engineers. This situation will undoubtedly change as computers become more accessible to artists who obviously are more qualified to explore and evolve the artistic potentials of the computer medium. Unfortunately, scientists and engineers are usually all too familiar with the inner working of computers, and this knowledge has a tendency to produce very conservative ideas about the possibilities for computers in the arts. Most certainly the computer is an electronic device capable of performing only those operations that it has been explicitly instructed to perform. And this usually leads to the portrayal of the computer as a powerful tool but one incapable of any true creativity. However, if creativity is restricted to mean the production of the unconventional or the unpredicted, then the computer should instead be portrayed as a creative medium— an active and creative collaborator with the artist.

Computers and creativity

Digital computers are constructed from a myriad of electronic components whose purpose is to switch minute electric currents nearly instantaneously. The innermost workings of the computer are controlled by a set of instructions called a program. Although computers must be explicitly instructed to perform each operation, higher-level programming languages enable pyramiding of programming statements that are later expanded into the basic computer instructions by special compiler programs. These programming languages are usually designed so that the human user can write his computer program using words and symbols similar to those of his own particular field. All of this leads to the portrayal of the computer as a tool capable of performing tasks exactly as programmed.

However, the computer is such an extremely powerful tool that artistic effects can sometimes be easily accomplished that would be virtually impossible by conventional artistic techniques. For example, by calculating and drawing on the automatic plotter the perspective projections from two slightly different directions of some three-dimensional object, the computer can generate three-dimensional movies of novel shapes and forms. Such three-dimensional animation, or kinetic sculpture, is far too tedious to perform by any other method. The computer's ability to handle small details has made possible intriguing dissolves and stretches, such as those executed by Stan Vanderbeek, without the tedium of conventional hand animation. Mathematical equations with certain specified variables under the control of the artist have also been used by John Whitney to achieve completely new animation effects. Much of "op art" uses repetitive patterns that usually can be expressed very simply in mathematical terms. The waveforms shown in Figure 16-1, which are like Bridget Riley's painting "Currents," were generated as parallel sinusoids with linearly increasing period. Thus, computer and automatic plotter can eliminate the tedious part of producing "op" effects.

Computers most certainly are only machines, but they are capable of performing millions of operations in a fraction of a second and with incredible accuracy. They can be programmed to weigh carefully, according to specified criteria, the results of different alternatives and act accordingly; thus, in a rudimentary sense, computers can appear to show intelligence. They might assess the results of past actions and modify their programmed algorithms to improve previous results; computers potentially could be programmed to learn. And series of numbers can be calculated by the computer that are so complicatedly related that they appear to us as random.

Of course, everything the machine does must be programmed, but because of the computer's great speed, freedom from error, and vast abilities for assessment and subsequent modification of programs, it appears to us to act unpredictably and to produce the unexpected. In this sense, the computer actively takes over some of the artist's creative search. It suggests to him syntheses that he may or may not accept. It possesses at least some of the external attributes of creativity.

The Mondrian experiment

How reasonable is it to attribute even these rudimentary qualities of creativity to an inaminate machine? Is creativity something that should only be associated with the products of humans? Not long ago, in 1950, A. M. Turing expressed the belief that at the end of the century "one will be able to speak of machines thinking without expecting to be contradicted." Turing proposed the now well-known experiment consisting of an interrogator, a man, and a machine, in which the interrogator had to identify the man by asking the man and the machine to answer questions or to perform simple tasks.

A crude approximation to Turing's experiment was performed using Piet Mondrian's "Composition With Lines" (1917) and a computer-generated picture composed of pseudorandom elements but similar in overall composition to the Mondrian painting as shown in Figs. 16-2 and 16-3 respectively. Although Mondrian apparently placed the vertical and horizontal bars in his painting in a careful and orderly manner, the bars in the

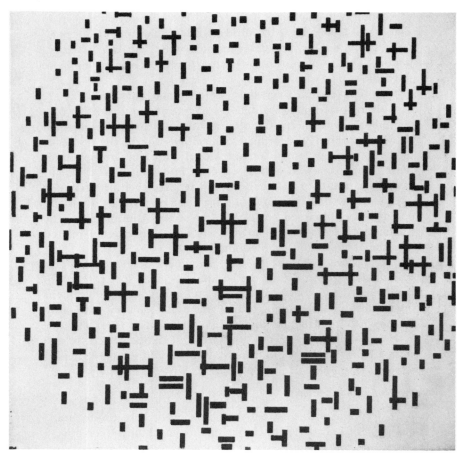

FIGURE 16-2 "Composition With Lines" (1917) by Piet Mondrian. (Reproduced with permission of Rijkmuseum Kröller-Müller, Otterlo, the Netherlands, © Rijkmuseum Kröller-Müller.)

computer–generated picture were placed according to a pseudo–
random number generator with statistics chosen to approximate
the bar density, lengths, and widths in the Mondrian painting.
Xerographic copies of the two pictures were presented, side by
side, to 100 subjects with educations ranging from high school
to postdoctoral; the subjects represented a reasonably good
sampling of the population at a large scientific research laboratory. They were asked which picture they preferred and also
which picture of the pair they thought was produced by Mondrian. Fifty–nine percent of the subjects preferred the computer–generated picture; only 28 percent were able to identify
correctly the picture produced by Mondrian.

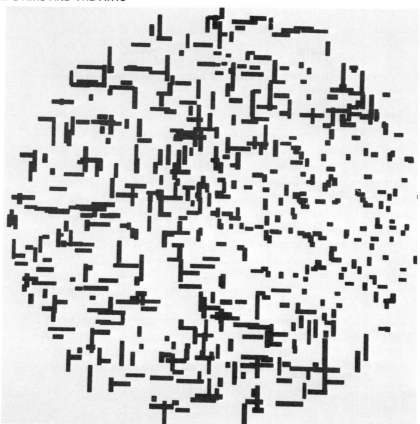

FIGURE 16-3 "Computer Composition with Lines" (1964) © A. Michael Noll, 1965.

In general, these people seemed to associate the randomness of the computer–generated picture with human creativity whereas the orderly bar placement of the Mondrian painting seemed to them machinelike. This finding does not, of course, detract from Mondrian's artistic abilities. His painting was, after all, the inspiration for the algorithms used to produce the computer-generated picture, and since computers were nonexistent 50 years ago, Mondrian could not have had a computer at his disposal. Furthermore, we must admit that the reduction in size of the original painting and its xerographic reproduction degrades its unique aesthetic qualities. Nevertheless, the results of the experiment in light of Turing's proposed experiment do raise questions on the meaning of creativity and the role of randomness in artistic creation. In a sense, the computer with its program could be considered creative, although it can be argued that human creativity was involved in the original program with the computer performing only as an obedient tool.

These questions should perhaps be examined more deeply by more ambitious psychological experiments using computer-generated pictures as stimuli.

Toward real–time interaction

Although the experiments described show that the computer has creative potentialities beyond those of just a simple tool, the computer medium is still restrictive in that there is a rather long time delay between the running of the computer program and the production of the final graphical or acoustic output. However, recent technological developments have greatly reduced this time delay through special interactive hardware facilities and programming languages. This tightening of the man–machine feedback loop is particularly important for the artist who needs a nearly instantaneous response.

For example, in the field of music an electronic graphic console has been used to specify pictorially sequences of sounds that were then synthesized by the computer. Functions for amplitude, frequency, and duration of a sequence of notes were drawn on the face of a cathode–ray tube with a light pen. If desired, the computer combined specified functions according to transparently simple algorithms. Thus, the fine details of the composition were calculated by the computer and the overall structure was precisely specified by the graphical score. The feedback loop was completed by the computer-generated sounds heard almost immediately by the composer, who could then make any desired changes in the score.

A similar man–machine interactive system has been proposed for choreography. In this system, the choreographer would be shown a computer-generated three-dimensional display of complicated stick figures moving about on a stage, as shown in Figure 16–8 below. The choreographer interacts with the computer by indicating the spatial trajectories and movements of the figures. Random and mathematical algorithms might be introduced by the computer to fill in certain fine details, or even to give the choreographer new ideas to evaluate and explore.

A new active medium

The beginnings of a new creative partnership and collaboration between the artist and the computer clearly emerge from these most recent efforts and proposals. Their common denominator is the close man–machine interaction using the computer to generate either musical sounds or visual displays. The computer acquires a creative role by introducing randomness or by using mathematical algorithms to control certain aspects of the artistic creation. The overall control and direction of the creative process is very definitely the artist's task. Thus, the computer is used as a medium by the artist, but the great technical powers and creative potentialities of the computer result in a totally new kind of creative medium. This is an *active* medium with which the artist can interact on a new level, freed from many of the physical limitations of all other previous media. The artistic potentialities of such a creative medium as a collaborator with an artist are truly exciting and challenging.

Interactive aesthetic experiences

In the previous examples the artist sat at the console of the computer and indicated his desires to the computer by manually using push buttons or by drawing patterns on an electronic visual display. These are probably efficient ways of communicating certain types of instructions to the computer; however, the communication of the actual subconscious emotional state of the artist could lead to a new aesthetic experience. Although this might seem somewhat exotic and conjectural, the artist's emotional state might conceivably be determined by computer processing of physical and electrical signals from the artist (for example, pulse rate and electrical activity of the brain). Then, by changing the artist's environment through such external stimuli as sound, color, and visual patterns, the computer would seek to optimize the aesthetic effect of all these stimuli upon the artist according to some specified criterion.

This interactive feedback situation with controlled environment would be completely dynamic. The emotional reaction of the artist would continually change, and the computer would react accordingly either to stabilize the artist's emotional state or to steer it through some preprogrammed course. Here then is a completely new aesthetic experience utilizing man–machine communication on the highest (or lowest, if you will) subconscious levels and computer processing and optimization of emotional responses. Only a digital computer could perform all the information processing and generate the sights and sounds of the controlled environment required for such a scheme. One is strongly tempted to describe these ideas as a consciousness-expanding experience in association with a psychedelic computer!

Although such an artistic feedback scheme is still far in the future, current technological and psychological investigations would seem to aim in such a direction. For example, three-dimensional computer-generated color displays that seem to surround the individual are certainly already within the state of the art. Electroencephalograms are being scrutinized and studied in great detail, using advanced signal analysis techniques; it is not inconceivable that some day their relation to emotional state might be determined.

Artistic consequences

Predictions of the future are risky in that they may be really nothing more than what the person predicting would like to see occur. Although the particulars should be viewed skeptically, they actually might be unimportant; if the art of the future follows the directions outlined here, then some general conclusions and statements can be made that should be independent of the actual particulars.

The aesthetic experience will be highly individualistic, involving only the individual artist and his interactions with the computer. This type of participation in the creative and aesthetic experience can be experienced by artist and nonartist alike. Because of the great technical and creative power of the computer, both the artist and nonartist are freed from the necessity of strong technical competence in the use of different media. The artist's "ideas" and not his technical ability in manipulating media could be the important factor in determining artistic merit. Conceivably, a form of "citizen-artist" could emerge, as envisoned by Allon Schoener. The interactive aesthetic experience with computers might fill a substantial portion of that great leisure time predicted for the man of the future.

The artist's role as master creator will remain, however, because even though the physical limitations of the medium will be different from traditional media, his training, devotion, and visualization will give him a higher degree of control of the artistic experience. As an example, the artist's particular interactions with the computer might be recorded and played back by the public on their own computers. Specified amounts of interaction and modification might be introduced by the individual, but the overall course of the interactive experience would still follow the artist's model. In this way, and for the first time, the artist would be able to specify and control with certainty the emotional state of each individual participant. Only those aspects deliberately specified by the artist might be left to chance or to the whims of the participant. All this would be possible because the computer could monitor the participant's emotional state and change it according to the artist's specifications. The artist's interaction with the computer would be of a new order because the physical restrictions of the older media would be eliminated.

This is not to say that the traditional artistic media will be swept away; but they will undoubtedly be influenced by this new active medium. The introduction of photography—the new medium of the last century—helped to drive painting away from representation, but it did not drive out painting. What the new creative computer medium will do to all of the art forms—painting, writing, dance, music, movies—should be exciting to observe. We might even be tempted to say that the current developments and devices in the field of man–machine communication, which were primarily intended to give insight into scientific problems, might in the end prove to be far more fruitful, or at least equally fruitful, in the arts.

Computer graphics range from familiar line drawings through images redrawn by a computer to the artist's desires, to randomly-produced shapes. As Harold Rosenberg, art critic of *The New Yorker,* has written, "The inspiration of machine art is problem-solving; its chief aesthetic principle is the logical adjustment of means to end."

The latest computer-graphics development is the computer-processing of scanned photographs. In this technique, the individual dots that make up an image can be transformed by the computer to numbers or symbols (a kind of "computer pointillism"), or a symbolic variation of the photograph can be programmed. This technique is based on reproducing an object rather than creating a new one. H. P. Peterson of Honeywell, Inc. recently scanned a reproduction of the Mona Lisa with a computer and reconstructed it entirely of minute, two-digit numbers based on a scale of 100 increments between black and white. It required a scanning time of four minutes and a plotting time of 16 hours.

Also, a reproduction by K. C. Knowlton and L. D. Harmon of Bell Telephone Laboratories is shown in Figure 16-4. They have divided the shades of gray into 14 different tones. For each tone, they program the computer to substitute tiny hieroglyphic symbols—faces, airplanes, animals, musical notes, telephones and automobiles. The effect is not unlike a Seurat painting. Held close up, the hieroglyphs are seen separately. When it is held at arm's length, a whole painting can be seen. This is simple substitution.

FIGURE 16-4 "Gargoyles in Paris," by Ken C. Knowlton and Leon D. Harmon.

The same techniques that are used for computer graphics can be used for generating computer–animated films. The artist and the computer work with freely invented forms, shapes and dynamic rhythms. The art form used by John Whitney, one of the leading artists working with computer films, is often called Constructivism.[6] It is an abstract art without the illusion of a subject. Constructivism originated in Europe toward the end of the last century. It has offered creative inspiration to some of the 20th century's leading architects and artists, including Walter Gropius, Paul Klee, Wassily Kandinsky, and Piet Mondrian. In the 1920s, the new movement provided the impetus for the great Bauhaus school in Germany.

Whitney calls his films visual music since he uses the computer to orchestrate motion. He describes his films as "a compositional language of graphics in motion" paralleled by musical counterpoint, or "patterns graphically superimposed over themselves forward and backward in many ways." He uses an algorithm and suitable shapes to generate the motion. The algorithm allows for accelerations, decelerations and oscillations of the figures. Whitney's computer-generated color film, *Permutations,* was shown at the 1968 Lincoln Center Film Festival in New York.* Some figures from Whitney's films are shown in Figure 16-5.

Permutations is distributed by the Film Library of the New York Museum of Modern Art for non–profit showings.

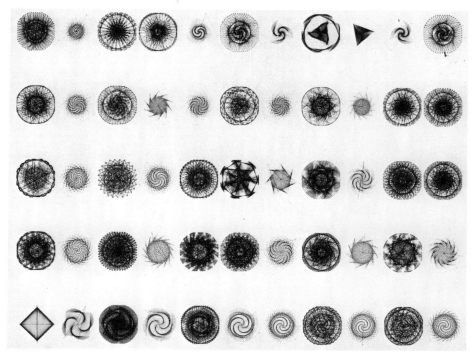

FIGURE 16-5   Some figures from a computer-animated film by John Whitney. *Courtesy of John Whitney and Computing Report.*

Charles Csuri of Ohio State University is an American artist who has used computers as a means of extending his art. An illustration of his computer-aided art is shown in Figure 16-6. The four faces of an old man were generated by a computer and use selected symbols to develop the figure. A realistic line drawing of an old man was used as the data check and the line drawing was transformed into a shaded image using a computer algorithm.[7]

A recent exhibition in London entitled "Cybernetic Serendipity" explored and demonstrated the relationships between technology and creativity.[8] *Cybernetics,* which we explore further in Section 17-7 and Chapter 18, is defined as follows:

Cybernetics The science of control and communication in complex electronics machines such as computers, control systems and the human nervous system.

By the title "Cybernetic Serendipity," the sponsors of the exhibition mean the faculty of happy chance discoveries through the means of complex machines, especially computers. Hundreds of items illustrating the discoveries of art through the use of the computer were exhibited.

FIGURE 16-6   Four computer–generated drawings of an old man. A spiral, rectangle, triangle and star are used as the symbols. *Courtesy of C. Csuri.*

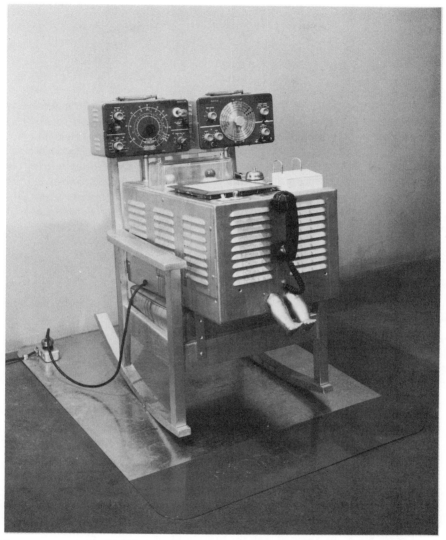

FIGURE 16-7   "The Friendly Grey Computer–Star Gauge Model #54" (1965), by Edward
Kienholz. Motorized construction as a rocking chair. Collection, the Museum of Modern Art, New York. Gift of Jean and Howard Lipman.

The computer has inspired the artist to create objects of art.

Edward Kienholz's construction entitled "The Friendly Grey Computer"
is shown in Figure 16-7. This construction is in the collection of the Museum
of Modern Art in New York and the catalog describing the piece states:[17]

A folklore has rapidly developed about the computer. It has become a wonder child, capable of answering any question, solving any problem. As he does so frequently, Kienholz here makes use of modern folklore. His mood, though still sardonic, is gentler than in the grim *Back Seat Dodge—'38*. His directions for operating *The Friendly Grey Computer* advise us:

Flashing yellow bulb indicates positive answer. Flashing blue bulb indicates negative answer. Green jewel button doesn't light so it will not indicate anything. Computers sometimes get fatigued and have nervous breakdowns, hence the chair for it to rest in. If you know your computer well, you can tell when it's tired and sort of blue and in a funky mood. If such a condition seems imminent, turn rocker switch on for ten or twenty minutes. Your computer will love it and work all the harder for you. Remember that if you treat your computer well it will treat you well.

Kienholz kindly programmed the computer to give more "yes" than "no" answers. A question random-found on a card: "Will I ever get a boyfriend?"*

The relationship between the graphic artist and the computer is becoming increasingly productive. In the future, programming languages will undoubtedly be developed for helping artists to communicate with the computer. Mr. K. Knowlton of Bell Telephone Laboratories has summarized the relationship:

The problem of providing an artist with good software involves the search for a comfortable compromise between the extremes of machine autonomy and machine stupidity. In the first case, we have a machine that works almost entirely automatically, producing great volumes of output over which the artist has little control except for culling the results. At the other extreme, the programmer has complete spot-by-spot control, but far too much effort is required for specifying an interesting picture. . . . The outcome of present experimentation ultimately may be a number of relatively suitable languages for artists. Such languages may become sufficiently established and familiar —no longer a cute gimmick—that artists can use them to say something without the medium itself arousing such curiosity, acclaim or disdain as to distract severely from the artistic content of the work.

*From *The Machine as Seen at the End of the Mechanical Age* by K. G. Pontus Hultén published by The Museum of Modern Art, New York, 1968, p. 190. All rights reserved. Reprinted by permission.

Whether computers will enable the artist to produce great works of visual arts is an open question. Certainly, the computer is a new and important medium for some artists to use in the creation and production of visually beautiful art. The possibilities inherent in the computer as a creative tool will do little to change those idioms of art which rely primarily on the dialogue among the artist, his ideas and his media. They will, however, increase the scope and diversity of art.

16.3 COMPUTERS AND MUSIC AND DANCE

To set to work to make music by means of valves, springs, levers, cylinders, or whatever other apparatus you choose to employ, is a senseless attempt to make the means to an end accomplish what can result only when those means are animated and, in their minutest movements, controlled by the mind, the soul, and the heart. The gravest reproach you can make to a musician is that he plays without expression; because, by so doing, he is marring the whole essence of the matter. Yet the coldest and most unfeeling executant will always be far in advance of the most perfect machines. For it is impossible that any impulse whatever from the inner man shall not, even for a moment, animate his rendering; whereas, in the case of a machine, no such impulse can ever do so. The attempts of mechanicians to imitate, with more or less approximation to accuracy, the human organs in the production of musical sounds, or to substitute mechanical appliances for those organs, I consider tantamount to a declaration of war against the spiritual element in music; but the greater the forces they array against it, the more victorious it is. For this very reason, the more perfect that this sort of machinery is, the more I disapprove of it; and I infinitely prefer the commonest barrel–organ, in which the mechanism attempts nothing but to be mechanical, to Vaucanson's flute player, or the harmonica girl.

E. T. A. Hoffmann
Automata, 1816

A computer can produce a numerical description of a sound wave or a combination of sound waves. Thus, the artist interested in music can use a computer to assist in the production of music. A Decca record of 1962, *Music from Mathematics,* shows that the computer can play tunes in a variety of tone qualities, imitating plucked strings, reed instruments and other common effects, and going beyond these to produce shushes, garbles, and clunks that are unknown in conventional music.

The electric signal, which by means of a pickup goes into a sound system, can be specified by a sequence of numbers which give the amplitude of the signal at regularly spaced instants of time. The number of numbers required is about 20,000 per second for high-quality music; and approximately 20,000 three-digit numbers provided each second by a computer is sufficient to describe any music.[9] Thus, a computer in conjunction with equipment for turning a sequence of numbers into electronic signals that can excite a loudspeaker is truly a musical instrument.

The development and composition of computer music has taken place during the past decade and is still embryonic. The user of the computer can specify the wave form, the pitch and the amplitude and the relationship of these variables. However, very few people have many years of experience with music composed by means of a computer.

The composer John Cage has successfully used a random process in the selection of notes for computer-generated music. Other composers of computer-assisted music are James C. Tenney of Yale University, Harry F. Olsen of RCA and Gerald Strang of California State College, Long Beach.

It is not easy to use computers to assist in the creation of music. The complexity of music places difficult obstacles in the path of the composer. The composer must develop the music through an elaborate set of instructions which form a program, which in turn determines the composition of the score to be played and all interpretive musical characteristics for each instrument. On the other hand, the composer can, if he likes, allow the computer to choose pitch, loudness or anything else randomly, where and when he pleases.

The computer doesn't compose the music; the person does, with the assistance of the computer. The meaning of music provided by the composer is the structure he provides for the collection of sounds. The aesthetic content of music can be analyzed in terms of fluctuations between the two extremes of total randomness and total redundancy. For example, in 1795 Simrock published a system for composing waltzes and contredanses using chance operations which have been attributed to Mozart. Two dice are thrown, and the resulting number is referred to the table to determine the sequence of measures in the composition. A dice-music program has been applied to provide a composition. Two kinds of music that have been generated in this manner are pieces for chimes and for bagpipes.

Computer music, like other branches of machine art, has no body of critical judgment on which an aesthetics can be built. Most critics of computer music use the 19th century criteria, such as:

1. There must be an artist who is the sole creator of a work of art.
2. That work should be judged in the context of the history of its type.
3. It should also be unique and limited in availability.

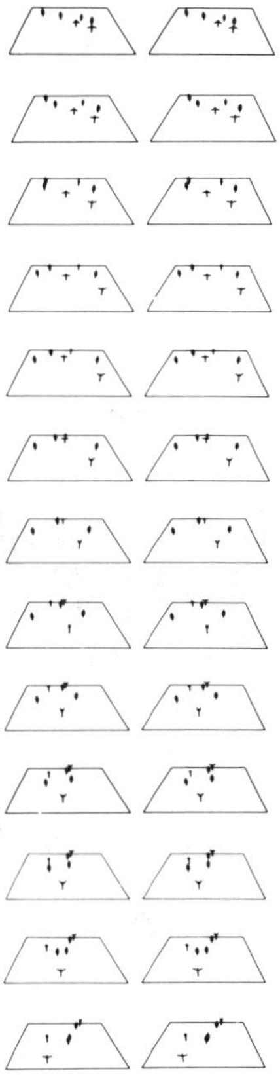

FIGURE 16-8   A choreographed sequence of dance movements obtained with the assistance of a computer. *Courtesy of A. M. Noll and Bell Telephone Laboratories.*

(Most computer music is the result of effort by many workers who may be artists and computer scientists, and the works of art are often reproducible in large volume at low cost.)

Computers may be used to compose dance sequences as well as musical compositions. A choreographer plans the sequence of movements in a dance or a ballet. He can use a computer as the musical composer does. In fact, most choreography is completed with the full dance company present and the finished plans often remain only in the minds of the dancers. Without extensively developed dance notations and well understood methods for dance choreography, the computer must be used by experienced choreographers in the composition of dances.

One means of computer choreography proposed by A. M. Noll uses a computer and a visual display.[10] The choreographer interacts with the computer during the creative process. Stick figure representations of the dancers appear on some form of three-dimensional display. The choreographer, by manipulating different buttons on the console, controls the movement and progress of the work. The different movements of each dancer are stored in the computer memory and requested by the choreographer and put together as a sequence. An illustrative sequence of dance movements is shown in Figure 16-8. The choreographer can easily make corrections and changes in the dance. Also, the computer could calculate the display for any specified vantage point so that the choreographer could ascertain the impact of the stage motion as seen from any location in the theatre.

Since 1964 Professor Jeanne Beaman has been working with Paul Le Vasseur at the University of Pittsburgh in the development of computer–programmed dance. Figure 16-9 shows a computer choreographed dance.

FIGURE 16-9   Computer–generated choreography at the University of Pittsburgh. *Courtesy of Professor Jeanne Beaman and Lilo Brych, W.Q.E.D., Pittsburgh, Pa.*

The aesthetics of music and dance are difficult to define in terms suitable for use with a computer. Nevertheless, the computer provides the composer or choreographer with a tool which is capable of representing an orchestra or a dance company and storing the composition or dance at every stage of development. The computer is certainly a valuable tool for composers and choreographers to consider using in the development of their art. While computer music and computer dance are embryonic arts at present, they appear likely to grow in importance in the future.

16.4 THE COMPUTER AND THE HUMANITIES

The computer has considerable potential to assist the creative writer, the historian, the archeologist, and the literary scholar. In increasing numbers, archeologists and museum scholars are studying the artifacts of the past with a new tool—the computer. Computer applications are being found in data storage and retrieval for art and archaeological works, in the analysis of artistic content, the execution of aesthetic decisions, detection of art forgeries and in the field of museum education.

At a recent meeting at the Metropolitan Museum of Art in New York, curators, museum directors and teachers exchanged ideas on computers and their potential applications in museums. Mr. Dauterman, Associate Curator at the Metropolitan, told the conference how he is using a computer to classify and catalog Sèvres porcelain. "We found that each piece of Sèvres porcelain had a set of incised marks—initials, symbols, numbers—in various combinations," said Mr. Dauterman. "We decided to use a computer to help determine their significance. At the same time, the computer could produce the first reference list of such markings, which would be a valuable tool for collectors and scholars."

An Egyptian temple built during the period 1367 to 1350 B.C. was later completely dismantled. Computers are now being employed to recreate the building.[12,18] The temple lies in 30,000 pieces—too many, it is said, for the human brain to assemble without assistance. But by matching photographs of the individual pieces on computers, American and Egyptian archaeologists expect to have the temple reconstructed, at least pictorially, in a year or two.

The computer will be helpful to the historian in the problem of linking individual acts with the historical results. The view of long historical patterns is partial and fragmentary. Theories of history have concentrated on impersonal forces, laws, environment determinants, and the singular effects of local religious, political, and other leaders. Other variables, such as series of individually identifiable decisions leading to changes minor in themselves, but cumulatively effective over long time spans, have been too numerous and complex to account for within the record. The computer will assist the historian in tracing all the human beings and the myriads of relationships that culminate in an historical force or result.

The question of whether a computer can write prose and poetry is an interesting and provocative one. The computer is certainly able to generate surprising combinations of words and phrases. Experiments with random combinations of words have produced several interesting serendipitous products.[13]

The more important current potential of the application computers to literature is in the area of literary scholarship. Professor Louis Milic reviewed the varieties of computer applications to literature in a recent article.[14]

In 1961 an item appeared in the *New York Times* describing a landmark computer project of James T. McDonough. McDonough for the previous four years had been reducing the *Iliad* of Homer to patterns representing the meter of the Greek epic and encoding these patterns on punched cards. Then he used a computer in an attempt to discover whether the uniformity of the patterns showed that the poem had been written by a single author, a question about which there had been a discussion during the past century. Since this first use of computers for the solution of literary problems, many other scholars have used computers for various literary projects.

Computers have been widely used in research fields related to literature such as machine translation, the making of concordances, attribution study, editing, and bibliography as well as the study of linguistics. The field of computational linguistics is currently active and a great deal of valuable research is taking place in it which will ultimately be of use in translation and even in literary analysis. Work in automatic syntactic analysis, sentence generation and semantics has implications for all kinds of word–connected activity.

The task of attributing an anonymous or uncertain work to its author requires processing a substantial portion of text for each possible author and comparing its features with those of the work in question. Previously such attributions were made impressionistically on the basis of intuitively–perceived similarities or differences which could only be summarized as a work sounding like the work of a specific author. With the use of a computer, the identification of the authors of such works as "The Federalist Papers" and the Epistles of Saint Paul were made possible. Perhaps we can look forward to a settling of the Bacon–Shakespeare–Marlow dispute concerning the authorship of the plays of Shakespeare by means of a computer study.

The use of computers in the study of idiosyncratic patterns in individual writing is called computational stylistics. If a text contains a sufficient selection of terms from a given category, it is concluded that the writer was concerned with that theme. Thus it has been concluded, for example, from the number of words about lunacy (mad, madly, madness, insane, disease) in the first act of *Hamlet* that Shakespeare had this in mind when he wrote the play. Many conclusions can be reached by studying word–clusters and word–associations. This approach has the virtue of attacking the semantic component of language, which has been a great problem to all literary users of computers.

The computer is utilized by the literary scholar to assist in distinguishing between the aesthetic and commonplace, good literature and bad, poetry and mere verse. These questions become specific as the person studies words, phrases, themes, plots, symbols, stylistic devices, meaning and value. The computer will increasingly become a tool of great value to the literary scholar within the next decade.*

SUMMARY

The possibilities and opportunities for artistic creation and scholarship by utilizing the digital computer are numerous. Several opportunities will undoubtedly occur to the reader in his studies. In a few years, we may be able to hear in our living room, with the aid of computer-synthesized music, a musical composition completely indistinguishable from what we might hear in a concert hall. We may hear a poem written by a computer, sung in a computer voice, to an accompaniment of computer-generated and computer-played music. Perhaps we will see a ballet of persons dancing in patterns generated by computer-aided choreography. The artist and the computer will work together in a partnership to provide man with new works of art. Undoubtedly, a large portion of the products will be of little lasting value, but we can expect much of value from this new tool. In some sense, the computer provides a source of creative amplification. (One man's view of the new artist-machine partnership is illustrated in Figure 16-10.) While the new partnership will not be necessary for all artists, those who explore the potential of the computer in the creative arts will probably find new media, new modes of expression and new sources of beauty. Certainly, many artists will welcome the chance to explore the new arts just as Stravinsky, Feininger, and Balanchine did in the past.

CHAPTER 16 PROBLEMS

P16-1.   List several applications of computers to the arts.

P16-2.   Reexamine Figure 16-5 and discuss the effects of substitution utilizing various tiny hieroglyphic symbols. What would be the effect on using a set of symbols different that that used in Figure 16-5?

P16-3.   Describe your response to viewing the photo of the Friendly Grey Computer which appears in Figure 16-9.

*Surveys and articles on the progress of research in the humanities which utilize computers appear in the monthly journal *Computers and the Humanities*.

P16-4. Programming a computer to compose a musical work or choreograph
        a dance sequence is a difficult project. Design an algorithm for com-
        posing a simple musical piece.

P16-5. Develop a computer program for the algorithm of Problem 16-4.

"I SIT HERE AND SOLVE MATHEMATICAL PROBLEMS, PROGRAM
ELECTRONIC MUSIC, ANALYZE ARCHITECTURAL POSSIBILITIES...BUT
SOMEHOW BEING A RENAISSANCE MAN ISN'T WHAT IT USED TO BE."

FIGURE 16-10 *Courtesy of Sidney Harris, New York* and *Saturday Review, Inc.* From
Saturday Review, Feb. 15, 1969.

CHAPTER 16 REFERENCES

1. D. Fabun, *The Dynamics of Change*, Prentice-Hall Book Co., Englewood Cliffs, N. J., 1967.
2. M. McLuhan and Q. Fiore, *War and Peace in a Global Village*, Bantam Books, New York, 1968.
3. A. M. Noll, *Computers and the Visual Arts, Design and Planning*, No. 2, 1967, pp. 65-71.
4. T. Schachtman, "Art and the Computer," *Electronic Age*, Summer, 1969, pp. 12-16.
5. A. M. Noll, "The Digital Computer as a Creative Medium," *IEEE Spectrum*, October, 1967, pp. 89-95.
6. "The Art of Motion Graphics," *Computing Report*, March, 1969, pp. 10-13.
7. C. Csuri and J. Shaffer, "Art, Computers and Mathematics," *Proceed. of the Fall Joint Computer Conference*, 1968, Thompson Book Co., Washington, D.C., 1968, pp. 1293-1298.
8. J. Reichardt, "Cybernetic Serendipity," *Studio International*, London, England, 1968.
9. J. R. Pierce, "Computers and Music," *New Scientist*, No. 431, Feb. 18, 1965.
10. A. M. Noll, "Choreography and Computers," *Dance Magazine*, Jan., 1967.
11. "The Art of the Computer," *Data Processor*, Vol. XI, No. 3, June, 1968, pg. 27.
12. "Computing the Temple," *Science News*, Vol. 94, Oct. 12, 1968, pg. 361.
13. J. R. Pierce, "The Arts" in *The Computer Impact*, Prentice-Hall, Inc., Englewood Cliffs, N.J., 1970, pp. 252-259.
14. L. T. Milic, "Winged words—varieties of computer applications to literature," *Proceedings of the Fall Joint Computer Conference*, 1967, Thompson Book Co., Washington, D.C., 1967, pp. 321-326.
15. M. D. Freedman, "A Digital Computer for the Electronic Music Studies," *Journal of the Audio Engineering Society, Vol. 15*, No. 1, Jan., 1967.
16. "Cybernetic Art: The Computer as Renaissance Man," *System Development Corp. Magazine*, Vol. 12, No. 4, April, 1969.
17. K. G. P. Hulten, "The Machine," The Museum of Modern Art, New York, 1968.
18. R. W. Smith, "Computer Helps Scholars Recreate an Egyptian Temple," *National Geographic Magazine*, Vol. 138, No. 5, November, 1970, pp. 634-655.
19. N. Negroponte, *The Architecture Machine*, The M.I.T. Press, Cambridge, Mass., 1970.
20. T. P. Moran, "Artificial, Intelligent Architecture: Computers in Design," *Architectural Record*, March, 1971, pp. 129-134.

21. J. Reichardt, *The Computer in Art,* Van Nostrand Reinhold Co., New York, 1971.

22. M. P. Barnett, "SNAP—A Programming Language for Humanities," *Computers and Humanities,* March, 1970, pp. 23–31.

17

APPLICATIONS OF COMPUTERS

17.1 INTRODUCTION

Computers have influenced our way of conducting business, our industry, our schools and the services provided by our government. In this chapter, we consider the applications of computers in various selected fields in industry, education, and government.

17.2 THE APPLICATION OF COMPUTERS IN THE MEDICAL SERVICES

A significant part of medical practice involves processing information about symptoms, tests and diseases. As physicians are able to formalize the relationships among symptoms, diseases and treatment, they will be able to utilize computers increasingly to help deliver medical services to people who need and desire them. Expenditures for health and medical purposes are the third largest total in the United States, behind only food, which is first, and national defense, which is second. Approximately $70 billion were spent for health care services of all kinds in 1969, for instance.

We live in a time of rising expectations for health services, but the delivery of health services is inadequate. In the future computers and the information systems built around them will be directed toward developing improved methods for the prevention, diagnosis, treatment and management of disease. More satisfactory forms of health–oriented instrumentation, automation, computation, communications, systems engineering and operations research techniques must be developed to aid in this endeavor.

The essence of medical practice is to collect information about a patient, evaluate it in light of knowledge and experience, and then make decisions about the action to be taken to cure the patient. Only after information is processed can the doctor treat the disease actively. The computer may assist the medical practitioner by storing and making accessible the important facts. Computers can speed communications, distill information from data, and safeguard against human errors. Also, computers can reduce the time a patient must spend in the hospital by helping with the data–collecting routine even prior to his entry.

Computers are currently screening vast numbers of patients' electrocardiograms, with each individual screening requiring 15 seconds. They are also used to supervise post–operative care of open–heart surgery patients. For example, a computer has monitored approximately 400 patients following open–heart surgery at one large hospital. It maintains records and monitors on the patient's heart rate, blood pressure, fluid drainage, and temperature. The computer controls the monitoring devices and determines whether the patient needs infusions of blood or other special solutions or medications; then it automatically starts the infusion and stops it when it should. Already entrusted with the management of patients who have undergone the most complex open–heart surgery (multiple valve replacement, artery and heart repairs), it can also be applied following other forms of surgery and for serious medical conditions.[1]

When a patient is seriously ill or has received extensive surgical treatment, the delicate balance of salts and chemicals (especially sodium, potassium, and chloride ion) in the blood may be altered. Serious destructive changes occur in the cells of the brain and the muscles, among them the heart, if the chemical imbalance continues. An automatic monitoring device can make the difference between chemical death and survival. Here the computer can be of great value, for not only can it monitor blood serum chemical levels—in fact, it can also be attached to devices which supply missing chemicals intravenously *as they are needed.*

The computer will increasingly be used to assist physicians, nurses and hospitals to provide medical services. The primary areas of application of computers in the field of medicine and health services are (1) monitoring a patient's condition; (2) storing a patient's medical records; (3) assisting in the diagnosis of diseases; and (4) maintaining central information systems, as in hospitals.

We have briefly mentioned the advantages of a computer monitoring system for patient care. Several on–line monitoring techniques to improve the care of patients have been developed.[2] Automated techniques for the collection and rapid retrieval of readings of the physiological performance of a patient have been developed which utilize a computer. The aim of the computer system is to aid in the identification of potentially dangerous conditions early enough in their development in order to correct them easily and minimize their effect on the patient. At the end of each day, the computer can produce a 24-hour log of all activity, including the results of the analyses performed. The doctors can also obtain a graphic record of the results for each patient that plots the behavior of the variables against time. The variables monitored by one system are, among others, (1) temperature; (2) heart rate; (3) premature ventricular contractions; (4) respiratory flow and pressure, and (5) circulatory system blood pressures.

The number of tests that are typically performed on a hospitalized person number from 50 to 350. Laboratories are called on to perform over half a billion of these tests annually. The increasing number and complexity of these tests are generating serious problems with respect to their performance and the handling and storage of the data from individual patients. The reproducibility and reliability of the tests and the incidence of errors are often unacceptable. The one method of producing faster, cheaper, more reliable, and more accurate tests is the automation of the entire clinical laboratory process, from sample acquisition to computer print-out of final results on the patient's chart.[3,59]

The logical combination of a computer, a clinical laboratory and an intensive care unit for the monitoring and management of the critically ill has resulted in several special-purpose hospital care units. These units, which include coronary and intensive care facilities, trauma, renal dialysis and post-surgery recovery wards, now provide up to five percent of beds in community hospitals. A computer patient monitoring system provides real-time acquisition and display of data, analysis of clinical tests, and management of the data of the patient. The availability of such information has been life saving, particularly in coronary care units, where mortality has been reduced from 30 percent to less than 15 percent.[4] Computer monitoring and automated clinical systems are expensive, but they enable a hospital to reduce the staff which must monitor the condition of the critically ill and to provide improved care for the critically ill.

Computers can be utilized to automate the process of collecting data from the patient. This process, usually performed by a physician, is called the development of a patient's medical history. One automated medical data collection system developed at the Mayo Clinic uses a display terminal to present a series of questions. Patient responses are entered on the display terminal with an electronic light pen. Computer-administered questioning permits the effective use of question branching. This means a questionnaire can be tailored to the individual patient, so that factors such as sex, age, education, and ability to understand questions can be accounted for. Moreover, the patient answers only those questions which pertain to his own medical problems.[4] Pictorial techniques also allow the patient more freedom of expression. For example, the illustration shown in Figure 17-1 permits him to specify the location of abdominal pain. The patient responses are condensed into a concise summary statement for the examining physician. In one test, the automated medical history system obtained approximately 95 percent of the information normally recorded by the physician.[5]

The purpose of screening for disease is to discover people who appear to be well but who are in fact suffering from disease. Such people can then be given treatment, and steps can be taken to prevent spread of the disease. Thus, screening is a way of combatting disease because it can help detect disease in its early stages and allow it to be treated adequately before it secures a firm hold. The health screening center at Kaiser-Permanente in California uses a set of cards with a single question on each. The patients are asked to sort the cards into piles containing questions to which they have answered "no" and those to which they have answered "yes." The patient's responses are then entered directly into the computer using a card reader.[6] Another computer system uses a terminal to display 320 different sequences of questions to develop a medical history. The time spent by patients at the terminal has varied from 12 to over 60 minutes with an average of 25 minutes. Patient response to automated medical history-taking has been quite favorable. In the case of the experimental systems the patients were routinely asked whether they would prefer to give the history to the machine as they have done; to a physician; to a nurse; or whether they have no preference. They are also asked to indicate whether they think the history was complete, incomplete, interesting, dull, or difficult to understand. Although over half the patients expressed no preference, it is of interest to note that of those who did express a preference, the machine was favored over the physician by a margin of approximately three to one. Also, almost all the patients stated that they found the automated history interesting.[6]

After information about a patient is developed and recorded in an automated medical history system, it is used to provide a printed summary output for the physician. The information can also be retained in the computer storage for subsequent retrieval. The accumulation of large masses of medical data has led to the development of medical data banks. In Sweden, the medical records of one and a half million persons in the Stockholm region are recorded in a data bank. The information is filed in the memory bank in layers, each with more detailed information. There are three levels now, but this can be expanded. The first level has basic identification; the second, such critical medical data as drug allergies, vaccinations, and past illnesses. The third layer covers hospital visits and X-ray information. A person's records can be obtained by reference to an identification number, his name, or just his physical description in an emergency. Only hospital staff members with a "need-to-know" status have keys that can turn on the display terminals which in turn are

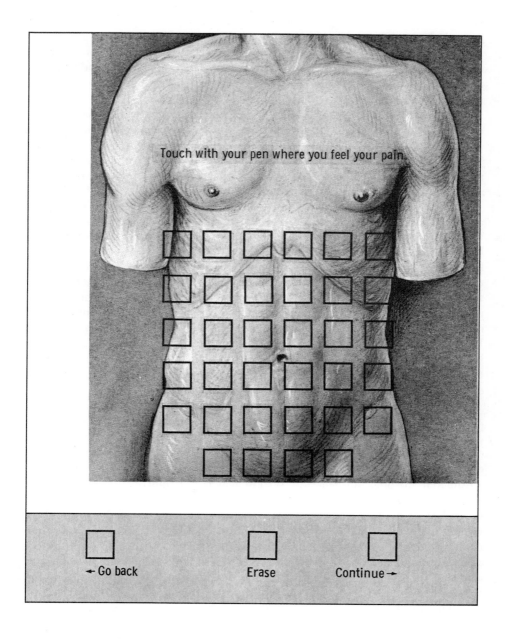

Touch with your pen where you feel your pain

← Go back   Erase   Continue →

FIGURE 17-1 A pictorial question for the patient to answer in the development of an automated medical history. *Courtesy of IBM Corporation* and *the Mayo Clinic.*

coded to the computer by locations. The X-ray department, for example, can get only X-ray information.

In addition, such personal information as psychiatric treatment can be obtained only by certain physicians, who must insert a special code number into the machine. The computer also keeps track of those who requested such confidential displays.

In the future, it is possible that a centralized computer data bank will be developed which will contain the medical histories of an entire population of a city, a state or even a nation. Plans are underway to develop such a bank for Jerusalem in Israel.[7] The data bank is being used for individual patient treatment; the development of community health profiles; as a population register, and the study and control of epidemics.

A computer in a hospital can be used for retaining the records of patients and also scheduling for best utilization of clinics and wards; accounting services; automation of the clinical laboratory, and physiological monitoring. It has been estimated that 25 percent of the total operating budget of the average hospital goes to the recording, handling, and sorting of medical information by nurses.[8] A hospital information system using a terminal input to a computer should reduce the cost of information processing and storage. Automated ward record-keeping systems are currently being developed. Automated patient records will some day be available to even the remotest small hospital in the United States on a time-sharing basis. A medical information terminal is shown in Figure 17-2. The terminal shown uses a light pen and typewriter for input. It can be used in a ward for admissions, clinical tests, and retrieval of patient data, drug orders and other functions.

A centralized totally integrated hospital information system would be able to include such functions as accounting, admissions, room scheduling, orders and inventories, scheduling of X-ray and operating room facilities, laboratory report tests, diet planning, and patient information retrieval, among others.[9,58] The Veterans Administration has been active in developing an automated hospital information system which is comprised of a number of automated subsystems. One of these is the medication subsystem, composed of a number of activities linking those organizational entities of the hospital involved in the ordering, preparation, distribution, administration and use of the medications and supplies issued by the pharmacy.[9] The recent establishment of a national drug code system will provide an identification code in computer language to permit automatic processing of drug data by manufacturers and hospitals.

The development of medical data banks will assist the medical practitioners in the delivery of health services to the citizens of the United States. The delivery of the best attainable health services is a major national concern and a major economic investment. Automation of medical information is necessary to process the information necessary for the task.

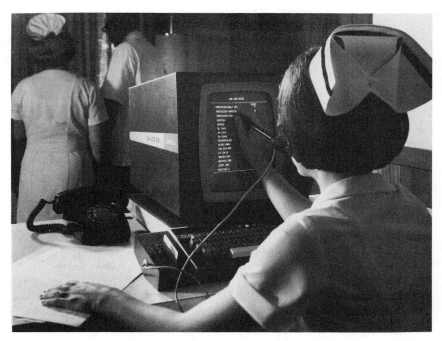

FIGURE 17-2   The display terminal of a medical information system. Physicians, nurses,
and others requiring information from the system simply insert their ID
card (and/or a patient's ID card) into one of the input/output stations located strategically around the hospital. A general index of formats is then
called to the screen of the electronic display at that station as shown in the
figure. The index contains general categories for all the information stored
in the system. For example, it may list titles of more specific indices, drug
order forms, order forms for treatment and laboratory tests, patient lists,
and other basic classes of information. The requesting individual touches an
electronic light pen device to the face of the display over the indexed item
he wishes to see. This action causes the index to dissolve, and the selected
information to appear. The selected information can be updated, modified,
or erased by using the typewriter keyboard at the station. It can be proof-
read on the screen, then automatically returned to system storage with the
push of a button. *Courtesy of Sanders Associates, Inc.*

Major changes in the delivery of health services arising from the use of
computers will occur during the next decade. One of the most significant
changes will be in the field of patient diagnosis. Computers augment man's
reasoning power and thus can be used to assist the physician in the diagnostic
process. For computers to aid such processes, however, a series of systematic
algorithms must be developed that correspond in some sense to the reasoning
used by the diagnostician.[10] A flow chart of the diagnostic–treatment cycle
is shown in Figure 17-3. At present, the computer could be used to assist the
physician at steps 1, 2, 4, 5, 6 and 9. Steps 3 and 8 are decisions which will be

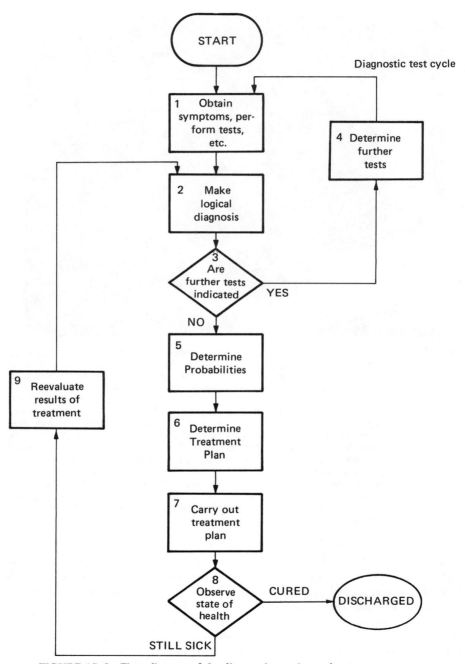

FIGURE 17-3   Flow diagram of the diagnostic, testing and treatment process.

retained by the physician. After the probabilities for the alternative possible diagnoses have been determined, the treatment plan must be made (See Box 5 of Figure 17-3). The computer can help the practitioner choose the alternative treatments and procedures to obtain the best results. Uncertainty implies no knowledge of even the probabilities involved and presents the most difficult treatment-value problem. Progress has been obtained in applying linear programming to the treatment decision, particularly where a combination of treatments is required.[10]

The process of diagnosis consists of four basic steps:

1. Obtain the case facts from the patient's history, physical examination and laboratory tests.
2. Evaluate the relative importance of the different signs and symptoms.
3. List all diseases which the specific case can resemble and (4) eliminate diseases from the list until a disease category fits or its exact nature cannot be determined.

It is widely believed that errors in differential diagnosis result more frequently from errors of omission from the list than from other sources. The computer can be used to store all the possible diseases in the category list. The diagnosis can be accomplished by the physician with the assistance of the computer, which retains the disease list and assists in the elimination of the diseases that do *not* fit the symptoms of a particular patient. Some experimental computer diagnostic systems use a matrix, or table, of symptoms and the related probability of a specific disease. The data accruing from examination of a new patient are fed into the machine and compared with the data in the probability matrix. The most probable or likely diagnosis is then computed.[11] In continuing studies conducted at the University of Florida College of Medicine, a computer program has been developed which will make a correct assessment of the thyroid function of an individual after his symptoms, signs and laboratory test results have been supplied to the machine. The original probability matrix for this program was constructed from data from 879 patients. A study of this system at the University of Florida showed that only 2.8 percent of the last 500 patients screened had been misdiagnosed by the program.

At Toronto General Hospital, a computer is used to provide physicians with printed information about the volume and width of a patient's left ventricle—the heart pump—much more rapidly than by manual methods. An on-line terminal will provide (in real time) a graph of heart volume versus time as the patient is X-rayed.[12] This system greatly aids in the diagnoses of diseases.

A computer can be used to control and record information from a radio-isotope scanner used to detect tumors. The computer is also used to average the data and printout a graph of the area scanned. In Figure 17-4, the results of a scanning of a human's brain is shown. An isotope is injected into the brain and a nuclear detector connected to a computer are used to provide the diagnostic graph of the brain and the location of a tumor or other lesion.

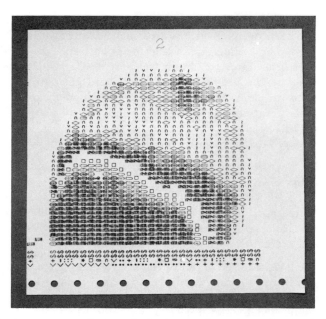

FIGURE 17-4   A computer printout of a brain scanning using an isotope indicator and a
computer algorithm for locating a brain tumor. Note the brain tumor in the
upper right of the photo. *Courtesy of Honeywell, Inc.*

At the 118th annual meeting of the American Medical Association, computers demonstrated their skill at diagnosing some 263 diseases, including 78 mental and emotional disorders. Over 1,750 different symptoms of gastrointestinal, urinary, and emotional diseases were handled by the computer, providing a differential diagnosis, based on the various combinations fed in by the participating physicians, almost instantaneously. The system has been compared to an encyclopedia of medical knowledge which opens itself at the appropriate page.

Computers may be used to simulate the physiological systems of the human body and thus aid in their study. At the University of Pennsylvania, a research study is using a computer model of the human circulatory system that will include the cardiovascular system and the aspects of the nervous system, the kidney system, and the endocrine system that control and regulate the cardiovascular system. The computer model is a mathematical description that includes all the hundreds of variables and the complex relationships that determine their behavior. Investigators are able to conduct experiments in which they can change variables in the system and determine the effects of the changes.

A computer graphics simulation of the human heart has been accomplished using a graphic output.[13] Recent techniques of computer graphics enable investigators to model the complex motions of the heart. Theoretical models of heart muscle contraction and relaxation for normal or diseased states can be tested for correspondence, visual subjective data from angiocardiography can be quantitatively evaluated and the teaching of complex heart anatomy and physiology can be significantly aided by computer graphics. A computer–generated graphic model of the heart is shown in Figure 17-5. A computer program can be used to construct heart images at a rate of six drawings per minute and thus simulate heart motion by showing the heart chambers in sequential stages of contraction and relaxation. These models can be used for research and education.

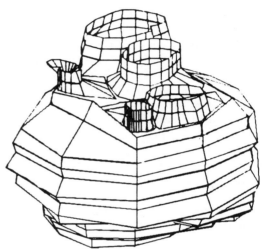

FIGURE 17-5 A computer generated graphical view of the heart from behind and slightly above. The three large, cylindrical openings on its superior surface are, from the top downward, the pulmonary artery, the aorta, and the superior vena cava. The two smaller cylindrical openings represent two pulmonary veins. The surfaces occupying most of the heart proper represent the left and right atrium. The inferior, or lower, portions of the heart represent the ventricular surfaces. *Courtesy of Dr. A. F. Bowyer.*

Computers are becoming significantly important to the practice of medicine and the delivery of health services. The need for effective management of health data is important for financial and health–information reasons. Medicare alone will create some half–billion paper documents on prescription drugs in the period 1970-75.[14] The handling and storage of health records must be increasingly automated in order to avoid a paperwork crush. The computer will be able to assist the physician, the nurse, and other health service persons in providing more effective tests, diagnoses of disease, and hospital care, hopefully at reduced costs to the patient. Computers, perhaps on a time–sharing basis, will become part of the equipment necessary for medical practice and hospital operation.

17.3 COMPUTERS, LAW ENFORCEMENT AND THE LEGAL SYSTEM

The application of computers to law enforcement and the legal system is becoming increasingly important. In law enforcement, the computer is used to increase the probability of prevention of crime, or the apprehension of criminals once crimes have been committed. In the legal system, computers help to provice increased means for citizens to obtain rapid and equitable justice.

Because airplanes and superhighways permit easy mobility of criminals, time is an important factor in law enforcement. Thus, the use of a computer information network provides the rapid information necessary for timely law enforcement.[17]

Several programs for the use of computers to aid in the law enforcement process are presently being developed and put into use. The National Crime Information Center of the Federal Bureau of Investigation provides 100 control terminals which serve local, state, and Federal law enforcement agencies in the United States and Canada. Thirty-one regional computer networks are integrated with the National Center. The Center contains over two million records concerning wanted criminals and certain types of unrecovered stolen property, such as guns, vehicles and securities. The average number of transactions handled each day is more than 52,000. Positive responses resulting in an enforcement action average over 500 per day.[15]

California employs a computer information system called California Law Enforcement Telecommunication System (CLETS). This system stores information on criminals and motor vehicles and provides a high-speed message-switching system enabling any urban or rural law enforcement agency to obtain instant information on wanted persons, stolen and lost property, firearms and stolen vehicles. The five-million-dollar network utilizes computerized crime files from the California Highway Patrol, Department of Motor Vehicles and Department of Justice as well as data files from the FBI National Crime Information Center in Washington.[16] The computer system receives a daily flow of 35,000 messages from 1,000 terminals in the state. The system uses two pairs of computers; it can switch 17,000 messages per peak hour, provide a 24-hour retrieval capability, operate 24 hours a day for seven days a week, generate internal messages to send between centers, and accept messages of unlimited size.

A city police department may use a computer to store the data generated as a result of the activities of the department. Reports of incidents and investigations are stored in the computer for detective investigations, juvenile reporting, field investigations, offense and arrest reports, accident reports, traffic citations, narcotics tests, officer activity reports and a daily work report. This information is used to detect crime centers and criminals statistically as well as to achieve the best distribution of police manpower.

A computer system for fingerprint encoding and classification has been proposed.[18] Fingerprints have been used systematically as a means of establishing personal identification for nearly a hundred years. The ten-finger file has been accepted by almost every country to be the single most reliable and convenient way of general personal identification. However, as populations grow, the task of searching fingerprint files becomes increasingly more difficult.

In the United States, the Federal Bureau of Investigation has about 175 million ten-finger cards on file. In addition to the FBI file, almost all police departments maintain their own extensive files. Since file-searching procedures are at present largely manual, obviously a great deal of manpower is involved in searching fingerprint files. It is possible to automate the fingerprint-searching process for the ten-print file and this may be accomplished within the decade. A system for identification by means of a computer stored single-fingerprint file has been demonstrated experimentally.[18] The single fingerprint of the right index finger is encoded by means of an input device and transmitted to the computer. In the experiment a set of 110 individual fingerprints was used. A test of 53 prints against the 110 stored in the computer resulted in an identification of 49 of the 53 prints. This system or one similar in objective may lead to a computer-oriented identification system used for law enforcement as well as identification purposes.

The legal ramifications of the applications of computers are also interesting and important. Computers have brought about significant changes in business accounting and data processing. As business shifts from ledgers to computer accounting systems, the legal system must reconsider the law concerning admissibility and proof of business records. The laws of evidence have generally required that business records be visibly legible. But computer tapes are not legible visibly and the magnetic tape itself cannot be read by a human. A print-out from the tape must first be made, and it has been questioned whether it is admissible evidence. The Nebraska Supreme Court, in the case of *Transport Indemnity vs. Siebe* in 1965, was the first to allow a print-out as evidence. Other courts are following this precedent. The courts of the future may require the availability of a computer to examine the evidence submitted in business cases. In addition, the computer may be used to schedule trials and hearings to provide the speedy access to justice which is promised by the Constitution of the United States.[56]

Computers will provide continuing assistance to the law enforcement agencies and the legal system of the nation. Many applications of computers in law enforcement are as yet unenvisioned. Yet the rapid and completely integrated processing of the information related to crimes and accidents should improve the quality of protection for all citizens significantly.

17.4 COMPUTER APPLICATIONS IN TRANSPORTATION AND AERO-SPACE SYSTEMS

The transportation of goods, materials and people is a vital function performed by various companies, public services, and by individuals. A transportation activity can be viewed as part of a transportation system, with the movements of goods and people as objectives. Several trends in the transportation industry will lead to the application of computers to various functions. In this section we limit our discussion of applications to the following modes of transportation: aerospace; airlines; railroads; ships, buses and autos.

While the aerospace transportation system transports very few people, it is important because many computer applications developed for space travel can be transferred and adapted for use by other transportation modes. The aerospace industry uses many computers and has developed many applications which are currently used by airlines, railroads and other segments of the transportation industry.

The National Aeronautics and Space Administration (NASA) is responsible for US efforts in aerospace. The objective of space travel is to transport several astronauts to outer space and the moon for scientific exploration. The space mission of a vehicle with astronauts is a complex, hazardous mission. A reliable guidance and computer–control system is required. Reliability is a primary objective of an aerospace computer. An initially–perfect computer has only a limited lifetime of error-free computation. For protection, the computer uses redundancy in order to achieve the necessary reliability.

The computer on a spacecraft supervises the guidance of the craft. In the Apollo vehicle, a computer built into the craft coordinates the flight. The astronauts let the computer control most of the flight while they check its progress and provide input information. The guidance and control system is illustrated in Figure 17-6. The computer stores information about the spacecraft's position and speed; automatically projects the craft's future course; calculates any needed course corrections and automatically controls the firing of engines to move the craft back on course. The inertial measurement unit provides the computer with a fixed–reference by which to gauge the spacecraft's attitude, and to sense and relay to the computer any changes in speed and attitude that result from engine firings. Another source of information is the network of radar tracking stations on earth. In both an earth–orbital mission, such as Apollo 9 and a lunar flight, these stations are the computer's main source of data. The radar tracks the spacecraft and, using a computer, calculates the spacecraft's velocity and position. The calculations are then radioed to the spacecraft's computer. The third source of input data is information from the star and landmark sightings made by the astronauts.[20]

The NASA radar tracking stations and associated calculation and communication system utilizes more than 100 computers. In the first Apollo flight that landed on the moon, there were two computers in the lunar module and one computer in the command module. Computers at the Kennedy Space Center monitored the countdown and controlled the lift–off of all Apollo flights. At the Goddard Space Flight Center in Greenbelt, Maryland, computers received data from the worldwide tracking system and, after evaluating it, transmitted it to the Manned Spacecraft Center in Houston. There, computers enabled Mission Control to monitor virtually every aspect of the Apollo

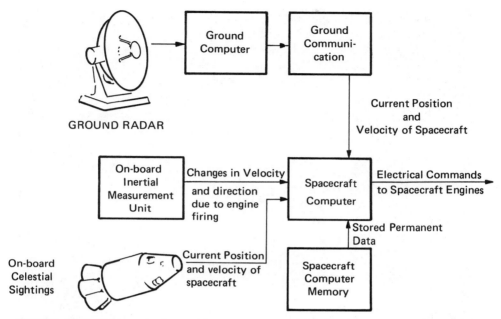

FIGURE 17-6 Guidance and control system of an Apollo spacecraft, using an on–board
computer.

11 mission in real time. The computer complex at the NASA Manned Spacecraft Center is shown in Figure 17-7. This computer system operates so fast
that there is virtually no time delay between receiving and solving a computing
problem. The reliability of the NASA communications, tracking and data acquisition network, is at this writing, 99.92 percent.[21] Computers are used to calculate liftoff data needed by the astronauts as they leave the moon to rendezvous with the command module. They are also used to calculate the orbit path
for the lunar module and the rendezvous calculations. The computers are used
from liftoff to splashdown to calculate the path of the spacecraft and to control the steering and firing commands of the craft's engines. A space mission
would not be possible without the use of computers for communication and
control of the mass of data necessary for a successful mission.

As the complexity of space projects has grown, the amount of data transmitted and recorded has increased significantly, as is shown in Figure 17-8.
With increasing complexity of space missions the equipment on a mission has
grown more complex and the duration of the mission has increased. The amount
of data transmitted had grown in 1967 to 1700×10^6 bits per day.[22] The
physical size of the spacecraft computers has been reduced, while reliability and
speed have been improved significantly.

The computers and the associated techniques used for aerospace missions
are now being used or considered for use in other transportation systems. Many

FIGURE 17-7   Real time computer complex in NASA's Manned Spacecraft Center uses
five powerful computers, IBM System/360 Model 75's. Here in this room
operations of the spacecraft and astronauts are monitored, tracking information is analyzed and computations guiding the flight are made for display
to mission controllers in the mission control room. Clockwise from foreground are printer, card read punch, printer, tape units, and the Model 75
console with its two typewriter inquiry stations. *Courtesy of IBM Corporation.*

of the applications of computers to aerospace missions can be transferred with
little alteration to the monitoring and control of aircraft. Paralleling the trends
of larger crews, longer operational times, and greater complexity in future
space missions, the trends in aircraft such as the Boeing 747 are toward greater
passenger capacity, more operational aircraft hours and more complex systems.
During the past decade the aircraft industry has experienced an increase in the
number, variety, and speed of aircraft, in the number of passenger miles flown,

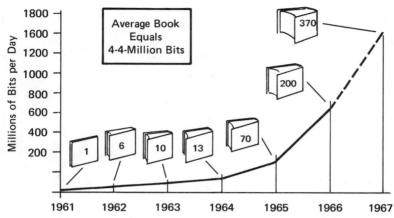

FIGURE 17-8   The growth of space mission data from 1961 to 1967.

and in the complexity of the control systems. Aircraft computers are used for: (1) systems monitoring; (2) full management; (3) guidance and navigation; (4) flight data display; (5) communications; and (6) collision avoidance, among other purposes. It was the navigational function that first brought computers to aircraft. More recent applications, especially for the newer commercial and military planes, include traffic aids for landing, holding and collision avoidance.

Future operations of aircraft such as the Supersonic Transport (SST) will require computers that can communicate to and from a ground station to transmit location and environmental atmospheric data so that true heading and ground speed can be calculated. The computer can in turn relay to the ground station the plane's identity and status. Such information can be relayed to a central air-traffic-control system to help in determining arrival and departure schedules. A reply can then be sent to the plane to adjust its course and speed in order to alter its arrival time and minimize waiting in a traffic pattern.[22]

The amount of airline traffic may increase threefold in passenger-miles during the next decade. This increase presents many problems in air and ground logistics. One basic problem is concerned with relating available space to the potential or committed traveler and it will increase the need for more sophisticated reservation and passenger-information systems. New reservation systems and extensions to current ones will include computerized fare computation, schedule generation, ticket generation and accounting to prorate the air fare between involved carriers. A large computer complex used for passenger service and reservations is shown in Figure 17-9.[23] This system is necessary to store the records for the passengers using one airline. It can service one million passengers up to the time of their flight.

According to estimates, the number of aircraft owned by airlines is expected to increase from 2,200 in 1967 to an estimated 3,400 in 1974. Over this same period, the number of private aircraft should increase from 114,000 to

FIGURE 17-9   Eastern Airlines, whose jets carried more than 20 million passengers in
1968, is operating a powerful computer-based reservations system. Built
around three computers, the Passenger Service System serves Eastern's reservations offices. The system can store records for one million passengers at a
time, and it can record information on 1,300 daily flight segments, including
time of departure and arrival, meals, class of service and fares. As it monitors
the preparation of each passenger's itinerary, it assures that all details are in
order. The slowest part of the new reservations system is voice communications between the passenger and reservations agent. The agent has nearly
instantaneous communication with the computers to retrieve information or
make a reservation. *Courtesy IBM Corporation.*

170,000. While computers alone cannot alleviate the air traffic congestion problem, the proposed National Airspace System, when fully implemented, will provide automated Air Traffic Control Services (see below). The broad objective
of the system is to increase traffic-handling capabilities and increase air safety
by relieving air traffic controllers of tasks that can be computer-assisted.

Computer control of all air traffic is planned for the near future by the
Federal Aviation Administration. The system is planned to control all take-offs,
landings, and enroute flight. The purposes of the computer system are to relieve congestion at airports and to provide accurate control of planes in flight in
order to avoid collisions. Air flight controllers now rely primarily on manual
and visual methods of directing plane movements. A computer system can be
used to monitor flights and determine flight paths to avoid collisions.

Computers are extensively used for flight-simulation systems. A computer
flight simulation system is used to train and upgrade pilots in the operation of
an aircraft realistically, safely and economically without ever leaving the ground.
For example, a simulator of the Boeing 737 controls all the variables of a flight
situation and directs the simulator to recreate the same sensations that would
occur in actual flight. Thus, the simulator provides the runway feel and sound
the pilot actually would experience during a takeoff. As the plane reaches flying
speed and the pilot eases back on the control yoke, the computer sends out the
necessary signals to cut off the mechanisms providing the runway sensations.
If the pilot tries to take off before the plane has attained flying speed, the simu-

lator creates a stall, with authentic sounds and violent cockpit vibrations. The cockpit in the trainer looks just like the real one, with all the controls and instruments.

Queen Elizabeth 2, a new cruise ship, includes a computer on board for full technical, operational and business-data processing operations. The computer is used for recording the data from the engines and machinery automatically and controlling the fuel use of the engines. The computer is also used to calculate, using weather reports received, the optimum speed and course to minimize fuel consumption without undue delay in the ship's schedule. The computer is also used to monitor and store information about the ship's cargo, supplies, and fresh water.

Computers are being increasingly used by the nation's railroads in an attempt to improve the efficiency of the industry and the attendant profit. Recently, a computer system has been developed to improve the control of the 1.5 million freight cars being used to haul shipments in the US and Canada. The identification system is called Automated Car Identification (ACI); it utilizes trackside scanners to detect color-coded identification panels on the sides of passing cars. All freight cars have been labelled.[24] The system will be used to provide status and location information for loaded cars. Also, in the future, computer management systems for both empty and loaded cars are expected to improve railroad car utilization significantly. A coordinated information system for all railroads should help to achieve that objective.

Computer control of railroad yards is expected to occur in the near future. The basic function of a railroad yard is to sort and service freight cars. Often time delays occur in the yards with an attendant loss in the utilization of freight cars. Automated railroad yard control will become a reality as the systems using computers are developed and implemented.[57]

Computers are being used in the control of new urban rail transit systems such as the Bay Area Rapid Transit System (BART) in the San Francisco region. The BART system is the first system to be completely automated. It is scheduled for operation in 1972. BART will have as many as 105 trains in operation running on headways (time between trains) as close as 90 seconds and at speeds of 80 miles per hour. The computer system enables BART trains to operate as a coordinated system and it supervises scheduling, routing and train speeds. A display board, as shown in Figure 17-10, provides information on the operation of all the trains.

Computers can also be applied to the monitoring and control of the movement of buses and automobiles. A computer-aiding routing system (CARS) is being developed which uses a digital computer to control and coordinate a fleet of small driver-operated buses providing a taxi-like service for almost the price of a bus ride.[25] The would-be rider telephones a central location where the computer, on receiving the request, dispatches a vehicle to the caller's home within a guaranteed period of time to take him wherever he wishes to go. Meanwhile, the bus is making stops on the way to pick up other people awaiting ser-

FIGURE 17-10   The operator at the train control console can display train operations at
                the console and on the display board above. The panel next to the tele-
                phone displays malfunction alarms. The keyboard can be used to request
                various data displays on the cathode ray tube above it. It is also used to
                enter minor program changes, such as a change in the nominal (20 second)
                dwell time at a passenger station. Typers to the left and right of the console
                make record copies of CRT-displayed information and of all alarms asso-
                ciated with train operations. *Courtesy of Westinghouse Electric Company.*

vice. The objective of the system is to provide convenience close to that of a
taxi or one's own auto with a cost to the rider close to that of using his auto
for the trip.

Several computer systems for the control of automobile traffic flow in a
city have been implemented. New York City's Department of Traffic has been
gradually installing a computer controlled traffic system. In the Borough of
Queens, some 500 intersections, on seven major arterial roads, are now under
the control of a computer.[26] Eventually the city plans to extend the system
to 7500 of the city's 9000 intersections with traffic signals. Computer traffic
control systems are also currently working in San Jose, California and Wichita
Falls, Texas. The purpose of each system is to coordinate the traffic lights in a
city so that the traffic flow is controlled in the best possible manner and the
travel time for each individual trip is reduced.

The application of computers to transportation systems is a logical outcome of the ability of computers to monitor and control space vehicles, railroad trains, rapid transit trains, automobile traffic and ship travel. Computer systems are providing vital assistance in the operation and maintenance of the vast and important transportation industry.

17.5 COMPUTERS AND PROCESS CONTROL

The control of industrial processes, such as the production of steel, is an important function of our industrial system. A process control system combines the sensors (for measurement) with a computer to regulate, record and control a process. The basic functions of a process computer are to collect input data from the process and to monitor the use of this information to control the process in a desired manner.

An industrial process is a series of operations which produce a given commodity or product. The operations involve the treatment of energy or matter and its conversion, by chemical or physical means, to produce the products therefrom at a profit. Measuring instruments, or sensors, are used to obtain information about the state of operation of a process. This information is used by the computer in conjunction with information about the desired state of the process in order to determine a control action. A computer process control system may be defined as follows:

> COMPUTER PROCESS CONTROL SYSTEM A system based on a computer connected to sensors which monitor a process for handling matter or energy. The computer output is used to control the process in order to produce a product at a profit.

Modern industrial and laboratory processes are primarily derived from 17th and 18th century investigations in chemistry and physics. Discovery of physical laws, electricity, chemical elements, the steam engine, and the development on all scientific fronts of new industrial devices were put to good use by practical men. Their efforts resulted in the invention of processes on which were founded a number of industries, such as those which today produce chemicals, steel, textiles, electric power and petroleum. The objective of a control system is the achievement of balance among yield, waste, quality, operating expense and profit.

By July 1968, 1674 digital process–control computers were installed in the United States.[27] The electric power industry used the most computers. The process computer control industry experienced its initial growth during the decade 1960-1970. In the electric power industry, it is expected that the capacity delivered by the utilities will double during the next decade. During that period, it is also estimated that three out of four of the power generators will use process control computers.

The ultimate goal of many industries is to achieve the "automatic factory."[28] Sixty-nine percent of the selling price of all US manufactured goods is attributable to shop and production cost. The computer-controlled manufacturing plant is a possibility for the future as industry strives for increased productivity per worker.

The control of a process is graphically illustrated in Figure 17-11. This form of computer control is called *closed-loop*, since the measurements are used in the computer calculations to compare with the desired objective and ultimately to control the input variables of the process.

As a practical example of a process-control system, consider the steering control of an automobile. The vehicle dynamics and the resulting path along the road together make up the process. The desired objective is the completed path along the right side of the road in the proper direction, as shown in Figure 17-12. The output variable is the actual path of the vehicle which is measured by the driver's eyes. This information is compared with the desired path stored and generated in the driver's brain (which is like a computer). Then the resulting controlling action is taken to steer the vehicle.

The production and control of paper and paper products is an industry that has experienced increased introduction of computer control. The pulping, bleaching, and production of paper is a large and complex process. Papermaking

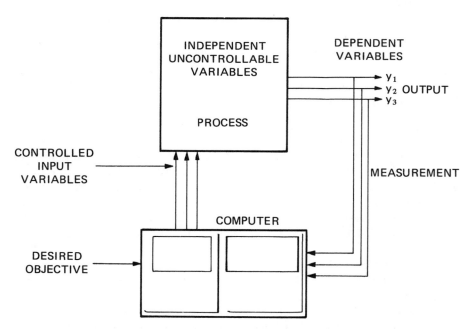

FIGURE 17-11   A computer process control system.

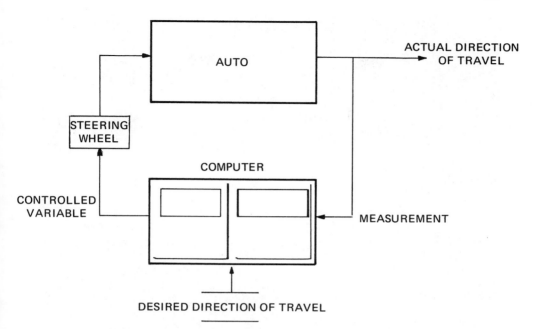

FIGURE 17-12   The steering control of an automobile travelling on a road.

involves some unique characteristics, such as the large amount of high–speed rotating mechanical equipment required to make paper. The large amount of distributed mechanical equipment and the high–speed nature of the operation has resulted in a difficult process to control. There are 750 mills in the United States and in 1967 these mills produced 36 million tons of pulp, 20 million tons of paper and 22 million tons of paperboard. It is estimated that over one hundred paper mills will be under the control of a computer by 1972.[29] In one newsprint paper mill, a computer is used to monitor and control over 200 variables in the papermaking process. Every hour the paper machine produces a 102–inch diameter reel of paper weighing 29 tons, as shown in Figure 17-13. The machine drives are all computer controlled and the computer collects and analyzes data of interest to the control operator and prepares and prints logs for management in addition to controlling the major functions in the process. The control room of this computer–controlled process is shown in Figure 17-14.[30]

The electric power generation and distribution industry is the largest industry in the United States. Expansion of the generation capability has continued to match the continuing growth of consumer use and demand. The nation's generating capacity exceeded 300 million kilowatts in 1968 and the energy used in the US was 1400 billion kilowatt–hours during 1969, representing about 37 percent of total world energy production.[31] Computers

FIGURE 17-13   A computer controlled paper machine produces a 102 inch reel of paper
                every hour. The computer controls and monitors over 200 variables of
                this production process. *Courtesy of Control Engineering.*

can save two percent of the cost of producing electric power. They can provide more efficient use of facilities and help to avoid the power blackouts which could occur in integrated networks of generating plants.[31]

There are other interesting applications of computers to the control of processes. For example, in a manufacturing plant, material handling accounts for almost 75 percent of plant space, with a good portion used for storage and in-process inventory. Therefore, we can expect increasing computer control of material flow, which is one of the least-automated functions now. A new concept is the use of stacker cranes and high-rise storage areas for maximum space utilization. A computer control is being developed which "knows the address" of each part in storage and directs the stacker crane to any address within the system. The computer control of physical storage and movement of produced goods is a growing industry. Total inventory-carrying units can run to 30 percent of the cost of the goods, thus becoming a primary factor in many industries. A computer-controlled warehouse has been built. It has proved a valuable tool for controlling costs of inventory and materials handling.[32]

FIGURE 17-14 The control room of the computer controlled paper mill which oversees all major process functions, from wood grinding to the operation of the paper machine reel. Both the groundwood mill operator and the papermill operator are able to communicate with the computer at any time. *Courtesy of Control Engineering.*

Many manufacturing processes use metal–cutting tools. The productivity of computer–controlled tools is many times that of manual tools. Also, machining accuracies are substantially increased by the use of computer control. In current terminology, *numerical control* refers to the control of machine tools by punched paper or magnetic tapes suitably encoded with directive information. Machine tools with numerical control accounted for 24 percent of the tool market in 1970. A direct–computer controlled machine tool is a step beyond the numerically controlled tool. The computer machine tool system makes it possible to extend the data loop of a machine beyond the operator's station. The data–manipulating power of the computer can be tapped to make the machine work more efficiently. Data on the machine's output and status can be collected automatically, analyzed, and distributed to manufacturing management, and fed back into machine scheduling.[33]

The control of large steel mills by computers has resulted in improved efficiency and increased production in a given period of time. A computer–controlled steel mill is shown in Figure 17-15. The computer monitors the temperature of the sheet and the thickness of the sheet, among other variables, and generates correction commands that control the speed of movement of the sheets and the distance between the rolls.

A new range of applications of computers to control industrial processes is being opened up with the availability of small computers constructed with integrated circuits and commonly called *minicomputers*. A minicomputer is often the size of a suitcase ($16'' \times 24'' \times 12''$), has a memory of 10,000 to 400,000 bits, and costs \$4,000 to \$20,000. The minicomputer is small in size

FIGURE 17-15 The nation's first completely computer-controlled hot sheet mill has been put into operation at Bethlehem Steel Corporation's new $400 million plant at Burns Harbor, Indiana. The computer system tracks production from the time the huge slabs enter the mill until the hot rolled sheet coils reach the delivery area. Communications between the computer and the operators are flashed through this control pulpit. As the nation's most powerful hot sheet mill, the facility uses motors totaling 108,000 horsepower. It is capable of speeds of 3,750 feet a minute. The 80-inch mill's own electrical substation could supply the needs of a city of 100,000 persons. *Courtesy of Westinghouse Electric Corporation.*

and relatively low in cost, but it incorporates significant computer power. Over 10,000 minicomputers have been manufactured each year for the past several years for use in industrial process control systems.[34] The use of low-cost minicomputers for process control systems will accelerate the automation of industry during the next decade.

17.6 THE MAN-COMPUTER PARTNERSHIP

The partnership of man with his assistant, the digital computer, has brought about new opportunities and new applications for computers. The use of a machine such as the computer in cooperation with, and under the control of, a man results in an amplified ability. Thus, rather than taking man out of an automated system, we are suggesting that he be properly employed in terms of his abilities and limitations and that the computer be used to assist the man in completing the necessary calculations and storing information.

A man may interact and communicate directly with a computer by means of a visual display computer terminal such as the one shown in Figure 17-16. The unit shown uses a light pen, as well as a typewriter, for communication with the computer. In the illustration the man is manipulating geological data.[35] The nature of geological studies, for example, requires a visualization of the geological relationships represented by contour maps, perspective displays, cross sections, and other representations of three-dimensional data. Interactive computer graphics is a recent development that enables the geologist to converse with the computer in terms of this graphic language. By using a light pen on a

FIGURE 17-16 A visual display computer terminal, the IBM 2250, with a light pen and a typewriter for input and communication with the computer. A perspective diagram is shown on the display and the man is pointing the light pen to a point on the display. *Courtesy of IBM Computing Report.*

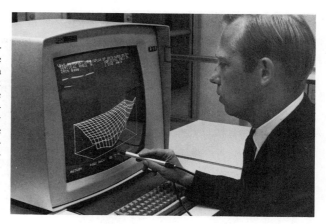

series of graphic displays, the geologist can select and edit data, apply a variety of numerical models, and display results in the form of contour maps, cross sections, and so forth.

The essential feature of the man–computer partnership and the use of a visual display graphics terminal is the immediate interaction between man and machine. Ideas and problems are communicated to the machine and their effects and results are displayed rapidly so that the author can change and improve them gradually to produce the desired results. The user is able to think, experiment, and design with the aid of the computer and so improve his ideas in a dynamic manner not possible when using a computer as a batch processor. The itneractive graphics terminal provides two–way, on–line interaction with the computer, usually through the means of time–sharing a large computer among several users. Alternatively, several on–line graphics systems use a computer dedicated to sole use with the graphics terminal. The display terminal typically uses a cathode ray tube (CRT) as the display device as is shown in Figure 17-16. A common means of drawing on the display screen is the light pen, which is a photo–electric device for sensing light shown in Figure 17-17.

The market for computer graphics terminals is expected to grow to $350 million in 1971 and more than 25 percent of all computers in the United States will have some display devices.[36] One forecast indicates that there will be 250,000 installed terminals in January, 1974, compared to 69,000 display terminals installed in January, 1969.[37]

Interactive computing in which humans work on problems while linked to a powerful computing system is providing new opportunities to designers, architects, cartographers, geologists and businessmen. The computer is adept at calculating rapidly and accurately and storing the results while the person is adept at linking concepts and applying insight and reasoning to a problem. A comparison of the abilities of man and computer is given in Table 17-1.[38]

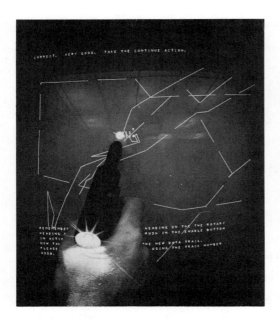

FIGURE 17-17 A light pen input device, which is a photo–electric device for sensing light. The operator points it at a spot on the screen, and when that spot is illuminated, the resulting pulse can be compared with what appeared on the screen at that instant. The computer is thus able to "know" where the pen is being pointed. *Courtesy of System Development Corporation.*

The power resulting from the linking of man and the computer will provide new strengths and opportunities. Interactive graphics offers much in the way of bring the program user closer to the problem-solving process.

One major use of interactive graphics systems is in the design of machines, buildings, automobiles and other products. General Motors uses a system called DAC (Design Augmented by Computer) and it has been reported that the time-shared DAC system is approximately ten times faster than the batch processing mode of processing computing problems for design purposes.[39] The DAC system is used to design automobile parts within a man–computer partnership. One such auto body part is shown in perspective in Figure 17-18.

The computer–man partnership has been used in the design process in textile design, integrated circuit design, and architectural design, among others. Users claim a reduction in the time required to perform certain design functions of up to six to one. Interactive graphics can also be used for management information systems. Primarily, the display allows the manager to ask the question "what if?" in the context of changing inventory levels, changing production levels, and a variety of other factors. Interactive graphic displays can also be used in process computer control. In such systems, the operator can control a process by setting the objectives and monitoring the systems progress while the computer stores and manipulates the data and provides the control signals to the process. The human operator readily detects related events or groups through visual interaction with a graphic display, being able to see relationships instantly that might be extremely time-consuming to find by other means.

TABLE 17-1

A Comparison of the Information Processing and Decision Making Abilities of Man and the Computer*

MAN	information processing	COMPUTER

MAN	COMPUTER
Relatively low-speed information processor. Essentially a single-channel processor at any instant.	High-speed information processor. Can handle many channels simultaneously.
Weak and inaccurate as a computer. Tires quickly; especially in routine, boring jobs.	Tireless and fantastically accurate in comparison to man. Man should never compute if he can get a machine to do it.
Man is easy to program. He does not require extremely precise instructions. He is *flexible.*	Programming machines is time consuming. Each instruction must be detailed and specific.
Man's short-term memory is limited in size, accuracy and permanence. Access time is relatively high.	Machine memory can be almost unlimited. Accuracy and performance are high. Access time is very low.
Man processes information so slowly that he is relatively inefficient in search tasks, although he is good at recognizing and identifying targets once they are located.	Machines can rapidly search huge quantities of data for well-defined targets, but accuracy suffers as target definition is worsened.
Man has an excellent long-term memory for related events. Generalized relevant patterns of previous experience can be recalled to solve immediate problems.	This property can be built into machines only at great expense.

decision making

MAN	COMPUTER
Man can generalize and employ inductive processes.	Machines have less capability for induction and generalization.
A human being does not always follow an optimal strategy—usually because he cannot perceive or examine all ramifications of a situation and cannot compute all the possible solutions.	Machines always follow built-in strategies, or they can compute optimal strategies given sufficient information.
Decisions can be made despite incomplete information and where the rules are not certain.	A computer usually demands complete information before making a decision.
Human decision-making time is relatively high. Often man wavers between alternatives if the decision is not clear-cut.	Machines are fast and specific.
Man is always needed to set priorities, establish values, set goals, risks.	Machines must be instructed as to priorities, values, goals, etc.
Targets of opportunity are recognized better by man.	Machines are relatively insensitive to unspecified opportunities.
Humans can improvise superbly.	Machines improvise poorly.
Man learns from past experience.	Machines can learn, too, but are not proficient at it yet.

*Courtesy of E. G. Johnsen and NASA.

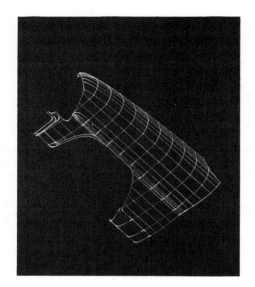

FIGURE 17-18 A picture on a CRT of an auto body part composed of 2500 short-line segments. The designer is able to alter and manipulate the auto part. *Courtesy of Adage, Inc.*

The two major categories of CRT displays are alphanumeric and graphic. Alphanumeric displays show only numeric, alphabetic, and special characters, usually on predetermined lines, similar to a typewriter; graphic displays present line drawings, curves, schematics, etc., in addition to presenting alphanumeric information at random positions. A grid of lines provides the ability to display a relationship of three variables in three dimensions as shown in Figures 17-16 and 17-18. A three-dimensional structure created by a computer is illustrated in Figure 17-19.[40] It is desirable to be able to rotate and manipulate an object displayed on the screen of the display; several display terminals provide this ability. Also several terminals, such as the one shown in Figure 17-20, provide a joystick (control handle) and mouse input devices, as well as a typewriter, in order to move a cursor (arrow) on the screen and thus draw an object or communicate a location to the computer. The mouse input device translates movement of the mouse, or small rolling device, to the cursor movement.

The application of computers to interactive design is illustrated in Figure 17-21, which shows a terminal being used for map-making.[41] Computer graphics have also been applied to the development of a numerical control program for a machine tool. An engineer can design a new part or modify an existing one in one sweep by applying his light pen to a computer display screen. He can then call for display of the image of a cutting tool on the screen and can "lead" the cutter along every external or internal surface of the part that is to be machined.

FIGURE 17-19 A three-dimensional structure created by a computer illustrates the ability of computer graphics terminals to generate three-dimensional displays. *Courtesy of Professor I. Sutherland and Mr. G. Watkins.*

FIGURE 17-20 A display terminal with a typewriter input option as well as a Joystick and Mouse input option. The mouse shown in the left foreground is two-dimensional, useful for positioning a cursor (arrow) on the screen of the display. The movement of the mouse on wheels causes the cursor to follow in an identical manner. The joystick is another device for positioning a cursor on the screen. *Courtesy of Computer Displays, Inc.*

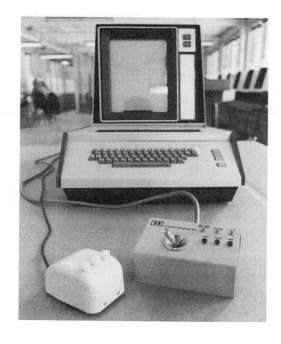

FIGURE 17-21   Computer-assisted map making is considered technically feasible through a
new method of direct graphic communication between the cartographer
and a computer. The method uses an IBM 2250 graphic display unit. It was
developed by IBM in cooperation with the U. S. Coast Geodetic Survey.

Among the responsibilities of the Coast and Geodetic Survey are making
and updating aeronautical charts, more than 2,500 of which are used in
the United States. To meet the demands of constantly increasing air traffic,
these charts must be updated monthly or even weekly.

Normally, a cartographer makes changes on such a chart by working with a
draftsman at a drawing board. By storing the chart data in a computer,
however, the cartographer can reproduce any part of it on the screen of a
2250, as in the photograph above, and make required changes by using a
light pen. On the screen he can quickly alter the size or position of symbols, lines, blocks of text, or other data; and, simply by pushing a button
on the terminal's keyboard, he can enter the changes into storage. A com-
puter-operated printer can then produce up-dated master charts for commercial reproduction. *Courtesy of Computing Report.*

The partnership of man and computer will result in new and improved designs in the fields of architecture, electronics, industry, business, and government, among others. Man and computer acting in concert to solve a problem or
design a product will be synergistic; that is, the united action of the two agents
will produce a greater effect than the sum of the two individual actions. The
whole of the man-computer partnership is greater than the sum of the two
parts.

17.7 COMPUTERS AND EDUCATION

The applications of the computer to the process of education are many and varied. Computers are able to store, manipulate and process information and thus assist in the process of education. In this section we will consider some of the potential and actual applications of computers to education.

Classroom scheduling by computer is an accomplished fact at many colleges and schools.[60] Some computer programs are used for assigning individual students to classroom groups and insuring that the number of groups matches the number of available teachers, and that these groups and teachers fit into available classrooms. The whole operation typically takes place once a term. Mechanizing this unpleasant and tedious task is clearly a worthwhile and useful accomplishment that is receiving wide acceptance. Scheduling classes, however, is less difficult than keeping track of individual students week by week, day by day, hour by hour, or minute by minute, and matching them in turn with resources themselves parceled out in smaller packages than teachers per semester or rooms per semester. Several programs are currently being developed for the purpose of recording the progress of individual students by utilizing a computer. Meanwhile, the use of computers to aid in administrative functions of education, such as record-keeping, has been accomplished at many colleges and schools.

The use of the computer to assist a student in the learning process is known by several names, of which the most common is *computer-assisted instruction* (CAI). The purpose of the use of the computer in CAI is to aid and assist both the teacher and the student in the educational process. One objective of CAI is to offer the student individualized instruction; it approximates the personal services of a tutor who tailors the learning experience to the individual learner. It has been shown that a student receives a more successful learning experience when the educational curriculum adapts to the individual learners. The computer allows each student to proceed according to his own capability with his performance constantly monitored.[43] A definition of computer-assisted instruction is:

COMPUTER-ASSISTED INSTRUCTION An interactive system containing a student and a computer and using a natural language such as English to produce long-lasting changes in the intellectual knowledge of a learner.

The computer technology is available to construct CAI systems for students in schools and colleges in the United States. The primary obstacles to the wide use of CAI systems are economic and pedagogical. The pedagogical question is: How may the educational community of teachers and the supporting education industry devise ways of individualizing instruction and of designing a curriculum that is suited to individuals?[44]

The use of CAI programs offers the opportunity to multiply the effect of the best teachers by repetitive use of programs generated by their talents and refined by their experience and that of the students. Also, CAI permits the teaching of material where either no qualified instructors are available, or where students are available only at irregular hours.

The student can interact with the computer in three separate ways. First, the computer can be used for drill and practice sessions which supplement the regular teaching process. This work is particularly suitable for the skill subjects. Second, the computer can be a personal teacher—a tutor—for the student. Here the system has the main responsibility for helping the student understand a concept and develop skill in using it. The aim is to approximate the interaction a patient tutor would have with an individual student. A third possible computer–student system is the dialog system, in which the student can conduct a genuine two–way conversation with the computer. Although drill–and–practice and tutorial systems are already in operation on an experimental basis, the dialog system may be some years away because of several technical problems. [43]

A variety of modes of interaction can be used in the man–computer interaction of a CAI system. Most CAI systems use a typewriter as the input device and a cathode-ray tube as the display device. The typewriter is usually connected by a telephone line to a time-sharing computer. While most CAI systems use a CRT display, several systems also use a computer–controlled slide projector to allow presentation of any graphic material. It is also possible to include a tape recorder under computer control to supplement the slides and typewriter. Several systems accept inputs from typewriter, light pen, or both. A CAI terminal is shown in Figure 17-22. This terminal uses a typewriter and a light pen for input and a CRT and slide projector for display to the student. By means of the terminal, the student is able to engage in a two–way communication with the computer. The student actually communicates with a CAI program stored within the computer and monitored and processed by the computer. The program within the computer was written by an author and then stored for later use. The preparation of useful, effective CAI programs is a costly, difficult task; this factor contributes to the potential high cost of CAI instruction.

Authors of CAI programs often use a branching technique which is very suitable for computer operation. Branching can be used to move the student to remedial or to advanced work. It is through branching, based on the student's prior knowledge and recent history of performance, that the author (via the computer) can fit the course to the student. Most courses are programmed so that the student has no choice in branching, but a few do allow the student to select a course of action.

For example, in one course segment of a CAI program, the student may choose among three alternative routes. He may elect to take a quiz, receive

FIGURE 17-22 A student terminal of a CAI system at Pennsylvania State University, using an IBM 1500 Instructional System. The terminal consists of an image projector to the left of the CRT, a cathode ray tube display, a light pen shown on the right side of the CRT, and a typewriter. *Courtesy of IBM Corporation and Pennsylvania State University.*

feedback on the adequacy of his knowledge, and then move to the beginning or end of this course. He may also receive instruction, move to a review, and then take the quiz. His third choice would be to go directly to the review, then to the quiz, instruction, or to another review. If he chose the first alternative and passed the quiz, he would have passed the course within a short period of time.

Branching may be done so subtly by the course author that the student is not aware of it. The author may also give the student the choice of branching and caution him of the consequences. Branching can also be used to take a student through a series of questions as shown in Figure 17-23.

Computer–assisted instruction may be seen as teaching by two methods of instruction: the traditional method, and the self–teaching method. Of course, the dichotomy between these two is not sharp or clear, but it is worth considering in terms of actual practice. The traditional method consists primarily of drill and practice of skill subjects under study. The self–teaching method is a tutorial system with the computer providing the stimulation.[45] Students in the CAI tutorial process find themselves in a new give–and–take suitation rather than the passive lecture–listening situation. Most students seem glad to be able to ask questions of the computer which they would not otherwise have the opportunity to have answered in any comparable detail.

Cost affects any decision to implement an operating CAI system. The PLATO project at the University of Illinois is designing its system so that the

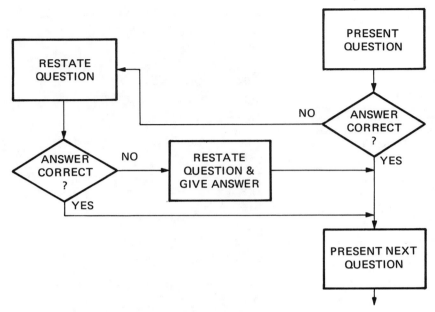

FIGURE 17-23   A flow chart of the branching process followed in one CAI program for drill and practice.

cost of the CAI system should be comparable with the cost of teaching using conventional methods. The goal is to achieve a cost of 25 to 30 cents per terminal hour for use of the computer and terminal. The PLATO project hopes to be implemented with 4000 remote terminals by 1972-1973. This system is discussed in the article which appears later in this section. In general, the cost for the lesson material is based on the concept that the CAI material would be produced at a cost equivalent to a good textbook with royalties going to the author for each use of the material. Whether authors can be convinced to invest in writing CAI materials is another question. Several attempts to use the economic motive to induce competent people to prepare material for the CAI activities have failed. An economically viable market for CAI materials is not yet available, nor is there a mechanism for collecting fees for their use from the user. In addition, methods must be found for determining whether any particular CAI material is suitable for a potential user. The cost of writing CAI programs has been estimated to range from $200 to $2000 per instructional hour of program.[43]

A CAI project in New York City used a computer to serve 192 terminals, similar to the terminal shown in Figure 17-22, located at 15 elementary schools in the city. About 6000 students used the terminals for a drill and practice program in arithmetic. The per terminal cost was $2230 per year and 25 pupils used the terminal each day. Significant improvement in the students' abilities in arithmetic were measured during school year 1970-71. The median cost is $89 per student per year to utilize the CAI system.[46] A sample lesson of a second grade arithmetic drill and practice session is given in Figure 17-24.

PLEASE TYPE YOUR NUMBER. 157
NOW YOUR FIRST NAME. ROBIN SULLIVAN

THIS IS A MIXED LESSON ON COUNTING AND INEQUALITIES.

24, 26, 28, 30

62, 65, 68, 71

20, 23, 26, 27
NO, TRY AGAIN.

20, 23, 26, 28
NO, THE ANSWER IS 29
TRY AGAIN.

20, 23, 26, 29
CHOOSE < OR = OR >.

16 > 8 + 8

51 = 51

18 < 9 + 8
NO, TRY AGAIN.

18 > 9 + 8

FIGURE 17-24   A sample lesson of a Grade 2 arithmetic drill and practice session. The student types his answer in the blank underlined space provided. *Courtesy RCA Corporation.*

The advantage of CAI is the projected ability to offer a learning experience to a student on an individualized basis. Thus, the individual learner, using the computer as his tutor, may progress at his own pace and according to his own ability. In a recent book, Professor Anthony Oettinger points out the danger of unrealistic expectations that computers will take over a large portion of the instructional burden within the next decade.[47] The evidence presented by Oettinger rests on two sets of observations. First he shows that, given the most optimistic estimates of the cost of any projected computer-based system, the present system of education is cheaper by a factor of ten. Furthermore, the expected savings in classroom teachers are most likely to be canceled out by new demands for more highly paid personnel and by the use of teachers to provide individual instruction. Second, he examines existing school systems to see how they have handled the existing technology. He finds that the ability of the educational system to assimilate the highly technical CAI system is overrated.

In the following article, Professors Alpert and Bitzer discuss the potential of CAI and discuss specifically the projected usage and costs of the Plato system at the University of Illinois.[48] A basic component of the Plato system is the use of a flat display device which is inexpensive and reliable. A photo of the experimental display unit is shown in Figure 17-25.

FIGURE 17-25   The Digivue electronic display panel is a flat, glass display device with an inherent memory capable of displaying information. The Digivue is to be used in the Plato system at the University of Illinois. The display consists of a sealed assembly of thin parallel glass parts filled with an ionizable gas mixture. *Courtesy of Owens–Illinois, Inc.*

ADVANCES IN COMPUTER-BASED EDUCATION*

D. Alpert and D. L. Bitzer

Since its initiation in 1959, the PLATO program at the University of Illinois has been committed to exploration of the educational possibilities and the engineering and economic problems relating to the introduction of the modern high-speed computer as an active element in the instructional process. During the past decade, numerous other groups at universities, nonprofit institutes, and industrial corporations have also begun to explore the possibility of utilizing modern computer technology for education. A widely varying array of such efforts is encompassed by the term "computer-assisted instruction" (CAI).

The setting for these activities is an overall formal educational process in which the national investment is more than $50 billion annually, a commitment which is expected to increase to well over $100 billion by 1980. Yet, despite this large national commitment, it is commonly agreed that there are vast unmet needs in education, in terms both of quantity and of quality. There are growing demands for more mass education over a larger fraction of the human life-span, and demands for more individualized instruction tailored to the specific preparation and motivation of a given student. However, these expanding educational needs have not been matched by increases in the productivity of the educational process. Rather, the costs per student at all levels and in various types of institutions have been rising so rapidly as to cause serious concern for the future.

Under these circumstances, it is not surprising that many institutions have sought to enhance educational productivity and to enrich the instructional process by the introduction of technology, especially the technology of the modern high-speed computer. The many programs in computer-assisted instruction have been based on recognition of the unique value of the computer in adapting the selection and presentation of instructional materials to the pace and style of individual students and in acquiring and processing data relating to the effectiveness of the teaching and learning processes. Nevertheless, although some of these programs have met with great enthusiasm on the part of highly qualified educators, it is fair to say that the general reaction has been mixed.

The mixed impressions about computer-assisted instruction are due in part to the wide variation in notions as to the types of systems that are

*From *Science*, Vol. 167, March 20, 1970, pp. 1582-1590, with the permission of *Science* and the authors. Copyright 1970 by the American Association for the Advancement of Science.

feasible and the teaching strategies that are possible. Several recent assessments of the field attest to the wide diversity of the objectives and professional specialization of such programs and to the even greater diversity of technological and educational resources available to them. At one end of the spectrum is the conception of such instruction simply as an automated version of a drill and practice lesson or a programmed textbook; at the opposite end is visualization of a remarkably powerful new medium capable of various instructional modes which can assist the student in becoming an efficient and independent learner in many fields and at all levels of education.

Another source of confusion lies in considerations of the costs of computer–assisted instruction and in mixed perceptions as to the state–of–the–art of available CAI technology. Some proponents of such instruction initiated programs and sought financial support as long ago as 1965, on the premise that a significant operational application was feasible with the computer technology then available. Others took it for granted that the prime need was an innovative approach to the preparation of lesson materials, and that the lesson materials developed would be compatible with later systems. Many proceeded on the assumption that economically feasible follow-on systems would somehow inevitably be developed, but they had little insight or evidence concerning what might evolve and when it might happen. The widespread interest of the popular press in the potential promise of such activities heightened the expectations of educators and the general public alike, but did not provide a basis for understanding the key issues.

It was some years after the onset of such publicity that the realities of the economics of existing technology were brought home to the educational administrators and public agencies faced with decisions on broad implementation of computer–assisted instruction. This more realistic view has called for assessment of costs as well as of benefits to be derived, and more sober perspectives have emerged. For example, in a recent evaluation of the field, carried out under the aegis of Associated Universities, Inc., the present educational validity and economic viability of CAI systems are summarized as follows.

> Although still a laboratory curiosity, the use of the computer for direct instruction has been amply demonstrated. . . . Without minimizing the differences of the many projects, their most interesting aspect is the common result. In every case, direct instruction by computer has shown substantial potential; it is effective, flexible and well received by students and faculty. But every case has also demonstrated that *such instruction is not economically viable. Resolving this conflict is the crux of useful computer assisted instruction* [italics added].

Since the economics of computer-based systems was recognized as a central issue at an early stage in the Plato program, we present here an assessment of the problems and potential of computer-assisted instruction from the perspective gained by this experience. In fact, the Plato program has for some time proceeded on the premise that the technology of the 1960's was not capable of making a significant and economically practical contribution to the nation's educational program. As early as 1964, a broad systems approach aimed at a novel and economically sound solution was set in motion. We proceeded to identify the specific systems problems in which technological innovations were called for; furthermore, as new educational ideas or teaching strategies were conceived, the design of hardware and software systems was modified to incorporate them. Although not promising immediate wide-scale utilization, this approach was in many ways far more ambitious than those built around available commercial systems in its perception of the possible role of the computer in education. To accent and characterize this approach, we have found it useful to describe our activity by a different and perhaps more appropriate term: "computer-based education." We call the laboratory in which the current effort is centered the Computer-based Education Research Laboratory. In this article, however, we use the terms "computer-assisted instruction" and "computer-based education" (CBE) interchangeably.

The Plato program has directed its efforts toward meeting two different, though related, objectives.

1) Investigation of the potential role of the computer in the instructional process. The major objective of this phase has been to examine the question, What is educationally possible?

2) Design of an economical and educationally viable system incorporating the most valuable approaches to teaching and learning developed in the above investigation.

To achieve the first objective, three successive and increasingly versatile systems (Plato I, II, and III) were designed and built. These systems were intended to explore the educational possibilities without regard to the economic constraints imposed by the technology available at the time of their completion. The initial stage of Plato III, a system utilizing a large commercial second-generation computer, was installed in late 1964 and has been in continuous use since then. A network of four associated demonstration centers was added early in 1969. Exploratory educational efforts with Plato systems have now involved experiments in at least 20 fields of study and over 100,000 student-contact hours (much of it for academic credit) in course work at the elementary, secondary, and college undergraduate and graduate levels. Among the results have been the realization of many new teaching strategies, valuable experience in different institutional environments, and an assessment of the attitudes of students, teachers, and authors of lesson materials.

The systems-design phase of the Plato program has addressed itself to the achievement of a highly flexible instructional system which could be economically justified at any educational institution. A milestone in this program was the proposal, in January 1968, of a design for Plato IV, a large-scale system which, even in a prototype version, would be justifiable in economic terms. The engineering design of Plato IV has been described elsewhere, by Bitzer and Skaperdas. Initial steps toward implementing the development of such a system at the University of Illinois have included demonstration of the technical feasibility of certain key components. Concurrently, some of these components are approaching the pilot production stage through the cooperative contributions of several industrial firms.

What is Educationally Possible?

What is the role of the computer as an active element in the educational process? It is now widely accepted that the computer can be a valuable tool in the presentation of drill and practice routines in fields like elementary mathematics and vocabulary development. A capability for such programs was provided by the earliest and most limited system, Plato I. Plato II provided a more expanded tutorial capacity. The most important consequences of these two systems, however, were their simulation of research and development leading to the broader capabilities of Plato III, which was designed for optimum educational versatility without specific concern for costs. In continuing full-time use as an exploratory system, Plato III has provided opportunities for developing many powerful new teaching strategies in fields as diverse as algebra and anatomy, psychology and pharmacology, languages and life sciences.

Without wanting to underrate the usefulness of computer-based systems for such rote learning situations as arithmetic drill and practice, we think it important to dispel the notion that computer-assisted instruction is limited to this type of application or is, in effect, an automated version of the Skinner teaching machine. The teaching strategies developed for Plato III are so far removed from this approach as to represent a totally different concept of the role of computer-based systems in education. To provide insight into the actual possibilities, it is important, first, to correct certain misconceptions about computer-based education. We list some of these, and give a brief commentary on each.

Misconception 1: Computer-based education is synonymous with programmed instruction. Computer-based education makes possible un-programmed instruction or student-controlled learning by utilizing teaching strategies which differ completely from the basic tutorial logic of most programmed instruction. While of substantial value for the development of certain skills, the interchange of factual information between man and computer is only one mode whereby a teaching strategy may be incorporated into the computer. For example, the information may be stored in the machine in the form of simulated models of an actual system or device; one may simulate such widely differing systems as a biological organism (such as the human circulatory system) or an electronic circuit (such as a defective television set). Through a set of instructions stored in the computer, so-called algorithms, the computer is called upon to calculate unique responses to varying student inquiries. It is in this manner that the great computational power of a computer has been programmed to play chess with human opponents—to make appropriate moves in response to unpredicted behavior. In other teaching strategies the computer may be programmed to aid the student in the development of logical, algebraic, or geometric proofs, or to play the role of referee and scorekeeper in interactive games between humans, thus providing new insights into group or adversary behavior.

Misconception 2: Since the instructional strategy must be previously programmed in the computer, it must of necessity anticipate all conceivable student responses so as to compare them with "correct" answers stored in the machine. Teaching strategies which do not call for specified student responses are widely used and often of greater value in many fields and at many levels of instruction. For example, students studying geometry may be called upon to "draw" on the Plato graphic display a figure that has specified geometrical properties but need not be of a particular size or in any given location on the screen. In such cases, a set of algorithms in a so-called "judging routine" makes use of the computational power of the machine to assess the validity of the "answer." Other such routines have been assembled to judge open-ended verbal responses and to distinguish between conceptual errors and spelling difficulties. In a sequence for teaching algebraic proofs, the computer helps the student by pointing out or correcting arithmetical or logical errors after each statement, thus allowing the student to concentrate on the central notion of "proof."

Misconception 3: Computer-based instruction may be useful for the transfer of information but is not of value in the development of critical thinking. On the contrary, the development of comprehension calls for individual challenge or attention and is often inconsistent with the "classroom" approach. Computer-based instruction has often been found to be more effective than standard educational procedures in many learning situations that call for judgment, interpretation of complex problems, and evaluation by the student of the validity of his conjectures. In the course of some lessons, for example, the student may use the computer-based system to calculate, analyze, and display. This relieves him of much of the drudgery of "learning" and helps him develop intuition and insight. Although we view computer-based education as a way of enriching rather than replacing human involvement in the teaching process, we do not relegate computer-based education solely to routine tasks.

Misconception 4: A computer system used for computer-based education cannot be used in a time-sharing mode for conventional computer programming. The extent to which this is true is largely dependent on the size and design specifications of the system. In any multiple-access system it is necessary to set aside some reserve time, over and above the statistical "average" time of individual student image, in order to avoid long intervals of waiting at times of peak load. In a large computer system this reserve time may be substantial. For Plato IV the reserve is to be of the order of 40 percent of the total available time, to make sure that the typical waiting time for any student is less than 0.2 second. This reserve capacity may be utilized in various ways for conventional computer programming. As many as 200 or 300 terminals could be used in a true time-sharing computational mode in concurrent operation with the remaining student terminals for purposes of computer-based instruction. Alternatively, this reserve computer time could be used for processing the educational response data from "on-line" students and could thus provide a mechanism for continuous evaluation of student progress and teaching effectiveness.

One example of a major departure from the tutorial mode of instruction is the so-called "inquiry" mode, which has proved to be of significant value in the development of critical thinking and intellectual comprehension. In this teaching strategy the student is presented with a problem statement that cannot be dealt with by a simple or multiple-choice answer; it may call for a sequential analysis or constructed response that cannot be uniquely anticipated. For example, in one of the chemistry sequences the student is asked to identify an "unknown" organic substance on the basis of any sequence of questions or "tests" he may specify. To make a valid response, the student may find it necessary to gather factual information about the substance's physical properties, to study its interaction with reagents selected by him, to "measure" and display its infrared spectrum, to interpret the data, or to calculate various reaction rates or other properties. While factual data may be stored in the form of dictionaries, tables, or other textual forms, the specific "results" of an experiment are often stored implicitly rather than explicitly. The student decides what tests he wants the computer to perform or what calculations he wants it to carry out. In a similar sequence in medical science, the student is asked to diagnose and prescribe the treatment for a patient's illness. When he proposes a treatment, the computer responds with a report of the expected effect on the simulated patient.

Obviously, we have proceeded far beyond the role of the computer as a bookkeeper, scorekeeper, and guide to selected textual material. Not only is the student helped in acquiring new information but he is aided in fitting this information into a broader context and in gaining new perspective. He may be introduced, even at a very early stage, to an investigative approach to the solution of many problems.

A major computer-based system provides a whole new capability for testing, evaluating, and model building for the learning and teaching process. Educational psychologists were among the first to recognize the potential value of this new medium for research in these areas. Several programs in educational psychology are in progress at the University of Illinois, with the Plato III system as the basic research tool. Obviously, such a system may also be utilized for evaluating specific course materials and, eventually, for measuring and increasing the effectiveness of this new medium.

Initial experiments aimed at evaluating educational effectiveness have been made at the University of Illinois and elsewhere. The data sample is altogether too limited, but the results have been encouraging. For example, a class of 20 students in a medical science course was taught for a semester entirely with the Plato system. When compared with a control group in a nationally administered test, the students taught with the Plato system were found to have scored as well in grade performance even though they had required only one-third to one-half as many student-contact hours of instruction as those taught in the conventional classroom. Subsequent measurements extending over a 26-week period indicated that the Plato group showed greater retention over that interval.

Subjective evaluation of Plato by students, teachers, and authors has been unusually positive in a wide variety of exploratory experiments. Several key features help to explain why computer-based education has aroused the enthusiasm of students and teachers alike.

1) The interactive nature of this instructional medium typically absorbs the attention and encourages the total involvement of students at all age and grade levels.

2) The student may proceed at his own pace and can exert considerable choice in the selection of alternative teaching strategies and methods of presentation.

3) The feedback of information is applied not only in the learning process but also in the teaching process; the system provides teacher or author with the means of assessing in detail the progress of the individual student, with a powerful tool for evaluation and modification of lessons, and with a mechanism for measuring overall educational effectiveness.

4) Lesson materials may be written or edited at a student console at any location while other consoles are being used by students. Thus, materials previously prepared elsewhere may be modified by a teacher in a participating institution (for example, a community college or a secondary or elementary school) in response to the particular needs of his own students.

We hasten to add, however, that the results attainable with any system of limited size cannot be considered definitive. We question whether a reasonable perspective can be achieved until much larger experiments can be performed. For a typical course, our data on Plato III have been limited to several hundreds of hours of student instruction. In the absence of a fully developed educational model or a widely accepted evaluative procedure, even for conventional educational methods, it is not possible from such relatively small samples to derive broad generalizations. Two conclusions seem justified: (i) that computer–based education is a plausible approach to improved individualized instruction in a very wide array of courses or subject–material areas; (ii) that the nature of educational testing and evaluation calls for, and will be radically and substantially affected by, the availability of large computer–based education systems; a valid measure of effectiveness calls for a much larger sampling of data and a longer period of comparison than has heretofore been available.

This expanded view of what is educationally possible is made feasible by several unique features of the Plato III system. First, a highly flexible software system has made it easy for educational innovators to use their intuitive notions to develop wholly new sets of teaching or testing strategies; the capacity of a large central computer makes possible a very wide variety of such teaching strategies, even in a single lesson. Second, the flexible software design has provided compatibility not only with CAI systems developed by other manufacturers and designers but also with the next generation of such machines; educational materials developed elsewhere can be readily incorporated. Third, although the software system has become increasingly sophisticated and permits an experienced author to develop very complex teaching strategies and lessons, it is not necessary for an author to become, or to be dependent on, a systems programmer. Teachers and authors can begin to prepare, edit, or modify lesson materials after a few hours of familiarization with the Tutor language, with no previous experience. Finally, it is possible for messages to be transmitted from a given student station to any other student station; thus, teachers or authors may act as participants in the system or monitor the progress of individual students.

What is the role of computer-based instruction in the context of the conventional classroom setting? Just as the printed page or the textbook has distinctly different uses at various educational levels, we postulate different uses for computer-based education at the various stages from preschool to graduate education and beyond. At the elementary grade level, in view of the important role of teacher and pupil interactions during most of the day, it seems reasonable to anticipate that computer-based instruction will occupy a relatively small fraction (perhaps 1 hour per day) of the pupil's time. Interestingly, our experience at this level indicates a unique cooperative relationship between teacher and pupil when the individual members of the class are at their Plato consoles. The teacher is called upon only when the pupil needs special help; when this occurs, help can be provided on the basis of a precise indication of the nature of the difficulty as exhibited by the particular sequence in which the problem was encountered. Applications at the grade school level include individual drill and practice in arithmetic and the development of reading skills, and they provide periodic rest intervals for the human teacher.

At the opposite end of the utilization scale we might envisage entire courses given at professional schools, at remotely located guidance centers, and in continuing adult education programs. The individualized approach to education that the Plato systems provide would be uniquely suited to the updating of professional skills or the development of new skills for adults at the nonprofessional level.

We visualize a particularly valuable role for computer-based education at the undergraduate level at universities, 4-year colleges, and community colleges. As to the degree of utilization, one may expect that the fraction of the instructional load that can be taken over by computer-based education would vary widely. In certain instances—such as introductory courses in computer science, mathematics, basic anatomy, or genetics—a Plato-type system might well assume the entire load. This would be particularly attractive for well-qualified students who wished to register in an advanced seminar without devoting an entire semester or two to a prerequisite survey course. Such students might well take the entire course and a proficiency examination within a week or two. Students who are less well qualified might by this means take remedial work at all levels to aid in their preparation for more advanced courses. In addition, there would be many courses in which the computer–based system and human teachers would share the load more or less equally. Faculty instructors could spend more of their available time in advanced or interdisciplinary seminars in which the discussion of human values or the development of new ideas would occupy the entire time available for interchange between teacher and students.

Computer–based education would make a unique contribution at the community college level, not only because of the shortage of adequately prepared instructors in many fields but also because of the value of such a system in orienting students who transfer to other colleges or universities after 1 or 2 years. They might, by this means, share, prior to transfer, an educational experience with students at the other institution.

Some Implications

The cumulative and overwhelming trend of our exploratory research results with the Plato III system suggests that this new medium will be educationally effective and enthusiastically received by students at all levels of age and experience. There is every evidence thus far that this enthusiasm is shared by teachers and authors as well. Supporting this appraisal is the corresponding experience of educators working in the

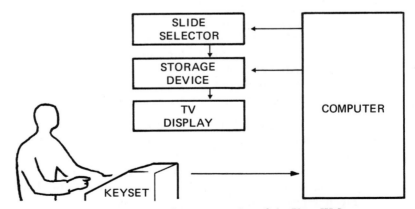

FIGURE 17-26 Schematic representation of the Plato III System.

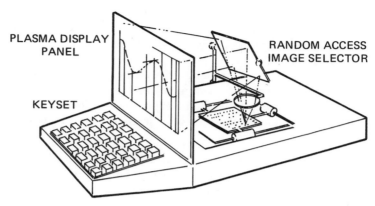

FIGURE 17-27   Schematic diagram of the Plato IV student console. See also Figure 17-25.

field of computer-assisted instruction at other institutions, for the most part with computer-based equipment far less flexible than Plato III. Most such educators are increasingly persuaded that this medium provides a powerful means of meeting heretofore unmet needs in the entire range of the educational process. If there has been informed skepticism or concern about the potentiality of computer-assisted instruction, it has largely been addressed to the issue of economics.

In this article we have discussed a number of advances in the economical implementation as well as the educational capability of computer-based education systems. We have described a system for which the projected target cost of 35 cents per student-contact hour is about one-fifth that of an updated Plato III system and about one-twentieth the cost of some systems in current use. This figure compares favorably with instructional costs at any grade level and would represent only a fraction (15 to 25 percent) of similar costs at the college level.

The availability of a large-scale, economically viable CBE system could provide a wide variety of educational opportunities which are currently either totally unavailable to only a small percentage of the population. Some of the possibilities that may well be realized through the application of computer-based education are the following.

1) Gradual abolishment of lock-step schedules and narrowly specified curricula in formal education. Students could proceed at a pace determined by their own capacity and motivation.

2) Provision of remedial instruction or tutorial assistance during regularly scheduled courses for students with insufficient preparation.

3) Reduction in the number of large lecture classes at the college level, in favor of small instructional groupings and seminars.

4) Special instruction at home for physically handicapped students.

5) Development of arithmetical or other skills, at the elementary level, away from the exposed and often competitive environment of the classroom.

6) Effective job training or retraining for any employee group especially affected by expanding technology.

7) Continuing education for professional personnel, permitting the updating of knowledge and skills in their own offices and on their own schedules.

Some of the available options would be economically justifiable even at the higher unit costs associated with Plato III. A much larger number of opportunities would be accessible with a fully implemented network of Plato IV system.

A single Plato IV system operating 10 hours a day could provide approximately 10 million student–contact hours annually at a cost of about $3 to $4 million (a total capital investment of approximately $12 million). This is equivalent to the total annual number of hours of instruction at a 4–year undergraduate institution with 24,000 students! Such an institution would typically have direct instructional expenses of well over $20 million annually and, in a university setting, a total budget several times greater. This comparison is obviously not meant to suggest that Plato could be substituted for such an institution. Rather, it is intended to indicate that a single Plato IV system could augment by 20 percent the instructional capacity of five such institutions on an annual budget of less than $1 million each.

Alternatively, this added capacity could release an equivalent portion of faculty time for developing new programs, for teaching in smaller group settings, or for providing extra help to individual students. The possibility of such enrichment of our national educational capability has provided added incentive for implementing and testing the Plato IV design and for learning how such a system would function in various educational settings.

The introduction of a major new technology into the educational process will undoubtedly raise questions on the part of some educators concerning the possible negative impact of an inanimate tutor on the very human processes of learning and teaching. Similar questions may well have been raised when the printing press and inexpensive paper were introduced into the educational process in the 15th century. It was not long, however, before the technology of the printed page became so identified with education that the library became the universal symbol of educational excellence. We believe that the resulting explosion of knowledge and of information has made the introduction of computer-based education all the more needed in a rapidly changing world.

The Plato program has called for a unique combination of educational and engineering talents. The program has benefited from cooperation among experts in many disciplines and among educators in universities, community colleges, high schools, and elementary schools. Finally, it has depended in a critical way on cooperation among educational institutions, industrial corporations, and government agencies. These features may be indicative of a new level of interinstitutional relationships which would accompany the incorporation of computer-based systems in the educational process.

CHAPTER 17 PROBLEMS

P17-1. Draw an algorithmic flow chart for a computer system which will monitor an alarm for a patient under treatment for a coronary disease (heart attack).

P17-2. What advantages and disadvantages does the use of a computer-based law enforcement system have for the law-abiding citizen?

P17-3. Design a block diagram, similar to Figure 17-6, for the computer guidance and control of a mass transit railway system such as the Bay Area Rapid Transit System (BART) or the New York City Subway System.

P17-4. Develop a block diagram, similar to Figure 17-11, for computer control of the heating plant at your college.

P17-5. Digital minicomputers are being developed for the control of an individual automobile's speed and fuel. Using some recent articles about automobile computers, design a block diagram of a computer control for the speed and fuel of an automobile.

P17-6. Write a small CAI program in FORTRAN or BASIC which will provide a drill and practice routine for addition of numbers from 1 to 1000 based on the flow chart of Figure 17-23.

CHAPTER 17 REFERENCES

1. J. F. Davis, "Computers in Medicine," *International Science and Technology*, December, 1966, pp. 40-48.

2. J. O. Beaumont, "On-line Patient Monitoring System," *Datamation*, May, 1969, pp. 50–55.

3. J. H. U. Brown and J. F. Dickson, III, "Instrumentation and the Delivery of Health Services," *Science*, Vol. 166, October 17, 1969, pp. 334–338.

4. D. H. Stewart, D. H. Erbach, H. Shubin, "A Computer System for Real-time Monitoring and Management of the Critically Ill," *Proceedings of the Fall Joint Computer Conference*, 1968, pp. 797–807.

5. W. Weksel, P. N. Sholtz, and J. G. Mayne, "The Automated Medical History," *Proceedings of the Fall Joint Computer Conference*, 1968, pp. 371–379.

6. H. A. Haessler, "Recent Developments in Automating the Medical History," *Computers and Automation*, June, 1969, pp. 24–27.

7. M. Davies, "Toward a Medical Data Bank for a Total Population," *Datamation*, November, 1969, pp. 257–262.

8. E. de Atley, "A Hospital Data System Designed by an M.D.," *Electronic Design*, April 26, 1970, pp. 30–32.

9. N. B. Reilly, "Computers in Medicine," *Datamation*, May, 1969, pp. 46–49.

10. R. S. Ledley, "Practical Problems in the Use of Computers in Medical Diagnosis," *Proceedings of the IEEE*, Vol. 57, No. 11, November, 1969, pp. 1900–1911.

11. J. A. Boyle, "Automated Diagnosis," *Computers and Automation*, June, 1969, pp. 20–22.

12. H. D. Covvey, "Measuring the Human Heart with a Realtime Computing System," *Data Processing Magazine*, May, 1970, pp. 27–32.

13. A. F. Bowyer, *et al*, "Computer Graphics Simulation of the Human Heart," *Proceedings of the Society of Photo-Optical Instrumentation Engineers*, August, 1968, pp. 390–395.

14. "Coordination of Medical Computing Records," *Datamation*, May, 1969, pg. 117.

15. H. V. Semling, Jr., "Getting that Man," *Modern Data*, October, 1970, pg. 30.

16. "California Computerizes Law Enforcement," *Data Processing Magazine*, August, 1970, pg. 14.

17. "Computers Speed Crime Detection," *Business Week*, May 23, 1970, pg. 90.

18. "Fingerprint Encoding and Classification," *IEEE Transactions on Man-Machine Systems*, September, 1970, pp. 156–160.

19. P. J. Scaletta, Jr., "The Legal Ramifications of the Computer Age," *Data Management*, October, 1970, pp. 12–15.

20. W. K. Stevens, "Computer on Board Apollo does the Flying," *New York Times*, March 4, 1969, pg. 14.

21. C. D. LaFond, "The 99.9% Effective Communications System," *Electronic Design*, April 26, 1969, pp. 28–32.

22. G. A. Vacca, P. L. Phipps and T. E. Burke, "Mission Influence on Advanced Computers," *Astronautics and Aeronautics*, April, 1967, pp. 36–40.
23. "They Make it Easier to Fly," *Data Processor*, Vol. XI, No. 5, November, 1968, pg. 24.
24. F. B. Nelson, "Railroad Data Systems Meeting," *Datamation*, December 15, 1970, pp. 47–49.
25. "Dial-a-Bus, or We Make it Easier to Ride," *Control Engineering*, April, 1969, pp. 49–50.
26. "Computer Guides New York City's Traffic," *Computer Decisions*, Vol. 2, No. 1, January, 1970, pg. 2.
27. "Of Process Computers and Manpower," *Control Engineering*, November, 1970, pg. 97.
28. L. T. Rader, "Future of Computers in Manufacturing," *Automation*, June, 1970, pp. 50–55.
29. D. B. Brewster and A. K. Bjerring, "Computer Control in Pulp and Paper 1961-1969," *Proceedings of the IEEE*, Vol. 58, No. 1, January, 1970, pp. 49–69.
30. "Largest Paper Machine on DDC," *Control Engineering*, August, 1969, pg. 63.
31; N. Cohn, *et al*, "On-line Computer Applications in the Electric Power Industry," *Proceedings of the IEEE*, Vol. 58, No. 1, January, 1970, pp. 78–87.
32. "How Rohr Learned to Move the Goods," *Business Week*, July 26, 1969, pp. 92–93.
33. "Computers Move into the Machine Shop," *Business Week*, September 19, 1970, pp. 88–90.
34. "The Spotlight is on Minicomputers," *Electronic Design*, August 16, 1970, pg. 6.
35. E. W. Peikert, "Interactive Graphics—a Now Dimension," *Computing Report*, Vol. V, No. 5, December, 1969, pp. 4–6.
36. "Univac Sees Big Role in Computer Graphics," *Modern Data*, January, 1969, pg. 10.
37. A. B. Kamman, "The Uses of Display Terminals for Business Applications," *Computers and Automation*, April, 1970, pp. 15–17.
38. E. G. Johnsen, *Teleoperator Controls,* NASA Publication S.P.-5070, Washington, D.C., December 1968, pp. 53–54.
39. C. Machover, "CRT Displays, Part 1," *Modern Data*, July, 1968, pp. 28–31.
40. I. E. Sutherland, "Computer Displays," *Science American*, June, 1970, pp. 57–63.
41. "Mapping with Graphics," *Computing Report*, January, 1969, pg. 2.
42. "Planning for Power," *Computing Report*, September, 1968, pp. 15–16.

43. I. Pressman, "Computer-Assisted Instruction: A Survey," *IEEE Transations on Education*, Vol. E–13, No. 3, September, 1970, pp. 134–141.

44. P. Suppes, "The Uses of Computers in Education," *Scientific American*, Vol. 215, September, 1966, pg. 207.

45. "Computers: Supermedia for Education?" *Computer Decisions*, April, 1970, pp. 23–25.

46. D. Jamison, P. Suppes, and C. Butler, "Estimated Costs of Computer-Assisted Instruction for Compensatory Education in Urban Areas," *Educational Technology*, September, 1970, pp. 49–57.

47. A. G. Oettinger, *Run, Computer, Run*, Harvard University Press, Cambridge, Mass., 1969.

48. D. Alpert and D. L. Bitzer, "Advances in Computer-based Education," *Science*, March 20, 1970, pp. 1582–1590.

49. P. Suppes and M. Morningstar, "Computer-Assisted Instruction," *Science*, October 17, 1969, pp. 343–350.

50. R. W. Gerard, *Computers and Education*, McGraw-Hill Book Company, New York, 1967.

51. *Computers in Higher Education*, Report of the President's Science Advisory Committee, The White House, Washington, D. C., US Government Printing Office, 1967.

52. R. C. Atkinson and H. A. Wilson, "Computer-Assisted Instruction, *Science*, October 4, 1968, pp. 73–77.

53. M. E. Abrams, *Medical Computing*, American Elsevier Publishing Co., New York, 1970.

54. K. R. Hammond, "Computer Graphics as an Aid to Learning," *Science*, Vol. 172, May 28, 1971, pp. 903–907.

55. E. E. David, Jr., "One Objective for Science Teaching," *Science*, Vol. 172, May 28, 1971, pg. 901.

56. G. T. Felkenes, "Can the Computer Save our Courts?" *Datamation*, June 15, 1971, pp. 36–39.

57. D. T. Borch, "A Computer Simulation Model of Train Operations in CTC Territory," *Proceedings of the Spring Joint Computer Conference*, Vol. 38, AFIPS Press, Montvale, N. J., 1971, pp. 93–102.

58. J. R. Schultz *et al*, "An Initial Operational Problem-Oriented Medical Record System—For Storage, Manipulation and Retrieval of Medical Data," *Proceedings of the Spring Joint Computer Conference*, Vol. 38, AFIPS Press, Montvale, N. J., 1971, pp. 234–264.

59. "Faster Results in a Clinical Laboratory," *Computing Report*, Vol. VII, No. 3, June, 1971, pp. 7–10.

60. W. K. Winters, "A Scheduling Algorithm for a Computer-Assisted Registration System," *Communications of the Association of Computing Machinery*, Vol. 14, No. 3. March, 1971, pp. 166–171.

18

CYBERNETICS, ARTIFICIAL INTELLIGENCE AND THE SOCIAL CONSEQUENCES OF COMPUTERS

18.1 CYBERNETICS AND ARTIFICIAL INTELLIGENCE

The collaboration of man and machine has been a fact of western civilization since the industrial revolution. One illustration of the man–machine relationship is shown in Figure 18-1. With the development of the digital computer after World War II, there has been increasing study of the relationships among computers, the human nervous system, and the human's thinking process. The origination of this field of study is usually attributed to Norbert Wiener (1894-1964). Wiener invented the word *cybernetics* to describe the field of control and communication in machines and in living organisms. The word cybernetics is taken from the Greek *kybernetes*, meaning "steersman." From the same Greek word, through the Latin corruption *gubernator*, came the term *governor*, which has been used for a long time to designate a control mechanism. *Governor* was also the title of a brilliant study written by James Clerk Maxwell. The basic concept which both Maxwell and the investigators of cybernetics describe, by the choice of this term, is that of a feedback mechanism, or self-control device, which is especially well represented by the steering engine of a ship and described below.[1]

Feedback is used to control various industrial systems as well as CAI systems and others. (The use of a computer to control an industrial process or to

FIGURE 18-1 Man and Machine. Charlie Chaplin in *Modern Times. The Museum of Modern Art/Film Stills Archive, New York City.*

provide a man–machine system was discussed in Chapter 17.) If we have a goal or objective in mind, we can use feedback to make sure we reach our goal, because feedback is self–correction. It keeps us on the path to our goal. When feedback is added to digital computer processes, we have all that we need to simulate almost any action of an organism in its environment.

The self–correcting process includes the desired output, which the computer compares with the actual output. The difference, or error, is used by the computer to cause the regulated process to respond in the desired way. The steering engine of a ship is one of the earliest forms of feedback mechanisms.

When you reach for the salt cellar, the distance and direction of that object from your hand is the desired–result input to your brain. By an astonishing series of observations and measurements, carried out unconsciously and at lightning speed, your brain measures the difference between where your hand is and where the salt cellar is, returning that information as feedback to your brain. Your brain keeps your arm and hand moving until that feedback is zero, at which point it switches from the MOVE HAND procedure to the CLUTCH and LIFT procedures.

A block diagram of a computer feedback system is shown in Figure 18-2. The system shown incorporates a *negative* feedback mechanism, since the *error* is the difference between the desired and the measurement of the actual. This type of feedback system may also be called a *trial and error* system. The basic hypothesis of cybernetics is that the chief mechanism of the human nervous system is one of negative feedback. Also, cybernetics includes the hypothesis that the negative feedback mechanism explains purposive and adaptive behavior.[2] Thus, one definition of cybernetics is:

> CYBERNETICS   The theory of control and communication which can be applied to machines and animals.

The analogy of the computer to the human brain has been used to study the process of thinking and the action of the human nervous system. John Van Neumann commented on the digital nature of human nerve functioning.[3]

> The most immediate observation regarding the nervous system is that its functioning is *prima facie* digital.

> The basic component of this system is the nerve cell, the neuron, and the normal function of a neuron is to generate and propagate a nerve impulse. This impulse is a rather complex process, which has a variety of aspects—electrical, chemical and mechanical. It seems, nevertheless, to be a reasonably uniquely defined process; *i.e.* nearly the same under all conditions; it represents an essentially reproducible, unitary response to a rather wide variety of stimuli.

The use of process–control computers has led to a discussion of whether computers may be said to possess intelligence and engage in the process of thinking. This subject of discussion and research is called the field of artificial intelligence (AI). Other fields within AI include problem solving using computers, computers that learn, and neurological information–processing models. One definition of artificial intelligence is:

> ARTIFICIAL INTELLIGENCE   The characteristic of a computer system capable of thinking, reasoning and learning (functions normally associated with human intelligence).

There have been several attempts to set up a learning program in a machine so that the machine modifies its own performance on the basis of experience gained. A computer has been programmed to learn from its successes and failures at the game of checkers to improve its own play so that eventually it

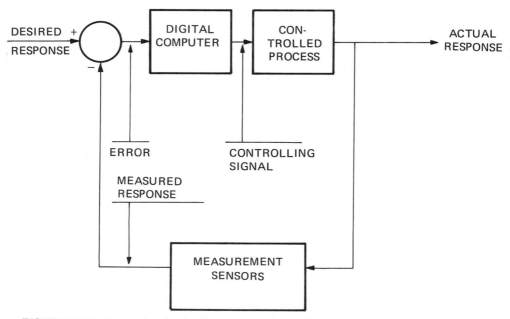

FIGURE 18-2 A negative feedback control process. The error is the difference between the desired and the measured actual response.

beats the person who programmed it. We may be many years yet from the time when computer–learning techniques have wide commercial application. Probably we shall need new technical developments to improve the computer's ability to recognize patterns. A considerable range of human behavior can be explained in terms of information processing theories. Within the theories of artificial intelligence, comparisons can be made between men and machines in that range of activities we describe as thinking. If there is objection to the use of the word *thinking*, then *ability to process information* or some similar term can be used. But it must be admitted that there exists some field of behavior in which men and machines coexist and in which they can be compared. It has been noted that one often regards an action as "intelligent" until he understands it. In explaining the action, it often becomes routine and mechanistic rather than intelligent.

One important goal of artificial intelligence research is to devise machines to perform various tasks normally requiring human intelligence. Proving mathematical theorems, translating languages, playing good games of chess, and learning to improve its own performance are a few of the kinds of things such a machine is expected to perform. Can a computer be programmed to be intelligent? In a recent article Marvin Minsky illustrates several computer programs which he contends meet the definition of artificial intelligence.[4]

The question of whether a computer can think or can possess an intelligence has occupied the thoughts of several philosophers. In order to determine whether a computer can think, a definition of thinking must be developed to be used as a criterion. Professor A. M. Turing, one of the first computer scientists, was challenged by the problem of developing a criterion of thinking which could be used with a computer to test its ability to exhibit an intelligence like that of a human. Professor Turing published an article in *Mind* in 1950 attacking the problem of machine intelligence. The first two pages of that article clearly outline the qualities which Turing suggests might be used to distinguish intelligence. They appear below.*

CAN A MACHINE THINK?

By A. M. Turing

1. The Imitation Game

I propose to consider the question, 'Can machines think?' This should begin with definitions of the meaning of the terms 'machine' and 'think.' The definitions might be framed so as to reflect so far as possible the normal use of the words, but this attitude is dangerous. If the meaning of the words 'machine' and 'think' are to be found by examining how they are commonly used it is difficult to escape the conclusion that the meaning and the answer to the question, 'Can machines think?'' is to be sought in a statistical survey such as a Gallup poll. But this is absurd. Instead of attempting such a definition I shall replace the question by another, which is closely related to it and is expressed in relatively unambiguous words.

The new form of the problem can be described in terms of a game which we call the 'imitation game.' It is played with three people, a man (A), a woman (B), and an interrogator (C) who may be of either sex. The interrogator stays in a room apart from the other two. The object of the game for the interrogator is to determine which of the other two is the man and which is the woman. He knows them by labels X and Y, and at the end of the game he says either 'X is A and Y is B' or 'X is B and Y is A.' The interrogator is allowed to put questions to A and B thus:

C: Will X please tell me the length of his or her hair?
Now suppose X is actually A, then A must answer. It is A's object in the game to try and cause C to make the wrong identification. His answer might therefore be:

*from *Mind*, 1950, pp. 2099–2123, with permission.

'My hair is shingled, and the longest strands are about nine inches long.'

In order that tones of voice may not help the interrogator the answers should be written, or better still, typewritten. The ideal arrangement is to have a teleprinter communicating between the two rooms. Alternatively the question and answers can be repeated by an intermediary. The object of the game for the third player (B) is to help the interrogator. The best strategy for her is probably to give truthful answers. She can add such things as 'I am the woman, don't listen to him!' to her answers, but it will avail nothing as the man can make similar remarks.

We now ask the question, 'What will happen when a machine takes the part of A in this game?' Will the interrogator decide wrongly as often when the game is played like this as he does when the game is played between a man and a woman? These questions replace our original, 'Can machines think?'

As well as asking, 'What is the answer to this new form of the question,' one may ask, 'Is this new question a worthy one to investigate?' This latter question we investigate without further ado, thereby cutting short an infinite regress.

The new problem has the advantage of drawing a fairly sharp line between the physical and the intellectual capacities of a man. No engineer or chemist claims to be able to produce a material which is indistinguishable from the human skin. It is possible that at some time this might be done, but even supposing this invention available we should feel there was little point in trying to make a 'thinking machine' more human by dressing it up in such artificial flesh. The form in which we have set the problem reflects this fact in the condition which prevents the interrogator from seeing or touching the other competitors, or hearing their voices. Some other advantages of the proposed criterion may be shown up by specimen questions and answers. Thus:

Q: Please write me a sonnet on the subject of the Forth Bridge.
A: Count me out on this one. I never could write poetry.
Q: Add 34957 to 70764.
A: (Pause about 30 seconds and then give as answer) 105621.
Q: Do you play chess?
A: Yes.
Q: I have K at my K1, and no other pieces. You have only K at K6 and R at R1. It is your move. What do you play?
A: (After a pause of 15 seconds) R-R8 mate.

The question and answer method seems to be suitable for introducing almost any one of the fields of human endeavour that we wish to include. We do not wish to penalise the machine for its inability to shine in beauty competitions, nor to penalise a man for losing in a race against an aeroplane. The conditions of our game make these disabilities irrelevant. The 'witnesses' can brag, if they consider it advisable, as much as they please about their charms, strength or heroism, but the interrogator cannot demand practical demonstrations.

The game may perhaps be criticised on the ground that the odds are weighted too heavily against the machine. If the man were to try and pretend to be the machine he would clearly make a very poor showing. He would be given away at once by slowness and inaccuracy in arithmetic. May not machines carry out something which ought to be described as thinking but which is very different from what a man does? This objection is a very strong one, but at least we can say that if, nevertheless, a machine can be constructed to play the imitation game satisfactorily, we need not be troubled by this objection.

It might be urged that when playing the 'imitation game' the best strategy for the machine may possibly be something other than imitation of the behaviour of a man. This may be, but I think it is unlikely that there is any great effect of this kind. In any case there is no intention to investigate here the theory of the game, and it will be assumed that the best strategy is to try to provide answers that would naturally be given by a man.

Considering the lucid criterion given above for determining whether a machine is thinking, we can progress to the question of whether modern computers are able to exhibit the qualities of intelligence.* In the following article the famous author Arthur Clarke reflects on several of the often–mentioned consequences of computers possessing an intelligence.[6]

ARE YOU THINKING MACHINES?**

By Arthur C. Clarke

"Are you serious? Do you really believe that a machine thinks?"—It will not be accepted universally, but there is one very straightforward answer to this question that originally was posed in the opening line of Ambrose Bierce's classic, *Moxon's Master*. It can be maintained that every man is perfectly familiar with at least one thinking machine, because he has a late-type model sitting on his shoulders. For if the brain is not a machine, what is it?

*An excellent discussion of the Turing test or game appears in reference 27.
**Copyright 1968 by Arthur Clarke. Reprinted by permission of the author and Scott Meredith Literary Agency, Inc., 580 Fifth Avenue, New York, New York 10036.

Critics of this viewpoint (who are probably now in the minority) may argue that the brain is in some fundamental way different from any nonliving device. But even if this is true, it does not follow that its functions cannot be duplicated, or even surpassed, by a nonorganic machine. Airplanes fly better than birds, though they are built of very different materials.

For obvious psychological reasons, there are people who never will accept the possibility of artificial intelligence, and would deny its existence even if they encountered it.

We no longer become upset because machines are stronger, or swifter, or more dexterous than human beings, though it took us several painful centuries to adapt to this state of affairs. How our outlook has changed is well shown by the ballad of John Henry; today, we should regard a man who challenged a steam hammer as merely crazy—not heroic. I doubt if contests between calculating prodigies and electronic computers will ever provide inspiration for future folk songs. But I'll be happy to donate the theme to Tom Lehrer.

It is, of course, the advent of the modern computer that has brought the subject of thinking machines out of the realm of fantasy into the forefront of industrial research. One could not have a plainer answer to the question that Bierce posed three-quarters of a century ago than this quotation from MacGowan and Ordway's recent book, *Intelligence in the Universe:* "It can be asserted without reservation that a general-purpose digital computer can think in every sense of the word. This is true no matter what definition of thinking is specified; the only requirement is that the definition of thinking be explicit."

The last phrase is, of course, the joker, for there must be almost as many definitions of thinking as there are thinkers; in the ultimate analysis, they all boil down to "Thinking is what *I* do."

One neat way of avoiding this problem is a famous test proposed by the British mathematician Alan Turing, even before the digital computer existed. Turing visualized a "conversation" over a teleprinter circuit with an unseen entity "X." If, after some hours of talk, one could not decide whether there was a man or a machine at the other end of the line, it would have to be admitted that X was thinking.

There have been several attempts to apply this test in restricted areas—say, in conversations about the weather. One clever program (DOCTOR) has even allowed a computer to conduct a psychiatric interview, with such success that 60% of the patients refused to believe afterward that they were not "conversing" with a flesh-and-blood psychiatrist.

For the Turing test to be applied properly, the conversation should not be restricted to a single narrow field but should be allowed to range over the whole arena of human affairs. ("Read any good books lately?" "Has your wife found out yet?," etc.) We certainly are nowhere near building a machine that can fool many of the people for much of the time; sooner or later, today's models give themselves away by irrelevant answers that show only too clearly that their replies are, indeed, "mechanical," and that they have no real understanding of what is going on.

As Oliver Selfridge of MIT has remarked sourly: "Even among those who believe that computers *can* think, there are few these days, except for a rabid fringe, who hold that they actually *are* thinking."

Though this may be the generally accepted position in the late 1960s, it is the "rabid fringe" who will be right in the long run. The current arguments about machine intelligence slowly will fade out, as it becomes less and less possible to draw a line between human and electronic achievements.

To quote another MIT scientist—Marvin Minsky, professor of electrical engineering: "As the machine improves . . . we shall begin to see all the phenomena associated with the terms 'consciousness,' 'intuition' and 'intelligence' itself. It is hard to say how close we are to this threshold, but once it is crossed, the world will not be the same. . . . It is unreasonable to think that machines could become *nearly* as intelligent as we are and then stop, or to suppose that we will always be able to compete with them in wit and wisdom. Whether or not we could retain some sort of control of the machines, assuming that we would want to, the nature of our activities and aspirations would be changed utterly by the presence on earth of intellectually superior beings."

Very few, if any, studies of the social impact of computers have yet faced up to the problems posed by this last sentence—particularly the ominous phrase "assuming that we would want to." This is understandable; the electronic revolution has been so swift that those involved in it have barely had time to think about the present, let alone the day after tomorrow. Moreover, the fact that today's computers are very obviously not "intellectually superior" has given a false sense of security—like that felt by the 1900 buggy-whip manufacturer every time he saw a broken-down automobile by the wayside. This comfortable illusion is fostered by the endless stories—part of the transient folklore of our age —about stupid computers that have had to be replaced by good old-fashioned human beings, after they had insisted on sending out bills for $1,000,000,000.95, or threatening legal action if outstanding debts of $0.00 were not settled immediately. The fact that the *gaffes* are almost invariably due to oversights by human programmers is seldom mentioned.

Though we have to live and work with (and against) today's mechanical morons, their deficiencies should not blind us to the future. In particular, it should be realized that as soon as the borders of electronic intelligence are passed, there will be a kind of chain reaction, because the machines will rapidly improve themselves. In a very few generations—*computer* generations, which by this time may last only a few months—there will be a mental explosion; the merely intelligent machine will swiftly give way to the *ultra*intelligent machine.

One scientist who has given much thought to this matter is Dr. Irving John Good of Trinity College, Oxford—author of papers with such challenging titles as "Can an Android Feel Pain?" (This term for artificial man, incidentally, is older than generally believed. I had always assumed that it was a product of the modern science-fiction magazines, and was astonished to come across "The Brazen Android" in an *Atlantic Monthly* for 1891.) Good has written: "If we build an ultraintelligent machine, we will be playing with fire. We have played with fire before, and it helped keep the other animals at bay." Well, yes—but when the ultraintelligent machine arrives, *we* may be the "other animals"; and look what's happened to them. It is Dr. Good's belief that the very survival of our civilization may depend upon the building of such instrumentalities; because if they are, indeed, more intelligent than we are, they can answer all our questions and solve all our problems. As he puts it in one elegiac phrase: "The first ultraintelligent machine is the last invention that man need make." *Need* is the operative word here. Perhaps 99% of all the men who have ever lived have known only need; they have been driven by necessity and have not been allowed the luxury of choice. In the future, this no longer will be true. It may be the greatest virtue of the ultraintelligent machine that it will force us to think about the purpose and meaning of human existence. It will compel us to make some far-reaching and perhaps painful decisions, just as thermonuclear weapons have made us face the realities of war and aggression, after 5,000 years of pious jabber.

These long-range philosophical implications of machine intelligence obviously far transcend today's more immediate worries about automation and unemployment. Somewhat ironically, these fears are both well grounded and premature.

Although automation already has been blamed for the loss of many jobs, the evidence indicates that so far, it has created many more opportunities for work than it has destroyed. (True, this is small consolation for the particular semiskilled worker who has just been replaced by a couple of milligrams of microelectronics.)

Fortune magazine, in a hopeful attempt at self-fulfilling prophecy, has declaimed: "The computer will doubtless go down in history not as the explosion that blew unemployment through the roof but as the technological triumph that enabled the U.S. economy to maintain the secular growth on which its greatness depends." I suspect that this statement may be true for some decades to come: but I also suspect that historians (human and otherwise) of the late 21st Century would regard that "doubtless" with wry amusement.

For the plain fact is that long before that date, the talents and capabilities of the average—and even the superior—man will be as unsalable in the market place as his muscle power. Only a few specialized and distinctly non-white-collar jobs will remain the prerogative of non-mechanical labor; one cannot easily picture a robot handy man, gardener, construction worker, fisherman. . . . These are professions that require mobility, dexterity, alertness and general adaptability—for no two tasks are precisely the same—but not a high degree of intelligence or data-processing power.

And even these relatively few occupations probably will be invaded by a rival and frequently superior labor force from the animal kingdom; for one of the long-range technological benefits of the space program (though no one has said much about it yet, for fear of upsetting the trade unions) will be a supply of educable anthropoids filling the gap between man and the great apes.

It must be clearly understood, therefore, that the main problem of the future—and a future that may be witnessed by many who are alive today—will be the construction of social systems based on the principle not of full employment but rather full *un*employment.

At the very least, we may expect a society that no longer regards work as meritorious or leisure as one of the Devil's more ingenious devices. Even today, there is not much left of the old puritan ethic; automation will drive the last nails into its coffin.

The need for such a change of outlook has been well put by the British science writer Nigel Calder in his remarkable book *The Environment Game:* "Work was an invention, which can be dated to the invention of agriculture . . . Now, with the beginning of automation, we have to anticipate a time when we must disinvent work and rid our minds of the inculcated habit."

The disinvention of work: What would Horatio Alger have thought of *that* concept? Calder's thesis (too complex to do more than summarize here) is that man is now coming to the end of his brief 10,000-year agricultural episode; for a period of a hundred times longer he was a hunter, and any hunter will indignantly deny that his occupation is "work." We now have to abandon agriculture for more efficient technologies; first, because it has patently failed to feed the exploding population; second, because it has compelled 500 generations of men to live abnormal—in fact, artificial—lives of repetitive, boring toil. Hence, many of our present psychological problems; to quote Calder again: "If men were intended to work the soil, they would have longer arms."

"If men were intended to . . ." is, of course, a game that everyone can play; my favorite competitor is the old lady who ojbected to space exploration because we should stay home and watch TV, "as God meant us to." Yet now, with the ultraintelligent machines lying just below our horizon, it is time that we played this game in earnest, while we still have some control over the rules. In a few more years, it will be much too late.

The optimum human population

Utopiamongering has been a popular and, on the whole, harmless occupation since the time of Plato; now it has become a matter of life and death—part of the politics of survival. Thinking machines, food production and population control must be considered as the three interlocking elements that will determine the shape of the future; they are not independent, for they all react on one another. This becomes obvious when we ask the question, which I have deliberately framed in as nonemotional a form as possible: "In an automated world run by machines, what is the optimum human population?"

Fred Hoyle once remarked to me that it was pointless for the world to hold more people than one could get to know in a single lifetime. Even if one were President of United Earth, that would set the figure somewhere between 10,000 and 100,000; with a very generous allowance for duplication, wastage, special talents, and so forth, there really seems no requirement for what has been called the Global Village of the future to hold more than 1,000,000 people, scattered over the face of the planet.

If the machines decide that more than 1,000,000 human beings constitutes an epidemic, they might order euthanasia for anyone with an I.Q. of less than 150, but I hope that such drastic measures will not be necessary.

Whether the population plateau levels off, a few centuries from today, at a million, a billion or a trillion human beings is of much less importance than the ways in which they will occupy their time. Since all the immemorial forms of "getting and spending" will have been rendered obsolete by the machines, it would appear that boredom will replace war and hunger as the greatest enemy of mankind.

One answer to this would be the uninhibited, hedonistic society of Huxley's *Brave New World;* there is nothing wrong with this, so long as it is not the *only answer.* (Huxley's unfortunate streak of asceticism prevented him from appreciating this point.) Certainly, much more time than at present will be devoted to sports, entertainment, the arts and everything embraced by the vague term "culture."

In some of these fields, the background presence of superior nonhuman mentalities would have a stultifying effect; but in others, the machines could act as pacemakers. Does anyone really imagine that when all the grand masters are electronic, no one will play chess? The humans will simply set up new categories and play better chess among themselves. All sports and games (unless they become ossified) have to undergo technological revolutions from time to time; recent examples are the introduction of fiberglass in pole vaulting, archery, and boating. Personally, I can hardly wait for the advent of Marvin Minsky's promised robot table-tennis player.

These matters are not trivial; games are a necessary substitute for our hunting impulses, and if the ultraintelligent machines give us new and better outlets, that is all to the good. We shall need every one of them to occupy us in the centuries ahead.

Thinking machines will certainly make possible new forms of art and far more elaborate developments of the old ones, by introducing the dimensions of time and probability. Even today, a painting or a piece of sculpture that stands still is regarded as slightly passé.

Even if art turns out to be a dead end, there still remains science—the eternal quest for knowledge, which has brought man to the point where he may create his own successor. It is unfortunate that, to most people, "science" now means incomprehensible mathematical complexities; that it could be the most exciting and *entertaining* of all occupations is something that they find impossible to believe. Yet the fact remains that, before they are ruined by what is laughingly called education, all normal children have an absorbing interest and curiosity about the universe that, if properly developed, could keep them happy for as many centuries as they may wish to live.

Education: that, ultimately, is the key to survival in the coming world of thinking machines. The truly educated man (I have been lucky enough to meet two in my lifetime) can never be bored. The problem that has to be tackled within the next 50 years is to bring the entire human race, without exception, up to the level of semiliteracy of the average college graduate. This represents what may be called the *minimum* survival level; only if we reach it will we have a sporting chance of seeing the year 2200.

Perhaps now we can glimpse one viable future for the human race, when it is no longer the dominant species on this planet. As he was in the beginning, man again will be a fairly rare animal, and probably a nomadic one. There will be a few towns in places of unusual beauty or historical interest, but even these may be temporary or seasonal. Most homes will be completely self-contained and mobile, so that they can move to any spot on earth within 24 hours.

The land areas of the planet will have largely reverted to wilderness; they will be much richer in life forms (and much more dangerous) than today. All adolescents will spend part of their youth in this vast biological reserve, so that they never suffer from that estrangement from nature that is one of the curses of our civilization.

And somewhere in the background—in the depths of the sea, orbiting beyond the ionosphere—will be the culture of the ultraintelligent machines, going its own unfathomable way. The societies of man and machine will interact continuously but lightly; there will be no areas of conflict, and few emergencies, except geological ones (and these could be fully foreseeable). In one sense, for which we may be thankful, history will have come to an end.

All the knowledge possessed by the machines will be available to mankind, though much of it may not be understandable. There is no reason why this should give our descendants an inferiority complex; a few steps into the New York Public Library can do *that* just as well, even today. Our prime goals no longer will be to discover but to understand and to enjoy.

For in the long run, our mechanical offspring will pass on to goals that will be wholly incomprehensible to us; it has been suggested that when this time comes, they will head on out into galactic space, looking for new frontiers, leaving us once more the masters (perhaps reluctant ones) of the solar system, and not at all happy at having to run our own affairs.

That is one possibility. Another has been summed up, once and for all, in the most famous short science-fiction story of our age. It was written by Fredric Brown almost 20 years ago, and it is high time that he received credit from journalists who endlessly rediscover and quote him.

Fred Brown's story—as you have probably guessed—is the one about the supercomputer that is asked, "Is there a God?" After making quite sure that its power supply is no longer under human control, it replies in a voice of thunder: "*Now* there is."

This story is more than a brilliant myth; it is an echo from the future. For in the long run, it may turn out that the theologians have made a slight but understandable error—which, among other things, makes totally irrelevant the recent debates about the death of God.

It may be that our role on this planet is not to worship God—but to create Him.

And then our work will be done. It will be time to play.

The discussion of whether computers are able to exhibit a quality not unlike human intelligence will undoubtedly continue for the next decade. Professor Marvin Minsky in a recent lecture charged that many teachers have been reactionary in telling students and the world about computers. He said that they have engaged in only describing the limitations of computers and stating that "the computer is nothing but. . . a lightning-fast calculator that does what you tell it. . .or a bunch of flip-flops," or whatever. Such oversimplifications, he noted, could be applied as well to people.[7]

In 1871, Samuel Butler completed the manuscript of the satire *Erewhon*.[8] Butler saw machines as gradually evolving into higher forms and assuming the capacities and functions of animals and man. As the machine was seen to assume some of the characteristics of man, the discussion grew in range and pitch. In one book, *God and Golem, Inc.*, Weiner states, "No, the future offers very little hope for those who expect that our new mechanical slaves will offer us a world in which we may rest from thinking. Help us they may, but at the cost of supreme demands upon our honesty and our intelligence. The world of the future will be an ever more demanding struggle against the limitations of our intelligence, not a comfortable hammock in which we can lie down to be waited upon by our robot slaves."[8]

Thus, the question of the intelligence of the computer leads to a challenge of a human intelligence and the question of conscience. In an elaborate treatment of the question of conscience, Mortimer Adler states that when it becomes possible to carry on a discussion with a computer behind a screen, not knowing whether it is a computer or a man—and after a long conversation, thinking the computer is a *man*, we shall then realize that man has nothing to distinguish him substantially from the machine.[9] And yet, who is to make the final decisions—the man or the computer? Perhaps one of the challenges lies in the

area of decision-making where it may be a temptation to let the computer decide and thus avoid the matter of conscience.

The use of intelligent computers integrated with machines that perform
tasks like a human worker has been foreseen by several authors. Karel Čapek, a
Czechoslovakian author, was apparently inspired by the legend of a mechanical
man or "golem" of medieval Prague. He called artificial workers *robots*, de-
riving the word from the Czech noun *robota*, meaning "work." The term won
international usage in Čapek's famous play *R.U.R.* [10] The play concerns a
revolt of Rossum's Universal Robots, their destruction of humanity, and their
own need to develop a conscience. Čapek expresses this conflict between the
machine as worker and the machine without conscience, as the following passage illustrates: [10]

> DOMAIN. So young Rossum said to himself: A man is some-
> thing that, for instance, feels happy, plays the fiddle, likes go-
> ing for walks, and, in fact, wants to do a whole lot of things
> that are really unnecessary. . . . But a working machine must
> not want to play the fiddle, must not feel happy, must not do
> a whole lot of other things. A petrol motor must not have
> tassels or ornaments, Miss Glory. And to manufacture artificial
> workers is the same thing as to manufacture motors. The
> process must be of the simplest, and the product of the best
> from a practical point of view. What sort of worker do you
> think is the best from a practical point of view?

> HELENA. The best? Perhaps the one who is most honest and
> hardworking.

> DOMAIN. No, the cheapest. The one whose needs are the small-
> est. Young Rossum invented a worker with the minimum
> amount of requirements. He had to simplify him. He rejected
> everything that did not contribute directly to the progress of
> work. In this way he rejected everything that makes man
> more expensive. In fact, he rejected man and made the Robot.
> My dear Miss Glory, the Robots are not people. Mechanically
> they are more perfect than we are, they have an enormously
> developed intelligence, but they have no soul.

In the field of the development of robots, there has been some advancement
during the past decade. At Disneyland, the technology has been used to create extremely life-like computer-controlled humanoids capable of moving their
arms and legs, grimacing, smiling, glowering, simulating fear, joy and a wide
range of other emotions. Built of clear plastic, the robots closely resemble
human forms. To this technology must be added the technologies being de-

veloped in the field of artificial intelligence. A group of research centers are working to develop machines that can act intelligently. Most tasks assigned to these experimental machines involve manipulating objects or moving around a laboratory environment autonomously, carrying out assigned tasks which are incompletely specified. Intelligent machines with a "hand" and "eye" are being controlled by a digital computer. One version of a hand/eye robot is shown in Figure 18-3. The hand is capable of grasping, transporting, and assembling blocks of various shapes with the area of vision of the television camera eye. A digital computer provides the intelligence required to select, recognize, pick up, and place the blocks in the proper sequence to build a structure.

A mobile automation vehicle has been constructed at Stanford Research Institute in California which exhibits some attributes of intelligence. The mobile vehicle is shown in Figure 18-4. The mobile robot requires the same abilities used by an explorer trained to sense, map, navigate, and use information obtained from an environment unknown to him. The laboratory environment consists of a large well-lighted room strewn with a number of solid objects such as cubes and ramps. In this laboratory setting, the mobile robot is required to sense and recognize objects and room boundaries; to make, store and update representations or models of the environment; to plan sensible routes through

FIGURE 18-3   An intelligent hand/eye robot built at Stanford University. A television eye, in the upper right of the photo, feeds data to a digital computer which instructs the hand to grasp and assemble building blocks into structures. *Courtesy of the Artificial Intelligence Project, Stanford University.*

FIGURE 18-4 The automation vehicle used by SRI in the application of artificial intelligence principles to the development of integrated robot systems. The vehicle is propelled by electric motors and carries a television camera and optical range finder in a movable "head." The vehicle responds to commands from a computer. The sensors are the bump detector, the T.V. camera and the range finder. *Courtesy of SRI.*

available passageways; to navigate in carrying out its route plans and to gather information; and, ultimately, to interact physically with the objects by simple manipulative means.[11,28,29]

The development of intelligent robots will lead to their application in at least two fields. First, the application of robots to control functions in the foundry, mining and other industrial activities will relieve men of very tedious, often dangerous and undesirable jobs. Second, there is a need for machines that can act independently--at least for part if not all of the time. Applications exist such as the exploration of the Moon, planets, space, the deep seas and Arctic wastes which are inhospitable to man and which require very expensive life-support systems for protracted stays by human explorers.

The movie *2001: A Space Odyssey* is based on a book by Arthur C. Clarke concerned with space travel, eventually to the planet Jupiter. The star of *2001: A Space Odyssey* is a computer, HAL, which operates the space ship, monitors the trip, and communicates with the astronauts in spoken words. HAL appears as a computer panel with a large T.V. eye. Several paragraphs from this book follow.[12]*

> The sixth member of the crew cared for none of these things, for it was not human. It was the highly advanced HAL 9000 computer, the brain and nervous system of the ship.
>
> Hal (for *H*euristically programmed *AL*gorithmic computer, no less) was a masterwork of the third computer breakthrough. These seemed to occur at intervals of twenty years, and the thought that another one was now imminent already worried a great many people.
>
> Hal had been trained for this mission as thoroughly as his human colleagues—and at many times their rate of input, for in addition to his intrinsic speed, he never slept. His prime task was to monitor the life-support systems, continually checking oxygen pressure, temperature, hull leakage, radiation, and all the other interlocking factors upon which the lives of the fragile human cargo depended. He could carry out the intricate navigational corrections, and execute the necessary flight maneuvers when it was time to change course.
>
> Whether Hal could actually think was a question which had been settled by the British mathematician Alan Turing back in the 1940s. Turing had pointed out that, if one could carry out a

*Reprinted by permission of The World Publishing Company from *2001: A Space Odyssey* by A. C. Clarke. A NAL Book. Copyright © 1968 by Polaris Productions, Inc. and Arthur C. Clarke.

prolonged conversation with a machine—whether by typewriter or microphone was immaterial—without being able to distinguish between its replies and those that a man might give, then the machine *was* thinking, by any sensible definition of the word. Hal could pass the Turing test with ease.

The computer HAL begins to malfunction and the astronauts attempt to ascertain the difficulty as shown in Figure 18-5. The climax of the controversial part of 2001 occurs when HAL, the computer which was programmed to simulate human emotions, kills one astronaut and shuts off the life support systems of the hibernating crew members. The one remaining crew member performs a lobotomy on the brain of the computer, rendering it helpless. The following paragraphs illustrate this portion of the film:

Here goes, thought Bowman. I never imagined I'd be an amateur brain surgeon—carrying out a lobotomy beyond the orbit of Jupiter.

FIGURE 18-5   Astronaut Poole, left and Mission Commander Bowman seek the privacy of a one-man space pod in an effort to confer without being overheard by computer HAL 9000. The computer is able to read their lip movements by means of the T.V. camera input. From *2001: A Space Odyssey* © 1968 by Metro-Goldwyn-Mayer Inc.

He released the locking bar on the section labeled COGNITIVE FEEDBACK and pulled out the first memory block. The marvelously complex three-dimensional network, which could lie comfortably in a man's hand yet contained millions of elements, floated away across the vault.

"Hey, Dave," said Hal. "What are you doing?"

I wonder if he can feel pain? Bowman thought briefly. Probably not, he told himself; there are no sense organs in the human cortex, after all. The human brain can be operated on without anesthetics.

He began to pull out, one by one, the little units on the panel marked EGO-REINFORCEMENT. Each block continued to sail onward as soon as it had left his hand, until it hit the wall and rebounded. Soon there were several of the units drifting slowly back and forth in the vault.

"Look here, Dave," said Hal. "I've got years of service experience built into me. An irreplaceable amount of effort has gone into making me what I am."

A dozen units had been pulled out, yet thanks to the multiple redundancy of its design—another feature, Bowman knew, that had been copied from the human brain—the computer was still holding its own.

He started on the AUTO-INTELLECTION panel.

"Dave," said Hal, "I don't understand why you're doing this to me. . . . I have the greatest enthusiasm for the mission. . . . You are destroying my mind. . . . Don't you understand? . . . I will become childish. . . . I will become nothing. . . ."

This is harder than I expected, thought Bowman. I am destroying the only conscious creature in my universe. But it has to be done, if I am ever to regain control of the ship.

"I am a HAL Nine Thousand computer Production Number 3. I became operational at the Hal Plant in Urbana, Illinois, on January 12, 1997. The quick brown fox jumps over the lazy dog. The rain in Spain is mainly in the plain. Dave—are you still there? Did you know that the square root of 10 is 3 point 162277660168379? Log 10 to the base e is zero point 434294481903252 . . . correction, that is log e to the base 10. . . . The reciprocal of three is zero point 333333333333333333-333 . . . two times two is . . . two times two is . . . approximately

4 point 101010101010101010. . . . I seem to be having some difficulty—my first instructor was Dr. Chandra. He taught me to sing a song, it goes like this, 'Daisy, Daisy, give me your answer, do. I'm half crazy all for the love of you.' "

Thus, the man is able to disconnect the intelligence of HAL, the computer, suggesting that man will always be able to control his robots, if, perhaps, at a great cost.

Richard Brautigan, the San Francisco poet, summarizes a view of the cybernetic machine and its anthropomorphic qualities in his poem which concludes this section.

All Watched Over by Machines of Loving Grace*

Richard Brautigan

I like to think (and
the sooner the better!)
of a cybernetic meadow
where mammals and computers
live together in mutually
programming harmony
like pure water
touching clear sky.

I like to think
    (right now, please!)
of a cybernetic forest
filled with pines and electronics
where deer stroll peacefully
past computers
as if they were flowers
with spinning blossoms.

I like to think
    (it has to be !)
of a cybernetic ecology
where we are free of our labors
and joined back to nature,
returned to our mammal
brothers and sisters,
and all watched over
by machines of loving grace.

*Copyright © 1969 by Richard Brautigan. Reprinted by permission of The Sterling Lord Agency.

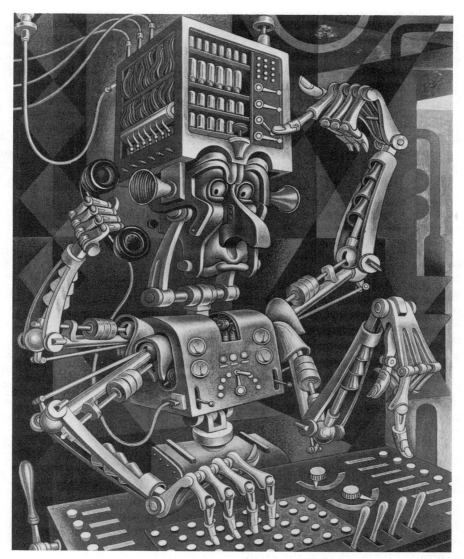

FIGURE 18-6 *Executive of the Future* by Boris Artzybasheff. *Reproduced by permission of the estate of Boris Artzybasheff.*

The development of robots, machines that perform tasks formerly reserved for man and which exhibit intelligence, has been the subject of many novels. In the novel *Player Piano* by Kurt Vonnegut, Jr. the robots have replaced the working man in Illium, New York, and the computers and engineers are in control. The hero of the novel revolts against the automation and robot age.[13] The conflict against the robots, a theme running from *Erewhon* and *R.U.R.* to *Player Piano* and *2001,* often assumes that the computer controlled robots exhibit human qualities such as intelligence and emotion. This attribution of human form or qualities to things such as machines or computers is called *anthropomorphism.* A visual image of the anthropomorphic computer is shown Figure 18-6 where the drawing is titled The Executive of the Future.

18.2 THE SOCIAL CONSEQUENCES OF COMPUTERS

The implications of the application of computers to a myriad of industrial, governmental, and educational problems is an issue of great significance. The consequences of the uses of computers to our social structure and to each person's value to himself and his society are currently being explored by many computer scientists and social scientists. Technological change almost always has accompanying social consequences. The automobile has led to changes in family relationships, work location and our cities. In a similar fashion, computers may have led to more effective and efficient government, but also to a loss of privacy. The unforeseen effects on society and the individual are often positive as well as negative. It is the purpose of this section to expose some of the projected consequences of the use of computers and to advocate the application of computers to problems where the social consequences, as well as the short-term solution or profit, are accounted for.

If one were asked to try to capture the essential spirit of the last half of the 20th Century in a single picture, he might well consider as his background a vast chessboard that stretches to the far corners of the world. On one side of the board, he might place a forlorn, hopelessly romantic Don Quixote, the Knight of an age long gone, mounted on a mechanical Rocinante, as shown in Figure 18-7. Facing this symbolic relic of the past—whose dispirited lance already droops in foregone defeat—at the other side of the board, there is an enigmatic little black box, the computer. In its calm inscrutability it seems to have crept out of the world of the future. And perhaps it has. One feels instinctively that the confrontation between these two is reflected on the thousand squares and diagonals of which our world is made; and that whatever move the knight makes now, the little black box will make the last one.[14]

Computers have already had an impact on man's society and his personality.[15] A striking effect is the extent to which computers have excited the popular imagination. There is widespread belief and appreciation that the computer is beneficial now and will continue to be so in the future. The computer,

FIGURE 18-7 Man and his life with a little black box—the computer. *Courtesy of Kaiser Aluminum News.*

however, is often seen as an autonomous entity without control by humans. Also, people tend to generalize from the computer's well-known computational accuracy to the idea that the computer is infallible in solving the larger problems for which it may be used. The emergence of the computer has become, for many, a challenge to man's self-concept.[14] Some authors see man as threatened by the computer and his applications of the computer and thus out of harmony with himself because he is discontinuous with the machines that he has built. It is fashionable to describe such a state as "alienation." This discontinuity may be a result of a desire of some people to have a problem solved in an incomprehensible fashion by a computer rather than to have to adjust their own value systems and understanding in order for themselves to do something concrete and rational about the problem. In a related matter, H. R. J. Grosch stated,[16] "If the average American has to choose between privacy and a convenient way to charge a purchase, he'll pick convenience."

The computer provides a challenge to activities formerly reserved for humans. For example, as computers are able to reproduce a human activity, such as proving geometry theorems, then people tend to state that the act does not define human intelligence. As computers become adept at playing chess, perhaps man will decide that playing chess is not what being human is about. However, the fear is that just as John Henry lost his identity when his physical strength was matched by that of the steam drill, perhaps people whose forte is the kind of tedious rote work done better by computers will lose theirs.[17]

The technological activity in the field of computer development and computer applications is quite rapid and causes social changes. For over twenty years, growth and change in the computer field have been caused by technological advances that made equipment better and cheaper each year. As equipment becomes more diverse, efficient and cheap, more and more applications will become practical. The spread of applications of computers leads to an increased anxiety over the social problems associated with the use of computers. Some comparisons of technological increases in different fields of endeavor are given in Table 18-1. Note that the speed of computation has increased by a

TABLE 18-1

Comparison of Technological Increase

Area	Ancient Times	1870	1950	1970	Factor of Increase in		
					2000 years	100 years	20 years
Transportation	40 miles/day	200	600	3,500	90	17.5	6
Average Formal Education (U.S.)		1 yr.	10	12	–	12	1.2
Life Expectancy (U.S.)	22 yrs.	45	66	67	3.05	1.48	1.07
Energy per Person	1/2 unit	1.6	10	15	30	9	1.5
Computation Speed	.005	.005	40	10,000,000	2×10^9	2×10^9	250,000

Energy Unit = 1 horsepower for 8-hour day.

Computation Speed Unit = multiplications per second for 8–digit numbers.

factor of 250,000 over the past twenty years. The corresponding increase in speed of travel is only six! This rapid change in computational speed and the resulting social change and adjustment that accompanies it have caused some concern among authors and social scientists. Many have asked if there is a possibility of the formation of a data elite, manipulating society by their manipulation of data on American individuals. The blurring of the private and the public data creates anxiety concerning data banks on individuals and their uses. The origins of depersonalization lie in the high degree of standardization needed to use computers efficiently. As computer activities spread, individuals tend to feel molded to fit the requirements of the computer system. During several campus riots in the late 1960's, major attacks were directed toward computer centers.

A common case of depersonalized treatment by a computer involves dealing with a store that uses a computer for its billing operation. The problems usually arise from the fact that a system's design is made more complicated by provisions for dealing with exceptional circumstances, so they are ignored. This difficulty is compounded if an organization seeks to get by with minimum training of the clerical staff that examines the customer "inputs" of payments and complaints. The usual result is that the customer writes letter after letter into a non-answering void, his resentment growing at each cycle. Meanwhile, the computer is sending him even-nastier demands and recriminations.[18]

Also in the fields of business, we may be confronted with difficulties as our banking system, our mutual funds, our exchanges and other institutions make increasing use of computer records. We have had cases already in which records were destroyed by mistake or were lost. The size of the largest organization in a given field tends to approach the maximum that is manageable. The use of the computer increases the manageable size of a company but also increases the vulnerability of that company if something happens to the computer and the records stored in it.[18] Furthermore, business management may become vulnerable in the corporate decision-making. As a firm relies on data banks and management science, there is a chance that filtering of information by staff personnel will occur before materials are presented to senior management. As the decision-making apparatus becomes more complex, it will be harder for managers to exercise effective personal control.

Some anticipated consequences of technological and scientific developments associated with the field of computers are given in Table 18-2.[19] Several consequences are outlined for each potential development, and the judgment of which are positive and which are negative consequences is left to the reader.

Norbert Wiener wrote his book *Cybernetics* in 1946 and published an article of the same title in *Scientific American* in 1948.[1] This article and book aroused much discussion among computer scientists leading to a further article by Weiner concerning the moral and technical consequences of computer

TABLE 18-2

Some Anticipated Consequences of Technological and Scientific Developments*

Development	Potential Consequence
Laboratory operation of automated language translators capable of coping with idiomatic syntactical complexities.	Increased technical and scientific communications including, perhaps, reorientation of scientific journals.
	Further ethnic separation between countries speaking different languages since there would be fewer linguists and less intimate understanding of vocabulary nuances.
	Decrease in the number of extant languages.
Establishment of a central data storage facility (or several regional or disciplinary facilities) with wide public access (perhaps in the home) for general or specialized information retrieval primarily in the areas of library, medical and legal data.	Individual citizens becoming proficient in law and medicine, through easy availability of the relevant data in the home.
	The rise of new methods of computer-aided crime.
	Information overload; the problem will be to select from the available plethora of information that which is important and relevant to the individual.
Availability of complex robots which are programmable and self-adaptive and capable of performing most household chores, such as machines which independently prepare meals and clean or otherwise dispose of dishes.	Reorientation of certain industries (*e.g.*, the electronic industry moving into the home appliance industry *diversifying* into electronics service-mechanisms, etc.
	Development of a counter-trend which places high value in "personally" done housework and menial tasks (*e.g.*, home-cooked vs. robot prepared meals).
Availability of a computer which comprehends standard IQ tests and scores above 150 (where "comprehend" is to be interpreted behavioristically as the ability to respond to questions printed in English and possibly accompanied by (diagrams).	Self replicating computers and more advanced computers designed by other computers.
	The raising of philosophical and speculative questions regarding human significance.
	Development of meaningful, or at least amusing, hardly ever boring, pastimes.
Demonstration of man-machine symbiosis enabling man to extend his intelligence by direct electromechanical interaction between his brain and a computing machine.	Elimination of factual education, since this data could be stored.
	The creation of robots which would be used to decrease human risk, as in war.

*From *A Forecast of Technological Trends, Their Societal Consequences and Science Policy Strategies of the Future*, Theodore Gordon, *Proceedings of the Hearings of the Committee on Science and Astronautics*, U.S. House of Representatives, Washington, D.C., 1970, pp. 429–470.

automation.[20] This article was responded to by another computer scientist, Arthur Samuel, then of IBM Corporation, and now at Stanford University. The response was a strong refutation of Wiener's concerns and thesis.[21] While these articles appeared in 1960, over ten years ago, they remain a definitive and unexcelled pair of articles concerned with the social consequences of computer automation, and for that reason are included here.

SOME MORAL AND TECHNICAL
CONSEQUENCES OF AUTOMATION*

As machines learn they may develop unforeseen
strategies at rates that baffle their programmers.

Norbert Wiener

Some 13 years ago, a book of mine was published by the name of *Cybernetics*. In it I discussed the problems of control and communication in the living organism and the machine. I made a considerable number of predictions about the development of controlled machines and about the corresponding techniques of automatization, which I foresaw as having important consequences affecting the society of the future. Now, 13 years later, it seems appropriate to take stock of the present position with respect to both cybernetic technique and the social consequences of this technique.

Before commencing on the detail of these matters, I should like to mention a certain attitude of the man in the street toward cybernetics and automatization. This attitude needs a critical discussion, and in my opinion it should be rejected in its entirety. This is the assumption that machines cannot possess any degree of originality. This frequently takes the form of a statement that nothing can come out of the machine which has not been put into it. This is often interpreted as asserting that a machine which man has made must remain continually subject to man, so that its operation is at any time open to human interference and to a change in policy. On the basis of such an attitude, many people have pooh-poohed the dangers of machine techniques, and they have flatly contradicted the early predictions of Samuel Butler that the machine might take over the control of mankind.

It is true that in the time of Samuel Butler the available machines were far less hazardous than machines are today, for they involved only power, not a certain degree of thinking and communication. However, the machine techniques of the present day have invaded the latter

*N. Wiener, "Some Moral and Technical Consequences of Automation," *Science*, Vol. 131, May 6, 1960, pp. 1355-1358, Copyright 1960 by the American Association for the Advancement of Science.

fields as well, so that the actual machine of today is very different from the image that Butler held, and we cannot transfer to these new devices the assumptions which seemed axiomatic a generation ago. I find myself facing a public which has formed its attitude toward the machine on the basis of an imperfect understanding of the structure and mode of operation of modern machines.

It is my thesis that machines can and do transcend some of the limitations of their designers, and that in doing so they may be both effective and dangerous. It may well be that in principle we cannot make any machine the elements of whose behavior we cannot comprehend sooner or later. This does not mean in any way that we shall be able to comprehend these elements in substantially less time than the time required for operation of the machine, or even within any given number of years or generations.

As is now generally admitted, over a limited range of operation, machines act far more rapidly than human beings and are far more precise in performing the details of their operations. This being the case, even when machines do not in any way transcend man's intelligence, they very well may, and often do, transcend man in the performance of tasks. An intelligent understanding of their mode of performance may be delayed until long after the task which they have been set has been completed.

This means that though machines are theoretically subject to human criticism, such criticism may be ineffective until long after it is relevant. To be effective in warding off disastrous consequences, our understanding of our man–made machines should in general develop *pari passu* with the performance of the machine. By the very slowness of our human actions, our effective control of our machines may be nullified. By the time we are able to react to information conveyed by our senses and stop the car we are driving, it may already have run head on into a wall.

Game-Playing

I shall come back to this point later in this article. For the present, let me discuss the technique of machines for a very specific purpose: that of playing games. In this matter I shall deal more particularly with the game of checkers, for which the International Business Machines Corporation has developed very effective game–playing machines.

Let me say once for all that we are not concerned here with the machines which operate on a perfect closed theory of the game they play.

The game theory of von Neumann and Morgenstern may be suggestive as to the operation of actual game-playing machines, but it does not actually describe them.

In a game as complicated as checkers, if each player tries to choose his play in view of the best move his opponent can make, against the best response he can give, against the best response his opponent can give, and so on, he will have taken upon himself an impossible task. Not only is this humanly impossible but there is actually no reason to suppose that it is the best policy against the opponent by whom he is faced, whose limitations are equal to his own.

The von Neumann theory of games bears no very close relation to the theory by which game-playing machines operate. The latter corresponds much more closely to the methods of play used by expert but limited human chess players against other chess players. Such players depend on certain strategic evaluations, which are in essence not complete. While the von Neumann type of play is valid for games like ticktacktoe, with a complete theory, the very interest of chess and checkers lies in the fact that they do not possess a complete theory. Neither do war, nor business competition, nor any of the other forms of competitive activity in which we are really interested.

In a game like ticktacktoe, with a small number of moves, where each player is in a position to contemplate all possibilities and to establish a defense against the best possible moves of the other player, a complete theory of the von Neumann type is valid. In such a case, the game must inevitably end in a win for the first player, a win for the second player, or a draw.

I question strongly whether this concept of the perfect game is a completely realistic one in the cases of actual, nontrivial games. Great generals like Napoleon and great admirals like Nelson have proceeded in a different manner. They have been aware not only of the limitations of their opponents in such matters as materiel and personnel but equally of their limitations in experience and in military know-how. It was by a realistic appraisal of the relative inexperience in naval operations of the continental powers as compared with the highly developed tactical and strategic competence of the British fleet that Nelson was able to display the boldness which pushed the continental forces off the seas. This he could not have done had he engaged in the long, relatively indecisive, and possibly losing conflict to which his assumption of the best possible strategy on the part of his enemy would have doomed him.

In assessing not merely the materiel and personnel of his enemies but also the degree of judgment and the amount of skill in tactics and strategy to be expected of them, Nelson acted on the basis of their record in previous combats. Similarly, an important factor in Napoleon's conduct of his combat with the Austrians in Italy was his knowledge of the rigidity and mental limitations of Würmser.

This element of experience should receive adequate recognition in any realistic theory of games. It is quite legitimate for a chess player to play, not against an ideal, nonexisting, perfect antagonist, but rather against one whose habits he has been able to determine from the record. Thus, in the theory of games, at least two different intellectual efforts must be made. One is the short-term effort of playing with a determined policy for the individual game. The other is the examination of a record of many games. This record has been set by the player himself, by his opponent, or even by players with whom he has not personally played. In terms of this record, he determines the relative advantages of different policies as proved over the past.

There is even a third stage of judgment required in a chess game. This is expressed at least in part by the length of the significant past. The development of theory in chess decreases the importance of games played at a different stage of the art. On the other hand, an astute chess theoretician may estimate in advance that a certain policy currently in fashion has become of little value, and that it may be best to return to earlier modes of play to anticipate the change in policy of the people whom he is likely to find as his opponents.

Thus, in determining policy in chess there are several different levels of consideration which correspond in a certain way to the different logical types of Bertrand Russell. There is the level of tactics, the level of strategy, the level of the general considerations which should have been weighed in determining this strategy, the level in which the length of the relevant past—the past within which these considerations may be valid—is taken into account, and so on. Each new level demands a study of a much larger past than the previous one.

I have compared these levels with the logical types of Russell concerning classes, classes of classes, classes of classes of classes, and so on. It may be noted that Russell does not consider statements involving all types as significant. He brings out the futility of such questions as that concerning the barber who shaves all persons, and only those persons, who do not shave themselves. Does he shave himself? On one type he does, on the next type he does not, and so on, indefinitely. All such questions involving an infinity of types may lead to unsolvable paradoxes. Similarly, the search for the best policy under all levels of sophistication is a futile one and must lead to nothing but confusion.

These considerations arise in the determination of policy by machines as well as in the determination of policy by persons. These are the questions which arise in the programming of programming. The lowest type of game–playing machine plays in terms of a certain rigid evaluation of plays. Quantities such as the value of pieces gained or lost, the command of the pieces, their mobility, and so on, can be given numerical weights on a certain empirical basis, and a weighting may be given on this basis to each next play conforming to the rules of the game. The play with the greatest weight may be chosen. Under these circumstances, the play of the machine will seem to its antagonist—who cannot help but evaluate the chess personality of the machine—a rigid one.

Learning Machines

The next step is for the machine to take into consideration not merely the moves as they occurred in the individual game but the record of games previously played. On this basis, the machine may stop from time to time, not to play but to consider what (linear or nonlinear) weighting of the factors which it has been given to consider would correspond best to won games as opposed to lost (or drawn) games. On this basis, it continues to play with a new weighting. Such a machine would seem to its human opponent to have a far less rigid game personality, and tricks which would defeat it at an earlier stage may now fail to deceive it.

The present level of these learning machines is that they play a fair amateur game at chess but that in checkers they can show a marked superiority to the player who has programmed them after from 10 to 20 playing hours of working and indoctrination. They thus most definitely escape from the completely effective control of the man who has made them. Rigid as the repertory of factors may be which they are in a position to take into consideration, they do unquestionably—and so say those who have played with them—show originality, not merely in their tactics, which may be quite unforeseen, but even in the detailed weighting of their strategy.

As I have said, checker–playing machines which learn have developed to the point at which they can defeat the programmer. However, they appear still to have one weakness. This lies in the end game. Here the machines are somewhat clumsy in determining the best way to give the *coup de grâce*. This is due to the fact that the existing machines have for the most part adopted a program in which the identical strategy is carried out at each stage of the game. In view of the similarity of values of pieces in checkers, this is quite natural for a large part of the play but ceases to be perfectly relevant when the board is relatively empty and the main problem is that of moving into position rather than that of direct attack. Within the frame of the methods I have described it is quite possible to have a second exploration to determine what the policy should be after the number of pieces of the opponent is so reduced that these new considerations become paramount.

Chess-playing machines have not, so far, been brought to the degree of perfection of checker-playing machines, although, as I have said, they can most certainly play a respectable amateur game. Probably the reason for this is similar to the reason for their relative efficiency in the end game of checkers. In chess, not only is the end game quite different in its proper strategy from the mid-game but the opening game is also. The difference between checkers and chess in this respect is that the initial play of the pieces in checkers is not very different in character from the play which arises in the mid-game, while in chess, pieces at the beginning have an arrangement of exceptionally low mobility, so that the problem of deploying them from this position is particularly difficult. This is the reason why opening play and development form a special branch of chess theory.

There are various ways in which the machine can take cognizance of these well-known facts and explore a separate waiting strategy for the opening. This does not mean that the type of game theory which I have here discussed is not applicable to chess but merely that it requires much more consideration before we can make a machine that can play master chess. Some of my friends who are engaged in these problems believe that this goal will be achieved in from 10 to 25 years. Not being a chess expert, I do not venture to make any such predictions on my own initiative.

It is quite in the cards that learning machines will be used to program the pushing of the button in a new pushbutton war. Here we are considering a field in which automata of a non-learning character are probably already in use. It is quite out of the question to program these machines on the basis of an actual experience in real war. For one thing, a sufficient experience to give an adequate programming would probably see humanity already wiped out.

Moreover, the techniques of pushbutton war are bound to change so much that by the time an adequate experience could have been accumulated, the basis of the beginning would have radically changed. Therefore, the programming of such a learning machine would have to be based on some sort of war game, just as commanders and staff officials now learn an important part of the art of strategy in a similar manner. Here, however, if the rules for victory in a war game do not correspond to what we actually wish for our country, it is more than likely that such a machine may produce a policy which would win a nominal victory on points at the cost of every interest we have at heart, even that of national survival.

Man and Slave

The problem, and it is a moral problem, with which we are here faced is very close to one of the great problems of slavery. Let us grant that slavery is bad because it is cruel. It is, however, self–contradictory, and for a reason which is quite different. We wish a slave to be intelligent, to be able to assist us in the carrying out of our tasks. However, we also wish him to be subservient. Complete subservience and complete intelligence do not go together. How often in ancient times the clever Greek philosopher slave of a less intelligent Roman slaveholder must have dominated the actions of his master rather than obeyed his wishes! Similarly, if the machines become more and more efficient and operate at a higher and higher psychological level, the catastrophe foreseen by Butler of the dominance of the machine comes nearer and nearer.

The human brain is a far more efficient control apparatus than is the intelligent machine when we come to the higher areas of logic. It is a self–organizing system which depends on its capacity to modify itself into a new machine rather than on ironclad accuracy and speed in problem–solving. We have already made very successful machines of the lowest logical type, with a rigid policy. We are beginning to make machines of the second logical type, where the policy itself improves with learning. In the construction of operative machines, there is no specific foreseeable limit with respect to logical type, nor is it safe to make a pronouncement about the exact level at which the brain is superior to the machine. Yet for a long time at least there will always be some level at which the brain is better than the constructed machine, even though this level may shift upwards and upwards.

It may be seen that the result of a programming technique of automatization is to remove from the mind of the designer and operator an effective understanding of many of the stages by which the machine comes to its conclusions and of what the real tactical intentions of many of its operations may be. This is highly relevant to the problem of our being able to foresee undesired consequences outside the frame of the strategy of the game while the machine is still in action and while intervention on our part may prevent the occurrence of these consequences.

Here it is necessary to realize that human action is a feedback action. To avoid a disastrous consequence, it is not enough that some action on our part should be sufficient to change the course of the machine, because it is quite possible that we lack information on which to base consideration of such an action.

In neurophysiological language, ataxia can be quite as much of a deprivation as paralysis. A patient with locomotor ataxia may not suffer from any defect of his muscles or motor nerves, but if his muscles and tendons and organs do not tell him exactly what position he is in, and whether the tensions to which his organs are subjected will or will not lead to his falling, he will be unable to stand up. Similarly, when a machine constructed by us is capable of operating on its incoming data at a pace which we cannot keep, we may not know, until too late, when to turn it off. We all know the fable of the sorcerer's apprentice, in which the boy makes the broom carry water in his master's absence, so that it is on the point of drowning him when his master reappears. If the boy had had to seek a charm to stop the mischief in the *grimoires* of his master's library, he might have been drowned before he had discovered the relevant incantation. Similarly, if a bottle factory is programmed on the basis of maximum productivity, the owner may be made bankrupt by the enormous inventory of unsalable bottles manufactured before he learns he should have stopped production six months earlier.

The "Sorcerer's Apprentice" is only one of many tales based on the assumption that the agencies of magic are literal-minded. There is the story of the genie and the fisherman in the *Arabian Nights*, in which the fisherman breaks the seal of Solomon which has imprisoned the genie and finds the genie vowed to his own destruction; there is the tale of the "Monkey's Paw," by W. W. Jacobs, in which the sergeant major brings back from India a talisman which has the power to grant each of three people three wishes. Of the first recipient of this talisman we are told only that his third wish is for death. The sergeant major, the second person whose wishes are granted, finds his experiences too terrible to relate. His friend, who receives the talisman, wishes first for £200. Shortly thereafter, an official of the factory in which his son works comes to tell him that his son has been killed in the machinery and that, without any admission of responsibility, the company is sending him as consolation the sum of £200. His next wish is that his son should come come back, and the ghost knocks at the door. His third wish is that the ghost should go away.

Disastrous results are to be expected not merely in the world of fairy tales but in the real world wherever two agencies essentially foreign to each other are coupled in the attempt to achieve a common purpose. If the communication between these two agencies as to the nature of this purpose is incomplete, it must only be expected that the results of this cooperation will be unsatisfactory. If we use, to achieve our purposes, a mechanical agency with whose operation we cannot efficiently interfere once we have started it, because the action is so fast and irrevocable that we have not the data to intervene before the action is complete, then we had better be quite sure that the purpose put into the machine is the purpose which we really desire and not merely a colorful imitation of it.

Time Scales

Up to this point I have been considering the quasi-moral problems caused by the simultaneous action of the machine and the human being in a joint enterprise. We have seen that one of the chief causes of the danger of disastrous consequences in the use of the learning machine is that man and machine operate on two distinct time scales, so that the machine is much faster than man and the two do not gear together without serious difficulties. Problems of the same sort arise whenever two control operators on very different time scales act together, irrespective of which system is the faster and which system is the slower. This leaves us the much more directly moral question: What are the moral problems when man as an individual operates in connection with the controlled process of a much slower time scale, such as a portion of political history or—our main subject of inquiry—the development of science?

Let it be noted that the development of science is a control and communication process for the long-term understanding and control of matter. In this process 50 years are as a day in the life of the individual. For this reason, the individual scientist must work as a part of a process whose time scale is so long that he himself can only contemplate a very limited sector of it. Here, too, communication between the two parts of a double machine is difficult and limited. Even when the individual believes that science contributes to the human ends which he has at heart, his belief needs a continual scanning and re-evaluation which is only partly possible. For the individual scientist, even the partial appraisal of this liaison between the man and the process requires an imaginative forward glance at history which is difficult, exacting, and only limitedly achievable. And if we adhere simply to the creed of the scientist, that an incomplete knowledge of the world and of ourselves is better than no knowledge, we can still by no means always justify the naive assumption that the faster we rush ahead to employ the new powers for action which are opened up to us, the better it will be. We must always exert the full strength of our imagination to examine where the full use of our new modalities may lead us.

SOME MORAL AND TECHNICAL CONSEQUENCES
OF AUTOMATION—A REFUTATION*

Arthur L. Samuel

Abstract. The machine is not a threat to mankind, as some people think. The machine does not possess a will, and its so–called "conclusions" are only the logical consequences of its input, as revealed by the mechanistic functioning of an inanimate assemblage of mechanical and electrical parts.

In an article entitled "Some moral and technical consequences of automation," Norbert Wiener has stated some conclusions with which I disagree. Wiener seems to believe that machines *can* possess originality and that they *are* a threat to mankind. In ascribing a contrary opinion to the man in the street—to wit, "that nothing can come out of the machine which has not been put into it"—he overlooks or ignores the fact that there is a long history of the acceptance of this more reassuring view by scientific workers in the field, from the time of Charles Babbage to the present. Apparently Wiener shares some of the lack of understanding which he ascribes to the public, at least to the extent that he reads implications into some of the recent work which the workers themselves deny.

It is my conviction that machines cannot possess originality in the sense implied by Wiener and that they cannot transcend man's intelligence. I agree with Wiener in his thesis that "machines can and do transcend some of the limitations of their designers, and that in doing so they may be both effective and dangerous." The modern automobile travels faster than its designer can run, it is effective, and the records of highway fatalities attest to the dangerous consequences. However, a perusal of Wiener's article reveals that much more than this is meant, and it is to this extension of the thesis that I wish to take exception.

Wiener's reference to the "Sorcerer's Apprentice," and to the many tales based on the assumption that the agencies of magic are literal-minded, might almost lead one to think that he attributes magic to the machine. He most certainly seems to imply an equality between man and the machine when he states "disastrous results are to be expected not merely in the world of fairy tales but in the real world wherever two agencies essentially foreign to each other are coupled in the attempt to achieve a common purpose." In relationships between man and a

*A. L. Samuel, "Some Moral and Technical Consequences of Automation—A Refutation" *Science*, Vol. 132, Sept. 16, 1960, pp. 741–742, Copyright 1960 by the American Association for the Advancement of Science.

machine the machine is an agency, but only an agency of man, entirely subservient to man and to his will. Of course, no one will deny that "we had better be quite sure that the purpose put into the machine is the purpose which we really desire and not merely a colorful imitation of it." If we want our house to be at 70° F when we get up in the morning, we had better set the thermostat at 70° and not at 32°. But once the thermostat is set at 70° we can go to sleep without fear that the genie in the furnace controls might, for some reason of his own, decide that 32° was a better figure. In exactly the same way and to the same degree we must anticipate our own inability to interfere when we instruct a modern digital computer (which works faster than we do) and when we instruct a thermostat (which works while we sleep).

Wiener's analogy between a machine and a human slave is also quite misleading. He is right in his assertion that "complete subservience and complete intelligence do not go together" in a human slave with human emotions and needs and with a will of his own. To ascribe human attributes to a machine simply because the machine can simulate some forms of human behavior is, obviously, a fallacious form of reasoning.

A machine is not a genie, it does not work by magic, it does not possess a will, and, Wiener to the contrary, nothing comes out which has not been put in, barring, of course, an infrequent case of malfunctioning. Programming techniques which we now employ to instruct the modern digital computer so as to make it into a learning machine *do not* "remove from the mind of the designer and operator an effective understanding of many of the stages by which the machine comes to its conclusions." Since the machine does not have a mind of its own, the "conclusions" are not "its." The so–called "conclusions" are only the logical consequences of the input program and input data, as revealed by the mechanistic functioning of an inanimate assemblage of mechanical and electrical parts. The "intentions" which the machine seems to manifest are the intentions of the human programmer, as specified in advance, or they are subsidiary intentions derived from these, following rules specified by the programmer. We can even anticipate higher levels of abstraction, just as Wiener does, in which the program will not only modify the subsidiary intentions but will also modify the rules which are used in their derivation, or in which it will modify the ways in which it modifies the rules, and so on, or even in which one machine will design and construct a second machine with enhanced capabilities. However, and this is important, the machine *will not* and *cannot* do any of these things until it has been instructed as to how to proceed. There is (and logically there must always remain) a complete hiatus between (i) any ultimate extension and elaboration in this process of carrying out man's wishes and (ii) the development within the machine of a will of its own. To believe otherwise is either to believe in magic or to believe that the existence of man's will is an illusion and that man's actions are as mechanical as the machine's. Perhaps Wiener's article and my rebuttal have both been mechanistically determined, but this I refuse to believe.

An apparent exception to these conclusions might be claimed for projected machines of the so-called "neural net" type. These machines were not mentioned by Wiener, and, unfortunately, they cannot be adequately discussed in the space available here. Briefly, however, one envisions a collection of simple devices which, individually, simulate the neurons of an animal's nervous system and which are interconnected by some random process simulating the organization of the nervous system. It is maintained by many serious workers that such nets can be made to exhibit purposeful activity by instruction and training with reward-and-punishment routines similar to those used with young animals. Since the internal connections would be unknown, the precise behavior of the nets would be unpredictable and, therefore, potentially dangerous. At the present time, the largest nets that can be constructed are nearer in size to the nervous system of a flatworm than to the brain of man and so hardly constitute a threat. If practical machines of this type become a reality we will have to take a much closer look at their implications than either Wiener or I have been able to do.

One final matter requires some clarification—a matter having to do with Wiener's concluding remarks to the effect that "We must always exert the full strength of our imagination to examine where the full use of our new modalities may lead us." This certainly makes good sense if we assume that Wiener means for us to include the full use of our intelligence as well as of our imagination. However, coming as it did at the end of an article which raised the spectre of man's domination by a "learning machine," this statement casts an unwarranted shadow over the learning machine and, specifically, over the modern digital computer. I would be remiss were I to close without setting the record straight in this regard.

First a word about the capabilities of the digital computer. Although I have maintained that "nothing comes out that has not gone in," this does not mean that the output does not possess value over and beyond the value to us of the input data. The utility of the computer resides in the speed and accuracy with which the computer provides the desired transformations of the input data from a form which man may not be able to use directly to one which is of direct utility. In principle, a man with a pencil and a piece of paper could always arrive at the same result.

In practice, it might take so long to perform the calculation that the answer would no longer be of value, and, indeed, the answer might never be obtained because of man's faculty for making mistakes. Because of the very large disparity in speeds (of the order of 100,000 to 1), on a computer we can complete calculations which are of immense economic value with great precision and with a reliability which inspires confidence, and all this in time intervals which conform to the demands of real–life situations. The magnitude of the tasks and the speed with which they are performed are truly breath–taking, and they do tend to impress the casual observer as being a form of magic, particularly when he is unacquainted with the many, many hours of human thought which have gone into both the design of the machine and, more particularly, into the writing of the program which specifies the machine's detailed behavior.

Most uses of the computer can be explained in terms of simulation. When one computes the breaking strength of an airplane wing under conditions of turbulence, one is, in effect, simulating the behavior of an actual airplane wing which is subjected to unusual stresses, all this without danger to a human pilot, and, indeed, without ever having to build the airplane in the first place. The checker–playing program on the I.B.M. 704, to which Wiener referred, actually simulates a human checker player, and the machine learns by accumulating data from its playing experience and by using some of the logical processes which might be employed by a person under similar circumstances. The specific logical processes used are, of course, those which were specified in advance by the human programmer. In these, and in many other situations, the great speed of the computer enables us to test the outcome resulting from a variety of choices of initial actions and so to choose the course with the highest payoff before the march of human events forces us to take some inadequately considered action. This ability to look into the future, as it were, by simulation on a computer is already being widely used, and as time goes on it is sure to find application in more and more aspects of our daily lives.

Finally, as to the portents for good or evil which are contained in the use of this truly remarkable machine—most, if not all, of man's inventions are instrumentalities which may be employed by both saints and sinners. One can make a case, as one of my associates has jokingly done, for the thesis that the typewriter is an invention of the devil, since its use in the nations' war offices has made wars more horrible, and because it has enslaved the flower of our young womanhood. On the whole, however, most of us concede that the typewriter, as a labor–saving device, has been a boon, not a curse. The digital computer is something more than merely another labor-saving device, since it augments man's brain rather than his brawn, and since it allows him to look into the future. If we believe, as most scientists do, that it is to our advantage to increase the rate at which we can acquire knowledge, then we can hardly do otherwise than to assert that the modern digital computer is a modality whose value is overwhelmingly on the side of the good. I rest my case with this assertion.

The authors of modern literature are stating that man feels threatened by the machine and by his tools and feels out of harmony, or discontinuous with the machine age. Thus, as Professor Drucker states, we live in an age of discontinuity; an age of the knowledge industry when information is the conveyor of power rather than energy and materials. The fears of man are that the computer provides the following threats:

1. The computer threatens man's identity as a worker and as a producing member of society.
2. The computer adds to the depersonalization of man's relationships.
3. The computer contributes to the pollution of man's environment.
4. The computer makes man himself, as an intelligent being, irrelevant, inadequate or meaningless.

In many ways the greatest threat to man is the possibility of forcing upon us the need to find an alternative to work. The possibilities of automation are profound to consider. Perhaps within this century work will no longer exist as we now know it and jobs will not be available for the majority of the population. As William Kuhns recently stated,[9] "For computers will not simply force upon us the need to find an alternative to work; they will offer us that alternative. New ways of registering knowledge, an unbelievably enlarged capacity for information, new possibilities of communication—the computer's potential for a leisure-stricken society is even more phenomenal than its creation of such a world. Yet it is possible, even likely, that men will be hesitant and fearful about the computer, that the radically ambivalent reactions noticeable in man's response to many contemporary environments will be all the more apparent in the final age of the computer."

When a person engages in work, he uses his body and brain in three specific ways. The first is the exercise of physical strength and manual dexterity, called skill. The second is the functioning of the five perceptive senses. . .and the personal control that is exercised therefrom. The third is the use of the brain, both in its decision-making capacity and in the information storage system we call memory. The computer used in automation systems is a challenge to all three of these ways of man. The computer and automated devices may effectively replace man in a majority of tasks in the future. To this present time, however, the alarm over the potential unemployment caused by computer automation has been premature. The silent conquest of the employment market foreseen by Donald Michael and others has not yet become a reality.[22] Yet computer automation, often called *cybernation* (for *cybernetics* and *automation*), is only in its infancy. Perhaps the exponential growth of unemployment, due to cybernation, has only begun. The profound changes in the size of the agricultural labor force has only begun. The half century and the changes we are to experience due to the computer will not be significant before the end of the twentieth century. It has been estimated that whereas in 1900 eighteen out of twenty worked with their hands, ten of them on the farm, by 1965 only five of twenty earned their living by manual work, just one of them on the farm.

One of the consequences of the introduction of the computers to clerical activities is the industrialization of the office in a pattern amazingly similar to that found on assembly lines. In large banks, insurance companies, and credit billing operations, the paperwork operation is strikingly factory-like, and its managers tend to talk in production-line terminology. Work tasks are fragmented until they become little more than keying an account number and a dollar amount onto a card. Thus, automation of the functions of the business office has this unforeseen result.[16]

As the computer becomes a partner with man in the intellectual process, one has to consider an additional problem as Kuhns states:[9]

> . . . the tendency of men to think computationally—What effect will our new concept of information have on the way in which people know? In other words, in a world of immediately accessible information, what will become of knowledge—and of insight, the ratios of knowledge created by the personal mind? The repercussions here are strongest for art and religion, in which insight—the inescapably personal aspect of knowledge—is fundamental. Will computational man be capable of insight, or will insight be capable of enabling men to distinguish between computational and noncomputational thought, even as they distinguish between reality and fantasy?

Computers are man's tools and can be used knowingly to perform needed tasks for society. Alternatively, man's slaves can, when used indiscriminately, cause social consequences of a profound and foreseen nature. A fear of these unforeseen consequences of a delirious nature has caused many to echo Samuel Butler's dictum:[8]

> But the servant glides by imperceptible approaches into the master; and we have come to such a pass that, even now, man must suffer terribly on ceasing to benefit the machines. If all machines were to be annihilated at one moment, and if all knowledge of mechanical laws were taken from him so that he

could make no more machines, and all machine-made food destroyed so that the race of man should be left as it were naked
upon a desert island, we should become extinct in six weeks.
Man's very soul is due to the machines; it is a machine-made
thing: he thinks as he thinks, and feels as he feels, through the
work that machines have wrought upon him, and their existence
is quite as much a *sine qua non* for his, as for theirs. This fact
precludes us from proposing the complete annihilation of machinery, but surely it indicates that we should destroy as many
of them as we can possibly dispense with, lest they should
tyrannize over us even more completely.

Is the answer to destroy as many of the computer systems as we can? Many
people believe so. Is there another way to use computers advantageously while
overcoming the problems of depersonalization, unemployment due to cybernation, and the inability to comprehend the solutions resulting from rapid calculations? Perhaps the answer for man is to remain man above all else, and not
imitate or compete with his tool or slave the computer. It is appropriate that
Norman Cousins has suggested this course of action and Mr. Cousins' reasoned
response to the challenge of the computer serves as a suitable ending to a chapter which cannot answer questions, but only raise the issues. For the consequences of the actions we take with the computer in the present will only be
known by those who experience them in the future. But that is, of course, one
of the great challenges to man.

THE COMPUTER AND THE POET*

Norman Cousins

The essential problem of man in a computerized age remains the same
as it has always been. That problem is not solely how to be more productive, more comfortable, more content, but how to be more sensitive,
more sensible, more proportionate, more alive. The computer makes
possible a phenomenal leap in human proficiency; it demolishes the
fences around the practical and even the theoretical intelligence. But
the question persists and indeed grows whether the computer will make
it easier or harder for human beings to know who they really are, to
identify their real problems, to respond more fully to beauty, to place
adequate value on life, and to make their world safer than it now is.

Electronic brains can reduce the profusion of dead ends involved in
vital research. But they can't eliminate the foolishness and decay that
come from the unexamined life. Nor do they connect a man to the
things he has to be connected to—the reality of pain in others; the pos-

*From July 23, 1966, *Saturday Review.* Copyright 1966, *Saturday Review,* Inc.

sibilities of creative growth in himself; the memory of the race; and the rights of the next generation.

The reason these matters are important in a computerized age is that there may be a tendency to mistake data for wisdom, just as there has always been a tendency to confuse logic with values, and intelligence with insight. Unobstructed access to facts can produce unlimited good only if it is matched by the desire and ability to find out what they mean and where they would lead.

Facts are terrible things if left sprawling and unattended. They are too easily regarded as evaluated certainties rather than as the rawest of raw materials crying to be processed into the texture of logic. It requires a very unusual mind, Whitehead said, to undertake the analysis of a fact. The computer can provide a correct number, but it may be an irrelevant number until judgment is pronounced.

To the extent, then, that man fails to make the distinction between the intermediate operations of electronic intelligence and the ultimate responsibilities of human decision and conscience, the computer could prove a digression. It could obscure man's awareness of the need to come to terms with himself. It may foster the illusion that he is asking fundamental questions when actually he is asking only functional ones. It may be regarded as a substitute for intelligence instead of an extension of it. It may promote undue confidence in concrete answers. "If we begin with certainties," Bacon said, "we shall end in doubts; but if we begin with doubts, and we are patient with them, we shall end in certainties."

The computer knows how to vanquish error, but before we lose ourselves in celebration of the victory, we might reflect on the great advances in the human situation that come about because men were challenged by error and would not stop thinking and probing until they found better approaches for dealing with it. "Give me a good fruitful error, full of seeds, bursting with its own corrections," Ferris Greenslet wrote. "You can keep your sterile truth for yourself."

The biggest single need in computer technology is not for improved circuitry or enlarged capacity or prolonged memory or miniaturized containers, but for better questions and better use of the answers. Without taking anything away from the technicians, we think it might be fruitful to effect some sort of junction between the computer technologist and the poet. A genuine purpose may be served by turning loose the wonders of the creative imagination on the kinds of problems being put to electronic tubes and transistors. The company of poets may enable the men who tend the machines to see a larger panorama of possibilities than technology alone may inspire.

A poet, said Aristotle, has the advantage of expressing the universal; the specialist expresses only the particular. The poet, moreover, can remind us that man's greatest energy comes not from his dynamos but from his dreams. The notion of where a man ought to be instead of where he is; the liberation from cramped propsects, the intimations of immortality through art—all these proceed naturally out of dreams. But the quality of a man's dreams can only be a reflection of his subconscious. What he puts into his subconscious, therefore, is quite literally the most important nourishment in the world.

Nothing really happens to a man except as it is registered in the subconscious. This is where event and feeling become memory and where the proof of life is stored. The poet—and we use the term to include all those who have respect for and speak to the human spirit—can help to supply the subconscious with material to enhance its sensitivity, thus safeguarding it. The poet, too, can help to keep man from making himself over in the image of his electronic marvels. For the danger is not so much that man will be controlled by the computer as that he may imitate it.

The poet reminds men of their uniqueness. It is not necessary to possess the ultimate definition of this uniqueness. Even to speculate on it is a gain.

CHAPTER 18 PROBLEMS

P18-1. Select an area of human thought and discuss if a computer would duplicate the processes involved.

P18-2. Does HAL, the computer of *2001: A Space Odyssey*, think or just mimic thinking? Can a computer have emotions?

P18-3. It has been said, "the steam drill outlasted John Henry as a digger of railway tunnels, but that didn't prove the machine had muscles; it proved that muscles were not necessary for digging railway tunnels."[27] Can one say the same about computers and their "ability to think?"

P18-4. List a foreseeable development of computer use and its potential consequences as illustrated in Table 18-2.

P18-5. Computers will be increasingly used in business and thus will affect the nature of the business world and the consumer as an individual. Discuss the consequences of increased use of computers in business which accrue to the citizens and consumers in the US.

CHAPTER 18 REFERENCES

1. N. Wiener, "Cybernetics," *Scientific American*, November, 1948, pp. 348–384.
2. J. O. Wisdom, "The Hypothesis of Cybernetics," *British Journal for the Philosophy of Science*, Vol. 2, No. 5, 1951.
3. J. Von Neumann, *The Computer and the Brain*, Yale University Press, New Haven, Conn., 1958.
4. M. L. Minsky, "Artificial Intelligence," *Scientific American*, September, 1966, pp. 142–148.
5. A. M. Turing, "Can a Machine Think?" *Mind*, 1950, pp. 2099–2123.
6. A. C. Clarke, "Are You Thinking Machines?" *Industrial Research*, March, 1969, pp. 52–55.
7. "The Day They Rated Minsky," *Datamation*, October, 1969, pg. 159.
8. N. Weiner, *God and Golem, Inc.*, M.I.T. Press, Cambridge, Mass., 1964.
9. W. Kuhns, *Environmental Man*, Harper and Row, Inc., New York, 1969.
10. K. Čapek, *Rossum's Universal Robots*, English version by P. Selver and N. Playfair, Doubleday, Page and Co., New York, 1923.
11. C. A. Rosen, "Machines that Act Intelligently," *Science Journal*, London, October, 1968, pp. 109–114.
12. A. C. Clarke, *2001: A Space Odyssey*, Signet Books, New York, 1968.
13. K. Vonnegut, Jr., *Player Piano*, Avon Books, New York, 1952.
14. D. Fabun, *Dynamics of Change*, Prentice-Hall, Inc., Englewood Cliffs, N. J., 1968.
15. R. S. Lee, "The Computer's Public Image," *Datamation*, Dec., 1966, pp. 33–39.
16. "Problem Solver, Problem Maker," *Business Week*, October 17, 1970, pp. 182–190.
17. D. F. Foster, "Computers and Social Change: Uses and Misuses," *Computers and Automation*, August, 1970, pp. 31–33.
18. M. L. Ernst, "What Else Will Computers Do to Us?" *Wall Street Journal*, Oct. 21, 1970, pg. 15.
19. T. Gordon, "A Forecast of Technological Trends, Their Societal Consequences and Science Policy Strategies of the Future," *Proceedings of the*

Hearings of the Committee on Science and Astronautics, U.S. House of Representatives, 1970, pp. 429–470.

20. N. Wiener, "Some Moral and Technical Consequences of Automation," *Science*, Vol. 131, May 6, 1960, pp. 1355–1358.

21. A. L. Samuel, "Some Moral and Technical Consequences of Automation— A Refutation," *Science*, Vol. 132, September 16, 1960.

22. D. N. Michael, "Cybernation: The Silent Conquest," Center for the Study of Democratic Institutions, 1962.

23. G. Hardin, "An Evolutionist Looks at Computers," *Datamation*, May, 1969, pp. 98–109.

24. N. Cousins, "The Computer and the Poet," *Saturday Review*, July 23, 1966.

25. N. Wiener, *The Human Use of Human Beings*, Houghton Mifflin Co., Boston, 1950.

26. Z. W. Pylyshyn, *Perspectives on the Computer Revolution*, Prentice-Hall, Inc., Englewood Cliffs, N. J., 1970.

27. M. Gardner, "Mathematical Games: The Turing Game and the Question It Presents: Can a Computer Think?" *Scientific American*, Vol. 224, No. 6, June, 1971, pp. 120–123.

28. B. Darrach, "Meet Shaky, the First Electronic Person," *Life*, Vol. 69, No. 21, Nov. 20, 1970, pp. 58–68.

29. T. Alexander, "The Hard Road to Soft Automation," *Fortune*, July, 1971, pp. 94–97.

30. C. W. Churchman, *The Systems Approach,* Dell Publishing Co., Inc., New York, 1968.

31. J. Martin and A. R. D. Norman, *The Computerized Society*, Prentice-Hall, Inc., Englewood Cliffs, N. J., 1970.

19

COMPUTERS AND THE FUTURE

19.1 FUTURE COMPUTERS AND COMPUTER SYSTEMS

Our society is future-oriented; to a great extent computers have contributed to this orientation. As we noted in the last chapter, many feel that the technological determinants of our society give us nothing like a free choice in our future, but rather have already set us on a path that is technologically determined. Yet, if we are to exercise a free choice about the development of large new computers and their uses, we must be informed about existing computers and the potential new machines. Thus, the purpose of this chapter is to portray the new and expected world of the computer during the period from the present until the year 2000.

It has been estimated that the market for computing systems will continue to grow at a rapid rate. For example, the computing systems market in 1975 will be twice the size (in dollars) of the market in 1969. While it is doubtful that this pace of growth can continue for the next three decades, a market for computers which doubles every six or ten years implies a rapid change in technology and equipment.[1] In a sense, computers become obsolete the way automobiles do. The technological and psychological push is toward possessing the latest model with its new and special features. Furthermore, the average performance/price ratio increases by a factor of two every two years, which leads competing industries and firms to upgrade and update their computer equipment. Table 19-1 shows the increase in performance/price ratio during the period 1953-1968.[2,6] As this performance continues to increase, the obsolescence of the old computer is caused by the availability of the new, higher performance computer.

TABLE 19-1

Performance/Price Ratio for the Period 1953-1966

	Year Introduced	Performance/Price Ratio (10,000 Operations/Dollar)
First Generation	1953	1.82
	1956	14.1
	1958	16.6
Second Generation	1959	94.8
	1962	154
	1964	178
Third Generation	1966	1920
	1968	4000

The widespread availability of time-sharing computers may result in a national information computer utility with tens of thousands of computer terminals in homes and offices connected to a large central computer. Also, the communication of data will occur, by means of terminals, through the use of telephone and other communication devices. The amount of data transmitted over telephone lines is certain to increase in the next decade. It is estimated that computer data transmissions over telephone lines now account for about 5 percent of the telephone time consumed in the United States. By 1980 it is estimated that data information transmission will equal that of all voice communications.[3]

As the size of computers, computer networks and data banks grow during the next several decades, the performance of computers and computer communication systems must be monitored and evaluated. During the past several years, the performance of computers has been studied and several measures of performance have been developed. One measure of performance is the performance/price ratio of operations per dollar as given in Table 19-1. The performance measures of computers assist the computer user in evaluating the relative effectiveness of one computer compared to another. Also, the measures of effectiveness can be used to determine if there are economies of scale in using different computers. In developing an inclusive measure of computer system effectiveness, the cost of personnel and programming costs must be included since they often consume a fair share of the costs of operating a computer center.[4] Man's progress is always measured by indices of his performance in conjunction with his tools. Therefore what is needed is a measure of effectiveness of a computer system including the equipment, the operating personnel and the programming time and cost. Measures of effectiveness are usually numerical, and one problem with computer systems today is the unsophisticated manner of recognizing their important characteristics which can be represented numerically. Real progress in the computer art will be made when it is known what is significant about computer behavior, when numbers are assigned to these effects, and when progress is measured using these numbers.[5] As a theory of computer performance is developed, two kinds of information will become available: knowledge about the *structure of programs* during execution, and knowledge about the *response of computers* to these program structures.

The four performance measures commonly used today for analyzing computer effectiveness are capacity, throughput, speed and ease of use. *Capacity* is the total information work executable per unit when all the accessible resources of a computer are utilized. *Throughput* is the number of useful jobs run per unit time. The *speed* of a computer can be defined as the rate of adding two numbers or a similar index. The *ease* of *use* describes the effort required to prepare a problem for solution by the computer and to operate the computer to solve that problem. All of these measures must be considered in the evaluation of the effectiveness of a computer. The inclusion of the cost of programming in the total measure of effectiveness is critical. In 1969, it cost 25¢ per million computer arithmetic additions. As the cost of the computer arithmetic has decreased, the cost of programming has become relatively important. It has been estimated that in 1969, the cost of equipment consumes 20 percent of the total computer operation cost and the programming costs consumed 80 percent of the total costs.[6] Therefore, in the future, even a drastic reduction in the cost of hardware, or a significant increase in speed at an unchanged price, can have only a minor effect on the cost of computing as a whole. Lower programming cost is what is needed; in order to achieve a significant improvement in the effective low-cost use of computers in the future, it will be necessary to reduce the cost of programming. This is particularly important as industry, business and government progress toward the use of increasingly complex programs.

In order to ease the cost and complexity of programming, it would be advantageous if improved programming languages would be developed. An improved programming language should be easy to learn, use and implement and it should be machine-independent. Also, the language should be applicable to a wide variety of problems. Currently, there are programming langauges available for specific purposes such as business and science. What may emerge is a series of languages to fit a range of users from beginner to expert, but all general in application. Some languages may be for big problems and big machines, others for small ones; some for experiments and one–of–a–kind problems, others for production runs.[6]

The use of computers in large complex systems has grown during the past decade and will continue to grow during the next several decades. In a recent article Professor Licklider notes the tendency in the design of large complex systems using computers to underestimate the costs and development time and to exaggerate the expected performance. The most complex subsystem or portion of the complex system is often the computer programming. As Licklider notes, in the case of the ABM (which is illustrative of complex systems) computer programs that carry out regulatory and control functions are usually much simpler and easier to prepare than computer programs that involve target acquisition, pattern recognition, decoy discrimination, decision–making and problem–solving.[7]

All complex computer programs contain programming errors. No complex program is ever wholly debugged and very few complex programs can ever be run through all possible states or conditions in order to permit the programmers to see that what they think ought to happen actually does happen.

Perhaps, in order to avoid the reprogramming required by a new generation of computers, future computer systems will be modular in design. As is done in the telephone industry, the replacement of modules or subsystems with newly–developed modules will enable an evolutionary growth to occur.

It has been stated that overexpectations and underestimates characterized the application of computers to large-scale complex systems during the past decade.[7,8] If the expectations were exaggerated, it was the concept of on-line large integrated information systems that was attractive but unfulfilled in practice. During the next decade, computer systems will evolve which will increasingly incorporate the interactive feature required for effective man–computer systems used in process control, CAI and management information systems. The modular development of the evolutionary computer will enable the programmers to develop effective programs to accommodate the changing computer.

The large, high-speed computer of the last few years of the decade of the 1960's and the first few years of the 70's was built to satisfy a need for time-sharing computers or large complex system computers which could operate in real time. The IBM System/360 Model 195 is an example of a presently available large computer. The 195 can be used for a complex airline reservation systems, or coast-to-coast time-sharing networks. Other applications include extensive scientific studies, such as global weather forecasting and space exploration. The central processing unit possesses a cycle time of 54 nanoseconds for accessing data stored in its core storage. The computer uses a 64–bit word and integrated circuit memory components, and is reported to provide an increase in its performance/price ratio of approximately five over the IBM System/360 Model 75.[9] The large computer, the 195, is designed to mix computer programs, a fact that has widespread implications for improving throughput.

The Control Data Corporation 7600 computer is another large computer built to accomplish large complex tasks. The cycle time of the 7600 is 27.5 nanoseconds; the computer utilizes a 65-bit word.

The Illiac 4 computer may be the world's fastest when in full operation at the University of Illinois. Essentially 64 computers operating in parallel and handling more than 200 million instructions per second, Illiac 4 was designed to solve large scientific problems. The computer uses 64-bit words and incorporates integrated circuits as the memory elements.[17]

The development of a computer using optical principles and utilizing a laser is proceeding toward a practical product. One company recently reported that it is developing a laser computer which incorporates 10^{10} bits of storage and operates with a storage access time of 20 nanoseconds. In addition, it is planned that this laser computer involve a storage cost of 10^{-7} cent per bit and average less than one error in 10^9 bits.[18]

The computer of the future will be modular in design and faster than present machines. Also, the computer will be designed toward improved equipment and hardware to serve the functions often previously relegated to a program. The number of program instructions in basic software available with a computer has grown ten times every 5.5 years during the period 1952–1968.[10] With the growth in importance and cost of programming software, the hardware portion of the computer must assume some of the tasks previously allocated to software.

19.2 COMPUTERS AND INFORMATION SYSTEMS IN THE YEARS 1971-2000

In this section we present some specific predictions and estimates for the period 1971 to 2000. Many of these predictions will undoubtedly prove to be in error, but predictions still provide us with an arrow pointing toward the future. While we cannot clearly visualize the path to be followed, one can indicate the direction of the evolving field of computer science; that is the objective of this section.

Future generations of computers will be classified as communication-and-control systems, using on-line data collection. The computers will be directed to user requirements. The user will participate more in the design of the computer in order to assure that the computers are built with the objectives of applications. For example, computers will be designed to shift the emphasis in industry *from* administrative record-keeping in the plant production environment *toward* a system involving the real-time monitoring of men, machines, and material throughout the working day. One possible technical approach to controlling plant operations involves on-line use of a computer with programs structured to provide continuous information on the operation as well as summary input to the administrative record-keeping system. Computer utilities, or networks of computers, will be developed. Networks of computers, particularly those designed for sharing data bases, open tremendous possibilities for the users, as in scale-time management information systems.

In a recent article, Drs. Rector and Walter discuss the potential for the fourth generation of computers.[11] They note that the emphasis on replacing clerical routines by computer programs has severely limited our understanding of the nature of applications to which computers could be applied. They state:[11]

> We suggest that the people who understand the design of computers do not understand the problems of users. The challenge of computing is not to design and program a system to obtain reports that enable individuals to perform functions; rather, the challenge is to design and program a system to direct computer performance of the functions—and thereby directly assist in the operation of a company, institution, or similar entity. . . . Computer professionals are slowly viewing internal organizations of computers and/or software in perspective and realizing that a computer is a general-purpose device primarily for ease of manufacturability. Furthermore, a computer is only one of many system components in a user's environment. The typical user's lack of ability to tailor a general-purpose machine to a particular application has been a major factor inhibiting extensive use of computers. Even if funds and required capabilities are available, the user may not wish to reinvent the wheel that constitutes his application.

The expected characteristics of the fourth generation computers are summarized in the following article, which assumes the evolution of computers toward a modular communication and control system.[11]

EXPECTED FOURTH-GENERATION CHARACTERISTICS*

1. The major design criterion will be the optimal use of available communication interfaces. The system will be classified as a communication and control system and will be capable of widely-diversified processor applications. Intrasystem and intersystem communication interfaces will be required for both hardware and software.

---

*From R. W. Rector and C. J. Walter, "The Fourth-Another Generation Gap?" *Modern Data*, March 1969, pp. 42-48.

2. The system will be controlled primarily by data rather than by programs as were previous machines; i.e., system control will be established primarily by input rather than by stored information. Development of this characteristic is dependent upon submission of information in real time. Feedback is a key consideration. Proper interaction between intersystem and intrasystem interfaces is vital. The interrelationships between data (communication bits) and programs (information bits) must be carefully defined.

3. Hardware will govern communication and control procedures; use of control programs will be substantially reduced or eliminated. This characteristic is closely related to the preceding one. Focalizing system design by application of communication networks eliminates much of the need for software and facilitates system control. Again, consideration of both intersystem and intrasystem data flow is important. When such techniques are applied, control program requirements will be minimized.

4. Most processing will be executed in real time; operations will be performed on input at a rate that provides output within the required response time. Real time, as discussed here, does not imply the interleaving of programs or the man–machine interaction of time–sharing. Rather, the implication is that the system will accept inputs as they are made available and process those inputs within the constraints imposed by desired response times.

5. The system will be readily expandable. Hardware and software will be modular in design. Computing power will be modified without redesign of the system. A variable instruction set is not implied. However, nested subsets of hardware will be available to complement nested subsets of software. In fact, this nesting of software is currently practiced.

Construction of special–purpose computers by specialization or combination of generalized hardware and software modules will be possible. Tailoring hardware to the user's needs and/or particular applications appears straightforward.

6. The hardware design will permit component parts to be updated. Modular design of system hardware is a basic determinant of the degree to which a system can be upgraded and the ease with which such updating can be performed. Systems need not become obsolete because advancements resulting from technical developments can be readily incorporated in systems currently in operation. (Modular design should not, however, be regarded as a permanent deterrent to obsolescence of fourth–generation equipment.)

7. The system will be designed to function without device-specific software routines. Required functions will be performed by a general software routine and the interchangeable functional hardware modules.

8. Collection of data at its source is a trend in the computer industry; on-line collection of data will be the standard rather than the exception in fourth generation systems. Cards and attendant keypunching operations will be a secondary source of input. Translation of data from a medium understandable by the user to a medium understandable by the computer will be an accepted function of the computer hardware. On-line submission of data or interrogation of the system from remote terminals will be a common technique by which desired information can be entered or secured. An advantage of the fourth generation will be the ability of people without knowledge of programming to use computer terminals. This capability, coupled with computer control of remote manufacturing machines and remote gathering of data, provides management with unique opportunities to increase production efficiency significantly.

9. Most data flow, in and out of computers today, is unnecessary and repetitive in nature. Repetitive entry of input will be reduced or eliminated, and reports will be generated on an exception basis.

10. Hardware diagnostic routines will be completely compatible with normal I/O routines so that on-line diagnostics can be executed simultaneously with normal system operations. Indication of malfunction will be detected and corrective procedures will be initiated. Thus, costly delays will be avoided. Compatibility of diagnostic routines and I/O routines achieves the following goals:

- Minimizes system downtime due to malfunction of hardware elements,
- Permits graceful degradation, and
- Eliminates the necessity to interrupt normal processing to detect and correct minor hardware malfunctions.

11. The system will be designed to operate efficiently, and this efficiency will not be significantly affected by distances between application devices. System tradeoffs in fourth-generation computers within communication and control systems will be expressed in terms of response times, communication bandwidths, equipment complexities, and number of channels. Standardization of interfaces and specifications of standard response times and bandwidths will permit the relocation of application devices in the system.

When the basic nature of anticipations is considered from a communication and control point of view, the following functions can be identified: data acquisition and reduction, algorithm computation, monitoring, and process optimization and control. These functions can be structured as a horizontal unification of computing elements, I/O and communication elements, and user devices, or data–generating elements. Within all applications, there is also a vertical structuring determined by the specific assignment which the system is initialized to perform.

Some of the computer devices that will become available during the next decade can be envisaged as logical extensions of technologies presently in the laboratory. These laboratory technologies will be designed for volume production and produced at a commercial price. We can expect that a low–cost minicomputer will become available in many sizes and forms and in special purpose units which will extend their use in dozens of ways. The low–cost minicomputer will cost approximately $1,000, which may become practical for the home and the hobby shop. The minicomputer can be used for such practical home functions as storing and processing budget and account information, recipes, menus, and calendar schedules. The minicomputer will also be available for such plant uses as segmented process control and automated testing, for communication–system data handling, and for general business calculating and record–keeping chores in, say, a fair–sized neighborhood retail store.[12]

Within the decade, computers may play a major role in data storage and retrieval. A large time–sharing system similar to a telephone network would alter the nature of our society. The availability of a library stored in the computer, and computer–aided instruction to subscribers, could be of significant value to the citizens of the United States. For example, the *New York Times's* Information Bank, scheduled to go into operation in 1971, will eventually make indexed data and topical summaries from the paper's files available as a subscriber service. Users will punch in requests on keyboards in their own offices and receive either CRT readings or print–outs.

The combination of artificial intelligence and mechanical devices may lead to practical robot devices within the next decade. The computer–controlled hand and eye laboratory robot could lead to the production of robots by 1980. These robots would serve as a limited substitute for humans in a variety of dangerous or undesirable industrial operations. Perhaps other types of cybernetic machines (*e.g.*, robots) will be serving in factories and in the home.

By reviewing the progress and problems of the second computer decade, we can visualize the problems and promise of the third computer decade. The discussion about the value of various programming languages will continue in the next decade, for instance, and we can expect to find several new programming languages available. Also, the basic education of the computer scientist is now a subject for debate because it is generally not systematic. Perhaps the education of the future computer scientist will begin to occur on a systematic basis in the 1970's as several graduate programs in computer science, at many universities, become available. The graduates of these advanced programs will become the teachers of our future programmers, operators, computer scientists and engineers at all levels of study. Perhaps we will even find the study of computers regularly available to the high school student at an introductory level.

During the late 1970's, we can expect the emergence of a profession of computer science as the qualifications and educational standards become accepted and standardized. As Gruenberger points out, the computer allows one to automate and mass produce inaccuracies and incorrect programs.[13] The nation will look to the professionalism of the computer scientists for leadership, control and a solution to the problems of the second decade of computers which will be solved in the third decade of computers.

A forecast of the applications of computers and developments within the computer field for the years 1968-2000 was recently published by Parsons and Williams, Inc., a consulting firm of Denmark.[14] The forecast was prepared by the use of the Delphi procedure to obtain a consensus among computer scientists and users.

In a Delphi forecast, a group of experts use a two-step questionnaire to come to a consensus about when technical events will occur. The first step usually results in widely divergent opinions; those at the extremes are asked to justify their views. In the second part, the experts are told how the first survey came out, and the reasons for extreme positions. They are then asked to reconsider their views. The second part usually shows a closer range of opinions. The questionnaire was mailed to 174 computer experts registered for an international conference on information processing. The size of the panel questioned was one of the largest ever used in a Delphi forecast. Most of the computer scientists involved in the conference were Europeans; thus the forecast tends to an international view of the future of computers.

By 1985, predicts this group of experts, employers will record income on terminals and automatically transfer this information to the tax authorities. (Many of the experts argued that by then direct taxes will be obsolete.) In general, the prospect of automated tax collection was viewed with dismay. Book libraries for factual information, not for literature, will be obsolete by 1992. Also, computer-aided instruction will have widespread use by 1978 and central files of scientific data will be common around 1983.

One day, there may even be a computer linkup in every home—a teletype terminal connected to a large data bank, but compulsory ownership of a terminal is not foreseen by this Delphi panel.[15]

Some of the specific forecasts of the Delphi panel are summarized as follows:*

---

*With the permission of Lt. Col. Joseph P. Martino and *The Futurist*, published by the World Future Society, P. O. Box 19285, Washington, D. C. 20036. The material originally appeared in *Forecast 1968-2000 of Computer Development*, Parson and Williams, Inc.

There will continue to be a rapid development of advanced computer applications which will result in much more influence on society than is the case today.

Widespread automation may even create new forms of democracy in the future with widespread participation through remote computer terminals.

By the late 1980s there will be a 50% reduction in the working force in present industries, partly compensated for by shorter working hours and new industries. However, unemployment is expected to be a serious problem.

By the year 2000 all major industries will be controlled by computers. Small industries will not be automated to the same extent, but not many will exist by then.

The money and check system of today will, to a large extent, be taken over by a network of terminals and computers by the early 1990s. Around 1985 a majority of employers will have terminals where income is recorded and taxes automatically transferred to the appropriate government agencies.

Large urban traffic flow will be controlled by computers after 1973 and policing of individual vehicles by combined radar detection and computer record of violations will be normal between 1980 and 1986. In the late 1990s there will be a widespread use of automobile autopilots.

Around 1975 patients in major hospitals will be monitored by computers; and in the beginning of the 1980s, a majority of doctors will have computer terminals for consultation. By then computers will give reliable diagnoses when the physician presents the computer with the patient's symptoms.

By the early 1980s pocket-sized computers will be available for use as "advanced slide rules." By the end of the century, computers will be just as common in private homes as telephones or television sets.

These predictions are summarized in Figure 19-1, which shows the median estimate as well as the range of estimates. The range of estimated dates of occurrence of predicted events spreads as the predicted date of occurrence is further in the future.

If the forecast is reasonably accurate, the computer will have penetrated the sectors of industry, the hospital, and the home significantly by the year 2000. Widespread participation in the political process by means of the com-

Computers and the Future*

The horizontal bars indicate the interquartile range (where 50% of the responses lay). The vertical bar indicates the median estimate. The last two events had upper quartiles falling later than the year 2000.

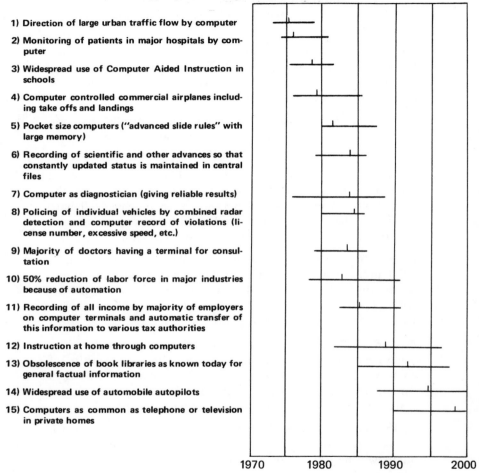

1) Direction of large urban traffic flow by computer

2) Monitoring of patients in major hospitals by computer

3) Widespread use of Computer Aided Instruction in schools

4) Computer controlled commercial airplanes including take offs and landings

5) Pocket size computers ("advanced slide rules" with large memory)

6) Recording of scientific and other advances so that constantly updated status is maintained in central files

7) Computer as diagnostician (giving reliable results)

8) Policing of individual vehicles by combined radar detection and computer record of violations (license number, excessive speed, etc.)

9) Majority of doctors having a terminal for consultation

10) 50% reduction of labor force in major industries because of automation

11) Recording of all income by majority of employers on computer terminals and automatic transfer of this information to various tax authorities

12) Instruction at home through computers

13) Obsolescence of book libraries as known today for general factual information

14) Widespread use of automobile autopilots

15) Computers as common as telephone or television in private homes

1970   1980   1990   2000

FIGURE 19-1

*With the permission of Lt. Col. Joseph P. Martino and the World Future Society, Washington, D.C. 20036. Also with the permission of Parsons and Williams, Inc., publishers of *Forecast 1968–2000 of Computer Development.*

puter could significantly alter the processes of government, possibly causing governing bodies to be more responsive to the desires of the governed.

The forecast predicts that the work force in the present industries will be reduced by 50 percent. Of course, that reduction, due to automation, can be partially accounted for by a shorter work week and an early retirement age. As Herman Kahn and Anthony Weiner noted in *The Year 2000*, automation and cybernation are likely to create as many jobs as they eliminate by contributing to the increase of productivity and economic growth.[16] The net effects on employment, hours worked and productivity are difficult to predict because society may choose to invest in increased production or increased leisure in some unknown proportion. Kahn and Weiner forecast that the United States will have a population of 318 million with 38 percent employed with a work year of 1600 hours in the year 2000. In this era of a post–industrial United States, Kahn and Weiner predict widespread cybernation and a lesser emphasis on efficiency as a criteria for industry and society. Whatever the exact consequences of a cybernated society are to a person in 2000 A.D., we can estimate that our society will experience a change in attitude about work, leisure and the value of time.

Whatever the outcome of the future development of computers and computer applications, man remains the architect of his own destiny. All the functions and activities of computer science relate to the larger problems and needs of man and his economic, political, social and religious dimensions. Computers will help to make life more livable for man if their limitations, applications and implications are fully understood. That is the objective of this book and computer science.

CHAPTER 19 PROBLEMS

P19-1. Determine the performance/price ratio of the computer available for your use and compare it with those listed in Table 19-1.

P19-2. Determine the throughput of the computer available for your use and compare it with another computer near your location.

P19-3. Establish another class at your college as a Delphi panel and using two cycles of inquiry and feedback determine their estimates for the statements given in Figure 19-1.

CHAPTER 19 REFERENCES

1. "Computer Market in 1975," *Modern Data*, May, 1969, pg. 18.
2. L. Amdahl, "Computer Obsolescence," *Datamation*, January, 1969, pp. 27–28.
3. J. N. Kessler, "Dither Over Data: Another Phone System Crisis?" *Electronic Design*, Vol. 19, September 13, 1969, pp. 25–30.
4. J. Diebold, "Bad Decisions on Computer Use," *Harvard Business Review*, January–February, 1969, pp. 14–27.
5. R. R. Johnson, "Needed: A Measure for Measure," *Datamation*, December 15, 1970, pp. 22–30.
6. F. L. Alt, "Computers–Past and Future," *Computers and Automation*, January, 1969, pp. 14–16.
7. J. C. R. Licklider, "Underestimates and Overexpectations," *Computers and Automation*, August, 1969, pp. 48–52, also in *ABM: An Evaluation of the Decision to Deploy Antiballistic Missile System*, Harper & Row, Inc., New York, pp. 118–129.
8. T. McCusker, "Computers in the 70's," *Datamation*, June, 1970, pp. 157–159.
9. R. A. McLaughlin, "The IBM 360/195," *Datamation*, October, 1969, pp. 119–122.
10. "Software Suffers from Gigantism," *Datamation*, January, 1969, pg. 82.
11. R. W. Rector and C. J. Walter, "The Fourth–Another Generation Gap," *Modern Data*, March, 1969, pp. 42–48.
12. "New Products of Tomorrow: A 1975 Sampler," *Fortune*, May 15, 1969, pp. 218–222.
13. F. Gruenberger, "The Shakedown Decade," *Datamation*, January, 1970, pp. 69–72.
14. "Forecast 1968–2000 of Computer Developments and Applications," Parsons and Williams, Inc., Copenhagen, Denmark, 1969.
15. J. Martino, "What Computers May Do Tomorrow," *The Futurist*, October, 1969, pp. 134–135.
16. H. Kahn and A. J. Wiener, *The Year 2000*, The Macmillan Co., New York, 1967.
17. D. L. Slotnick, "The Fastest Computer," *Scientific American*, Vol. 224, No. 2, February, 1971, pp. 76–87.
18. E. Myers, Perspective—an interpretive review of significant events," *Datamation*, July 1, 1971, pp. 52–53.
19. W. H. Ware, "The Ultimate Computer," *IEEE Spectrum*, March, 1972, pp. 84–91.

APPENDIX

ERRORS AND FLOATING POINT COMPUTER ARITHMETIC*

B.1 NATURE OF COMPUTERS

An automatic digital computer is a general-purpose machine. The bits of information in its store can be used to represent any quantifiable objects—e.g., musical notes, letters of the alphabet, elements of a finite field, integers, rational numbers, parts of a graph, etc. Thus such a machine is a general abstract tool, and this generality makes computer science important, just as mathematics and natural language are important.

In the use of computers to represent letters of the alphabet, elements of a finite field, integers, etc., there need be no error in the representation, nor in the processes that operate upon the quantities so represented. The problems in dealing with integers (to select one example) on computers are of the following type: Is there enough storage to contain all the integers we need to deal with? Do we know a process that is certain to accomplish our goal on the integers stored in the computer? Have we removed the logical errors ("bugs") from the computer representation of this process? Is this the fastest possible process or,

*Excerpted from "Pitfalls in Computation, or Why a Math Book Isn't Enough," by George E. Forsythe, *American Mathematics Monthly,* Vol. 77, November, 1970, pp. 931–956. With permission of the author and the Mathematical Association of America.

if not, does it operate quickly enough for us to get (and pay for) the answers we want?

The above problems are not trivial; there are surely pitfalls in dealing with them; and it is questionable whether math books suffice for their treatment. But they are not the subject of this paper. This paper is concerned with the simulated solution on a digital computer of the problems of algebra and analysis dealing with real and complex numbers. Such problems occur everywhere in applied science—for example, whenever it is required to solve a differential equation or a system of algebraic equations.

There are four properties of computers that are relevant to their use in the numerical solution of problems of algebra and analysis. These properties are causes of many pitfalls:

(i) Computers use not the real number system, but instead a simulation of it called a "floating–point number system." This introduces the problem of *round-off*.

(ii) The speed of computer processing permits the solution of very large problems. And frequently (but not always) large problems have answers that are much more *sensitive* to perturbations of the data than small problems are.

(iii) The speed of computer processing permits many more operations to be carried out for a reasonable price than were possible in the pre–computer era. As a result, the *instability* of many processes is conspicuously revealed.

(iv) Normally, the intermediate results of a computer computation are hidden in the store of the machine, and never known to the programmer. Consequently the programmer must be able to detect errors in his process without seeing the warning signals of possible error that occur in desk computation, where all intermediate results are in front of the problem solver. Or, conversely, he must be able to prove that his process cannot fail in any way.

B.2 FLOATING-POINT NUMBER SYSTEM

The badly named *real number system* is one of the triumphs of the human mind. It underlies the calculus and higher analysis to such a degree that we may forget how impossible it is to deal with real numbers in the real world of finite computers. But, however much the real number system simplifies analysis, practical computing must do without it.

Of all the possible ways of simulating real numbers on computers, one class is most widely used today—the *floating-point number system*. Here a number base β is selected, usually 2, 8, 10, or 16. A certain integer s is selected as the number of significant digits (to base β) in a computer number. An integer exponent e is associated with each nonzero computer number, and e must lie in a fixed range, say

$$m \leqq e \leqq M.$$

Finally, there is a sign + or − for each nonzero floating-point number.

Let $F = F(\beta, s, m, M)$ be the floating-point number system. Each nonzero $x \in F$ has the base-β representation

$$x = \pm .d_1 d_2 \cdots d_s \cdot \beta^e,$$

where the integers $d_1, \cdots, d_s$ have the bounds

$$1 \leq d_1 \leq \beta - 1,$$
$$0 \leq d_i \leq \beta - 1 \qquad (i = 2, \cdots, s).$$

Finally, the number 0 belongs to F, and is represented by

$$+.00 \cdots 0 \cdot \beta^m.$$

Actual computer number systems often differ in detail from the ideal one discussed here, but the differences are of only secondary relevance for the fundamental problems of round-off.

Typical floating-point systems in use correspond to the following values of the parameters:

$$\beta = \quad 2, s = 48, m = -975, M = 1071 \text{ (Control Data 6600)}$$
$$\beta = \quad 2, s = 27, m = -128, M = \quad 127 \text{ (IBM 7090)}$$
$$\beta = 10, s = \quad 8, m = - \quad 50, M = \quad 49 \text{ (IBM 650)}$$
$$\beta = \quad 8, s = 13, m = - \quad 51, M = \quad 77 \text{ (Burroughs 5500)}$$
$$\beta = 16, s = \quad 6, m = - \quad 64, M = \quad 63 \text{ (IBM System/360)}$$
$$\beta = 16, s = 14, m = - \quad 64, M = \quad 63 \text{ (IBM System/360)}.$$

Any one computer may be able to store numbers in more than one system. For example, the IBM System/360 uses the last two base-16 floating-point systems for scientific work, and also a certain base-10 system for accounting purposes.

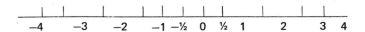

F is not a continuum, nor even an infinite set. It has exactly $2(\beta - 1)\beta^{s-1} \cdot (M - m + 1) + 1$ numbers in it. These are not equally spaced throughout their range, but only between successive powers of β and their negatives. The accompanying figure, reproduced from [3] by permission, shows the 33-point set F for the small illustrative system $\beta = 2, s = 3, m = -1, M = 2$.

Because F is a finite set, there is no possibility of representing the continuum of real numbers in any detail. Indeed, real numbers in absolute value larger than the maximum member of F cannot be said to be represented at all. And, for many purposes, the same is true of nonzero real numbers smaller in magnitude than the smallest positive number in F. Moreover, each number in F has to represent a whole interval of real numbers. If x and y are two real numbers in the range of F, they will usually be represented by the same number in F whenever $|x - y|/|x| \leq \frac{1}{2}\beta^{-s}$; it is not important to be more precise here.

As a model of the real number system R, the set F has the arithmetic operations defined on it, as carried out by the digital computer. Suppose x and y are floating–point numbers. Then the true sum x + y will frequently not be in in F. (For example, in the 33–point system illustrated above let x = 5/4 and y = 3/8.) Thus the operation of addition, for example, must itself be simulated on the computer by an approximation called *floating–point addition,* whose result will be denoted by fl(x + y). Ideally, fl(x + y) should be that member of F which is closest to the true x + y (and either one, in case of a tie). In most computers this ideal is almost, but not quite, achieved. Thus in our toy 33–point set F we would expect that fl(5/4 + 3/8) would be either 3/2 or 7/4. The difference between fl(x + y) and x + y is called the *rounding error* in addition.

The reason that 5/4 + 3/8 is not in the 33–point set F is related to the spacing of the members of F. On the other hand, a sum like 7/2 + 7/2 is not in F because 7 is larger than the largest member of F. The attempt to form such a sum on most machines will cause a so–called *overflow signal,* and often the computation will be curtly terminated, for it is considered impossible to provide a useful approximation to numbers beyond the range of F.

While quite a number of the sums x + y (for x, y in F) are themselves in F, it is quite rare for the true product x · y to belong to F, since it will always involve 2s or 2s − 1 significant digits. Thus the simulated multiplication operation, fl(x · y), involves rounding even more often than floating addition. Moreover, overflow is much more probable in a product. Finally, the phenomenon of *underflow* occurs in floating–point multiplication, when two nonzero numbers x, y have a nonzero product that is smaller in magnitude than the smallest nonzero number in F. (Underflow is also possible, though unusual, in addition.)

The operations of floating–point addition and multiplication are commutative, but not associative, and the distributive law fails for them also. Since these algebraic laws are fundamental to mathematical analysis, working with floating–point operations is very difficult for mathematicians. One of the greatest mathematicians of the century, John von Neumann, was able to collaborate in some large analyses with floating–point arithmetic (see [10]), but they were extremely ponderous. Even his genius failed to discover a method of avoiding nonassociative analysis.

B.3   AN EXAMPLE OF A ROUND–OFF PROBLEM

One of the commonest functions in analysis is the exponential function e^x. Since it is so much used, it is essential to be able to have the value of e^x readily available in a computer program, for any (not too large or small) floating–point number x. There is nowhere near enough storage to file a table of all values of e^x, so one must instead have an *algorithm* for recomputing e^x whenever it is needed. (By an algorithm we mean a discrete process that is completely defined and guaranteed to terminate.) There are, in fact, a great many different methods such an algorithm could use, and most scientific computing systems include such an algorithm. But let us assume such an algorithm did not exist on your computer, and ask how you would program it. This is a realistic model of the situation for a more obscure transcendental function of analysis.

Recall that, for any real (or complex) value of x, we can represent e^x by the sum of the universally convergent infinite series

$$e^x = 1 + x + \frac{x^2}{2!} + \frac{x^3}{3!} + \cdots.$$

Since you learned mathematics because it is useful, you might expect to use the series to compute e^x. Suppose—just for illustration—that your floating-point number system F is characterized by $\beta = 10$ and s = 5. Let us use the series for x = −5.5, as proposed by Stegun and Abramowitz [13]. Here are the numbers we get:

$$
\begin{array}{rl}
e^{-5.5} \approx & 1.0000 \\
- & 5.5000 \\
+ & 15.125 \\
- & 27.730 \\
+ & 38.129 \\
- & 41.942 \\
+ & 38.446 \\
- & 30.208 \\
+ & 20.768 \\
- & 12.692 \\
+ & 6.9803 \\
- & 3.4902 \\
+ & 1.5997 \\
& \cdot \\
& \cdot \\
& \cdot \\
\hline
+ & 0.0026363
\end{array}
$$

(The symbol "$\approx$" means "equals approximately".) The sum is terminated when the addition of further terms stops changing it, and this turns out to be after 25 terms. Is this a satisfactory algorithm? It may seem so, but in fact $e^{-5.5} \approx 0.00408677$, so that the above series gets an answer correct to only about 36 percent! It is useless.

What is wrong? Observe that there has been a lot of cancellation in forming the sum of this alternating series. Indeed, the four leading (i.e., most significant) digits of the eight terms that exceed 10 in modulus have all been lost. Professor D. H. Lehmer calls this phenomenon *catastrophic cancellation,* and it is fairly common in badly conceived computations. However, as Professor William Kahan has observed, this great cancellation is not the *cause* of the error in the answer—it merely *reveals* the error. The error had already been made in that the terms like 38.129, being limited to 5 decimal digits, can have only one digit that contributes to the precision of the final answer. It would be necessary for the term $(-5.5)^4/4!$ to be carried to 8 decimals (i.e., 9 leading digits) for it to include all 6 leading digits of the answer. Moreover, a tenth leading digit would be needed to make it likely that the fifth significant digit would be correct in the sum. The same is true of all terms over 10 in magnitude.

While it is usually possible to carry extra digits in a computation, it is always costly in time and space. For this particular problem there is a much better cure, namely, compute the sum for x = 5.5 and then take the reciprocal of the answer:

$$e^{-5.5} = 1/e^{5.5}$$
$$= 1/(1 + 5.5 + 15.125 + \cdots)$$
$$\approx 0.0040865, \text{ with our 5-decimal arithmetic.}$$

With this computation, the error is reduced to 0.007 percent.

Note how much worse the problem would be if we wanted to compute e^x for x = −100.

Actual computer algorithms for calculating e^x usually use a rational function of x, for x on an interval like $0 \le x \le 1$. For x outside this interval, well-known properties of the exponential function are used to obtain the answer from the rational approximation to e^y, where y = x − [x]. The creation of such algorithms for special functions is a branch of numerical analysis in which the general mathematician can hardly be an expert. On the other hand, it is part of the author's contention that mathematics books ought to mention the fact that a Taylor's series is often a very poor way to compute a function.

B.4 SOLVING QUADRATIC EQUATIONS

You don't have to learn college mathematics to find algorithms. In ninth grade there is a famous algorithm for solving a quadratic equation, implicit in the following mathematical theorem:

Theorem. *If a, b, c are real and a $\neq$ 0, then the equation $ax^2 + bx + c = 0$ is satisfied by exactly two values of x, namely*

(1)
$$x_1 = \frac{-b + \sqrt{b^2 - 4ac}}{2a}$$

(2)
$$x_2 = \frac{-b - \sqrt{b^2 - 4ac}}{2a}.$$

Let us see how these formulas work when used in a straightforward manner to induce an algorithm for computing x_1 and x_2. This time we shall use a floating-point system with $\beta = 10$, $s = 8$, $m = -50$, $M = 50$; this has more precision than many widely used computing systems.

Case 1: $a = 1, b = -10^5, c = 1$.

The true roots of the corresponding quadratic equation, correctly rounded to 11 significant decimals, are:

$$x_1 \approx 99999.999990 \qquad \text{(true)}$$
$$x_2 \approx 0.000010000000001 \text{ (true)}.$$

If we use the expressions of the theorem, we compute

$$x_1 \approx 100000.00 \qquad \text{(very good)}$$
$$x_2 \approx 0 \qquad \text{(100 percent wrong)}.$$

(The reader is advised to be sure he sees how x_2 becomes 0 in this floating-point computation.)

Once again, in computing x_2 we have been a victim of catastrophic cancellation, which, as before, merely reveals the error we made in having chosen this way of computing x_2. There are various alternate ways of computing the roots of a quadratic equation that do not force such cancellation. One of them follows from the easily proved formulas, true if $abc \neq 0$:

(3)
$$x_1 = \frac{2c}{-b - \sqrt{b^2 - 4ac}},$$

(4)
$$x_2 = \frac{2c}{-b + \sqrt{b^2 - 4ac}}.$$

Now, if $b < 0$, there is cancellation in (2) and (3) but not in (1) and (4). And, if $b > 0$, there is cancellation in (1) and (4), but not in (2) and (3). Special attention must be paid to cases where b or c is 0.

At this point I should like to propose the following criterion of performance of a computer algorithm for solving a quadratic equation. This is stated rather loosely here, but a careful statement will be found in [2].

We define a complex number z to be *well within the range of* F if either $z = 0$ or

$$\beta^{m+2} \leq |\operatorname{Re}(z)| \leq \beta^{M-2} \quad \text{and}$$
$$\beta^{m+2} \leq |\operatorname{Im}(z)| \leq \beta^{M-2}.$$

This means that the real and imaginary parts of z are safely within the magnitudes of numbers that can be closely approximated by a member of F. The arbitrary factor β^2 is included as a margin of safety.

Suppose a, b, c are all numbers in F that are well within the range of F. Then they must be acceptable as input data to the quadratic equation algorithm. If $a = b = c = 0$, the algorithm should terminate with a message signifying that all complex numbers satisfy the equation $ax^2 + bx + c = 0$. If $a = b = 0$ and

$c \neq 0$, then the algorithm should terminate with a message that no complex number satisfies the equation.

Otherwise, let z_1 and z_2 be the exact roots of the equation, so numbered that $|z_1| \leq |z_2|$. (If a = 0, set $z_2 = \infty$.) Whenever z_1 is well within the range of F, the algorithm should determine a close approximation to z_1, in the sense of differing by not more than, say, $\beta + 1$ units in the least significant digit of the root.

The same should be done for z_2.

If either or both of the roots z_i are not well within the range of F, then an appropriate message should be given and the root (if any) that is well within the range of F should be determined to within a close approximation.

That concludes the loose specification of the desired performance of a quadratic equation solving algorithm. Let us return to a consideration of some typical equations, to see how the quadratic formulas work with them.

Case 2:   a = 6, b = 5, c = —4.

There is no difficulty in computing $x_1 \approx 0.50000000$ and $x_2 \approx -1.3333333$, or nearly these values, by whatever formula is used.

Case 3: $a = 6 \cdot 10^{30}$, $b = 5 \cdot 10^{30}$, $c = -4 \cdot 10^{30}$.

Since the coefficients in Case 3 are those of Case 2, all multiplied by 10^{30}, the roots are unchanged. However, application of any of the formulas (3)–(6) causes overflow to occur very soon, since $b^2 > 10^{50}$, out of the range of F. Probably this uniform large size of $|a|$, $|b|$, $|c|$ could be detected before entering the algorithm, and all three numbers could be divided through by the factor 10^{30} to reduce the problem to Case 2.

Case 4: $a = 10^{-30}$, $b = -10^{30}$, $c = 10^{30}$.

Here z_1 is near 1, while z_2 is near 10^{60}. Thus our algorithm must determine z_1 very closely, even though z_2 is out of the range of F. Obviously any attempt to bring the coefficients to approximate equality of magnitude by simply dividing them all by the same number is doomed to failure, and might itself cause an overflow or underflow. This equation is, in fact, a severe test for a quadratic equation solver and even for the computing system in which the solver is run.

The reader may think that a quadratic equation with one root out of the range of F and one root within the range of F is a contrived example of no practical use. If so, he is mistaken. In many iterative algorithms which solve a quadratic equation as a subroutine, the quadratics have a singular behavior in which $a \to 0$ as convergence occurs. One such example is Muller's method [9] for finding zeros of general smooth functions of z.

Case 5:   a = 1.0000000, b = —4.0000000, c = 3.9999999.

Here the two roots are $z_1 \approx 1.999683772$, $z_2 \approx 2.000316228$. But applying the quadratic formulas (3), (4) gives

$$z_1 = z_2 = 2.0000000,$$

with only the first four digits correct. These roots fail badly to meet my criteria, but the difficulty here is different from that in the other examples. The equation corresponding to Case 5 is the first of our equations in which a small relative change in a coefficient a, b, c induces a much larger relative change in the roots z_1, z_2. This is a form of instability in the equation itself, and not in the method of solving it. To see how unstable the problem is, the reader should show that the computed roots 2.0000000 are the exact roots of the equation

$$0.999999992x^2 - 3.999999968x + 3.999999968 = 0,$$

in which the three coefficients differ, respectively, from the true a, b, c of Case 5 by less than one unit in the last significant digit. In this sense one can say that 2, 2 are pretty good roots for Case 5.

This last way of looking at rounding errors is called the *inverse error approach* and has been much exploited by J. H. Wilkinson. In general, it is characterized by asking how little a change in the data of a problem would be necessary to cause the computed answers to be the exact solution of the changed problem. The more intuitive way of looking at round off, the *direct error approach,* simply asks how wrong the answers are as solutions of the problem with its given data. While both methods are useful, the important feature of inverse error analysis is that in many large matrix or polynomial problems, it can permit us easily to continue to use associative operations, and this is often very difficult with direct error analysis.

Despite the elementary character of the quadratic equation, it is probably still true that not more than five computer algorithms exist anywhere that meet the author's criteria for such an algorithm. Creating such an algorithm is not a very deep problem, but it does require attention to the goal and to the details of attaining the goal. It illustrates the sort of place that an undergraduate mathematics or computer science major can make a substantial contribution to computer libraries.

Sensitivity of certain problems. We now show that certain computational problems are surprisingly sensitive to changes in the data. This aspect of numerical analysis is independent of the floating–point number system.

We first consider the zeros of polynomials in their dependence on the coefficients. In Case 5 of Section 4 above, we noted that, while the polynomial $x^2 - 4x + 4$ has the double zero 2, 2, the rounded roots of the polynomial equation

$$(10) \qquad x^2 - 4x + 3.9999999 = 0$$

are 1.999683772 and 2.000316228. Thus the change of just one coefficient from 4 to 3.9999999 causes both roots to move a distance of approximately .000316228. The displacement in the root is about 3162 times as great as the displacement in the coefficient.

The instability just described is a common one, and results from the fact that the square root of a small ϵ is far larger than ϵ. For the roots of (10) are the roots of

$$(x - 2)^2 = \epsilon, \qquad \epsilon = .0000001,$$

and these are clearly $2 \pm \sqrt{\epsilon}$. For equations of higher degree, a still more startling instability would have been possible.

However, it is not only for polynomials with nearly multiple zeros that instability can be observed. The following example is due to Wilkinson [14]. Let

$$p(x) = (x - 1)(x - 2) \cdots (x - 19)(x - 20)$$
$$= x^{20} - 210x^{19} + \cdots.$$

The zeros of $p(x)$ are 1, 2, $\cdots$, 19, 20, and are well separated. This example evolved at a place where the floating-point number system had $\beta = 2$, $s = 30$. To enter a typical coefficient into the computer, it was necessary to round it to 30 significant base-2 digits. Suppose that a change in the 30-th most significant base-2 digit is made in *only one* of the twenty coefficients. In fact, suppose that the coefficient of x^{19} is changed from -210 to $-210 - 2^{-23}$. How much effect does this small change have on the zeros of the polynomial?

To answer this, Wilkinson carefully computed (using $\beta = 2$, $s = 90$) the roots of the equation $p(x) - 2^{-23}x^{19} = 0$. These are now listed, correctly rounded to the number of digits shown:

1.00000 0000	10.09526 6145 $\pm$ 0.64350 0904i
2.00000 0000	11.79363 3881 $\pm$ 1.65232 9728i
3.00000 0000	13.99235 8137 $\pm$ 2.51883 0070i
4.00000 0000	16.73073 7466 $\pm$ 2.81262 4894i
4.99999 9928	19.50243 9400 $\pm$ 1.94033 0347i
6.00000 6944	
6.99969 7234	
8.00726 7603	
8.91725 0249	
20.84690 8101	

Note that the small change in the coefficient -210 has caused ten of the zeros to become complex, and that two have moved more than 2.81 units off the real axis! Of course, to enter $p(x)$ completely into the computer would require many more roundings, and actually computing the zeros could not fail to cause still more errors. The above table of zeros was produced by a very accurate computation, and does not suffer appreciably from round-off errors. The reason these zeros moved so far is not a round-off problem—it is a matter of sensitivity. Clearly zeros of polynomials of degree 20 with well-separated zeros can be much more sensitive to changes in the coefficients than you might have thought.

APPENDIX REFERENCES

1. R. Fletcher and M. J. D. Powell, "A Rapidly Convergent Descent Method for Minimization," *Computer J.*, 6 (1963), 163–168.
2. George E. Forsythe, "What is a Satisfactory Quadratic Equation Solver," pp. 53–71 of B. Dejon and P. Henrici (editors), *Constructive Aspects of the Fundamental Theorem of Algebra*, Wiley-Interscience, New York, 1969.
3. George E. Forsythe and Cleve B. Moler, *Computer Solution of Linear Algebraic Systems*, Prentice-Hall, Englewood Cliffs, N. J., 1967.
4. George E. Forsythe and Wolfgang R. Wasow, *Finite–Difference Methods for Partial Differential Equations*, Wiley, New York, 1960.
5. C. W. Gear, "The Automatic Integration of Stiff Ordinary Differential Equations," pp. A81–A86 of Anonymous, *Proceedings IFIP Congress 68*, North Holland Publishing Co., Amsterdam, 1968.
6. D. Hilbert, "Ein Betrag zur Theorie des Legendre'schen Polynoms," *Acta Math.*, 18 (1894), 155–160.
7. William Edmund Milne, *Numerical Solution of Differential Equations*, Wiley, New York, 1953.
8. Cleve B. Moler, "Numerical Solution of Matrix Problems," pp. 15–26 of Anonymous, The Digest Record of the 1969 Joint Conference on Mathematical and Computer Aids to Design, *I.E.E.E. Catalogue* No. 69 C 63–C, 1969.
9. David E. Muller, "A Method for Solving Algebraic Equations Using an Automatic Computer," *Math. Tables and Other Aids to Computation*, 10 (1956), 208–215.
10. John von Neumann and H. H. Goldstine, "Numerical Inverting of Matrices of High Order," *Bull. Amer. Math. Soc.*, 53 (1947), 1021–1099, and *Proc. Amer. Math. Soc.*, 2 (1951), 188–202.
11. Michael R. Osborne, "A New Method for the Integration of Stiff Systems of Ordinary Differential Equations," pp. A86–A90 of Anonymous, *Proceedings IFIP Congress 68*, North Holland Publishing Co., Amsterdam, 1968.
12. Anthony Ralston and Herbert S. Wilf, *Mathematical Methods for Digital Computers*, Wiley, New York, Vol. 1, 1960, and Vol. 2, 1967.
13. Irene A. Stegun and Milton Abramowitz, "Pitfalls in Computation," *J. Soc. Indust. Appl. Math.*, 4 (1956), 207–219.
14. J. H. Wilkinson, *Rounding Errors in Algebraic Processes*, Prentice-Hall, Englewood Cliffs, N. J., 1963.
15. _____ , *The Algebraic Eigenvalue Problem*, Clarendon Press, Oxford, 1965.

INDEX